HAYDN

AND HIS WORLD

OTHER PRINCETON UNIVERSITY PRESS VOLUMES
PUBLISHED IN CONJUNCTION WITH
THE BARD MUSIC FESTIVAL

Brahms and His World
edited by Walter Frisch (1990)

Mendelssohn and His World
edited by R. Larry Todd (1991)

Richard Strauss and His World
edited by Bryan Gilliam (1992)

Dvořák and His World
edited by Michael Beckerman (1993)

Schumann and His World
edited by R. Larry Todd (1994)

Bartók and His World
edited by Peter Laki (1995)

Charles Ives and His World
edited by J. Peter Burkholder (1996)

Haydn
and His World

Edited by Elaine Sisman

PRINCETON UNIVERSITY PRESS
PRINCETON, NEW JERSEY

The article, "Joseph Haydn's Library: An Attempt at a Literary-Historical Reconstruction" by Maria Hörwathner, was orginally published in German under the title "Joseph Haydn's Bibliothek—Versuch einer literarhistorischen Rekonstruktion," © 1976 *Jahrbuch für österreichische Kulturgeschichte*, which was kindly granted permission for its publication here in English translation.

Published by Princeton University Press, 41 William Street,
Princeton, New Jersey 08540
In the United Kingdom: Princeton University Press,
Chichester, West Sussex

Library of Congress Cataloging-in-Publication Data

Haydn and his world / edited by Elaine Sisman.
p. cm.—(Bard Music Festival series)
Includes bibliographical references and index.
ISBN 0-691-05798-2 (cl: alk. paper).—ISBN 0-691-05799-0 (pb: alk. paper)
1. Haydn, Joseph, 1732–1809—Criticism and interpretation.
I. Sisman, Elaine Rochelle. II. Series.
ML410.H4H318 1997
780'.92—dc21 97-19850

This publication has been produced by the Bard College Publications Office:
Ginger Shore, Director
Juliet Meyers, Art Director

This book has been composed in Baskerville
by Juliet Meyers

Music typeset by Don Giller

Princeton University Press books are printed on acid-free paper and meet the guidelines for permanence and durability of the Committee on Production Guidelines for Book Longevity of the Council on Library Resources

Printed in the United States of America

1 3 5 7 9 10 8 6 4 2

1 3 5 7 9 10 8 6 4 2
(Pbk.)

Designed by Juliet Meyers

FOR ARIELLE AND DANIEL

Contents

PART II
DOCUMENTS

Preface and Acknowledgments

The year 1997 marks the two-hundredth anniversary of the composition of Haydn's six string quartets Op. 76, an extraordinary group of works that comprised his last completed instrumental opus. Although he was to write two more string quartets (Op. 77, 1799), he never finished the third that would have completed the set (Op. 103, ca. 1802). The only other work of 1797 occupying Haydn was his ongoing composition of *The Creation*. These pieces seem to cover all the available modes of expression at the end of the eighteenth century. The quartets include some of Haydn's most well-known and accessible movements—like the variations on "God Save Franz the Kaiser," the Austrian National Hymn he had just written, in no. 3—as well as some rather esoteric explorations of harmony and texture, like the haunting Fantasia of no. 6. This distinction—between accessible and esoteric—underlies some of the fundamental ways by which the later eighteenth century conceived of music and its contexts, and consequently the ways in which we too have learned to make sense of this period. Some of these distinctions are too simple, but they are useful nonetheless. Both the audience and the musical patrons were thought to comprise connoisseurs and amateurs (*Kenner* and *Liebhaber*), while the concerts they listened to were performed by both virtuosos and dilettantes. Performances took place in either a public or a private sphere, with musical gestures and genres appropriate to each. Styles could be broadly designated as the accessible and esoteric already mentioned, or galant (the "basic" style of Classicism) and learned (the complex forms of older counterpoint). A composer might choose an elevated, serious level of discourse or a plain, even comic, style, and to suit this rhetorical notion would seek appropriate musical topics in order to communicate intelligibly with the audience.

Several of the essays in this volume explore oppositional paradigms in a new way—to resituate Haydn's music and cultural world—while others complicate the poles of the opposition in the first place. Their contextualizing strategies focus on aesthetic categories, decorum, rhetorical argumentation, modes of listening, aristocratic culture, and the role of theater in Haydn's time, and critical reception in his time and thereafter. The essays that deal with the broadest issues of compositional meaning and reception are mine and Leon Botstein's, and it is appropriate that these two frame Part I of the book. My essay connects critics' comparisons of Haydn to Shakespeare with the larger issue of Haydn's vaunted "originality," as well as the ways in which both Shakespeare and Haydn were seen to violate "the rules." Certain remarks by critics, adaptations of Shakespeare plays in Haydn's milieu, and the pronounced theatrical strain in a number of his works lead to a consideration of character and rule in several of his later works. Botstein examines the ways in which nineteenth-century critics and musicians lost the tools to understand Haydn as the eighteenth century had; their desire for greater emotional verisimilitude occluded their ability to see beyond Haydn as a formalist. Only the understanding of music in its philosophical and moral richness can restore the intensity of the earlier response.

Although the musical sublime was first applied to vocal works in the eighteenth century—specifically Handel's oratorios—recent studies have sought to study its effect in instrumental music. James Webster's study of the sublime as a category centrally bound up with Haydn's late oratorios and masses seeks to analyze and evaluate both the category and its application. It also offers a new understanding of types of sublime experience. Two essays on instrumental music follow. Mary Hunter finds that the question of public and private musical gesture is more complex than a simple assignment of performance venues and domestic/"feminine" or concert/"masculine" genres (piano trio and string quartet, respectively). The essay by Mark Evan Bonds takes up the public side of this opposition by returning to the question of the symphony and sublimity—the essence of the comparison between symphonies and the Pindaric ode—and explores aesthetics, criticism, and the music itself to ascertain what the eighteenth-century listener heard in the "grand" and "overwhelming" experience of the symphony.

The essays by Rebecca Green and Tom Beghin themselves form a kind of opposition in their detailed examinations of exterior and interior worlds. Green provides a rich portrait of the Esterházy establishment and the new palace of Eszterháza, especially as it geared up for a princely wedding. Haydn's opera *Le pescatrici,* to a libretto by the great Italian playwright Goldoni, actually reveals an emerging paradigm shift in the representation of the aristocracy. Beghin evaluates the unusually unbalanced proportions of the finale of a two-movement sonata by Haydn and discovers, through a densely argued chain of rhetorical and logical analyses, that the structure of the second movement could not be otherwise because it stands in a logical relation to the first movement. The work is thus exceptional testimony to Haydn's intricate rhetorical skill in persuading the listener.

Oppositional thinking has its attractions. Although its primary pitfall is a closing off of possibilities, it may retain a sense of fluidity between its poles. At a lecture given in the early 1980s, the late Haydn scholar Jens Peter Larsen (often called "the father of modern Haydn research") said "Beethoven uses music to express his feelings about Time and Fate; Haydn uses music to rise above Time and Fate." This subjective-objective opposition has the effect of elevating Haydn's achievement to a position of transcendence vis-à-vis Beethoven; the latter is seen as an exemplar merely of Romantic subjectivity. But many recent studies that explore oppositions, including those in this volume, do not necessarily assign relative values to each pole: the side that is "more so"—more difficult, more complex, higher, more intense—is not necessarily better. The ability to maintain a more value-neutral stance to these oppositions derives at least in part from the identification of valid musical topics—identifiable and characteristic styles, gestures, techniques—on both sides. For example, the two sides of the serious-comic divide might be characterized by learned-fugal or elevated-chordal topics on the one side, and dance-like (e.g. contredanse, minuet) or folklike topics on the other. At the same time, a piece of music or an element in the musical culture is nearly always at the intersection of several sets of oppositions, which has the effect of enriching its meanings while mitigating possible value judgments.

Part II of the book presents three large documents from Haydn's lifetime. First is the listing of patrons, musicians, and concert series in Vienna in 1796, published in the indispensable almanac, *A Yearbook of Music in Vienna and Prague 1796*. We see Haydn take his place among a host of composers and performers, including young "Bethofen." The compiler of the almanac, Johann Ferdinand von Schönfeld, is not above taking potshots at some members of the list, and the occasional hapless member who simply "spielt gut" (plays well) looks a little undernourished next to the panegyrics for the great performers and composers. The listing of over two hundred "virtuosos and amateurs" in Vienna is especially interesting in what it reveals about the musical specialties of men and women at the time. With very few exceptions (three violinists, a harpist, and a mandolin-player out of seventy-four female musicians), the women are virtually evenly divided between singers and pianists. Only about one-sixth of the men are pianists, however, and even fewer are singers, while nearly one-quarter are violinists; other instruments are well-represented. Moreover, the forty-two composers culled from this list (appearing in the seventh chapter of the Yearbook) include only three women.

The second document is the first English translation of a lengthy serialized article that appeared in 1801, surveying the entire eighteenth century in German music. Interesting oppositions are created by Pastor Triest: we read of the distinctions between pure and applied music and between rhetorical and poetic music, for example. Triest was important for appreciating Johann Sebastian Bach earlier than most writers and setting up Mozart and Haydn as the epitomes of, respectively, vocal and instrumental music at the end of the century. Longer than most articles in the *Allgemeine musikalische Zeitung,* which was published in Leipzig by Breitkopf & Hartel, Triest's study was clearly considered important by Friedrich Rochlitz, the founding editor of the journal.

The final document is an annotated listing of the contents of Haydn's library, based on the manuscript of Haydn's collection in the Vienna City Library (Stadtbibliothek) and published in 1976. This absorbing list reveals that Haydn owned a wide array of books on many topics (from the arts to economics, medicine, and geography) and in several languages, including Ovid's *Metamorphoses* and Martial's epigrams in German, Aesop's Fables in Italian, and works by Moses Mendelssohn, Edward Young (*Night Thoughts,* in German), and Shakespeare, in addition to the Schönfeld *Jahrbuch 1796* and the *Allgemeine musikalische Zeitung* in which Triest's article appeared. These three documents in translation now join the wealth of translations provided by the indefatigable H. C. Robbins Landon in the five-volume *Haydn: Chronicle and Works* (Bloomington, 1976–80) and in the *Haydn Yearbook.*

We are all in debt to Emil Katzbichler Verlag (Salzburg and Munich) for its 1976 republication of Schönfeld's *Yearbook* in a facsimile edition, and to Otto Biba, who provided the afterword and index for that edition. Readers interested in the other chapters that we were unable to translate here should consult the Schönfeld under its original title, *Jahrbuch der Tonkunst Wien und Prag 1796.* Similarly, fascinating articles and reviews besides Triest in the *Allgemeine musikalische Zeitung* may be found in the facsimile of the entire run of the journal (1798–1848) published by N. Israel and Fritz A. M. Knupf (Amsterdam, 1964). Here I would also like to thank the editors of the *Jahrbuch für österreichische Kulturgeschichte* for granting permission to publish Maria Hörwarthner's work of bibliographic sleuthing, "Joseph Haydn's Bibliothek—Versuch einer literarhistorischen Rekonstruktion," which originally appeared in 1976 in Volume 6 of that publication.

Since 1990 the Bard Festival has fostered the opportunity for intensive reexamination of a great composer, and I am grateful to Leon Botstein for asking me to help him push the boundaries of the Festival back into the eighteenth century for the first time; his vision has been critical to the endeavor. Mark Loftin and Robert Martin have provided stimulating collaboration in recontextualizing Haydn. In addition, many people worked very hard to see this book through its punishing production schedule. I would like to thank Ginger Shore and Juliet Meyers of the Bard Publications Office for their roles in organizing, coordinating, and designing the book; Paul De Angelis for expert and sympathetic copyediting; Don Giller for the attractive musical examples; Elliot Linzer for preparing the index; and Susan Gillespie and Kathrine Talbot for their faithful yet idiomatic translations of the documents. Malcolm Litchfield, Kenneth Reed, and Linda Truilo shepherded the book through Princeton University Press.

This book is dedicated to my children, Arielle Amanda Fridson and Daniel Wolfe Fridson, who have developed an interest in Haydn despite my intense involvement in the project.

Elaine Sisman
20 May 1997

Part I

Essays

Haydn, Shakespeare, and the Rules of Originality

ELAINE SISMAN

This essay's point of departure is Haydn's celebrated description, late in life, of how he came to be "original." To Griesinger, who was interviewing him for a biography, he put the best face on his years as Kapellmeister to Nicolaus Esterházy:

> My Prince was satisfied with all of my works; I received applause. As head of an orchestra, I could make experiments, observe what created an impression and what weakened it, and thus improve, add, make cuts, take risks. I was isolated from the world; no one in my vicinity could make me lose confidence in myself or bother me, and so I had to become original.[1]

This is a remarkable claim, in both meaning and context. To take the context first, we see that Haydn's claim of originality is based first on his ability to make experiments and second on his isolation. By linking his position as "head of an orchestra" with the idea of trying things out ("experiments . . . add . . . cuts . . . risks"), he implies that his main interest was in the audience's (and his own) reactions to orchestral effects or musical details and forms filtered through orchestral sonorities and textures. He needed to know *how* his audience heard, and when he scribbled "This was for entirely too learned ears" over a few rejected measures in the slow movement of Symphony 42, we understand that his attempt to thin out the texture, to make the music "lose steam" between statements of the second theme, had failed to "create an impression" or indeed had actively weakened it, in performance at Eszterháza in 1771.[2] By mentioning both his isolation and freedom from distracting criticism, Haydn finessed several questions, however:

he was nearly thirty when he went to work for the Esterházys, and had already written symphonies, string quartets, and sonatas; he was obviously exposed to and participated in the musical society he found while the court was in Vienna each winter, enabling him to hear considerable amounts of new music and interact with fellow composers and intellectuals in the salons of the day; and there was also both an extensive Esterházy musical library and keen interest on the part of his patrons to hear music by other composers.[3]

This brings us to the question of meaning: what did Haydn mean both by "original" and by "becoming original"? One possible interpretation is his clear interest in asserting priority in developing a musical style. Haydn's traditional kindly image makes this seem uncharacteristically ungenerous, yet in Haydn's own time he was considered not the merely humorous "Papa" the nineteenth century understood him to be, but a "father and reformer of noble music" and the "patriarch of new music."[4] Indeed, the *Allgemeine musikalische Zeitung* in 1798 asked younger composers to stop copying Haydn's characteristic symphonic techniques so that the style would not be diluted and devalued.[5] Haydn was always careful about which composers he claimed had influenced him: he was happy to tell Griesinger that "only Emanuel Bach was his model [*Vorbild*]" and to reject the rumor that Sammartini's influence can be heard in his earlier string quartets. Haydn went so far as to say that he had indeed heard Sammartini's music but thought he was a hack writer [*Schmierer*]. Griesinger himself claimed to be surprised when he heard the rumor from "a reliable source," because he "had never heard Haydn's originality doubted, especially in quartets."[6] Giuseppe Carpani mentioned the anecdote in his own biography, but assumed that the source of the rumor, the composer Josef Myslivecek, "went too far. Haydn's style, considered in its totality, is completely his own, completely new . . . "[7] Carpani even suggests that one reason for Haydn's originality is that he could not find a "maestro" willing to teach him counterpoint *gratis* during his early days in Vienna, but that this was a boon because "Haydn with such a teacher might have avoided some of the errors that befell him when writing for church or theater, but I respond: then he would have turned out to be less original in everything."[8]

Finally, we must ask: if studying the works of other composers and the rules of counterpoint would have made Haydn less "original," what did Haydn's originality mean to the many contemporary critics who commented either favorably or unfavorably upon it? How was the term generally understood in this period? Originality was linked, in the second half of the eighteenth century, with far-reaching debates about imitation, imagination, and genius, about the relationship between following one's fantasy and "following the rules." Yet at the same time it could be seen as mere eccentricity, as a taste for the bizarre, Haydn's desire to see what "created an impression" interpreted as the straining after effect. Thus, when the earliest English biographical notice of Haydn appeared in 1784, his music was praised as "*original, masterly,* and *beautiful.*" But the context for this praise was a defense against the criticisms of northern German pamphlets, "alledging his works [to be] too flighty, trifling, and wild, and accusing him at the same time as the inventor of a new musical doctrine, and introducing a species of sounds totally unknown in that country."[9] Those critics argued not only that his music was too eccentric but that it was incorrect, especially in breaking rules about parallel octaves and in breaching decorum by mixing comic and serious styles in the same work. To German critics, the moral of Carpani's anecdote would have been the opposite: there is no advantage in not having had a good teacher.

Although arguments over "following the rules" go back to antiquity—there are quite a few rhetorical figures which depend for their effect upon breaking rules—and arguments pairing genius and rules go back at least to the Renaissance,[10] the principal focus of such debates in their eighteenth-century incarnation was Shakespeare.The vogue for translations and performances sweeping Europe during the second half of the century forced critics in an era obsessed with dramatic proprieties to confront Shakespearean breadth, structure, morality, and characters. Commentators who tested Shakespeare against the rules of drama, especially the unities, split one of two ways: in the French-influenced precincts of Gottsched (and Frederick the Great), Shakespeare was found wanting; by the lights of Lessing or in the *Sturm und Drang*-associated notions of original genius (*Originalgenie*) promulgated by Herder and Goethe, he was found vastly to supersede the classical rules. Shakespeare was a touchstone: critics' reactions to him instantly place them within the larger debates of the time. In fact, it is remarkable the degree to which critical responses to Shakespeare among German writers (an absorbing tale in itself, with echoes elsewhere in Europe), correlate with critical responses to Haydn. Moreover, the features of Haydn's "originality" that elicited the strongest responses—his mixture of serious and comic elements, of high and low styles, in a single instrumental work—are precisely the features of Shakespeare's plays that eighteenth-century critics had most difficulty confronting. Haydn and

Shakespeare were regarded with suspicion in the same quarters for largely the same reasons, including an inappropriate "caprice."

This essay will first examine Haydn's attitudes to rules, as well as the apparent conflict between genius and rule and the ways in which originality intersects with both. I will then chart the changing responses to Shakespeare and to Haydn and discuss the comparisons made between Haydn and Shakespeare by both German and English critics, especially as they relate to originality. Then I will explore Haydn's connection to theatrical productions, especially of Shakespeare plays, as one important source for Haydn's "original" style. Finally, I will consider several works in which Haydn deliberately cast aside "rules," in order to explore rhetorical ideas of originality that call attention to themselves in this way. To anticipate my conclusions, I will suggest that the "rules" plot a continuum from the narrowly defined and venerable "laws" (dissonance treatment or voice leading, for example) to broadly conceived senses of decorum which would be violated by, say, antithetical uses of serious and comic elements; that this continuum embodied precisely the kinds of rules operating in rhetoric and the theater; and that Haydn, at the end of his composing life and in the era of Beethoven's ascendancy, was seeking not only priority, but recognition of his own status as a genius.

Haydn and Rules

Haydn, in conversations with his biographers Georg August Griesinger and Albert Christoph Dies, struck several contradictory poses about rules. His remarks about actual instances of composing see him invoking rules, but his more general aesthetic remarks suggest that he found them both insufficient and petty. As we will see, there appear to be at least two kinds of rules and three sources of rules, two of them legitimate. Here he is, composing at the keyboard, conjuring with rules:

> I sat down and began to fantasize, according to whether my mood was sad or happy, serious or playful. Once I had caught hold of an idea, my entire effort went toward working it out and sustaining it according to the rules of art.[11]

But he also told Griesinger that he was able to withstand criticism by "strict theoreticians" who objected to many things but especially his "comical trifling," for he

> soon convinced himself that an anxious compliance with the rules often produces works that are the most lacking in taste and feeling, that mere arbitrariness had branded many things as rules, and that in music the only thing absolutely forbidden is what offends a delicate ear.[12]

Similarly, when told that Albrechtsberger wanted to banish fourths from the strict style, Haydn responded:

> What does that mean? Art is free, and will be limited by no artisan's fetters [*Handwerksfesseln*]. The ear, assuming that it is educated, must decide, and I hold myself to be as competent as anyone to give rules here.[13]

Significant here is his opposition of art and craft (*Kunst* and *Handwerk*), of what guides the artist but constrains the artisan. He had come a long way from the remark in his autobiographical sketch of 1776 that "I wrote diligently, but not quite correctly, until at last I had the good fortune to learn the true fundamentals of composition from the celebrated Herr Porpora."[14]

Several other comments in the biographies of Griesinger and Dies reflect Haydn's sense that rules were arbitrary, small-minded, or excessively restrictive to a "free spirit." Here Haydn again uses the term *Fesseln*, fetters, to describe his objections to Kirnberger's treatise on strict composition. Haydn aimed to touch the heart, according to Dies, and although he wanted his music to be "correct," he was willing to bend the rules:

> If I found something to be beautiful, so that the ear and the heart in my opinion could be satisfied, and I would have had to sacrifice such beauty to withered pedantry, then I would rather let stand a little grammatical slip.[15]

Clearly, beauty must take precedence over correctness. This venerable idea goes back to antiquity: Longinus asked the rhetorical question, in *On the Sublime*, "Which is the better in poetry and in prose, grandeur with a few flaws or correct composition of mediocre quality, yet entirely sound and impeccable?"[16] Even Rameau, associated in later minds with the rules of harmony, wrote "There is a world of difference between a music without fault and a perfect music."[17] When asked point-blank by Dies about whether he relied on a system or even made up his own rules to ensure popular approval, Haydn replied:

> I never thought about that in the heat of composing; I wrote what seemd to me good, and corrected it afterward according to the laws of harmony. Other tricks I have never used. Several times I took the liberty not of offending the ear, of course, but of breaking the usual textbook rules, and wrote above those places with the words *con licenza*.[18]

Of those critics who decried his errors and pointed to the Austrian musical theorist and composer Fux, Haydn continued, he asked if their ears could discern the mistakes; they were forced to admit they could not. Dies triumphantly concluded that, since Haydn's con licenza was applauded by connoisseurs abroad—indeed, evoked the wonderment that works of genius inspire—and smiled at by local composers, he could properly be thought of as the free artist praised by Horace and Schiller, unconstrained by the past or by academicism.

Finally, Griesinger identified what Haydn considered to be the requirements for a good piece of music:

> His theoretical raisonnements were very simple: a piece of music should have a flowing melody [*Gesang*], coherent ideas, no superfluous ornaments [*Schnörkeleyen*], nothing overdone, no confusing accompaniment, and so forth. How to satisfy these requirements? That, he confessed himself, cannot be learned by rules, and simply depends on natural talent and on the inspiration of inborn genius.[19]

In this respect, Haydn joined many eighteenth-century voices, among them Rameau and Heinrich Christoph Koch, who considered melody to be difficult or impossible to teach because it was dependent upon innate qualities.[20]

Thus there are two kinds of rules: the rules of art, which are true, broad, and deep, and the "guild" rules of strict counterpoint and harmony. Moreover, there are two *legitimate* sources of rules: the realm of art [*Kunst*] and the artist himself and his educated ear. The tradition and texts that sanctioned the laws of counterpoint and harmony may be invoked only selectively, lest they lead to a narrowing of vision. A composer's originality, then, may be connected to his willingness to depart from "textbook rules" for aesthetic reasons and on the basis of his "free spirit," even "genius"—a word Haydn stopped short of actually applying to himself, but which was certainly applied to him by Dies and many others. Indeed, genius [*Genie*] and spirit (*Geist*) are semantically and philosophically linked.

Originality and Genius

Kant memorably put genius together with both rules and originality in his *Critique of Judgment* of 1790:

> Genius is the talent (natural endowment) which gives the rule to art . . .
> (1) Genius is a talent for producing something for which no determinate rule can be given, not a predisposition consisting of a skill for something that can be learned by following some rule or other; hence the foremost property of genius must be *originality*.
> (2) Since nonsense too can be original, the products of genius must also be models, i.e., they must be *exemplary*; . . . they must serve . . . as a standard or rule by which to judge.
> (3) Genius itself cannot describe or indicate scientifically how it brings about its products, and it is rather as nature that it gives the rule. That is why, if an author owes a product to his genius, he himself does not know how he came upon the ideas for it; . . . Indeed, that is presumably why the word genius is derived from (Latin) *genius*, [which means] the guardian and guiding spirit that each person is given as his own at birth, and to whose inspiration [*Eingebung*] those original ideas are due.
> (4) Nature, through genius, prescribes the rule not to science but to art, and this also only insofar as the art is to be fine art.[21]

Thus, rhetorical *invention*, the source of artistic ideas, cannot be explained; even the genius does not know how his ideas arose. Griesinger claimed "in Haydn there was complete confirmation of Kant's observation" on this point.[22] In the attitude toward rules in this discussion, Kant might have been following the lead of Lessing, whose brilliant criticism in the ground-breaking *Hamburg Dramaturgy* had argued over twenty years before that genius "laughs at boundary lines drawn by critics": "O you manufacturer of rules, how little do you understand art, and how little do you possess of genius which creates the ideal, on which you make [the rules] and which can break [the rules] as often as it likes!" Genius, Lessing asserted, is the "only source for perfection in drama."[23]

The most important and widely-read discussion of originality in the eighteenth century was Edward Young's *Conjectures on Original Composition*, which appeared in English in 1759 and within a year had been twice translated into German. In England its topic was quite familiar, part of an ongoing debate, but in Germany it was all news.[24] To Young, author also of the influential series of poems *Night Thoughts*, which Haydn owned in German, originality emerged as the "fairest flower" of the mind of a man of genius, though it has not escaped notice that Young never is able to define it.[25] He can, however, compare it favorably to imitation, which comprises imitation of nature and of authors:

> An *Original* may be said to be of a *vegetable* nature; it rises spontaneously, from the vital root of Genius; it *grows*, it is not *made*: *Imitations* are often a sort of *manufacture* wrought up by those *Mechanics*, *Art*, and *Labour*, out of preexistent materials not their own.[26]

Modern artists have a choice about whether they will follow models and follow rules; in order to be original they need to look within and cultivate their own genius. Young proclaims an opposition between Genius and Learning: the latter is the "instrument" leading to knowledge of the past and its imitation. Learning is a "great Lover of Rules, and Boaster of famed Examples" but is clearly not enough: "For unprescribed beauties, and unexampled Excellence, which are Characteristics of *Genius*, lie without the Pale of *Learning's Authorities*, and Laws. . . . Rules, like Crutches, are a needful aid to the Lame, tho' an Impediment to the Strong."[27] Not only is Learning placed second to Genius, but its purpose is to "fling light on the works of Genius, and point out its Charms." And finally, "Learning is borrowed knowledge; Genius is knowledge innate": here is the distinction between the original and the imitation in a nutshell.[28] Thus we have an organic model of genius, from which originality blossoms, although Genius is also compared to a radiant star (which Learning points out); such a "Star of the first magnitude among the Moderns was *Shakespeare*; among the Antients, *Pindar*." Moreover, Shakespeare was lucky not to be hampered by too much learning, because he might have "thought less, if he had read more," or been partly extinguished by the "oppression" of it. Young concludes that Shakespeare was "as learned as his dramatic province required; for whatever learning he wanted, he was master of two books, unknown to many of the profoundly read . . . the book of Nature, and that of Man."[29] In this way, he exemplified the "Adult Genius [who] comes out of nature's hand," unlike the "Infantine Genius [who] must be nursed and educated."

The notion of being "oppressed" by learning is memorably expressed in the first person by the writer and artist Salomon Gessner, author of the celebrated prose *Idylls* (1756), who admitted in a "Letter on Landscape Painting":

> Yet when I applied myself long to the study of particular masters, I found too great a degree of timidity oppress my native powers. Occupied by their beauties, and impressed with the humblest idea of my own talents, I despaired of equalling, or even approaching the excellence they had attained. My imagination, filled by their images, and occupied by their scenery, lost its inventive powers. I observed how imitation suppresses the warmth of genius and the boldness of fancy.[30]

Although in some respects Young elaborates arguments already made by Addison nearly fifty years before—the distinction between the natural and learned genius, and the burden that learning places on developing genius—the critical nexus between natural genius and Shakespeare was not formed in Germany until the first German translations of the *Spectator* in 1739–43 and Pope's *Essay on Criticism* in 1741. These translations, together with the first translation of Shakespeare in the same year (*Julius Caesar*, 1741), prepared the field to receive both the first attacks on Shakespeare and what turned out to be Young's and then Lessing's thunderbolts. Explorations in German of genius, originality, and rules now had Shakespeare as their measure.

Shakespeare in Germany and Austria

The period I want to demarcate in Shakespeare criticism is almost exactly that of Haydn's lifetime, from Gottsched in 1730 to Schlegel in 1809.[31] Johann Christoph Gottsched (1700–66) was an extraordinarily influential if posthumously ridiculed figure, who claimed that the French neoclassical tragedies of Corneille and Racine and their rationalist underpinnings should be the model for German drama because the transmission of moral values is the most important goal for drama. The rigidity of the rules by which such plays were written, especially the unities of place, time, and action, had an impeccable pedigree: Aristotle's call for unity of action was elevated to an elaborate series of unities in the Italian Renaissance, and then formulated further by late seventeenth-century theorists like Boileau. But

Gottsched's project was not only moral uplift. According to Nicholas Boyle, Gottsched's *Critical Art of Poetry* of 1730

> is the moment at which the drama emerges as Germany's alternative to the novel, the alternative, that is, to the literary form in which England's increasingly confident bourgeoisie learns in the eighteenth century to represent and interpret itself to itself and for which the social foundation is simply non-existent in Germany at the time. . . . Gottsched did more than advocate the courtly virtues of propriety and regularity for a theatre characterized by crudity and improvisation. He also . . . identified the drama . . . as the focal point for several different national ambitions: the moral and intellectual edification of all, the improvement of the German language, and the establishment of a national literature of European status.[32]

Gottsched was appalled by *Julius Caesar* in Caspar Wilhelm von Borcke's translation (1741), to the point of saying "the vilest improvised burlesque [*Haupt- und Staatsaktion*] of our common Comedians is scarcely so full of blunders and errors against the rules of drama and sound reason as this play by Shakespeare."[33] He was especially critical of the "throwing-together" of farcical scenes involving "workmen and rabble," "rogues and scalawags" with serious scenes in which the "greatest Roman heroes" are occupied with affairs of state. Because the French cultural model held sway in German lands from Berlin to Vienna, Gottsched's view was considered normative even when attacked, as it was in sustained fashion from 1759 on. But it did not die; consider this extreme echo from Frederick the Great's book on German literature, published in 1780:

> To convince yourself of the lack of taste which has reigned in Germany until our day, you need only go to the public spectacles. There you will see presented the abominable works of Shakespeare, translated into our language; the whole audience goes into raptures when it listens to these ridiculous farces worthy of the savages of Canada. I describe them in these terms because they sin against all the rules of the theater, rules which are not at all arbitrary.
>
> Look at the porters and gravediggers who come on stage and make speeches worthy of them; after them come the kings and queens. How can such a jumble of lowliness and grandeur, of buffoonery and tragedy, be touching and pleasing?

> One can pardon Shakespeare for these bizarre errors; the beginning of the arts is never their point of maturity.
>
> But then look at [Goethe's] *Götz von Berlichingen* making its appearance on stage. A detestable imitation of these bad English pieces, while the public applauds and enthusiastically demands the repetition of these disgusting stupidities.[34]

Because of the growing interest in English literature throughout the century, other more positive voices were raised throughout the 1750s, voices that began to see virtues in Shakespeare that reflected English criticism in such venues as Addison's *Spectator*. Addison had described two categories of geniuses, the "natural genius" who is "born not made"—a category including Homer, Pindar, the poets of the Hebrew Bible, and Shakespeare—and the geniuses "that have formed themselves by rules, and submitted the greatness of their natural talents to the corrections and restraints of art"—a group including Plato, Virgil, and Milton.[35] This thought was echoed by Pope in his edition of Shakespeare, that "If ever any author deserved the name of an *Original*, it was Shakespear [sic]. . . . [H]e is not so much an Imitator, as an Instrument of Nature. . . . "[36] An anonymous German pamphlet of 1753 appeared in Frankfurt and Leipzig that described Shakespeare in the same terms, virtually quoting Pope (in the sequel to the quotation above) that he does not speak through nature, she speaks through him.[37] Moreover, he can't be judged by the rules of Aristotle because they were unknown to him. Nicolai referred to him in 1755 as a man "without knowledge of the rules, without erudition, without orderliness, [who] owes the greater part of his fame to the diversity and strength of his characters."[38] Even the philosopher Moses Mendelssohn wrote about Shakespeare, citing his "sublimity" arising from unsuspected and surprising moments and the fact that in a play like *Othello* there isn't a single rule from Horace's *Ars poetica* left standing.[39]

With Lessing's attack on Gottsched and the "rules" of drama, Shakespeare criticism enters a new phase. As Herder wrote in his obituary of Lessing in 1781, "I believe that no recent writer has had more impact in Germany concerning matters of taste and the finer basic judgment of literature than Lessing."[40] Gotthold Ephraim Lessing (1729–81) threw out Corneille and Racine as a model for German drama, finding that Shakespeare is a better exemplar of the cathartic effect of tragedy and hence, ironically, closer to the ancients.[41] In the course of wide-ranging discussions of virtually every topic relevant to a thoughtful national theater, he compared Voltaire unfavorably to Shakespeare and invoked Lope de Vega and Wieland to praise the mixture of serious and comic characters as a reflection of nature. He also spoke passionately on the kind of music needed for plays, in the twenty-sixth and -seventh parts of the *Hamburg Dramaturgy*.

The profound effect of Lessing's writings on theater in general and Shakespeare in particular was enhanced by the translations of twenty-two plays made by Christoph Martin Wieland between 1762 and 1766.[42] Yet Wieland's literal and often heavyhanded and over-explanatory prose (only *A Midsummer's Night's Dream* was done in verse) was not ideal for performance, and his translations were hardly ever ventured in that form. A single example will transmit their flavor. The famous line in Hamlet's soliloquy, "To die, to sleep; to sleep, perchance to dream," is easily rendered literally, as in Schröder's slightly later translation: "—Sterben, schlafen. — Schlafen? Vielleicht auch träumen." But Wieland has it: " — Sterben — Schlafen — Doch vielleicht auch etwas mehr — wie wenn es träumen wäre?"[43] The first full review of Wieland, by Heinrich Wilhelm von Gerstenberg—the poet and playwright who was later to set Hamlet's soliloquy to a keyboard fantasia by C. P. E. Bach—is a remarkable defense of Shakespeare that at the same time roundly criticizes the translation. Emphasizing Shakespeare's central contribution as the full and passionate representation of character, Gerstenberg "suggests a revision of the relationship between author, play and audience. . . . Instead of being the passive object of the writer's eloquence, the audience by this new theory [of being carried away by the drama's illusion, the creation of illusion being the province of genius] is called on to take part, imaginatively, in the events shown in the play."[44]

Just as Lessing was concerned with the principles of theater and drama and the formation of a national theater in Hamburg, the Viennese intellectual Joseph von Sonnenfels (1732–1817) also wrote a series of responses to productions of the day, in a series of journalistic articles published in the 1760s, as *Letters on the Viennese Stage*.[45] Theater in Austria was contested ground in the 1750s and 60s: Maria Theresia moved in several steps toward the imposition of full censorship in 1765. After various restrictions since the early 1750s failed to bring the freewheeling comedies of *Hanswurst* and other popular clownlike figures sufficiently under Imperial control, she finally banned improvisation in the theater in 1769. In 1770 she appointed Sonnenfels himself as censor. [46] Sonnenfels was a supporter of the unities, as were Viennese critics generally, but he was willing to loosen them somewhat: twenty-four hours could be extended to thirty-six hours, and the unity of place might be expanded to include adjacent spaces if the change took place during the intermission.[47] And while he was less than thrilled by Shakespeare, especially his abandonment of the rules of drama and the unfortunate mixtures of heroism and slapstick, Sonnenfels was cognizant of his "venturing genius" [*abenteuerliche Genie*], as when he notes the "daring and beautiful" features of *Macbeth* or gives a mixed report like this:

> Shakespeare's plays are always monsters where the hero, who only just now appeared [dressed] in gold and purple, turns toward the tavern with the most vulgar speech, wherein verisimilitude, morals, and propriety are violated; [the plays] should, with all the fire of [their] tragic genius, be admired rather than imitated.[48]

It is interesting to see a Viennese critic thus giving vent to a modified Gottschedian view, because it reminds us of the tenacious hold of French theater in Vienna. Sonnenfels' desire for a German national theater in Vienna was realized in 1776, when Joseph II opened what was to be its short-lived incarnation in the Burgtheater.

Perhaps an appropriate assessment of the state of Shakespeare criticism at this moment requires the sober English words of Hugh Blair, whose *Lectures on Rhetoric and Belles Lettres*, given at Edinburgh in the 1750s and 1760s, were published in 1783:

> Instances, I admit, there are, of some works that contain gross transgressions of the laws of Criticism, acquiring, nevertheless, a general, and even a lasting admiration. Such are the Plays of Shakespeare, which, considered as dramatic poems, are irregular in the highest degree. But then we are to remark, that they have gained the public admiration, not by their being irregular, not by their transgression of the rules of art, but in spite of such transgressions. They possess other beauties which are conformable to just rules; and the force of these beauties has been so great as to overpower all censure, and to give the public a degree of satisfaction superior to the disgust arising from their blemishes. Shakespeare pleases, not by his bringing the transactions of many years into one play; not by his grotesque mixture of tragedy and comedy in one piece; nor by the strained thoughts, and affected witticisms, which he sometimes employs. These we consider as blemishes, and impute them to the gross-

> ness of the age in which he lived. But he pleases by his animated and masterly representations of characters, by the liveliness of his descriptions, the force of his sentiments, and his possessing, beyond all writers, the natural language of passion: Beauties which Criticism no less teaches us to place in the highest rank, than nature teaches us to feel.[49]

One wonders, is "pleasingness" really strong enough to counter "disgust"? Are we being told that Brutus is an honorable man? And who is "the public," as a standard-bearer of taste?

With Herder and Goethe, we enter the period of the *Sturm und Drang*, the so-called *Geniezeit*, in which Shakespeare is seen as a force of nature, and is adduced in the service of far-ranging theories of the origins of language and art. Here we do not read of Shakespeare's "pleasingness." Johann Gottfried Herder's (1744–1803) writings on poetry, and the German language and folk music, connect such elements as *Kraft* (power, as in the essential power of man and poetry), *Besonnenheit* (the power of reflection, self-possession), *Ursprünglichkeit* (originality in the sense of springing up from origins, the primitive originary state), and *Genie* (creating from origins, whether genius of a language or of a people, on the one hand, or *Originalgenie*, on the other).[50] Herder also introduces a new term into German criticism, namely *Volkstümlichkeit*, or popularity: standards for art and for criticism should be drawn not merely from the taste of a literary elite but from congruence with "the essence, the conception, the feelings of the uncultivated, naive people."[51] This has real meaning for an era in which composers sought the norms of tastes outside the court and were forced to reconcile the two strands of their audience, the so-called *Kenner* (connoisseurs) and *Liebhaber* (amateurs). In the last of three versions of a Shakespeare essay (1771), Herder was at pains to show how drama arises from its social and historical circumstances: the simplicity of Greek life, times, religion led to a naturally evolved series of living rules for drama.[52] Shakespeare may be seen as a similar product of his times:

> Shakespeare found around him anything but that simplicity of national customs, deeds, tastes, and historical traditions, that formed the Greek drama. . . . Shakespeare found no chorus there; but he did find historical and marionette plays—well then! Out of such historical and marionette plays, such poor clay! he moulded the splendid creation that stands and lives before us![53]

One must conclude, then, that the messiness of Shakespeare's plays reflects his times and genres, and that the resulting sense of eventfulness (*Begebenheit*, as opposed to the smaller treatment of action, or *Handlung*, in Greek drama) is what helps to overwhelm the audience with "the illusion of truth."

For the young Goethe, reading Shakespeare was the stuff of blinding revelation, not "orderly" thoughts. In a speech about him at a birthday tribute in 1771, he said: "The first page I read made me a slave to Shakespeare for life. And when I had finished reading the first drama, I stood there like a man blind from birth whom a magic hand has all at once given light."[54] After a diatribe about the "burdensome fetters on our imagination" that observing the unities mandates, and about the "self-parodying" French, Goethe defended Shakespeare against charges that his characters are offensive, crying "Nature! Nature! Nothing is so like Nature as Shakespeare's figures. . . . Shakespeare competes with Prometheus, imitating him by forming human beings feature by feature, but on a colossal scale—that is why we don't recognize them as our brothers. Then he brings them to life by breathing his spirit into them. He speaks through them all, and we recognize the kinship."[55] Indeed, with subjectivity of this magnitude, the only way to approach Goethe is by quotation. His ringing conclusion shows the centrality both of Shakespeare and of art to the life of a young artist:

> To work, gentlemen! Take your trumpets and drive forth those noble souls from the Elysium of so-called good taste, where, drowsy in monotonous twilight, they live, yet do not live; have passions in their hearts but no marrow in their bones, and, because they are not tired enough to rest and yet too lazy to act, they stroll aimlessly among the myrtles and laurels, idling and yawning away their shadowy lives.[56]

Shakespeare thus represents artistic commitment. He was also a convenient source of character and of such paradigmatic scenes as balcony and graveyard.[57]

In the ensuing decades, Shakespeare remained a preoccupation for Goethe and Schiller, although their attitude changed somewhat, partly as a result of their producing some of his plays at Weimar, and partly as an issue in their own writings. Goethe wrote extensively about *Hamlet* in his *Wilhelm Meister* books (the earlier version, *Wilhelm Meisters theatralische Sendung*, finished before 1783, introduced most of the commentary that appeared in the later version, *Wilhelm Meisters*

Lehrjahre of 1795–96). And in his production of *Julius Caesar*, Goethe added a pageant-filled funeral procession for Caesar, in order to help the "masses" understand the play.[58] At various times, Goethe's remarks suggest that he found aspects of Shakespeare, especially his forms, troubling, and that perhaps it would be better simply to read him. Schiller actually admitted, in his *Naive and Sentimental Poetry* of 1795–96, that he did not need to apologize for his critical youthful view of Shakespeare—"incensed by his coldness, the insensitivity which permitted him to jest in the midst of the highest pathos, to interrupt the heart-rending scenes in *Hamlet*, in *King Lear*, in *Macbeth*, etc., with a Fool; restraining himself now where my sympathies rushed in, then coldbloodedly tearing himself away where my heart would have gladly lingered"—because the critics of the time had published similar views.[59] Yet he came fully to appreciate the artistry of Shakespeare.

To the Romantic generation of Ludwig Tieck and August Wilhelm Schlegel, among other important critics born at the beginning of the *Sturm und Drang*, Shakespeare's value is never in question. In an essay of 1793, Tieck describes his "treatment of the marvelous," looking at the ways in which Shakespeare creates the illusion of spirit realms in *The Tempest* and *Midsummer's Night's Dream*, as well as in *Hamlet* and *Macbeth*. In the former two a complete alternate world is created, with a profound sense of almost dreamlike unreality, while in the tragedies the spirit world is a more menacing background presence.[60] Schlegel also discussed oppositions, though not between the real and the marvelous: his essay on *Romeo and Juliet*, published in Schiller's journal *Die Horen* in 1797, sees it as "one great antithesis,"[61] produced by a supremely reflective artist who is deliberate, self-conscious, and systematic. For example, the problematic characters Mercutio and the Nurse act as foils to Romeo's and Juliet's characters and situations, respectively, which mitigates the comic/tragic dichotomy, just as the antagonism of the minor characters balances that of the feuding families.[62] Thus for Schlegel, who went on to make verse translations of seventeen plays and give a series of lectures in 1809 (published and widely translated), Shakespeare is an artist fully aware of his art and craft, not an instinctive, uncultivated genius. The wild original has come in from the state of nature.

After the early Romantics, Shakespeare's plays were no longer considered an issue; one didn't have to take sides or to offer a synthesis of their meaning. The striking parallels to Haydn's posthumous influence and reputation make this assessment by Roy Pascal rather poignant:

> [Shakespeare] ceases to enthrall writers [after 1815]. A taste for Shakespeare existed side by side with a quite different taste in contemporary literature. He is studied for the depth of his knowledge of human nature, for the artistry of his technique. . . . But while many authors still show traces of his influence, in their best works they emancipate themselves from him. . . . Above all, the growing popularity of the problem play, of plays composed round the needs of each generation, makes the practice of the nineteenth century more and more remote from the method of Shakespeare.[63]

The primary image we develop, in evaluating the course of Shakespeare reception from Gottsched to Schlegel, is that of the life cycle of a person: Shakespeare grows up. He starts out an unruly rule-breaking disobedient youth; grows into a brilliantly uncultivated young man with extraordinary instincts and untutored originality; emerges into a maturely reflective artist; and subsides into a venerated old age.

Haydn's Critics and Haydn as Shakespeare

Mixed in with the growing acclaim for Haydn's works in the 1760s and 1770s were a number of nay-saying responses primarily emanating from the centers of the German periodical literature in the north—Berlin, Hamburg, and Leipzig. Rarely written by such cogent, witty, and wide-ranging intellects as the commentators on Shakespeare, they stung him just the same. And the fact that laudatory writers made reference to these attacks (for example, the *European Magazine* in 1784, Charles Burney's *A General History of Music* in 1789, and Ernst Ludwig Gerber's *Tonkünstler-Lexikon* in 1790) suggests that they created a *cause célèbre*. The decade from 1766 to 1776 was particularly full of such criticisms, ranging from mild reproach to frontal assault. In a number of these, the whole Viennese style is condemned, with Haydn merely given pride of place. The same period is demarcated by two defensive strikes, beginning with the lengthy article in the *Wiener Diarium* detailing the glories of "the Viennese Taste in Music" (1766), and ending with Haydn's autobiographical sketch (1776). Both were critical of the critics and forthright in singing Haydn's praises: in the former Haydn is called "the darling of our nation"; in the latter Haydn asserts that "in the chamber style" he had pleased almost all nations except the Berliners, who "in one weekly paper . . . praise me to the skies, whilst in another they dash me sixty fathoms deep into the earth. . . ."[64]

It is interesting to consider that this decade was also precisely coextensive with Haydn's first as full Kapellmeister after the death of his predecessor Werner, to whom he had been second in command for five years; the period in which Nicolaus built and then moved the court to isolated Eszterháza, with a concomitant expansion in theatrical life; and the period enclosing the so-called *Sturm und Drang* style, a period whose boundaries and meanings are still contested by scholars (who can agree only that many works reveal quirky passion and original effects).[65] A retrospective view of the problem various critics had with the Viennese and Mannheim style is given by Charles Burney, in his *General History of Music* in 1789:

> [Haydn's] innumerable symphonies, quartets, and other instrumental pieces, which are so original and so difficult, have the advantage of being rehearsed and performed at Esterhasi under his own direction. . . . . Ideas so new and so varied were not at first so universally admired in Germany as at present. The critics in the northern parts of the empire were up in arms. And a friend at Hamburg wrote me word in 1772, "the genius, fine ideas, and fancy of Haydn, Ditters, and Filtz, were praised, but their mixture of serious and comic was disliked, particularly as there is more of the latter than the former in their works; and as for rules, they knew but little of them. . . ."[66]

The principal rule-based objections to Haydn included his invention of melodies played in parallel octaves between the first violin and a lower stringed instrument (like "father and son begging")[67] and "errors of composition, especially of phrase-rhythm, and for the most part a great ignorance of counterpoint."[68] The larger stylistic objection can be summed up in a single rhetorical idea: an inappropriate combination of levels, which violates decorum. Johann Adam Hiller's *Weekly Reports on Music* calls it Haydn's "odd mixture of styles, of the serious and the comic, of the lofty and the vulgar, so often found side by side in one and the same piece." This thought is echoed by several other writers.[69] Like many of his colleagues, Hiller does not like minuets in larger works because they break up the mood, and is even more put out when those minuets display learned technique, such as canon. Symphonies, the composer Johann Abraham Peter Schulz argued in 1774, exemplify the grand style, and its movements must have characters suited to the "dignity" of the symphony;[70] clearly, representations of the world of dance did not qualify, and we typically find no minuets in symphonies by C. P. E. Bach and his North-German contemporaries.

Gretchen Wheelock has identified a review from Hiller's *Musical Reports and Observations from the Year 1770* to be the first actually to apply these concerns to specific Haydn works (Symphonies 17, 29, 28, 9, and 3, plus one spurious symphony rightly suspected by the reviewer), and she shows exactly what offended against "correct stylistic manners."[71] These include the "laughable manner" in which the melody is split up between the first and second violins in the Andante of Symphony 29 (an attractively cooperative venture which would have been interpreted, according to Wheelock, as tampering with the idea of "melody as song; fragmentation of a tune in motivic play violates its vocal integrity, and thus, by North German standards, its expressive coherence");[72] overlapping phrases without clear tonic arrival (in the "silly trio" of Symphony 28); and abuses of decorum in the contrast of comic and serious styles in the Poco Adagio of Symphony 28 (the middle-register main theme with walking bass giving way, phrase after phrase, to high-register, staccato, dotted rhythms that later accelerate).

These charges, considered serious in Germany, were turned into a greater *cause célèbre* by the glowing biography of Haydn published in the *European Magazine and London Review for October, 1784*. As mentioned in the first section of this essay, Haydn was defended against these charges:

> [W]e now behold Haydn outstrip all his competitors. And as envy never fails to pursue merit, the masters in Germany were so jealous of his rising fame, that they entered into a combination against him in order to decry his works and ridicule his compositions; nay they even carried it so far as to write against him; and many pamphlets in the German language appeared in print to depreciate him in the public esteem, alledging his works were too flighty, trifling, and wild, accusing him at the same time as the inventor of a new musical doctrine, and introducing a species of sounds totally unknown to that country. In the last position they were perfectly right: he had indeed introduced a new species of music: it was his own, totally unlike what they had been used to—*original, masterly*, and *beautiful*.[73]

The writer went on to claim that C. P. E. Bach attacked Haydn as well, and that Haydn took revenge upon his enemies by parodying their styles in his Sonatas Hob.XVI:21–26 and 27–32 (singled out in the biography are Nos. 22/ii and 23). When this biography was published in German the following year, C. P. E. Bach refuted the unfounded charges in a letter to a Hamburg newspaper, writing "I must believe that this worthy gentleman, whose work still gives me much pleasure, is certainly my friend in the same way as I am his." Whether Haydn intentionally copied and "burlesqued" the styles of Bach and others is a matter of debate.[74]

Hiller also provides a remarkable and explicitly theatrical metaphor for the mixture of styles, based on his evident distaste for the stock character of Viennese improvised comedy: "Nowadays we hear so many concertos, symphonies, etc., that in their measured and magnificent tones allow us to perceive the dignity of music; but before one suspects it, in springs Hans Wurst, right into the middle of things; and the more serious the emotion that had immediately preceded his arrival, the more he arouses our sympathy with his vulgar antics."[75] Hiller thus hears or interprets the staged entrance of an actual comic character in a piece of instrumental music, rather than a topical reference to a particular style. Whether he would be willing to personify the "dignified" character of the opening is unclear. Does he mean that one may listen to the serious music without having to swerve into a type of "spectatorship" until Hans Wurst uncomfortably appears and makes it impossible not to do so? But he does imply a mode of "theatrical listening" in which musical segments become agents of the drama by causing interruptions in tone. This reflects a profound understanding—however couched in disparaging language—of one of Haydn's most original developments.[76]

A similar conclusion may be drawn from a radically different critique of Haydn, the comments by Karl Ludwig Junker (1748–1797) published in 1776 in his *Twenty Composers: A Sketch.* These comments are somewhat hostile, even though Junker supports Haydn in both his supposed "transgressions against the rules of counterpoint," claiming that rules can be too inhibiting to an artist, and his "octave doublings," which he finds makes things clearer. The importance of his evaluation (which was reprinted anonymously nearly twenty years later)[77] lies in its linkage of Haydn and Shakespeare, the earliest such reference known to me outside of the association of Haydn as composer of music to Shakespeare's plays (to be considered below). Junker's remarks appear in the article on Dittersdorf as well as on Haydn himself and are couched in language that is somewhat off the beaten path:

> (1) Since Hayde [sic] altered the tone of Viennese music, or set a new fashion, it is truly more characteristic than before, but it has sunk too much, from the dignity preserved by Wagenseil, to the trifling. Since Hayde, music has perhaps undergone the same change that the theater has endured, but it has certainly gained less in doing so.

> To arouse laughter was the latter's a
> the point when a Sonnenfels dared to po
> and proposals for the throne. . . . The co
> been banished from the theatrical sphe
> begged acceptance into music; the priest [Hay
> seems to be made for humor, was softened—se
> thing—and shoved her into his temple;—and eve
> laugh at Viennese music.[78]
>
> (2) No one will deny that the single governing sentime (because we are speaking of music) that the single governing feeling in Hayden [sic] is wayward, bizarre;—that it expresses itself without restraint. Does someone wish to refer to Hayden's *adagio*? Good, because it is serious, interest-engaging humor [*Laune*]; like the tragic sentiments of a Schakespear. . . .[79]

Junker thus explicitly connects Haydn's most characteristic moods with theater both comic, as in (1), and serious, even Shakespearean, as in (2), implying that theater always had comic and serious elements, whether because the Hanswurst reform which banned improvisation brought a greater degree of comedy into "regular plays," or because a play was by Shakespeare who always mixed them.[80] Junker personifies the comic figure as the "droll thing" now in the temple of music, where she calls attention to herself. And the sense of "caprice" contained in the word *Laune* used in conjunction with "bizarre" and "tragic" suggests a new kind of amalgam: a protean piece in which the audience will be engaged in figuring things out as well as reacting to them. Moreover, Junker links these ideas to the slow movement, the site for some of Haydn's most arresting ideas; in London, the slow movements were the most frequently encored parts of his symphonies. Mark Evan Bonds finds that humor is the way for the composer to insert himself into the music, and that contemporary comparisons of Haydn with Laurence Sterne reveal the permeability of artistic borders and the end of "aesthetic illusion."[81] I would like to argue that Hiller's and Junker's comments suggest that Haydn's contemporaries were aware that Haydn wrote music inspired by spoken plays, and that in such theatrically inspired pieces the composer may regard some of his instrumental movements as "scenes," and populate or interrupt them with active characters, sometimes conceived oppositionally.

Later writers who compare Haydn to Shakespeare, the majority of them English, include journalists and critics who write "Haydn, the Shakespeare of Music" as an automatic conferral of greatness, as part of their campaign to bring in audiences, or who genuinely believe

…n his breadth and power to be on the elevated plane of the …d. Two are more explicit, and reveal some of the range of the analogy. In the London *Morning Chronicle* of 12 March 1791 we read about the "first musical genius of the age":

> It is not wonderful that to souls capable of being touched by music, HAYDN should be an object of homage, and even of idolatry; for like our SHAKSPEARE, he moves and governs the passions at his will."[82]

And when Haydn received an honorary doctorate from Oxford, the correspondent for the *European Magazine* described him as:

> this musical Shakespeare—this musical Drawcansir, who can equal the strains of a Cherub, and enchant in all the gradations between those and a ballad—a genius whose versatility comprehends all the powers of harmony, and all the energy, pathos, and passion of melody! Who can stun with thunder, or warble with a bird![83]

Thus, Haydn had become the epitome of original genius: not only the Bard but also an adventurer, his works on a continuum from the most elevated (Cherub's singing) to the commonest (ballad), from the most scientific and learned (harmony) to the most inspired rule-free invention (melody), from the sublime (thunder) to the beautiful (birdsong).

There is a single anecdotal thirdhand report of Haydn comparing himself to Shakespeare. The French flautist Louis Drouet (1792–1873) visited Beethoven during a concert tour in 1816, and published a report of his meetings in a Hamburg newspaper many years later, in 1858. The article included this report of an exchange between Haydn and Beethoven:

> [Haydn to Beethoven, who had asked for an honest opinion about his first works:] [In] my opinion there will always be something—if not eccentric [*Verschrobenes*], then at any rate unusual in your works: one will find beautiful things in them, even admirable passages, but here and there something peculiar, dark, because you yourself are a little sinister and peculiar, and the style of the musician is always that of the person himself. Look at my compositions. You will often find something jovial about them, because that's the way I am; next to a serious thought you will find a cheerful one, as in Shakespeare's tragedies.[84]

The idea that the work reflects the person comes originally from the rhetorical idea of *ethos*, or character. Aristotle had identified three means of persuasion: *ethos*, arising from the speaker's personal qualities or character; *pathos*, arising from the audience's emotions as they react to the speech; and *logos*, the words of logical argument or proof.[85] Haydn was one of the first composers to be identified in these terms, as a person whose character—perceived as humorous, sunny—is manifested in his compositions. This view of course drastically simplifies, even falsifies, the picture.

The life-cycle nature of the Haydn criticism, which strikingly resembles the trajectory of Shakespeare reception in eighteenth-century Germany, worked ultimately to his detriment. As the critics caught up with his popularity, he went from being an error-ridden decorum-violator to being an original, mature, complex, elevated, yet always accessible artist.[86] The terms of his success laid the basis for the subsequent decline of his reputation. His very originality and priority, on the one hand, and *ethos* of good-humored character, on the other, led to his being relegated to "founder" status—kicked literally downstairs, as two images will reveal—where he would live on as the only earthbound member of the Viennese Classical Three. In 1808, the composer, traveller, and journalist Johann Reichardt, who had already proclaimed Haydn's new maturity in 1782, visited Vienna and compared Haydn, Mozart, and Beethoven in their string quartets. The image he uses is architectural: Haydn is the lovely summer house, Mozart the palace, Beethoven the defiant towers. Needless to say, each built in successive stages on top of the last.[87] In 1838 the writer Wolfgang Griepenkerl used a more musical image to describe the Three as part of a triad: "Haydn is the creator, the root, Mozart is the beautiful third, Beethoven the powerful fifth which impetuously rushes to all regions."[88] As with Shakespeare, Haydn was venerated, but had ceased to be a force.

Haydn and Shakespeare

Hiller and Junker placed the most original features of Haydn's style squarely in the theater, adducing the virtual polar opposites of Hanswurst and Shakespeare to characterize his unsettling innovations. In this, they help to remind us of two related and rather extraordinary facts. First, plays were put on at Eszterháza every day for six months of the year (April to October), beginning at least in 1769, and that Haydn was responsible for finding or composing appropriate orchestral music to be used as overtures and entr'actes. Drama-obsessed Nicolaus Esterházy hired some of the best companies to stage everything from improvised comedy to elevated tragedy; even before the court moved to Eszterháza, acting troupes visited Eisenstadt regularly. Second, Haydn was the first composer to be mentioned in conjunction with the first great flourishing of Shakespeare on the German stage. Not only did Nicolaus hire the celebrated company of Carl Wahr from 1772–1777 and sponsor the production of Shakespeare's tragedies, including *Hamlet, Macbeth, Othello,* and *King Lear*, but contemporary reports assert that Haydn wrote orchestral music for *Hamlet* in 1774. This music has never turned up. But it is highly probable that much of Haydn's symphonic music of that period was either originally destined for the stage, or composed with a view to possible later use as overtures and entr'actes, and that important dramatic and rhetorical features of his style can be understood in this light.[89]

Haydn's single known piece of theater music, to Regnard's 1694 comedy *Le distrait* (*Il distratto, Der Zerstreute*, the absent-minded man), was written for the Carl Wahr troupe in 1774; its overture, four entr'actes, and finale were immediately turned into a six-movement symphony, no. 60 in C major. The dramatically effective musical details have been evaluated elsewhere, in studies by Robert Green, Gretchen Wheelock, and myself, and here I will simply summarize the ways in which theatrical music required both breaking rules and the insertions of various active characters.[90] These techniques include inappropriate treatments (for example, expressive disparity between successive phrases, such as lyrical/martial or folk/"exotic," excessive extensions of phrase lengths or single chords); concatenations of melodies; linear successions of musical ideas without clear recapitulatory functions and with unrelated concluding passages; and abrogation of conventional tonal and formal arrangements. In effect, these are all violations of "rules" of convention and expectation.

Theatrical documents suggest that Haydn had either a friendship or a close professional relationship with Carl Wahr, who was by all accounts an extraordinary actor.[91] Wahr had played in Germany and even with Joseph Kurz (Bernardon) in Vienna, becoming principal of his own company in 1770 or 1771; because he was reputed never to perform improvised burlesques, his experience with Kurz is usually glossed over. Some accounts suggest that Wahr and Haydn were good friends, while theater journals identified Haydn as the music director of Wahr's troupe.[92] The *Gotha Theater-Kalender* of 1775 even commented that Haydn supplied the troupe with "appropriate music for the entr'actes of nearly every noteworthy play."[93] Moreover, the

Pressburger Zeitung featured an article from a correspondent at Eszterháza dated July 6, 1774, which implies that Haydn had either just written or was expected to write music for Shakespeare's *Hamlet*:

> Eszterhaz, 30 June: Persons of high rank from abroad . . . will stop at Eszterhaz for two days, inspecting everything of interest. . . . This evening there will be a German comedy, *Der Triumph der Freundschaft*, followed by a serenade and dinner. . . . Tomorrow evening is the Italian opera *L' infedeltà delusa*. The music is by Herr Kapellmeister Joseph Hayden. This outstanding musician recently composed, for Herr Wahr's company, original music to the comedy *Der Zerstreute*; connoisseurs consider it a masterpiece. One notices, this time in music intended for a comedy, the same spirit that elevates all of Hayden's work. His masterful variety excites the admiration of experts and is nothing short of delightful for the listener. . . . —We still look forward to hearing original music [*Man erwartet noch eigene Musik*] to Shakespeare's Hamlet by this adept composer.[94]

But the *Hamlet* performed in Haydn's milieu was quite different from the one familiar to modern audiences, and in order to bring full circle the connection made in this essay between Haydn and Shakespeare—from parallels in the history of criticism, to overt comparisons, to Haydn's actual experience with the "originality" of Shakespeare's plays—we need to imagine his Shakespeare, not our own. In fact, not until the early nineteenth century, with the Schlegel translations, were Shakespeare's tragedies seen in anything like their original version. Adaptations, often rather free ones, were the norm: imagine a *Romeo and Juliet,* as did playwright Christian Felix Weiße in 1767, that begins after Tybalt's death and after the marriage of the title characters.[95] Let us take *Hamlet* as a case in point.

The very first production of *Hamlet* on the German stage was the adaptation made by Franz von Heufeld that premiered in Vienna at the Kärntnerthortheater on January 16, 1773, during the same theatrical season that saw Viennese premieres of four other Shakespeare plays: *Macbeth* (adapted by Gottlieb Stephanie the younger, which opens with Malcolm and the English lords already in Scotland), *Romeo und Julia* (Weisse's version, further altered by Heufeld), *Die ländliche Hochzeitsfest* (*Midsummer Night's Dream* very loosely adapted by Christian Moll), and *Die lustigen Abentheuer an der Wien* (*The Merry Wives of Windsor*, given a new Viennese locale and context by Joseph Bernard Pelzel).[96] Heufeld, a bureaucrat and playwright, knew how to satisfy the public and the censor. His *Hamlet* was a success, repeated six times that season and staying in the repertory as a "Lieblingsstück."[97] It was also seen as more faithful to Shakespeare than some of the other adaptations in that he based the text on Wieland's prose, except for the rhyming verse in Alexandrines for the play-within-a-play, "The Murder of Gonzaga." Heufeld adapted the play to accord with the prevailing Viennese taste, which included observance of the unities, a happy ending, a manageable number of characters, and a reduced body count. All the action takes place in a single day in and around the palace of Elsinore. Besides abandoning the trip to England, Heufeld omits Rosencrantz, Fortinbras, the gravediggers, and, most surprising of all, Laertes. Heufeld also took the opportunity to pare some of the flowery language of both Shakespeare and Wieland: in his Act I, scene 7, for example (Shakespeare's I.i), Hamlet's "But look, the morn, in russet mantle clad,/Walks o'er the dew of yon high eastern hill," rendered by Wieland as "Der Morgen, in einem roten Mantel eingehüllt, wandelt über jenen emporragenden ostlichen Hügel durch den Tau," becomes, to the laconic Heufeld, "Aber seht, der Morgen bricht an."

Shakespeare's Act I provides the material for Heufeld's Acts I and II (omitting the Polonius-Laertes-Ophelia scene in the absence of Laertes), and his Act II for Heufeld's III (doing without both the political dealings and bantering with the players). The most profound changes occur in Heufeld's last two acts, which compress and completely recast Shakespeare's Acts III, IV and V. Ophelia never goes mad or drowns—she simply does not appear again after Hamlet consigns her to a nunnery. And if she does not die, and her brother does not exist, there is no opportunity for a gravediggers' scene, a burial, or a duel. The final scenes are these: the King tells Guildenstern that Hamlet must die. During the toast to Hamlet's forthcoming trip to England, the Queen accidentally drinks from the poisoned cup meant for Hamlet, Hamlet stabs the King, and as the outraged Danes come toward Hamlet, the dying Queen confesses her guilt and that of the King in murdering the late King, Hamlet's father. Hamlet accedes to the throne, calling, in the last line, for the Danes to take note of his honor and his vindication.[98]

An early review in the *Realzeitung* praised Heufeld's "sharp critical sense" for tightening up Shakespeare's loose and irregular episodic construction, and took pride in the smaller number of deaths onstage (three, instead of the eight in the English original).[99] In fact, Hamlet's character lost many of its contradictions and ambiguities. Heufeld cut the ironic undertones, political overtones, and sexual innuendoes, leaving only a serious-minded and melancholy young man caught in a family drama and grimly doing the ghost's bidding. The Viennese *Hamlet* thus joined the prose "middle-class tragedies" of German theater, the so-called "bürgerliches Trauerspiel."[100] Yet this version seems closer to Shakespeare than the first French stage *Hamlet*, adapted by Jean-François Ducis in 1769. Rigorously observing the unities, and wafting the dignity and virtue of French Classical tragedy over all, Ducis reduces *Hamlet* to a "claustrophobic palace intrigue" in which Ophelia is Claudius's daughter, Claudius is no longer Hamlet's uncle but merely a vile usurper, and Gertrude, not yet married to Claudius, immediately and continuously regrets her role in the King's death.[101] Thus we see two attempts to take "original genius" and subject it to the rules of taste; the Viennese *Hamlet* was by no means as rule-bound as the French. The irony is that these tamed versions of Shakespeare are staged at the same time that Herder and Goethe are proclaiming his "wild" genius. By the late 1770s, Schröder's widely performed revision of Heufeld had restored both Laertes and the gravediggers to *Hamlet*, setting sensibility and rude wit side by side in the same piece, while still allowing Hamlet to remain standing at the end.

Haydn's Rules of Originality

The final section of this essay seeks, in a few musical examples, to recover some part of the "Shakespearean" Haydn: the capricious juxtapositions of high and low, serious and comic, that reflect his deepest proclivities, the theatrical effects of "character" and "scene" that reveal his extensive experience in the playhouse, the casting aside of rules in original ways. I begin with the question of expressive disparity, taking the opening movement of Symphony 80 (1783 or 84) and the closing movement of String Quartet Op. 76, no. 1 (1797), which begin in agitated drama and end in frivolous comedy, and comparing them to works in which the disparity is either tighter (within a single theme) or looser (between rather than within movements). Then I turn to three slow movements that call attention to their own irregularities: two with the title Capriccio, the Adagio of the C major String Quartet, Op. 20, no. 2 (1772), and the Largo of the Symphony in D major, no. 86 (1786), and one with a licenza marking, the Andante con moto of the E-flat major String Quartet, Op. 71, no. 3 (1793).[102] Finally, I consider the effect in performance of disparate characterizations within a piece, the case in point being the tiny Alternativo to the Minuet in the String Quartet Op. 76, no. 6 (1797).

Symphony 80, one of three works Haydn wrote at Eszterháza and immediately had published in Vienna and London in 1784, opens with a violence intensified by irregular phrase rhythm. In fact, it appears to have no theme at all, just a frenzy of activity punctuated by a brief sighing appoggiatura (Example 1a). The first "coherent"—that is, periodic—theme appears already in the relative major, F, in m. 25, hence "too early," and conflates the ascent and appoggiatura of the first theme (Example 1b). This F-major passage introduces harmonic and rhythmic excursions which propel the music right into a trill cadence (m. 53) and a closing based on the opening music, until it is cut off at the moment we expect a repetition of the closing and cadence. Instead, we hear a melody described by Landon as "waltz-like frivolity" and by Webster as a "cheap tune."[103] Indeed, this little oompah dance, with pizzicato chords and ingratiating scotch-snap dotted rhythms, appears to have wandered in from another piece (Example 1c).

Example 1. Haydn, Symphony no. 80/i; (a) main theme, (b) F major theme, (c) "oompah" tune.

This melody is the principal subject of the development, framing it with a double statement at beginning (D-flat major, E-flat major) and end (A major, F major, the same key as the end of the exposition). In between these statements is a contrapuntal recasting of the opening idea. The ostensible beginning of the recapitulation in fact turns that material (m. 128) into a retransition with lengthy dominant pedal, and turns the original F-major theme into the "real" return, in

D major. And, in a priceless example of Haydn's pungent instrumental wit, the scoring of the oompah tune, basically for strings, changes every time: exposition: flute doubles violin on melody, pizzicato oompahs; development: D-flat, oboe oompahs; E-flat, bassoon oompahs; A, bassoon plus arco string oompahs; F, flute doubles melody; recapitulation, oboe doubles melody, horn and violin oompahs. The ballroom equivalent of Hanswurst enjoys himself greatly, especially in these surroundings; Haydn may beautifully recompose the oompahs in the Trio of his Symphony 97, but in that piece there is no strident *agitato* to make of them a comic framing device, worthy of a theatrical revelation.

Two things alert us to the fact that something is wrong at the beginning of the finale of the G major quartet Op. 76, no. 1. First of all, it starts in G minor, when every other movement to this point has been in a major key, even the Trio. Second, the dramatic unison phrase ends on E♭–D ($\hat{6}$–$\hat{5}$) with a trill on the E♭ for all four instruments that lasts a full measure; this gesture may be seen as portentous or mock-sinister, depending on the performance (Example 2a). These signals advise the listener to be alert to nuance especially of mode and harmony, while the prevalence of contrapuntal texture also announces a special kind of serious style. The exposition is surprisingly unbalanced in that the G-minor thematic area lasts for only seventeen measures before turning to the relative major, B-flat, where it will remain for another fifty-five bars. Without benefit of "second theme," the second key area nonetheless has an important articulation in a remote-key excursion (mm. 54–63, B-flat minor–D-flat major via an E♭ minor-seventh chord [IV$^6_5$]). This presages a lengthy and extraordinary enharmonic passage in the development section, that ends up in the equivalent of B𝄫 major. The recapitulation turns to G major in the expected place (m. 139, the beginning of the second key area). But nothing prepares us for the coda (m. 180, Example 2b), which executes a serenely comic turn, the quartet turned into a folky tune for violin plus strumming instrument: its lower strings execute a pizzicato chordal accompaniment to a melody based on the triplet upbeat of the main theme. Often minor-to-major conclusions elevate the tone of the proceedings, casting on them a triumphant or even transcendent ray of light. Here, however, we can make out the sound and image of strolling players.

Symphony 80 and Op. 76, no. 1, obviously differ in the frequency and placement of their comic turns. In both, comedy functions as a peroration, a *lieto fine*, but in the former the close of the exposition cannot yet be a happy ending while it still has a significant structural and expressive role to play in the movement.[104] In the latter, on the other hand, it closes both movement and quartet in an enchanted realm in which we can almost see Monostatos and the animals dancing to Papageno's magic music box.

Example 2. String Quartet in G, Op. 76, no. 1/iv. (a) beginning, (b) coda.

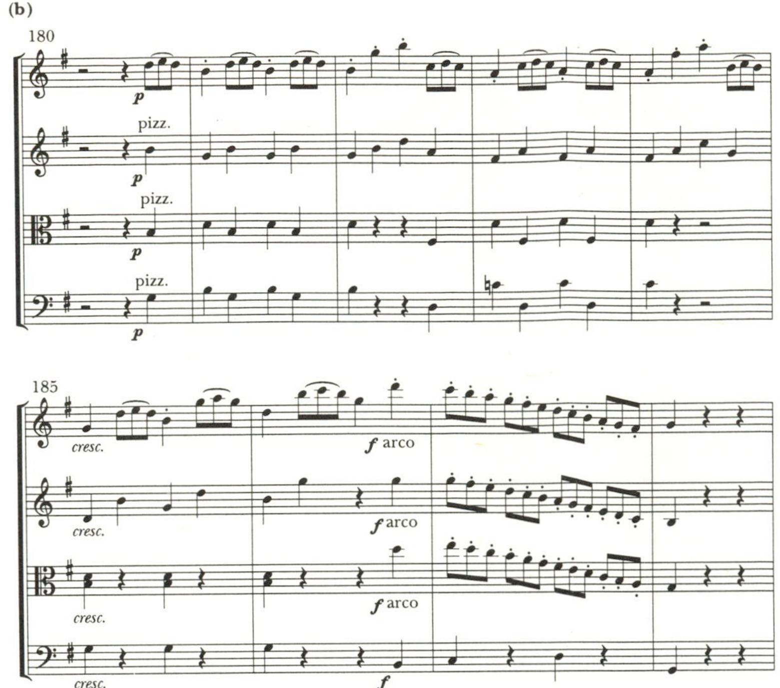

Example 2, continued.

Expressive disparities also occur on more local levels—the themes which combine lyrical and martial material, for example. Some of these movements are explicitly theatrical, like the Andante of Symphony 60 (*Il distratto, Der Zerstreute*), and others speculatively so, like the Adagio of Symphony 65 (Example 3) or even of Symphony 28 (where both melody and fanfare are set for strings).[105]

In such a theme type, the music seems to embody a scene or situation in which characters come and go in conflict or intrigue. But subsequent treatment may separate the characters or complicate their relationship. For example, in Symphony 65, the initial disparity is exacerbated by the introduction of a unison figure (mm. 21–24) which not only causes separation between the parts of the theme (mm. 28–31) but also dissociates the two segments completely during the recapitulation. In Symphony 82 ("L'ours"), the very topical richness of the theme creates a disparity between the grand styles of the opening gesture (mm. 1–4) and closing fanfare (mm. 8–20), and the delicate minuet "middle section" (mm. 5–8).[106] Finally, there are movements constructed entirely as antitheses, for example Haydn's alternating variations on a major and a minor theme, in which scoring, texture, affect, and dynamics may all serve to create oppositions in level that go beyond what is expected of each mode.[107]

Example 3. Symphony no. 65/ii.

Example 3, continued.

Haydn's characteristic and original disparities in style also work at the level of the movement, not just the theme. The anomalous juxtaposition of movements which embody very different stylistic levels ultimately raises issues not only of decorum but larger ones about the meaning of the cycle. To the German critics, of course, nearly any minuet could be an annoyingly jovial intruder, detracting from the serious tone. The G major String Quartet Op. 33, no. 5, follows up its motivically dense first movement with a passionate G minor aria for first violin, complete with cadenza. Abruptly cancelling the progression to greater seriousness is the succeeding Scherzo, with its rocketing hemiolas, off-kilter pauses, and insistently delayed cadences. Whether in 1782 critical opinion might still have found this an inappropriate instance of Hanswurst springing in, or merely a model comic episode with "deviant manners,"[108] is an open question.

Although the terms capriccio and fantasia have long been linked because of their association with extemporaneous performance, only in definitions of capriccio do we find words like "bizarrerie" or *Laune* (humor, caprice).[109] And only in discussions of fantasia can one distinguish elements of the rhetorical figure *phantasia*, or vivid image of an absent thing.[110] Neither capriccio nor fantasia is common as a title for a movement within a larger work, and both are but rarely used by Haydn.[111]

The Capriccio of Op. 20, no. 2, is a complex, elevated open-ended movement in C minor (Example 4). It is usually referred to as a *scena,* meaning there are declamatory segments like recitative and arioso in addition to a melody-oriented section that acquires the connotation of "aria" by following the others. The movement falls into two large sections, each ending with a nearly identical half cadence on the dominant of C minor, but these sections do not simply oppose a "recitative" with an "aria" nor a "declamatory" with a "lyrical" section. If that were the case, as it is in *Le midi*, for example, Haydn could easily do without the capriccio designation. Instead, in the first section, assertive *accompagnato* chords give way to meandering, quasi-improvisatory violin solos, in which neither the mode of articulation (legato, staccato, groups of slurs, all carefully marked in the autograph manuscript) nor dynamics (strikingly rendered from *ff* to *pp*) nor the number and point of entry of the accompanying instruments can be predicted. The type of improvisatory writing is quite different from Haydn's other instrumental recitatives, which mimic vocal models much more literally: slow movements of Symphony no. 7 (*Le midi,* 1761), String Quartets Op. 9, no. 2 and Op. 17, no. 5, Divertimento Hob.II:17, and the finale of the *Concertante* (Hob.I:105).[112] Not only does the tone of "voice" of the melodic protagonist keep changing, in register and degree of independence, but there appear at times to be several competing or cooperating voices; the stage is populated, and the speakers turn now this way and now that. The sense of physical gesture is palpable, if rendered abstract.

One of the "freest," least rule-bound aspects of the movement is that each half succeeds only in achieving its dominant. The declamatory half does this via a chord progression in which the bass line ascends chromatically, between mm. 14 and 22, from A♮–B♭–B♮–C, then back down to A♭ (m. 23) and then to the G-minor statement of the cello's arioso theme (m. 26). The "aria" section in E-flat major presents a leisurely three-phrase construction: 4 mm. to I, 4 mm. to half cadence in V, 4 mm. to full cadence in V, followed by a cadenza and cadence (mm. 46–50). Now the rhetoric of declamation overwhelms the aria, and its two remaining two-measure statements of the opening melody, a sequence from F minor to E-flat major, each give way to strong-arming by the unison scales.[113] The aria is nowhere near ending when it is forced to: its concluding half cadence (m. 63), rhyming with the earlier structural half cadence (m. 33), invites us to hear the limping minuet as a declamatory sequel to the aria.[114] As Junker stated, the "single governing feeling . . . is expressed without restraint." The movement's capriciousness paradoxically reinforces the seriousness of its expressive values.

Example 4. String Quartet in C, Op. 20, no. 2/ii. (a) part 1, (b) part 2.

Example 4, continued.

The Largo of Symphony no. 86, one of Haydn's "Paris" symphonies, is an extraordinary movement, not least because its opening thematic gesture features "sunrise" dynamics and a suspension at its dynamic and melodic peak (Example 5). It is also one of the very few slow movements whose opening measures resemble the rhetoric of the slow introduction, especially that of Haydn's Symphony 92 (1789, "Oxford"). The reasons for its Capriccio designation appear to be the shocking, unprepared *ff* digression in mm. 25–28 (and its aftershocks in mm. 47 and 85), the repetition of the main theme in different keys at unpredictable moments, and, as a result of both of these, a rather submerged sonata structure. Indeed, most of Haydn's works labelled capriccio and fantasia will reiterate the same melody in different keys, sometimes with material between the statements that could be described as filler, transitional, or episodic; the surprising result is that conventional formal patterns are abrogated.

Example 5. Symphony no. 86/ii.

In the G major Largo of Symphony 86, the exposition features two themes in the tonic (1a and 1b); the second of these modulates and forms the second-group theme in m. 20. A deceptive cadence on ♭VI in the dominant slightly siphons off the surprise of the forte digression in the next measure, and then the dotted chords effect a retransition to the tonic (mm. 29–32). The return of the opening theme thus sounds like a rondo-like return as well as a repeat of the exposition, but its deceptive cadence heralds the development, as does the immediate repetition of the theme in A minor. Here a second deceptive cadence anticipates the comparable moment in the finale of

Beethoven's Ninth when the cello and bass recitative gives way to a recall of the first movement. In Symphony 86, the unearthly C♯-major chord ushers in a profound suspension-laden passage in learned style, F-sharp minor (mm. 41–46), with a flute countermelody that looks forward to the *Creation's* "Chaos" (Example 6). A return of the digression precipitates a repeat of the opening theme in E minor and finally in G major as the beginning of the recapitulation. Thus, the development is framed by statements of the first theme just as the first movement

Example 6. Symphony no. 86/ii, dev.

Example 6, continued.

of Symphony 80 is framed by statements of the oompah tune. But after the recapitulation of 1b and 2 in G major, 1a returns in G minor, revisiting 1b and 2 all over again. Could this be a second recapitulation? The point is that circularities are capricious and confusing, that a formal hybrid of sonata, rondo, and possibly strophic form results, and that complications arise from simple avoidance of the proper harmonic resolution.

Haydn lets us know there are parallel octaves in the theme of the Andante con moto of Op. 71, no. 3. Labelling the measure "licenza," he telegraphs his knowledge and the intentional breaking of a rule his ear allows him to contravene (Example 7). Interesting here is that unlabelled parallel octaves occur in nearly every reprise of the piece, including the *minores*, which do not follow the theme literally.

Example 7. String Quartet in E♭, Op. 71, no. 3/ii.

Also by confessing and making a virtue of his error at the outset—that is, by making it a rhetorical figure—he deflects attention from the extremely odd structures (phrase, cadence, variation) and textures found in the movement. In this six-part piece (A B A A_1 B_1 A_2), the poignant and expressive minor (B) sections vary the major theme rather than each other, and their interior cadences similarly do not match. The second (B_1) is quite a bit more contrapuntal than the first, and also prepares the transformation of the theme's texture in the final section, an extraordinary high-register variation in which every part of the texture has accelerated to sixteenth notes, not merely the melodic voice. Dissolving the theme's melody and texture (Example 8) and finally its structure, this ethereal yet bizarre passage prepares the final coda-like return of the theme in which the A melody confronts contrapuntal elements from B.

Example 8. Op. 71, no. 3/ii. Second minor variation (B1) and final major variation (A2).

Example 8, continued.

My final example is the Alternativo (Trio to the Minuet) in Op. 76, no. 6. Each movement in the quartet is based on repetition, particularly repetition without decoration but with new contrapuntal, topical, and harmonic surroundings, and there are ways in which it does the whole an injustice to look at only one of the parts.[115] Yet the Alternativo gives us a clearer sense of ensemble "acting" than any of the other movements. The hilariously banal subject, an E-flat major scale, is handed

Example 9. String Quartet Op. 76, no. 6/iii. Alternativo.

from one player to another, in a rigidly prescribed order (Example 9): first, descending scales beginning with the cello and moving up one by one, then ascending scales beginning with the cello, et. seq. Then the instrument order changes: descending scales starting with the first violin and moving down one by one, then ascending scales, beginning with the violins. Finally, a return to the original order: descending, then ascending, scales; cellos through first violins.

The originality of this movement stems not only from its ground plan, but from the discrete, closed theme, which makes all the counterpoints themselves discrete, far from the continuous rhetoric of a canon or fugue. Indeed the countersubjects have to reinvent themselves with each statement of the scale, creating a virtual theater of responses. These responses range from species counterpoint (the very first entry, m. 64) to elaborated accompaniment (m. 89), from an entirely new dance (m. 113, Example 10a) to a single statement of a fugal-style countersubject (m. 128, the only time the scale moves without stopping into something new, Example 10b). The ventures are also cooperative, since succeeding statements must fit in with each other. Every time a new series of scales begins, the first instrument plays alone, thereby appearing to announce a new moment of invention, the space where genius holds sway and gives the rule to art. Thus, in one of his last string quartets, we see at once Haydn as the paragon of invention and as man of the theater, creating tiny scenes of group improvisation, each member taking the theme and creating its context anew.

Example 10. Op. 76, no. 6/iii. Alternativo. (a) Dance-like countermelody, and (b) fugal countersubject.

Just as Shakespeare criticism in the 1790s saw him as the man of true artistry and noble craftsmanship, so Haydn was viewed as both genius and servant of the art. The scene of cooperative invention in Op. 76, no. 6, is a reminder. Haydn's originality in discovering the means of "staging" an E-flat major scale recalls these words by William Duff, in his *Essay on Original Genius* of 1767: "[B]y the word original, when applied to genius, we mean that Native and Radical power which the mind possesses, of discovering something New and Uncommon in every subject."[116] Moreover, Haydn from the 1780s on was perceived as having such a mastery of counterpoint that he could conceal artifices at will. It must have given him great pleasure, after his early snubbing for infractions against the rules, to see a reference to his "well-known learned manner" in a 1799 review of his E-flat major Piano Trio, Hob.XV:30, as well as to his "ability to give to such artificial passages, which some might hold to be empty schoolroom stunts, a *pleasing* aspect."[117] Haydn, like Shakespeare, was perceived as commanding the entire range of style, technique, and emotion—from common to elevated, from natural to learned, from beautiful to sublime. It is not surprising that Haydn himself should try to maintain that position in his words to his biographers. Image matched substance, and he knew it.

NOTES

1. Georg August Griesinger, *Biographische Notizen über Joseph Haydn* (Leipzig, 1810; facs., ed. Peter Krause, Leipzig, 1979), p. 24. My translation differs from that in Vernon Gotwals, *Haydn: Two Contemporary Portraits* (Madison, 1968), p. 17. The original reads: "Mein Fürst war mit allen meinen Arbeiten zufrieden, ich erhielt Beyfall, ich konnte als Chef eines Orchesters Versuche machen, beobachten, was den Eindruck hervorbringt, und was ihn schwächt, also verbessern, zusetzen, wegschneiden, wagen; ich war von der Welt abgesondert, Niemand in meiner Nähe konnte mich an mir selbst irre machen und quälen, und so mußte ich original werden." In the following citations I use my own translations but refer the reader also to the relevant page numbers in Gotwals, because it is widely available.

2. Haydn's notation reads *Dies war vor gar zu gelehrten Ohren*; the measures are given in, among other places, H. C. Robbins Landon, *Haydn: Chronicle and Works*, vol. 2: *Haydn at Eszterháza, 1766–1790* (Bloomington, 1978), p. 279. On their significance, see Elaine R. Sisman, "Genre, Gesture, and Meaning in Mozart's 'Prague' Symphony," in *Mozart Studies* 2, ed. Cliff Eisen (Oxford, in press).

3. See Ulrich Tank, *Studien zur Esterházyschen Hofmusik von etwa 1620 bis 1790* (Regensburg, 1981); János Harich, "Inventare der Esterházy-Hofmusikkapelle in Eisenstadt," *Haydn Yearbook* 9 (1975): 5–125.

4. Statements from the Viennese Tonkünstler-Sozietät (1797) and the Leipzig journal *Allgemeine musikalische Zeitung* (1800), respectively, quoted by Georg Feder, "Haydn

als Mensch und Musiker," in *Joseph Haydn und seine Zeit, Jahrbuch für Österreichische Kulturgeschichte* 6 (1972): 46.

5. "F . . .", "Bescheidene Anfragen an die modernsten Komponisten und Virtuosen," *Allgemeine musikalische Zeitung* 1 (1798), cols. 152–55.

6. Griesinger, *Biographische Notizen*, p. 15.

7. Giuseppe Carpani, *Le Haydine* (Milan, 1812), pp. 62–63, quoted by Gotwals, *Haydn*, pp. 217–18, who suggests that Carpani must have told Griesinger.

8. Carpani, *Le Haydine*, p. 25f., quoted in Landon, *Haydn: Chronicle and Works*, vol. 1: *Haydn: The Early Years, 1732–1765* (Bloomington, 1980), pp. 67–68.

9. "An Account of Joseph Haydn, a Celebrated Composer of Music," in *European Magazine and London Review; for October 1784*, quoted in A. Peter Brown, "The Earliest English Biography of Haydn," *Musical Quarterly* 59 (1973): 343.

10. On the idea of genius in music history, see Lowinsky, "Musical Genius—Evolution and Origins of a Concept," *Musical Quarterly* 50 (1964): 321–40, 476–95; on rules and rhetoric, see J. Peter Burkholder, "Rule-Breaking as a Rhetorical Sign," in *Festa Musicologica: Essays in Honor of George J. Buelow*, ed. Thomas J. Mathiesen and Benito V. Rivera (Stuyvesant, N.Y., 1995), pp. 369–89. See also George J. Buelow, "Originality, Genius, Plagiarism in English Criticism of the Eighteenth Century," *International Review of the Aesthetics and Sociology of Music*, 21 (1990): 117–28.

11. Griesinger, *Biographische Notizen*, p. 114. (Compare Gotwals, *Haydn*, p. 61.)

12. Griesinger, *Biographische Notizen*, p. 16. (Compare Gotwals, *Haydn*, p. 13).

13. Griesinger, *Biographische Notizen*, p. 114. (Compare Gotwals, *Haydn*, p. 61; *Handwerksfesseln* is translated as "pedestrian rules.")

14. This sketch was written in letter form for inclusion in *Das gelehrte Oesterreich*, ed. Ignaz de Luca (vol. 1, 1776), trans. in Landon, *Haydn Chronicle*, vol. 2, p. 398. Nicola Porpora (1686–1768) was a celebrated composer of Italian opera.

15. Albert Christoph Dies, *Biographische Nachrichten von Joseph Haydn* (Vienna, 1810), p. 91. (Compare Gotwals, *Haydn*, p. 125.)

16. *'Longinus' on the Sublime*, trans. and ed. W. Hamilton Fyfe, Loeb Classical Library (Cambridge, Mass., 1927), ch. 33, p. 217.

17. Rameau, *Traité de l'Harmonie* (Paris, 1722), Livre II, chap. XXI, p. 147, quoted by Lowinsky, "Musical Genius," pp. 329–30.

18. Dies, *Biographische Nachrichten*, p. 64–65. (Compare Gotwals, *Haydn*, p. 109.) For a passage marked *con licenza*, see the slow movement of the E-flat major string quartet Op. 71 no. 3, discussed below.

19. Griesinger, *Biographische Notizen*, p. 113–14; trans. in Gotwals, *Haydn*, p. 60.

20. This point is discussed in Mark Evan Bonds, *Wordless Rhetoric: Musical Form and the Metaphor of the Oration* (Cambridge, Mass., 1991), pp. 47, 49, 71.

21. Immanuel Kant, *Critique of Judgment*, trans. Werner S. Pluhar (Indianapolis, 1987), Part I, §46, p. 175.

22. Griesinger, *Biographische Notizen*, p. 113; Gotwals, *Haydn*, p. 60.

23. Gotthold Ephraim Lessing, *Hamburgische Dramaturgie* (Hamburg, 1769), ed. Otto Mann (Stuttgart, 1958), respectively pp. 31, 191–92, 133. Ernst Cassirer, *Kant's Life and Thought*, trans. James Haden (New Haven and London, 1981; first pub. 1918), p. 321, suggests that Kant "adheres to this conclusion of Lessing's," that in genius "is shrouded an inner lawfulness and purposiveness, which, however, appears and leaves its imprint nowhere else than in the concrete and individual art form itself." Thus, new forms always go together with original genius. Johann Georg Sulzer, on the other hand, differentiated between originality in content and in form throughout the article on *Originalgeist* in his *Allgemeine Theorie der schönen Künste* (Leipzig, 1771–1774; 2nd ed.

1793; rept. Hildesheim, 1967), pp. 625–28. For example, p. 626: "In poetry, Horace is an original spirit who imitated venerable forms; Klopstock invented new forms; in music our [Carl Heinrich] Graun was indisputably an original spirit, but he had nothing new in form; in painting Raphael was certainly original but in forms he undoubtedly retained more of the conventional than did Hogarth." Sulzer also uses Graun as an exemplar of the sublime; see the essay by James Webster in this volume.

24. John Louis Kind, *Edward Young in Germany* (New York, 1906), p. 11.

25. On the "blank at the center" of the *Conjectures*, and other scathing criticisms of it, see Joel Weinsheimer, *Imitation* (London, 1984), p. 54.

26. Edward Young, *Conjectures on Original Composition* (London, 1759), reprinted in Alois Brandl, "Edward Young. On Original Composition. Ein Beitrag zur Geschichte der Shakespeare-Kritik im 18. Jahrhundert," *Jahrbuch der Deutschen Shakespeare-Gesellschaft* 39 (1903): 1–42, at §12, p. 19.

27. Young, *Conjectures*, §27–28, pp. 22–23.

28. Ibid., §29 and 36.

29. Ibid., §30 and 81.

30. "Letter on Landscape Painting," in *The Works of Salomon Gessner*, trans. Rose Lawrence (Liverpool and London, 1802), vol. 1, pp. 186–87.

31. This section is indebted to the important studies by Roy Pascal, *Shakespeare in Germany, 1740–1815* (Cambridge, 1937); Nicholas Boyle, *Goethe: the Poet and the Age*, vol. 1: *The Poetry of Desire* (Oxford, 1991); Ernst Cassirer, *The Philosophy of the Enlightenment*, trans. Franz C. A. Koelln and James P. Pettegrove (Princeton, 1951; first pub. 1932); Robert A. Kann, *A Study in Austrian Intellectual History: Baroque to Romanticism* (New York, 1960); M. H. Abrams, *The Mirror and the Lamp: Romantic Theory and the Critical Tradition* (Oxford, 1953); and Ernst Leopold Stahl, *Shakespeare und das deutsche Theater* (Stuttgart, 1947).

32. *Goethe: The Poet and the Age*, vol 1, pp. 21–22. The complete title of Gottsched's treatise is *Versuch einer Kritischen Dichtkunst für die Deutschen* (Leipzig, 1730).

33. Gottsched, *Beiträge zur critischen Historie der Deutschen Sprache* (1741), vol. 7, p. 516, quoted in Pascal, *Shakespeare in Germany*, p. 39. My translation. But a translation in rhyming couplets would hardly give a modern audience the sense of "disorder" experienced by Gottsched; Marc Antony's funeral oration is rendered by von Borcke this way: "Römer, Landes-Leute, / Und Freunde, neigt das Ohr zu mir, und hört mich heute. / Ich komme, Cäsars Leich anjetzt, o! glaubet mir, / Nur zu beerdigen, nicht ihn zu preisen hier. / Das Uebel lebt nach uns, was wir begangen haben, / Und was wir Gutes tun, wird oft mit uns begraben. . . ." (Pascal, p. 167)

34. *De la littérature allemande* (1780), quoted by Norbert Elias, *The Civilizing Process*, trans. Edmund Jephcott (Oxford and Cambridge, Mass., 1994; first pub. 1939), pp. 11–12. My thanks to Robert Hymes for the reference.

35. *Spectator* no. 160 (1711), quoted by Abrams, *The Mirror and the Lamp*, p. 187.

36. Alexander Pope, Preface to *Works of Shakespeare* in *Works of Alexander Pope* (London, 1778), vol. 3, pp. 270–72, 285, cited in Abrams, *The Mirror and the Lamp*, p. 188.

37. Anon., *Neue Erweiterungen der Erkenntnis und des Vergnügens* (Frankfurt and Leipzig, 1753), excerpted in Pascal, *Shakespeare in Germany*, p. 47.

38. Friedrich Nicolai, *Briefe über den itzigen Zustand der schönen Wissenschaften in Deutschland* (1755), excerpted in Pascal, *Shakespeare in Germany*, p. 48.

39. Moses Mendelssohn, "Ueber das Erhabene und Naive in den schönen Wissenschaften," in *Bibliothek der schönen Wissenschaften* (1758) and *Briefe die neueste*

Litteratur betreffend, no. 84 (1760), excerpted in Pascal, *Shakespeare in Germany*, pp. 48–50.

40. *Herders sämtliche Werke*, ed. B. Suphan (Berlin, 1877ff.), vol. 15, p. 486, quoted by Klaus L. Berghahn, "From Classicist to Classical Literary Criticism, 1730–1806," in *A History of German Literary Criticism*, ed. Peter Uwe Hohendahl, trans. by Franz Blaha et al. (Lincoln, Neb., 1988), p. 49.

41. Lessing, *Briefe die neueste Litteatur betreffend* no. 17 (1759), excerpted in Pascal, *Shakespeare in Germany*, pp. 50–51.

42. Christoph Martin Wieland, *Shakespear: Theatralische Werke*, 8 vols. (Zurich, 1762–66). For responses to this and other translations, see Hans Wolffheim, *Die Entdeckung Shakespeares. Deutsche Zeugnisse des 18. Jahrhunderts* (Hamburg, 1959).

43. *Hamlet* appears in vol. 8 of Wieland's *Shakespear*. The topic of texts for performance is discussed in Jürgen Wertheimer, "Schlegel's *Hamlet*: a Textual Translation in its Historical Context," *Shakespeare Translation* 10 (1984): 15–18. Apparently only one stage production, in Biberach, was ventured using Wieland's text, and that was directed by himself. See Wilhelm Widmann, *Hamlets Bühnenlaufbahn, 1601–1877*, Schriften der deutschen Shakespear Gesellschaft, Neue Folge (Leipzig, 1931), pp. 46–47. A modern edition of Friedrich Ludwig Schröder's 1776 translation is *Die Aufnahme Shakespeares auf der Bühne der Aufklärung in den Sechziger und Siebziger Jahren*, ed. Franz Brüggemann, Deutsche Literatur in Entwicklungsreihen, Reihe Aufklärung, 2 (Darmstadt, 1966), pp. 165–233.

44. Pascal, *Shakespeare in Germany*, p. 10.

45. *Briefe über die Wienerische Schaubühne* (Vienna, 1767–1769; rept. ed. by Hilde Haider-Pregler, Graz, 1988). On Sonnenfels see Kann, *A Study in Austrian Intellectual History*, pp. 146–258, especially 203–24.

46. Already in 1752, Maria Theresia had banned Joseph Kurz from performing his popular improvised comedies, in which he created a character derived from *Hanswurst* known as Bernardon; had brought the Kärntnerthortheater under the control of the court; and had prohibited "Teutsche Comoedien" from being performed during fifty "Norma-Tage," most of them religious holidays. See Gustav Zechmeister, *Die Wiener Theater nächst der Burg und nächst dem Kärntnerthor von 1747 bis 1776*, in *Theatergeschichte Österreichs*, III/2 (Vienna, 1971), pp. 50–62, for the history of increasing censorship. The actor J. H. F. Mueller noted in his memoirs that in Vienna in about 1763, regular plays were performed twice a week (a comedy on Tuesday, a tragedy on Thursday), with improvised burlesques the rest of the time (*Abschied von der k.k. Hof- und National-Schaubühne* [Vienna, 1802], pp. 46–7). For a more detailed survey, see Franz Hadamowsky, "Ein Jahrhundert Literatur- und Theaterzensur in Österreich (1751–1848)," in *Die österreichische Literatur: ihr Profil an der Wende vom 18. zum 19. Jahrhundert* (1750–1830), ed. Herbert Zeman (*Jahrbuch für österreichische Kulturgeschichte* 7-9 (1977–79): 289–305.

The character *Hanswurst* ("Jack Sausage"), created by the great actor Josef Anton Stranitzky (1676–1726), achieved dynastic status when Stranitzky picked Gottfried Prehauser (1699–1769) to be his successor. The death of Prehauser furnished Maria Theresia's pretext for banning improvised theater entirely.

47. Kann, *Austrian Intellectual History*, pp. 206–7.

48. Sonnenfels, *Briefe*, II, 7th section, 23rd letter, 14 May 1768, p. 137.

49. Hugh Blair, *Lectures on Rhetoric and Belles Lettres* (Edinburgh, 1783; Brooklyn, 1807), pp. 28–29.

50. Eric A. Blackall, *The Emergence of German as a Literary Language, 1700–1775*, 2nd ed. (Ithaca, 1978), pp. 471–73.

51. *Grimms Deutsches Wörterbuch*, 12:499, quoted by Berghahn, "From Classicist to Classical," p. 76.

52. Herder, "Shakespear," in *Von Deutsche Art und Kunst* (1773), excerpted in Pascal, *Shakespeare in Germany*, pp. 76–77. See also Roy Pascal, *The German Sturm und Drang* (Manchester, 1953), p. 257.

53. Herder, "Shakespeare," in Pascal, *Shakespeare in Germany*, pp. 78–79; trans. in Pascal, *The German Sturm und Drang*, p. 259.

54. Goethe, "Shakespeare: A Tribute," in *Goethe: Essays on Art and Literature*, Collected Works, vol. 3, ed. John Gearey, trans. Ellen von Nardoff and Ernest H. von Nardoff (Princeton, 1994), p. 163.

55. Ibid., p. 165.

56. Ibid.

57. Pascal, *Shakespeare in Germany*, pp. 12–13.

58. Ibid., p. 20.

59. Friedrich Schiller, *Naive and Sentimental Poetry*, trans. and ed. Julius A. Elias (New York, 1966), pp. 106–107.

60. René Wellek, *A History of Modern Criticism, 1750–1950*, vol. 2: *The Romantic Age* (Cambridge, 1981; first pub. 1955), pp. 94–95; Pascal, *Shakespeare in Germany*, p. 26.

61. *Schillers Werke*, vol. 7, p. 97, quoted by Wellek, *History of Modern Criticism*, p. 64.

62. Pascal, *Shakespeare in Germany*, p. 27.

63. Ibid., p. 36.

64. Translated in Landon, *Haydn Chronicle*, vol. 2, pp. 130 and 399 respectively. For a rhetorical reading of Haydn's autobiographical sketch which identifies this refutation of the Berlin critics as the *confutatio* of a classic rhetorical structure (the refutation of one's enemies' arguments), see my *Haydn and the Classical Variation* (Cambridge, Mass., 1993), p. 24.

65. On *Sturm und Drang* as a musical style or period, see Barry Brook, "Sturm und Drang and the Romantic Period in Music," *Studies in Romanticism* 9 (1970): 269–84; Landon, *Haydn Chronicle* vol. 2, pp. 266–83; R. Larry Todd, "Joseph Haydn and the *Sturm und Drang*: A Revaluation," *Music Review* 41 (1980):172–96; Joel Kolk, "'Sturm und Drang' and Haydn's Opera," in *Haydn Studies*, ed. Jens Peter Larsen, Howard Serwer, and James Webster (New York, 1981), pp. 440–45; Elaine R. Sisman, "Haydn's Theater Symphonies," *Journal of the American Musicological Society* 43 (1990): 292–352; James Webster, *Haydn's "Farewell" Symphony and the Idea of Classical Style: Through-Composition and Cyclic Integration in His Instrumental Music* (Cambridge, 1991).

66. Charles Burney, *A General History of Music* (London, 1789), vol. 2, 958–59, quoted in Gretchen Wheelock, *Haydn's Ingenious Jesting with Art: Contexts of Musical Wit and Humor* (New York, 1992), p. 35.

67. From the *Hamburgische Unterhaltungen* 1 (1766), quoted in Landon, *Haydn Chronicle*, vol. 2, p. 132, as the description of "minuets in octaves." Johann Adam Hiller describes the same technique as "those repellent octaves in the second violin or another lower part together with the first violin" also found in "Hofmann, Ditters, Fils, etc." *Wöchentliche Nachrichten und Anmerkungen, die Musik betreffend* (Leipzig, 1768), p. 107, quoted by Landon, *Haydn Chronicle*, vol. 2, p. 154. Leopold Hoffman and Karl Ditters von Dittersdorf worked in or near Vienna, Anton Filtz in Mannheim. Landon gives extracts from many of the relevant critical documents.

68. Johann Christoph Stockhausen, *Critische Entwurf einer auserlesenen Bibliothek für die Liebhaber der Philosophie und schönen Wissenschaften* (Berlin, 1771), quoted by Klaus Winkler, "Alter und neuer Musikstil im Streit zwischen den Berlinern und Wienern zur Zeit der Frühklassik," *Die Musikforschung* 33 (1980): 40; included in this indictment are

also Toeschi, Cannabich, Filtz, Pugnani, and Campioni. Stockhausen is writing about trios and quartets.

69. Johann Adam Hiller, *Wöchentliche Nachrichten* (Leipzig, 1768), p. 107, quoted by Wheelock, *Haydn's Ingenious Jesting with Art*, p. 43. Stockhausen (see n. 68) wrote that even "half-connoisseurs" could see the "vacuity, the strange mixture of comic and serious, trifling and moving."

70. Johann Abraham Peter Schulz, "Symphonie," in Johann Georg Sulzer, *Allgemeine Theorie der schönen Künste* (Leipzig, 1771–74).

71. Wheelock, *Haydn's Ingenious Jesting with Art*, pp. 40–45.

72. Ibid., p. 41.

73. "An Account of Joseph Haydn, a Celebrated Composer of Music," in *European Magazine, and London Review; for October, 1784*, pp. 252–54, quoted in Brown, "Earliest English Biography," p. 343–44. A facsimile is given in Landon, *Haydn Chronicle*, vol. 2, pp. 496–97.

74. See A. Peter Brown, *Joseph Haydn's Keyboard Music: Sources and Style* (Bloomington, 1986), Essay VII: "Joseph Haydn and C. P. E. Bach: The Question of Influence," pp. 206–29. The C. P. E. Bach letter is translated in Brown, "Earliest English Biography," p. 345.

75. Hiller, *Wöchentliche Nachrichten* (1767), p. 14, quoted by Mark Evan Bonds, "Haydn, Laurence Sterne, and the Origins of Musical Irony," *Journal of the American Musicological Society* 44 (1991): 83; translation slightly modified. Wheelock, *Haydn's Ingenious Jesting with Art*, chap. 2, gives an excellent summary of the critical commentary about Haydn.

76. This kind of mixture correlates especially well with the way serious plays were performed in Vienna. The first Viennese performances in 1763 of Lessing's tragedy, *Miss Sara Sampson*, featured Gottfried Prehauser, the Hanswurst specialist, as Norton, the servant. It is unlikely that this master of improvisation played the role as written. See Zechmeister, *Wiener Theater*, p. 121. And George Lillo's melodrama, *The London merchant; with the history of George Barnwell* (1731), that found such extraordinary popularity on the German stage as *Der Kaufmann von London*, was performed in Vienna in 1754 and 1759 with the two original servants (Lucy and Blunt) now replaced by three stock comic figures: Columbina, "Scapin, ein Lohnlackey," and "Hanns Wurst, ein Kaufmannsjung." The comic characters do not appear after the first act, and they were purged entirely from the new production put on in Vienna in 1767. Johann Wilhelm Mayberg (Meiperg), who translated and adapted the play, was an actor in Kurz's company. See Alexander von Weilen, "Der 'Kaufmann von London' auf deutschen und französischen Bühnen," *Beiträge zur Neueren Philologie. Jakob Schipper zum 19. July 1902 Dargebracht* (Vienna and Leipzig, 1902), pp. 220–34; Lawrence Marsden Price, "George Barnwell on the German Stage," *Monatshefte für Deutschen Unterricht* 35 (1943): 205–14.

77. Junker, *Zwanzig Componisten: eine Skizze* (Bern, 1776); rpt. *Portfeuille für Musikliebhaber* (Leipzig, 1792); excerpts translated in Landon, *Haydn Chronicle*, vol. 3, pp. 189–91 and more accurately in Gretchen Wheelock, "Wit, Humor, and the Instrumental Music of Joseph Haydn" (Ph.D. diss., Yale University, 1979), pp. 100–102; German originals are given in the Appendix, pp. 279–81.

78. Junker, "Ditters," in *Zwanzig Componisten*, p. 28; trans. in Wheelock, "Wit, Humor," p. 100.

79. Junker, "Haydn," in *Zwanzig Componisten*, pp. 64–67; trans. slightly adapted from Wheelock, "Wit, Humor," pp. 101–102. Landon always translates *Laune* as "caprice," which was doubtless one of its meanings, but Bonds argues convincingly for the broader term in the "older sense of the term, signifying one's general disposition as

determined by the mixture of bodily humors"; "Haydn, Laurence Sterne, and the Origins of Musical Irony," p. 61. The original reads: "Das wird niemand in Abrede seyn, dass die einzig herrschende Gesinnung, (oder weil von der Tonkunst die Rede ist) die einzig herrschende Empfindung Haydens abstechend, bizarr sey;—dass sie sich ohne Zurueckhaltung äussre. Will man sich auf Haydens Adagio berufen?—gut denn ists ernsthafte, interessirende Laune; wie bey den tragischen Gesinnungen eines Schakespear."

80. Junker has been something of a bête noire among Haydn scholars—Landon refers to his "nauseating verbosity"—but he receives sympathetic treatment from Bellamy Hosler, *Changing Aesthetic Views of Instrumental Music in Eighteenth-Century Germany* (Ann Arbor, 1981), pp. 168–77.

81. Bonds, "Haydn, Laurence Sterne, and the Origins of Musical Irony," especially pp. 69–72.

82. Cited in Landon, *Haydn Chronicle*, vol. 3, p. 49. Mozart was also sometimes compared to Shakespeare, but critics in that instance were primarily thinking of operas with "the language of ghosts," like *Don Giovanni*. A propos of the graveyard scene in *Don Giovanni*, one critic wrote: "Mozart seems to have learnt the language of ghosts from Shakespeare"; *Dramaturgische Blätter* (Frankfurt, 1789), quoted in Otto Erich Deutsch, *Mozart: A Documentary Biography* (Stanford, 1965), p. 341. Other comparisons are discussed in Gernot Gruber, *Mozart and Posterity*, trans. R. S. Furness (Boston, 1991), pp. 87–90; Mozart was even taken to task by Pastor Triest in 1801 for his mixtures of comic and tragic; see the translation in this volume.

83. *European Magazine and London Review*, 15 July 1791, quoted in Landon, *Haydn Chronicle*, vol. 3, p. 93. Wheelock corrects his mention of "Drawcausir," and reveals that the *OED* identifies Drawcansir as "a swashbuckling, impetuous character in a [George] Villiers play of 1672 modeled after Dryden." Wheelock, *Haydn's Ingenious Jesting with Art*, p. 214 n. 40.

84. *Zeitung für Gesangvereine und Liedtafeln*, quoted in Landon, *Haydn Chronicle*, vol. 4, p. 63.

85. See my "Pathos and the *Pathétique*: Rhetorical Stance in Beethoven's C Minor Sonata, Op. 13," *Beethoven Forum* 3 (1994): 86–87.

86. See the picture painted by Wheelock in her examination of the later criticism, in *Haydn's Ingenious Jesting with Art*, pp. 48–51.

87. Johann Reichardt, *Vertraute Briefe geschrieben auf einer Reise nach Wien . . . 1808/9* (Amsterdam, 1810), quoted by Wheelock, *Haydn's Ingenious Jesting with Art*, p. 51.

88. Wolfgang Robert Griepenkerl, *Das Musikfest oder der Beethovener* (Braunschweig, 1838), quoted by Gernot Gruber, *Mozart und die Nachwelt* (Salzburg and Vienna, 1985), p. 157.

89. I have made the case for this in "Haydn's Theater Symphonies." The material in this section is largely summarized from that article.

90. See Sisman, "Haydn's Theater Symphonies," pp. 311–20; Robert A. Green, "Haydn's and Regnard's *Il distratto*: A Re-examination," *Haydn Yearbook* 11 (1980): 183–95; Gretchen Wheelock, *Haydn's Ingenious Jesting with Art*, chap. 7, "The Paradox of Distraction." The plays of Jean-François Regnard (1655–1709) remained popular through the eighteenth century.

91. On Wahr, see Mátyás Horányi, *The Magnificence of Eszterháza* (London, 1962), pp. 72–117, passim; Landon, *Haydn Chronicle*, vol. 2, p. 176 and passim in chapter 2 among the documents for 1772 to 1777. His early career received mixed notices: he was probably hooted off the stage in Augsburg for his Romeo in 1770, (Schmid, *Chronologie*

der deutschen Theaters, 1775) but he was a success in Vienna (*Theaterjournal für Deutschland*, 1779).

92. *Theater-Kalender auf das Jahr 1776* (Gotha, [1776]), p. 252: "Wahrische Gesellschaft. Schau- und Singspiel. Aufenthalt: Esterhaz in Ungarn und Pressburg. Musikdirector H. Haydn fürstl. Esterhazyschen Kapellmeister."

93. Cited in Teuber, *Geschichte des Prager Theaters*, 2, p. 48: "Der Capellmeister Herr Haydn verfertigt der Truppe für fast jedes merkwürdige Stück eine passende Musik für die Zwischenakte."

94. *Pressburger Zeitung* 54, 6 July 1774, given in Pandi and Schmidt, "Musik in der Preßburger Zeitung," *Haydn Yearbook* 8 (1971): 170, trans. on p. 270; cited in full in "Haydn's Theater Symphonies"; I have slightly modified the translation of the last sentence.

95. See Stahl, *Shakespeare und das deutsche Theater*, p. 60.

96. For details of these productions, see Heinz Kindermann, "Shakespeares Tragödien im Spielplan des frühen Burgtheaters," in *Österreich und die angelsächsische Welt*, ed. Otto Hietsch (Vienna, 1961), pp. 457–73 and Stahl, *Shakespeare und das deutsche Theater*, pp. 73–82, among many other sources. The previous two seasons saw productions of *Richard III* and *Othello*. Stephanie was later Mozart's librettist for *Die Entführung*.

97. Stahl, *Shakespeare und das deutsche Theater*, p. 80; *Almanach des Theaters in Wien*, (Vienna, 1774), n.p.

98. The only modern edition of the Heufeld version is *Die erste deutsche Bühnen-Hamlet. Die Bearbeitungen Heufelds und Schröders*, ed. Alexander von Weilen (Vienna, 1914). See also Rudolph Genée, *Geschichte der Shakespeare'schen Dramen in Deutschland* (Leipzig, 1870; rept. Hildesheim, 1969), pp. 230–31.

99. Although the second of these items is widely quoted, the entire review is found only in Adolf Winds, *Hamlet auf der deutsche Bühne bis zur Gegenwart*, Schriften der Gesellschaft für Theatergeschichte 12 (Berlin, 1909), pp. 32–34. See also Herbert Foltinek, "Franz von Heufeld und seine Beziehung zur englischen Literature," *Die österreichische Literature: ihr Profil an der Wende vom 18. zum 19. Jahrhundert (1750–1830)*, ed. Herbert Zeman, *Jahrbuch für österreichische Kulturgeschichte* 7–9 (1977–79): 459.

100. For an account of German eighteenth-century tragedy, including the middle-class tragedies, see Robert R. Heitner, *German Tragedy in the Age of Enlightenment* (Berkeley and Los Angeles, 1963).

101. See J. D. Golder, "'Hamlet' in France 200 Years Ago," *Shakespeare Survey* 24 (1971): 79–86.

102. I leave out of account the early keyboard trio in A, Hob.XV:35/i and the single-movement capriccio Hob.XVII:1 (1765), which participate in different traditions. See Brown, *Joseph Haydn's Keyboard Music*, pp. 221–29. I address Haydn's capriccios and fantasias in detail in a separate study.

103. Landon, *Haydn Chronicle*, vol. 2, p. 566; Webster, *Haydn's "Farewell" Symphony*, p. 167.

104. On comic tunes in closing sections, see Wye J. Allanbrook, "Mozart's Tunes and the Comedy of Closure," in *On Mozart*, ed. James M. Morris (Cambridge, 1994), pp. 169–86.

105. I have suggested that Symphonies 64 (*Tempora mutantur*) and 65 are connected to Haydn's theatrical responsibilities, plausibly even to *Hamlet*; "Haydn's Theater Symphonies," pp. 326–30.

106. On the topics in this theme, see my *Mozart: The "Jupiter" Symphony* (Cambridge, 1993), pp. 47–48.

107. See my *Haydn and the Classical Variation*, pp. 158–62, for a discussion of the alternating variation as antithesis, as well as Tom Beghin's essay in this volume.

108. Wheelock, *Haydn's Ingenious Jesting with Art*, p. 111.

109. The former appears in the entry by Pierre-Louis Ginguené in *Encyclopédie méthodique: Musique*, ed. Nicolas-Étienne Framery, et al., 2 vols. (Paris, 1792–1818; repr. New York, 1971), vol. 1, p. 547, s.v. "Fantaisie"; the latter in Heinrich Christoph Koch, *Musikalisches Lexikon* (Frankfurt am Main, 1802), s.v. "Capriccio."

110. The extensive literature on fantasia cannot be cited here. See Elaine R. Sisman, "After the Heroic Style: *Fantasia* and the 'Characteristic' Sonatas of 1809," *Beethoven Forum* 6 (1997), in press.

111. One each for solo piano (Hob.XVII:1 and 4), three movements called capriccio (the two mentioned above plus the A major keyboard trio Hob.XV:35), and one movement called fantasia (the Adagio of the E-flat major String Quartet Op. 76, no. 6). In his correspondence, Haydn sometimes refers to the Fantasy Hob.XVII:4 as a capriccio.

112. On types of instrumental recitative, see David Charlton, "Instrumental Recitative: A Study in Morphology and Context, 1700–1808," *Comparative Criticism: A Yearbook* 3 (1982): 149–68.

113. Janet M. Levy speaks of the "aura of authoritative control" of unison texture in "Texture as a Sign in Classic and Early Romantic Music," *Journal of the American Musicological Society* 35 (1982): 507.

114. Webster reads the entire quartet as through-composed, moving toward a fugal culmination-finale; see *Haydn's "Farewell" Symphony*, pp. 296–300.

115. I have discussed this issue in *Haydn and the Classical Variation*, pp. 178–85.

116. William Duff, *An Essay on Original Genius* (London, 1767; ed. J. L. Mahoney, Gainesville, Fla., 1964), p. 86, quoted in *Historisches Wörterbuch der Philosophie*, ed. Joachim Ritter and Karlfried Gründer (Basel and Stuttgart, 1984), s.v. "Original, Originalität," vol. 6, col. 1374.

117. *Allgemeine musikalische Zeitung* 1 (1799): col. 601. My translation.

The *Creation*, Haydn's Late Vocal Music, and the Musical Sublime

JAMES WEBSTER

In recent years, many "newer" musicologies have turned away from the ideal of absolute music, which had been dominant since the late nineteenth century, in favor of what I would call the various contextual aspects of music. Although this "turn" has primarily affected the understanding of nineteenth- and twentieth-century music, as well as opera, scholars of eighteenth-century instrumental music have not been immune. Regarding Haydn, several recent studies have focused on his musical rhetoric;[1] the symphonies in particular have been interpreted in terms of their employment in the theater, extramusical associations, and "moral enlightenment."[2] However, these treatments reflect the traditional emphasis on his instrumental music. And yet for Haydn himself, and his contemporaries, vocal music was primary. If we are really interested in contextual aspects of music, vocal music would seem to be the natural starting point. In this study I will focus on a central contextual aspect of Haydn's late vocal music: the category of the sublime.

The musical sublime (in the sense I will discuss) developed in the period bounded roughly by the mid-1780s and the death of Beethoven: in Mozart's and Haydn's late orchestral music, in *Don Giovanni* and *The Magic Flute*, in Beethoven's "heroic phase" and, later, the *Missa Solemnis* and the Ninth Symphony. Squarely in the middle of this process stood the sacred vocal music of Haydn's last creative period, following his return to Vienna from London in 1795, when he produced the *Creation*, the *Seasons*, and the six late masses. In these works he raised the sublime into a central aesthetic category.

*

During the eighteenth century, the sublime was understood in two different ways.[3] In the first sense it was treated as an aspect of rhetoric; it was considered traditional, indeed derived from Classical authors, especially the influential first-century tract *Peri Hupsous*, attributed to Longinus.[4] According to this view, the sublime is that which is raised up above the ordinary; that which is grand, majestic, "high" in style.[5] Longinus states, "The *Sublime* is a certain eminence or perfection of language," and that its effect

> not only persuades, but even throws an audience into transport. . . . In most cases it is wholly in our power, either to resist or yield to persuasion. But the Sublime, endued with strength irresistible, strikes home, and triumphs over every hearer. . . .

Of the five qualities Longinus enumerates of the sublime,

> The *first* and most excellent . . . is a boldness and grandeur in the *Thoughts*. . . . The *second* is call'd the *Pathetic*, or the power of raising the passions to a violent and even enthusiastic degree; and these two being genuine constituents of the *Sublime*, are the gifts of nature, whereas the other sorts depend in some measure upon art.[6]

—that is, upon rhetoric.

By contrast, the newer sense of the sublime lay on the boundary between aesthetics and psychology; indeed it formed part of the emerging sensibility of Romanticism. Like Romanticism, it was oriented towards the vastness of untamed Nature, and represented a turn away from the everyday, in favor of the boundless, of the inexpressible, of transcendence. It also shared the Romantic tendency towards the blurring of boundaries: the sublime mediates between historical and cultural context, philosophical concepts applied to art, and aesthetic qualities in individual art works.

We may distinguish three phases in the development of this newer aspect of the sublime during the second half of the eighteenth century. They are represented, respectively, by Edmund Burke's *A Philosophical Enquiry into the Origins of our Ideas of the Sublime and the Beautiful* (1757), Kant's *Critique of Judgement* (1790), and the emergent Romantic aesthetics at the turn of the nineteenth century.[7] Burke codified the long-standing distinction between the sublime and the beautiful. For him, beauty was allied with symmetry and form; it was both limited and pleasurable. By contrast,

> Whatever is in any sort terrible, or is conversant about terrible objects, is a source of the *sublime*. . . . The passion caused by the great and sublime in *nature* . . . is *Astonishment*; and astonishment is the state of the soul, in which all its motions are suspended, with some degree of horror. In this case, the mind is so entirely filled with its object, that it cannot entertain any other, nor by consequence reason on that object that employs it. Hence arises the great power of the sublime, that far from being produced by them, it anticipates our reasonings, and hurries us on by an irresistible force. . . .[8]

Burke thus privileges nature over art as a source of the sublime. (Indeed the most common metaphor for the sublime throughout the century, again deriving from Longinus, was the thunderbolt: a phenomenon that linked nature and myth.) Hence Burke grants music no higher status than the beautiful: "the beautiful in music will not bear that loudness and strength of sounds which may be used to raise other passions, nor notes which are shrill or harsh or deep; it agrees best with such as are clear, even, smooth and weak."[9]

Kant goes beyond Burke, in that he distinguishes between two different aspects of the sublime, which he calls respectively the mathematical and the dynamic. The mathematical sublime is connected with the idea of the infinite: it is "that in comparison with which everything else is small"; or, more precisely, "that which, merely by [our] capacity to conceive it, demonstrates a faculty of mind that transcends all empirical standards."[10] The dynamic sublime, on the other hand, arises from fear, especially the fear of Nature:

> Towering stormclouds from which come lightning flashes and thunderclaps . . . , volcanoes in all their destructive violence, hurricanes leaving devastation in their trail, the boundless, raging ocean . . . all render our capacity to resist insignificantly small in comparison to their sheer power. But their aspect becomes all the more attractive, the more frightening it is, if only we remain in a position of security; and we gladly call these objects sublime, because they raise [our] spiritual power above its usual average level, and allow us to discover in ourselves a capacity of resistance of quite another kind. . . .

> So sublimity is contained, not in any natural object, but in our mind and spirit, in so far as we can become aware of being superior to nature in ourselves, and thereby to nature outside of ourselves as well.[11]

Thus (to oversimplify somewhat), while Burke located the sublime primarily in the awe-inspiring phenomena of untamed Nature and saw its effect on us as a consequence of our encounter with it, Kant located it in the human subject; i.e., in the domain of psychology. Its distinguishing feature is what he calls a "*movement* of the mind or spirit,"[12] namely from "the feeling of a momentary check to the vital forces" to "an immediately following, and all the more powerful, discharge of those forces."[13] This stance is already proto-Romantic. However, with respect to the fine arts, Kant remained skeptical: "The sublime in art [is] of course restricted to the conditions of being consonant with nature."[14] And he still maintained the traditional distinction between the sublime and the beautiful, and hence did not work out a full-fledged theory of the aesthetic sublime—least of all with respect to music.[15]

The principle of imitation (*mimesis*), which governed virtually all eighteenth-century aesthetic thought, marginalized music, especially instrumental music; owing to its supposed lack of conceptual content, music necessarily occupied a low rung in the artistic hierarchy. Hence eighteenth-century aestheticians were no more capable than philosophers of imagining a genuine musical sublime; they remained wedded to the rhetorical concept of the sublime: as grandeur, the marvelous, and so forth. For example, Johann Georg Sulzer wrote in 1771: "The sublime . . . works on us with hammer-blows; it seizes us and irresistibly overwhelms us. . . . It . . . must be used whenever admiration, awe, powerful longing, high courage, and also fear or terror are to be aroused.[16] Like Burke, Sulzer assigned no special role to the sublime in music. He referred to it only in connection with sacred vocal music by Handel and Carl Heinrich Graun, and only in traditional senses: "Music too does not lack the sublime; it commands the sublime of the passions, as well as peaceful greatness of soul. Handel and Graun often achieved it."[17]

Indeed, musicians and aestheticians stayed within the traditional rhetorical concepts even when they described the sublime in contemporary instrumental music. This can be seen most obviously in the common analogy of the symphony and the Pindaric ode as potentially sublime genres, a point emphasized by Carl Dahlhaus.[18] But it is also evident in their rhetoric and argumentation;[19] for example, in the often-cited essay on the symphony by Johann Abraham Peter Schulz, which appeared in 1774 in the second part of Sulzer's *Allgemeine Theorie*. In fact, Schulz uses the term "sublime" only twice (and only once as a noun), and in contexts that clearly perpetuate the traditional rhetoric of "high" style: "The symphony is excellently suited for the expression of the grand, the festive, and the noble."[20] The other passage likens the opening allegro of the symphony to the ode: "Such an allegro . . . lifts and stirs the soul of the listener and requires the same spirit, the same elevated powers of imagination, and the same aesthetics in order to succeed."[21] The dependence of these sentiments on Sulzer, and ultimately on Longinus, is obvious.

For this reason, I do not agree with the recent contention that these eighteenth-century concepts of the sublime were more or less equivalent to those of the early nineteenth; that, in Dahlhaus's words, "not until Beethoven did the symphony become that which it had always claimed to be, but without actually being so." [22] (In fact, the analogy between the ode and instrumental music was not applied to instrumental music alone. Johann Nikolaus Forkel, in his well-known 1783 essay on C. P. E. Bach, compared it instead to the sonata, in markedly similar terms to those used by others regarding the symphony: "A series of very lively concepts, strung together according to the principles of an inspired imagination, is an *ode*. Similarly, a series of lively, expressive musical ideas (sentences), if they are strung together according to the rule of a musically inspired imagination, is a *sonata*."[23] On the contrary: later views of the musical sublime were no longer rhetorical, but precisely Kantian (indeed more Kantian than Kant's own). It is the latter views, I will argue, that do justice to the music of late Haydn and Mozart, as well as Beethoven's.[24]

• • •

The earliest important discussion of the musical sublime in its newer sense seems to be that of Christian Friedrich Michaelis, in an 1801 article that enjoyed wider currency in a related version from 1805.[25] (Michaelis was a follower of Kant; earlier, he had published *Ueber den Geist der Tonkunst mit Rücksicht auf Kants "Kritik der Urteilskraft."*[26]) Here, he begins by framing the question in dualistic terms:

> Music can either seek to arouse the feeling of sublimity through an inner structure that is independent of any emotional expression, or portray the state of mind aroused by such a feeling. In

> the first case the music can objectively be called sublime, like untamed nature, which arouses sublime emotions; in the second case, the music portrays what is pathetically sublime. The former resembles epic poetry, the latter lyric poetry.[27]

In and of themselves, these distinctions—especially the generic analogy—also go back to Longinus. Immediately thereafter, however, Michaelis actually defines the musical sublime, in terms that are unmistakably Kantian:

> In music, only that can be sublime which exceeds the conceptual powers of the imagination: which appears too large and significant, too foreign and strange, for the imagination to grasp it easily. . . .[28]
>
> The feeling of sublimity in music is aroused when the imagination is elevated to the plane of the limitless, the immeasurable, the unconquerable. This happens when such emotions are aroused as . . . prevent the integration of one's impressions into a coherent whole.

This is no longer merely proto-Romantic; it differs but little from the descriptions that E. T. A. Hoffmann, later in the same decade, would give to all genuinely "romantic" instrumental music. Indeed, in his 1805 piece Michaelis, again for the first time, relates the concept of the sublime to the symphonies of Haydn, Mozart, and Beethoven in general; that is, to what seems to us the appropriate musical repertory.[29]

But Michaelis also discusses—again for the first time, as far as I see—the *means* by which the musical sublime can be created. He distinguishes two principal ones:

> Firstly, by uniformity so great that it almost excludes variety: by the constant repetition of the same note or chord . . . by long, majestic, weighty, or solemn notes, and hence by very slow movement; by long pauses holding up the progress of the melodic line, or which impede the shaping of a melody, thus underlining the lack of variety. Secondly, by too much diversity, as when innumerable impressions succeed one another too rapidly and the mind is too abruptly hurled into the thundering torrent of sounds, or when (as in many polyphonic compositions involving many voices) the themes are developed together in so complex a manner that the imagination cannot

> easily and calmly integrate the diverse ideas into a coherent whole without strain. Thus in music, the sublime can only be that which seems too vast and significant, too strange and wonderful, to be easily assimilated by it.[30]

Thus Michaelis construes the musical sublime as a species of Kant's mathematical sublime. Its sign is the musically abnormal, organized under the mutually opposed headings of excessive uniformity and unfathomable diversity. This is clearest in his reference to passages of contrapuntal complexity, a relationship emphasized in Elaine Sisman's interpretation of the finale of the "Jupiter" Symphony.[31]

Not even Michaelis offers a musical analogue to Kant's dynamic sublime. But his description implies an essential quality of the sublime in art, one that does provide such an analogue: the *incommensurable*. This concept opens up central paradoxes of art. An art work is the creation of poor human beings, yet often perfect (or treated as such); bound to its time and place, yet often transcending them; the expression of an individual author's personality, yet understandable to many. An art work is finite in aims, extent, and resources, yet boundless, inexhaustible, perpetually suggesting new interpretations. By the same token, it is through the use of incommensurable or apparently incommensurable categories that art works, notwithstanding their finitude, can suggest unimaginable vastness or depth. Sulzer had already suggested as much:

> Since the sublime invariably arouses astonishment through its size, but since a sense of size originates only when we realize how big something is, the size of the sublime object should not be totally beyond our conception: for admiration of size arises only from the ability to compare. We are moved as little by the wholly inconceivable as if it never existed. If we are told that God created the world ex nihilo, or that God rules the world by His Will, we experience nothing at all, since this lies totally beyond our comprehension. But when Moses [sic] says, "And God said: 'Let there be light; and there was light,'" we are overcome with astonishment because we can at least form some idea of such greatness; we hear to some extent words of command and feel their power. . . . Hence we must have a yardstick by which we seek to measure the extent of the sublime, even if unsuccessfully. Where this is lacking, its grandeur evaporates or degenerates into mere bombast.[32]

The pertinence of these remarks to artistic contexts is self-evident. An art work can invoke the sublime, not by mere vastness of scale, but only indirectly: by violent or unexpected contrasts, or by means of incongruity or mixture: for example, in an epic poem, by a conflation of the formulaic, the grand, and the marvelous; or in a painting by Poussin, where a few poor humans wander in a vast landscape of ruined Classical temples.[33]

In music, by contrast, sublime effects depend precisely on temporal phenomena—phenomena that can arouse dynamic effects, indeed in a far more immediate manner than the other arts. In particular, the musical sublime can arise even through the effects of a single moment: such a moment can "reverberate" long afterwards, on different musical and hermeneutic planes. It is this multi-layered temporality that constitutes the analogy to Kant's *Bewegung* of the spirit, and therefore generates the musical sublime.

• • •

Now let us turn to the sublime in Haydn's late sacred vocal music. My first point may seem elementary, but it is crucial. These works set canonical or allegorical texts, which had specific, highly charged religious content and associations, which in turn enabled his audiences easily to grasp his point. Haydn's primary means of invoking the incommensurability that is the hallmark of the sublime is musical contrast (see Table 1). The contrasts are based on common stylistic elements of the time: musical topics, performing forces, gesture and rhythm, harmony, and so forth. Such features cannot create the sublime in their own right; they must either occur in an unusual and exposed context, or many of them must appear together in unusual or "pointed" combination.

To illustrate, one can hardly do better than to cite Haydn's creation of Light. Ever since Longinus, the Creation story in Genesis had served as the touchstone of the sublime (compare Sulzer, as quoted just above).[34] Haydn himself was aware of this:

> The [story of the] Creation has always been considered the sublimest and the most awe-inspiring image for mankind. To accompany this great work with appropriate music could certainly have no other result than to heighten these sacred emotions in the listener's heart, and to make him highly receptive to the goodness and omnipotence of the Creator. . . . It is not

> unlikely that [audiences] will have been touched far more by my oratorio than by [any] cleric's sermon.[35]

Even in the 1830s, when Haydn's music was rapidly becoming *passé*, the aesthetician Gustav Schilling wrote:

> The concept of the sublime transcends all physical reality. . . . In music too the sublime achieves its most perfect expression and greatest power when it links the finite and the phenomenal, so to speak, with the infinite and divine. . . . Thus there is still no music of greater sublimity than the passage "And There Was Light" which follows "and God said" in Haydn's *Creation*.[36]

Note again that the incommensurable serves as the touchstone.

Table 1
Invocation of the Sublime through Contrast

- Topics or ideas (ideational; textual; musical)
  - Majesty vs. submission
  - Sin vs. resurrection
  - (Etc.)
- Performing forces
  - Voices vs. instruments
  - Soloist(s) vs. chorus
  - Unisons/octaves vs. full harmony
- Rhythm and gesture
  - Dynamics
    - Loud vs. soft
    - Sound vs. silence
  - High vs. low (especially: extremes of range)
  - Fast vs. slow
  - Long vs. short notes
  - Syncopated vs. on-beat rhythm
  - Variations in phrasing
- Harmony
  - Major vs. minor
  - Consonance vs. dissonance
  - Diatonic vs. chromatic

Haydn's creation of Light is of course preceded by his "representation"/"idea" (the German *Vorstellung* entails both meanings) of Chaos. The idea operates on two different, nested levels. First, it is sublime in its own right: the notion of Chaos is literally unthinkable; it implies both going beyond limits, and an unnameable fear, and in a sense thus combines Kant's mathematical and dynamic sublime. As both Donald Tovey and Heinrich Schenker emphasize, however, Haydn's paradoxical composition is everything but "chaotic"; it uses the means of art to frustrate the effects of art,[37] and thus superbly renders this "impossible" concept through music.[38] In the larger context, however, Haydn's blaze of light resolves the disjunction and mystery of the entire Chaos music that has preceded it. The sublime effect depends on his integration of three separate movements—overture, recitative, chorus—into a single progression that moves from paradoxical disorder to triumphant order. As a whole, the process therefore offers a perceptible and memorable analogy to that which is unfathomable, unthinkable: the origins of the universe and of history.[39]

Several features of this passage touch on general aspects of Haydn's style. In his late sacred vocal music he often integrated distinct but related movements in run-on or through-composed fashion specifically to create sublime effects (see Table 2). In fact, this technique had been one of his most powerful means of creating extraordinary effects on a large scale at least since around 1770. But (again) this process has so far been studied almost exclusively with respect to his instrumental music.[40]

Second, as already stated, the creation of Light is based locally on the simplest contrasts: soft vs. loud, minor vs. major, unison vs. full harmony, "dry" pizzicato vs. full orchestra. The majority of Haydn's sublime passages arise from unusual or "pointed" combinations of just such contrasting features (see again Table 1). The fact that the stylistic elements are familiar allows him to have his cake and eat it too: the effect of the incommensurable is powerful, and we are duly astonished; nevertheless, the passage as a whole dimly remains coherent. This point too has general import: it relates to the need for the artist possessed by the sublime muse to retain his sense of coherence, or *Besonnenheit* (self-possession), to cite E. T. A. Hoffmann's famous expression applied to Beethoven in respect to the Fifth Symphony.[41]

Table 2

Compound Movements and Run-on Movement-Pairs

The second (and subsequent) text incipits give the location(s) of the change(s) of meter/tempo/key. Accompanied recitatives are omitted, unless they precede concerted numbers run-on to them. Chaos in (1) is not literally, but psychologically run-on to recitative.

Creation	
1	Chaos—"In the beginning . . . and God said" — "And There Was Light"
2	Aria and chorus: "Now vanish before the holy beams . . . Afflighted fled Hell's spirits . . . Despairing rage . . . A new created world"
6	Aria: "Rolling in foaming billows . . . Softly purling"
13	Chorus: "The Heavens Are Telling" (Allegro — Più allegro)
18–19	Trio and chorus: "Most beautiful appear . . . The Lord is great"
26–28	Chorus: "Achieved is the glorious work . . . Trio: On thee each living soul awaits . . . Chorus: Achieved is the glorious work"
30	Duet and chorus: "By thee with bliss . . . Of stars the fairest . . . Hail, bounteous Lord!"
32	Duet: "Graceful consort! . . . The dew-dropping morn"
Seasons	
6	Trio and chorus: "Sei nun gnädig . . . Uns spriesset Überfluss"
8–9	Trio and chorus: "O wie lieblich" (progressive tonality; then:) Chorus: "Ewiger Gott . . . Von deinem Segensmahle . . . Ehre, Lob und Preis sei dir"
11	Aria and recitative: "Der munt're Hirt . . . Die Morgenröthe"
12	Trio and chorus: "Sie steigt herauf . . . Heil, o Sonne! . . . Dir danken wir . . . Heil, o Sonne!"
17	Aria: "Welche Labung . . . Die Seele wache auf"
18–19	Recitative and chorus: "O seht! es steiget . . .Ach! das Ungewitter naht"
20	Trio and chorus: "Die düst'ren Wolken . . . Vom oben winkt" (progressive tonality as well)
23	Trio and chorus: "So lohnet die Natur . . . O Fleiss, o edler Fleiss"
25	Duet: "Ihr Schönen aus der Stadt . . . Welch' ein Glück . . . Lieben und geliebet werden"
27	Aria: "Seht auf die breiten Wiesen hin . . . Dem nahen Feinde zu entgehn"
29	Hunting chorus (progressive tonality)
31	Drinking chorus: "Juhe, der Wein ist da . . . Nun tösen die Pfeifen"

36	Aria: "Hier steht der Wand'rer nun . . . Da lebt er wieder auf"
42	Aria: "Erblicke hier, bethörter Mensch . . . Wo sind sie nun?"

Masses
(Excludes pairs exhibiting slow introduction-allegro [symphonic] pattern, and transitions to "Osanna" from Sanctus and/or Benedictus.)

Missa in tempore belli	Et incarnatus—Et resurrexit—Et vitam venturi
	Agnus dei—Dona nobis pacem
Heiligmesse	Et resurrexit—Et vitam venturi
	Agnus dei—Dona nobis pacem
Nelson Mass	Qui tollis—Quoniam
	Agnus dei—Dona nobis pacem
Theresienmesse	Gloria—Gratias agimus—Qui tollis—Quoniam
	Et resurrexit—Et vitam venturi
	Sanctus—Pleni sunt coeli
	Agnus dei—Dona nobis pacem
Schöpfungsmesse	Gloria—Miserere nobis
	Et incarnatus—Et resurrexit—Et vitam venturi
	Sanctus—Pleni sunt coeli
	Agnus dei—Dona nobis pacem
Harmoniemesse	Gratias—Quoniam
	Et resurrexit—Et vitam venturi
	Sanctus—Pleni sunt coeli
	Agnus dei—Dona nobis pacem

Remarkably, however, the same contrasts—if made to seem incongruous rather than profound—constitute a primary source of musical humor as well. Michaelis (who wrote on musical wit as well as the sublime) noted the role of incongruity in producing both comic and sublime effects.[42] And the novelist Jean-Paul, who was often compared to Haydn in this period, wrote in his *School of Aesthetics* (1804) that his preferred brand of "annihilating humor" precisely "inverts the sublime."[43] Unlike the similar comparison between Haydn and Laurence Sterne, however, this one implies the need to seek a *rapprochement* between the two ostensibly opposed aspects of Haydn's style: his special brand of humor (*besondere Laune*) and his moral earnestness.[44] In fact, from the point of view of musical "topics," this odd couple makes good sense.[45] Like individual topics, the "surprising juxtaposition" of ostensibly unrelated ones is not a fixed, immutable effect, but malleable, capable of creating differing associations according to the means of employment and the context.[46] Indeed it appears that it was Jean-Paul himself who first insisted on the need for Besonnenheit—in the context of his discussion of humor![47]

A final respect in which Haydn's creation of Light is typical of his late vocal style is the inclusion of frequent abrupt contrasts between successive text phrases of differing import. This point might seem to open up my argument to the potential objection that the sublime effect of the passages under discussion in his oratorios depends primarily on the meaning and associations of their sacred texts. But the objection would be short-sighted, as becomes clear when we turn to the broader question of how texts function in Haydn's late sacred vocal music. Even after bracketing the issue of intertextuality (references and relationships to other works), we can distinguish at least six relevant senses of "text":

(1) The oratorios are, in the literal meaning of the term, settings of textbooks.[48] (2) At the same time, like the majority of oratorios, they are in large part narratives; that is, a variety of epic. This explains the textual layering characteristic of the genre, whereby expository recitatives alternate with dramatic or lyric arias and grand choruses. (3) Both oratorios (and the masses as well) favor passages of "musical pictorialism," as it has been called in a detailed study.[49] However, this characteristic goes far beyond word-painting in the narrow sense of bird songs, croaking frogs, and all the other literalistic imitations that in Haydn's time were already falling into disfavor, to encompass what I would call musical conceptualization. This category includes analogies to non-acoustical phenomena (e.g., long notes on the word "Ewigkeit", eternity),[50] musical topics (march, hunt, dance, etc.), "semantic" associations of all sorts (such as the flute with the pastoral), key-characteristics,[51] and many others. (4) The texts of the oratorios display an ideational content with cultural-historical significance. The *Creation* links the *Ur*-story of our culture that begins with the first words of Genesis to Milton's great epic *Paradise Lost*. The *Seasons* is arguably the last great manifestation of the pastoral tradition in our culture (unless one places Beethoven's "Pastoral" Symphony on the same level).[52] (5) These textual associations are, as one might expect, incorporated in much of Haydn's music. (6) Finally, the music of this period, in all its aspects, above and beyond the texts and even beyond their larger meanings, is itself writing cultural history. (I will return to this last point briefly in my conclusion.)

• • •

The most common types of sublime passage in Haydn's late vocal music are listed in Table 3.

Table 3
Classes of Sublime Passage

Gestural shock
Majesty (sublime as "grand," not terror/astonishment)
Foregrounding of key text-phrase
Tonal or generic discontinuity
Climax

1. Preparation (often: disruption of structural cadence)
   a. chromatic or weird harmonic progression
      relatively fast harmonic rhythm
      complex, "opaque" counterpoint
   b. unison chorus (high voices) on long notes and/or pedal
   c. "one more time": first "normal," then "more so"
2. Apotheosis (the "moment"): sudden, unexpected sonority or event
3. Denouement: fast, unmediated drive to cadence.

The type I call "gestural shock" appears most frequently in two contexts: slow initial sections in Mass movements (Kyrie, Sanctus, Agnus Dei), and the middle of other movements. Although in the latter case they are usually motivated by the text, they can be articulated by the orchestra. Perhaps the most astonishing stroke of this kind occurs in the *Seasons*, in Winter, in the recitative no. 33 (see Example 1): Hanne's reference to "the stormy dark winter now strides down from Lapland" is illustrated by a blast of cold wind, in the form of a shockingly remote *ff* chord.

Many of Haydn's Kyrie and Sanctus mass movements begin with slow initial sections that resemble the slow introductions in his London symphonies, especially nos. 102–104 of 1795[53]—the context in which he first developed the musical sublime to any considerable extent.[54] In these introductions, he often avoided clear melodies and periodic phrasing, in favor of short, irregular phrases and contrasting motives, juxtaposed in unexpected or apparently incommensurable ways. In Symphony no. 102 in B-flat (see Example 2a), the long, unfathomably deep unison tonic contrasts with the very high phrase that follows; when the thematic motive migrates to the bass, things become downright mysterious. Beethoven was presumably inspired by this opening in the introduction to his Fourth Symphony, also in B-flat (see Example 2b).

Example 1. The *Seasons*, Winter, no. 33 (recitative), mm. 18–29.

Example 2a. Symphony no. 102, beginning.

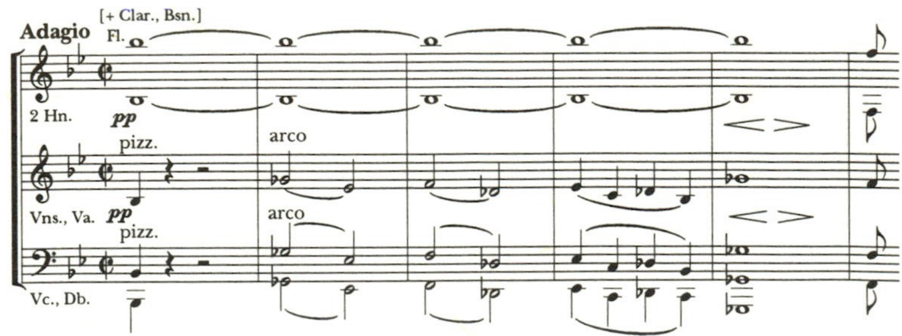

Example 2b. Beethoven, Symphony no. 4, beginning.

Haydn's most overt invocation of the sublime in an instrumental introduction is found in the "Drum Roll" Symphony, no. 103 in E-flat (see Example 3a). The drum roll is nothing if not astonishing; indeed it overtly invokes a thunderbolt. The ensuing bass theme, with its mysterious low, bare octaves, splendidly illustrates Michaelis's notion of long, slow, even notes creating an atmosphere of mystery and foreboding. Finally, at the end of the introduction (Example 3b), the mysterious low octaves not only return, but cadence off the dominant, such that the allegro con spirito enters by tonal indirection: a multifarious shock of key, tempo and meter, rhetorical topic, and register.

This complexly layered introduction almost seems to introduce, not merely the allegro con spirito, but the entire symphony, an effect amply confirmed in the course of both fast outer movements. On the other hand, as he always does even at his most disruptive, Haydn maintains a substrate of intelligibility: in the clear motivic links between the bass melody and the Allegro headmotive, and the continuity of the third scale degree.[55]

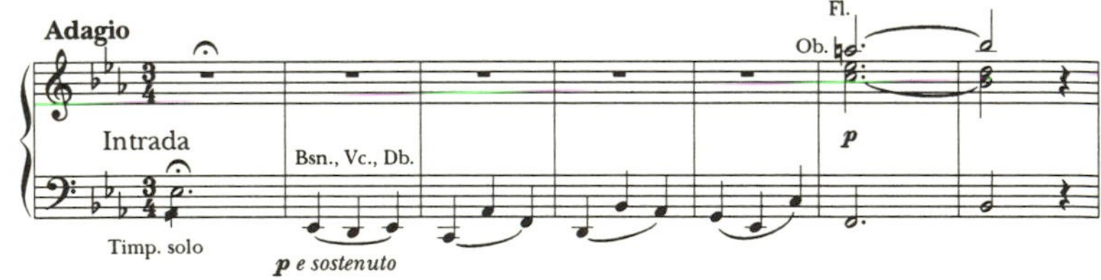

Example 3a. Symphony no. 103 ("Drum Roll"), introduction: mm. 1–7.

Example 3b. Symphony no. 103 ("Drum Roll"), introduction: mm. 34–43.

Doubtless the most striking "introductory" shock in Haydn's late vocal music is found in the Kyrie of his last completed composition, the *Harmoniemesse* of 1802. The work is in B-flat, and begins with a rather long orchestral introduction. Note the unceasing contrasts between soft and loud, and the unexpected entry of G-flat, the flat submediant, in the fifth bar. Things then proceed more or less normally for ten more bars, until, in the middle of a quiet descending sequence, the entire chorus and large orchestra burst in, *ff*, on an unexpected diminished-seventh chord.

The outburst subsides at once—but this only enhances the sublime effect. Like Longinus's thunderbolt, it is as astonishing as it is inexplicable; it resonates long afterwards, both in our inner ear and in its consequences for the music. (Such strokes occur even in Haydn's late secular music; see the lieder "O tuneful voice" and "She never told her love.").[56]

The second category of musical sublime is majesty; it too occurs most commonly in slow introductory movements. However it is associated, not with terror and the incommensurable, but with the traditional sublime topic of lofty grandeur; its musical representation usually involves trumpets and drums and dotted rhythms. Perhaps Haydn's most overwhelming example is the beginning of the complex, multipart chorus that closes Spring in the *Seasons*, no. 9, "Ewiger, mächtiger, gütiger Gott"—an effect that is only enhanced by the return of this motive, on the same words, in both later sections of this huge chorus.

The third category, foregrounding of a key text phrase, is, obviously, a general feature of vocal style; hence such foregrounding

Example 4. *Harmoniemesse*, Kyrie, beginning.

counts as sublime only when the treatment is extraordinary. Often the effect depends on a sudden change of performers and texture, most commonly from chorus to soloists or vice-versa. The key words are often emphasized by one or more fermatas. The most familiar example from Haydn's late oratorios is doubtless the line "keiner Zunge fremd" ("ever understood") in "The Heavens Are Telling," at the end of Part I of the *Creation* (see Example 5). Note the sudden forte outburst on "keiner" ("ever"), the equally sudden stop, and then the heavenly solo caress—I can think of no better word—of the simple C-major triad in root position and first inversion, with the remarkable slur from the soprano's fermata C to the passing-tone C-sharp, and then the rush to the cadence and the abrupt choral entry.

Example 5. The *Creation*, no. 13 (chorus and trio), "The Heavens Are Telling," mm. 84–95.

Example 5, continued.

A similar and equally splendid example of textual highlighting occurs at the end of the trio, no. 18, "Most beautiful appear." The angels exclaim, "How many are thy works, O God!" in beautiful imitative counterpoint; then they ask rhetorically, "Who may their numbers tell?"—and pause, on a remote augmented-sixth chord, as they repeat the question: "Who?" The answer, of course, is a repetition of "O God"—indeed, God alone can count His works—as the augmented-sixth resolves, over the characteristic fermatas. A repetition works around to the tonic, with the fermatas on even "better" harmonies; and soon we reach the home dominant and the run-on chorus, "The Lord is Great."

These techniques of verbal emphasis appear in secular works as well as sacred ones, mirroring the close relationship between the sublime and the comic noted above. For example, the late part-songs of 1796–99 (Hob.XXVb–c) include many similar textual emphases. In no. 9, "Betrachtung des Todes" (Contemplation of Death), the word "keiner" (in the context of the pointed last line, "None of them perceives his error") is analogously highlighted (see Example 6), both by rhythmic isolation and repetition, and by a shocking modulation from C to the vastly remote C-sharp minor.

Example 6. Part-Song no. 9 (Hob.XXVb:3), "Betrachtung des Todes," mm. 17–24
Translation of the text: "And none of them perceives his error."

Example 6, continued.

And the comic-beautiful no. 11, "An die Frauen" ("Ode to Women") sets the key word "Schönheit"—indeed it is only "beauty" that Daphne lacks—with a caress of the C-major triad that is almost identical to that in "The Heavens Are Telling" (see Example 7).

Example 7. Part-Song no. 11 (Hob.XXVb:4), "An die Frauen," mm. 9–17 Translation of the text: "But to men, [Nature] gave wisdom." / "To men? / "Not to women?" / "What did she give them?"/ "Beauty! Instead of all our swords, instead of all our shields, ..."

Example 7, continued.

The fourth class of sublime passage comprises tonal and especially generic discontinuities or disruptions. They differ from those I have called gestural shocks primarily in that they seem to function on a larger scale: for example, an unexpected and violent contrast between entire large sections or movements. They are more common in Haydn's masses than the two oratorios; I will again take my example from the *Harmoniemesse* in B-flat. The Agnus Dei begins in the remote key of G major, but after modulating widely it works its way to the dominant of G minor, where the pianissimo close is run-on without pause to the Dona nobis pacem (see Example 8).

Example 8. *Harmoniemesse*, transition from Agnus Dei to Dona nobis pacem.

The tonal transition is based on D, the common tone between the dominant of G and the overall tonic B-flat. The *ff* outburst in the winds is at once mysterious and astonishing: the dominant of G is stripped down to D; after three bars, F is added on top (the sonority remaining incomplete); only after three more bars do the chorus and strings enter on "Dona nobis pacem," on a complete B-flat triad. However, the timpani anticipate this resolution by entering on B-flat one bar "too soon," at once grounding the passage in what we instantaneously know to be the tonic, and yet—again—at first cannot quite grasp. Surely Haydn intended this overwhelming moment as an invocation of the idea of revelation—of the Last Judgment itself.

*

My final category is the most important: the sublime as climax. These passages usually come at or near the end of a movement (which, in turn, often concludes an entire large section); thus they often seem retrospectively to organize a very long stretch of music. Three features tend to combine to create the effect, as noted in Table 3: preparation, apotheosis, and denouement. The movements in Haydn's late vocal music that exhibit passages of this type are listed in Table 4.

Table 4
Sublime Climaxes

Number	Text incipit	Remarks
Creation		
1	"And There Was Light"	Cf. text.
13	The Heavens Are Telling	Ends Part I. All features present, especially "one more time".
19	The Lord is Great	Ends Fifth Day. Similar to no. 13, except second progression is not intensification.
28	Achieved is the Glorious Work	Ends Part II. Multiple intensifications (pedals; harmonies; high-points g^2–ab^2; brass dissonances).
30c	Hail, bounteous Lord	Long high pedals; many abrupt contrasts (esp. major/minor, dynamics); apotheosis surprisingly on diatonic supertonic (cf. *Seasons*, final chorus).

34	Sing the Lord	Final chorus. Climax-progression alternates with solo roulades. Apotheosis on V^6/ii (*not* V^6_5/ii) (cf. *Heiligmesse*; *Harmoniemesse*, In Gloria Dei Patris).
Seasons		
9	Ewiger ... Gott	Ends Spring. Arguably Haydn's grandest chorus; perhaps majestic rather than dynamic sublime.
23b	O Fleiss, o edler Fleiss	"One more time"; sudden high A over V/ii; chromatic rise to F# over A#(!); continued rise to A over G (V^9).
44	Dann bricht der grosse Morgen an	Cf. text.
Masses		
Heiligmesse	Et vitam venturi	302–3: V^7/IV(fermata)–V^6/ii (cf. *Creation*, no. 34).
Theresienmesse	Dona nobis pacem	150–68: huge half-cadence; 150ff. "one more time" at 169ff.; solo high B♭; chorus syncopated *fz*'s, high G pedal over chromatic mystification.
Schöpfungsmesse	In gloria Dei Patris	331ff.: high syncopated B♭ pedal over (familiar) chromatic motive; unison chorus to chromatic *fz*.
	Dona nobis pacem	139ff.: high pedal; sudden chromatics (cf. 93–101 in V); unison chorus–minor–sudden slow *piano*.
Harmoniemesse	In gloria Dei Patris	316ff. leads to IV; offbeat unison chorus + minor; soloists subvert cadence; 331 break off on 4th beat; chorus V^6/vi (cf. *Creation*, no. 34); syncopated.
	Dona nobis pacem	178: chromatic stasis, troubled soprano; 189 minor *f–p–f*, bass G♭/G; sudden syncopated diatonic chorus *ff*; 203 unison to high B♭.

These moments of sublimity begin with a passage of preparation, which often subverts what appeared to be the drive towards a structural cadence. Typically, this preparatory passage is difficult or obscure: harmonically remote or complex, contrapuntally dense, often with rising chromatic motion and extremes of range. Simultaneously, however, these same elements contrast with long-held notes, either a high pedal in the sopranos and/or the violins, or unison chorus against the orchestra. (As we will see, in some cases this passage is further emphasized in that it begins as a varied repetition of an earlier, simpler one, creating a "one more time" effect.)

Then comes the apotheosis: the difficult passage suddenly culminates in a single, astonishing moment—the "thunderbolt" so characteristic of the sublime. But the apotheosis is surprising in a complex way: it simultaneously releases the tension *of* the buildup, and projects a new and unexpected light *on* the buildup. The moment of astonishment is at one and the same time the briefest event in the passage, and the one that resonates most deeply; this double temporal effect produces the effect of incommensurability required for the dynamic sublime. In such passages Haydn exploited *avant la lettre* an aesthetic category ordinarily associated with Mahler, which Adorno described as the aesthetic of the "moment," of breakthrough.[57]

Finally comes the denouement: a rapid drive to the long-postponed structural cadence, often accompanied by indirect confirmations of the extraordinary event just heard, for example a unison chorus and extremes of range. The very terseness of the conclusion confirms the proportional disjunction that is essential to the overall effect. It also ensures that the immediately preceding moment of astonishment will dominate the impression we carry away with us after the work is over.

The most familiar of these passages in late Haydn is the end of "The Heavens are Telling"; it is based on the "one more time" procedure (see Example 9). The first wave follows a strong cadence in the tonic C; the bass rises to a dissonant B-flat, which immediately descends to an augmented-sixth chord on A-flat, and on to a dominant pedal. The pedal soon leads to another cadence, from where the second, climactic wave takes off. The basses again rise to B-flat; however, instead of resolving, it is maintained underneath a mystifying chromatic alteration. More astonishingly, the bass suddenly begins to rise chromatically, with "unfathomable" harmonies above. Finally, over the highest bass note, the music comes out the other side, as it were, onto a plain supertonic D-minor triad, signaled by a striking 9–8 suspension: the mystery literally resolves into intelligibility.

Example 9. The *Creation*, "The Heavens Are Telling," mm. 175–96.

Example 9, continued.

Example 9, continued.

Moreover, the latter progression is immediately repeated in sequence onto the tonic C itself, from where we immediately move to the long-lost augmented-sixth chord on A-flat, and on to the final cadence.

Example 10. The *Creation*, no. 34 (chorus), "The Lord is Great," mm. 68–77.

There is actually a double moment of apotheosis in this passage: the resolution of the chromatic mystification onto the plain supertonic, and the recapture of the augmented-sixth chord, which retrospectively anchors the entire passage in its initial, ordinary context. (As is well known, Beethoven included an unmistakable intertextual recall of this passage near the end of the first movement of his Second Symphony.)[58]

Another superb example of this type of passage is found in the final chorus of the *Creation*, "Sing the Lord, ye voices all" (see Example 10). Here the process features an "unfathomable" harmonic progression underneath a long choral pedal on "Ewigkeit" (eternity), leading however to an astonishing resolution onto V^6/ii (m. 74)—and *not* V^6_5/ii, as would ordinarily be the case with a secondary dominant; the astonishment derives in large part from this remarkable conflation of dia-

Example 11. The *Seasons*, no. 44 (trio and double chorus), "Dann bricht der grosse Morgen an," mm. 1–8.

tonic and chromatic function—and on to the cadence. This treatment of "Ewigkeit," again, goes beyond mere word painting; it participates in the sublime effect conceptually as well as analogically.[59]

My last example is drawn from the final number of the *Seasons*, which concludes Winter; its apotheosis at the end seems to me the most tremendous passage of this kind Haydn ever composed. The number is in C, and is a double chorus—the only one Haydn ever composed, as far as I can see—with soloists.

Overall, this finale contains five sections. First, a splendid example of the majestic sublime (see Example 11), constructed as a substantial double period for solo tenor and bass.

Then the choruses enter for the *second* section (mm. 30–48, Example 12a), during which they ask a series of four questions, each time answered by the soloists. The first of these question-response pairs clearly recalls *Die Zauberflöte* (see Example 12b, p. 91): "Wer darf durch diese Pforten gehn?" intone the singers, in C minor (think of

Example 12a. "Dann bricht der grosse Morgen an," mm. 30–34.

Example 12a, continued.

Tamino and the three portals in the Act I finale), whereupon the soloists answer, "Der Arges mied und Gutes tat," in radiant E-flat and accompanied by clarinets, bassoons, and horns (Mozart's wind-complement for *Heiligtum*; see the same finale, mm. 88–89).

This is by no means the only recall of Mozart's sublime operatic masterpiece in Haydn's late oratorios, or even in this number. The four question-response pairs rise in sequence, and lead to unexpected harmonic regions (especially E minor), until the line "O seht, der grosse Morgen kommt" (mm. 49–52) effects a transition to the third section in the tonic (mm. 53–76), a varied and intensified repetition of the first, which also recalls the sufferings of the winter of life. Important for later events is a passage marked by the first entry of the trombones (mm. 61–64), in which a rising motive on the C-major triad ("An eternal Spring reigns") leads to a *ff* outburst on the subdominant.

At its expected conclusion (m. 74), this section cadences deceptively onto V/V and leads directly to the fourth section (mm. 75–115). This is a fugue, and an unusual one (Example 13). The subject is odd

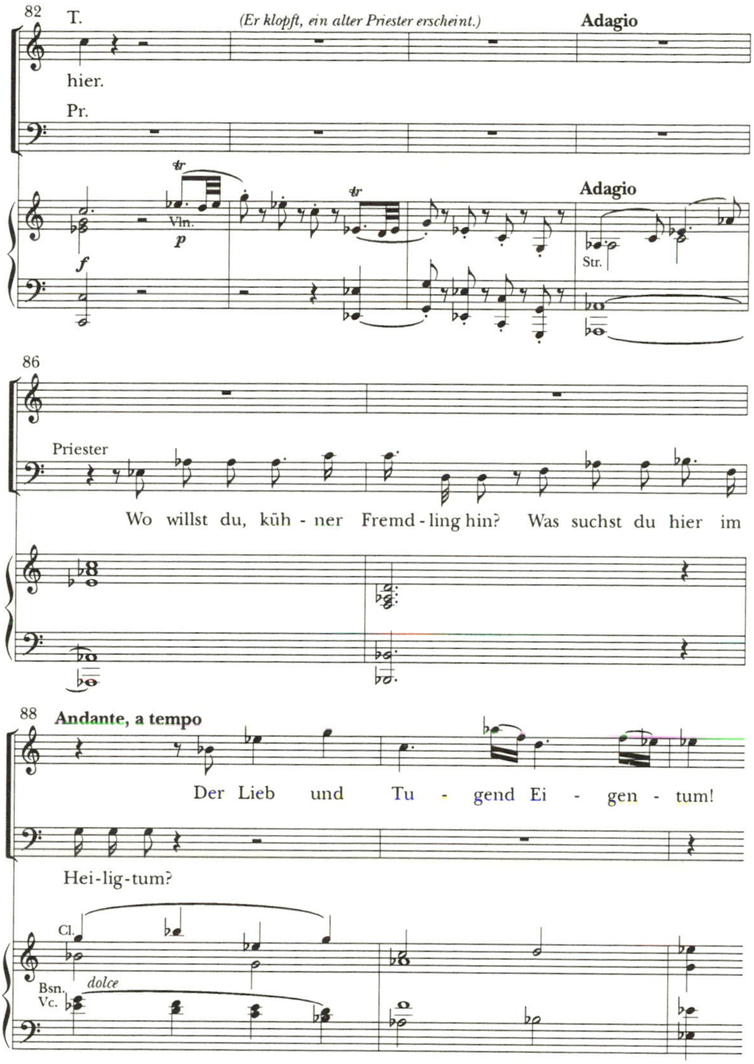

82 T. (Er klopft, ein alter Priester erscheint.) Adagio

hier.

Pr.

tr Vln. p tr

f

Adagio

Str.

86

Priester

Wo willst du, küh - ner Fremd - ling hin? Was suchst du hier im

88 Andante, a tempo

Der Lieb und Tu - gend Ei - gen - tum!

Hei-lig-tum?

Cl.

Bsn. Vc. dolce

Example 12b. Mozart. *Die Zauberflöte,* Act I Finale, mm. 77–79.

Example 13. "Dann bricht der grosse Morgen an," mm. 77–79.

indeed; it—again—rises sequentially, this time by upward sixths, including a difficult leap to an implicitly dissonant B-flat.

The countersubject is lightly chromatic as well. The fugue is not only densely contrapuntal, but harmonically difficult: another example of Kant's mathematical sublime. Two passages go so far as to embellish (mm. 90–91) or chorally sequence (104–05) those awkward rising-sixth leaps; the latter is ratcheted up to an almost impossibly high and intonationally difficult climax, again in E minor (the sopranos' octave-leaps "want" to achieve high B; they may be grateful that it was not Beethoven who composed this passage). However, we immediately fall back into F major, *ff*, and again with trombones, as the submediant of A minor, and cadence in the latter key (m. 107); this F may foretell the apotheosis at the end. Following this complexity, however, the fugue soon returns to the home dominant (m. 112) and cadences in the tonic.

And now comes our reward, in the fifth and final section (Example 14); a gigantic recomposition of the earlier climax in mm. 61–64. The final couplet, "Then we will sing; then we will enter into Thy realm's glory," is sung without text repetitions. While the trombones sustain, the winds and brass intone a massive, three-fold buildup of the C-major triad—one thinks inevitably of the Trinity—with each phrase punctuated by the chorus.[60] But the third phrase enters sooner than we think, and the sopranos rise higher as well, all the way to B-flat. And then, on the climactic word "Herrlichkeit" (glory), the entire world resolves, *fortissimo*, onto a plain root-position subdominant triad, where all motion stops.

The mortal coils of the difficult chromatic fugue have suddenly opened out, sooner than we realized and yet with unimaginable breadth and power, onto the heavenly gates through which we are about to pass; and this miraculous resolution is anchored in the subdominant, the most stabilizing of all sonorities. The final cadence, which Tovey called "one of the most overwhelmingly energetic" in all music,[61] follows immediately, with breathtaking swiftness. Haydn's final utterance in any oratorio was also his greatest representation of the sublime as an end—as salvation.

• • •

In conclusion, I would like to touch on some connections between the historical situation around 1800—when the new, Romantic sense of the sublime was first flowering—and Haydn's triumph with the *Creation*. As he and many others said, its subject was the most sublime

Example 14. "Dann bricht der grosse Morgen an," mm. 116–29.

Example 14, continued.

Example 14, continued.

story known to man. He also said that this work, above all others, would ensure the survival of his reputation after his death. However, this prediction turned out to be somewhat wide of the mark. Since early in the nineteenth century, the music of Haydn's that has been most performed and written about, that has occupied the pride of place in our image of his art and his historical position, has been his instrumental works. And these have been valued primarily for wit and humor, freedom of form, and part-writing and instrumentation—that is, as canonic exemplars of "absolute" music.

By contrast, Haydn believed that "instead of so many quartets, sonatas, and symphonies, [I] should have written more vocal music."[62] If so, he would surely have left us even more musical representations of the sublime, though it may be doubted whether he could have enjoyed a greater triumph than the *Creation*. But as we have just seen, Haydn's sublime is associated not merely with beginnings—not merely with the Creation of Light—but with endings as well: with "last things," the Day of Judgment, the end of time. Indeed, the sublime endings of the *Creation* and *Seasons* can stand for the general sublimity of Haydn's last style. Moreover, these endings, coming as they do at the end of a long and illustrious career, recall Longinus's notion that, in the artistic sublime, the spirit of the work becomes fused with the persona of its author.[63]

Certainly Haydn's contemporaries responded thus. For example, in 1800 Christoph Martin Wieland (Haydn's favorite poet) composed an ode entitled "To Haydn on the Performance of his Cantata *The Creation of the World"*; it concludes, "How beautiful is this earth, / Nay, more beautiful, now that the Lord has summoned you to life / To complete His work!"[64] Closer to the usual level of kitsch was the effort by Gabriele von Baumberg, distributed as a broadsheet at the 1799 Burgtheater premiere: "Now you have created your 'Let there be!' . . . The entire Creation for the second time. . . Thus we pay tribute to . . . the omnipotence of your magic tones / And to you, the God of harmony!"[65] An 1801 letter accompanying a medal given to him by the musicians of the Paris *opéra* stated, "When imitating, in [The *Creation*], the *fires of light*, Haydn appeared to portray himself, and to prove to us all that his name will shine as long as the stars whose rays he seems to have appropriated."[66]

Indeed, Haydn himself harbored such feelings about his last vocal works. According to Sigismund von Neukomm, Haydn said of the great bass aria that immediately precedes the final chorus of the *Seasons*, "Erblicke hier, betörter Mensch": "'This aria refers to *me*!' . . . And one must assume that this was the decisive point when the Lord,

Who giveth and Who taketh away, closed Haydn's glorious career, and allowed him to see 'his life's image and his open grave'."[67]

In the *Creation*, Haydn's music created history as well. It helped to found music's new-found status as the highest and most romantic art, albeit in a form that simultaneously maintained its traditional aesthetic function as mimesis. Among the elements that made this triumph possible, the musical sublime was arguably the most important. From this perspective, Haydn's final triumph itself almost seems sublime, not only in elementary human terms, but in historical ones as well. For his triumph was the artistic touchstone of an entire historical period: a period for which we have no name, because it links, rather than divides, the Enlightenment and Romanticism.[68] We could do far worse than to think of the entire great flowering of music between 1780 and 1815 as the age of Haydn's sublime.

NOTES

This study was initially presented at the University of North Carolina at Chapel Hill in 1991 at a symposium on Haydn's *Creation* in honor of Howard M. Smither. Thereafter it was presented at Princeton University and the University of Notre Dame. A somewhat different German version was given at the international conference of the Gesellschaft für Musikforschung, "Musik als Text," Freiburg im Breisgau, 1993, and will appear in the proceedings of that conference, edited by Hermann Danuser et al.

1. László Somfai, "'Learned Style' in Two Late String Quartet Movements of Haydn," *Studia musicologica* 28 (1986): 325–49; Hartmut Krones, "Rhetorik und rhetorische Symbolik in der Musik um 1800: Vom Weiterleben eines Prinzips," *Musiktheorie* 3 (1988): 117–40; Mark Evan Bonds, *Wordless Rhetoric: Musical Form and the Metaphor of the Oration* (Cambridge, Mass., 1991); Elaine R. Sisman, *Haydn and the Classical Variation* (Cambridge, Mass., 1993).

2. Sisman, "Haydn's Theater Symphonies," *Journal of the American Musicological Society* 43 (1990): 292–352; James Webster, *Haydn's "Farewell" Symphony and the Idea of Classical Style: Through-Composition and Cyclic Integration in his Instrumental Music* (Cambridge, 1991), chaps. 4, 7, 8; Richard J. Will, "Programmatic Symphonies of the Classical Period" (Ph.D. diss., Cornell Univ., 1994); David P. Schroeder, *Haydn and the Enlightenment: The Late Symphonies and their Audience* (Oxford, 1990).

3. There are relatively few treatments of the musical sublime in the eighteenth century. Many primary sources are conveniently translated and annotated in Peter LeHuray & James Day, *Music and Aesthetics in the Eighteenth and Early-Nineteenth Centuries* (Cambridge, 1981). Other references are given in context below.

4. Discussions of the corresponding variety of musical sublime center on Handel; see Claudia L. Johnson, "Giant HANDEL and the Musical Sublime," *Eighteenth-Century Studies* 19 (1985–86): 515–33; Alexander J. Shapiro, "'Drama of an Infinitely Superior Nature': Handel's Early English Oratorios and the Religious Sublime," *Music and Letters* 74 (1993): 215–45. See also Luca Zoppelli, "Lo 'stile sublime' nella musica del Settecento: Premesse poetiche e recettive," *Recercare* 2 (1990): 72–93. Modern editions

of Longinus include *Aristotle, Horace, Longinus: Classical Literary Criticism*, trans. T. S. Dorsch (Harmondsworth, Middlesex, 1965), and the Loeb Classical Library edition (vol. XXIII), trans. W. Hamilton Fyfe (Cambridge, Mass., 1927).

5. This sense corresponds to the (rather curious) etymology: *sub* + *limen*, that which is raised up just "under" a "lintel"; i.e., as high as possible.

6. *On the Sublime*, trans. William Smith, 4th ed. (London, 1770), pp. 3, 4, 21; quoted from Samuel H. Monk, *The Sublime: A Study of Critical Theories in XVIII-Century England* (Ann Arbor, 1960), pp. 12–13.

7. Sisman treats the subject of the later eighteenth-century musical sublime in two important studies: *Mozart: The "Jupiter" Symphony* (Cambridge, 1993), chap. 2; and "Learned Style and the Rhetoric of the Sublime in the 'Jupiter' Symphony," in Stanley Sadie, ed., *Wolfgang Amadè Mozart: Essays on his Life and his Music* (Oxford, 1996), pp. 221–26, 233–36. See also Michela Garda, *Musica sublime: Metamorfosi di un'idea nel Settecento musicale* (Milan and Lucca, 1995; I thank Dr. Garda for supplying me with this volume immediately upon publication); Michael Fend, "Literary Motifs, Musical Form, and the Quest for the 'Sublime': Cherubini's *Eliza ou le Voyage aux glaciers du Mont St Bernard*," *Cambridge Opera Journal* 5 (1993): 17–38. Notwithstanding the close connection between sacred vocal genres and ideas associated with the sublime, no general study of the musical sublime in this period known to me deals with sacred vocal music.

8. Burke, *Philosophical Enquiry*; quoted in LeHuray and Day, p. 71.

9. Ibid., p. 72.

10 Kant, *Kritik der Urteilskraft*, ed. Karl Vorländer (Hamburg, 1924; Philosophische Bibliothek, 39a), §25, p. 94; trans. LeHuray and Day, pp. 224, 225. (I have tacitly modified their translations from the German to make them reflect the original more accurately.)

11. §28, pp. 107, 110 (LeHuray and Day, p. 227).

12. "*Bewegung* des Gemüts" (emphasis original): §24, p. 91 (LeHuray and Day, p. 224).

13. §23, p. 88 (LeHuray and Day, p. 223). For an acute analysis of the psychological implications of this formulation, see Neil Hertz, "The Notion of Blockage in the Literature of the Sublime," in Geoffrey H. Hartman, ed., *Psycholanalysis and the Question of the Text* (Baltimore, 1978), pp. 62–85.

14. §23, p. 88 (LeHuray and Day, p. 224).

15. §51, pp. 180–182 (LeHuray and Day, pp. 220–21).

16. Johann Georg Sulzer, *Allgemeine Theorie der schönen Künste*, 2d ed. (1786–87), s.v. "Erhaben," vol. 2, p. 84, col. 2 (LeHuray and Day, p. 138).

17. Ibid., p. 89, col. 1.

18. Dahlhaus, "E. T. A. Hoffmanns Beethoven-Kritik und die Ästhetik des Erhabenen," *Archiv für Musikwissenschaft* 38 (1981): 79–92. See the essay by Mark Evan Bonds in this volume.

19. Indeed, as early as J. A. Scheibe's 1739 *Critischer Musicus* (cited by Dahlhaus, p. 82).

20. Johann Abraham Peter Schulz, "Symphonie," in Sulzer, *Allgemeine Theorie*, 4th ed., 1792–94, vol. 4, p. 478; trans. Bathia Churgin, "The Symphony as Described by J. A. P. Schulz: A Commentary and Translation," *Current Musicology* 29 (1980): 11.

21. Schulz, "Symphonie," p. 479; Churgin, "The Symphony," p. 12 (with the last quoted phrase given erroneously as "to be happy therein").

22. Dahlhaus, "Hoffmann's Beethoven-Kritik," p. 90; similar views are given by English-language scholars, e.g., Judith L. Schwartz, "Periodicity and Passion in the First Movement of Haydn's 'Farewell' Symphony," in Eugene K. Wolf and Edward H. Roesner, eds., *Studies in Musical Sources and Style: Essays in Honor of Jan LaRue* (Madison, 1990), pp. 293–338, §4 (although I do not agree with her interpretation of the "minuet"-like interlude in the development of the allegro assai of Haydn's "Farewell" Symphony as exemplifying the sublime).

23. Forkel, "Ueber eine Sonate aus Carl Phil. Emanuel Bachs dritter Sonatensammlung für Kenner und Liebhaber, in F moll," in Forkel, *Musikalischer Almanach für Deutschland auf das Jahr 1784* (Leipzig, 1783), p. 27. (It is clear from the context that Forkel means specifically the solo sonata, not the broader sense of "sonata" as designating all elaborate instrumental works, which is occasionally encountered in eighteenth-century writings on music.)

24. Mozart's early biographer Franz Xaver Niemetschek noted the presence of the sublime in the "Prague" symphony, albeit still in the older, rhetorical sense: Niemetschek, *Ich kannte Mozart: Leben des K. K. Kapellmeisters Wolfgang Gottlieb Mozart nach Originalquellen beschrieben*, ed. Jost Perfahl, 2d ed. (Munich, 1985), p. 27; cf. Sisman, *"Jupiter" Symphony*, p. 10.

25. Christian Friedrich Michaelis, "Ueber das Erhabene in der Musik," in the *Deutsche Monatsschrift* (Leipzig, Jan. 1801); and in "Einige Bemerkungen über das Erhabene der Musik," *Berlinische musikalische Zeitung* 1 (1805), no. 46, pp. 179–81.

26. Michaelis, *Ueber den Geist der Tonkunst mit Rücksicht auf Kants "Kritik der Urteilskraft,"* 2 vols. (Leipzig, 1795–1800).

27. Michaelis, "Bemerkungen," p. 180, col. 1 (LeHuray and Day, p. 289).

28. Michaelis, "Bemerkungen," p. 180, col. 1; p. 179, col. 2 (LeHuray and Day, p. 290).

29. Michaelis, "Bemerkungen," pp. 180–81 (LeHuray and Day, annotation p. 289).

30. Michaelis, "Bemerkungen," p. 179 (LeHuray and Day, p. 290).

31. Sisman, "Learned Style in the 'Jupiter'," pp. 235–36, *"Jupiter" Symphony*, chap. 8.

32. Sulzer, "Erhaben," pp. 84–85 (LeHuray and Day, pp. 138–39). See n. 16.

33. As in the common operatic treatment of abandoned heroines; see Mary Hunter, "Landscapes, Gardens, and Gothic Settings in the *Opere Buffe* of Mozart and his Italian Contemporaries," *Current Musicology* 51 (1993): 94–104.

34. See Sisman, "Learned Style," pp. 222–23, and *"Jupiter" Symphony*, pp. 14, 16.

35. 24 July 1801: *Joseph Haydn: Gesammelte Briefe und Aufzeichnungen*, ed. Dénes Bartha (Kassel, 1965), p. 373; English translation adapted from H. C. Robbins Landon, *Haydn: Chronicle and Works*, vol. 5, *Haydn: The Late Years, 1801–1809* (Bloomington, 1977), pp. 70–71.

36. Schilling, *Encyclopädie der gesammten musikalischen Wissenschaften, oder Universal Lexikon der Tonkunst*, 7 vols. (Stuttgart, 1834–38), vol. 2, p. 617 (LeHuray and Day, p. 474).

37. Donald Francis Tovey, *Essays in Musical Analysis*, vol. 5, *Vocal Music* (London, 1937), pp. 114–18; Heinrich Schenker, "Haydn: Die Schöpfung: Die Vorstellung des Chaos," *Das Meisterwerk in der Musik* 2 (1926): 159–70 (translation forthcoming from Cambridge Univ. Press). For an interpretation of "Chaos" as generated by a paradox-

ical combination of genres—ricercar and fantasy—see A. Peter Brown, "Haydn's Chaos: Genesis and Genre," *Musical Quarterly* 73 (1989): 18–59.

38. Compare Handel's passage in *Samson* (in some ways analogous but in more important ones not) cited by Brown, "*The Creation* and *The Seasons*: Some Allusions, Quotations, and Models from Handel to Mendelssohn," *Current Musicology* 51 (1993): 28–30.

39. On the cultural and literary context of this inspiration, see Hans-Jürgen Horn, "Fiat lux: Zum kunsttheoretischen Hintergrund der 'Erschaffung' des Lichts in Haydn's Schöpfung," *Haydn-Studien* 3 (1973–74): 65–84.

40. See Webster, *Haydn's "Farewell" Symphony*; Ethan Haimo, *Haydn's Symphonic Forms: Essays in Compositional Logic* (Oxford, 1995).

41. As Dahlhaus points out ("Hoffmann's Beethoven-Kritik," pp. 80–81, 84), eighteenth-century discussions of the sublime had already emphasized the need for underlying coherence in such passages.

42. "Ueber das Humoristische oder Launige in der musikalischen Komposition," *Allgemeine musikalische Zeitung*, vol. 9, no. 46 (12 August 1807), cols. 725–29 (LeHuray and Day, pp. 291–92).

43. Jean-Paul (Johann Paul Friedrich Richter), *Vorschule der Aesthetik*; trans. in Kathleen M. Wheeler, ed., *German Aesthetics and Literary Criticism* (Cambridge, 1984), pp. 174, 177–78. See Alfred Brendel, "Must Classical Music Be Entirely Serious? (1) The Sublime in Reverse," in Brendel, *Music Sounded Out* (New York, 1990), p. 15; William Kinderman, "Beethoven's High Comic Style in Piano Sonatas of the 1790s; or, Beethoven, Uncle Toby, and the 'Muckcart-Driver'," *Beethoven Forum* 5 (1996): 120–21.

44. The oft-quoted comments by Johann Karl Friedrich Triest ("Bemerkungen über die Ausbildung der Tonkunst in Deutschland im achtzehnten Jahrhundert (Fortsetzung)," *Allgemeine musikalische Zeitung*, vol. 3, no. 24 (11 March 1801), cols. 405–10, specifically link Haydn with both Sterne and Jean-Paul, with careful distinctions among humor (Laune), and related concepts. Among the many recent treatments of Haydn and humor, the most insightful seem to me Mark Evan Bonds, "Haydn, Laurence Sterne, and the Origins of Musical Irony," *Journal of the American Musicological Society* 44 (1991): 57–91 (for Triest see pp. 61–63); Gretchen A. Wheelock, *Haydn's Ingenious Jesting with Art: Contexts of Musical Wit and Humor* (New York, 1992). On Haydn's moral earnestness see Webster, *Haydn's "Farewell" Symphony*, pp. 234–36, 247–49 et passim. See the translation of Triest in this volume.

45. On musical topics see Leonard G. Ratner, *Classic Music: Expression, Form, and Style* (New York, 1980), parts I–II; Wye Jamison Allanbrook, *Rhythmic Gesture in Music: 'Le nozze di Figaro' and 'Don Giovanni'* (Chicago, 1983), introduction and part 1; V. Kofi Agawu, *Playing with Signs: A Semiotic Interpretation of Classic Music* (Princeton, 1991).

46. This point is especially clear in opera; see Webster, "The Analysis of Mozart's Arias," in Cliff Eisen, ed., *Mozart Studies* (London, 1991), §II.1, "Aria Types," esp. pp. 109–12.

47. See Kinderman, "Beethoven's High-Comic Style," p. 120, n. 5.

48. That is, encompassing the entire realm of "word-tone relations," which cannot be further addressed here.

49. See Anke Riedel-Martiny, "Das Verhältnis von Text und Musik in Haydns Oratorien," *Haydn-Studien* 1(1965–67): 205–40, esp. p. 224 ff..

50. In the *Creation*, "ewig" and "Ewigkeit" are interpreted in this way, with sublime effect, in Nos. 19[b], "The Lord is Great"; 30[c], "Hail to Thee, O God"; and 32, "Sing the Lord." (The last of these is shown below as Example 10.)

51. Rita Steblin, *A History of Key Characteristics in the Eighteenth and Early Nineteenth Centuries* (Ann Arbor, 1983).

52. On the eighteenth-century pastoral see *Die Vier Jahreszeiten im 18. Jahrhundert: Colloquium der Arbeitsstelle 18. Jahrhundert, Gesamthochschule Wuppertal, Universität Münster, Schloß Langenburg vom 3. bis 5. Oktober 1983* (Heidelberg 1986). The *Creation* is also suffused with pastoral associations, not only in arias such as "With verdure clad," but especially in the Adam and Eve sections of Part III.

53. See Landon, *The Symphonies of Joseph Haydn* (London, 1955), chap. xiv; Martin Chusid, "Some Observations on Liturgy, Text and Structure in Haydn's Late Masses," in Landon and Roger E. Chapman, eds., *Studies in Eighteenth-Century Music: A Tribute to Karl Geiringer on his Seventieth Birthday* (New York, 1970), pp. 125–35. (The analogy has in fact been exaggerated; but that is a topic for another study.)

54. Webster, *Haydn's "Farewell" Symphony*, pp. 163, 248 et passim.

55. Ibid., pp. 330–31.

56. The earliest example I have noticed is the *Salve regina* in G minor of 1771, a passage that (again) determines much of the course of the entire multimovement composition. See Webster, "Haydns Salve Regina in g-Moll (1771) und die Entwicklung zum durchkomponierten Zyklus," *Haydn-Studien* 6 (1986–94): 245–60.

57. See Wolf Frobenius, "Momentum/Moment, instans/instant, Augenblick," in Hans Heinrich Eggebrecht et al., ed., *Handwörterbuch der musikalischen Terminologie*; idem, "Über das Zeitmaß Augenblick in Adornos Kunsttheorie," *Archiv für Musikwissenschaft* 36 (1979): 279–305. (I thank Berthold Hoeckner for these references.) On the brevity of the sublime experience, see Sisman, "Learned Style," pp. 235–36.

58. Cited by Tovey, *Essays in Musical Analysis*, vol. 5, *Vocal Music* (London, 1937), pp. 132–33; and many other observers.

59. Michael Haydn singled out this passage for praise: "Here and there you will be surprised; and what my brother contrives in his choruses with 'Ewigkeit' etc. is something extraordinary." Cited from Albert Christoph Dies, *Biographische Nachrichten von Joseph Haydn* (1810), ed. Horst Seeger, 2d ed. (Berlin, 1962), p. 179.

60. The authentic sources for the text give both "singen" (to sing) and "siegen" (to triumph). See Horst Walter, "Gottfried van Swietens handschriftliche Textbücher zu 'Schöpfung' und 'Jahreszeiten,'" *Haydn-Studien* 1 (1965–67): 277; Landon, *Haydn: The Final Years*, p. 113; Landon, ed., *The "Creation" and the "Seasons": The Complete Authentic Sources for the Word-Books* (Cardiff, 1985; including facsimiles of van Swieten's recently discovered handwritten libretto), pp. 124, 190. I prefer the associations of "to sing." It is noteworthy that Swieten suggested avoiding text repetitions in setting the creation of Light; i.e. in sublime contexts. See ibid., pp. 14, 84; London, *Haydn Chronicle*, vol. 4, *The Years of "The Creation" 1796–1800* (Bloomington, 1977), p. 351.

61. Tovey, *Essays*, vol. 5, p. 161.

62. Georg August Griesinger, *Biographische Notizen über Joseph Haydn* (Leipzig, 1810), pp. 118; trans. Vernon Gotwals, *Joseph Haydn: Eighteenth-Century Gentleman and Genius* (Madison, 1963), p. 63.

63. See Sisman, *"Jupiter" Symphony*, pp. 13–14.

64. "Wie schön ist diese Erde, / Und schöner, nun der Herr auch dich ins Daseyn rief, / Auf daß sein Werk vollendet werde!" Quoted from Landon, *The Years of "The Creation,"* p. 583. Many contemporary encomiums and reviews are quoted ibid., pp. 453–57, 572–601 et passim.

65. "Jüngst schuf Dein Schöpferisches WERDE! . . . Die Schöpfung ganz—zum Zweitenmal. . . . So huld'gen wir . . . Der Allmacht deiner Zaubertöne / Und Dir, dem Gott der Harmonie!" (quoted ibid., p. 457). I thank Susan Youens for providing a copy of its later, anthologized, publication in *Sämtliche Gedichte Gabrielens von Baumberg* (Vienna, 1800), pp. 268–69. On Baumberg see Youens, *Schubert's Poets and the Making of Lieder* (Cambridge, 1996), chap. 1.

66. Griesinger, *Biographische Notizen*, pp. 73–74 (emphasis original); Gotwals, *Joseph Haydn*, pp. 41–42.

67. Horst Seeger, "Zur musikhistorischen Bedeutung der Haydn-Biographie von Albert Christoph Dies," *Beiträge zur Musikwissenschaft* 1/3 (1959): 30; the concluding internal quotation is drawn from the text of the aria in question ("seines Lebens Bild und sein offenes Grab"). Cf. Webster, *Haydn's "Farewell" Symphony*, pp. 228–32.

68. Of course, this implies a disprivileging of the traditional sense of "Classical Style." The essential continuity between all music from c. 1750 to c. 1900 was argued by Friedrich Blume, *Classic and Romantic Music* (New York, 1970); and, in the more restricted sense of late Beethoven returning to his late eighteenth-century "roots," by Charles Rosen, *The Classical Style: Haydn, Mozart, Beethoven* (New York, 1971). I have adumbrated the concept "first Viennese modern Style" for what I see as the period c. 1750–c.1815 (or –1830); see Webster, *Haydn's "Farewell" Symphony*, p. 357; idem, "The Concept of Beethoven's 'Early' Period in the Context of Periodizations in General," *Beethoven Forum* 3 (1994): 25–27.

Haydn's London Piano Trios and His Salomon String Quartets: Private vs. Public?

MARY HUNTER

It is a truism of the Haydn literature that the six string quartets of 1793 are "public" pieces, while the twelve late piano trios of 1795–1796 belong to a "private" musical sphere. That is, the string quartets Op. 71 and 74 were intended at least in the first instance for professional performance by Johann Peter Salomon and his quartet before London's large paying concert audiences. By contrast, the piano trios Hob.XV:18–29, also published in London, are chamber music in a more literal sense, written largely for amateurs (however accomplished) to perform in rooms to which no admission was charged and before a much smaller audience, or no audience at all. The social associations of these particular works in these genres were by no means unique. In the London of the 1790s, as Simon McVeigh points out in his study of concert life in the latter part of the century, string chamber music was normal fare for (male) professional performance, while accompanied sonatas, a genre that includes piano trios, were an "amateur domestic medium."[1] It is consistent with these associations that the Haydn trios in question are all dedicated to women[2] (two of them accomplished amateur performers) while the quartets were dedicated to their commissioner, Haydn's long-standing patron Count Apponyi.[3]

Scholars who have made much of the different intended or ideal performance venues of these works have found certain aspects of these venues reflected relatively literally in the music. László Somfai, for example, remarks on the utilitarian "noise killer" beginnings to some of the public quartets, while H. C. Robbins Landon and others have pointed to the "symphonic" presence of slow introductions, rare in Haydn's previous quartets.[4] Most students of these works have also noted that the formal processes and sonic qualities of the Op. 71/74 quartets (in effect a single opus) are well-adapted to the listening circumstances of large audiences. Singled out in this respect are the quartets' blocks of clearly contrasted material,[5] their "conspicuous" tonal shifts,[6] and their use of "orchestral" sound effects like tutti tremolos.[7] These qualities are typically said to contrast with the trios' tendency to unfold subtly, which is sometimes described as improvisatory and informal,[8] or as having spontaneous, "almost disorganized" aspects.[9] In addition, both Landon and Charles Rosen refer to the "popular" character of some of the quartet tunes, again associating this with their function as public works.[10]

There is less writing about the non-public expressive features of the trios; Landon often mentions their "personal" qualities, and words like "intimate" and "intricate" are not infrequent in the literature. These terms, however, are markedly less objective than "popular" or "orchestral." They emerge from a modern critical-biographical lexicon rather than from a sense of late-eighteenth-century rhetoric. Interestingly, they also interpret the trios as expressions of the composer's inner life rather than as utterances aimed at a particular set of listeners, however small or exclusive: "private" in these comments about the trios comes to mean "personal" (and by implication without social function) rather than "performed in non-public social circumstances and fulfilling needs different from those of concerts for large paying audiences." One reason for the paucity of explanatory literature about the trios is that they are not as canonic a genre as the quartets even within musicology, let alone on stage or in recordings.[11] But the absence of socially-based criticism may also result from the comparative difficulty of relating "private" musical gestures and rhetoric to venue and audience. There is, for example, no obvious private equivalent to (or inverse of) the inherently public "noise killer" gesture, and the absence or infrequency of other apparently "public" attention-grabbing maneuvers in the trios does not bespeak "private" in the way that their presence and frequency in the quartets bespeaks "public."

My aim here is not to deny the validity of expressive and formal musical reflections of context in these two genres; indeed, I think one can find here a rich trove of expressive topics and formal devices denoting clearly opposed domains of behavior and relationships.[12] But to parcel out the expressive attributes of the two genres between an absolutely "public" and an absolutely "private" domain does justice neither to the historically-grounded complexity of the relation between public and private, nor to the richness with which music can embody social structures and relations—relations which both include and transcend the private/public continuum.

The Interdependence of Public and Private: Audiences and Concerts

That "public" did not mean in late-eighteenth-century London what it means now is clear from Simon McVeigh's magisterial work. The modern understanding of a "public" concert is a musical occasion to which anyone, regardless of social standing, may buy a ticket. McVeigh has shown that concert life in London operated on what he (following William Jackson) has called a "principle of exclusivity," by means of which only people in the upper reaches of society (defined variously by birth and money) were able or expected to attend the more prestigious concerts—and Haydn's appearances always counted among these.[13] Thus although Haydn's concert appearances were public in the sense of being widely advertised and for sale, they were not what we might now think of as "fully" public in the sense of being realistically available to more than the highest echelons of society. As McVeigh notes, price was not the only thing used to confirm the exclusivity of a musical event; performances by certain musicians were restricted in number, and a general understanding about the social status of various concerts discouraged people below "the quality" from attending certain events.[14]

Thus even on the relatively straightforward level of accessibility, certain public concerts in London at this time had strong elements of "the private." Indeed, as McVeigh points out, anecdotal and fictional accounts of the highest level of concert life at the time often give it the characteristics of a moveable party. Audience members looked out for and conversed with friends and associates. Certain concerts—even whole series of concerts—were *de rigueur* for keeping up with the social whirl. Conversely, although there were undoubtedly many fully private musical occasions, "private" concerts—salons, birthday celebrations for important people, some court occasions—had a public aspect. They were often widely known about, guests might gain admittance through quasi-official introductions even though they were not known to the hosts, and the occasions occasionally merited public review or commentary afterwards.[15]

Adding historical qualifications to the terms "public" and "private," while complicating their modern meanings, allows us to paint a more accurate picture of the context for these chamber works of Haydn. But it does not change the fact that the intended setting for the original performances of Op. 71/74 was large, publicly advertised (and thus at least relatively anonymous), and run for financial benefit, whereas the settings for the earliest performances of the late trios seem to have been smaller, and were certainly unadvertised. Nor does it inevitably lead to a change in the way we consider the music of these works. The commercial, professional, and male-dominated world of the quartets is still fairly clearly opposed to the domestic (or quasi-domestic), amateur, female-centered world of the trios. However, the historical complications mentioned suggest the pervasive interpenetrations of public and private that characterized the changing musical and cultural scene of this period; and to take these abstract structures seriously suggests a new or at least a more nuanced evaluation of how these works of Haydn reflect and embody their context.

The most insightful discussion I have found on the subject, Jürgen Habermas's *The Structural Transformation of the Public Sphere*,[16] stresses the total dependence of the public and private domains on each other, indeed, not only dependence, but constant intersection. Concerning the eighteenth-century explosion in letterwriting and the contemporaneous popularity of the epistolary novel, for example, Habermas notes that "Subjectivity, as the innermost core of the private, was always already oriented to an audience."[17] In other words the eighteenth-century literary interest in creating an illusion of insight into the innermost feelings of a subject depended on the existence of a public ready to be taken in by the illusion. Michelle Dulak has noted an analogous phenomenon in the Op. 71/74 quartets, which inflate and dramatize "conversational" gestures, like passing the melody among the parts, so that even minimally attentive members of a large and physically distant audience will "get" the interactive topos.[18] One could add to this observation that however "public," broadly-conceived, concerto-like, or "orchestral" these pieces are in comparison to some of Haydn's earlier quartets (some of which were performed in London before Op. 71/74, though they were not composed for performance there),[19] they clearly retain their identity as chamber music in such techniques as the delicate dovetailing of the parts, and the multiple-accompaniment texture so uncharacteristic of Haydn's writing for the orchestra. These works re-enact the elaborate courtesies of the chamber much as the epistolary novel re-enacted immediacy and intimacy for enormous, ravenous audiences.

Leonard Ratner has offered another interpretation of the private/public spheres in noting that one social function of private chamber music was to bring other genres and styles within the domain of the domestic and to "deliver [them] to the rapidly growing musical public of the late eighteenth century in neat and manageable packages."[20] This notion of the domestic consumption and replication of "public" music—evident not only in the countless arrangements of operatic excerpts and symphonies but also in music composed expressly for the chamber—makes sense of the many "public" gestures in Haydn's late piano trios. Such "public" gestures include opening moments like the "noise-quelling" three chords at the beginning of the A major Trio no. 18[21] and the single introductory chords at the beginnings of the D major Trio no. 24 and the E-flat major Trio no. 29. The broad contrast between the fanfare arpeggio at the beginning of the C major Trio no. 27 and its immediate tender continuation in measure 2 also falls into this category (Example 1); the double gesture is repeated on the dominant in measures 3–4, as in Mozart's "Jupiter" Symphony.

Example 1. C Major Trio, Hob.XV:27/i, mm. 1–2.

Though not a beginning, the tutti tremolo sixteenth-notes at the end of the last movement of the same C major Trio are just as "orchestral" as the similar instances in the quartets. But examples need not be limited to texture. The famous "Gypsy Rondo" finale to the G major Trio no. 25 is scarcely an intimate piece, with its modular construction and rattling textures, and the largely unaltered reappearance of the F-sharp-major slow movement of Trio no. 26 in Symphony no. 102, with but a single reorchestrated reprise, reveals the permeability of generic boundaries.[22] Thus, although on the face of it they seem an odd couple, Ratner the historicist and Habermas the political theorist join in pointing out the confluence of private and public in this repertory.

If public and private are conceived as venues and as economic structures of performance whose characteristics can be accommodated or reflected in music, then it is probably indisputable that the differing proportions of "public" and "private" musical gestures and processes in the quartets and trios place them at different points on the continuum from the parlor to the public concert hall. There is a clear analogy here with the way the public-but-exclusive audiences for, say, the Professional Concerts in Hanover Square and the personally-invited audiences for certain publicized courtly concerts represent different way stations on the continuum from the unadvertised private occasion to the purely commercial concert. But the power of Habermas's model is that it takes us beyond the characteristics of an actual performance venue or fully-realized set of economic arrangements to the more abstract question of how private and public reception, consumption, and comprehension relate to each other.

When we change to these terms, "public" and "private" function more as simultaneous and contrapuntal strands of experience than as the two poles of a single continuum. To take the circumstances of listening as an example, the institution of the public concert hall removes—or at least diminishes—the audience's obligation to respond in a way calculated to please the concert's "host" partly by making the terms of entry at least putatively commercial rather than personal, and thus by figuring its audience as at least putatively or partially "anonymous." It also frees each member of the audience to respond individually, a trend reinforced by the increasingly anti-conversational arrangement of seats, the increasing expectation that audiences would be quiet, and, eventually (though not in Haydn's time) by the darkening of the auditorium. The London audiences for Haydn's concerts were, of course, not uniformly quiet, attentive, or anonymous, but Habermas's insights allow us to see the beginnings of concert-giving and -going structures which would facilitate the "publicly private" consumption of music, and reconfigure the relations among composer, performer, and listener, much as the published novel reconfigured the relations between author and reader. Simon McVeigh's observation that public performance in London became increasingly professionalized at the end of the century lends material confirmation to this theoretical hypothesis. McVeigh associates the demonstrable preference for highly-trained performers with the increasing "passivity" of London audiences: those who played and those who listened became increasingly distinct, and the experiences of playing and listening became ever more specialized.[23]

Along with the increasing specialization of performing and listening came a strengthening of the separation between composing and performing—a separation that, among other things, increasingly figured the performer (of instrumental more than of vocal music) as a vessel for, or window to, the product of the composer's mind, rather than a co-creator. This reorganization in the relationship between composing and performing also affected listening, as the ideal primary communication in certain genres was now increasingly understood as an almost direct link between composer-as-embodied-in-the-work and listener, much as the novel (read silently) communicates directly between the author and the reader.[24] Habermas observes that with the rise of the novel, especially of the epistolary sort:

> The relations between author, work, and public changed. They became intimate mutual relationships between privatised individuals who were psychologically interested in what was "human," in self knowledge and in sympathy.[25]

In the remainder of this essay I hope to demonstrate that while Haydn's Op. 71/74 quartets adumbrate this model of the "direct" communication of a largely fixed text from an author to a receiver, the London trios suggest a different social context for the creation, performance, and reception of music. The main evidence for this assertion is that the quartets and the trios exemplify markedly different relations between performer and composer: the former represent a cultural world with relatively clear distinctions between the functions of composition and performance, and the latter serve to model a world in which these distinctions are less clear. Rosen has already suggested the "improvisatory" quality—the sense of thinking at the keyboard—conveyed by the trios: the following remarks are in part an attempt to put that observation into the social context it deserves.[26]

Social Modeling in the London Trios and Op. 71/74 Quartets

To ask what it means for a piece of music to "model" the relationships between composer and performer partly involves asking what the composer leaves to the performer's discretion, especially in the realm of ornamentation and improvisation. However, on a more significant but also less tangible level it also involves asking whether the work draws attention to the act of performance as something separate from, or somehow integrated with, the act of composition. Virtuosic or "brilliant" passages, for example, may reveal that the composer has clearly constructed a moment in which the audience's attention is meant to be directed to the performer's capacity to reproduce the difficult passagework he has written (as they are in Haydn's London quartets), or they may, by being more capriciously or inconspicuously woven into the flow of the music (as they are in his London trios), suggest that composing and performing are more seamlessly co-extensive. One might ask whether, for example, the parts are so complexly related to one another that they "would have had" to be fully composed, or whether they are sufficiently routine, subsidiary, or (improbably) independent that extemporary performance could be imagined as a possibility even if all the notes are in fact written out. Unlike the question of the actual amount of improvisation allowed or encouraged, which gets at the literal relation between the actual composer and the actual performer(s) in a given piece, these less tangible questions always deal in the conditional, and suggest the relation between an *implied* performer and the composer, a relation fully written into the musical text, if not consciously intended as such by the composer. Noticing the differences in the way this implicit relation plays out in Haydn's London quartets and piano trios sheds light on the different social locations and meanings of these works.

In general, the trios model the act of performance as more continuous with the act of composition than do the quartets. On the most literal level, they allow considerably more room for improvisation. The thirty-six movements of these works contain thirty-five ornamentable fermatas with the potential for completely free ornamentation.[27] They also offer the possibility of rhythmic improvisation in the seven written-out but unmeasured, ornamented cadences.[28] There are also nine fully written-out ornamented cadences that give the impression of improvisation.[29] No such passages exist in the Op. 71/74 quartets; the closest Haydn comes in these works is a single group of ten thirty-second-notes in the slow movement of Op. 74, no. 3. And in the twenty-four movements of these quartets there are only thirteen ornamentable fermatas.[30] It may be worth noting in this context Donald Tovey's implicit suggestion that cadenzas in chamber music are decidedly old fashioned. He writes about Op. 9, no. 4: "in a quartet otherwise astonishingly mature . . . Haydn not only leaves a blank space for a cadenza at the end of a slow movement, but represents its conventional 6/4 chord by a bare fourth." Tovey's main point here is Haydn's retrogressive musical behavior in writing the cadential moment as though a continuo player would fill in the missing notes, but the presence of the cadenza itself is not immune from criticism.[31]

The second demonstrable way in which the trios much more than the quartets model performance as a creative (or semi-creative) act is in their much greater use of decorative variation, or of what Elaine R. Sisman calls "melodic outline variation."[32] Fully half the movements of the London piano trios include decorative variations or decorated repeats or returns of melodic material. The decorations go beyond *agréments*, but are typically very much the sort of thing that a perhaps overzealous performer might improvise. In the second phrase of the first movement of the E major Trio no. 28, the piano repeats the melody with lovely chromatic ornaments (Example 2). Now it is true that these chromatic elements turn out to have longer-range significance, as the chromatic semitone, and to a lesser extent the chromatic scale, recur throughout the movement (for example, in mm. 29–32 and the beginning of the development). But their structural embeddedness does not, I think, prevent mm. 5–6 from sounding improvised.

Example 2. E Major Trio, Hob.XV:28/i, mm. 1–8.

In the reprise of the A-minor slow movement of Trio 18 in A major (Example 3), three things help the music sound extemporised. The simplest of the three is the unmeasured material in m. 42, and the sextuplet rush at the end of m. 43 to arrive at the right note in m. 44. More interesting is the almost constant and always literal presence of the unadorned tune, at pitch, in either the piano or the violin (whichever one is not ornamenting); this virtual heterophony highlights the fact of ornamentation. The presence of a melody together

Example 3. A major Trio, Hob.XV:18/ii, mm. 37–42.

with the variation of its main notes is quite different from the quartets' use of fast and genuinely contrapuntal countersubjects to the theme, as in the finales of Op. 71, no. 3 or 74, no. 1. It is also to be distinguished from the use of an ornamented accompaniment, such as that in the slow movement of the E-flat major Trio, no. 29 (Example 4). The third "extemporary" aspect of the reprise in the slow movement of the A major trio is the relative brevity of the decorating flourishes. This decorated reprise insightfully represents a performer's somewhat irregular spurts of decorative inspiration. Moreover, the substance of these decorations relies on the staple formulae of division work: scales, turns, arpeggios, and measured trills. This highly "performative" combination of apparently capricious invention and reliance on stock patterns is quite characteristic of the trios but can be found nowhere in the quartets. The written notes in these works imply that performance is an activity co-extensive with creation.

Example 4. E♭ major Trio, Hob.XV:29/ii, mm. 9–12.

Example 5. Op. 71, no.3/ii, mm. 1–8.

A third and final distinction in how the two genres represent composition and performance emerges from the slower movements' handling of wit and caprice. In moments where the slow quartet movements evidence something akin to wit, they draw attention to the act of composition. By contrast, the oddities or capricious aspects of the trio movements in slow tempi typically highlight the act of performance, or the aspects of composition closest to performance. In particular they emphasize the capacity of performance to breathe life and passion into routine structures. My first example concerns the variation-form slow movement of Op. 71, no. 3,[33] and the opening variation movement of Trio 23. The quartet movement presents a number of instances of a particularly felicitous eighteenth-century definition of wit: namely, "the dextrous performance of a legerdemain trick, by which one idea is presented and another substituted."[34] The sudden turn to the mediant minor at the end of the first phrase is the first such substitution (Example 5). This spawns a second half of the theme which begins not on what would have been the predictable dominant, but on the dominant of the supertonic (V/ii). The second

Example 6. Op. 71, no.3/ii, mm. 90–94.

"legerdemain trick" is the astonishing excursion into homophonic staccato sixteenth-notes in the third bar (i.e. at neither the beginning of the phrase nor at a respectable hiatus point) of the return of the major key theme after the last minor episode (Example 6). The last example of this sort of wit is the final appearance of the theme, in which the harmonic irregularities of the original version have been ironed out, though in the process the phrase rhythm has been wrinkled. The wit of switching the interest of the theme from its harmony to its phrase rhythm is wonderfully encapsulated in the little cello echoes in mm. 122 and 125 (Example 7). These are not the only instances of wit in this movement, but they are the most immediately audible, and serve well for comparison with the variation movement of the D minor Trio.

The minor-key theme of Trio 23 is not without its harmonic surprises (e.g. the diminished-seventh chord vii7/C in m. 6 moving to F major), but more striking as an overall characteristic is the capriciousness (and detail) of the performance markings — the accents in mm. 2, 3 and 6 and especially the combination of offbeat accents and an extremely spiky melody in mm.17ff. (Example 8). The major-key theme in this alternat-

Example 7. Op. 71, no.3/ii. mm. 109–128.

Example 8. D minor Trio, Hob.XV:23/i, mm.1–17.

ing set continues the capriciousness, with offbeat sforzandos followed immediately by marked accents. Indeed, although the two minor variations (a stormy unison perpetual motion in sixteenth-notes and an alla zoppa, or limpingly syncopated one) are strongly marked in character, the major mode variations are the more surprising ones, given what Sisman calls the "radiant" character of the basic pitch material.[35] The first of these begins with a series of almost declamatory upward-rushing scales for the piano that only gradually settle in to the more predictable and decorative thirty-second notes (Example 9a), while the last one starts with fairly conventional thirty-second-note divisions on the tune—and even continues with them, as might be expected, but very loudly and with the violin and piano in raucous unison (Example 9b). This is striking and even bizarre, but it is not a "legerdemain trick of substitution." Indeed, one of the remarkable things about this movement is that with pitch material of a relatively unremarkable sort, and indeed within the confines of a perfectly regular structure (unlike that of the variations in Op. 71, no. 3), Haydn has created a movement full of surprise and caprice (though not exactly wit) by deploying the an cillary characteristics of volume, accent, and selective doubling—

Example 9a. D minor Trio, Hob.XV:23/i, mm. 65–70.

Example 9b. Hob.XV:23/i, mm. 108–112

features that, by virtue of their auxiliary relation to the notes themselves, could be considered part of the *performer's* domain.

If this pair of pieces suggests that the quartets highlight the wit of the composer, while the trios highlight the comic or capricious potential of the act of performance (if not of the actual performers), another pair reveals that even when performance or performers are the subject of the joke, the two genres differ in the way they present the relations between composers and performers. In the other variation set of the quartets, the slow movement of Op. 74, no. 2, the binary form theme is in perfectly regular four-measure units until the return of the opening material, which begins with the second violin, and then is taken over and re-started by the first (Example 10). This "false" start by the second violin and viola presages a series of gentle witticisms about who plays what. Starting in m. 27, the first variation begins with the tune played in the same register as the second violin's and viola's false start in m. 17, but with the cello on top and viola playing a third below. At the "false start place" in the second half of this variation (m. 43) the second violin plays ornamentation above the cello and viola's tune, but once again the first violin asserts its right to the dominant material, and that

Example 10. Op. 74, no. 2/ii, mm. 1–26.

Example 11. Op. 74, no. 2/ii, mm. 43–47.

material's right to the higher register (Example 11). However, in the happy ending to this series of snubs, the second violin gets the main voice in the *minore* variation, which ends *not* with the return of A, with its second-violin false start, but with the B section of the theme, expanded by two measures. One might argue that not only would the return of A with its double start be formally superfluous at this point, but also "performatively" *de trop*—that is, the joke does not need to be repeated at this moment of longer lasting and more impressive domination (Example 12). This is wit that plays on the group roles of the performers, but it is a discourse presented as totally controlled; indeed, literally orchestrated, and made clearly audible (as well as visible in live performance)—by the composer.

The "instrument joke" in the London trios occurs in the G-major strophic variation movement of the B-flat major Trio no. 20, where Haydn instructs the pianist to play the two-part theme with the left hand alone (Example 13). In its opening appearance it is hard to know what to make of this; is it a special sonic effect like the on-one-string fingering in the Ländler-like second group of the first

Example 12. Op. 74, no. 2/ii, mm. 53–70.

movement of the G minor quartet Op. 74, no. 3? If modern performances, in which the one-handedness of the theme is inaudible, are any measure, then sonic effect is not the point. It would, rather, seem to be a humorous comment about the role of the piano. This becomes clearer in the first variation, where the violin doubles the tune in the thumb-end of the piano's left hand, while the right hand does the decorative work that might normally be expected from the violin (Example 14). The second variation is also surprising in its texture or division of labor, with a sixteenth-note division of the tune in the left hand of the piano over the bass line played with the remaining fingers of the same hand while the right hand sits idle, and the violin plays a slow countermelody (Example 15). In the last variation, the right hand of the piano makes up for lost time by playing thirty-second-note divisions, while strings and left hand play the harmonic skeleton (Example 16).

Example 13. B♭ major Trio, Hob.XV: 20/ii, mm. 1–4

Example 14. B♭ major Trio, Hob.XV:20/ii, mm.21–24.

Example 15. B♭ major Trio, Hob.XV:20/ii, mm. 39–46

Example 16. B♭ major Trio, Hob.XV:20/ii, mm. 61–63

Like the D-minor variations of Trio 23, the form of this movement, and of every phrase in the movement, is utterly regular, and the increase from plain eighths in the tune, through sixteenths to thirty-seconds in the variations is also quite unexceptional. (Indeed, in his comments on this piece, A. Peter Brown notes the similarity of this procedure to hack work.[36]) The oddity of the piece lies almost entirely with the deployment of the piano; and what is more, this oddity is not easily audible. It is not a comment from a composer to a physically distant but mentally and psychologically connected audience about the ambitions of subordinates (as is the quartet movement); it is, rather, a witticism to be shared by the performers among themselves, and possibly with a couple of audience members who have a good view of the pianist's hands. There is no obviously compositional feature (like phraseological irregularity or harmonic surprise) pointing the listener to the piano joke. It is also such a peculiar instruction that it would not be unreasonable for an audience member who could see to assume that it was the performer's own choice. Once again in these trios, the line between the act of composition and the act of performance is blurred.

If the quartets in all their relevant aspects signify a world in which performers re-create music in such a way as to communicate a composer's concepts as faithfully as possible, regardless of whether the composer is physically present or not, the trios model a world in which the composer is perpetually present. Such a world might be that of the court composer whose presence in the establishment of his patron was essentially constant, and whose successive presentation of new works under his own direction ensured the inextricable entanglement of composition and performance, an entanglement particularly tightly knotted when the compositions were not routinely or officially available for publication, as Haydn's were not until the re-writing of his contract in 1779.

Texture, Social Models, and the Market

The social model I am proposing for the London quartets is analogous to the one that Habermas describes for the eighteenth-century novel. Not only do these quartets enact an apparently direct communication from the composer (author) to the listener (reader), but they are also "about" intimate dialogue or discourse among fully characterized individuals speaking, as it were, for themselves (there being no narrator). The illusion of conversation is an important part of this model, not only because of the way it enacts intimacy in public, but also because it requires that the actual performers become subsumed within the line they perform. Theodor W. Adorno remarks in his *Introduction to the Sociology of Music*:

> Even great chamber music [and he obviously means the string quartet] has to pay tribute to the primacy of the thing; [chamber music's] native hour coincides with the abolition of the figured bass, and thus of the modest remains of improvisation, the irrational spontaneity of players.[37]

Adorno here imagines chamber music as the simulacrum of a meaningful private sphere to be reproduced by performers who are technically proficient, spiritually prepared, but not given to treading on the composer's sacred ground. According to Adorno's model, Haydn's London quartets can be seen as calculated in broad formal conception not only for the virtuosic display of the concert hall, but also for the "publicly private" listening marketplace that was analogous to the developing market for the novel.

Not surprisingly, the trios' relation to the market is less self-explanatory. It is equally unsurprising that Adorno, who was wedded to the notion that the string quartet fully embodied the spirit of chamber music, dismisses private music involving the piano as distinctly secondary. However, just as the quartets' conversational texture is congruent with their social location and meaning, the performance-as-composition texture of the London trios can be understood as a crucial part of the way they depict the social relations of their imagined world.[38] As many commentators have noticed, they are only rarely conversational in the same sense as the quartets. Where the violin and the right hand of the piano (the two most frequent and most equal interlocutors) do engage in the sort of free yet connected exchange that might reasonably be construed as conversation, it is almost always in an exchange of ornamental figures—a practice based in improvisatory performance—rather than the "substantial" exchange of primary thematic material. The typical texture in these late trios is a sort of exfoliation of the piano part, in which the violin's relation to the piano is much more heterophonic than contrapuntal (when it is not playing a melody to the piano's straightforward accompaniment). Even when the violin melody diverges from the piano's in interesting ways in the middle of a phrase, it will often return to double the piano at the end. And when it is indisputably the preeminent voice, that pre-eminence usually lasts for at least a whole phrase; there is almost no illusion of interruption or even of competition between the voices. As W. Dean Sutcliffe writes, "Haydn's three instruments . . . seem to have reached a prior agreement as to the significance of the material they are to perform."[39] The social dynamic this suggests is not the interaction of "fully constituted individuals," but, rather, that of a single will projected in several voices. Whereas the conversational mode is often taken to represent a sort of democracy, however conditional or confined, the obvious social referent for the projection of a single will is the court. Norbert Elias, in his classic *The Court Society* notes, "The king brings his subjects to a point where, as Montesquieu once put it, they think *comme il veut*." [40]

I am not proposing here that the trios were intended for court performance; indeed, the dedication of the last two sets to Therese Jansen and Rebecca Schroeter would make such a proposal absurd. What I want to suggest is that in certain ways these pieces evoke the world of courtly social relations, and not just because they mirror the fundamental structure of the court itself. The way they interweave composition and performance also aptly represents the system of courtly patronage that bound court and court composer. However bound to their era, it would do these trios a grave disservice to mark them as simply old-fashioned, aesthetically, socially, or commercially. Not only do the extraordinary modulations (third-related and enharmonic) match the most advanced of Haydn's music; not only do many of these tunes breathe a warmth Landon hears as anticipating Schubert,[41] but these pieces took their place in the market right along with the quartets. The trios are just as "composed" as the quartets; the actual performers are essentially as "vessel-like" as their quartet counterparts. By invoking a social and musical order different from, and older than, that of the emerging specialized commercial concert hall with its audience of consumers of putatively permanent artworks, these trios might well have provided a British audience with the simulacrum of a culture both recognizable and distant, whose demise or at least decline at the very end of the eighteenth century was being both celebrated and regretted.[42] For Haydn, they may have functioned in part as an opportunity to relive, with a conflicting mixture of strong feelings, his years of service at Eszterháza. And for us, their curious but moving mixture of modernity and antiquity, of passion and quaint gentility, of ritualized social relations and a marvelous improvisatory informality, should evoke music's power to embody social relations in all their complexity.

NOTES

1. Simon McVeigh, *Concert Life in London from Mozart to Haydn* (Cambridge, 1993) , p. 104.

2. Hob.XV:18–20 are dedicated to the Dowager Princess Esterházy, widow of Prince Anton Esterházy; nos. 21–23 to Maria Hermenegild Esterházy, wife of Nicholas II; nos. 24–26 to Rebecca Schroeter, and nos. 27–29 to Therese Jansen. The Esterházy dedications are the traditional indications of patronage ties and indicate next to nothing about the practical relation between the dedicatees and the particular works, although Maria had received the dedication of the sonatas Hob.XVI:40–42 in 1784. Rebecca Schroeter and Therese Jansen, however, were both fine pianists (though not "professional"), and the works were evidently intended for them to play.

3. H. C. Robbins Landon, *Haydn: Chronicle and Works,* vol. 3: *Haydn in London, 1791–1795* (Bloomington, 1976), p. 459, notes that Apponyi reserved the Viennese performing rights for a period, but that despite the dedication of Op. 71/74 to this patron, Haydn's "eye was on Salomon and the Hanover Square Rooms rather than Apponyi and his chamber."

4. Ibid., pp. 459–60; László Somfai, "Haydn's London String Quartets," *Haydn Studies: Proceedings of the International Haydn Conference, Washington D.C. 1975*, ed. Jens Peter Larsen, Howard Serwer and James Webster (New York and London, 1981), pp. 389–91.

5. Somfai, "Haydn's London String Quartets," p. 390.

6. McVeigh, *Concert Life,* 159. McVeigh makes the point about the "public" quality of the quartets implicitly, by discussing their harmonic language together with that of the symphonies.

7. Landon, *Haydn Chronicle*, vol. 3, p. 459; Reginald Barrett-Ayres, *Joseph Haydn and the String Quartet* (New York, 1974), p. 281. Barrett-Ayres points out the different and "magical" effect of an orchestral texture in its new home.

8. James Webster, liner notes to Titanic recording of Trios 19, 27 and 29, played by Sonya Monosoff, Malcolm Bilson, and John Hsu.

9. Rosen, *The Classical Style*, (New York, 1971), p. 352.

10. Ibid., pp. 335–36; Landon, *Haydn Chronicle*, vol. 3, p. 460.

11. James Webster pointed this out in "Haydn's Piano Trios at the Crossroads," unpublished paper delivered at Amherst College, March 1995.

12. One could start with the two E-major slow movements of works in G (Op. 74, no. 3 and Hob.XV:25) where one might read the quartet movement as a mixture of hymn-like, elevated (and by implication public, even civic) oratorical *topoi* (topics or commonplaces) and the trio as a representation of domestic song.

13. McVeigh, *Concert Life in London*, pp. 11–12.

14. Ibid. On p. 11, McVeigh quotes a "crude" 1789 rendering of the hierarchy of concerts and their audiences; this moves from the Professional Concerts aimed at "the Quality" to those held at the Anacreontic Society, apparently aimed at "Folks." McVeigh also notes instances where the audience was explicitly restricted to members of certain classes.

15. McVeigh, *Concert Life*, p. 5, lists the regularly scheduled "private" concerts. Mary Sue Morrow, *Concert Life in Haydn's Vienna* (Stuyvesant, N. Y., 1989), presents a whole chapter on private concert life in that city, though with appropriate caveats about the incompleteness of the records.

16. Jürgen Habermas, *The Structural Transformation of the Public Sphere: An Inquiry into a Category of Bourgeois Society*, trans. Thomas Burger, with Frederick Lawrence (Cambridge, Mass., 1989).

17. Ibid., p. 49.

18. Michelle Dulak, "Audience, Texture, and the Evolution of Haydn's Late Quartet Style," unpublished paper delivered at Amherst College, March 1995..

19. Simon McVeigh shows that quartets from Haydn's Op. 64 set were performed in March 1791; "The Professional Concert and Rival Subscription Series in London, 1783–1793, *Royal Musical Association Research Chronicle* 22 (1989): 98. In *Concert Life in London*, p. 214, he notes that some from Op. 54 were performed in 1789.

20. Leonard Ratner, *Classic Music: Expression, Form, and Style* (New York, 1980), p. 142.

21. These numbers correspond to the Hoboken catalogue (Antony van Hoboken, *Joseph Haydn: Thematisch-Bibliographisches Werkverzeichnis*, vol. 1 (Mainz, 1957), used in the complete edition *Joseph Haydn: Werke*, vol. 17/3, ed. Irmgard Becker-Glauch (Munich, 1984), and assume the designation Hob.XV before the indicated number.

22. Though see Friedhelm Krummacher, "Klaviertrio und sinfonischer Satz: Zum Adagio aus Haydns Sinfonie no. 102" in *Quaestiones in Musica: Festschrift Franz Krautwurst zum 65. Geburtstag*, ed. Friedhelm Brusniak and Horst Leuchtmann (Tutzing, 1989) on the differences made by the orchestration and the repetition of the first period in the orchestral version.

23. *Concert Life in London*, Epilogue, pp. 223–24.

24. The decreasing importance of the performer in the conception of "the work" is connected to, but not identical with, the rise of the notion of "absolute music." Carl Dahlhaus' *The Idea of Absolute Music*, trans. Roger Lustig (Chicago, 1989) has been the starting point for a growing body of work on the political and cultural grounding of this notion. On the emergence of the "work-concept" in this period, see Lydia Goehr, *The Imaginary Museum of Musical Works* (Oxford, 1992).

25. Habermas, *The Structural Transformation*, p. 50.

26. Rosen, *The Classical Style*, p. 352: "Haydn was a composer who needed the piano in order to write music: these trios seem to give us Haydn at work."

27. Hob.XV:18/i, mm. 71–2, 119–120, 180, ii, m. 4, iii, m. 69; no. 19/iii, m. 48; no. 20/i, m.12, iii, mm. 24, 66, 98; no. 22/ ii, end; no. 23/ii, mm. 35, 53, end, iii, mm. 50, 151; no. 24/i, mm. 29, 72, 127; no. 26/ i, m. 62, iii, mm. 32, 71–72, 104,119; no. 27/ii, m. 52; no. 28/i, m. 59, iii, mm. 31, 53, 58–59, 89, 120, 157; no. 29/iii, mm. 154, 271–72, 285. I have not counted fermatas on initial chords or at the end of introductions, or on single final chords of movements.

28. The following ornamented cadences consist entirely of, or include, unmeasured notation: Hob.XV:22/iii, m. 167; no.23/i, end, and ii, m. 49; no. 27/ii, mm. 64–66; no. 28/i, m. 20, and iii, mm. 186–89; and no. 29/i, m. 41.

29. Hob.XV:20/i, m. 65; no. 22/i, m. 224, and iii, m. 106; no. 24/i, mm. 172–78, and no. 27/ii, mm. 13 and 19, 61 and 63; no. 28/ii, end.

30. Op. 71, no. 1/i, m. 20, ii, m. 18, 52; Op. 71, no. 2/iv, mm. 74, 94, Op. 74, no. 1/ii, mm. 148–49. iv, mm. 48–49, 183–84, 248; Op. 74, no. 2/i, m. 20, iii, mm. 23–24, iv, m. 271; Op. 74, no. 3/ iv, m. 99 (note the fermatas on pauses in mm. 72, 74, 76).

31. Sir Donald Francis Tovey, "Haydn's Chamber Music," in *Essays and Lectures on Music*, ed. Hubert J. Foss (London, 1949), p. 7. Haydn's Op. 9 was written c. 1769–70.

32. Elaine R. Sisman, *Haydn and the Classical Variation* (Cambridge, Mass. 1993), p. 112.

33. Landon, *Haydn Chronicle*, vol. 3, p. 471, calls this form double ABA, but Sisman, *Haydn and the Classical Variation*, refers to it as alternating variation (p. 268), identifying it further as an "unusual mode-alternating movement whose *minore* variations are based on the melody of the major theme" (p. 156).

34. William Jackson, quoted in Gretchen Wheelock, *Haydn's Ingenious Jesting with Art* (New York, 1992), p. 21.

35. Sisman, *Haydn and the Classical Variation*, p. 186.

36. A. Peter Brown, *Joseph Haydn's Keyboard Music: Sources and Style* (Bloomington, 1986), p. 359.

37. Theodor W. Adorno, *Introduction to the Sociology of Music*, trans. E. B. Ashton (New York, 1988), p. 87.

38. Rosen, *The Classical Style*, p. 352, mentions the general complaint about the cello's lack of independence in all of Haydn's trios. See also Katalin Komlós, "Haydn's Keyboard Trios, Hob.XV:5–17: Interaction between Texture and Form," *Studia Musicologica* 28 (1986): 353–400.

39. "Haydn's Piano Trio Textures," *Music Analysis* 6 (1987): 320.

40. Norbert Elias, *The Court Society*, trans. Edmund Jephcott (Oxford, 1983), p. 71.

41. Landon, *Haydn Chronicle*, vol. 3, p. 421.

42. Hester Lynch Piozzi, for example, in *Observations and Reflections Made in the Course of a Journey Through France, Italy, and Germany* , ed. Herbert Barrows (Ann Arbor, 1967), p. 37, wrote: "I have a notion there is much less of those distinctions at Milan than at London, where birth does so little for a man, that if he depends on *that*, and forbears other methods of distinguishing himself from his footman, he will stand a chance of being treated no better than him by the world." At the same time as Mrs. Piozzi regretted the efforts the more democratic English had to make to keep social distinctions clear, she found the combination of "obsequiousness" and familiarity of some of the serving class in Milan quite appalling.

The Symphony as Pindaric Ode

MARK EVAN BONDS

Recent decades have witnessed great advances in our understanding of how Haydn's symphonies were performed during his lifetime, yet we still know relatively little about how the composer's contemporaries actually perceived this music. What did Haydn's original audiences hear in his symphonies? In one sense, there ought to be as many answers to this question as there were individual listeners. But virtually none of those listeners recorded their views for posterity, so that the paucity of direct evidence makes it difficult to reconstruct even the basic, consistent attitudes toward Haydn's symphonies during the late eighteenth and early nineteenth centuries, let alone the idiosyncratic ones. Concert reviews from the time are few in number, and the brief notices we do have rarely go beyond such bland generalities as "bold," "original," "spirited," or "moving." Indeed, we scarcely know which of Haydn's London symphonies were premiered at which concerts, so vague is the record from even one of the best-documented periods of the composer's life. Private correspondence and diaries are equally uninformative on this count. The idea of recording one's responses to a specific work of music in any kind of detail would not begin to take hold until later in the nineteenth century.

With so little to go on in the way of direct testimony, we must look to other kinds of evidence in order to reconstruct contemporaneous perceptions of Haydn's symphonies. Among the most revealing sources of this kind are the half dozen or so descriptions of the symphony as a genre that appeared during the composer's lifetime. Brief as they are, these accounts identify specific elements that distinguished the symphony from all other genres. In so doing, they suggest the particular qualities to which an informed eighteenth-century listener might have given special attention while hearing a symphony. Genres are more than just categories: they guide perception. By its very nature, the generic designation of a work predisposes listeners to hear and judge that work against a tradition of similarly-named works. Consciously or unconsciously, audiences of the day anticipated—and heard—certain specific features in a symphony that they did not expect in other genres like the string quartet or the piano sonata. A genre can of course change over time and almost always does in at least some way; but there seems to have been a fairly stable set of expectations for the chamber symphony in the German-Austrian tradition of the late eighteenth century. Contemporaneous accounts of the genre of the symphony—particularly those that go beyond such basic external criteria as "a large work for orchestra in three or four movements"—can thus provide important (if indirect) clues about what late eighteenth-century audiences heard when they listened to a symphony. By combining these accounts with other, more general commentaries on Haydn's instrumental music, we can at least begin to reconstruct an outline of what particular features eighteenth-century listeners found so appealing in Haydn's symphonies.

By far the most detailed account of the symphony in the second half of the eighteenth century appears in Johann Georg Sulzer's *Allgemeine Theorie der schönen Künste* of 1771–74. Sulzer's "General Theory of the Fine Arts" encompasses literature, painting, sculpture, architecture, and dance as well as music. It was not a radical work in its time and yet for this very reason can be understood as documenting the more or less conventional wisdom of its day. Sulzer's encyclopedia was popular enough to appear in three different editions and several reissues over the next twenty-five years, with new bibliographies added to many of the entries in later editions.[1] Beethoven is known to have used this source on at least one occasion.[2] And when Heinrich Christoph Koch produced his lengthy and highly influential musical dictionary in 1802, he still considered Sulzer's entry on the symphony worth quoting at length.[3]

Most of Sulzer's three-page article necessarily concerns itself with the external characteristics of the symphony, such as the number of instruments, the sequence of movements, and the traditional distinction among the three types of symphony according to the intended place of performance: in the church (the *sinfonia da chiesa*), the theater (the opera overture), or the concert hall (the chamber symphony). Although of considerable interest, these points need not detain us here. What is of greater import for our purposes is the manner in which Sulzer describes the "true spirit" of the chamber symphony.

Symphonies in general, according to Sulzer, are "especially suited to the expression of the grand, the solemn, and the sublime." While the purpose of a theater symphony—an overture—"is to prepare the listener for an important musical event," the purpose of a chamber symphony, "which constitutes a self-sufficient entity, without reference to any following music," is to "exhibit the full splendor of the orchestra." A chamber symphony can achieve this end

> only by means of a full-toned, brilliant, and fiery manner. The allegros of the best chamber symphonies contain grand and bold ideas, free handling of compositional techniques, apparent irregularity in the melody and harmony, strongly-marked rhythms of various sorts, powerful bass melodies and unisons, concerting middle voices, free imitations, often a theme handled fugally, sudden transitions and shifts from one key to another, which are the more striking the weaker the connection is, bold shadings of *forte* and *piano*, and particularly the *crescendo*, which has the greatest effect when used with a rising melody and its climax. To this is added the art of weaving all the voices in and out of one another in such a way that all parts, when played together, create a single melody that is incapable of accompaniment, but rather one in which every voice is making its own particular contribution to the whole. Such an Allegro in a symphony is like a Pindaric ode: it elevates and moves the soul of the listener in the same way, and it requires the same spirit, the same sublime imagination, and the same knowledge of art in order to achieve this effect.[4]

The culminating analogy to Pindar's odes is striking and resonates with many of the features emphasized not only here, in Sulzer's account, but in many other contemporaneous discussions of symphonies in general and of Haydn's symphonies in particular. Even though Sulzer's evocation of Pindar is unique within the eighteenth century, it is by no means isolated or eccentric, for this richly suggestive simile unites essentially all of the attributes that other writers of the day consistently associated with the genre of the symphony. The connection of the ode and symphony, moreover, extended into the nineteenth century, culminating in the finale of Beethoven's Ninth.

The Prestige of Artifice

Late eighteenth-century accounts of genres in all the arts are almost invariably presented within an aesthetic hierarchy of value, even if that hierarchy was not always made explicit.[5] From this perspective, instrumental music as a whole had long stood in the shadow of all vocal genres, particularly opera and oratorio. Because it lacked a text and any specific object of representation, instrumental music was seen as vague and somehow incomplete. Sulzer himself repeatedly emphasized the decided superiority of vocal music on the grounds that instrumental music, although pleasing and at times moving, was indeterminate. Even Koch, whose compositional manual of 1782–1793 devotes unprecedented space to the forms of instrumental music, insisted on the fundamental superiority of vocal music. Instrumental music, to use Kant's celebrated phrase of 1790, was "more pleasure than culture" because it could not transmit concepts. Music without a text could move the passions but not the mind.

Against this backdrop, Sulzer's analogy of the symphony to a Pindaric ode is all the more striking, for no genre of instrumental music had ever been compared to such an elevated literary form. Music had long been understood as a kind of language in its own right, and it was by no means unusual for critics of the eighteenth century to compare an instrumental work to a poem, a drama, or (most commonly) an oration.[6] But the analogy to the Pindaric ode is particularly significant because of this genre's prestigious standing among literary forms. The ode in general, according to Sulzer, was too diffuse a category of poetry to tolerate any concise characterization: no one element common to all odes could differentiate this genre from all others. The only point that critics could agree on about the ode, Sulzer maintained, was that it represented "the highest form of poetry" because it demanded the greatest degree of poetic artifice. It is not the greatness of the ode's object that sets it apart, but rather its expression, its manipulation—which is to say, its poetic artifice. And the "high Pindaric ode," in Sulzer's account, stands as the most musical and most prestigious exemplar of this highest poetic form. The ostensible subjects of these particular odes, as Sulzer points out, actually hold very little interest for us in and of themselves. Why should anyone, Sulzer asks, really care about the winners of various pan-Hellenic athletic competitions from the fifth century, B.C.?[7]

Pindar was not a universally admired figure in late eighteenth-century Germany. Because his victory odes—the large majority of his surviving poetry—were written on commission from aristocrats wishing to honor themselves, Pindar's detractors were quick to dismiss him as a "flatterer," a hired pen. More egregious still, in the opinion of these critics, was the poet's propensity toward garrulousness, digression, and obscurity.[8] But a more discerning generation of German critics and poets was beginning to take up his cause in the second half of the eighteenth century, and many leading figures of the *Geniezeit* looked to Pindar as the paradigm of the poetic genius. For Lessing, Herder, Goethe, Hölderlin, and others, Pindar's works embodied a synthesis of both extreme originality—a product of inspiration, of nature—and extreme artifice. His daunting syntax, neologisms, and seemingly disordered line of thought were seen as assets rather than as liabilities, as complications that richly rewarded those who made the effort to come to terms with them.[9] Pindar's admirers valued his odes for their richness of voice and imagery, and for the manner in which they weave myth, history, current events, and praise of the gods into a richly textured narrative. In the end, the athletes whose triumphs are celebrated in these odes were seen as figures of secondary importance; what resonated for later generations, in the words of one modern scholar, were the poetic "webs of connotation, implication, and association [that] branch out indefinitely in every direction."[10]

Haydn's admirers similarly emphasized his synthesis of natural genius and technical skill. Critics repeatedly praised the composer's ability to integrate the highest degree of artifice into a work that on the surface, at least, remained easily apprehensible. Pointing to the symphonies and string quartets as the genres in which Haydn had made his greatest impression, Ernst Ludwig Gerber observed that Haydn "possesses the great art" of presenting that which "often appears to be familiar." And "in spite of all contrapuntal artifices" to be found in his works, his music remains "popular and pleasing to every amateur."[11] Johann Karl Friedrich Triest concluded his review of Haydn's music along the same lines by noting that "if one wished to define further, with two words, the character of Haydn's compositions, it would be—so it seems to me—artistic popularity or a popular (perceptible, penetrating) fullness of art."[12]

Aside from the most obvious and audible of technical artifices—polyphony—Haydn's contemporaries acknowledged the synthesis of genius and artifice most openly in their comments on his ability to make so much out of such seemingly insignificant thematic ideas. Over and over again, critics of Haydn's symphonies noted a pleasing disparity between the subject at hand—the opening theme of a movement—and its subsequent artistic elaboration. Haydn was rarely lauded for his powers as a melodist (as well he might have been), but he won consistent praise for his ability to transform an apparently simple idea into something that was at once both pleasing and profound. The London *Morning Herald*'s review of Salomon's concert of 23 March 1792 is typical in this regard. Most of this brief review is given over to an evaluation of the performances by the soloists in the evening's arias and concertos. Alone among all the program's many works, Haydn's symphony (no. 94) is evaluated not in terms of its performance, but in terms of its design, and specifically the first movement's "subject," which "was remarkably simple, but extended to vast complication, exquisitely modulated, and striking in effect. Critical applause was fervid and abundant."[13] In essence, the entire movement was perceived as one vast elaboration of a seemingly modest idea.

Along much the same lines, the *Mercure de France* had already identified the composer's ability to develop a single subject in a rich and varied manner as the one characteristic that set Haydn apart from those "sterile composers who pass continually from one idea to another, without knowing how to present one idea in varied forms, . . . and jumping from effect to effect, without connections and without taste."[14] This view is remarkably similar to Haydn's own account of how he composed, as recorded by one of his early biographers, Georg August Griesinger:

> I sat down [at the keyboard] and began to fantasize, according to whether my mood was sad or happy, serious or playful. Once I had seized an idea, my entire effort went toward elaborating and sustaining it according to the rules of art. . . And this is what is lacking among so many of our young composers: they string together one little bit after another, and they break off before they have barely begun, but nothing remains in the heart when one has heard it.[15]

Haydn's contemporaries clearly perceived the result of this method. After summarizing the composer's life in his biographical dictionary of 1790, Gerber began his evaluation of Haydn's music by crediting him with "giving to our instrumental music, and in particular to quartets and symphonies, a perfection that never before existed. Everything speaks when he sets his orchestra in motion." Haydn's themes "consistently bear the mark of genius, and the attentive listener will immediately recognize them as Haydn's own among thousands of others." But at the same time, his themes often seem almost haphazard, and at first glance appear to "have nothing to say." Yet "in the hands of this master," they take "remarkable turns," and in the end, "one is swept up in them."[16] Gerber would amplify these remarks four years after Haydn's death in an important essay devoted to the idea of basing an entire symphonic movement on a single theme, and again, it is Haydn's symphonies that are held up as paradigms of this technique.[17]

Haydn's art of "making something out of nothing" also comes in for special attention in Jérôme-Joseph de Momigny's *Cours complet d'harmonie et de composition* of 1805. In an unusually detailed technical analysis of the first movement of the Symphony in E-flat major, no. 103 ("Drumroll"), Momigny places great emphasis on motivic connections and the coherent unfolding of ideas. At m. 14 of the slow introduction, for example, he points out how Haydn "always remains faithful to variety without ever detracting from unity" by avoiding the easy introduction of another theme and instead repeating the "same theme, but with other instruments, and with modifications that give the effect of something new." At the close of the exposition, in turn, Haydn "derives his idea from the preceding material rather than finishing the section with something banal or foreign." In Haydn's music, "all appears simple, for his art is infinite"—which is to say (in part) that his apparently "natural" themes are subjected through his artifice to seemingly infinite expansion and manipulation.[18]

A similar outlook is evident in Triest's extended retrospective on eighteenth-century music, written in the first year of the nineteenth. Triest contrasts the empty artistry of concertos and much chamber music with the genre of the symphony, which "uses an entire mass of instruments for the development of the beautiful and the significant, which lies in the main idea, which is easily grasped and often seems to be simple."[19] A few short paragraphs later, Triest identifies Haydn as the greatest symphonic composer of his (and all) time. E. T. A. Hoffmann valued this same quality in Haydn's symphonies. Reviewing a new symphony by Friedrich Witt in the last month of Haydn's life, Hoffmann declared that he missed in its finale "those profound elaborations, those always new turns of the theme" one finds in Haydn's music. In spite of their "loose arrangement," it is precisely these turns of the theme that constitute the "thread of the work" in Haydn's symphonies, and it is this thread that "holds the listener in constant suspense until the final measures." A year later, Hoffmann would celebrate the genius of such thematic transformations even more explicitly in his celebrated review of Beethoven's Fifth Symphony.[20]

That the symphony—as opposed to, say, the sonata—should be singled out for its propensity to manipulate an opening idea is at least in part a function of the simple fact that orchestral players were not able to embellish or improvise to any substantial degree. With more than one performer to most parts, the symphony was a genre that precluded such performative freedom. Sulzer explained this distinction by means of a secondary metaphor, in which he called the symphony a choral work for instruments and contrasted it with the sonata, which he likened to a cantata for solo voice and instruments. In the latter,

> the melody of the leading voice can be constructed in such a way that it will accommodate (or indeed, as is often the case, demand) ornamentation. In the symphony, by contrast, in which each voice is performed by many instruments rather than by a single instrument, the melody must be capable of making its greatest impression at once, in the notes written on the page; no voice can tolerate even the slightest embellishment or coloratura. Unlike the sonata, which is a piece to be practiced, the symphony must also allow for sight-reading by the performers and therefore may not include any difficulties that cannot be performed simultaneously and clearly by many different players.

One effect of these restrictions in writing a symphony was to place greater weight on the perceived role of the composer in the ultimate success of the artwork. The aesthetic impression of a solo work (or a work like a concerto, whose central line is performed by a soloist) depends in large measure on the performer's skill, particularly his ability to improvise and embellish. More often than not, as Sulzer pointed out, such performative elements are not only permissible but essential. The symphony, by contrast, neither demands nor permits such latitude. The virtuosity demanded by the symphony is compositional rather than performative and thus demands a correspondingly higher degree of poetic—compositional—artifice.

Sulzer's analogy manifests no small change in aesthetics. One need only glance at a typical eighteenth-century opera libretto to be reminded that it was the performers who took center stage, both literally and figuratively. The composer, if mentioned at all, is often listed alongside the choreographer, the costume designer, and the master of swords. The great instrumental virtuosos of the day, in turn, could make a name for themselves as soloists in the sonata and concerto repertoires. But the growing art of instrumental music for large ensembles with no soloists at all—manifested most notably by the symphony—opened the way for the composer to emerge as the principal agent of artistic achievement, equal to if not of even greater importance than the performer.

The Sublime

Sulzer's pronouncement that the symphony is like a Pindaric ode is foreshadowed in his more general observation that the symphony is "especially suited to the expression of the grand, the solemn, and the sublime." No other poet was as consistently and as quickly associated with the sublime as Pindar, whose odes are full of the grand, bold strokes that "elevate" and "move the soul of the listener" to a higher, almost spiritual kind of aesthetic ecstasy.[21]

From a musical perspective, a good part of this effect depended on the sheer size of the symphonic orchestra. In our own time, period ensembles that perform Haydn's symphonies seem small to us because we inevitably hear them in contrast to the larger orchestras of Brahms or Mahler. But it is important to remember that by eighteenth-century standards, Haydn's ensembles were very large and very loud indeed. And it is scarcely coincidental that the musical genre most closely associated with the sublime in the late eighteenth century was the oratorio, whose forces of chorus, vocal soloists, and orchestra constituted what at the time were the largest indoor ensembles of any kind. The term "sublime" surfaces over and over again in accounts of Handel's oratorios, particularly the monster performances that took place during the Handel celebration at Westminster Abbey in 1784. To our late twentieth-century ears, historically-informed performance practice has made Haydn's music sound less monumental and less loud, whereas to his contemporaries, the perceived effect was precisely the opposite.

Among instrumental genres, then, only the symphony could sustain the analogy to Pindar's odes. The string quartet, although prized as the "purest" of genres—a "conversation among four rational individuals" with a minimum of timbral contrast—was almost never described in terms of the sublime because its sonic dimension was too limited, its tone too intimate. And while the concerto could project a sound as forceful as that of the symphony, it was never able to free itself entirely from the specter of empty virtuosity. Self-serving display was simply not consistent with the idea of the sublime. The sublime may have been complex and loud, but it was never vapid or bombastic.

Not all symphonies passed this test, of course, and a number of eighteenth-century critics bemoaned the tendency of grandeur to devolve into grandiloquence. Even Triest, a sensitive and sympathetic admirer of the "grand and bold gestures" in newer symphonies, conceded that at least some of these works "deafen us through their chaotic noise, in which the timpani increasingly play the main role (for who still composes symphonies without timpani?)"[22] William Jackson of Exeter, writing in the year of Haydn's arrival in London (1791), was more blunt. Recent composers, in order "to be grand and original, have poured in such floods of nonsense, under the sublime idea of *being inspired*, that the present SYMPHONY bears the same relation to good music, as the ravings of a bedlamite do to sober sense."[23]

Jackson's complaint about "floods of nonsense" relates to another element of the poetic sublime, the notion that ideas are to be presented not in a painstaking, logical order, but in a sequence that might seem random or at times even chaotic. The sublime appeals to a level of the soul that stands above and beyond reason. While the beautiful could appeal to contemplation, the sublime relied on the effect of sheer and immediate impact. A storm at sea provided eighteenth-century critics with one of their favorite illustrations of the sublime because it combined force with unpredictability. And even if most of Europe had only a secondhand knowledge of Pindar, many of Sulzer's readers would have been directly familiar with Horace's celebrated description of the Pindaric ode as "a powerful mountain torrent, swelled by strong rains, which with irresistible power sweeps up everything along with it."[24] Here we sense the importance of the poet's frenzy—the *furor poeticus*—in the creation of a sublime work of art. At times, this quasi-ecstatic state threatens to overwhelm the work, and the result is a torrent of ideas that cannot be rationalized in every detail.

Horace's image of the Pindaric ode as a rushing, swollen river is implicit in other contemporaneous accounts of the symphony. As Michael Broyles has demonstrated, eighteenth-century distinctions between the "symphony" and "sonata" styles emphasize the rhythmic propulsion of the symphony and its tendency to elide cadences for the sake of forward motion. Cadences in the sonata style, by contrast, are more frequent and distinct and have the effect of dividing the music into relatively discrete units.[25] The symphony, in short, was heard as the more propulsive and rhythmically irregular of the two genres.

These same qualities of forward motion and unpredictability are evident in Sulzer's entry on the symphony, which points specifically to the genre's "apparent irregularity of melody and harmony" and to "sudden transitions and shifts from one key to another, which are the more striking the weaker the [harmonic] connection is" between the two keys. Originality and surprise are of course two of the qualities most commonly identified in Haydn's music by his contemporaneous critics, and not only in his symphonies. Burney considered "the most sublime Idea in Haydn's work" to be the depiction of chaos in *The*

Creation by means of "dissonance & broken phrases."[26] But in the realm of instrumental music, it was the symphony alone that was seen to integrate these qualities within the sublime. All of these elements are neatly subsumed in *The Times* report on the premiere of Haydn's Symphony no. 93 in D Major: "Novelty of idea, agreeable caprice, and whim combined with all *Haydn's* sublime and wonten grandeur, gave additional consequence to the *soul* and feelings of every individual present."[27] The very newness, strangeness, and disorder of Haydn's symphonies made them all the more sublime to his original audiences.

The Central Role of Texture

Sulzer's analogy of the symphony to the Pindaric ode occurs immediately after his account of ideal texture in a symphonic first movement. Texture, oddly enough, is a term for which the German language lacks any concise equivalent, even today. But texture is clearly what Sulzer has in mind when he describes how all the voices in a symphony should weave "in and out of one another in such a way that all parts, when played together, create a single melody that is incapable of accompaniment, but rather one in which every voice is making its own particular contribution to the whole." In this sense, a symphony is not merely an orchestrated sonata, but a work conceived from the beginning for *all* the instruments of the orchestra.

Sulzer illustrates his ideas on this point through a critique of symphonies by three of the most noted composers of his time: Johann Gottlieb Graun (1702 or 1703–1771), Carl Heinrich Graun (1703 or 1704–1759), and Johann Adolph Hasse (1699–1783). Noting that the "opera symphony"—the overture—"has more or less the characteristics of the chamber symphony," Sulzer praised the overtures of the elder Graun for their

> exceptional degree of artistry and character. . . [B]ut his delicate soul lacked the fire they also require. The beautiful melodies that he never ceased to write, no matter how admirable they are, always have a feeble effect in every one of his symphonies. One thinks one is hearing a fiery operatic aria performed by instruments. Graun was surpassed in this respect by his brother, the late concert master, who found the true spirit of the symphony in some of his chamber symphonies. Hasse also surpassed him [Johann Gottlieb Graun], even though his opera symphonies also have a number of aria-like qualities to them.[28]

By this account, a "fiery operatic aria performed by instruments" was precisely what a symphonic first movement should *not* be. An essentially homophonic texture—melody and accompaniment—was perfectly appropriate to the aria, but the first movement of a symphony called for a more polyphonic style of writing in which the resulting melody was "incapable of accompaniment," and in which "every voice is making its own particular contribution to the whole." Only occasionally, according to Sulzer, did the Grauns and Hasse succeed in achieving the "true spirit of the symphony," which is to say, a predominantly polyphonic texture in which all the voices contribute more or less equally.

This emphasis on texture relates at once to both the multi-faceted richness of the Pindaric ode and its status as the most "artful" of all literary genres. For polyphony, in the end, is a function of counterpoint and harmony: these were techniques that could be codified and taught, and scarcely a year went by in the second half of the eighteenth century without the publication of at least one new treatise on these subjects. Melody, by contrast, was perceived to be a product of inspiration and as such beyond the bounds of that which could be codified. It is for this reason that we have so few treatises on melody from the eighteenth century. The supreme accolade of any eighteenth-century melody, after all, was the epithet of "natural"—that is, spontaneous and unforced. For eighteenth-century critics, the ideal melody was artless in the best sense of the term.

Sulzer's emphasis on the importance of texture to the "true spirit of the symphony" can be read in part as an oblique criticism of Johann Adolph Scheibe's earlier (1745) emphasis on the importance of melody in this genre. Scheibe had pointed specifically to the symphonies of Hasse and Graun (presumably Johann Gottlieb) as exemplary in their use of melody. Still, even Scheibe had conceded that a chamber symphony must be worked out in manner more "fully voiced" than a theater symphony (overture), and that "one must give the middle voices more to do and allow them to come forward in an artful manner every now and again."[29]

Scheibe's acknowledgment of the necessity for a richer texture in the chamber symphony would figure in almost every subsequent account of the genre throughout the eighteenth century—and, for that matter, well into the nineteenth. Even in the briefest of eighteenth-century accounts of the symphony, it is texture that stands out as the genre's most important distinguishing characteristic. "The German symphonists," according to François Jean de Chastellux in his *Essai sur l'union de la poësie & de la musique* of 1765, "are less concerned with finding simple musical motives than they are with producing beautiful effects through the harmonies they draw out of the large number of different instruments they use and through the manner in which these instruments work in succession."

> Their symphonies are a type of *Concerto*, in which the instruments shine in turn, in which they provoke each other and respond; they dispute and reconcile among themselves. It is a lively and sustained conversation. But throughout all these contrasts, one always recognizes, particularly in good works, one motive that constitutes the basis of the entire edifice. Each part, it is true, occupies itself with this edifice in its turn. This passage is destined for the horn, that one for the oboe; it is a period that is shared among all the parts of the orchestra, a canvas on which each instrument executes a small amplification.[30]

This kind of texture is evident in virtually every symphonic first movement Haydn ever wrote (and a great many other movements). The opening presto of his Symphony no. 54 in G major, written the same year Sulzer's "Symphony" article appeared, offers a good example of the kind of "melody incapable of accompaniment" that so impressed Haydn's contemporaries (Example 1). When we first hear the theme (which enters after a brief slow introduction), our ear is drawn to the active rhythms of the strings; the winds, at least initially, seem to be there merely to "fill out" the sound of the orchestra. But after a few measures, we begin to realize that the held notes of the winds are actually the beginning of a melodic line, and that the repeated string motive is in fact more accompanimental than melodic. Yet the figure in the strings remains something more than mere underpinning, and in the end, the "accompanimental" line of the strings turns out to be no accompaniment at all, but rather an essential element of the whole. The very identity of this theme rests on its integration of contrasting lines, rhythms, and timbres between winds and strings.

The widely popular Symphonies no. 85 ("La Reine," 1785), no. 88 (ca. 1787), and no. 91 (1788) all use a similar interweaving of voices in the opening measures of their respective allegros. Such examples could be multiplied at will. This kind of writing offers up not an "ostentatious bustling of instruments," as Triest would put it in his description of symphonies by some composers other than Haydn, but rather a genuine polyphony in which "an entire mass of instruments" is used for the "development of the beautiful and the significant, which lies in the main idea, which is easily grasped and often seems to be simple."[31]

The technical commentary from Haydn's own time, sparse as it is, repeatedly calls attention to this textural quality in his symphonies. In the account mentioned earlier, Gerber observes that "all the subsidiary voices—which in the works of other composers are mere accompaniment—often become decisive principal voices in his hands." Even in Italy, where the chamber symphony had declined greatly in popularity by the end of the eighteenth century, the distinctive texture of the genre continued to be an object of comment. In his textbook on composition published in 1796, Francesco Galeazzi devotes a mere three sentences to the chamber symphony, yet in these three sentences, he asserts that it is a genre "written with the greatest artifices of the art of music"; that the symphonies of Haydn serve as "a perfect model" for such works; and that the formal structure of the symphony is much like that of the string quartet, "with the sole dif-

Example 1. Haydn, Symphony no. 54/i.

Example 1, continued.

ference of a quite extensive interlacing that must emanate from the various parts."[32] Thus we see, even in this very brief account, the demands of artifice, the paradigmatic status of Haydn's symphonies, and the deciding quality of an essentially polyphonic texture.

August F. C. Kollmann, a German émigré working in London during Haydn's years there, similarly proclaimed Haydn to have provided the best models of the genre, particularly in matters of texture. In his compositional manual of 1799, Kollmann recommends that "a symphony's principal themes" be written in such a way that "all Instruments can *execute* them, or at least *join* in them in the principal Key. If this rule is not attended to, a Symphony cannot answer the purpose of employing the whole Orchestra to advantage"—which, it will be recalled, was Sulzer's *raison d'être* for the chamber symphony. Kollmann goes on to note that "Haydn will be found very particular in attending to this rule, for the subjects of most of his best Symphonies are not only calculated for the Horn and Trumpet, but

Example 1, continued.

even for the Kettle Drums," as in the Symphony no. 97, with its insistent tonic-dominant opening.[33]

A more or less equal-voiced texture is a quality we associate more readily nowadays with the string quartet than with the symphony. Yet eighteenth-century critics were equally inclined to hear this texture in the symphony, perhaps because the very size and diversity of its requisite performance forces made this quality all the more striking. When listening to a well-blended string quartet, one can at times imagine that one is hearing a single instrument. No such illusion is possible when hearing a symphony. To the contrary: it was the synthesis of such highly diverse timbres within an essentially equal-voiced texture that stood out for earlier listeners as the genre's most immediately audible feature.

The Quality of Massed Expression

Sulzer's secondary analogy of the symphony to an instrumental chorus is entirely consistent with his image of the Pindaric ode, a genre that itself had originally been sung (and danced) by a large chorus. The texts of Pindar's odes contain numerous internal references to their choric nature and at times even refer to accompanying instruments and the chorus master.[34]

In this respect, Pindar's odes are closely related to the choruses of ancient Greek tragedy. Indeed, the perceived similarity of function between the chamber symphony and the Greek chorus had grown in part out of the earlier tradition of the theater: Lessing, for one, had already made such a comparison in his drama reviews of the 1760s, noting that "the orchestra at our stage plays takes the place, as it were, of the ancient choruses."[35] In the latter part of the eighteenth century, this tradition would be transferred to the chamber symphony by Bernard Germain, Comte de La Cépède, who in 1785 likened the individual instruments in a symphony to the characters in a drama, with the tutti orchestra representing the Greek chorus.[36] Heinrich Christoph Koch also accepted the analogy of the chorus and went on to note that the symphony "therefore has as its goal, like the chorus, the expression of a sentiment of an entire multitude." The portion of Sulzer's article on the symphony that Koch quoted at length in his own *Musikalisches Lexikon* of 1802 includes, significantly enough, the comparison to the Pindaric ode.[37]

In this sense, both the symphony and the Pindaric ode were perceived as expressions of a communal—as opposed to personal—sentiment. The size of the requisite ensemble and the size of the performance venue combined to play an important role in both the production and perception of symphonies in Haydn's lifetime. The symphony was choric not only by virtue of the size of the orchestra performing it, but also by the nature of the genre's very "tone."

The idea of hearing a symphony as the "voice" of a large body may seem somewhat foreign to us today, yet it was too widespread in Haydn's time to be dismissed as idiosyncratic. Sulzer's analogy in fact resonates with many later writers. In the late 1770s, for example, Christian Friedrich Daniel Schubart praised a symphony by Christian Cannabich on the grounds that he could hear in this work "not the mere uproar of the rabble, shrieking in a tumult, but rather a musical whole, whose parts, like emanations of spirit [*Geisterausflüsse*], reconstitute to make themselves a whole. The listener is not merely deafened, but rather shaken by and permeated with humbling, lasting effects."[38] Schubart's account thus directly links complexity and the variety of parts to the aesthetics of the sublime: the listener is "shaken," "permeated," and "humbled" by the experience of listening in part because the symphony projects the voice of a large and diverse community rather than that of a mere individual.

Nineteenth-century writers sustained this idea of the genre's communal tone. "Destined for a large gathering of persons," Momigny argued in 1805, the symphony "must have at once both grandeur and popularity. The composer should choose his subject from among scenes of nature, or from among scenes of society that are most capable of moving and engaging the multitude, without however descending at any time to that which is base and trivial. Those who have read our preliminary discourse will perhaps remember that we have cited the symphonies of Haydn" as exemplary in this regard.[39] And indeed, Momigny's analysis of the first movement of Haydn's Symphony 103 conjures up a large gathering of persons assembled to pray for relief against the terrors of thunder (the opening drumroll). The group rejoices at the arrival of sunny weather and cowers collectively at the resumption of the thunder when the slow introduction makes its unexpected return at m. 202. Momigny's analysis of a chamber work, by contrast—Mozart's String Quartet in D Minor, K. 421—focuses on Dido's grief at Aeneas's departure from Carthage. The emotional anguish we hear is that of an individual, not of an entire community. Later in the nineteenth century, virtually all the programmatic interpretations of Beethoven's Seventh Symphony would evoke images of some kind of communal gathering, ranging from a peasant dance or wedding (the first and third movements) to a priestly ceremony (the second movement) to a bacchanal (the finale).[40]

Haydn himself was well aware of the communal implications of the genre. In a letter to a Parisian publisher of 28 August 1789, shortly after the beginning of the French Revolution, he announced his intention to call one of four symphonies he proposed to write a "National" Symphony.[41] Such a title would have been unthinkable for a new quartet or concerto, for among instrumental genres, only the symphony could convey this quality of massed expression. The personification of the orchestra (and of instruments in general) is of course a venerable trope, extending back many centuries and forward to our own time, and it is applicable to virtually all genres. But the distinctive element here is the sense of a large group engaging in a quasi-public dialogue. This is not an intimate conversation among friends, as the formulation most frequently applied to the string quartet would have it, but the deliberative discourse of a large populace, to be performed by a large body of musicians for a large audience.

It is scarcely coincidental, after all, that the most celebrated expression of communal ideals is to be found in a symphony—Beethoven's Ninth—and that this symphony bases its finale on an ode, Schiller's "An die Freude."[42] While the idea of incorporating vocal forces into a symphony may have been novel, the idea of projecting a sense of communal expression was not. Even before Beethoven's Ninth, one anonymous German critic, writing in 1820, had asserted that in the symphony, as in a work for large chorus, there appears "the universality of humanity, in which everything that is individual finds itself melted as discrete entities within the whole."[43]

In the wake of the Ninth, commentators would take this idea still further, maintaining that the true symphony represents not the self-expression of an individual composer, but rather the expression of a larger society. When Adolf Bernhard Marx likened the solo sonata to the ode (in the general sense, not to the Pindaric ode), he went on to compare the symphony to the hymn. Unlike the solo sonata, performed by one player on one instrument, the symphony was seen to express the emotions of a large body of individuals, a veritable chorus, and in this regard, the Pindaric ode and hymn are in fact closely related.[44] It is not a question of the depth of expression that is possible in either genre, but rather the tone and nature of that expression. Marx praised the profundity of such works as Beethoven's Piano Sonatas Opp.110 and 111, but distinguished the expression of the "individual-subjective piano" from that of the chorus and the symphony, which address general conditions "in the grand sense of ancient tragedy."[45] The critic Gottfried Wilhelm Fink, writing a decade later (1835), argued that a symphony is "a story, developed within a psychological context, of some particular emotional state of a large body of people." Such sentiments prevailed through the end of the century. As August Reissmann pointed out in 1878, a true symphony does not present the subjective spirit of the individual, but rather "that objective spirit fulfilled by the manifest supremacy of the world-spirit." Only if the composer sublimates his personal ideas and emotions to the good of the larger whole could a symphony realize its full potential.[46] And in a conversation with his wife, Cosima, shortly before his death in 1883, Wagner emphasized the distinction between Beethoven's symphonies, on the one hand, and his sonatas and quartets on the other. In the sonatas and quartets, Cosima reports Wagner as having said, "Beethoven makes music; in the symphonies, the entire world makes music through him."[47]

These are nineteenth-century formulations, to be sure, and it would be anachronistic to read such interpretations into eighteenth-century descriptions of the symphony as a genre. At the same time, it would be equally mistaken to overlook the origins of these ideas in the earlier (if fragmentary) comments about the communal "tone" of the symphony.

• • •

The remoteness of Sulzer's image of the symphony as Pindaric ode reminds us that it is not only performance practice that has changed over the past two centuries, but also the very act of listening itself. In a sense, Haydn's symphonies—at least the late ones—are too familiar to us: they have come down in an unbroken line of tradition since the composer's own time, and they seem far more approachable than any number of later works by subsequent composers. Yet few of us today are as conscious of the elements that seem to have captured the imaginations of Haydn's original audiences: the synthesis of nature and artifice, the aesthetic of the sublime, the centrality of an integrated texture, and the perception of a communal voice in the symphony as a whole. Admittedly, the evidence for these eighteenth-century perceptions rests on fewer sources than we would like. The breadth and richness of newly heard or newly interpreted voices from Haydn's era make plain how the symphony came to occupy such a central place in the cultural imagination of the nineteenth century. We will surely gain by the attempt to hear in these symphonies something of what Haydn's own audiences might have heard in them.

NOTES

1. On the intellectual background and publication history of Sulzer's *Allgemeine Theorie*, see Johan van der Zande, "Orpheus in Berlin: A Reappraisal of Johann Georg Sulzer's Theory of the Polite Arts," *Central European History* 28 (1995): 175–208.

2. See Richard Kramer, "Beethoven and Carl Heinrich Graun," in *Beethoven Studies* [1], ed. Alan Tyson (New York, 1973), pp. 18–44. On the currency of Sulzer's *Allgemeine Theorie* in musical circles of the late eighteenth and early nineteenth centuries, see Owen Jander, "Exploring Sulzer's *Allgemeine Theorie* as a Source Used by Beethoven," *The Beethoven Newsletter*, 2/1 (Spring, 1987): 1–7.

3. *Musikalisches Lexikon* (Frankfurt am Main, 1802; reprint, Hildesheim, 1964). The entry on the symphony in Sulzer's encyclopedia was actually written either wholly or in

part by the composer Johann Abraham Peter Schulz, whom Sulzer had commissioned to help with the articles on music. For the sake of simplicity and consistency, however, I shall refer throughout the present essay to Sulzer as the author of this entry, on the grounds that it clearly reflects the format, style, and tone of his encyclopedia as a whole. Sulzer went to great lengths to integrate the fine arts within his accounts of their individual elements: entries abound in cross-references linking literature to music, painting to dance, etc. As van der Zande and Christensen (see note 4, below) have argued, moreover, Sulzer was an active collaborator on earlier musical entries in the encyclopedia that had been prepared by Schulz's teacher, Johann Philipp Kirnberger. It is clear, in other words, that Sulzer did not merely transmit what Kirnberger or Schulz provided him in the way of articles on music.

4. Sulzer, *Allgemeine Theorie*, s.v. "Symphonie." The translation here is my own; for two other, different translations of the entire entry, see Bathia Churgin, "The Symphony as Described by J. A. P. Schulz (1774): A Commentary and Translation," *Current Musicology* 29 (1980): 7–16; and Thomas Christensen, "Johann Georg Sulzer: *General Theory of the Fine Arts* (1771–74): Selected Articles," in Nancy K. Baker and Thomas Christensen, eds., *Aesthetics and the Art of Musical Composition in the German Enlightenment: Selected Writings of Johann Georg Sulzer and Heinrich Christoph Koch* (Cambridge, 1995), pp. 105–8.

5. See Klaus R. Scherpe, *Gattungspoetik im 18. Jahrhundert: Historische Entwicklung von Gottsched bis Herder* (Stuttgart, 1968), pp. 18–26.

6. See my *Wordless Rhetoric: Musical Form and the Metaphor of the Oration* (Cambridge, Mass., 1991).

7. Sulzer, *Allgemeine Theorie*, s.v. "Ode," "Pindar."

8. See Malcolm Heath, "The Origins of Modern Pindaric Criticism," *Journal of Hellenic Studies* 106 (1986): 85–98. Even in the twentieth century, Ezra Pound could proclaim Pindar to be "the prize wind-bag of all ages"; see D. S. Carne-Ross, *Pindar* (New Haven, 1985), p. 1. I am grateful to Professor William H. Race for his helpful guidance on the reception of Pindar's works.

9. On Pindar's reputation in eighteenth-century Germany, see Sigmund Lempicki, "Pindar im literarischen Urteil des xvii und xviii Jahrhunderts," *Eos: Comentarii societatis philologae polonorum* 33 (1930–31): 419–74; Jochen Schmidt, *Die Geschichte des Genie-Gedankens in der deutschen Literatur, Philosophie und Politik, 1750–1945*, 2 vols. (Darmstadt, 1985), vol. 1, pp. 179–92; Thomas Gelzer, "Pindarverständnis und Pindarübersetzung im deutschen Sprachbereich vom 16. bis zum 18. Jahrhundert," in *Geschichte des Textverständnisses am Beispiel von Pindar und Horaz*, ed. Walther Killy, Wolfenbütteler Forschungen, 12 (Munich, 1987), pp. 81–115.

10. Thomas Hubbard, *The Pindaric Mind: A Study of Logical Structures in Early Greek Poetry* (Leiden, 1985), p. 164.

11. Ernst Ludwig Gerber, *Historisch-Biographisches Lexikon der Tonkünstler* (Leipzig, 1790), col. 610: "Er besitzt die grosse Kunst in seinen Sätzen öfters bekannt zu scheinen. Dadurch wird er trotz allen contrapunktischen Künsteleyen, die sich darinne befinden, populair und jedem Liebhaber angenehm."

12. "Bemerkungen über die Ausbildung der Tonkunst in Deutschland im achtzehnten Jahrhundert," *Allgemeine musikalische Zeitung* 3 (1801): 407.

13. *Morning Herald*, 24 March 1792, quoted in H. C. Robbins Landon, *Haydn: Chronicle & Works*, 5 vols. (Bloomington, 1976–80), vol. 3, *Haydn in London, 1791–1795*, p. 149. See also the review in the *Morning Chronicle*, 5 March 1794, quoted in Landon, ibid., p. 241: ". . . having found a happy subject, no man knows like HAYDN how to produce incessant variety, without once departing from it."

14. *Mercure de France*, 5 April 1788, quoted in Landon, *Haydn Chronicle*, vol. 2, *Haydn at Eszterháza, 1766–1790*, p. 593.

15. Georg August Griesinger, *Biographische Notizen über Joseph Haydn*, ed. Karl-Heinz Köhler (Leipzig, 1975; 1st ed. 1810), p. 78. My translation.

16. Gerber, *Historisch-Biographisches Lexikon*, col. 610.

17. Gerber, "Eine freundliche Vorstellung über gearbeitete Instrumentalmusik, besonders über Symphonien," *Allgemeine musikalische Zeitung* 15 (1813): 457–63.

18. Momigny, *Cours complet d'harmonie et de composition*, vol. 2 (Paris, 1805); the translation here is from Ian Bent, ed., *Music Analysis in the Nineteenth Century*, vol. 2: *Hermeneutic Approaches* (Cambridge, 1993), pp. 130, 132, 133

19. Triest, "Bemerkungen," p. 400. [See the translation in this volume.]

20. E. T. A. Hoffmann, review of Friedrich Witt, Symphony in D Major, *Allgemeine musikalische Zeitung* 11 (1809): 516; idem, review of Beethoven's Fifth Symphony, *Allgemeine musikalische Zeitung*, 12 (1810): 630–642, 652–659. Both reviews are available in translation in *E. T. A. Hoffmann's Musical Writings*, ed. David Charlton (Cambridge, 1989).

21. The aesthetics of the symphonic sublime have already been well explored by a number of scholars. My account here is deeply indebted to Carl Dahlhaus, "E. T. A. Hoffmanns Beethoven-Kritik und die Ästhetik des Erhabenen," *Archiv für Musikwissenschaft* 39 (1981): 80–92; Nicolas Waldvogel, "The Eighteenth-Century Esthetics of the Sublime and the Valuation of the Symphony," Ph.D. diss., Yale University, 1992, chaps. 3 and 4; and Elaine R. Sisman, *Mozart: The "Jupiter" Symphony* (Cambridge, 1993), pp. 13–20. For an account of Sulzer's concept of the sublime as applied to the symphonies of Beethoven, see Carl Dahlhaus, *Ludwig van Beethoven: Approaches to his Music*, trans. Mary Whittall (Oxford, 1991), pp. 67–80. See also James Webster's essay in this volume.

22. Triest, "Bemerkungen." pp. 400–1.

23. William Jackson, *Observations on the Present State of Music in London* (London, 1791), p. 23. Charles Burney's amusing review, reproduced in Landon, *Haydn Chronicle*, vol. 3, pp. 100–4, shows that Jackson's viewpoint was decidedly in the minority in his time.

24. From Horace's Odes, Book IV, no. 2. The paraphrase here is taken from Sulzer's entry on "Pindar" in the *Allgemeine Theorie*.

25. Michael Broyles, *Beethoven: The Emergence and Evolution of Beethoven's Heroic Style* (New York, 1987), chap. 1.

26. Burney, undated letter to Christian Ignatius Latrobe, quoted in David P. Schroeder, *Haydn and the Enlightenment* (Oxford, 1990), p. 126.

27. *The Times*, 20 February 1792, quoted in Landon, *Haydn Chronicle*, vol. 3, p. 134.

28. Sulzer, *Allgemeine Theorie*, s.v. "Symphonie."

29. Scheibe, *Der critische Musikus*, new ed. (Leipzig, 1745), p. 620 (originally published 15 December 1739). For a more detailed discussion of Scheibe's critique of counterpoint in the symphony, see Waldvogel, "Eighteenth-Century Esthetics," pp. 168–81.

30. Chastellux, *Essai sur l'union de la poesie & de la musique* (Paris, 1765), pp. 49–50. My translation.

31. Triest, "Bemerkungen," p. 400.

32. Francesco Galeazzi, *Elementi teorico-pratici di musica*, vol. 2 (Rome, 1796), p. 289.

33. August Friedrich Christoph Kollmann, *An Essay on Practical Musical Composition* (London, 1799), p. 17.

34. See William H. Race, *Pindar* (Boston, 1986), p. 13.

35. See Elaine R. Sisman, "Haydn's Theater Symphonies," *Journal of the American Musicological Society* 43 (1990): 304–6. Wagner would later press this metaphor into service as a justification for his own theory of music drama.

36. Bernard Germain, Comte de La Cépède, *La poétique de la musique*, 2 vols. (Paris, 1785), vol. 2, pp. 332–33.

37. Koch's acceptance of this image becomes all the more significant in light of the fact that he took exception to other portions of Sulzer's account of the symphony. See Carl Mennicke, *Hasse und die Brüder Graun als Symphoniker* (Leipzig, 1906), 97–98.

38. Schubart, *Leben und Gesinnungen*, 2 vols. (Stuttgart, 1791–1793), vol. 1, p. 211: "Es ist nicht blos Stimmengetöss, wie der Pöbel im Aufruhr durcheinander kreischt, es ist ein musikalisches Ganzes, dessen Theil wie Geisterausflüsse wieder ein Ganzes Bilden. Der Hörer wird nicht blos betäubt, sondern von niederstürzenden, bleibenden Wirkungen erschüttert und durchdrungen." Although not published until the 1790s, Schubart dictated his memoirs in 1778–79.

39. Momigny, *Cours complet*, vol. 2, pp. 584–85.

40. See Thomas Grey, "Metaphorical Modes in Nineteenth-Century Music Criticism: Image, Narrative, and Idea," in *Music and Text: Critical Inquiries*, ed. Steven Paul Scher (Cambridge, 1992), pp. 99–103. In this regard, Berlioz's *Symphonie fantastique* and *Harold en Italie* are on one level anomalous as symphonies, for they focus on a single individual; yet on another level, they probe the gulf between those individuals and society as a whole. See my *After Beethoven: Imperatives of Originality in the Symphony* (Cambridge, Mass., 1996), chap. 2.

41. See Landon, *Haydn Chronicle*, vol. 2, p. 726; the original German is given in Landon, "Haydniana (II)," *Haydn Yearbook* 7 (1970): 317.

42. Although Schiller himself never called this poem an ode, it was widely circulated as such during his lifetime, particularly in musical settings, and Beethoven preserved this designation on the title page of the Ninth's first edition, published by B. Schotts Söhne of Mainz in 1826 (*Sinfonie mit Schluss-Chor über Schillers Ode: "An die Freude"*).

43. Anonymous, review of two symphonies by J. Küffner, *Allgemeine musikalische Zeitung* 22 (1820): 273.

44. Marx, "Etwas über die Symphonie und Beethovens Leistungen in diesem Fach," *Berliner Allgemeine musikalische Zeitung* 1 (1824): 168. On the long-standing connection between the ode and the hymn, see Kurt Schlüter, *Die englische Ode: Studien zu ihrer Entwicklung unter dem Einfluss der antiken Hymne* (Bonn, 1954); Paul H. Fry, *The Poet's Calling in the English Ode* (New Haven, 1980), pp. 5–10; Stuart Curran, *Poetic Form and British Romanticism* (New York, 1986), chap. 4.

45. A. B. Marx, *Die Musik des neunzehnten Jahrhunderts und ihre Pflege* (Leipzig, 1855), pp. 162–63.

46. Hermann Mendel and August Reissmann, *Musikalisches Conversations-Lexikon*, vol. 10, article "Symphonie" (Berlin, 1878).

47. Cosima Wagner, *Die Tagebücher*, vol. 2, ed. Martin Gregor-Dellin and Dietrich Mack (Munich, 1977), p. 1103, entry for 30 January 1883. This idea of the symphony as a genre of communal expression would find its most eloquent exponent in the early twentieth century in the writings of the German critic and historian Paul Bekker, particularly in his *Die Symphonie von Beethoven bis Mahler* (Berlin, 1918).

Representing the Aristocracy: The Operatic Haydn and *Le pescatrici*

REBECCA GREEN

This essay is dedicated to Sarah Green, with gratitude and admiration.

The subject of "Haydn" usually summons up the composer of instrumental music, a father whose progeny was generic rather than genetic, an artist whose musical authority is taken for granted, and an early middle-class success story: wheelwright's son discovers fame and fortune in the concert halls of London. The operatic Haydn is a different subject altogether, a figure still only dimly recognizable despite the considerable time and energy he invested in dramatic music at Eszterháza. Indeed, he has proven to be something of an embarrassment, a kind of disappointing *doppelgänger* to the father of the symphony and string quartet: for Giuseppe Carpani, "Haydn in teatro non è più Haydn."[1]

What makes Haydn disappear in the opera house? Certainly not a lack of evidence. While in the service of the Esterházys, Haydn composed at least twelve Italian operas, and at least five Singspiels for the marionette opera, arranged dozens of other operas for production, and conducted over one thousand opera performances.[2] Even if few would agree with Carpani today, the operatic Haydn is still criticized for his stodgy pacing, lack of vivid characterization and what has been perceived as an inadequate sense of drama in the theater.[3] The comparison with Mozart is always at least implicit. What is rarely acknowledged is that Haydn, unlike Mozart, composed on demand for a private court theater. Each of Haydn's Italian operas for the Esterházys received its premiere in connection with a particular celebration associated with the dynastic rhythms of Eszterháza: family name-days and weddings. As such, Haydn's operas were originally conceived for the social and political purposes of a particular occasion, before becoming part of a regular repertoire.[4] With this in mind, it seems more appropriate to compare opera at Eszterháza with the private court opera of the Habsburgs than with operas at public theaters such as the Burgtheater. The similarity in repertoire between Eszterháza and the Burgtheater notwithstanding,[5] they operated under very different conditions that required distinct modes of spectatorship, even though the seats of these theaters were often filled with many of the same people.

In this essay, I will not attempt to demonstrate that Haydn was a competent and up-to-date composer for the stage—that much I will assume. Nor will I call for the inclusion of Haydn in the operatic canon. Rather, I want to consider the conditions under which he produced his operas, and how he responded musically within this compositional and sociopolitical context: in other words, how Haydn *represented* the aristocracy. A particular occasion, the wedding celebration of 1770 for which Haydn composed the opera *Le pescatrici*, will provide the focus.

Authorship and Authority at Eszterháza

Haydn's failure to measure up to his instrumental self is surely, in part, a function of his employment. As a retainer of Prince Esterházy, his primary task was to satisfy the demands of the prince, a situation which is incompatible with the notion of the artist as autonomous individual. Ultimately, his authorship was subjected to the prince's authority. A closer look at the operatic Haydn active at Eszterháza reveals a valued servant working within a feudal system of power and obligation that is far removed from the bourgeois world of the public concert in which the instrumental Haydn was to thrive. In order to understand Haydn's operas, it is essential to consider the palace itself as a site for the circulation of power through the theatrical spectacle of courtly life with all its ceremonies, processions, and representations, of which opera was only the most formal, and evidently the most lavish.[6] The eponymous palace of Eszterháza was much more than a place to live; it was an architectural testament to the continuing feudal power of its author.[7]

Nicolaus "the Magnificent" assumed the hereditary title of prince of the Holy Roman Empire when his older brother, Paul Anton, died in 1762. His ancestor, the first Nicolaus Esterházy (1582–1645), had accumulated land and wealth through shrewd marriages, and was rewarded with the title of baron, and then count, for his support of the Habsburgs against the Turks and Hungarian nationalists. From that time, the Esterházys had been loyal supporters of Habsburg interests in Hungary, and gradually became the most wealthy and powerful of the Hungarian magnates. By the time Haydn came into service with the family in 1761, they had an average yearly income of 600,000 florins, and owned over half of the urbarial land in Sopron county.[8] When Nicolaus became *Majoratsherr* upon his brother's death, he embarked on an ambitious project to transform his favorite residence, Süttör castle at the edge of the marshy Neusiedlersee, into his main residence, a process that took approximately twenty years and twelve million florins.[9] The prince took an active interest in the construction of Eszterháza, from specifications of the furniture to the planning of the garden. Through the imprinting of numerous coats of arms and princely initials, he literally placed his stamp upon the palace.

Eszterháza was a spectacular accomplishment, even in an era in which one of the burdens of wealth was an obligation to display it. In addition to the magnificent rooms and sumptuous furnishings of the palace itself, the grounds held fabulous pleasures for the delight of the prince and his guests. Flanking the palace were twin galleries for the contemplation of nature and culture: exotic plants in the Wintergarten, and exquisite pictures in the Bilder Galerie. The park featured a cultivated garden dotted with temples, statues, and even an artificial waterfall, but the wilder side of nature was available in the Tiergarten, stocked with game. Among the splendors of the park were the twin jewels of the opera house and the marionette opera house, located on the east and west sides of the park respectively. On numerous occasions during the 1770s, the prince hosted magnificent fêtes at his palace. One such occasion was the wedding of Countess Lamberg, the daughter of Nicolaus' sister, to Count Pocci in September of 1770. A report of this event, which appeared in both the *Pressburger Zeitung* and the *Wiener Diarium*, described three days of festivities, including fireworks displays, splendid banquets and masquerade balls, military maneuvers, a popular festival in the park, and an opera by Haydn. Says the author, "one can easily imagine what a deep impression these truly Princely fêtes made on all those who had the honour to be present."[10]

Like its French counterpart, the "Hungarian Versailles" was articulated around a focal point—the main section of the palace, which had formed the original castle, contained the magnificent sala terrena as well as the apartments of the prince and princess. The rest of the palace extended on either side to form a horseshoe, enclosing a courtyard and a fountain. To the rear, the geometric patterns of the park converged on the central portion of the palace. This physical structure emphasized the importance of the prince, or, quite literally, his gravity. In a plan printed in 1784,[11] the north-south orientation is inverted in order to allow the node of the prince's apartments to anchor the entire palace. (See Plate 1. The Neusiedlersee would be located just below the bottom of this plan, that is, just north of the palace itself.) In the plan, the palace and gardens appear to impose a rational control on an unruly countryside: a network of roads and sightlines emanates from the palace, situated at the lower center. Indeed, Esterházy's authority as a prince of the Holy Roman Empire spilled over from his seat at Eszterháza to the surrounding county of Sopron, of which he was lord high sheriff, also a hereditary position.

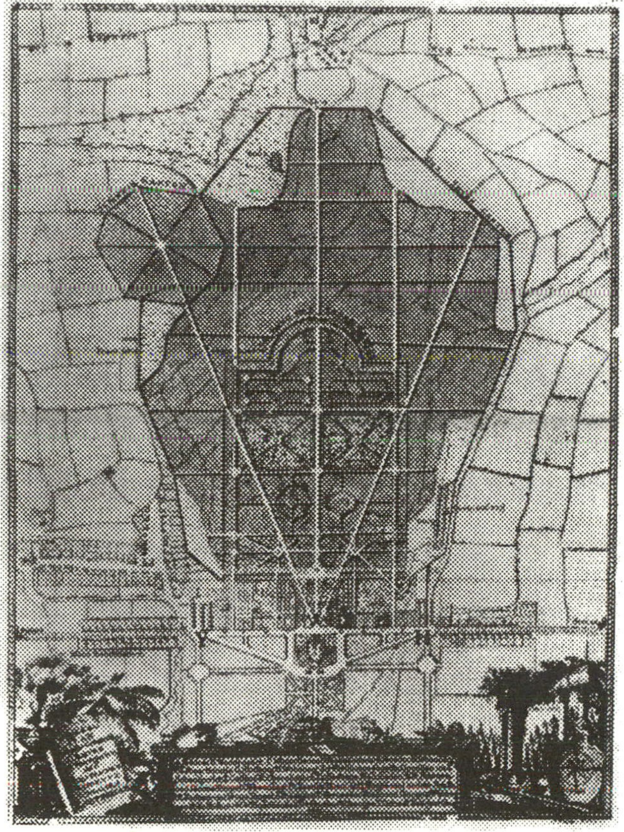

Plate 1. Ground plan of Eszterháza, from *Beschreibung des hochfürstlichen Schlosses Esterhass im Königreiche Ungern* (Pressburg: Anton Löwe, 1794).

The location of the opera house in a separate building in the park is a testament to the prominence given to opera at Eszterháza.[12] In many ways, it could be considered a simulacrum of the princely residence. Like the palace, it was decorated in red and green with lavish gilding, and the boxes and adjoining rooms were appointed with fine furniture, porcelain, fireplaces and clocks. Just as the prince's apartments could be found at the hub of the palace, the princely box was situated at the center of the balcony: both were accessible by a double staircase. The arrival of the prince signaled the beginning of the performance:

> At six o'clock, everyone goes to the theater and takes one's place in the parterre without formalities. As soon as the prince appears in his box, the *coup d'archet* [first down-bow] is given and after a symphony in the latest fashion, one is enchanted by the evening's entertainment.[13]

Thus, the prince presided over the opera house as symbolic "conductor" of the performances. From the balcony of the palace, the prince commanded a view of his domain, not only the geometric patterns of the park, but the church steeples of the neighboring villages, which were visible at the vanishing points of the allées.[14] The princely theater box likewise provided a view of the stage, but rather than gazing at a landscape of cultivated nature, the prince could observe a cultured view of human nature. The picturesque association between the theater and the park was a conceit actually built into some aristocratic theaters in Hungary. According to Géza Staud, in some cases the back wall of the theater could even be opened to reveal a perspective view of the park itself, as if to dissolve the boundary between "art" and "life".[15] During the wedding festivities of 1770, the picturesque settings of *Le pescatrici* were complemented by a rural pastoral scene staged by the prince in his own park. The guests were taken by carriage to a clearing with a fountain and trellises:

> But soon another spectacle drew the attention of the company: a large crowd of peasants, men and women, appeared quite unexpectedly and contributed no little to the company's diversion by their peasant dances and songs, and by the great joy to be seen in their faces.[16]

This event was probably meant to indulge an aristocratic penchant for courtly fantasies of peasant life. The *Bauernhochzeit*, in which nobles dressed in peasant costumes, was a typical feature of imperial wedding celebrations. In this case, the wedding guests did not actually "play" peasants, but were invited to participate in the spectacle of peasant life itself, albeit in a highly constructed form.

The spontaneous appearance of contented peasants was no doubt also politically motivated, since the Esterházys did not have the most sterling reputation for their treatment of their serfs. Their land was home to two-thirds of the peasant population in Sopron county, and in a letter, Maria Theresia named them (along with the Batthyánys) as "the most hardened oppressors."[17] During the period in which Eszterháza was erected, Maria Theresia and Joseph II[18] attempted to introduce a number of reforms aimed at improving peasant conditions, most notably the *Urbarium* of 1767, only three years prior to the wedding of 1770. This regulation was an attempt to limit the demands landlords could make on their peasants and to prevent them from evicting tenants. Such reforms also had the effect of transferring power from the Hungarian landlords to the central government, and so served Maria Theresia's strategy of modernizing the empire.[19]

In the eighteenth century, Hungary was still governed in a feudal manner by powerful magnates who jealously protected their traditional privileges, the most sacred of which was freedom from taxation. Landlords such as the Esterházys extracted a wide range of goods, labor, taxes, and other forms of wealth from peasants, Jews, and petty nobles, and they enjoyed a number of prerogatives, from the right to collect tolls and dispense wine to sweeping judicial powers, including the death penalty.[20] Despite Maria Theresia's official title as king [*sic*] of Hungary,[21] the serfs were essentially subject economically and legally to the powerful seigneurs rather than the monarch. Esterházy's various positions, including lord high sheriff, proprietor of a military regiment, and captain of the Hungarian Bodyguard gave him immense influence in spheres far beyond his actual estate.

Introducing reforms and enforcing them were two different matters however. Hungary was the only province to have its own parliament (diet), and enforcement of imperial initiatives depended on the cooperation of large landowners. The pace of reform was slow. Maria Theresia needed the support of traditional allies like the Esterházys in order to win over the more intransigent gentry to her plans, but most of her initiatives were patently not in their best interest. Thus, this period was a delicate one for relations between the Esterházys and the Hofburg, as Maria Theresia attempted to encroach on aristocratic powers while retaining support for her reforms.

This ambivalence can be read in a portrait of Nicolaus made by Ludwig Guttenbrunn in 1770. (See Plate 2.) Resplendent in the vestments of military and aristocratic status, the prince is pictured amidst symbols of both the battlefield and the court. The helmet and sword are reminders of Nicolaus' military achievements[22] while the horn alludes to the civilized bloodshed of the hunt, and is perhaps also a reference to musical activity. The name and titles of the prince are given in courtly French: "Nicolas le Prince Esterhazy/ de Galantha Chevalier de la Toison D'or Comendeur de/ L'Ordre Millitaire de Marie Therese General Feld Marechal/ Capitaine de la Noble Garde Hongroise au Service de S.M.T. et R.Ap." Nicolaus' magnificence is thus construed in terms of his military prowess and his relationship with Maria Theresia. While the portrait affirms the majesty of a prince, it also reminds us that his might is derived from a greater political source. He is both protector and servant, sovereign power and imperial subject.

Plate 2. Engraving from portrait by Ludwig Guttenbrunn of Nicolaus Esterházy, 1770.

It is well known that music played an important role at Eszterháza; what is rarely discussed is its function in this feudal court where music-making facilitated the assertion of power as well as provided pleasure. This becomes more evident if one considers the connections between the musical and military forces at Eszterháza. The sword and the horn, which helped to construct Nicolaus' identity in the Guttenbrunn portrait, had a physical symmetry in the architectural plan of Eszterháza—the music house, where many of the musicians and singers lived, was matched by a military barracks on the other side of the park, indicated as H and Y respectively in Plate 1. Both the grenadiers and the Kapelle represented the prince through their distinctive livery and uniforms, and were renowned for the precision of their performances. The ceremonial changing of the guard was one of the highlights of Eszterháza in no small part because of the accompanying *Harmoniemusik* :

> The service and military parade, accompanied by a band of oboists, is performed with all imaginable regularity and precision. At eleven o'clock, the members of the guard rise, make some movements, parade in excellent order before the windows of the Prince, and go to take up their posts. The musical march, which is extremely rhythmic and very harmonious, is composed by Haydn: that is all that needs to be said.[23]

The grenadiers symbolized the military power that Nicolaus could muster. The impression of discipline must have been enhanced considerably by the precision of the court orchestra: in the description above it is difficult to separate the musical performance from the military exercise. This distinction becomes even more blurred by the performance of the grenadiers on the operatic stage at Eszterháza as extras, or occasionally in military maneuvers presented as theater. One such display occurred following the performance of Haydn's opera *Le pescatrici*, at the 1770 wedding:

> After the theatre the princely Grenadier Guards presented a warlike spectacle, quite remarkable in its own way, demonstrating the proficiency of well-trained soldiers, as shown in types of attack and defence; the illumination of the star-shells, the exciting sounds of military music and the noise of cannon added greatly to the sight.[24]

In such performances, music enhanced the symbolic rehearsals of military might; on both sides of the footlights, the spectacle of power was constantly being presented and represented.

On at least one occasion, the prince exerted his power over these representations by disciplining one of his singers who caused a disruption in the theater. The event occurred in 1776 during a performance of *Il finto pazzo per amore* by Carl Dittersdorf. As reported by Ludwig Peter von Rahier, Esterházy's estates director:

> It occurred that at a certain moment when [Catharina Poschva] sings an aria during which she has to act in a lunatic fashion, [Benedetto] Bianchi leaning over and bending down, had a cane in his hand and lifted [Poschva's] skirt and shirt once and then again, despite the fact that she, as she continued to sing the aria, protested by negative signs with her hands. Moreover, he was warned by waves of the hand, whispering and calls from various members of the public, including her husband, to desist, but at the third attempt, to the anger of the whole audience and to her utter shame, she was totally denuded . . .[25]

Bianchi was ordered to give a public apology on stage, was placed under arrest for two weeks, and was threatened with fifty lashes to be given on stage should the event ever occur again. Kristina Straub's work on the politics of the eighteenth-century stage is instructive here for understanding the intersection of various power relations in this event, including the symbolic rape of Poschva, and the subsequent humbling of Bianchi. Because the spectator is emblematic of a "mode of discursive authority,"[26] she views the forced apology as an assertion of aristocratic control over what one sees in the theater. The Bianchi incident is a reminder of Esterházy's power over the representations in his theater, and illustrates the high stakes of departing from the script.

More often, however, the prince rewarded his singers with bonuses of gold ducats for their opera performances. As Landon has suggested, Nicolaus' patriarchal power expressed itself both in the harsh discipline he imposed and in his fatherly interest in his musicians.[27] Service in the Esterházy house brought many advantages, such as security against poverty and hunger; however, Esterházy exerted a degree of control over his musicians that seems repressive by the standards of twentieth-century individualism. Roger Hellyer notes that "one of the first requirements of the oboists and bassoonists was to sell their instruments to the prince, which both ensured that the *cappella* possessed instruments of some quality, and at the same time made it more difficult for a musician to resign his position."[28] Once in the princely service, musicians required permission to travel, and even to marry. Clauses in Haydn's contract of 1761 placed restrictions on conduct, moral character, personal relationships with the other musicians, and laid claim to the material results of his labor. The fourth clause of the contract of 1761 reads as follows:

> 4. The said vice-Kapellmeister shall be at all times obliged, on command of His High-princely Serenity, to compose such music as shall be required by His Highness and thereupon to make new compositions known to no-one, still less allow them to be copied, but to reserve them solely and exclusively for His Serene Highness and, in particular, to compose nothing for anyone else without the foreknowledge and gracious permission of His Highness. [29]

This particular contract was made between Paul Anton and Haydn, but it remained in effect when Nicolaus assumed the title after Paul Anton died in March 1762. Subsequently, some of these restrictions were removed, but the injunction forbidding Haydn's music to circulate was not officially lifted until the revised contract of January 1779. Although Haydn eventually forged an identity as an autonomous author in the public concert halls and publishing houses, he never had the opportunity to create a reputation for himself as an opera composer in the public sphere.[30] As a servant in livery, his works belonged artistically and legally to the prince; even his early biographer, A. C. Dies, was to claim that "Haydn's existence in the world of art is the creation and sole property of His Serene Highness Prince Esterházy."[31]

The prince's authority over the feudal palace of Eszterháza placed severe limits on Haydn's authorship; as the princely *Kapellmeister*, Haydn represented the Esterházys and enhanced their reputation as musical patrons. But Haydn also represented the Esterházys on stage, and even if Haydn was ultimately subject to his prince, his dramatic representations of the aristocracy in *Le pescatrici* produced a new kind of operatic subject at odds with the ideological expectations of his audience. This opera offers a glimpse of a moment when Haydn's role as princely Kapellmeister began to overlap with his emerging identity as autonomous author.

Courtship, Marriage, and Spectacle

Upper-class marriage in the eighteenth-century Habsburg empire was still based on the economic and political interests of a family rather than the emotional attachments of individuals. Johann Pezzl, who chronicled Viennese customs in the late eighteenth century, found that love had disappeared in the upper classes, where "all attachments are determined by calculating fathers or ambitious mothers, and the young pair are simply the means by which the parents realize their intentions."[32] The fate of Victoire Jabornigg, the adopted daughter of Paul Anton and his wife, Maria-Aloisia, illustrates that family interest still took precedence over personal sentiment in marriage practices of the Esterházy family. Jabornigg's opposition to the match made by her family, to one Baron Prandau, is said to have been so great that it hastened her death at the age of 25.[33] Because aristocratic weddings dramatized the perpetuation of dynastic lines, upholding traditional privilege and reinforcing the wealth and power of a family house, the forging of political bonds in a marriage gave rise to different forms of "play," from the solemn taking of vows by the bride and groom to the licentious feasting of popular festivals. Hence, dramatic entertainments cannot be isolated from the symbolic associations of the other performances that constituted the wedding celebrations as a whole.

Imperial weddings were among the few occasions during this period that still called for lavish ceremony and gala court festivities, and as Maria Theresia's numerous children reached a marrying age no expense was spared to celebrate their arranged marriages. Festivities often stretched over several months while the bride made her way, with great fanfare, to the imperial city, accompanied by a glittering retinue of distinguished escorts. The wedding itself was celebrated over three gala days of illuminations, banquets, balls, and performances of opera. There were also entertainments for the middle and lower ranks, including free admission to the theaters, popular out-of-door feasts and the distribution of gold ducats. These weddings were elaborate state affairs recalling an earlier era of pomp and ceremony, and were often overburdened with the demands of protocol and official ceremony. For example, when Maria Theresia decided on a bride for her son (the future Joseph II), Prince Liechtenstein was dispatched to Parma as imperial ambassador. Arriving incognito, he made a festive procession the next day to make a formal offer of marriage to Isabella of Parma. According to Spanish court etiquette, a picture of Archduke Joseph was pinned to the breast of the prospective bride before she had a chance to glance at the image of the man who was to be her husband.[34]

Although opera seria was rarely heard at the Burgtheater any more as part of the regular fare, imperial wedding operas called for a spectacular mode of self-representation characteristic of an earlier era, called the *festa teatrale*. Featuring mythological subjects, virtuosic singing, impressive choruses, and lavish scenery, this festive allegorical form reinforced the powerful claims of imperial majesty through the conventions of opera seria. As suggested in Martha Feldman's recent essay, the ritualistic aspects of opera seria helped to construct a mythic distance that prevented the spectator from identifying with the dramatic representations too closely while allowing for participation in the spectacle of power.[35] Dazzling vocal display, fantastic scenic proportions, and narrative unfoldings of a stable hierarchy of kinship relationships made claims to power by fiat, appealing to magical effects rather than logical argument. It is surely significant that the trope of enchantment figured prominently in descriptions of the magnificence of Eszterháza, whose "fairy-tale" luster was enhanced by the accretion of diverse amusements, the most spectacular of which was the opera.[36]

For an example of the way opera was embedded in the courtly celebration of the wedding festivity, we can turn to the entertainments at Archduke Joseph's first wedding, to Isabella of Parma, in 1760, an event that perhaps served as a model to ambitious princes. The main opera was *Alcide al Bivio* ("Hercules at the Crossroads") by two fixtures of the imperial court: Metastasio, the venerable court poet, and Johann Adolf Hasse, reputedly the favorite composer of the empress. In the plot of this opera, the hero, Alcides, is faced with a difficult decision between pleasure and virtue and chooses the latter—demonstrating his moral rather than physical strength. This dramatic resolution seems an unusual choice in a wedding opera, until we remember that the bridegroom was also the future emperor. Between the acts and at the conclusion of the main opera, ballets by Angiolini were performed. The second opera, *Tetide*, set by Gluck to a libretto by Migliavacca, also featured a mythological allegory in which the sea deity (Tetide) arranges for the marriage of her son (Achilles) in order to ensure peace; after all, Isabella of Parma was the granddaughter of Louis XV. The scenery must have been spectacular: a seascape with rocky cliffs and a crystal palace decorated with coral, shells and marine plants, designed by Servandoni.[37]

Although allegorical readings of these feste teatrale were encouraged by the tradition in which the imperial principals impersonated the gods and goddesses themselves,[38] on this occasion the operatic roles were taken by professionals. Daniel Heartz has suggested that the title role of Tetide, sung by Caterina Gabrielli, was particularly demanding, and would have dazzled the audience with a display of virtuosity that "reflects the virtù of all those Habsburgians sitting in the first row."[39] It is interesting to note that even Gluck seems to lose his identity when composing court opera. Heartz remarks that "in his zeal to serve the Italian virtuosi better than Hasse, Gluck effaced himself to the point where we scarcely recognize the genial master of Viennese Opéra-comique that Gluck had become by 1760."[40] Thus, although Gluck is usually associated with other styles of opera, on this occasion he produced precisely what was required: a string of lustrous da capo arias punctuated by recitative and capped with splendid choruses.

Aesthetically, opera seria reproduced the regulated norms and polished contours of courtly behavior. In commenting on the relationship between French tragedy and court life, Norbert Elias could have been describing opera seria:

> What must be hidden in court life, all vulgar feelings and attitudes, everything of which "one" does not speak, does not appear in tragedy either. People of low rank, which for this class also means of base character, have no place in it. Its form is clear, transparent, precisely regulated, like etiquette and court life in general.[41]

The symmetrical, harmonically self-supporting pillars of the da capo aria, which securely enclose its unstable elements, suggest the restraint and decorum demanded of the courtier. Similarly, Feldman's imaginative recreation of the performance of a Mozart aria suggests the way in which the "changing levels of repose and tension"were regulated by the formal parameters of the da capo aria.[42] Virtuosic flourishes erupted at moments of harmonic arrival, but these periods of ecstatic singing were punctuated securely by instrumental ritornellos which safely circumscribed the improvisatory aspects of the performance.

In the context of a wedding opera, then, it is still appropriate to think of the stage as a mirror, not reflecting in exact correspondence, but refracting at oblique angles the glories of the patron,[43] through allegorical readings of the plots, the use of virtuosity as a metaphor for *virtù*, and the reproduction of the aesthetic of the court.

These same conditions would have structured the performance of Haydn's first wedding opera, *Acide e Galatea*, for the wedding of the prince's heir in 1763. The marriage of Prince Nicolaus' eldest son (Paul) Anton to Countess Maria Theresia Erdödy in January 1763 closely followed this imperial model. The official report in the *Wiener Diarium* emphasized the close ties with the Hofburg.[44] The ceremony took place in the imperial palace in Vienna, and was followed by a luncheon with Empress Maria Theresia and her consort Franz Stephan. During the official procession south to Eisenstadt, a portion of the road was illuminated, as was the suburb and Jewish ghetto in Eisenstadt, and, of course, the Esterházy palace there as well. The wedding party was greeted by an honor guard of grenadiers and a *Triumphpforte* was erected in the courtyard. A *Te Deum* in the chapel followed, and a banquet of over sixty dishes "during which the guns were fired, a well trained exercise performed by the Princely Guard, and grenades were exploded, for the amusement of the spectators."[45] On the second day, a performance of Haydn's festa teatrale *Acide e Galatea* took place, followed by a masked ball. Twenty-four musicians were obtained from Vienna, and guests were entertained by acrobats, jugglers, and tightrope walkers as well as illuminations in the castle gardens. An opera buffa was performed on the third day, again followed by a ball. Nor were the peasants neglected; for them, a Neapolitan-style *cuccagna* featured roast hams, sausages, and bread as well as wine.[46]

Daniel Heartz has pointed out a number of links between the production of *Acide e Galatea* and the imperial wedding operas of 1760.[47] The liaison between the two events seems to have been none other than Count Giacomo Durazzo, later the architect of Gluck's operatic reform, who supervised arrangements for the imperial wedding music in his capacity as *cavagliere di musica*. He was also a relative of the Esterházy family. His protégé, Gianambrosio Migliavacca, who had penned the libretto of *Tetide*, also provided the libretto for *Acide e Galatea*. The character of Tetide even makes a *dea ex machina* appearance in Migliavacca's libretto, as if to recall the imperial event.[48] The arias of Haydn's opera are all in da capo or dal segno form, with proportions that emphasize the stately ritornellos and repetitive vocal statements of the A sections. The key of C major and heroic vocal style of Acide's opening aria would have painted a flattering picture of the Esterházy heir. Even the Empress might have received a compliment, for Tetide's aria is the longest and most elaborate.

It is revealing that the description of this Esterházy wedding in the *Wiener Diarium* does not even mention the name of the composer, who was, at any rate, merely the vice-Kapellmeister at this time: "there was a beautiful Italian Opera entitled *Acide*, performed by the virtuosi in the actual service of His Princely Grace: the princely musicians were all in identical, dark-red uniforms trimmed with gold."[49] On this occasion, the qualities of the work seemed to yield to the impression made by a performance of princely splendor, the musicians resplendent in their livery. By 1770, however, the name of Haydn carried considerable weight. In the lengthy account that appeared in both the *Pressburger Zeitung* and the *Wiener Diarium* describing the three days of festivities at the wedding of Prince Nicolaus's niece, Countess Lamberg, to Count Pocci in September of that year, the success of Haydn's *Le pescatrici* was enthusiastically reported:

> [After the wedding ceremony] the whole company repaired to the theatre, where a comic opera in Italian, Le Pescatrici, was performed with all possible skill and art by the princely singers and instrumentalists, to universal and well-deserved applause. The princely Kapellmeister, Herr Hayden, whose many beautiful works have already spread his fame far and wide, and whose flaming and creative genius was responsible for the music to the Singspiel [*sic*], had the honour to receive the most flattering praise from all the illustrious guests.[50]

Although the cachet of Haydn's name ultimately serves to enhance the prince's reputation, this passage suggests a greater authorial voice for Haydn. The composer's circumstances had clearly changed since *Acide* was performed in 1763: he had been promoted to Kapellmeister (in 1766, after the death of Gregor Werner), the princely residence had moved to Eszterháza, where the opera house was opened in 1768, and Haydn had begun to compose comic opera.[51]

Le pescatrici was Haydn's first full-length opera, and by far the most lavish production of any of his works to date. No expense was spared during this first grand fête at newly built Eszterháza. The libretto calls for a total of nine scene changes, with seven separate sets, including a beach with a ship.[52] Additional painters were hired from Vienna to complete the sets, and the carpenter Augustin Haunold submitted bills for work on a moveable ship complete with mast and rudder.[53] The libretto of *Le pescatrici* tells the story of a young noble, Lindoro, prince of Sorrento, who arrives on the shore of an idyllic fishing village to search for the lost princess of Benevento. (In order to protect her from the enemies of her father, who was murdered, the princess had been raised in this village, innocent of her noble origins.) By claiming this princess as his bride, Lindoro hoped to assume her father's title.

The identification of a princess who is fit to rule parallels the political concerns of the wedding itself, in which the continuation of an aristocratic line is consolidated by the marriage of two noble persons. Thus, the plot of *Le pescatrici* might seem to possess the attributes of a wedding opera (noble love in pastoral setting) but as a genre, the dramma giocoso—a term for comic opera sometimes used interchangeably with opera buffa—represents a dramatic departure from the courtly festa teatrale.

Genre, Gender, and Genealogy

The librettist of *Le pescatrici* was Carlo Goldoni, also the author of *Lo speziale*, which Haydn had set in 1768. Goldoni had an important role in the development of dramma giocoso, especially during the period of his reform of the spoken theater, 1748–53. The hybrid qualities of the genre are suggested etymologically in the term dramma giocoso: as Daniel Heartz has observed, "*dramma* by itself signified at the time the grander, heroic world of opera seria, while *giocare* means to play or frolic, also to deceive or make a fool of."[54] The friction caused by the proximity of wooden nobles and buffooning servants gave dramma giocoso the potential for parody of the high style, deflating the elevated utterances of opera seria. Whereas the festa teatrale relied on the dignity of opera seria, dramma giocoso chose greedily from a cornucopia of musical forms and styles both high and low.[55] Incorporating more flexible musico-dramatic forms (such as binary arias in two tempos, and the multi-sectioned finale, which combines stage action and lyrical reflection), the dramma giocoso and opera buffa generally contributed to the mid-century reforms which "began to displace the spectacular nature of seria's formal frames by pulling its set numbers into a more continuous, quasi-narrative flow."[56] Feldman correlates the dissolution of seria's ritual aspects with the imposition of greater behavioral restrictions on the modern spectator, but the infusion of progressive, dynamic forms was just as much an agent of change.[57]

The mirror of Goldoni's stage reflected the harsher light of verisimilitude. In place of the virtue and honor of the aristocracy, shown by means of allegory with mythological and historical characters from an ennobled past, Goldoni's comic theater aspired to present a faithful representation of the contemporary life and customs of the Venetian people through "a reasonable reflection of their problems, their merits and even their defects."[58] True, the librettos retreat to a world permeated with fictions, but Goldoni's librettos are far from the idealized realm of the beneficent ruler-gods of opera seria. Instead they are populated with dissolute and impoverished nobles, lecherous fathers and prodigal wives, the very figures which posed a threat to the stability of Goldoni's society.

Goldoni wrote his plays and librettos during a period when the patrician nobility of Venice was in decline, placing economic and political stability in jeopardy.[59] The mirror metaphor has also been pressed into service by Goldoni scholars to describe the ideological work of Goldoni's reform-period comedies:

> [T]he theatre proposes itself as a corrective "mirror" of vice and virtue, it separates the world reflected on stage into a series of simple dichotomies (vice/virtue, order/disorder, rationality/passion, frugality/prodigality, moderation/excess, etc.) and exorcises the negative half of the equation by expelling or absorbing it, triumphantly affirming the imposition of a bourgeois order on a threatening disorder.[60]

Although Goldoni's criticism of the nobility in his librettos has become conventional wisdom, Franco Fido has pointed out that Goldoni never satirizes the class as a whole. His wit is directed towards those elements which would threaten the stability of Venetian social and political structures: on the one hand, impoverished nobles who led parasitic and unproductive lives, and, on the other, the newly rich who pretended to the nobility associated with their improved economic status.[61] Much of the comic action in this libretto involves the materialist greed of Nerina and Lesbina, the genuine *pescatrici*, who are ready to abandon their humble stations and their local lovers at the slightest appearance (and promise) of wealth. In this aspect, they closely resemble Pezzl's description of the "female Viennese dandy": "She loves any man who pretends to be a count or a baron; everyone who wears boots and spurs, and understands horses; and every male hand bearing a diamond ring."[62]

While this libretto does not ridicule the aristocratic characters, it does reconfigure the basis upon which nobility is discernible. Since even the princess herself is ignorant of her high birth, she reveals her identity through a refinement of sensibility rather than manners. In Act II, Lindoro offers gifts to the villagers in return for their hospitality; while the others choose jewels, fine porcelain and money, Eurilda is mysteriously drawn to the dagger which killed prince Casimiro, her father. Her choice of this object, provoked by immaterial intuition rather than material greed, reveals her as the lost princess. A secondary aspect of the libretto is Eurilda's awakening to sexual passion, which begins from the moment when she first glimpses Lindoro. The theme of passion is an unusual feature of this libretto, since "passions of all sorts are seen as a danger to the stability of the *ragion borghese*, and they must be suppressed in order to protect the rational equilibrium of Goldoni's bourgeois ideology."[63] But even Goldoni was unable to resist the sway of sensibility, which permeated aspects of eighteenth-century life and thought from physiology to philanthropy.[64]

Sensibility began as a term of science and ultimately became indispensable to aesthetics. It was used by Albrecht von Haller (1708–77) and Robert Whytt (1719–66) in experiments for determining the capacity of response in a living organism to sensory stimulation. As a conduit between the body (sensation) and the mind (animation), the "nerve"—the source of feeling—was crucial to changes in epistemology: "If indeed the soul is limited to the brain, as [Thomas] Willis and his followers in the 1660s contended, then nerves alone can be held responsible for sensory impressions, and consequently for knowledge."[65] Central to the "nerve paradigm" was the figure of John Locke, whose assertion that individuals received their ideas from outside the mind depended upon the notion of the nerve as a conduit from the physical sensations of the world to the passive "tabula rasa" of the mind. The process of thinking became, in Locke's epistemology, a form of touching whereby ideas were impressed on the brain via sensory conductors. Once "feeling" came to denote the intersection of physical sensation and moral sentiment in the nerves,[66] fictional characters in the sentimental novels of Samuel Richardson, Lawrence Sterne, and Henry MacKenzie began to exhibit evidence of their highly refined sensibility through a language of feeling, expressed not only in a vocabulary of the nerves (thrill, excite, throb etc.) but in bodily signs such as tears, blushing, and swooning. Although these novels included both male and female sentimental characters, it was the female heroines, such as Richardson's Pamela, who were particularly associated with a propensity for feeling and hence virtue. Traditionally the more unstable vessel, the female body became a locus for sensibility; because of the finer tuning of her nerves, the physical "weakness" of women was reinterpreted as a moral virtue.

Goldoni made his own contribution to the cult and culture of sensibility in his comedy *La Pamela*[67] of 1750, and the libretto *La buona figliuola* of 1756. Both were based on the Richardson novel *Pamela, or Virtue Rewarded* (1740). The setting of *La buona figliuola* by Niccolò Piccinni (Rome 1760) was enormously influential, spawning a subgenre of sentimental opera.[68] Emery has argued that the differences in Goldoni's treatment of the Pamela story suggest a progression from the problem of passion in the comedy toward an aesthetic of sensibility in the libretto in which the viewer is aroused by the tender but uncomplicated feelings of the heroine.[69] Situated chronologically in Goldoni's oeuvre between Pamela and Cecchina of *La buona figluola*, Eurilda can perhaps be seen as a midwife to the birth of the sentimental heroine in the latter.

In the eighteenth century, the story of a servant girl who is sexually pursued by her master was hardly remarkable, although it is perhaps an aspect of the greater realism of comic opera.[70] What seems to have made the Pamela story so compelling, "a kind of spiritual rain-gauge," was the nature of Pamela's resistance to her aggressor, Mr. B.[71] By refusing to acknowledge Mr. B's claims to her body, even in exchange for money, by redirecting Mr. B's desire away from her physical body towards her "self," Pamela redefines the terms of the sexual (and political) contract between servant and master. As Nancy Armstrong has argued persuasively, the emphasis on a feminine domain of feeling established the basis for a new kind of political authority.[72] Value was placed on the internal worth of an individual rather than her claims to membership in a group based on external signs such as heraldic crests and property deeds: "If a servant girl could claim possession of herself as her own first property, then virtually any individual must similarly have a self to withhold or give in a modern form of exchange with the state."[73]

The volatile political implications of Richardson's story were not lost on the audience of Venice where the movement between classes was less fluid.[74] In *La buona figliuola,* the problem of interclass marriage is therefore resolved by the revelation at the end of the opera of Cecchina's true parentage; she is actually the daughter of a German baron. Just such a discovery animates the retrieval of the lost princess in *Le pescatrici.* If this libretto was chosen on the basis of the popularity of comic opera (and Goldoni[75]) in Vienna, thus allowing Esterházy to demonstrate his fashionable taste, it is also ideologically removed from the world of opera seria. The greater realism and more flexible forms of the dramma giocoso deflate the magical aura projected by the festa teatrale whose allegorical mythologies could be seen to overlap with the mythical timelessness of a stable family line, stretching back for generations. And the notion of a princess whose noble virtue rests on feminine feeling rather than regal bloodlines poses a challenge to the very grounds on which social and political prestige were claimed. Genre and gender undermine the traditional entitlements of genealogy. The presentation of *Le pescatrici* on the occasion of an aristocratic wedding suggests not merely that operatic tastes had changed, but also that the aristocracy were ever more comfortable with representations of a more complicated hierarchy of social interactions. Indeed, Nicolaus had proved this in his passion for spoken drama, to the point where, as those newspapers had it, "two short German plays with arias" were put on at the wedding. Before considering what happens when Haydn enters this mix, we will take a look at some aspects of previous and subsequent settings of the same libretto in order to gain an appreciation of the particular choices made by Haydn.[76]

Convention and Class

Ultimately, the degree to which particular elements of Goldoni's libretto emerge depends on the way the text is shaped by a specific composer's musical setting. Because of its pastoral context, *Le pescatrici* does retain something of the idyllic remove of a festa teatrale. Haydn's version contains a great number of choruses and ensembles conducive to the leisurely place of a festive opera, particularly in Acts I and III, and these create an aural landscape of pastoral tranquility. "Bell'ombra gradita," accompanied by the dulcet tones of English horns in E-flat, is a hymn to the pleasures of nature, and its rich harmonies call for a suspension of the action. Caryl Clark has observed that the finales of this opera are the least dramatic of Haydn's oeuvre.[77] Indeed, the static quality of many of the scenes is antithetical to the sparkling comic action expected of opera buffa. Silke Leopold describes Haydn's music in this opera as stemming from an "oratorio concept" of opera as opposed to the "scenic concept" of Leopold Gassmann's setting of the same text for Vienna in the following year for the Burgtheater.[78] But if Haydn composed music that created tableau-like scenes rather than the vivid dramatic pacing we have come to expect from Mozart, it is likely that he was responding to the particular festive occasion for which the opera was intended.

As was the convention in the 1750s when Goldoni wrote the libretto, *Le pescatrici*'s aristocratic characters do not participate in the comic business of the finales, and Goldoni's satirical barbs are aimed at the class pretensions of Nerina and Lesbina. The polarities of class are emphasized by Ferdinando Bertoni's setting in 1752: Eurilda's nobility is represented as an attribute of her birth, not her character, and her social station is mediated by the conventions of eighteenth-century opera.[79] The *naïveté* of Lindoro, who professes not to know the identity of the princess, is pitted against the savvy of the audience, which would recognize the princess immediately in the elevated musical behavior of Eurilda. Like Lindoro, Bertoni's Eurilda sings da capo arias with opportunities for virtuosic display, a musical style borrowed from the opera seria.[80] The other fisherwomen sing less demanding binary arias emphasizing local motivic patterns and metric contrast rather than large-scale formal design. The serious and comic characters are also distinguished through orchestration, horns and oboes being reserved for Eurilda and Lindoro. An exception to this occurs when Lesbina and Nerina pose as princesses in Act II, awash in the sound of oboes and horns,[81] but despite their attempts at a regal musical pose, they are ridiculed musically as it becomes clear that neither of these fisherwomen knows how to express herself in the manner of opera seria, the badge of nobility.

The topical rhythmic gestures in Bertoni's score also contribute to the social positioning of these characters. Eurilda is elevated through the minuet rhythms of "La bella calma"[82] while Lesbina and Nerina move to the more common strains of the contredanse (Example 1). This distinction in musical carriage responds to contemporary notions of difference in a culture in which "bearing reflected class, and thus, by extension, character."[83] The opposition between the exuberant but untutored movements of rural dance and the disciplined elegance required to execute the quintessential dance of the court is evident in the following comments by Nicolas Framery (1791):

> The slow minuet, which employs only two people and does not allow the spectators any occupation except admiring the dancers, could only be born in the cities, where people dance for the sake of amour-propre. In the village people dance for the sole pleasure of dancing, to move limbs accustomed to violent exercise; they dance to breathe out a feeling of joy which grows constantly in proportion to the number of dancers, and has no need for spectators.[84]

By means of rhythmic gesture, Nerina and Lesbina are associated with naive, instinctual responses to movement, while Eurilda conducts herself with the self-control and discipline of a courtier. Since she too was raised in the fishing village, Eurilda's refined manners can only be the result of her gentle birth. Bertoni's use of musical conventions both reflects and replicates the hierarchy of social conventions which associated worthiness with blood.

Example 1. Comparison of rhythmic profiles of "La bella calma," "Un pescatore me l'ha fatta brutta," and "Son furba la mia parte," F. Bertoni (F-Pc).

The passage of time between Venice in 1752 and Eszterháza in 1770 caused considerable erosion in Bertoni's coded representation of social class through musical conventions. By the time Haydn came to set Goldoni's libretto, it would have been extremely unfashionable to employ da capo arias in a dramma giocoso. Though general statements about the aria forms of Haydn's setting are difficult to make because of the fragmented nature of the source material, [85] it is nevertheless clear that Haydn's *Le pescatrici* presents an unusual democracy of musical form, rather than a musical index of social status; musical complexity is not limited to the serious characters. Needless to say, there are no da capo arias. Even Goldoni's two-verse texts (which received ternary da capo treatment in Bertoni's hands) are set in binary forms, often involving a change in tempo. Almost all of the arias begin with lengthy ritornellos, and each of the singers is given an opportunity for the display of vocal skill whether it is virtuosic passaggi, daunting leaps, or an impressive range. One of the more developed forms of the opera is found in the aria "Fra tuoni, lampi e fulmini," sung by Burlotto, one of the fishermen.

A sonata-form aria with two distinct thematic areas and an extended development, "Fra tuoni" (Example 2) is also very demanding technically, with large leaps and passaggi. A comparison of Haydn's setting of the first two lines with those of both Bertoni and Gassmann suggests how differently a musical setting can shape a text. Bertoni's version outlines a triad ascending from the tonic, but the interpolation of rests suggests the bluster of buffo phrasing. Likewise, the threefold repetition of line 2 ("andro per te a pescar") in short phrases establishes the tonic by insistence rather than persuasion. In contrast, Haydn's setting incorporates both lines into a long-breathed phrase. His phrase also outlines a triad, but with an urgency created by a digression to the fourth degree in the second measure. The repetition of the low F sets the line in motion as if spiraling out from the B-flat and reaching its peak in the penultimate measure. This energy propels the line forward and is finally released in the huge leaps just before the cadence. While Gassmann's setting of 1771 seems to acknowledge Haydn's setting in the first few measures, its phrasing is much closer to Bertoni's setting of twenty years earlier.

Example 2. Comparison of settings of "Fra tuoni, lampi e fulmini," by Bertoni (F-Pc), Haydn, and Gassmann (A-Wn).

Haydn's music resists the mapping of musical sophistication onto social status, and therefore does not naturalize the claim to nobility through operatic practice. On the contrary, in Lesbina's mock-serious aria, "Che vi par?," Haydn's parody of the elevated style criticizes the very convention by which opera seria operates as a sign of nobility. Wondering if she could possibly be the lost princess for whom Lindoro seeks, Lesbina sings this aria at the beginning of Act II, scene 6:

Che vi par? Son io gentile?
Sembro nata a comandar?
Son civile? Ah che vi par?
Aspettate, voglio andarmi
Nella Fonte ad ispecchiar.
(Frattanto, ch'Ella va ad ispecchiarsi, l'Orchestra suona.)

Son Maestosa;
Sembro orgogliosa:
Ma sarò docile,
Mi farò amar.
Ah? che vi par?[86]

What do you think? Am I not genteel?
Am I not born to rule?
Am I not civilized? Ah, what do you think?
Wait, I want to see my reflection in the fountain.
(*As she goes to the fountain and gazes at her reflection, the orchestra sounds.*)

I am majestic;
I appear proud:
but I will be gentle,
I will make them love me.
So? what do you think?

The text of this aria is unconventional, even for comic opera, in at least two ways: it incorporates stage action, and the two verses are in different meters, giving the aria a progressive, dramatic quality alien to the dramaturgy of opera seria. Another unusual aspect is the saturation of interrogatives in the first verse, making it more conducive to recitative than a lyrical setting, and giving Lesbina's utterance a tone of insecurity. Bertoni's setting of the text underlines this hesitancy; the vocal line skirts with uncertainty around the tonic, tending to hover on the dominant in the first two phrases (Example 3). The second verse (andante 3/8) glosses "majesty" with a dotted figure that is undercut by the rhythmic hiccup on "Son maestosa" and the ungainly meter of 3/8. By the return of "Che vi par?" at the end of the second verse, Lesbina's music has provided the answer to her own question.

Example 3. "Che vi par?" F. Bertoni (F-Pc), mm. 23–72, voice and bass.

Example 3, continued.

In contrast to Bertoni, Haydn provides Lesbina with a miniature scena, beginning with accompanied recitative. As a kind of expression reserved for serious characters, the use of accompanied recitative not only elevates Lesbina's character, but lends a greater weight and dramatic power to her fragmented speech.[87] After a lengthy opening ritornello, which could have been the beginning of one of Haydn's D major symphonies, the orchestra settles on a G-sharp diminished seventh chord in first inversion. This both prompts Lesbina's first utterance, as if requesting her to speak, and provides a context for the unstable position from which she begins—even as Lesbina asks the question "Che vi par?" she answers one by moving to the key implied by the orchestral chord. The instrumental interpolations not only provide continuity, but unify the interrogative fragments and lend them a certain musical logic. The same two lines which seemed so hesitant in Bertoni's setting are dispatched with rhetorical confidence here in a definite move towards the dominant, clinched by seven measures of the new key. This tonal move poses the question ("Sembro nata a comandar") which can then be answered by a move to the tonic as Lesbina resolves to go to the fountain (mm. 35–38). Although she has hardly sung more than a few phrases, Lesbina's utterance has been invested with eloquence by the end of the recitative section; indeed, the tremendous scope suggested by this lengthy preparation calls for an aria of heroic proportions.

Haydn's choice of common time and an allegro di molto tempo for the aria suggests that he treats Lesbina seriously. The aria begins with a restatement of the opening ritornello, now overlaid with Lesbina's vocal line in "white notes" (Example 4). Her vocal utterance is inflated

Example 4. "Che vi par?" Haydn, *Le pescatrici,* mm. 48–75.

Example 4, continued.

and supported by the orchestra until m. 58, where the independent instrumental accompaniment drops out to follow her lead in octaves. Suddenly on her own, Lesbina has difficulty delivering at this rhetorically crucial moment. Expectations heightened by the repetition of her first phrase are deflated when she merely descends to the lower tonic by inverting the opening fourth interval, but the moment is partially salvaged by an impressive series of leaps (mm. 61–65). The exaggerated bravura of these gestures is undercut however by the turn to the submediant at "ma sarò docile" (m. 68). Repetition and a kind of panic in the strings follows, and the text and motive of the recitative passage return. With a statement on the dominant of "Son maestosa" (m. 76), Lesbina appears to be rallying the orchestra, but this repetitive gesture suggests a poverty of expression. At m. 79, the orchestra finally comes to her aid, but with a motive that echoes the hesitancy of Bertoni's Lesbina and prompts the return of "Che vi par." In retrospect, the bravura posturing of the opening has a hollow ring. After a ritornello in the dominant, the second vocal section begins with a repetition of the aria text in the tonic, but the energy again flags, collapsing into the subdominant at the text "ma sarò docile, mi farò amar." She ends the aria as she began (singing "Che vi par?) and the aria is abruptly truncated with Lesbina stranded in the dominant key.

Thus, like Bertoni, Haydn composes music for Lesbina that demonstrates her inability to converse in the language of princesses; however, Haydn's aria produces a critical, ambivalent effect typical of parody.[88] In this parody of seria style, Lesbina gets the sound right, but she is incapable of formal manipulation; there is a comic discrepancy between her topical representation and her rhetorical competency. As long as Lesbina stays under the cloak of the instrumental texture, she projects the appearance of nobility. But when she is deprived of her majestic accompaniment, her musical expression falters, as if to suggest that nobility can be obtained merely by assuming the accoutrements of seria style. In parodying opera seria in this way, Haydn also exposes its very conventionality, the way that it operates as an arbitrary sign of class, a sign which, like a piece of clothing (or a ritornello), can be put on and taken off, thereby rendering its meaning unstable.

The Prince, the Princess, and Passion

In *Le pescatrici,* the aristocratic characters are configured in a way that does not draw on conventions of opera seria style. Instead of expressing passion in ritual outpourings of song, Lindoro and Eurilda share a musical language that opens up the individual world of the self.

As we have seen, the temporal and the sociogeographical gap between 1752 Venice and 1770 Eszterháza opened up a space for dramatic realignment in the libretto set by Haydn. It was customary to make some revisions in the text of a libretto when it received a new setting, but in the 1770 Eszterháza libretto they were particularly extensive. In five arias new texts were substituted, five other pieces were cut, and the recitative was shortened in several places.[89] These revisions were most likely the work of Carl Friberth, a tenor in the Kapelle who also sang the role of Frisellino in this opera. He was especially kind to Lesbina (sung by his wife, Magdalena Friberth), who survived the numerous cuts and even received an extra aria, at Nerina's expense.[90]

Perhaps in keeping with her enlarged role, Lesbina appears, initially, to share a musical language with Eurilda rather than with Nerina, the other true *pescatrice*. In their initial arias, Eurilda and Lesbina both express their desires in the sentimental language of the heart: a filigreed texture of appoggiaturas and dotted rhythms spread over a heavily divided beat, accompanied by pairs of winds and violins in thirds (Example 5).

The lexical and syntactical congruences of the new aria text written for Lesbina further emphasize the stylistic similarities between the two utterances:[91]

Lesbina: *Voglio amar, e vuò*
scherzare
Con ogn'un di fè, e d'amor:
Ma ad un solo vuò serbare
Tenerino questo cor.
[parte]

I want to love and to play
with everyone who is faithful
and loving:
but I want to keep the
tenderness
of my heart for only
one man.
(exit)

Act I, Scene 4

Eurilda: *Voglio goder contenta*
La pace, ed il riposo;
Non vuò per dolce Sposo;
Smarrir la libertà.

Sarria rischiar il certo
Per un incerto bene;
E paventar conviene,
D'inganni, e infedeltà.
[parte]

I want happily to enjoy
peace and repose;
I don't want to forfeit liberty
for a sweet husband.

It would be to risk certainty
for an uncertain good;
and it behooves one to fear
deceptions and infidelities.
(exit)

Act I, Scene 5

Example 5a. Opening of "Voglio amar" (Haydn).

Example 5b. Opening of "Voglio goder contenta" (Haydn).

Semantically, however, these texts could not be more different. Unlike the lusty Lesbina, who dedicates herself to pursuing love, Eurilda eschews it. In the scene preceding "Voglio goder contenta," Eurilda borrows the language of political liberty in order to declare her freedom from emotional involvement, much to the chagrin of her putative father, Mastricco, who despairs of finding a suitable match for her.

Oh cara libertà, quanto sei grata?	Oh dear liberty, how welcome!
Tenga pur fra catene oppresso il cuore	Let the heart which is the unfortunate
Chi è vassallo infelice al Dio d'amore.	vassal of the God of love remain oppressed by chains.

Act I, Sc. 5

But in "Voglio goder contenta," Eurilda invokes Amore (Cupid) musically even as she forswears him verbally, and the result is a conflicted relationship between music and text. Since "Voglio goder contenta" is one of the incomplete arias in this score,[92] it is impossible to compare the arias of Eurilda and Lesbina in their entirety, but it is perhaps not surprising that the profusion of appoggiaturas and ornamental trills conceals two very different musical structures. Example 6 gives a harmonic reduction of the ritornellos in "Voglio amar" and "Voglio goder contenta."

Example 6. Harmonic reduction of ritornellos, "Voglio amar" and "Voglio goder contenta" (Haydn).

While each of Lesbina's four phrases is harmonically static, Eurilda's ritornello is dynamic, consisting of two overlapping phrases moving to the dominant and back to the tonic. Her second phrase leads towards a registral, dynamic and harmonic climax on a fortissimo tonic seventh chord in measure 13. This surprisingly forceful juncture seems not only intense but even violently so (given the coordination of musical elements) compared with the harmonic simplicity of Lesbina's utterance. Although both arias reveal the ripplings of desire in the appoggiaturas and dotted figures, Eurilda's expression points towards turmoil at a deeper structural level, as if to carve out a musical space for the representation of emotional depth. In comparison with the transparency of Lesbina's utterance, its topical association glossing seamlessly the meaning of the text, Eurilda seems to possess an emotional surplus. Her psychological complexity is indicated in the contradiction between what she says and sings, and in the more complex harmonic scaffolding "below" the musical surface. Rather than flaunting the identity of the princess, Haydn conceals it in Eurilda's potential for powerful feeling.

The delicacy of Eurilda's sensibility begins to emerge when she beholds Lindoro. Compare the reactions of the three *pescatrici* upon seeing Lindoro in Act 1, Scene 12:

Nerina. *(Oh quanto egl'è bellino!)*	Nerina. (Oh how handsome he is!)
Lesbina.*(Oh quant'è graziosino!)*	Lesbina. (Oh how graceful!)
Eurilda. *(Ahimè quel vago aspetto,*	Eurilda. (Alas, this beautiful sight
Un insolito ardor mi desta in petto)	awakens an unusual ardor in my breast)

Eurilda's "nervousness" is expressed to a greater extent when she beholds the fatal dagger in Act II, Scene 12. Upon seeing the object, she is overcome by "un doloroso affetto" and, in a quintessentially sentimental response, she faints. Since it is one of the missing numbers from Act II, one can only imagine the kind of music Haydn composed for "Quanti diversi affetti," sung shortly after her recovery, but Eurilda's volatile sensibility is given full rein in her Act III aria "Questa mano e questo core" in which she finally submits to Amore by extending her hand and heart to Lindoro:

Questa mano e questo core	This hand and this heart
Tutto vostro ognor sarà.	will always be yours.
A voi giuro eterno amore	To you I swear eternal love
E costante fedeltà.	and steadfast faithfulness.
Ma sia pari il vostro affetto,	But let your affection be the same,
Pari in voi sia l'onestà.	let your honesty equal mine.
Il tradirmi, o mio diletto,	To betray me, my darling,
Saria troppa crudeltà.	would be too cruel.
(parte)	*(exit)*

Act III, Scene 2

The text imitates the stylized, literary expression of Metastasian opera, with the opposition of *fedeltà/crudeltà* underlining the contrast between the first and second verses. This opposition recalls the *libertà/infedeltà* construction on which "Voglio goder contenta" is hinged. The textual structure of "Questa mano" would seem to demand a ternary setting in order to dispel the cloud of doubt raised in the second verse. In his setting, however, Haydn seems almost to work *against* the elements of the text, creating a vehicle for the profound expression of individual emotion where a conventional expression of love is all that is suggested.

As the only aria in Act III, this one is highlighted as a solo musical utterance in the midst of several choruses and ensembles. Its textual formality is immediately undercut by the modest beginning of the aria, which plunges directly into a cantabile melodic line. Since "Questa mano" is the only aria in the opera which dispenses with an opening ritornello, this seems a deliberate attempt to establish the kind of intimate context created for a sentimental heroine. The tender sweetness of this type of character is also suggested in the combination of periodic symmetry and simplicity of texture in which Eurilda pledges her hand to Lindoro.

Formally as well, this aria is very modest: a cavatina in which the two verses are repeated (AB AB) in a simple binary form (I–V V–I). In order to affirm the harmonic goals of the two sections, however, it is the B section that receives repetition, shifting the rhetorical emphasis towards the ambivalent second verse. The disappearance of these two formal frames, the ritornello and the ternary da capo form, allows for a radical shift in the meaning of this text, and the reconfiguration of this dramatic moment. Rather than containing Eurilda's apprehensions within a closed musical form, this aria exposes, even highlights, Eurilda's conflicted emotions, which erupt in this aria in an episode of nervous sensibility, perhaps even of *Sturm und Drang*.

At the statement of the second verse (beginning at m. 23), Haydn allows the almost hymn-like serenity of the opening theme to disintegrate under the pressures of doubt expressed in the text. With the last two lines of verse two, the consequent phrase of the theme staggers through eight measures infused with chromatic details and sforzando accents, cadencing on the dominant (mm. 31–38). Here, the accompaniment splits open into two contrapuntal voices that tonicize E major in a circular holding pattern (E: V^6_5–I–♭II–V^6_5 etc.). As the theme becomes increasingly fragmented and distorted by the chromatic voice-leading and violent dynamic markings, the movement towards the dominant is highlighted as a harmonic event marked with dissonance and turmoil rather than inevitability.

The second section of the aria (returning to the tonic) opens with the text of verse 1 set to a variation of the opening theme, now refracted through a chromatic lens (m. 64). A pedal on the dominant prepares for the eventual recovery of the tonic at measure 93, but the consequent phrase again becomes mired in a thicket of chromatic voice-leading, violent accents, dynamic contrasts, and sudden harmonic diversions. Although harmonic resolution is obtained through the eventual restatement of the tonic, the dissonant harmonic vocabulary and the contrasting dynamic articulations exert a kind of resistance to D major which persists to the final eighth-note chord. Eurilda has become the "unfortunate vassal" whom she regarded with such contempt in Act I.

The event dramatized in *Le pescatrici* in which Eurilda enters into a marriage symbolizing social continuity and political stability intersects of course with the occasion for which Haydn's opera was composed, especially since the guests at such wedding entertainments were used to viewing them allegorically. Rather than celebrating this moment, however, Haydn's music marks the event with conflict: the resolution of the final chord is won through struggle rather than consent. If the members of Esterházy's audience expected to *see* themselves in this opera, they might well have been perplexed by the *sound* of a princess entering marriage enslaved to her feelings. This representation of aristocratic marriage diverges pointedly from Adolf Freiherr von Knigge's observation that "the very elegant and the very rich rarely have a sense for domestic bliss, feel no stirrings of the soul, live for the most part on a strange footing with their spouses."[93] Although Esterházy marriages "appear to have been based on mutual affection as well as contracts,"[94] Prince Nicolaus and his wife, Maria-

Elisabeth Weissenwolf, each maintained separate households with their own servants, the princess preferring to stay in Eisenstadt for the summer months. The prince's fondness for his wife did not prevent him from taking a mistress, which was hardly unusual among members of his class, even during the strict moral atmosphere of Maria Theresia's reign.[95] The representation of Lindoro also departs radically from conventional musical images of aristocratic passion, and also seems to belie Pezzl's assurance that "no Viennese of fine society will ever play the Werther."[96]

Again, the particular changes made to Haydn's libretto highlight this shift in representation. Whereas Lesbina's role is considerably amplified, that of the prince, Lindoro, is oddly muted. After the cuts, he was left with only a single aria (and a solo part in the chorus "Fiera strage") and much of his recitative was also removed. Hardly a trace remains of the Goldoni-Bertoni Lindoro, who cut an impressive figure of swaggering bravura. Arriving on the shore, that prince claimed a privileged alliance with the heavens in his first aria, "Scorso abbiam l'instabil mare":

Scorso abbiam l'instabil mare *Col favor d'amica stella,* *Né di scoglio o di procella* *Fui costretto a paventar.*	In the past, we have, with the favor of the stars, looked at the unstable sea and had to fear neither rocks nor storms.
Or lo stesso astro felice *Mi consola, e al cor mi dice* *Che alla patria più contenti* *Potrem lieti ritornar.* (partono)	Now the same heavenly bodies comfort me and tell me that we will be able to return to our country more blessed and contented. *(exit)*
Act I, Scene 8[97]	

Goldoni's text, which also echoes Metastasian vocabulary and prosody, was set by Bertoni as a da capo aria in the high style, with a heroic "white note" melodic line accompanied by a throbbing bass accompaniment, the harmonic pillars of the aria ornamented with the display of vocal agility (Example 7).[98] Lindoro's mastery over the seas and his claim to heavenly favor is also reinforced by the way in which modal stability is established in Bertoni's music. The key of G major is outlined through the elaboration of a tonic triad in a balanced pair of phrases (4 + 4mm.), forming an arch. Stability and symmetry are presented with grace and elegance.

Example 7. Opening of "Scorso abbiam," F. Bertoni (F-Pc).

While Goldoni's text, "Scorso abbiam," has all the hallmarks of the Metastasian style, it is replaced in Haydn's libretto with the real thing: "Varca il mar" is taken from Metastasio's *La Galatea* of 1722, the libretto which served as Migliavacca's model for Haydn's first wedding opera, *Acide e Galatea*. While this intertextual detail is probably a coincidence, it highlights the difference in the representation of aristocracy in these two operas. Indeed, anyone who knew the Metastasian text would recognize it as one sung by Galatea, in a scene with her confidante, Glauce:

Varca il mar di sponda in sponda	He crosses the sea from shore to shore,
Quel nocchier, ne si sgomenta[;]	this helmsman, yet he is not bewildered.
Ed allor, che meno il teme	And then, when he is least afraid,
Sorger vede il vento, e l'onda *Le sue vele a lacerar.* (parte)	he sees the wind and the waves rise and tear at his sails. *(exit)*

Act I, Scene 8

Whereas "Scorso abbiam" looked towards the heavens, this aria dwells on the unpredictable violence of the sea. In the context of the Metastasio libretto, the sea functions as a metaphor for love's arrows, which take the unsuspecting by surprise, but in *Le pescatrici*, it has a dramatic correlation in the setting. The image of a helmsman at the mercy of a chaotic sea sits uncomfortably with Lindoro's heroic moment of arrival on shore in his vessel. While the turbulent passion of this aria is obviously drawn from its depiction of a stormy sea, it also refers inward, to Lindoro's emotional state following his declaration "[f]ra speranza, e timor dubbioso ondeggio" ("Between hope and doubtful fear I waver"). Prepared in this way, "Varca il mar" is weighted towards gloomy pessimism rather than the confident hopes projected in "Scorso abbiam." The ominous dangers adumbrated in the text are heightened by various musical signs of instability including the minor mode,[99] and syncopated rhythmic figures. Undoubtedly, there is a sense of power projected in this aria, but this aristocratic figure inspires awe through the unruly instability of his expression, which threatens to exceed its formal boundaries. Lindoro enters on an ethereal *messa di voce* on $\hat{5}$, in a phrase that settles into the tonic only in the last measure. The mediant is immediately approached, but not secured even after a lengthy passage of vocalizing (mm. 35–46) in which Lindoro negotiates a series of treacherous leaps. Just as the arrival of the secondary key area is established, however, the aria trails off, tantalizingly, in one of the breaks in the source material. Hence, it remains an open question whether and how the restless energy of this aria is contained by its formal contours, and Lindoro is not granted another opportunity for a concerted musical utterance.

All the evidence suggests that Haydn represented the aristocracy well in this opera. Prince Esterházy gave him thirty ducats as a bonus, and each of the singers received twelve. In 1776, Haydn proudly referred to this opera as one of the works which had "received the most approbation,"[100] perhaps a reference to the incendiary phrase in the wedding report which singled out his "flaming and creative genius." Presumably, this referred in part to the intense expressions of passion of Haydn's aristocratic characters. If so, there is a certain irony here: the individuality of Haydn's style in this opera, which garnered prestige for his patron, also allowed him to represent the aristocracy in a way that undermined the traditional values of his spectators. Flattered by a mode of representation that intersected with the emerging culture of sensibility, they were perhaps unaware of its subversive power.

Both Eurilda and Lindoro are situated as characters of powerful passions, in a musical style that modern writers have associated with the literary movement known as *Sturm und Drang*: the minor mode, violent dynamic contrasts, disjunct melodic lines, and syncopated rhythmic figures are thought to suggest the intensity of the emotions explored in German plays and novels by Goethe, Lessing and others.[101] But the particular characteristics of the *Sturm und Drang* literary movement figure even more distinctly in the way that Haydn's music substitutes the passionate life of the emotions for the impersonal coventions of form. In its exploration of the inner life of feeling,

Sturm und Drang can be situated within the larger phenomenon of sensibility, but it takes on characteristics unique to the social and political factors of German-speaking lands. In part, it addressed the dearth of political outlets for members of society who were well-educated but lacked wealth and aristocratic connections. The retreat to the inner world of feeling and intuition has frequently been interpreted as their response to the superficiality of courtly behaviour and the artificiality of its ceremonies and norms. While this literary movement was not overtly political, it contained the "lineaments of a new cultural age, the bourgeois successor to the culture of 'polite society'."[102] As Norbert Elias has expressed it, the challenge to aristocratic society was not conducted directly on social and political privilege, but on the terrain of behavior: depth of honest feeling was contrasted with the superficial falsity of politeness as "civilization" gave way to "Kultur."[103]

As we have seen, Haydn finds many ways to dispense with convention in this opera, and even parodies the way that seria style functions as a badge of nobility. In "Questa mano" a conventional text is twisted into an individual expression of feeling that unsettles the opera at what should be its most stable moment. "Varca il mar," while ostensibly emphasizing Lindoro's lofty literary pretensions, actually destabilizes the character considerably, not only through its volatile musical elements, but also by the way that the trope of the sea oscillates between its literal reference to the setting and its metaphorical reference to Lindoro's emotional state. While I do not mean to propose that Haydn consciously sought to challenge the ideological assumptions of his audience, the "mirror" of his setting for this wedding no longer dazzles its audience with the spectacle of heroic *virtù*. Rather, it reflects a new kind of operatic subject who speaks to the interests of an emerging bourgeois spectator in the inner voice of feelings. Remarkably, the aristocratic audience responded.

In *Le pescatrici*, Haydn is poised between two overlapping modes of operatic spectatorship: in the pastoral setting, static dramatic pacing, and some of its formal conventions (such as the opening ritornello), this opera looks backward to the festive tradition of the wedding opera and hence is unlikely to appeal to later audiences accustomed to the more naturalistic rhythms of Mozartian drama; but in its reinterpretation of texts through dynamic, open forms and in the articulation of musical space suggesting psychological depth, this work looks forward to a modern concept of drama centered on individual character in which the role of music in the mediation of passion begins to dissolve. Placing Haydn's accomplishment on these terms, surely we too can appreciate "the flaming and creative genius" of the operatic Haydn.[104]

NOTES

1. *Le Haydine ovvero Lettere sulla vita e le opere del celebre maestro Giuseppe Haydn*, 2nd ed. (Padua, 1823), p. 138, quoted in Mary Kathleen Hunter, "Haydn's Aria Forms: A Study of the Arias in the Italian Operas Written at Eszterháza, 1766–1783" (Ph.D. diss., Cornell University, 1982), p. 21.

2. See Peter Branscombe and Caryl Clark, "Haydn," in *The New Grove Dictionary of Opera*, ed. Stanley Sadie, vol. 2 (London, 1992). The most comprehensive documentary study of Haydn in the opera house remains Dénes Bartha and László Somfai, *Haydn als Opern-kapellmeister: die Haydn-Dokumente der Esterházy-Opernsammlung* (Budapest, 1960). Haydn also composed two Singspiels (now lost) during his early years in Vienna, and an Italian opera on the Orfeo legend for his first visit to London, never performed there (or anywhere during his lifetime; see n. 30).

3. For a thorough review of the early literature, see Hunter, "Haydn's Aria Forms," pp. 21–40. Caryl Clark discusses some issues of Haydn opera research that emerged from the 1982 Haydn Congress in Vienna in "New Directions for Haydn Research," *Journal of Musicology* 6 (1988): 248–55. Both Clark and Hunter stress the positive side of Haydn the dramatist; see Caryl Clark, "The Opera Buffa Finales of Joseph Haydn," (Ph.D. diss., Cornell University, 1991) and Mary Hunter, "Text, Music, and Drama in Haydn's Italian Opera Arias: Four Case Studies," *Journal of Musicology* 7 (1989): 29–57.

4. In 1776, a repertory opera season was established at Eszterháza. The circumstances surrounding the composition of *La vera costanza* are unclear, however.

5. See Mary Hunter, "Eszterháza," in *The New Grove Dictionary of Opera*, ed. Stanley Sadie (London, 1992) , vol. 2, pp. 81–82.

6. Apparently, Nicolaus economized in some ways in order to support his musical projects. H. C. Robbins Landon, *Haydn: Chronicle and Works*, vol. 2, *Haydn at Eszterháza 1766–1790* (Bloomington, 1978), p. 30.

7. The following discussion is based on Rebecca Gates-Coon, *The Landed Estates of the Esterházy Princes: Hungary during the Reforms of Maria Theresia and Joseph II* (Baltimore, 1994), ch. 1; János Harich, "Das fürstlich Esterházy'sche Fideikommiss" *Haydn Yearbook* 4 (1968): 5–35; Mátyás Horányi, *The Magnificence of Eszterháza*, trans. András Deák (London, 1962); Landon, *Haydn Chronicle*, vol. 2, pp. 23–39.

8. Gates-Coon, *Landed Estates*, pp. 3, 63. Urbarial land was owned by a landlord, but used by peasants and petty nobles in return for various rents, service, and obligations.

9. Previous descriptions of the castle as a hunting lodge are somewhat misleading. See the contemporary description of the castle in 1760 in "Documents from the Archives of János Harich," *Haydn Yearbook*, 18 (1993): 7–13.

10. *Pressburger Zeitung*, 29 September 1770, quoted in "Music in Haydn's and Beethoven's Time as reported in the Pressburger Zeitung," compiled by Marianne Pandi and Fritz Schmidt, trans. Eugene Hartzell, *Haydn Yearbook*, 8 (1971): 269. The identical report appeared in *Wiener Diarium*, Wednesday, 26 September 1770.

11. In *Beschreibung des hochfürstlichen Schlosses Esterhass im Königreiche Ungern* (Pressburg, 1784).

12. More commonly, theatres were built in a wing of the palace buildings. See Géza Staud, *Adelstheater in Ungarn (18. und 19. Jahrhundert), Theatergeschichte Österreichs*, vol. 10 no. 2 (Vienna, 1977), pp. 28–29. The original opera house at Eszterháza was opened in 1768, but was destroyed in a fire in 1779. The only description we have refers to the new theater, which was erected the following year. See *Beschreibung*, excerpted in Landon, *Haydn Chronicle*, vol. 2, pp. 27–28.

13. "A six heures chacun se rend à la salle des spectacles, & on y prend place au parterre sans le moindre compliment; a l'instant que le Prince paroit dans sa loge, le coup d'archet se donne & aprés une Simphonie dans le dernier goût, on est enchanté par le spectacle." *Excursion à Esterhaz en Hongrie en Mai 1784*, (Vienna, 1784), p. 11; a facsimile appears in Landon, *Haydn Chronicle*, vol. 2, pp. 104–16. My translation.

14. See "Documents from the Archives of János Harich," *Haydn Yearbook* 18 (1993): 7.

15. Staud, *Adelstheater*, p. 33.

16. *Pressburger Zeitung*, quoted in *Haydn Yearbook* 8 (1971): 269.

17. Quoted in R. J. W. Evans, "Maria Theresa and Hungary," in *Enlightened Absolutism: Reform and Reformers in Later Eighteenth-Century Europe*, ed. H. M. Scott (Ann Arbor, 1990), p. 193. Occasionally, peasants were maimed or even killed by Esterházy officials (Gates-Coon, *Landed Estates*, p. 91).

18. During the period from 1765 until 1780, Maria Theresia ruled jointly with her son, although his actual powers were highly circumscribed. After her death in 1780, Joseph ruled alone as emperor until he died in 1790.

19. On the history of Hungary and the Habsburg empire during this period, see Gates-Coon, *Landed Estates*, esp. ch. 2; Derek Beales, *Joseph II*, vol. 1, *In the Shadow of Maria Theresa*, 1741–1780 (Cambridge, 1987), Franz A. J. Szabo, *Kaunitz and Enlightened Absolutism 1753–1780* (Cambridge, 1994), esp. ch. 8; Evans, "Maria Theresa and Hungary."

20. See Gates-Coon, *Landed Estates*, p. 96. This book offers a rich picture of the complexity and breadth of Esterházy's special privileges and powers.

21. In fact, this was the only title that Maria Theresia actually held. See Evans, "Maria Theresa and Hungary," p. 357, n. 1.

22. Nicolaus Esterházy achieved the rank of field marshal and was a member of the Maria Theresia Order. He particularly distinguished himself at the battle of Kolin in 1757. See Gates-Coon, *Landed Estates*, pp. 36–37.

23. "Le service & la parade militaire, accompagnée d'une bande de Hautboistes, s'y fait avec toute la regularité & la precision imaginable. La Garde monte a onze heures, fait quelques mouvements, defile en très bon ordre devant les fenêtres du Prince & va occuper les postes. La Marche musicale est exactement cadencée, fort harmonieuse & de la composition de Hayden [*sic*]: c'est tout dire." *Excursion*, p. 11. My translation. Unfortunately, it is not possible to identify the actual repertoire of the grenadier band from this period. See Roger Hellyer, "The Wind Ensembles of the Esterházy Princes, 1761–1813," *Haydn Yearbook* 15 (1984): 77–79 for some speculations.

24. *Pressburger Zeitung*, quoted in *Haydn Yearbook* 8 (1971): 269.

25. "Documents from the Esterházy Archives in Eisenstadt and Forchtenstein", ed. János Harich, part 2, *Haydn Yearbook* 19 (1994): 176.

26. Kristina Straub, *Sexual Suspects: Eighteenth-Century Players and Sexual Ideology* (Princeton, 1992), p. 3. On the forced apology, see ch. 7.

27. Landon, *Haydn Chronicle*, vol. 2, p. 36.

28. Hellyer, "The Wind Ensembles," p. 6.

29. "The Acta Musicalia of the Esterházy Archives (Nos. 36–100)," *Haydn Yearbook* 14 (1983): 116.

30. *L'anima del filosofo, ossia Orfeo ed Euridice*, the opera Haydn wrote for his first visit to London (1791), was never performed because of difficulties with the theater management.

31. Vernon Gotwals, *Haydn: Two Contemporary Portraits* (a translation and commentary of the *Biographische Notizen über Joseph Haydn* by G. A. Griesinger [Leipzig, 1810] and the

Biographische Nachrichten von Joseph Haydn by A. C. Dies [Vienna, 1810]), (Madison, 1968), p. 73.

32. Johann Pezzl, "Sketch of Vienna," trans. H. C. Robbins Landon in *Mozart and Vienna* (New York, 1991), p. 111.

33. See Gates-Coon, *Landed Estates*, p. 13. The source is Johann Josef Khevenhüller-Metsch, the *Obersthofmeister* of the imperial court.

34. See Andrea Sommer-Mathis, "*Tu felix Austria nube*": *Hochzeitsfeste der Habsburger im 18. Jahrhundert* (Vienna, 1994), p. 89. Details of the imperial wedding arrangements, including the musical entertainments, are given here in fascinating detail.

35. Martha Feldman, "Magic Mirrors and the *Seria* Stage: Thoughts toward a Ritual View," *Journal of the American Musicological Society* 48 (1995): 423–84.

36. For example, see the passage from the *Historisch-kritische Theaterchronik von Wien* (1774), which uses the expression "enchanted castle," quoted in Landon, *Haydn Chronicle*, vol. 2, p. 207.

37. See Sommer-Mathis, "*Tu felix Austria nube*," p. 103.

38. In her youth, Maria Theresia took the stage on a number of occasions, a tradition that continued well into the century. In 1765, the wedding opera for Joseph's second marriage, *Il parnasso confuso* (Metastasio/Gluck) was performed by four of Joseph's sisters, archduchesses Elisabeth, Maria Amalia, Maria Josepha and Maria Carolina, with the future Leopold II at the harpsichord.

39. Daniel Heartz, "Haydn's 'Acide e Galatea' and the Imperial Wedding Operas of 1760 by Hasse and Gluck," in *Joseph Haydn: Bericht über den internationalen Joseph Haydn Kongress 1982*, ed. Eva Badura-Skoda (Munich, 1986), p. 340.

40. Heartz, "Haydn's 'Acide'," p. 335.

41. Norbert Elias, *The History of Manners*, trans. Edmund Jephcott, vol. 1, *The Civilizing Process* (London, 1978), p. 16.

42. Feldman, "Magic Mirrors," p. 463.

43. On the (mis)use of the mirror metaphor, see Feldman's comments in "Magic Mirrors," pp. 423–25.

44. Quoted in Landon, *Haydn Chronicle*, vol. 1, *The Early Years 1732–1765* (Bloomington, 1980), pp. 382–83.

45. *Wiener Diarium*, quoted in Landon, *Haydn Chronicle*, vol. 1, p. 382.

46. For documents related to the wedding, see "Documents from the Archives of János Harich," 31–42.

47. See Heartz, "Haydn's 'Acide,'" pp. 333–36.

48. Could the appearance of this sea-goddess be a reference to Maria Theresia? Perhaps, although this character also appears in Metastasio's version of the legend, *La Galatea* (1722), on which Migliavacca modelled his libretto. See "Vorwort," *Acide und andere Fragmente Italienischer Opern um 1761 bis 1763*, ed. Karl Geiringer and Günter Thomas, *Joseph Haydn Werke* XXV/i (Munich, 1985), p. ix.

49. *Wiener Diarium*, quoted in Landon *Haydn Chronicle*, vol. 1, p. 382.

50. *Pressburger Zeitung*, quoted in *Haydn Yearbook* 8 (1971): 268–69.

51. *La canterina* (intermezzo, 1766) and *Lo speziale* (dramma giocoso, Carlo Goldoni, 1768), in which the serious parts were cut.

52. The scene changes are listed in the printed libretto of this production, located in Trieste, Civico Museo Teatrale di Fondazione Carlo Schmidl (I-TSmt).

53. See documents 38–41 in "Documents from the Archives of János Harich," 96–101.

54. Daniel Heartz, "Goldoni, *Don Giovanni*, and the *Dramma Giocoso*," in *Mozart's Operas*, ed. Thomas Bauman (Berkeley, 1990), p. 196.

55. See Mary Hunter, "Some representations of *opera seria* in *opera buffa*," *Cambridge Opera Journal* 3 (1991): 89–108.

56. Feldman, "Magic Mirrors, " p. 445.

57. Indeed, permissive conditions of spectatorship already seemed to have disappeared at Eszterháza, where the prince seemed less inclined to tolerate the stage antics of singers. In this respect, Eszterháza resembles more closely the elitist theatres of courts like Parma than the more raucous public houses of Venice, Rome and Naples.

58. "[Un] ragionevole specchio dei loro problemi, dei loro meriti, e perfino dei loro difetti." Franco Fido, *Guida a Goldoni: Teatro e società nel Settecento* (Turin, 1977), p. 8. My translation.

59. For an interesting discussion of this situation, see James Cushman Davis, *The Decline of the Venetian Nobility as a Ruling Class* (Baltimore, 1962). A classic work on Goldoni's relationship with society is Fido, *Guida a Goldoni*.

60. Ted Emery, *Goldoni as Librettist: Theatrical Reform and the* drammi giocosi per musica (New York, 1991), p. 38. See also Bartolo Anglani, *Goldoni: il mercato, la scena, l'utopia* (Naples, 1983) and "Le passioni allo specchio: Sentimenti e ragione mercantile nel teatro goldoniano," *Studi Goldoniani* 6 (1982): 7–55.

61. See "I borghesi e i cavalieri" in Franco Fido, *Guida a Goldoni*, pp. 13–20.

62. Pezzl, "Sketch of Vienna," p. 78.

63. Emery, "Goldoni," p. 131.

64. The literature on this subject is vast. I have found the following particularly useful: G. J. Barker-Benfield, *The Culture of Sensibility: Sex and Society in Eighteenth-Century Britain* (Chicago, 1992); Louis I. Bredvold, *The Natural History of Sensibility* (Detroit, 1962); R. F. Brissenden, *Virtue in Distress: Studies in the Novel of Sentiment from Richardson to Sade* (New York, 1974); John Mullan, *Sentiment and Sociability: The Language of Feeling in the Eighteenth Century* (Oxford, 1988); Janet Todd, *Sensibility: an introduction* (London, 1986); Ann Jessie Van Sant, *Eighteenth-century sensibility and the novel* (Cambridge, 1993).

65. George S. Rousseau, "Nerves, Spirits, and Fibres: Towards Defining the Origins of Sensibility," *Blue Guitar* 2 (December 1976): 136.

66. For discussions of the salient terms "sensibility", "sentiment" and their relationships, see R. F. Brissenden, "'Sentiment': Some Uses of the Word in the Writings of David Hume," in *Studies in the Eighteenth Century: Papers presented at the David Nichol Smith Memorial Seminar Canberra 1966*, ed. R. F. Brissenden (Toronto, 1968), pp. 89–107; Erik Erämetsä, *A Study of the Word 'Sentimental' and of Other Linguistic Characteristics of Eighteenth-Century Sentimentalism in England* (Helsinki, 1951); and Georgia J. Cowart, "Sense and Sensibility in Eighteenth-Century Musical Thought," *Acta Musicologica* 56 (1984): 251–66.

67. This play was also known by a number of other names. See Ted A. Emery, "Goldoni's *Pamela* from Play to Libretto," *Italica* 64 (1987): 581, n. 3.

68. For a description of this repertoire, see Mary Hunter, "'Pamela': the Offspring of Richardson's Heroine in Eighteenth-Century Opera," *Mosaic: A Journal for the Interdisciplinary Study of Literature* 18 (1985): 61–76. Previous settings of *La buona figliuola* by Egidio Duni (Parma 1756) and Salvatore Perillo (1760) were far less successful.

69. See Emery, "*Pamela*," p. 579.

70. For example, Prince Nicolaus' second son, also named Nicolaus, was embroiled in a similar situation in the mid-1770s, around the time of his wedding to his cousin Maria Anna Weissenwolf. See Gates-Coon, *Landed Estates*, p. 17.

71. E. Purdie, "Some Adventures of 'Pamela' on the Continental Stage," *German Studies Presented to Professor H.G. Fiedler* (Oxford, 1938), p. 353.

72. See Nancy Armstrong, *Desire and Domestic Fiction: A Political History of the Novel* (New York, 1987), especially chaps. 1 and 2.

73. Armstrong, p. 118.

74. See Emery, "*Pamela*," p. 574.

75. Goldoni operas had been performed with some regularity in Vienna and at Laxenburg beginning in 1763. *La buona figliuola* was performed at Laxenburg in May 1764, in Vienna (Summer 1768) and (in French) at the Kärntnertortheater in 1776; Gustav Zechmeister, *Die Wiener Theater nächst der Burg und nächst dem Kärntnerthor von 1747 bis 1776, Theatergeschichte Österreichs*, vol. 3/2 (Vienna, 1971), p. 306. *La buona figliuola* was produced at Eszterháza in 1776. *La buona figliuola maritata* (Goldoni/Piccinni) was also given in Vienna in 1764, according to a libretto in H-Bn. On Goldoni reception, see Arnold E. Maurer "The Reception of Goldoni's Comedies in 18th Century Germany," in *Classical Models in Literature. Proceedings of the IXth Congress of the International Comparative Literature Association*, ed. Zoran Konstantinovic, Warren Anderson and Walter Dietze (Innsbruck, 1981), pp. 97–101; John A. McCarthy, "'Humanitas' on the Popular Stage: Goldoni, Comedy, and German Idealism," in *Aufnahme-Weitergabe: Literarische Impulse um Lessing und Goethe*, (Hamburg, 1982), pp. 31–51. Geza Staud, "Rappresentazioni e Edizioni Goldoniane in Ungheria" *Studi Goldoniani* 5 (1979): 151–58, shows that the Goldoni operas produced at Eszterháza were among the earliest performances of Goldoni in Hungary.

76. The text was first set by Ferdinando Bertoni for the 1752 carnival season in Venice. It was also set by Florian Leopold Gassmann for the Vienna Burgtheater in 1771. For a comparison of the Haydn and Gassmann settings, see Silke Leopold "'Le pescatrici' —Goldoni, Haydn, Gassmann," *Joseph Haydn: Bericht über den Internationalen Joseph Haydn Kongress 1982*, ed. Eva Badura-Skoda (Munich, 1986), pp. 341–49.

77. Clark, "Haydn Finales," p. 95.

78. Leopold, "Le pescatrici," p. 341.

79. To my knowledge, there is no extant score of the actual Venetian production. Neither of the two scores I consulted matches the Venice libretto of 1752 exactly, although P-La comes closest with one replacement aria and three deleted numbers; F-Pc, which contains arias only, is most likely connected to a performance in Dresden in 1754. My comments will take both scores into consideration; therefore references to the "Bertoni" score should be taken in a general way that embraces the variations between productions that were typical of eighteenth-century operatic practice. The history of the libretto and its settings are discussed in greater detail in my dissertation "Power and Patriarchy in Haydn's Goldoni Operas, " (Ph.D. diss., University of Toronto, 1995), pp. 124–29.

80. With the following qualifications: Eurilda's "Quanti diversi affetti" (P-La) has an A section only. In F-Pc, there are no *passaggi* for Eurilda until her Act III aria "Ch'io mai vi possa."

81. P-La indicates flutes rather than oboes in Lesbina's "Che vi par?" and horns only in Nerina's "Pescatori, pescatrici." The use of horns in Burlotto's aria "Fra tuoni, lampi e fulmini" is probably meant to suggest thunder.

82. This aria appears in F-Pc only. The arias for Eurilda in P-La employ march-like rhythms with dotted figures.

83. Wye Jamison Allanbrook, *Rhythmic Gesture in Mozart:* Le Nozze di Figaro *and* Don Giovanni (Chicago, p. 1983), p. 69.

84. s.v. "Contredanse" in *Encyclopédie Méthodique*, vol. 1 (1791), quoted in Allanbrook, p. 62.

85. At some point, several folios of the autograph score were removed, leaving wholesale gaps in the middle of numbers. The incomplete numbers are "Voglio goder" (Eurilda), "Compatite la vechiezza" (Mastricco), "Varca il mar" (Lindoro), "Ti miro fisso fisso," (Lesbina) and "Pescatori, Pescatrici" (Nerina). The intervening recitative is also lost, and two numbers are missing in their entirety: "Quanti diversi affetti" (Eurilda), and the chorus "Nel mare placidi." The opera was "reconstructed" by Landon, a performance of

which was given at the Holland Festival in 1965. See Landon, *Haydn Chronicle*, vol. 2, pp. 246–48. More recently, a recording of *Le pescatrici* has been made by Olga Géczy and the Orchestra of the Lithuanian Opera for the Drive label (3801).

86. This and subsequent texts are taken from the Eszterháza libretto (I-TSmt). In preparing the translations, I received helpful suggestions from Anna Gaspari and Manuela Scarci.

87. The following reading was inspired in part by David Lewin, "Musical analysis as stage direction," in *Music and Text: Critical Inquiries*, ed. Steven Paul Scher (Cambridge, 1992), pp. 163–76.

88. See the discussion in Margaret A. Rose, *Parody: Ancient, Modern, and Post-modern* (Cambridge, 1993), ch. 3.

89. The new aria texts were: for Frisellino, "Fra cetre, e cembali;" for Lesbina, "Voglio amar e vuò scherzare," "Ti miro fisso, fisso," and "Già si vede i vezzi e vanti"; and, for Lindoro, "Varca il mar."

90. The substantiality of Lesbina's role is probably due as much to Magdalena Friberth's vocal gifts as to Carl Friberth's bias. Haydn wrote several challenging roles for her, including Vespina in *L'infedeltà delusa* and Princess Rezia in *L'incontro improvviso*. Her high salary suggests that she was the prima donna of the Kapelle at the time. Compare the yearly salaries of Haydn, 782fl, 30 xr; Magdalena Friberth, 500 fl; Gertrude Cellini (Eurilda), 412fl, 20xr; and Barbara Dichtler (Nerina), 100 fl. (Dichtler also received a greater amount of payment in kind), as listed in the *Conventionale* of 1769. See J. Harich, "Haydn Documenta (IV)," *Haydn Yearbook* 7 (1970): 61–62.

91. Because of the sequence of arias in the operas (Lesbina, then Eurilda), it is Eurilda who appears to adopt Lesbina's musical language; however, the source material indicates that Lesbina's aria was a late addition. Written on different paper (Larsen 8 and 9) than the rest of the opera (Larsen 7), "Voglio amar" was inserted into the score after the numbering of the gatherings (in Haydn's hand) but before the libretto was printed. Lesbina's original aria "Un pescatore me l'ha fatta brutta" had already been cut and the two scenes composed together with recitative. Hence, it was clearly Haydn's intention to represent Eurilda as a sentimental heroine before he composed "Voglio amar."

92. Only the opening ritornello remains.

93. "Die sehr vornehmen und sehr reichen Leute haben selten Sinn für häusliche Glückseligkeit, fühlen keine Seelenbedürfnisse, leben mehrenteils auf einem sehr fremden Fuß mit ihren Ehegatten . . . " Adolf Freiherr von Knigge, *Über den Umgang mit Menschen* (Hanover, 1788; reprint, ed. Gert Ueding, Frankfurt am Main, 1977), p. 179. My translation.

94. Gates-Coon, *Landed Estates*, p. 13.

95. See Landon, *Haydn Chronicle*, vol. 2, p. 36.

96. Pezzl, *Sketch of Vienna*, p. 112. The allusion is to the hero of Goethe's novel, *Die Leiden des jungen Werthers (The Sorrows of Young Werther)*, of 1774.

97. Giuseppe Ortolani, ed., *Tutte le Opere di Carlo Goldoni* (Milan, 1935-56), vol. 10, p. 1069.

98. In F-Pc, the B section is omitted.

99. The contemporary associations of the minor mode with femininity combined with the origins of this aria for a female character would suggest a complex situation with respect to gender, which unfortunately is beyond the scope of this article. For a discussion of gender and the minor mode, see Gretchen A. Wheelock "*Schwarze Gredel* and the Engendered Minor Mode in Mozart's Operas," in *Musicology and Difference: Gender and Sexuality in Music Scholarship*, ed. Ruth A. Solie (Berkeley, 1993), pp. 201–21. Haydn's use of the minor mode differs considerably from Mozart's, however.

100. From an autobiographical sketch that appeared in *Das gelehrte Oesterreich*. See Landon, *Haydn Chronicle*, vol. 2, pp. 397–98.

101. The subject has provoked a wide range of opinion. See Barry S. Brook, "Sturm und Drang and the Romantic Period in Music," *Studies in Romanticism* 9 (1970): 269–84; Joel Kolk, "'Sturm und Drang' and Haydn's Operas," in *Haydn Studies*, ed. Jens Peter Larsen, Howard Serwer, and James Webster (New York, 1981): 440–45; Landon, *Haydn Chronicle*, vol. 2, pp. 266–84; Sisman, "Haydn's Theater Symphonies"; R. Larry Todd, "Joseph Haydn and the *Sturm und Drang*: A Revaluation," *Music Review* 41 (1980): 172–96; and Webster, *Haydn's "Farewell" Symphony and the Idea of Classical Style: Through-Composition and Cyclic Integration in His Instrumental Music* (Cambridge, 1991).

102. Roy Pascal, *The German Sturm und Drang* (New York, 1953), p. xiii.

103. Elias, *History of Manners*, passim.

104. My research was generously supported by the Social Sciences and Humanities Research Council of Canada, and by a Killam Postdoctoral Fellowship at Dalhousie University, Halifax, Nova Scotia.

Haydn as Orator: A Rhetorical Analysis of his Keyboard Sonata in D Major, Hob.XVI:42

TOM BEGHIN

After Princess Maria Hermenegild married Haydn's future patron Prince Nicolaus II Esterházy in 1783, Haydn dedicated three piano sonatas to her, publishing them with Bossler the following year. All three (Hob.XVI:40–42) are in two movements, a type called the "ladies' sonata" by László Somfai, and all have fast, brilliant, and capricious finales.[1] Of the three finales, that in no. 42 handily beats the others in capriciousness. It is a scherzo in 2/4 with highly unusual proportions: the first section contains eight and the second ninety-three measures! Moreover, each section has a repeat sign, leading Franz Eibner to conclude that Bossler must have overlooked a repeat sign before the upbeat to m. 26, which would "normalize" the proportions from a "monstrous" binary 8/93 to a ternary 8/17/76.[2] Yet Haydn apparently passed up an opportunity to amend the score: he played the three sonatas and gave a copy of the Bossler edition to his brother Michael's friend Father Rettensteiner, but this extant copy has no emendations, only the recipient's delighted comment that "the following 3 sonatas were given to me as a present by Herr Joseph Haydn at Esterhasz on June 3 1785 at a long and entertaining visit, and they were played by him."[3] Why would Haydn not have rectified the ostensible omission of a repeat sign on Rettensteiner's copy?

Instead of dismissing the proportional imbalance as a problem, I align myself with authors such as Somfai or Elaine Sisman, who, while describing the movement as "a rather broad joke" or "the most unbalanced [two-reprise form] ever written," do not become suspicious of, but, on the contrary, praise Haydn's originality.[4] Both Somfai and Sisman, furthermore, link the finale with the first movement of the sonata. In its inventiveness, Somfai finds the finale "a worthy partner to the first movement."[5] And Sisman notes:

> How can Haydn follow up such a [i.e., the first] movement? With a restless Vivace assai that establishes no clear tonic at the onset—indeed, moving immediately to the dominant—and remains harmonically in motion.[6]

Although admiring Haydn's skill in pairing the two movements, neither author inquires into a specific overall plan of the sonata.

The working hypothesis of the following analysis is that such a plan exists and that, furthermore, it is rhetorical by nature: certain ideas are invented, ordered and executed, memorized and performed in such a way as to make the strongest possible effect on the listener. In other words, Haydn followed the rhetorical process of

1. *inventio*, or the finding of ideas (res),
2. *dispositio*, or the ordering of the ideas,
3. *elocutio*, or the expression of the invented ideas through appropriate words (verba),
4. *memoria*, or memorization of the words, and
5. *pronuntiatio* or *actio*, the delivery of the oration.

The premise of my analysis is that the pianist-orator is responsible for all stages; as an all-round musician, he performs his "own" music, in the same way that an orator delivers his own speech. "Haydn," "the pianist," "the composer," or "the orator," therefore, must all be read as synonyms for one and the same person. It is this person who addresses an audience.[7] Although the analysis of Sonata 42 will mainly examine its first three stages of *inventio*, *dispositio*, and *elocutio*, the two stages of performance, *memoria* and *pronuntiatio*, will always be latently present: if the performer wishes successfully to deliver the "elocuted" score, he first has to recapture what the orator-composer wanted to say.

• • •

In 1783—almost simultaneously with the publication of Haydn's no. 42—Johann Nikolaus Forkel published an account of C. P. E.

Bach's Sonata in F Minor, Wq. 57/6 (H.173), in which he put his theory of "musical rhetoric" into practice.[8] Attached to the example of Bach's sonata were more general observations on the sonata as a genre (*Betrachtungen über die Sonate überhaupt*). Surprisingly, this historical precedent of viewing a sonata as an integrated cycle of movements has but rarely inspired recent scholars to rhetorical analyses of whole sonatas by Mozart, Haydn or Beethoven.[9] Thus far, detailed analyses have been of passages or single movements only.[10] My analysis of Sonata 42 attempts to fill the gap.

Although inspired by Forkel's account, I am influenced by his theory of musical rhetoric only indirectly. Forkel's notions of musical rhetoric were firmly rooted in his knowledge of classical rhetoric, and one should seriously ask whether both disciplines can be separated at all.[11] Therefore, rather than drawing on Forkel's writings, I will, through the course of the analysis, call on Forkel's sources: Aristotle, Quintilian, the [*Rhetorica*] *Ad Herennium* once attributed to Cicero, Longinus, and others.[12] After all, these authors—and not Forkel—laid the foundation of an intellectual frame of mind, which was shared by Forkel's readers and Haydn's listeners alike.

But I must first examine the validity of the two basic premises of my analysis: first, that rhetoric was a pervasive factor in the cultural environment at the end of the eighteenth century; and, second, that a reappreciation of it—at the end of the twentieth century—allows for a more authentic understanding of Haydn's music. I am here anticipating the two common objections that rhetoric as a discipline was very much "in decline" at the end of the eighteenth century,[13] and that, even if rhetoric were still alive, it may not have influenced the music of Joseph Haydn, who after all was "an illustrious idiot" with a "singularly musical mind, not tempted by distractions such as reading literature."[14]

Rhetoric: A Dying Discipline?

From a broad historical standpoint, the "end of rhetoric" has been attributed to the eighteenth-century Enlightenment, on the one hand, and nineteenth-century Romanticism, on the other.[15] One notable opponent was Immanuel Kant, who, in his *Critique of Judgment* (1790), not only objected to rhetoric on philosophical grounds, but wished to ban oratory from public life altogether:

> Rhetoric, in so far as this means the art of persuasion, i.e. of deceiving by a beautiful show (*ars oratoria*), and not mere ele-

> gance of speech (eloquence and style), is a dialectic which borrows from poetry only so much as is needful to win minds to the side of the orator before they have formed a judgment and to deprive them of their freedom; it cannot therefore be recommended either for the law courts or for the pulpit.[16]

Is this condemnation at the end of the eighteenth century representative of the "decline," "dethronement," or even "death" of rhetoric?[17] Let us, with Carl Joachim Classen, draw some distinctions:

> In view of the thesis, often repeated and yet questionable, that rhetoric was neglected, even attacked since the end of the eighteenth century at least in Germany, it has to be emphasized that one has to distinguish between 1) the practice of oratory, 2) the general attitude towards rhetoric as a theoretical discipline and 3) the actual interest in rhetorical instruction.[18]

As to the "practice of oratory," which I take here in its original form of public speaking, it may be true that, in eighteenth-century European politics and society, there was little room left for the two privileged kinds of classical oratory, namely deliberative, political speeches and forensic, judicial ones. However, without even mentioning the art of preaching (*ars praedicandi*), there remained ample opportunity for the third, epideictic kind of oratory—the laudative speech. Such speaking took the form of congratulatory speeches (on the occasion of a birthday, engagement, marriage, etc.), welcome speeches (for guests of a state, court, city etc.), festive speeches (at the inauguration or departure of a mayor, council, professor etc.; upon anniversaries; for state celebrations), homage speeches, speeches in school, and so on.[19]

As to the "general attitude towards rhetoric as a theoretical discipline," one should ask whether anti-rhetorical works in the seventeenth and eighteenth centuries, from Bacon's *Novum Organum* (1620) to Kant's *Critique of Judgment* (1790), did not represent an ongoing debate among a small group of philosophers rather than reflect a changing (let alone changed) "general attitude." But more importantly, whereas rhetoric may, in principle, have been ousted by science and logic, empiricism and rationalism, it was, as a theoretical discipline, by no means yet removed from the learned body of knowledge. Its theory was, moreover, still firmly rooted in the study of Aristotle, Cicero, Quintilian, and Longinus.[20]

Finally, as to the "actual interest in rhetorical instruction," if it is true that "[t]he history of rhetoric has always been entwined with the history of education," the continuing publication and reprints of numerous schoolbooks at the end of the eighteenth and well into the nineteenth century hardly hints at a "dead" discipline.[21] Rhetoric, it appears, kept its firm grip on humanistic education, of which it still constituted a crucial part.[22] Through orations by Cicero or Demosthenes and by reading poetry of, for instance, Virgil or Homer, the European pupil was introduced to rhetorical terminology. Among other things, he learned to recognize rhetorical figures, not only for the sake of labeling them but in order to apply them in his own writing. For instance, in his *De utraque verborum ac rerum copia* (1512), designed as a Latin textbook for the schoolboys of St. Paul's Cathedral and republished numerous times until 1824, Erasmus advises while "perus[ing] good authors night and day . . . , [to] note all figures in them, store up in our memory what we have noted, imitate what we have stored up, and by frequent use make it a habit to have them ready at hand."[23]

We may conclude, then, that through practice, study, and instruction, rhetoric was still very much alive, despite some dissident voices then and alarming reminders of its decline now. Even rhetoric's most ardent opponents must still have had a thorough knowledge of what rhetoric stood for; they may have, in their oral and written diatribes, used the very methods of the discipline they attacked. How ironic that of all people it is Jean-Jacques Rousseau who in his *Projet pour l'éducation de Monsieur de Sainte-Marie* prescribes to his prospective pupil the study of Bernard Lamy's *De l'art de parler,* as well as "the abridged Quintilian of Monsieur Rollin." The latter textbook, although a so-called "short version" of Quintilian's twelve-volume *Institutio oratoria*, was still eight hundred pages long and in Latin. Not only did the boy have to read the work, he "was to learn it by heart"![24]

Haydn: A Musical Orator

In 1812, Giuseppe Carpani commented on Haydn's symphonies:

> The music of this composer is a true arsenal of the arms of oratory, covering the whole range of what is possible within today's theory of music. ([Footnote]: Only in instrumental music can the maestro be an orator; in vocal music he does nothing but translate the discourse of the poet into musical language and

> therefore he cannot nor is he allowed to be more than a translator, imitator, or paraphraser.) You find in it, as in orations by Cicero, almost all rhetorical figures applied; among them are gradatio, antitheton, dubitatio, isocolon, repetitio, congeries, epilogus, synonymia, suspensio; but very special is his usage of reticentia and aposiopesis, which, when used in one of his incomparable fast movements, create a marvelous effect.[25]

Carpani's comments were directed to an erudite reader, and, given that he is the one who made the "illustrious idiot" remark about Haydn, he may have assumed that Haydn himself did not know by name the very figures he was applying. Haydn could be, as Johann Mattheson said of those who used rhetorical figures but proclaimed their ignorance of rhetoric, like "the *bourgeois gentilhomme* of Molière, who did not know that he was using a pronoun when he said, "I, thou, or he," or that he was using the imperative when he said to his servant, 'Come here.'"[26] Still, Carpani clearly expected his reader to find his comparison of Haydn's with Cicero's figures illuminating. Just as one cannot prove that Shakespeare consciously applied an array of rhetorical figures, Haydn may not have been able "to name his tools."[27] But the myth of "Papa Haydn," who could not speak any foreign language, who did not read literature, in short who did not have a general education to speak of, has been destroyed once and for all by Herbert Zeman, Georg Feder, David Schroeder, James Webster, Sisman and others.[28] The general non-musical education that Haydn received at St. Stephen's in Vienna must not have been much different from that offered by any other respected school at the time. He certainly knew how to write in Latin, judging by the numerous annotations in his copy of Fux's *Gradus ad Parnassum*.[29] Even if he received instruction in Latin grammar only,[30] he would still have been introduced to rhetoric. Indeed, as Sisman notes, "it might have been difficult to learn any Latin without also learning some rhetoric."[31] Were his grammar teacher to quote Cicero's opening line "Quousque tandem abutere, Catilina, patientia nostra" in order to demonstrate that the verb *uti* requires an ablative case, he would not have failed to declare this example as a real rhetorical question: "In heaven's name, Catiline, how much longer will you take advantage of our forebearance?"[32]

But, we might ask, even if Haydn knew a standardized rhetorical terminology, did he use what he knew? Sisman has analyzed Haydn's autobiographical sketch (1776), particularly its order or *dispositio*, which in compliance with the rules of the *ars dictaminis* (the art of letter writing), consists of an *exordium* (introduction, including a *captatio benevolentiae* or securing of good will), a *narratio* (narration), a *corroboratio* (supporting evidence), a *confutatio* (refutation) and a *peroratio* (conclusion).[33] And Jürgen Neubacher has related Haydn's apology for contrapuntal or harmonic liberties, marked "con licenza" in his scores, with the rhetorical figure *licentia*—the begging of the audience for (artistic) liberty to say something that might be offensive to some.[34]

Another such rhetorical act is Haydn's often cited letter of February 25, 1780 to Artaria, in which he asks the publisher to print a notice in the edition of the "Auenbrugger" sonatas, Hob.XVI:35–39 and 20:

> Incidentally, I consider it necessary, in order to forestall the criticism of any witlings, to print on the reverse side of the title page the following sentence, here underlined:
>
> *Avertissement*
>
> *Among these 6 sonatas there are two single movements*[35] *in which the same idea [*einerley Idee*] occurs through several bars: the author has done this intentionally, to show different methods of execution [*Ausführung*].*
>
> For of course I could have chosen a hundred other ideas instead of this one; but so that the whole opus will not be exposed to blame on account of this one intentional detail (which the critics and especially my enemies might interpret wrongly), I think that this avertissement or something like it must be appended, otherwise the sale might be hindered thereby.[36]

With this "warning," eventually printed in Italian, Haydn is employing the rhetorical figure of anticipating objections known as *anticipatio*. The place where Haydn asks Artaria to print the *anticipatio*, namely on the reverse side of the title page, is rhetorically appropriate: anticipation, Quintilian writes, "is especially useful in the introduction."[37]

The content of the same letter to Artaria has aesthetic implications.[38] It brings us yet one level further: did Haydn describe his own compositional process in rhetorical terms? In fact, this letter may be connected with another famous statement of Haydn's, made to Georg August Griesinger:

> I sat down [at the keyboard], began to fantasize depending on whether my mood was sad or happy, serious or playful. When

> I got hold of an idea [*eine Idee*], my entire effort went toward executing [*auszuführen*] and sustaining [*souteniren*] it according to the rules of the art.[39]

The twofold process of finding an idea, on the one hand, and executing it, on the other, resembles the rhetorical distinction between *res* (ideas) and *verba* (words). And the clothing of res in verba, in turn, is materialized through the three stages of invention, disposition, and elocution, referred to by Haydn himself as *phantasieren*, *componieren* and *setzen*.[40]

These examples by no means enable us to "prove" Haydn's knowledge of rhetoric. Nor do I believe that a systematic list would bring us any further towards doing so. Indeed, as Sisman notes, "the reason composers did not leave documentation about their own use of rhetoric is that it was completely assimilated and natural."[41]

Rhetorical Analysis of Sonata 42

The unusual second movement of Sonata 42 will serve as my point of departure. Its irregular proportions will have to be accounted for, but they are only one "symptom" of an underlying problem. Diagnosing such symptoms at the level of *elocutio*—musical ideas translated into figures—will be my preliminary task. Next I will broaden the scope and look at the *dispositio* and *inventio* of the sonata as a whole. In particular, I will ask whether the second movement fits in with the disposition or ordering of the entire sonata and whether that disposition reflects what we can reconstruct about the level of invention. Finally, I will again take up the thread of *elocutio*. Thus my working process is bi-directional: first, I will work as an archaeologist, who, uncovering an artifact, scrapes off layer after layer—in this case *elocutio*, *dispositio,* and *inventio*; then, armed with my "discoveries," I will re-evaluate the *elocutio* and assess whether the words used (*verba*) indeed match the intended ideas (*res*). If the analysis seems at times somewhat esoteric, involving close reading of both musical and rhetorical argumentation, I ask the reader to bear with the details until my "excavation" is complete.

A quick tour of the second movement is necessary before even the preliminary assessment of its *elocutio*. Example 1 gives the entire movement, annotated as follows:

1. The two principal motivic units, unveiled in the opening measures, are marked **x** and **y**. Motive **x** is the initial eighth-note pattern

that can be read both as a sequence of descending thirds (**x1**), and as the underlying four-note descending scale (**x2**). Motive **y** is the down-and-up pattern of sixteenth notes that can be seen partly as a diminution and inversion of **x2** and partly as an expansion of the circle-figure (see below). Moreover, **y** elaborates a two-note group, an upwardly resolving leading-tone-figure (**y1**). In light of this, we might hear **x** as including two-note groups based on the upbeat. Motives **x** and **y** recur throughout the piece.

2. The principal divisions of the movement, articulated by cadences and their attendant pauses, are periods numbered **1** through **6**. The first section, a single eight-measure period, is the first division to end with a cadence (in A, the dominant), while the second section contains five more expanded periods, each with some kind of cadence in D major, as follows: **2**, 17 mm., half-cadence in m. 25; **3**, 20 mm., deceptive cadence in m. 45; **4**, 15 mm., half-cadence in m. 60; **5**, 27 mm., full cadence in m. 87; **6**, 14 mm., full cadence in m. 101.

Vivace assai: *elocutio*

I begin with an unusual moment in the second section. At the beginning of period **5**, mm. 61–66, the left hand insistently repeats the **y** motive, alternating between f♯ ($\hat{3}$) and g. Example 2 (p. 213) shows a reduction of these measures, revealing the two-note motive **y1** underlying **y**.

The right hand reiterates the same motive, but ascending registrally. The harmonic progression is: V–I–ii–I–V–I. The constant reminders of the tonic D major create a static moment. When in m. 66 the final I_6 is reached, and the left hand rises into the right hand's register, it appears as if the pianist finally reduces the tension and allows a descending parallel motion of sixths free play. The sixths rush down and linger on ii, V and I, this time in their usual cadential order, although not yet fulfilling their cadential role. What does the insistence on the third degree ($\hat{3}$) tell about the whole movement? (It might remind us that the very first notes in the movement are f♯–g, as are the first notes in period **4**.) Does something happen later that would not have been possible without this insistence; or, has something happened earlier that necessitates it?

An earlier passage at the end of **3**, mm. 40–45, displays a descending parallel motion similar to mm. 66–71. Unlike mm. 66–71, this passage seriously attempts to cadence, but the attempt fails with a deceptive vi chord in m. 45. Why is the attempt not successful?

Example 1. Haydn, Sonata in D, Hob. XVI:42/ii.

Example 1, continued.

Example 1, continued.

Example 1, continued.

Let us reconsider the movement's proportions (||:8:||:93:||); Somfai calls them "grotesque" and adds that "[t]hese seemingly absurd formal contours are surely against all 'rules.'"[42] A. Peter Brown also expresses surprise about the second part which "has an expansive section in five divisions that stretches the material to more than ninety measures"; this is especially unexpected after a first part that "presents two compact four-measure phrases that prepare one for a miniature along the lines of Hob.XVI:26/3."[43] Somfai similarly relates this finale to that of the A major sonata Hob.XVI:26, both scherzos in fast duple meter (2/4, vivace assai and presto respectively).[44] The finale of no. 26, however, he calls "grotesquely short,"[45] with its first section of 8 and a second of 18 measures (10 + 8). Thus, although these two movements are linked formally and by "type," they differ strongly in both overall dimensions and internal proportions. Where the finale of 26 is grotesquely—some would say embarrassingly[46]—short, the finale of 42 is "grotesquely" expansive. Why is the BA part (of an A:||:BA form) in 26 so short, and, by the same token, why must the second section of the other scherzo be so long?[47]

Example 2. Sonata 42/ii, mm. 61–66: resolution (reduction).

The first section of 26/iii consists of a straightforward period. The antecedent ends on $\hat{2}$ with a half-cadence; after an interruption, the consequent recaptures $\hat{3}$ and closes with $\hat{2}$ and $\hat{1}$. In contrast to this prototype of simplicity, the opening period of 42/ii, in Somfai's words, "resembles a puzzle or a labyrinth game in information theory."[48] The upbeat eighth note, typical not only for Haydn's scherzo movements but for his fast finales in general, is obscured by two elided slurs. On the one hand, the first slur brings weight to the upbeat note f♯; on the other hand the second slur takes up the downbeat note g as the first of a four-note group. The second slur is unusual: it connects two descending-third figures which would usually have one slur each. A diminuendo, therefore, is implied from the beginning of m. 1 to the end;[49] in addition, the long slur over the second measure suggests that it should be played more softly than the first. The metrical ambiguity—there is no clear first downbeat, and the upbeat two-note figure contradicts the descending-third figure—is joined by a harmonic one, as the underlying descent to the tonic note (g–f♯–e–d) is contradicted by the slurring. After the d♯, suggestive of E minor, for example, the following c♯–d–b might be thought of as harmonized in B minor. On the other hand, at this tempo, we might not have time to think anything about the harmony, and merely accept that the measures are in transit. After them, m. 3 comes as a relief: the sixteenth-note right-hand motive (**y**), accompanied by pulsing left-hand repeated notes, articulates the ascending half-step g♯–a to complete the ascending f♯–g of the opening upbeat. Thus, the first two measures starting with the f♯–g "suspended" the opening of the movement, which finally takes off in m. 3 (*suspensio*).[50] But surely, picking up from where the suspension started, we perceived the g of m. 1 as the seventh of a dominant seventh in D Major which requires resolution to f♯. How can it be pulled up to g♯, as dominant to the dominant? "Never mind," one hears the listener think, "let me ignore this disturbing thought and enjoy my first bit of certainty." And enjoy it we do. The figure of the right hand in m. 3 is what Marpurg would call a *vermischte Figur*.[51] That is, it combines the "half circle" (*Halbzirkel*, Example 3a), a four-note rolling figure of which the second and fourth notes are the same, with the "running figure" (*lauffende Figur*, Example 3b), sixteenth-note scalar extensions of the pattern.

Example 3a. Sonata 42/ii, mm. 3–4. half-circle figure (*Halbzirkel*).

Example 3b. Sonata 42/ii, mm. 3–4. running figure (*Lauffende Figur*).

Rhetorically, this half-circle is periphrasis on the smallest scale. Periphrasis, Quintilian writes, occurs "when we use a number of words to describe something for which one, or at any rate only a few words of description would suffice . . . , that is, a circuitous mode of speech."[52] The extra neighbor notes of the half-circle do not alter the meaning of the underlying g♯–a motive, harmonized as V^4_2–I_6 in A. They are decorative, which is quite all right, but the line between a necessary or decorative periphrasis and an excessive or redundant one is fluid and slippery. Thus Quintilian:

> But it is only called *periphrasis* so long as it produces a decorative effect: when it passes into excess, it is known as *perissologia*: for whatever is not a help, is a positive hindrance.[53]

The half-circle is repeated, even extended (m. 6, octave a^1–a^2), without bringing anything new. On the contrary, the ii_6 chord serves to confirm the cadence on A. The eighth-note motive g♯–a, nicely articulated under a slur (m. 8), restates what we have known from m. 3 onwards.

But what is it we know? The progression in m. 3 is a dominant-tonic one but in what key? It is hard to believe that, by the end of the opening phrase (m. 4), we have already reached the dominant; yet when the bass finally plays the long overdue d in m. 3, it is treated as a dissonant neighbor in the dominant key. The timing of this "wrong" harmonic treatment of the tonic—it comes when even a hint of stability would be welcome—is such that the listener embraces it as correct. The repetition of the periphrasis-figure endorses the harmonization and prepares a strong cadence in A major.

The resulting "period" may be somewhat puzzling but is still acceptable. If, with Brown, we discern "two compact four-measure phrases that prepare one for a miniature along the lines of Hob.XVI:26/3," then those two phrases would form a closed period in A Major, in which the second phrase would start the same way the first one ends—the elegant figure of speech *reduplicatio* or *anadiplosis* (/...x/x.../)[54]—and would close on the root-position tonic. (An example of such a period construction is found in the theme of 31/i.) This is precisely the point: the pianist presents to his audience something that is deceptively correct, but will, in the course of the movement, appear not to be a "help" but a "hindrance." After all, sooner or later, the piece will have to close in the right key. Thus, the opening period of 26/ii is "right" and that of 42/ii is "wrong." Moreover, one realizes why the attempt to cadence in mm. 44–45 fails: without a proper opening, there is no proper ending. Why, then, did Haydn not compose a simple, clear and correct opening period?

Beer's Discourse

To answer the question we have to broaden the scope and investigate the *dispositio* and *inventio* of the sonata as a whole. First, however, I introduce a short text by Johann Beer,[55] entitled "Whether a castrato sings with a natural or with a falsetto voice?" from his "Musical Discourses" published posthumously in 1719.[56] I first present an analysis of Beer's text in its own right. This preliminary step will supply me with both implicit and explicit reference points for subsequent analysis of Haydn's "text." In the context of this essay—a rhetorical analysis of a complete Haydn sonata—Beer's discourse seems a happy choice for several reasons. First, for what it is worth, Haydn himself owned a copy of Beer's little book.[57] Second, the text itself, albeit very short, is of a remarkable completeness and unity; its structure and content offer an appealing example of rhetorical *dispositio* and *inventio*. Third, the text itself is argumentative. Argumentation is, after all, the very heart of rhetoric, and will have to be addressed in Haydn as well. Fourth, the text is witty and parodistic. This aspect will be explored further after the actual analyses.

The following is Beer's complete text about castrati:

1	Ob die *Castraten* mit natürlicher oder mit einer *falsed* Stimme singen?	1	Whether castrati sing with a natural or with a falsetto voice?
2	*Affirmo posterius.* Denn was mit unnatürlichen Mitteln gesuchet wird	2	I affirm the latter. Because what is achieved by unnatural means,
3	das ist unnatürlich	3	is unnatural
4	(*qualis causa, talis effectus.*) Nun wird ihre Stimme durch unnatürliche Mittel *procuriret*; *ergo*. Hätten Sie	4	(thus the cause, so the result). Now their voice is procured by unnatural means; hence. Assume they had,

nun ausser der *Castration* eine andere Stimme	in spite of castration,[58] another [kind of] voice,
5 so ist dieses nicht die natürliche	5 then this would not be the natural one
6 welche sie nach der *Castration* haben. Man wird einwerffen: Wer nach der *Castration* eben dieselbe Stimme behält	6 that they have after castration. One will object: who after castration keeps exactly the same voice
7 welche er vor der *Castration* gehabt	7 that he had before castration,
8 der behält die natürliche; nun behält der *Castrat* nach der *Castration* eben die Stimme	8 keeps the natural one; now the castrato, after castration, indeed keeps the voice
9 die er zuvor gehabt	9 that he had before;
10 *ergo &c. Concedo prius, nego posterius*, denn der *minor* kan mit dem Widerspiel ümgestossen werden	10 hence etc. I concede the former but deny the latter, because the *minor* can be refuted by the contrary example
11 welches man an ihrer tausenden fleissig *observi*ret hat.	11 that one has diligently observed in thousands of cases.

Before proceeding to discuss the formal structure of Beer's discourse and its use of syllogisms and *Maior* and *minor* premises, it is of interest to look at its content. The issue under discussion is formulated by Lorenz Christoph Mizler in his *Musikalisch-kritische Bibliothek* (1737), a work also owned by Haydn.[59] The following is Mizler's description of the phenomenon of castration and of a castrato voice:

> The aim of castration is not to procure a new voice, but only to keep the already existing one. This is realized by taking away the little boy's masculine power so that the windpipe does not enlarge itself as it usually does with adult males, and [so that] they can, because of their narrow throat, produce high tones in an ordinary and natural way, whereas those who, on the contrary, have a wider throat, sing lower tones in a normal way. I

> say "in an ordinary or natural way." For someone who by nature sings lower tones can also in an extraordinary or artificial way produce high tones if he endeavors to do so by forcing and narrowing his throat. This way of singing is called *falsetto*. On the other hand, nobody who by nature sings higher tones can sing in a deeper or bass voice, because, although the throat is able to contract itself, it is hardly—if at all—capable of widening itself.[60]

Mizler's is a scientific approach. From this angle the answer to Beer's question would be that, of course, castrati sing with a natural voice, since—in order to produce high tones—they do not have to resort to the artificial technique of falsetto or narrowing the throat. Beer opposes this view, or at least feigns doing so (cf. line 2). In his contention that castrati sing with a falsetto voice, he paradoxically links "falsetto" with "castrato." The term falsetto, however, is used only in the question, or title of the discourse. In the actual argumentation, Beer uses the terms "unnatural" or "not natural" in opposition to "natural" (cf. lines 2, 3, 4, and 5). By this shift in terminology from a technical and neutral term designating vocal register and quality to a general, normative one—the discussion shifts from scientific to philosophical discourse. The fundamental question becomes: are castrato voices natural, real, beautiful, human, aesthetically or even ethically valuable? The resulting discourse takes on the form of a scholastic disputation, very much like those on the location of God before the creation, or the gender of angels. And like those disputations, in which terms like "location" and "gender" are never accurately defined, Beer never provides an actual definition of the term "natural," requiring us to assume that "a natural voice" means "the type of voice that is normal for a certain sex and age," while "natural" in general means "belonging to nature." The latter is contradicted in line 5, however, where "natural" appears to mean "naturally resulting." This pun provokes a puzzling fallacy of equivocation, which I will examine later.

First, I will examine the overall structure of Beer's argumentation. It is neatly marked by standard clauses and terms, either in Latin (*affirmo*, *posterius*, *ergo* etc.) or in a literal, German translation (*ob*, *nun*, *man wird einwerffen* etc.). The order Beer painstakingly follows is a textbook example of the scholastic *disputatio* or forensic *oratio*, which, although differing in purpose and content, have essentially the same arrangement (*dispositio*). The difference lies mainly in the degree of elaborateness of the parts: the disputation is much less elaborate than the forensic oration, and at the beginning of the former it is best not to spend too much time on engaging the audience's emotions with ethos or pathos—as in an *exordium* (introduction)—but to strike to the heart of the *quaestio*, the one-sentence question (*utrum . . . sit*; whether . . . is) at once.[61]

In the following outline, I adhere to the rhetorical *dispositio* as closely as possible.[62] The separate arguments have been labeled from A to D. A and B belong to the *probatio*; they are Beer's own arguments in favor of his proposition. C and D belong to the *refutatio*; C is the opponent's argument, which is refuted by D.

exordium/quaestio

Whether castrati sing with a natural or a falsetto voice.

propositio

I affirm the latter (they sing with a falsetto, i.e. unnatural voice)

probatio

Argument A: Because they get their voice by unnatural means, and

Argument B: Even if they had another voice after castration this would equally be unnatural (given that they were castrated).

refutatio

One will object (**Counter-argument C**) that castrati keep their former voice and consequently have a natural voice.
but I refute this by pointing to the (empirical) observation (**Argument D**) of so many voices of castrati.

conclusio

[Therefore, I re-affirm: castrati sing with an unnatural voice.]

As to the internal structure of the separate arguments, one is struck by the formulation as syllogisms of at least two of them: A and C. A syllogism is a logical proof, consisting of two premises—a major (*Maior*) and minor (*minor*)—and a conclusion (*conclusio*).[63] In rhetorical argument, a syllogism may also be *ratiocinatio*, enthymeme, epicheireme, or rhetorical syllogism. There are two main differences between a logical and a rhetorical syllogism: the former is concerned with truth, the latter with probability and credibility; the former is presented completely, the latter "is content to let its proof be understood without explicit statement."[64]

The following is Quintilian's example of a syllogism, laid out in such a way to illustrate its threefold structure.[65] I have made explicit the connection between major and minor premises by adding the adverb *nun* (now). The top line is the proposition in need of proof:

propositio:		Solum bonum virtus
syllogismus:	Maior	**nam** id demum bonum est, quo nemo male uti potest
	minor	[**nun**] virtute nemo male uti potest;
conclusio:		bonum est **ergo** virtus.

proposition/conclusion:	Virtue is a good thing
enthymeme:	because no one can put it to a bad use.

proposition:		Virtue is the only thing that is good,
syllogism:	Major	**for** that alone is good which no one can put to a bad use;
	minor	[**now**,] no one can make a bad use of virtue;
conclusion:		virtue **therefore** is good.

An incomplete, shortened version of the same syllogism (which would be called an enthymeme) could read:

proposition/conclusion:	Virtue is a good thing
enthymeme:	because no one can put it to a bad use.

Instead of shortening, the syllogism can be lengthened to become an *epicheireme*, e.g. by including an *approbatio propositionis* (grounds for the proposition) to the major premise or an *approbatio assumptionis* (backing of the assumption) to the minor premise.[66] However, both the extended and shortened version can be logically reduced or reconstructed into a threefold structure, which is, so to speak, the *Ur*-form of any deductive syllogism. Thus Quintilian:

> Personally however I follow the majority of authorities in holding that there are not more than three parts. For it follows from the very nature of reasoning that there must be something to form the subject of enquiry and something else to provide the proof, while the third element which has to be added may be regarded as resulting from the agreement of the two previous elements. Thus the first part will be the major, the second the minor premise and the third the conclusion.[67]

Beer's argument A is a straightforward syllogism; all three steps are spelled out. The "etc." after *ergo* is not a logical abbreviation that would turn the syllogism into an enthymeme but a rhetorical figure, an ellipsis; the reader is invited to supply the conclusion for himself.[68] Between brackets, the *approbatio propositionis* is added to turn the syllogism into an epicheireme: *qualis causa, talis effectus*. The structure of argument A can be rendered as follows:

Maior	All	things caused by unnatural means	are	unnatural
approbatio propositionis		*thus the cause, so the result*		
minor	All	*castrato* voices	are	things caused by unnatural means.
conclusio	All	castrato voices	are	unnatural.

Argument B is not a complete syllogism but an enthymeme. Its interpretation is extremely tricky. Being the second proof in the *probatio*, one expects it to reach the same conclusion as argument A, confirming that castrati sing with an unnatural voice. It indeed does so, but with a remarkable twist. The inattentive reader, who recognizes "not . . . the natural one" of line 5, might remain unaware of danger and link "unnatural" with "castrato voice." However, "not . . . the natural one" refers not to the castrato voice but to "another [kind of] voice." Indeed, the argument is based on a speculation of a contrary type: suppose they had another, not a castrato voice. This hypothetical voice, Beer contends, would not be the normal consequence of castration; i.e., not the "natural" voice after castration.

At the very core of an intricate argument, which is in itself difficult to grasp, Beer introduces a fallacy of equivocation: in argument B, "natural" acquires a different meaning than previously in argument

A. There, it meant "without any artificial intervention;" i.e., without castration. Now, "natural" is paired with the very process of castration. As a result of this semantic transformation, argument B ends up concluding that, after castration, voices *other* than the castrato voice would not be natural. As indicated before, after reading the "not natural" clause, the inattentive reader is comforted and prepared for the *refutatio*. The more attentive reader, on the other hand, infers that, if other voices are not natural, then castrato voices must be natural . . . and gets confused, as it does not make any sense that argument B would not confirm but contradict argument A. The very attentive reader, who pinpoints the fallacy of equivocation and successfully couples the two arguments, reaches an acceptable conclusion, albeit a paradoxical one: the only natural voice, i.e., normal after castration, is the one which, according to argument A, is unnatural; in other words, the castrato voice is "naturally" unnatural. This threefold degree of attentiveness—inattentive, more attentive, very attentive—does not so much imply different readers than consecutive stages of one and the same reader, who evolves from unawareness of, to puzzlement by, and, finally, disentanglement of the equivocational fallacy. In rhetorical terminology, one may describe the process as follows: after the reader is passively struck by the "pun" (*traductio*) between two meanings of the word "natural," he must actively make a distinction (*distinctio*) between two different uses. In other words, *traductio*, which is a figure of speech, has to be upgraded to a *distinctio*, a figure of thought.[69] If the reader fails to follow, the chain of arguments may still appear holding a sound formal structure, but would be logically nonsensical.

I now proceed from the *probatio* to the *refutatio*. Beer states argument C, i.e. the argument of his opponents ("one will object"), and does so, in all fairness, in exactly the same form as he presented his own argument A, the opening of the *probatio*.[70] The syllogism can be read as follows:

Maior	All	voices remaining the same after castration	are	natural voices.
minor	All	castrato voices	are	voices remaining the same after castration.
conclusio	All	castrato voices	are	natural voices.

Argument D refutes this counter argument. One would expect it to do so by a devastatingly definitive syllogism. Instead, Beer turns away from deductive-philosophical reasoning. This move can be interpreted in a number of ways. One option, which remains close to logic, would be induction: the *minor* of the deductive syllogism of argument C is annihilated by the empirical evidence of "thousands of cases" (of castrati who did not keep their natural pre-castration voice). Indeed, if "some" castrati do not keep their natural voice, one can no longer maintain that "all" castrati keep their natural voice. A second option, in line with rhetorical terminology, is to consider argument D as an *exemplum*. In fact, Beer himself uses the word "contrary example" (*Widerspiel*). The number—"thousands of cases"—is a sweeping exaggeration, the figure uses *hyperbole*;[71] one counter example would have sufficed to prove the invalidity of the opponent's syllogism. A third interpretive option would be an argument *a dissimile* ("castrato voices do not sound like any natural voice") or *a contrario* ("castrato voices sound like an unnatural voice"). One may, finally, go so far as to consider argument D as not belonging at all to the *genus artificiale* of proofs but to the *genus inartificiale*.[72] The refutation, then, appeals to bare facts: not the orator but many witnesses have observed that voices of castrati do not sound like any boy's voice, nor like any woman's for that matter; they have their own, typical unnatural voice.[73]

Whatever genus of persuasive means one reads into the refutation part of Beer's discourse, the author seems eager to put an end to it. He does not even re-affirm his opening proposition. All four interpretations that I have suggested boil down to: no more syllogisms, no more sophisms, no more rhetoric: back to plain observation. This shift resembles the line of thought upon which twentieth-century ordinary language philosophy is based: "don't think, but look."[74] The following chart offers a summary of the *inventio* and *dispositio* of Beer's text:

---

exordium/*quaestio*

Whether castrati sing with a natural or with a falsetto voice?

propositio

I affirm the latter: [unnatural voice].

probatio

Syllogism A

Maior Unnatural means = unnatural

approbatio propositionis	thus the cause, so the result
minor	castrato voices = unnatural means
conclusio	castrato voices = unnatural

Syllogism B

Maior	"natural" after-castration voices = castrato voices
minor	castrato voices ≠ other voices
conclusio	other voices ≠ "natural" after-castration voices (castrato voices are "natural")

refutatio

Syllogism C (opponent's syllogism)

Maior	after castration same voices = natural
approbatio propositionis	the same as before
minor	castrato voices = after castration same voices
conclusio	castrato voices = natural

Refutation of the *minor* of opponent's syllogism by observation of voices of castrati

conclusio

[Therefore, I re-affirm: castrati sing with unnatural/ falsetto voice.]

Haydn's "Discourse"

If we want to interpret Hob.XVI:42 as a "musical discourse," we must examine how its musical arguments are ordered and to what purpose—in other words—one must reconstruct the *dispositio* and uncover the *inventio* of the whole sonata.

The first movement of Hob.XVI:42 is one of four opening variation movements in Haydn's sonata output. The others are Hob.XVI:39, 40, and 48. Each of the latter three alternates mode: the first is a rondo variation with episodes in tonic and relative minors, the second is an alternating variation movement, while the third has two minor variations on the major theme.[75] In no. 42 however, as Somfai points out,

Haydn "delays the statement of the minor theme and does not compose a variation of it."[76] This delay, Somfai suggests, allows Haydn to create "the feeling of a real recapitulation"; indeed, after a short transition and fermata on the dominant, m. 62 brings in the opening theme in its unembellished version again.[77] The form of the first movement could be represented schematically as AA_1BA_2, in which B stands for the minor "variation" and A_2 for a literal repeat or recapitulation of the theme, along with new internal varied repetitions.

The opening theme of 42 is hardly a conventional one for a variation movement.[78] Koch's first requisite for successful variations, "a cantabile melody . . . which is already interesting in and of itself,"[79] seems not at all germane. On the contrary, numerous rests appear to hinder our speaker in his consecutive attempts to produce a coherent opening statement. It is, Sisman observes, as if the theme "is caught in the act of its own invention."[80] Only in m. 5, at the forte D-major arpeggiation, the highest and most outspoken so far, does the music seem finally to take off; instead of 1 +1 + 2 (mm. 1–4), mm. 5–8 are more or less linked in a single, coherent four-measure phrase (Example 4a).

Example 4a. Sonata 42/ii, mm. 1–8.

Exordium and *quaestio/propositio*

How, then, are the four opening measures to be interpreted? Forkel asserted that a sonata should start with the main proposition or *Hauptsatz* right away.[81] This, one expects, must be all the more true for a theme of a variation movement, since the theme there is supposed to constitute a proposition, which the consecutive variations will argue for (or possibly against).[82] But the hesitancy, almost shyness, in these opening measures hardly seem appropriate for an assertive affirmation of a proposition, as in Beer's "I affirm the latter." It therefore seems preferable to read the four opening measures as combining two different dispositional functions; they are both exordium or introduction, and *propositio*.

Introductory is the definition of the opening key. A D-major triad is unfolded, first by simple arpeggiation (a–d–f# in m. 1), then in a more complex way: the lower pitches a^1 and d^1 are reflected above, on a^2 (m. 2) and d^3 (m. 5). Although seemingly hesitant, this unfolding (see Example 4b) procures a firm tonal framework in which the next part, the *probatio* (proofs), can be cast. (It will be recalled that this kind of framework is conspicuously absent at the beginning of the second movement.)

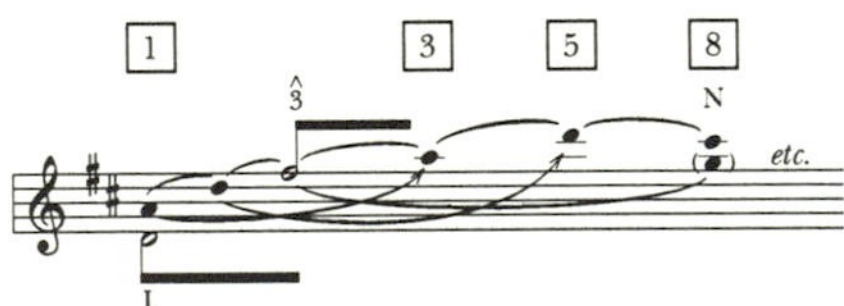

Example 4b. Sonata 42/ii, mm. 1–8. reduction.

Propositional, on the other hand, are the first two measures. Not only do they establish $\hat{3}$, but the inner voice also introduces the simple neighbor-note motion f#–g–f# over tonic support d. If one had to verbalize a proposition, it could read: "If $\hat{3}$ in D opens into neighbor g, the latter should resolve." Measures 3–4 create a half-cadence. The inner voice a (from the last beat of m. 2), having been transferred up an octave, initiates a series of descending parallel sixths. These move towards a cadential perfect fifth, as if marking the end of a *quaestio*: "Is my proposition true?" Example 5 shows, in a reduction, this *propositio* and *quaestio*. The proposition sounds like a musical axiom, even a truism, hardly in need of any consecutive proof. But, as we saw, not observing this simple truth will lead to catastrophic results in the second movement (see also below: *refutatio*).

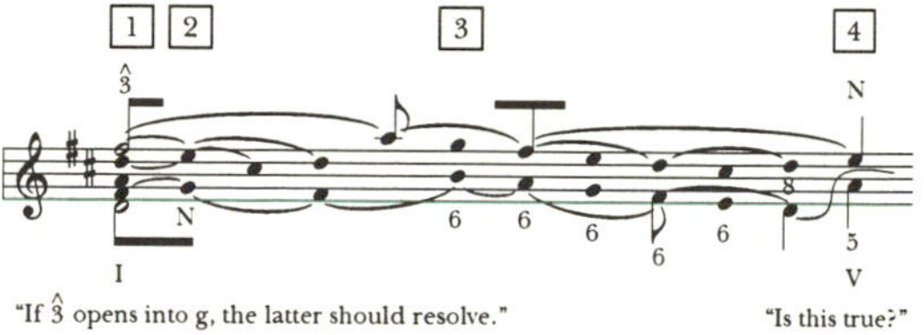

Example 5. Sonata 42/i, mm. 1-4: *propostio* and *quaestio.*

Probatio

The high D (d^3) on the first beat of m. 5 has a double function: it both rounds off the introductory unfolding of the D-major triad and marks the beginning of a new phrase. With this new phrase, the pianist-orator launches himself into the next part of his discourse: the *probatio*. This dispositional shift is accompanied by a change of tone: not only is d^3 the highest note so far, the dynamics also change from a cautious piano to an extroverted forte. From the proposition, followed by a question ("Is it true?"), the pianist proceeds to the first proof.

Mm. 5–8 constitute the *Maior* of a first syllogism in favor of the proposition. It will be followed by a *minor* in m. 17. Both will lead to their *conclusio* on the third beat of m. 19.

Maior

Mm. 5–8 can be seen as a distribution (*distributio*) of the original proposition: the proposition is revisited and its members amplified individually.[83] Neighbor-note g is now spread out over six beats. In the proposition, g was accompanied by e and c#. C# now shows up in the top voice and forms an augmented fourth with g, unfolding to a diminished fifth before resolving to the third f#–d. In the proposition, e was presented as an alternative to c# (m. 2), both being part of a dominant harmony. Now, it is harmonized as E Minor or ii in D Major, but remains a parenthesis within the opening and closing of neighbor g. The soprano descends through the notes that fill up the sixth between d and f#: [d]–c#–c♮–b–a–g–[f#]. After the resolution to $\hat{3}$ in the soprano, the bass, as if responding to that chromatic descent, ascends chromatically towards a half-cadence.

Minor

In m. 17 the two-chord progression that opened the *Maior* now returns to open the *minor*. This parallel opening resembles, one could say, the beginning of both *Maior* and *minor* with a quantifier ("all"—as in Beer's discourse—or "some"). However, m. 18 proceeds differently from m. 6. First, the neighboring dominant chord is repeated. This repetition, already emphatic in itself, launches a series of emphasized chords in which the bass diatonically ascends from tonic to dominant. Above this steady progression, the soprano fulfills the same descent as before: d, c♯, c♮, b, a. On the latter note, harmonized as V^6_4, the orator pauses: he leaves his audience in suspense about the outcome (*suspensio*). As an *emphasis*, the expected resolution follows: neighbor g—the next note in the descent of the soprano—is transferred one octave lower and resolves to $\hat{3}$ in the alto register.

Although *Maior* and *minor* use the same material, they apply it differently. Still similar to the opening *propositio*, the *Maior* took it as its task to distribute the process of opening and closing neighbor g. The harmonization of the quasi-chromatically descending soprano was a parenthesis and involved only middle voices. In the *minor*, these processes are integrated: while the bass now participates in the overall harmonization of the descent, the opening and closing of neighbor g is not neglected; on the contrary, g is emphatically resolved on the third beat of m. 19.

Conclusio

With this resolution not only the *minor* in itself but the whole syllogism, (the combination of *Maior* and *minor*), has reached its conclusion: $\hat{3}$, $\hat{2}$, $\hat{1}$. The circle is complete. Every possible aspect—texture (three voices), register, dynamics, touch—refers back to the very first measure of the piece. As in the second measure of the proposition, c♯ and e are juxtaposed as accompanying neighbors, this time in reversed order. The conclusion is very brief and, especially after the *suspensio* of the *minor*, sounds almost casual. Is Haydn creating a similar effect to Beer's *ergo*, leaving it up to the listener to fill in the ellipsis? The full conclusion, indeed, could read: "Hence, my initial proposition that every neighbor should return to its main note proves to be correct."

Example 7 (pp. 231–32, left column) is a schematic presentation of the three important members of the orator's syllogism in an abstracted form, in the same spirit as that in which Beer's arguments were formalized before. In the logical foreground, so to speak, there are two remaining steps in the chain of arguing. One need not invoke a rhetorical, five-step *epicheireme* to explain them. The first extra step concerns the return of the opening material of the ||:a:||:ba:|| form in m. 13. Rhetorically, this return constitutes a repeat of the orator's proposition, again followed by a question. The orator, for the sake of clarity, recapitulates his starting point before concluding his syllogism.

Another step has occurred in mm. 9–12. Although these measures formally are a middle phrase separating the opening period (mm. 1–8) and its repeat (mm. 13–20), their content is almost identical to the parenthesis of the *Maior* (mm. 6–7): ii (E Minor) is highlighted in mm. 9–10; then, a stepwise descent in the treble from c♮ through f# ($\hat{3}$) leads to the half cadence in m. 12, confirmed by the same chromatic ascent in the bass. Thus, this connective phrase not only traverses the same material of the *Maior*, it also reaches the same concluding point. This simple observation becomes an intriguing one when we compare the two ending points, m. 8 and m. 12. If we imagine the d and c# in m. 8 an octave higher, then the soprano's descent beginning in m. 9 can be read back to m. 8, making it the full quasi-chromatic descent (d–c#–c♮–b–a–g–f#) that it had just completed. The end of mm. 5–8, then, equals the beginning of mm. 8–12: a *reduplicatio*, which creates an impression of circularity. Conceivably, the orator could repeat the *Maior* a third or fourth time. However, he would soon find himself stuck in the useless enterprise of confirming the half cadence again and again.

The beginning and end of the *Maior*, unlike those of hypothetical, circular statements, are crucially different. Example 6 isolates both of them. Whereas, at the beginning (m. 5), the motive d–c# is firmly rooted within a tonic chord, played forte and with a thick texture, at the end (m. 8), the same notes loosely "float" around a dominant chord, are spoken in a soft voice, and have a thin texture. Harmonically, we observe a shift of hierarchy: the main note–neighbor relation becomes a neighbor–main note one. This shift is underlined metrically: strong–weak (m. 5) becomes weak–strong (upbeat to and m. 8).

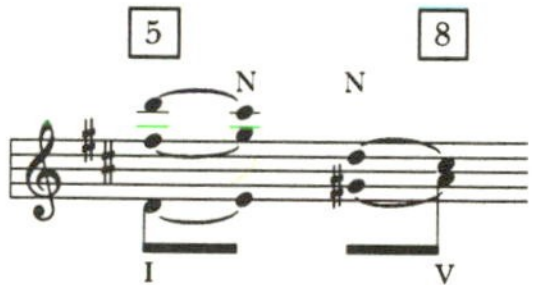

Example 6. Sonata 42/i, mm. 5–8: beginning and end of the *Maior*.

Slyly, however, the speaker seems to mislead his listener and make him believe that beginning and end might indeed be the same: harmonically, by continuing m. 9 in the same vein as before; metrically, by stressing weak parts of the measure both in m. 5 (neighbor g), and, at the end of m. 7 (sforzando on g# and d). It is with this layer of ambiguity, I would argue, that Haydn sows the seed for the puzzle of the beginning of the Vivace assai. And this process is very similar to the ambiguous character of Beer's pun on the word "natural."

Indeed, both beginning and end of the *Maior* may be loosely interpreted as a pun or *traductio*. Like Beer's reader, Haydn's listener may take pleasure in his recognition of the orator's playfulness. However, in the second movement, he will be forced to revisit his perception and be intellectually challenged to make an active distinction (*distinctio*) between the two meanings of beginning and end respectively.

The question therefore becomes: how does the *traductio* or the rather innocent seed of ambiguity in the orator's syllogism (two meanings of the same musical motive) develop into the outrageously "wrong" opening period of the second movement?

Refutatio

We can now answer the question posed at the beginning of this section: why did Haydn, at the beginning of the second movement, not write something simple, clear, and correct? *Because the opening period of the finale are not the orator's words but his opponent's.* They can be labeled as the "opponent's syllogism" and could, as in Beer's text, be preceded by: "One will object." Example 7 "confronts" the opponent's syllogism with the speaker's own syllogism. Although they have striking similarities, their differences are more important. (Similarly, in Beer's discourse, the form of his own and his opponent's arguments is identical[84] but their content, i.e. their respective terms, is different.) Melodically, the *Maior* of the vivace assai is modeled after the middle voice of the original *Maior* (cf. the circled notes in Example 7). Even the confusing articulation mark at the beginning of the second movement—the overlapping slur on neighbor g in m. 1—is traceable: it is a contraction of two notes. Implied in the main proposition (mm. 1–2) are two possible meanings of neighbor g: it can belong to a dominant or a subdominant chord. Indeed, in the *Maior* of the orator's syllogism these two meanings were juxtaposed: g (dominant) of m. 5 is repeated in the next measure in a new context of ii (subdominant). At the beginning of the second movement, however, these two meanings are contracted: the first slur from f# to g ($\hat{3}$ to its neighbor) implies a tonic–dominant relationship, which is immediately overruled when g, in its turn, is slurred to e and E minor is suggested. This articulatory

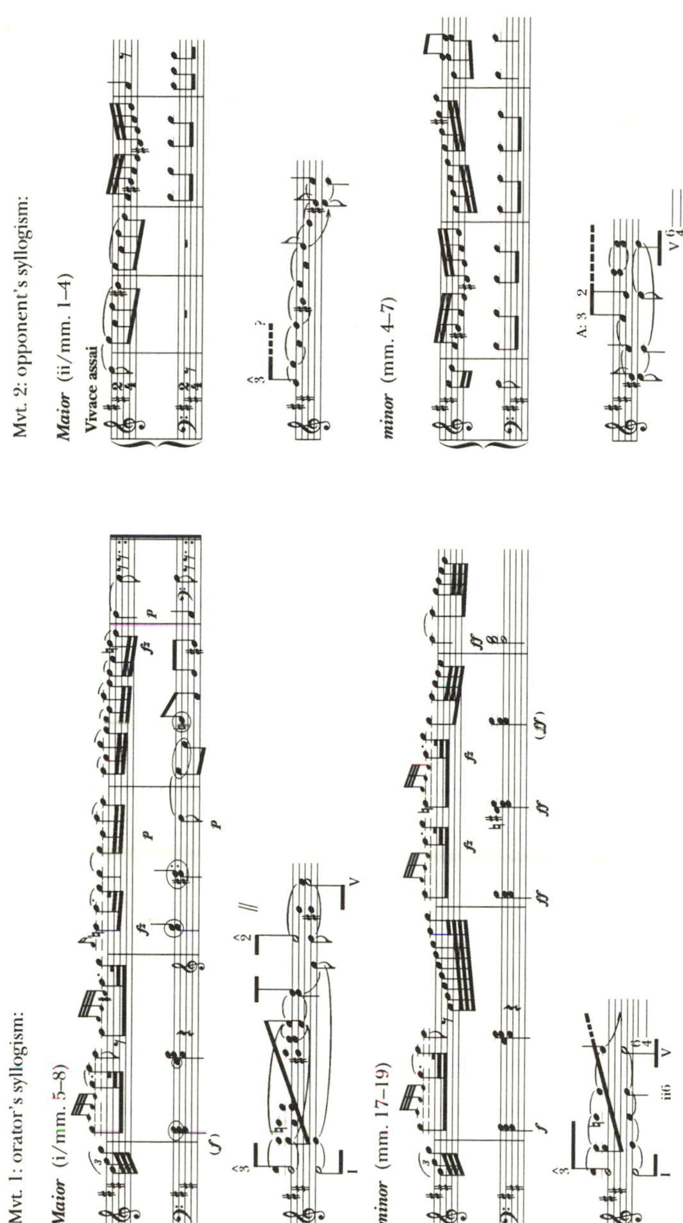

Example 7. Comparison of Sonata 42/i and ii, mm. 1–8, continued on top of next page.

Example 7, continued.

change of mind (*dubitatio*)[85]—"f# is the beginning of the slur, or no, rather, g is the beginning"—also problematizes the harmonic hierarchy of main note/neighbor (f#/g) as it existed at the beginning of the *Maior* of the orator's syllogism.

If one unfolds the parallel thirds of the first movement's m. 6, the reference is almost literal. In fact, the *Maior* of the second movement is not puzzling at all if one combines the unison middle voice with an imaginary top voice, as "remembered" from the first movement (Example 8). However, instead of proceeding to the cadential formula f#–g–g#–a as before, the finale-theme extends the descending thirds, and takes a short-cut to g#, dominant of the dominant. By presenting as the sole unison melody what was originally only a middle voice, the orator deliberately plants ambiguity in his opponent's reasoning. Taken out of context, the middle voice now creates its own tonal world: it steps out of D Major, touches on E minor, and ends up in A Major. Even the most perceptive listener, who can hear the opening as rooted in D Major, would be perplexed when d–c# enter, not in the melody (the start of a chromatic descent as in i/m. 5), but in the bass, in ii/m. 3. This entrance, as we observed, endorses the "wrong" tonality of the dominant A major. After this endorsement, the *minor* prepares a full cadence in that key, and the *conclusio* delivers: $\hat{3}$, $\hat{2}$, $\hat{1}$.

Example 8. Sonata 42/ii, mm. 1–4: "remembrance" of top voice.

Having confronted the opponents with the orator's syllogism, it is now possible to make the link between the *reduplicatio* of the opponent's

Maior and *minor* (ii/mm. 3–4) and the one that connected the *Maior* of the orator's own syllogism to a possible chain of repetitions. There, we noticed the danger of taking the end of the *Maior* statement (on a dominant harmony) for the beginning of a next one, which could result in pointless circularity. What remained a mere danger, is now, in the second movement, materialized. The *conclusio* of the adversary's syllogism is, indeed, an authentic cadence in A Major. If there is a *conclusio* in A Major, then there must have been a beginning in A Major. But, of course, this beginning has never taken place! It is this fallacy that will constitute the keystone of the orator's refutation or *refutatio*.

For our speaker, as well as for Beer, it is sufficient to deny either of the two premises in order to disprove the conclusion. Beer contested the *minor*; Haydn will have to contest the *Maior* of his opponent's syllogism: the opponent's error, indeed, lies not in the continuation and cadence of the dominant key (the *minor* and the *conclusio* of his syllogism), but in his failure to establish D Major in the *Maior*.

At this point, the following crucial difference between Beer's and Haydn's texts should be raised: whereas Beer set apart the refutation by "some will object," there was no such line at the beginning of the vivace assai. How, then, is the listener supposed to know that the orator spoke not in his own, but in his opponent's name? There is only one possible way: the orator needs to shake the listener's confidence and, slowly but steadily, distance himself from his own expression, making the listener eventually realize that all he is doing is "quoting" his opponent. In m. 9, the right hand raises pitch A, the arrival point of the first period, one step higher, to B. The bass then resumes the opening of the piece and rolls, as before, into V^4_2 of A Major. Instead of accompanying the *Halbzirkel* (m. 13) with a chord tone, the right hand answers with the same *Halbzirkel* around c#. As before, the pattern is repeated. However, whereas the repetition of the *Halbzirkel* in mm. 4–6 was embellished and could be interpreted as a stylistic *reduplicatio* between two four-measure phrases, now the repetition of the half-circles occurs *within* a single four-measure phrase. One can hardly describe this repetition as a stylistic *geminatio*, or the repetition of a word within one phrase (/...xx.../). It is a flagrant *tautologia*, a redundant repetition of the same word. *Tautologia* is the corresponding fault or vice to *geminatio*.[86] The situation calls for correction; the corresponding figure is *correctio*, by which one retraces one's steps.[87] The left hand takes initiative: in m. 16 g# is turned into g natural, V^4_2–I6 in D major. The right hand contributes as well: the left hand's periphrasis figure (the *Halbzirkel*) is turned into a *lauffende Figur*, a descending figure of four sixteenth-notes arriving at a different quarter note than the one that initiated the run. The thirds of the right hand in m. 19 not only underline the important shift in motivic direction (from rolling to running) but also a shift in harmonic stability. M. 19 is the first measure in which the tonic of D major in root position is heard. (M. 12, second beat, only touched upon the tonic passingly and with a suspension in the alto voice.) A half-cadence follows: ii–V in D Major.

After the pianist-orator has temporarily talked the listener into accepting A Major, he now, by the *correctio*, reminds him that D Major is the proper tonality, in which A Major functions as a half cadence. But there is still room for doubt: at least motivically, A major maintains its grip on the situation by incorporating the motive that opened this first division of the second part (period **2**, mm. 9–25): a–b–g#–a in both mm. 8–9 and mm. 22–23. Bracketing repetition is *redditio* or epanalepsis (/x...x/).

In the next division, **3**, from mm. 26 to 45, two figures of thought are at work: *evidentia* (mm. 26–39) and *permissio* (mm. 40–45). *Evidentia,* or more familiarly *hypotosis* (word painting, in music) is a vivid and detailed description, "appealing to the eye rather than the ear."[88] The facts or actions described can be in the past or present. They can also be imagined in the future while presented in a present tense. Such a description is usually preceded, as Quintilian says, by: "Imagine that you see." In mm. 28–39 the circling figure is allowed free play. All kinds of keys and registers are traversed. It is as if the pianist says to the audience: "Look, if you follow my opponent in not defining a clear starting point [in D Major] and having the periphrasis figure take over, this is what might happen." It must be especially this passage that Somfai had in mind when he wrote that "[t]he eight-note motive has an unpredictable winding motion while the sixteenth-note curling motive strengthens any key on which it happens to land."[89] In m. 26, the **y1** motive is pulled up even one step higher: b–c♮. Then, from its familiar presentation on the dominant of A major (m. 28), the curling figure passes through several keys. The register of each successive entry is unpredictable: first a big leap upwards (m. 31–32), then a gradual sequence up and then down again (mm. 33–39); these registral changes on the keyboard appeal to the eye as well as to the ear. The overall picture is one of extreme redundancy. Similar motives, in themselves already periphrastic, are chaotically heaped up on top of one another (*congeries*).[90]

The passage in mm. 40–45 (the end of **3**) attempts to bring direction to the unpredictably winding motion. At first it seems to succeed. Of the full circling figure, the first half alone now functions as a running figure (compare m. 18). The advantage is that instead of each time having to roll back to the starting note, a stepwise descent is now possible. In m. 43 the urgency of the descending run is intensified: the four sixteenth notes now run from light to heavy (instead of). At the very last moment, however, the attempt fails: the cadence is deceptive; even the bass now states motive **y1** in powerful octaves, again ending this division as it began.

I propose to link the effect of this failed attempt to the rhetorical figure of *permissio*. Against his own better judgment, the orator permits his opponent to act as he pleases, gambling that the latter will, by doing so, realize his mistake.[91] In our case, anybody who has not yet realized that the pianist began with something deceptively correct and which needs to be refuted, is now explicitly faced with the problem: "You want to cadence? Well, go on, try it. You'll see: it won't work."

The deceptive cadence rounds off the first part of the refutation: the orator has sufficiently distanced himself from his opponent's argument. He can now proceed to the next stage: the confirmation of his own argument. This takes place from m. 46 to m. 87 (periods **4** and **5**). First, in m. 46, he makes a fresh start with the material that opened the opponent's *Maior* (Example 9). The compactness of these two measures—note the voice exchange (*chiasmus*), which tightly holds the two voices together—strikingly resembles a rhetorical *sententia*, "a brief statement of an important maxim inserted into a speech."[92] The general truth of this musical *sententia* would be: "If you open, you have to close", and conversely: "In order to close, you first have to open."

This short maxim should not be confused with the original proposition of the sonata ("if $\hat{3}$ in D opens into neighbor g, the latter should resolve"). Whereas the proposition applied itself only to the concrete situation of D Major, the general truth of the *sententia* is valid for any key, not only for D but also, for instance, for dominant A: mm. 46–47. If there is a lesson to be drawn from the *sententia*, it is the following: if we follow an opening motive **y1**, for instance f♯–g, by another opening motive, g♯–a, we may forget what we opened in the first place and risk becoming sidetracked. Next, the orator puts the *sententia* into practice: the entire next passage from m. 50 to m. 71 is a huge amplification of the *sententia*.

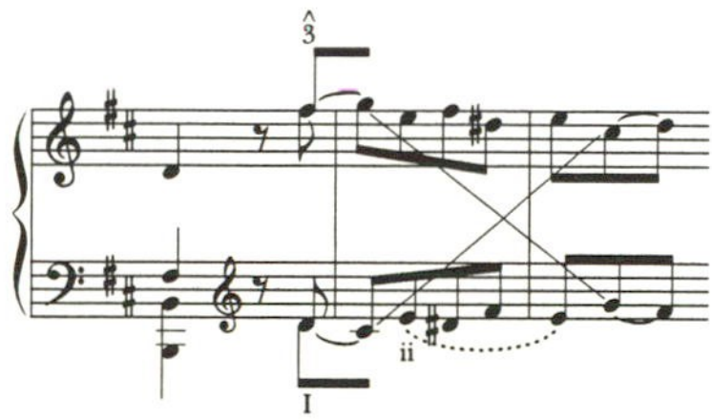

Example 9. Sonata 42/ii, mm. 46–47, beginning of [4].

Apart from procuring a strong middle-ground framework (f#–g–f# and d–c#–d over I–V^7–I), the *sententia* fulfills a specific role in the orator's argumentation. It serves as an *approbatio propositionis* (cf. Beer's "thus the cause, so the result") and enables the orator to confirm his original *Maior* in mm. 52–55. Above the dominant pedal, the middle voice plays a "normalized" version of the theme: it is now articulated in groups of two (instead of four) notes. The upper voice is the very top voice that the listener was challenged to supply in the opponent's *Maior*, albeit in a varied form; these sixteenth-note diminutions are no longer periphrasis for its own sake (as the curling sixteenth note motion before) but clever embellishment. Finally, the cadential formula (f#–g–g#–a) from the orator's original *Maior* is used again and unambiguously prepares a half-cadence in D Major.

The orator has contested his opponent's *Maior* and replaced it by his own. The path is cleared for his own *minor* and *conclusio*. Before proceeding to them, however, he recapitulates: mm. 72–82. All material that the orator presented before in order to refute his opponent, is repeated, not in a ridiculing way, but with regained confidence: the same periphrasis figures, which formerly degenerated into a chaotic *congeries*, now naturally flow into one another; the tautological repetition of mm. 13–17 is omitted in mm. 73–74; the running figures graciously prepare the half cadence (m. 82), which was so ill-prepared before. This cadence is perceived as the structural half-cadence ($\hat{2}$) and makes up for what should have been the caesura after an antecedent phrase, or a proper *Maior*, at the beginning of the movement. The listener now expects the long-awaited consequent, and he is not disappointed. The pianist playfully changes a in m. 82 to a#, a passing note to b. Also the e in m. 84 is turned into the leading tone e#. However, whereas the leading tones in the opponent's theme puzzled us, now they seem natural. Indeed, they simply are the corresponding *minor* and *conclusio* to the orator's *Maior*. Not only has the orator's syllogism been confirmed, the whole *refutatio* has now come to an end. Perhaps the parallel sixth chords in the *minor* of the confirmed syllogism (mm. 83–84), which contrast with the voice exchanges in contrary motion of the *sententia* (mm. 46–47), make a contrapuntal connection all the way back to the initial question after the proposition (mm. 3–4): "Is it true?"—"Yes, it is true!"

Peroratio

The *peroratio* or conclusion, from m. 88 (period **6**), celebrates this "all's well that ends well" feeling. The cause of and solution to the previous trouble are harmoniously joined together: the periphrasis figure, with g♯, and the two descending running figures, with g♮. The two hands, which before were all too eager to take over each other's word, now politely await their turn. And all this while the dominant seventh chord alternates with the tonic, harmonizing the neighboring motive g–f♯, the third scale degree which we were so deprived of at the beginning of the second movement. Then comes m. 98, set off by rests; does the case open all over again? No; in the two last measures the figure is inverted, in order to end with a descending $\hat{5}$, $\hat{4}$, $\hat{3}$, $\hat{2}$, $\hat{1}$. (In the same register, they resolve the $\hat{2}$ which was left unresolved by the deceptive cadence in m. 45.) These measures, despite their piano dynamics, are powerful; with this emphasis the orator rests his case.[93]

Example 10 summarizes the *elocutio* of the second movement. As revealed in the foregoing discussion, the principal rhetorical figures concern the deployment of neighbor-note motives that virtually overflow the piece. There is the opponent's statement, cadencing in A major (period **1**); the first attempt at a correction (period **2**); the chaotic *congeries*, which could go on as a *perpetuum mobile* as demonstrated in the *evidentia* (period **3**); in the same period the failed attempt to cadence (*permissio*); then the two forms of the same *sententia*, presented in tight chiasmi in periods **4** and **5**; period **5** also stabilizes scale degree three, makes the dominant behave, reinstates the orator's *Maior,* and moves over known territory to the structural half cadence, thus finally completing the major premise, or antecedent phrase. The minor premise (consequent phrase) with conclusion answers (mm. 82–88, end of period **5**), after which comes the *peroratio* (period **6**).

At the beginning of the analysis, the principal question framed the dimensions of the movement as a problem: why must the second section of the scherzo be so long? This initial question can now be countered by responding that it is, on the contrary, quite short. Indeed, the division of the second part into several periods is misleading. This entire part actually constitutes a reshaping of a fallacious antecedent. This reshaping is necessary in order to "earn" a proper consequent. According to this interpretation, the movement consists of a single period and a coda. And so we arrive at the following paradox: the structural outline of the second movement of Sonata 42, although much longer in number of measures, is much shorter than the straightforward finale of Sonata 26 in A major, which consists of a period A, a digression B, and period A again.

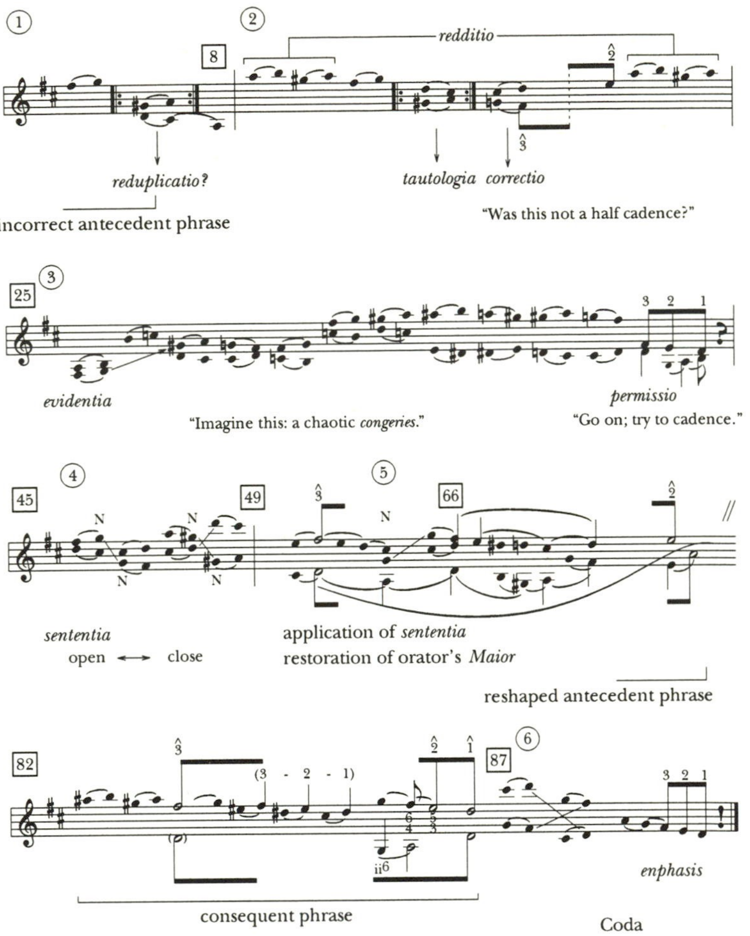

Example 10. Sonata 42/ii: *Elocutio.*

The Complete Oration

In order to view all of Sonata 42 as a fully rhetorical structure, we must at last take up the variations of the first movement as variations of the orator's syllogism, because these act as proofs in favor of the proposition, and are as such part of the *probatio.*[94] The first variation (mm. 21–40) may be called "similar" or *a simile*, the *minore* variation (mm. 41–58) "contrary" or *a contrario*, and the third (mm. 62–101)—

which also entails a literal recapitulation—"dissimilar" or *a dissimile*.[95] Since all of these include variations on the orator's syllogism, which I will henceforth label syllogism A, I label them as syllogisms in their own right: B, C and D. Each has its own structural integrity, but they are in fact more than syllogisms. Indeed, each of the variations includes a version of the proposition as well. The first variant (B), one octave lower, connects the previously disjointed parts by arpeggios in triplet motion. The second (C) keeps the idea of connective triplets, however not as arpeggios but as diatonic descending and ascending passaggi *(lauffende Figuren)*; the earlier melodic fragments have become decisive, French-overture-like chords. The third variant (D), finally, combines the outspokenness of the second with the registral span of the first while returning to the fragmented presentation of the original proposition.

What makes B "similar," C "contrary" and D "dissimilar"? Syllogism B *(a simile)* or var. 1 remains very close to its model, except for some registral and, what Somfai calls "textural and fioritura variants."[96] Sisman calls it a "simple pleonastic variation."[97] Syllogism C *(a contrario)* or var. 2 Brown finds "difficult to classify, for it is really a developmental variation that approaches in form the structure of the theme but could also be seen as an episode of the ternary structure."[98] His invocation of "development" resonates with Somfai's observing a "recapitulation" from m. 62. However, I prefer the very different reading of an argument *a contrario*. In fact, the term "a contrario" in this regard was coined by Sisman for alternating variations in major and minor keys.[99] Here, however, we are dealing with only one minor variation. It is a variation in favor of the main proposition, not to be confused with the opponent's argument (which is stated at the beginning of the *refutatio*; that is, at the beginning of the second movement). Characteristic for an *a contrario* is that, although traversing a different (contrary) route, it reaches the same conclusion as the original syllogism, here mm. 57–58. What makes the path of syllogism C "contrary" to A? First, of course, is its minor mode. Second, contrary to A's fragmentary presentation, C is coherent and outspoken: coherent, because of the overall arpeggiation in the bass (d–f–a) of the major premise; outspoken, because of its overall character of a French overture. And third, neighbor g, treated with all harmonic respect in A, now plays a rather insignificant role in the new context of F major.

After a transition, the orator recapitulates his opening proposition and original argument in syllogism D *(a dissimile)*, var. 3. Recapitulation is a rhetorical device useful at the beginning of an orator's *per-*

oratio, "both to refresh the memory of the judge and to place the whole of the case before his eyes."[100] Quintilian, however, advises, not to recapitulate too literally:

> [T]he points selected for enumeration [at the end of one's speech] must be treated with weight and dignity, enlivened by apt reflections and diversified by suitable figures; for there is nothing more tiresome than a dry repetition of facts, which merely suggests a lack of confidence in the judges' memory.[101]

Our orator's recapitulation is, indeed, not literal; it is combined with a varied repeat. This is not to say that each of the previous arguments would not have been varied in performance themselves, in line with the contemporary practice of varying repeats, but those variants are likely to have remained closer to the text than this written-out one, which is not only textural and registral—as the *a simile* argument of syllogism B/var. 2—but also gestural. For example, in m. 70, the initial shyness gives way to a self-confident display of passagework, and the *Sturm und Drang* arpeggios, starting in m. 90, imply a new extrovertedness.

The last three measures of the first movement—a reiteration of the final cadential phrase, mm. 102–105—constitute a provisional *peroratio*. They round off the chain of arguments A, B, C and D, all of which belong to the *probatio*. In the overall disposition of the sonata these measures function as a transition to the *refutatio* in the second movement; that is, they are both concluding and anticipatory.[102] As conclusion, they remind the listener of the main points of major and minor premises and their conclusion, which are reiterated in piano. It is as if the *quaestio* from the beginning (mm. 1–4) is now addressed directly: "When $\hat{3}$ of D opens to neighbor g it also needs closure. Is this true? ($\hat{3}$, $\hat{2}$?) Yes, so far, it appears to be true ($\hat{3}$, $\hat{2}$, $\hat{1}$)." And one small detail gives a hint of what is to follow in the second movement: the augmented fourth a–d♯ (m. 103) will soon recur as the periphrastic figure that overflows the vivace assai.

This anticipation sets the tone for a new departure in the *dispositio*. Soon, the orator will reveal himself able to make his listeners doubt what he made them carefully believe so far. This observation, valid for the *refutatio* in Hob.XVI:42, finds attractive general support in the words of one of Haydn's earliest biographers, Ignaz Theodor Ferdinand Arnold (1810):

Haydn acts like a sly orator, who, when he wants to persuade us of something, starts off with a statement universally recognized to be true, which everyone accepts, which everyone must understand. Soon, however, he skillfully molds this statement in such a way that he can persuade us of anything he wishes to, even if it were the contrary of the opening statement.[103]

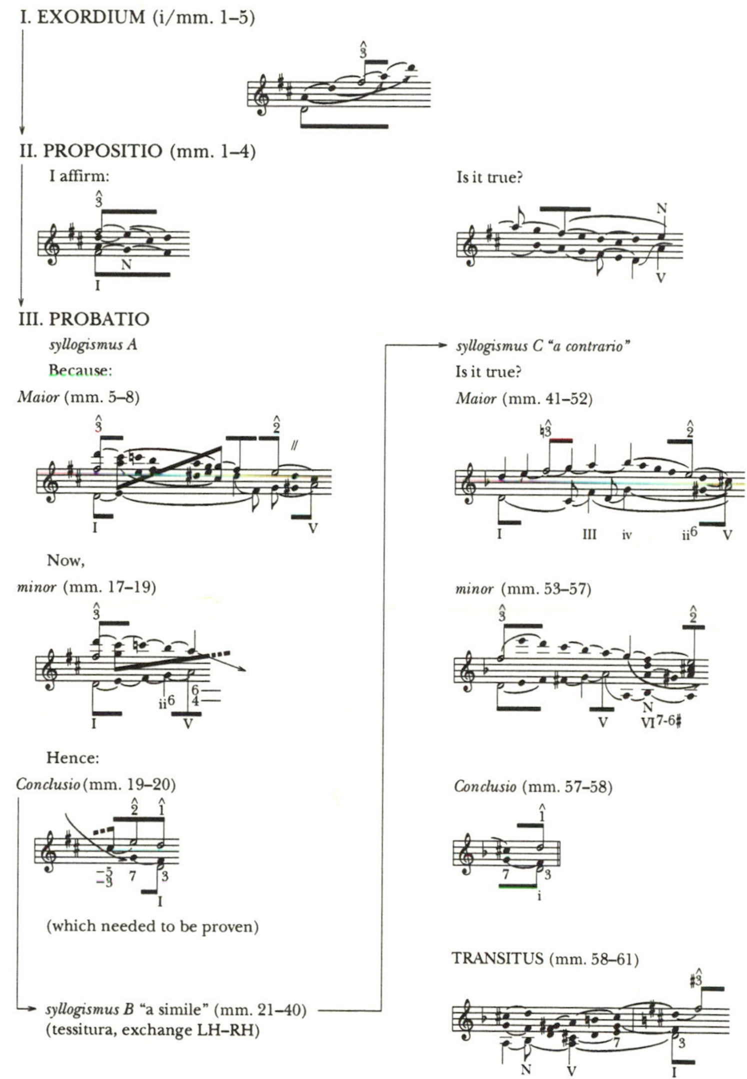

Example 11. Sonata 42/i and ii: *Dispositio* and *Inventio.*

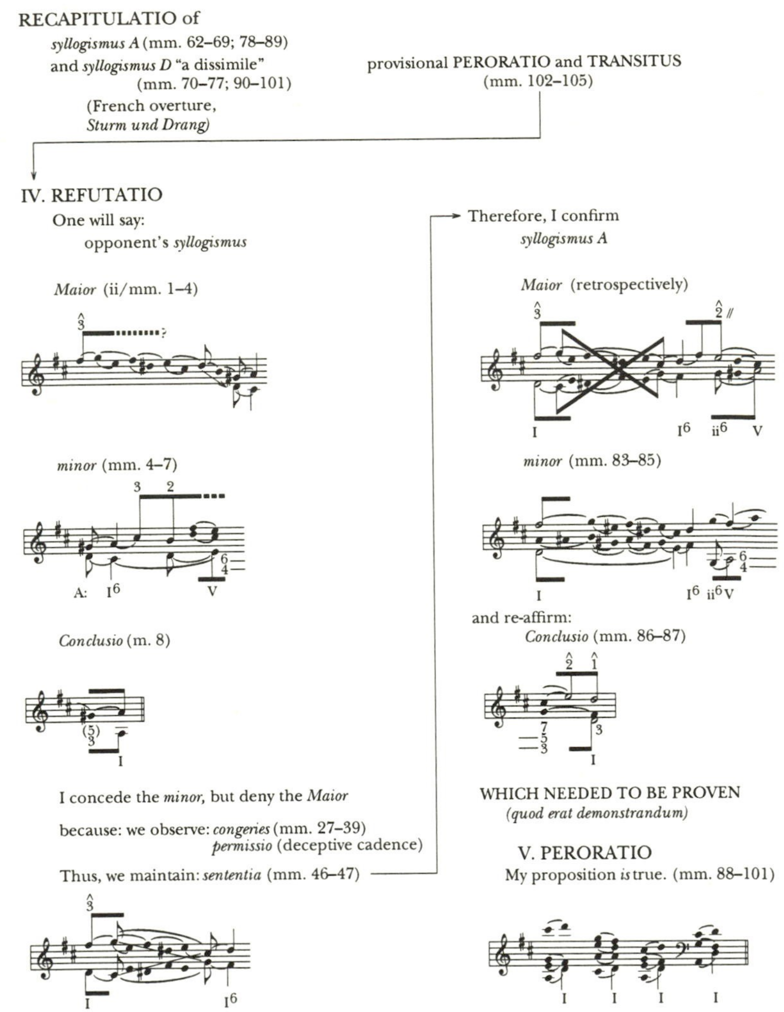

Example 11, continued.

Indeed, what was called a truism at the beginning of the analysis, namely the main proposition, will soon be turned into a puzzling sophism, the resulting proposition of which will be refuted and eventually replaced by the original one. Example 11 presents an overview of the disposition and invention of the entire Sonata Hob.XVI:42.

Conclusion

The finale, a scherzo of very unusual proportions, constituted the starting point of my rhetorical analysis of Hob.XVI:42. Its peculiarity at the level of *elocutio*, I argued, could not be explained without laying bare the *dispositio* and *inventio* of the sonata as a whole. Within this broadened scope the puzzling opening statement of the scherzo turned out to be the responsibility of the opponent, not of the orator. A model for the overall rhetorical disposition and invention of Haydn's sonata was provided by Beer's discourse. This model, however, should not be interpreted as a specific one which Haydn might have actually copied. That Hob.XVI:42 and "Whether castrati sing with a natural or falsetto voice" ended up displaying a similar structure, has everything to do with the fact that Beer's discourse itself follows a model of scholastic rhetoric and dialectics. Thus, at most, the following, modest conclusion may be formulated: both Haydn and Beer knew the rules of rhetorical invention and disposition.

A comparative analysis, however, cannot stop here. Beer does not merely display his knowledge of the rules, he does so in a jesting way. I already hinted at this aspect in my reading of the text. I now explicitly point at some of its jesting characteristics, and, at the same time, categorize them as being either humor *in* rhetoric or humor *of* rhetoric.

Humor *in* rhetoric (*le comique dans la rhétorique*)[104] is the normal oratorical kind.[105] In judicial oratory, Quintilian writes, humor "dispels the graver emotions of the judge by exciting his laughter, frequently diverts his attention from the facts of the case, and sometimes even refreshes him and revives him when he has begun to be bored or wearied by the case."[106] In Beer's *Musikalische Diskurse*, the short column on such a suggestive subject as "Whether castrati sing with a natural or with a falsetto voice"—for example, his hinting at the actual emasculation ("thus the cause, so the result")—may be interpreted as a humorous note among slightly more serious discussions on "What musicians adjudicate of themselves as well as what other people of them?" or "Whether a *composer* of necessity should be educated."[107] The orator, Quintilian continues, may also "seek to raise a laugh . . . [to] either reprove or refute or make light of or retort or deride the arguments of others."[108] Thus, Beer checkmates his opponent by a realistic-empirical twist ("don't think, but look!") after a set of philosophical-deductive arguments. Where one counter-example would have sufficed, Beer invokes "thousands of them."

More interesting is Beer's humor *of* rhetoric (*le comique de la rhétorique*). Whereas an orator uses "humor in rhetoric" only as yet another aid to his overall goal of persuasion, "humor of rhetoric" is not used to persuade at all, but to "amuse" the listener or reader by a display of argumentative schemes and other techniques of rhetoric.[109] Beer's column abounds with rhetorical devices. Not only is its structure a standard disposition, in which each of the parts is clearly delineated by clauses such as *affirmo posterius* or "one will object," also the arguments are presented as full-fledged syllogisms. Beer, it seems, is here complying with the practice of *syllogisando*, or the practice of clothing arguments into threefold syllogisms to make them appear stronger.[110] The result is a structure so predictable that, sometimes, the reader is invited to fill in gaps on his own: *ergo etc.*; the conclusion is simply omitted. Startling, however, is that, within this so perfectly laid-out argumentation, Beer plants a fallacy, not in his opponent's argument but in his own second argument in favor of the proposition, by using the word "natural" in two senses. Thus undermining his own *probatio*, he appears to make fun not only of this particular method of persuasion, i.e. the syllogistic proof, but of rhetoric altogether. Beer's "humor of rhetoric," therefore, becomes a "parody of rhetoric."[111]

In the scherzo of Sonata 42 we certainly find plenty of humor *in* rhetoric. Somfai calls the movement "a rather broad joke";[112] indeed, it sets a high-spirited tone after the preceding, rather serious variation movement. But the orator not only diverts the listener; he also sneers at his opponent by chaotically heaping the latter's periphrasis figures on top of each other (*congeries*) and granting him permission to cadence (*permissio*).[113]

But does one find humor *of* rhetoric in the sonata? Having interpreted the opening period of the finale as the statement of the orator's opponent, I must answer in the negative. Although the planting of the fallacy in the opponent's argument is sly, the disentanglement of it is serious and complicated; the orator executes both tasks primarily not to "amuse" his audience but to convince them of his own point of view. However, in order to demonstrate that a fallacy has been planted in the first place—there is no "one will object" to make this clear—Haydn is forced to go against the listener's expectation of the very genre he is using, namely that of a scherzo. The finale, indeed, may have ended with an authentic cadence in D major in m. 45; such an ending would certainly have rendered the scherzo's proportions more usual. But this ending would have been premature, even senseless, without the refutation of the opening statement. By confronting the listener with an overtly failed attempt to cadence, the orator drastically makes the listener abandon his expectancy of a "normal" scherzo, in favor of a rhetorical structure that, in one sudden stroke, is superimposed onto the scherzo. Precisely in this conflict between two structures—the formal convention of a scherzo and a rhetorical *dispositio* of a sonata—lies the strength of the refutation not only within the finale itself but, more importantly, within the sonata as a whole. To perceive everything beyond m. 45 as "expansive" or "excessive" would be to have missed the point of this superimposing of layers. All these measures are necessary ingredients of a strong refutation, which, in its turn, is a prerequisite for the eventual conclusion. And this conclusion, from m. 88 to the end, rounds off not only a scherzo but the entire sonata.[114]

Thus, in my rhetorical reading, there is no room for "humor *of* rhetoric"; m. 45 is not so much a humorous as a bewildering event, which results in the shift from one layer—the musical scherzo—to another. Still, identifying the second layer as rhetorical provides in itself a moment of recognition (charmingly rendered in German as an *Aha!-Erlebnis)* that would gives a listener a new, deeper dimension of his musical amusement. This new understanding stands or falls with the listener's musical wit to perceive (dis)similarities, as described by Nikolaus Forkel:

> Musical *wit* consists in comparing remote similarities, which are not easily perceived by everybody. Its expression is best realized through different methods of imitation and is mostly based on the art of double counterpoint. We therefore delight ourselves in musical wit mostly because our mind is entertained when it perceives those similarities that it has not suspected at all, and is incited to exercise, even strain its powers.[115]

But wit, as defined by Forkel, is not enough, given that some of the similarities we perceive are meant to deceive us. The listener also needs judgment in order to "detect the differences of things seemingly alike.[116] Haydn not only persuades his listeners with a full display of "the arms of oratory," then, he also remains a master at actively engaging the talents of those listeners.

In investigating an anomaly—the proportions of the finale of a single sonata—this essay has uncovered both its networks of rhetorical strategies and the complex interactions between composer and listener necessary to fulfill its meaning.

NOTES

Except as otherwise noted, all English translations in this essay (and the notes that follow) are my own.

1. Somfai, *Joseph Haydn: Instruments and Performance, Practice, Genres and Styles*, trans. Charlotte Greenspan and the author (Chicago, 1995), pp. 170–80. The numbering of the Hoboken catalogue has been retained in the complete edition (*Joseph Haydn Werke*), published by Henle, ed. Georg Feder (Munich, 1972). The Universal edition by Christa Landon (Vienna, 1964–66) uses a different numbering system, according to which these sonatas are numbered 54–56. The Hoboken numbers will be used throughout this essay. See Antony van Hoboken, *Thematisch-Bibliographisches Werkverzeichnis*, vol. 1 (Mainz, 1957).

2. Franz Eibner, "Die Form des 'Vivace Assai' aus der Sonate D-dur Hob.XVI:42" in Eva Badura-Skoda, ed., *Joseph Haydn: Proceedings of the International Joseph Haydn Congress Wien 1982* (Munich, 1986), pp. 190–201.

3. Georg Feder deduces from this note that "Haydn, to some extent, confirmed the authenticity of the Bossler edition." See *Joseph Haydn Werke*, XVIII/ 3, p. VII. No autograph is extant.

4. See Somfai, *Keyboard Sonatas*, p. 302; Elaine R. Sisman, "Haydn's Solo Keyboard Music," in Robert Marshall, ed., *Eighteenth-Century Keyboard Music* (New York, 1994), p. 292.

5. Somfai, *Keyboard Sonatas*, p. 303. Somfai examines groups of movements of Haydn's sonata output, such as all first-movement sonata forms, all sonata forms in slow tempos, minuets, all scherzo forms in the finale, etc. Sisman, on the other hand, treats the sonatas one by one. The first approach has the definite advantage of classification and sheds light on Haydn's developing or changing habits in handling a certain "type"of movement; the second has the advantage of being able to focus more on the individual traits of a certain sonata, such as tonal, motivic, gestural, and other similarities or dissimilarities that may exist between movements of an individual piece.

6. Sisman, "Haydn's Solo Keyboard Music," p. 291.

7. In the genre of a keyboard sonata, this relationship remains similar to traditional deliberative oratory: one orator or performer tries to persuade an assembly or concert audience. When analyzing chamber music, e.g. a string quartet, one would have to construe an "orator": are the four string players speaking as one persona (the composer?) or are they conversing with each other? In the latter case, is their conversation noncommittal, or is it rhetorical, in the sense that the one tries to convince the other, and if that is the case, may it be even dialectical, in that all four are striving, through dialogue, for one truth?

8. See Johann Nikolaus Forkel, "Ueber eine Sonate aus Carl Phil. Emanuel Bachs dritter Sonatensammlung für Kenner und Liebhaber, in F moll," in *Musikalischer Almanach für Deutschland auf das Jahr 1784* (Leipzig, 1783, facs. ed. Hildesheim, 1974). For a translation of the essay and a critical commentary on Forkel's theory of musical rhetoric, as outlined in his lecture *Über die Theorie der Musik: insofern sie Liebhabern und Kennern nothwendig und nützlich ist* (1777) and his "Einleitung" to the *Allgemeine Geschichte der Musik* (Leipzig, 1788), see the first part of my dissertation "Forkel and Haydn: A Rhetorical Framework for the Analysis of Sonata Hob.XVI:42 (D)" (D.M.A. diss., Cornell University, 1996), pp. 16–183.

9. The idea of the integrated cycle has been taken up by Wilhelm Seidel, "Schnell—Langsam—Schnell. Zur 'klassischen' Theorie des instrumentalen Zyklus," in *Musiktheorie* 1 (1986): 206, and James Webster, *Haydn's "Farewell" Symphony and the Idea of Classical Style: Through-Composition and Cyclic Integration in His Instrumental Music* (Cambridge, 1991), p. 179. In Elaine R. Sisman's "Pathos and the *Pathétique*: Rhetorical Stance in Beethoven's C Minor Sonata, Op. 13," *Beethoven Forum* 3 (1994): 81–105, the concept of "the pathetic" is admirably traced throughout the sonata, but the actual analysis remains of selected passages only.

10. One would have to combine two analyses of Haydn's sonata in A Major, Hob.XVI:30, by James Webster (*Haydn's "Farewell" Symphony*, pp. 288–294) and Elaine R. Sisman (*Haydn and the Classical Variation* [Cambridge, Mass., 1993], pp. 40–47), to come up with a rhetorical analysis of a complete work. Apart from the rhetorical aspect, my endeavor to examine the inner relations of a work as a whole is inspired by Webster's work on cyclic integration and through-composition.

11. I have developed this argument elsewhere. See my "Forkel and Haydn," especially my "letter to Forkel," pp. 177–183.

12. I am here taking up the gauntlet thrown by rhetorician Brian Vickers, who criticized not only historical music theorists but also modern musicologists for mistranslating rhetorical into musico-rhetorical terms: "Modern musicologists who simply endorse the unsupported analogies and begged questions of their eighteenth-century predecessors build on equally flimsy foundations." See his review of George Barth, *The Pianist as Orator: Beethoven and the Transformation of Keyboard Style* in *Rhetorica* 13 (1995): 100, as well as his "Figures of Rhetoric/Figures of Music?" in *Rhetorica* 2 (1984): 1–44. An excellent and rigorous introduction to classical rhetoric is Heinrich Lausberg, *Handbuch der literarischen Rhetorik: Eine Grundlegung der Literaturwissenschaft*, 2 volumes (Munich, 1960).

13. See, for example, the heading "The Decline of Neoclassical Rhetoric," in George A. Kennedy, *Classical Rhetoric and Its Christian and Secular Tradition from Ancient to Modern Times* (Chapel Hill, 1980), pp. 240–41.

14. David Schroeder, *Haydn and the Enlightenment; the Late Symphonies and their Audience* (Oxford, 1990), p. 21, gives the latter as the "historical view" and cites Giuseppe Carpani for the paradoxical characterization of Haydn as "an illustrious idiot." *Le Haydine* (Milan, 1812).

15. See the Introduction to S. IJsseling and G. Vervaecke, eds., *Renaissances of Rhetoric* (Leuven, 1994), p.1: "Rhetoric was . . . declared dead by two—at first sight apparently opposing—trends in Western culture. On the one hand there was the 'rational' school of thought, which demanded 'objectivity,' i.e., laws, structures, predictability and verifiableness, and fixed order. . . . On the other hand, there was the 'romantic' drift, which demanded absolute freedom and originality in the name of the individual."

16. Immanuel Kant, *Critique of Judgement* (1790), trans. J. H. Barnard (New York, 1951), p. 171.

17. See, for example, the subheading "The End of Rhetoric: A Historical Sketch" in John Bender and David E. Wellbery, "Rhetoricality: On the Modernist Return of Rhetoric" in their *The Ends of Rhetoric: History, Theory, Practice* (Stanford, 1990), pp. 3–39; Jane Sutton, "The Death of Rhetoric and Its Rebirth in Philosophy" in *Rhetorica* 4 (1986): 203–22; Marilyn Sides, "Rhetoric on the Brink of Banishment: D'Alembert on Rhetoric in the Encyclopédie" in *Rhetorik* 3 (1983): 111–24; Josef Kopperschmidt, "Rhetorik nach dem Ende der Rhetorik: Einleitende Anmerkungen zum heutigen Interesse an Rhetorik," in Kopperschmidt, ed., *Rhetorik*, vol. 1: *Rhetorik als Texttheorie* (Darmstadt, 1990), pp. 1–34.

18. Carl Joachim Classen, "The Role of Rhetoric Today," in S. IJsseling and G. Vervaecke, eds. *Renaissances of Rhetoric*, p. 29.

19. Ursula Stötzer, *Deutsche Redekunst im 17. und 18. Jahrhundert* (Halle, 1962), pp. 92–93. In 1759, Gottsched lists the three classical kinds of oratory, but then says that in view of the "totally changed system of rulership" (*die ganz veränderte Regimentsform*) in Germany only the epideictic kind is still in use. He proceeds by offering a new but again threefold division of oratory into "laudatory speeches towards persons of high rank," "speeches of teaching in church and school," and "complimentary speeches ordered by the principal." See Johann Christoph Gottsched, "Ausführliche Redekunst, nach Anleitung der alten Griechen und Römer" (Leipzig, 1759) in P. M. Mitchell, ed., *Johann Christoph Gottsched. Ausgewählte Werke* vol. 7/1 (Berlin, 1975), p. 67. See also Gert Ueding, *Einführung in die Rhetorik: Geschichte, Technik, Methode* (Stuttgart, 1976), pp. 100–5.

20. See Johann Georg Sulzer, in his *Allgemeine Theorie der schönen Künste* (1771–74), for instance: "Modern authors have left the theory of this art more or less there, where the ancient ones have stopped. At least, I would not know which newer writings I would recommend for further study to him who has studied Cicero and Quintilian." Quoted by Gert Ueding, *Einführung*, p.111. Also Christian Fürchtegott Gellert: "I believe that whoever in oratory has read the rules of Aristotle, Cicero, Quintilian and Longinus, has read the most excellent in this art," in his lecture on "The Use of the Rules in Oratory and Poetry" (*Wie weit sich der Nutzen der Regeln in der Beredsamkeit und Poesie erstrecke*) in W. Jung, J. F. Reynolds, B. Witte, eds., *Christian Fürchtegott Gellert: Gesammelte Schriften* vol. 5 (Berlin, 1994), p. 201.

21. See Thomas O. Sloane, "Schoolbooks and Rhetoric: Erasmus's *Copia*," in *Rhetorica* 9 (1991): 1. For a historical list of German handbooks on rhetoric from 1750 to 1900, see Dieter Breuer and Günther Kopsch, "Rhetoriklehrbücher des 16. bis 20. Jahrhunderts: eine Bibliographie," in Helmut Schanze, ed. *Rhetorik. Beiträge zu ihrer Geschichte in Deutschland vom 16.–20. Jahrhundert* (Frankfurt am Main, 1974), pp. 293–337.

22. In Belgium, classical-humanistic education prevailed, although probably in a less rigid form, until very recently. My own three last high school years in the early 1980s were still called respectively "syntaxis," "poesis," and finally—as the crown on the work—"rhetorica."

23. Desiderius Erasmus of Rotterdam, *On Copia of Words and Ideas* (De utraque verborum ac rerum copia), trans. D. B. King and H. D. Rix (Milwaukee, 1963), pp. 17–18. See Patricia Bizzell and Bruce Herzberg, eds., *The Rhetorical Tradition: Readings from Classical Times to the Present* (Boston, 1990), pp. 499–500.

24. See Peter France, "Quintilian and Rousseau: Oratory and Education," *Rhetorica* 13 (1995): 306.

25. Carpani, *Le Haydine ovvero lettere sulla vita e le opere del celebre Maestro Giuseppe Haydn*, 2nd ed. (Padua, 1823; facs. ed. Bologna, 1969), p. 71.

26. See Hans Lenneberg, "Johann Mattheson on Affect and Rhetoric in Music" in *Journal of Music Theory* 2 (1958): 204; Johann Mattheson, *Der vollkommene Capellmeister* (Hamburg, 1739; facs. ed. Kassel, 1954), p. 17.

27. "For all a Rhetorician's Rules/ Teach nothing but to name his Tools." Samuel Butler, *Hudibras* (1663, 1664, 1678), ed. John Wilders (Oxford, 1967), The First Part, Canto I, 89–90.

28. Georg Feder, "Joseph Haydn als Mensch und Musiker" in *Joseph Haydn und seine Zeit*, Jahrbuch für Österreichische Kulturgeschichte 2 (Eisenstadt, 1972); Herbert Zeman, ed., *Joseph Haydn und die Literatur seiner Zeit*, Jahrbuch für Österreichische Kulturgeschichte 6 (1976), and especially Maria Hörwarthner's "Joseph Haydns

Bibliothek—Versuch einer literarhistorischen Rekonstruktion," pp. 157–207 [translated in this volume]; Schroeder, *Haydn and the Enlightenment*; Webster, *Haydn's "Farewell" Symphony*; Sisman, *Haydn and the Classical Variation*.

29. See Alfred Mann, "Haydn as Student and Critic of Fux" in H. C. Robbins Landon, ed. *Studies in Eighteenth-Century Music: A Tribute to Karl Geiringer on his Seventieth Birthday* (New York, 1970), pp. 323–32, and "Haydn's Elementarbuch: A Document of Classic Counterpoint Instruction," *The Music Forum* 3 (1973): 197–237. Feder also points out Haydn's "striking preference for Latin *sententiae*" and his part songs on texts by Horace (in Latin) and Anakreon (translated from Greek). See Georg Feder, "Joseph Haydn als Mensch und Musiker," p. 47.

30. Griesinger writes: "Besides the scant instruction usual at the time in Latin, in religion, in arithmetic and writing, Haydn had in the Choir School very capable instructors on several instruments, and especially in singing." See Georg August Griesinger, *Biographische Notizen über Joseph Haydn* (1810), trans. Vernon Gotwals in *Haydn: Two Contemporary Portraits* (Madison, 1968), p. 10.

31. See Sisman, *Haydn and the Classical Variation*, p. 24.

32. Cicero, *In Catilinam* I, 1, quoted by Quintilian as an example of a rhetorical question; Marcus Fabius Quintilianus, *Institutio Oratoria*, 4 vols., trans. H. E. Butler (Cambridge, Mass., 1920), vol. 3, IX.ii.7.

33. See Sisman, *Haydn and the Classical Variation*, pp. 24–25.

34. Haydn said to his biographer Dies, "Several times I took the liberty of not offending the ear, of course, but breaking the usual textbook rules, and wrote beneath these places the words 'con licenza.'" Albert Christoph Dies, *Biographische Nachrichten von Joseph Haydn* (1810), trans. Gotwals in *Haydn*, p. 109. See Jürgen Neubacher, *Finis coronat opus. Untersuchungen zur Technik der Schlußgestaltung in der Instrumentalmusik Joseph Haydns, dargestellt am Beispiel der Streichquartette. Mit einem Exkurs: Haydn und die rhetorische Tradition* (Tutzing, 1986), p. 179.

35. The second movement of the C-sharp minor Sonata Hob.XVI:36 and the first movement of the G major Sonata Hob.XVI:39. Both are types of alternating variation movements.

36. Dénes Bartha, ed. *Joseph Haydn. Gesammelte Briefe und Aufzeichnungen* (Kassel, 1965), pp. 90–91, trans. Landon, *Collected Correspondence and London Notebooks of Joseph Haydn* (London, 1959), p. 25 (slightly altered).

37. Quintilian, *Institutio oratoria*, vol. 3, IX.ii.16.

38. Sisman and Neubacher have explored this in more detail. See Sisman, *Haydn and the Classical Variation*, pp. 120–21 and Jürgen Neubacher, "'Idee' und 'Ausführung.' Zum Kompositionsprozeß bei Joseph Haydn," *Archiv für Musikwissenschaft* 41 (1984): 187–207.

39. Georg August Griesinger, *Biographische Notizen*, in Gotwals, *Haydn*, p. 61.

40. See Hollace Ann Schafer, "'A Wisely Ordered Phantasie': Joseph Haydn's Creative Process from the Sketches and Drafts for Instrumental Music" (Ph.D. diss., Brandeis University, 1987), pp. 1–5.

41. Sisman, *Haydn and the Classical Variation*, p. 25.

42. Somfai, *Keyboard Sonatas of Joseph Haydn*, pp. 302–3.

43. A. Peter Brown, *Joseph Haydn's Keyboard Music*, p. 330.

44. Somfai's discussion of Haydn's four scherzo-type finales includes two scherzi in triple meter (3/4): the Presto of Hob.XVI:51 (D) and the Allegro molto of Hob.XVI:50 (C). See Somfai, *The Keyboard Sonatas of Joseph Haydn*, pp. 299–303.

45. Ibid., p. 302n; Somfai, "Opus-Planung und Neuerung bei Haydn," *Studia Musicologica* 22 (1980): 91n.

46. Somfai comments that "the whole movement is no longer than a rondo theme" (*Keyboard Sonatas of Joseph Haydn*, p. 302n). In conversation, Malcolm Bilson has expressed his suspicion about the completeness of this movement. However, the work was published with Haydn's consent in an opus dedicated to Prince Esterházy, a venue hardly suggestive of carelessness or lack of zeal. Moreover, an earlier scherzo with similar contour (||:8:||:16:||) is found in Hob.XVI:9 in F Major. Even if Haydn were eager to finish the Prince Esterházy set and opted for a hasty solution (and the recycling of the earlier *a rovescio* minuet from Symphony no. 47 as second movement could support this view), we still have no choice but to accept the published form as complete.

47. The formal paradox between the two movements is that the finale of 42 has the more "normal" absolute length of the two: 101 measures as opposed to 26; no. 26, however, has the more "normal" proportions: 8 + 18 as opposed to 8 + 93.

48. Somfai, *Keyboard Sonatas of Joseph Haydn*, p. 302.

49. According to Leopold Mozart, one should "attack the first of the slurred notes somewhat more strongly and connect the others quite gently and ever more softly." See his *Versuch einer gründlichen Violinschule*, 3rd ed. (Augsburg, 1787), p. 136.

50. An orator uses a *suspensio* to keep his audience in suspense about the outcome of something. As is often the case, Quintilian's definition of *suspensio* (or *sustentatio*) originates from a court situation: "Sometimes, . . . in such forms of communication we may add something unexpected, a device which is in itself a figure, as Cicero does in the *Verrines*: 'What then? What think you? Perhaps you expect to hear of some theft or plunder.' Then, after keeping the minds of the judges in suspense for a considerable time, he adds something much worse." Quintilian, *Institutio oratoria*, IX.ii.22.

51. Marpurg uses the term "figure" in the non-rhetorical or "mechanical" sense of "motive." See Friedrich Wilhelm Marpurg, *Anleitung zum Clavierspielen*, 2nd ed. (Berlin, 1765; facs. ed. New York, 1969), p. 39. For his definition of *vermischte Figur*, *Halbzirkel*, and *lauffende Figur*, see pp. 42–43.

52. See Quintilian, *Institutio oratoria*, VIII.vi.59.

53. Ibid., VIII.vi.61.

54. Rhetorical figures are divided into two groups: figures of speech (*figurae elocutionis*) and figures of thought (*figurae sententiarum*). Quintilian writes: "It is . . . agreed by the majority of authors that there are two classes of *figures*, namely *figures of thought*, that is of the mind [*mentis*], feeling [*sensus*] or conceptions [*sententiarum*], since all these terms are used, and *figures of speech*, that is of words [*verborum*], diction [*dictionis*], expression [*elocutionis*], language [*sermonis*] or style [*orationis*]: the name by which they are known varies, but mere terminology is a matter of indifference." *Institutio oratoria*, IX.i.16. This distinction cannot simply and wholly be reduced to the one between *inventio* and *elocutio*. It is true that figures of thought have more affinity with *inventio* than figures of speech, but the difference mainly lies in their verbal expression: whereas figures of speech "stand or fall" with their verbal formulations, figures of thought have a choice among many possibilities of verbal expression. See Heinrich Lausberg, *Handbuch der literarischen Rhetorik*, § 755.

55. Johann Beer or Bähr (1652–1700) is listed in Johann Mattheson's *Grundlage einer Ehren-Pforte woran der tüchtigsten Capellmeister, Componisten, Musikgelehrten, Tonkünstler [etc.] Leben, Wercke, Verdienste [etc.] erscheinen sollen* (Hamburg, 1740), ed. Max Schneider (Kassel, 1969), pp. 14–16. See also Adolf Schmiedecke, "Johann Beer und die Musik" in *Die Musikforschung* 18 (1965): 4–11. A remarkable figure in 17th-century German literature, Beer was "discovered" by Richard Alewyn only some 65 years ago. See James Hardin, *Johann Beer* (Boston, 1983); Johann Beer, *Sämtliche Werke*, ed. Ferdinand van Ingen and Hans-Gert Roloff (Bern, 1981).

56. *Musikalische Diskurse (*Nüremberg, 1719; facs. ed. Leipzig, 1982), ch. XV.

57. See Otto Erich Deutsch, "Haydns Musikbücherei" in R. Baum and W. Rehm, eds. *Musik und Verlag: Karl Vötterle zum 65. Geburtstag am 12. April 1968* (Kassel, 1968), p. 220.

58. *Außer der Castration* is difficult to interpret. I take "outside of the castration" to mean: "not taking into account the castration" or "in spite of the castration." Another possibility, which differs only in nuance, would be to assume an *ellipsis* of "Stimme": 'apart from the castrated [voice].' Yet another option is "uncastrated." Although the latter would still display the same kind of arguing from assumption, I find it more likely that Beer's assumption happens within the context of "being castrated."

59. Listed as number (92) in Maria Hörwarthner, "Joseph Haydns Bibliothek." Only the second volume was present.

60. Quoted in Hubert Ortkemper, *Engel wider Willen: die Welt der Kastraten* (Berlin, 1993), pp. 26–27.

61. Sometimes even in forensic rhetoric, however, it may be found convenient to state and answer a *quaestio* in a straightforward way, especially if one is to convince a perspicacious judge. See Quintilian, *Institutio oratoria*, IV.i.72.

62. A *quaestio* is either definite or indefinite (Quintilian III.v.4ff.). If definite, it is concerned with particular facts, persons, etc, as in Quintilian's example: "Should Cato marry?" Its typical context is forensic oratory. The indefinite *quaestio* is abstract and belongs to the realm of philosophers, as in Quintilian's example: "Should a man marry?" Furthermore, a *quaestio* can be either simple ("whether a man is dead") or complex ("whether he died of poison or some internal disease"). See Quintilian III. v.4 ff. Beer's *quaestio* is both indefinite and complex. A finite *quaestio* could have been: "With what voice does Farinelli sing?" A simple, indefinite *quaestio* could have been: "Whether castrati sing with a natural voice?"

63. In German treatises of the seventeenth and eighteenth centuries, these terms are *Obersatz, Untersatz,* and *Schlußsatz.*See Ursula Stötzer, *Deutsche Redekunst*, p. 49 and, as an example, Gottsched, *Redekunst*, pp. 263–64.

64. On credibility, see Quintilian, *Institutio oratoria*, V, x, 19; on the enthymeme, see ibid., V.xiv.24.

65. See Quintilian V.xiv.25.

66. See Cicero, "De inventione" I.xxxiv.58–59 in Cicero, *De Inventione, De Optimo Genere Oratorum, Topica*, trans. H. M. Hubbell (Cambridge, Mass., 1949). Analyzed in Frans H. van Eemeren, Rob Grootendorst, Tjark Kruiger, *Argumentatietheorie*, 2nd ed. (Utrecht, 1981), p. 93.

67. Quintilian, *Institutio oratoria*, V.xiv.6.

68. Ellipsis is the omission of one or more words, which can be easily understood. Gottsched gives the following example: "'O weakness!' stands for: 'O what a weakness that is!'" See Gottsched, *Redekunst*, p. 346.

69. *Traductio* is the traditional "pun." The equality in material of two words is coincidental, as in Pascal's *Le coeur a ses raisons que la raison ne connaît pas* ("The heart has its reasons [causes], that reason [*ratio*] does not know"; Pensées 277). In *distinctio*, however, one makes a distinction between two interpretations of a meaning of a word, as Corneille does in *Votre raison n'est pas raison pour moi* ("Your reason is not a reason for me"; Le Cid 2, 6, 599).

70. Both syllogisms are of the so-called "barbara-type," consisting of three universal-affirmative propositions. See W. de Pater and R. Vergauwen, *Logica: formeel en informeel* (Louvain, 1992), p. 113.

71. Quintilian calls this figure "an elegant straining of the truth"; *Insitutio oratoria*, VII.vi.67–68.

72. Since Aristotle, proofs (*pisteis*) or *probationes* have generally been divided into inartificial and artificial ones. "To the first class belong," according to Quintilian, "decisions of previous courts, rumors, evidence extracted by torture, documents, oaths, and witnesses [.]" These proofs are provided by the case itself. The artificial proofs, on the other hand, belong to the art of rhetoric and are to be provided by the orator. The orator, as Quintilian formulates it, "deduces or, if I may use the term, begets [them] out of his case." Artificial proofs are divided into "indications, arguments [and] examples." See Quintilian, *Institutio oratorai*, V.i.2; V.i.1; V.ix.1.

73. "Finally, that the sound of a castrato voice considerably distinguished itself from the character of a child's or woman's voice by its unnaturalness, was caused by the fact that, while the larynx remained small (almost childish), the whole apparatus (windpipe, breath volume, chest and resonance spaces) was at its disposal." Translated from Hans Fritz, *Kastratengesang. Hormonelle, konstitutionelle und Pädagogische Aspekte* (Tutzing, 1994), p. 59.

74. See Ludwig Wittgenstein, *Philosophical Investigations*, trans. G. E. M. Anscombe (Oxford, 1953), I, § 66.

75. See Sisman, *Haydn and the Classical Variation*, pp. 120–21, 186–91.

76. Somfai, *Keyboard Sonatas of Joseph Haydn*, p. 334.

77. Ibid., p. 335.

78. The numerous rests in this theme and that of 48 are often referred to as "rhetorical." "Rhetorical" in this context, it seems to me, means "speech-like," rather than "argumentative" or "persuasive." This speech-like style might indeed embody, in Sisman's words (about 48), "a conscious attempt to please a north-German audience, hitherto very critical of [Haydn's] work." See her "Haydn's Solo Keyboard Music," p. 292.

79. Koch, *Musikalisches Lexikon* (1802), quoted in Sisman, *Haydn and the Classical Variation*, p. 73.

80. Sisman, *Haydn and the Classical Variation*, p. 189.

81. *Allgemeine Geschichte der Musik*, vol. 1, p. 51.

82. Elaine Sisman analyzes 30/iii in such a way in *Haydn and the Classical Variation*, pp. 43–47.

83. *Distributio* takes up single parts of a whole and expands on each of them. Lee A. Sonnino gives the following example from Wilson: "He apparelleth himself with great distinction. For the stuff, his clothes were more rich than glittering; as for the fashion, rather usual for his sort than fantastical for his invention; for colour, more grave and uniform than wild and light; for fitness, made as well for ease of exercise as to set forth to the eye those parts which in him had most excellency." See Sonnino, *A Handbook to Sixteenth-Century Rhetoric* (London, 1968), p. 81.

84. They both were of the "barbara-type."

85. *Dubitatio* is an utterance of doubt or uncertainty. It "offers a certain faith in truth [*adfert aliquam fidem veritatis*], when we pretend [*simulamus*] to be searching where to begin, where to end; what preferably needs to be said or whether it needs to be said at all." See Quintilian, *Institutio oratoria*, IX.ii.19. His example is from Cicero, *Pro Cluentio*: "As for myself, I know not where to turn. Shall I deny that there was a scandalous rumor that the jury had been bribed, etc.?"

86. Before discussing ornament, Quintilian treats "its opposite, since the first of all virtues is the avoidance of faults." *Institutio oratoria*, VIII.iii.51.

87. Quintilian writes (IX.ii.17): "There is a form of self-correction [*emendatio*] such as, "I beg you to pardon me, if I have been carried too far." The Latin *correctio* is the equivalent of the Greek metanoia (metanoia), "repentence" for what one has just said.

See Lausberg, *Handbuch*, § 785.

88. See Quintilian, *Institutio oratoria*, IX.ii.40.

89. See Somfai, *The Keyboard Sonatas of Joseph Haydn*, p. 303.

90. *Congeries* is an accumulation or piling up of words, as in "The woman, the savage cruelty of the tyrant, love for his father, anger beyond control, the madness of blind daring," an example given by Quintilian, *Institutio oratoria*, IX.iii.48. Concerning this example Lausberg notes that "the tendency for chaotic enumeration is apparent." *Handbuch*, § 671, n. 1.

91. See Lausberg, *Handbuch*, § 426.

92. As "Every beginning is difficult." The definition is from Susenbrotus. See Sonnino, *Handbook*, p. 167. The example is from *Ad Herennium* (IV.xvi.24).

93. Steven E. Paul quotes these measures, along with Hob.XVI:39/iii and 40/ii, as an example of a "quiet, understated ending." See Steven E. Paul, "Comedy, Wit and Humor in Haydn's Instrumental Music," in *Haydn Studies*, ed. Jens Peter Larsen, Howard Serwer, and James Webster (New York, 1981) p. 454. Emphasis, Quintilian says (VIII. iii. 83), "succeeds in revealing a deeper meaning than is actually expressed by the words. There are two kinds of emphasis: the one means more than it says, the other often means something which it does not actually say. An example of the former is found in Homer, where he makes Menelaus say that the Greeks 'descended' into the Wooden Horse, indicating its size by a single verb. . . . The second kind of emphasis consists either in the complete suppression of a word or in the deliberate omission to utter it." Interesting to the performer is Peacham's 16th-century definition (cited in Sonnino, *Handbook*, p. 201): "A form of speech which signifieth that which it does not express, the signification whereof is understood either by the manner of the pronunciation, or by the nature of the words themselves." Conveying the full impact of mm. 100–101 through pronunciation is a challenge indeed.

94. A more detailed examination of the first-movement variations appears in my "Forkel and Haydn," pp. 241–52.

95. Proofs can be *a simile*, *a dissimile* or *a contrario*. Quintilian explains (V.xi.6–7): "We argue from the like [*simile*] when we say, "Saturninus was justly killed, as were the Gracchi"; from the unlike [*dissimile*] when we say. "Brutus killed his sons for plotting against the state, while Manlius condemned his son to death for his valor"; from the contrary [*contrarium*] when we say, "Marcellus restored the works of art which had been taken from the Syracusans who were our enemies, while Verres took the same works of art from our allies."

96. See Somfai, *The Keyboard Sonatas of Joseph Haydn*, p. 340

97. See Sisman, *Haydn and the Classical Variation*, p. 189

98. A. Peter Brown, *Joseph Haydn's Keyboard Music. Sources and Style*, p. 327.

99. "In those sets with related themes, one may also speak of the figure *contrarium*, or *reasoning by contraries*, which uses one of two opposing statements to prove the other." Sisman, *Haydn and the Classical Variation*, p. 159.

100. See Quintilian VI.i.1.

101. See Quintilian VI.i.2.

102. "Transition [*transitio*] . . . reminds the hearer of what the speaker has said, and also prepares him for what is to come." See *Ad Herennium*, IV.xxvi.35.

103. "Haydn macht es wie ein schlauer Redner, der, wenn er uns zu etwas überreden will, von einem allgemein als wahr anerkannten Sazze ausgeht, den jeder einsieht, jeder begreifen muß, bald aber diesen Saz so geschikt zu wenden versteht, daß er uns zu allen überreden kann, wozu er will, und wärs zum Gegentheil des aufgestellten Sazzes." See Ignaz Theodor Ferdinand Arnold, *Gallerie der berühmtesten Tonkünstler des*

achtzehnten und neunzehnten Jahrhunderts. Ihre kurzen Biografieen, karakterisirende Anekdoten und ästhetische Darstellung ihrer Werke. Erster Theil (Erfurt, 1810; facs. ed. Buren, The Netherlands, 1984), p. 110.

104. The distinction between "le comique *dans* la rhétorique" and "le comique *de* la rhétorique" was introduced by Charles Perelman and Lucie Olbrechts-Tyteca, the godparents of the Brussels school of *Nouvelle Rhétorique*: See their *Traité de l'Argumentation: la nouvelle rhétorique*, 2nd ed. (Brussels, 1970), p. 253; in English as *The New Rhetoric: A Treatise on Argumentation* (Notre Dame, 1969). The distinction is elaborated upon by Olbrechts-Tyteca in her *Le comique du discours* (Brussels, 1974).

105. We make use of "humor" in a broad sense, without taking into account distinctions among terms such as humor, wit, joke, jest etc., let alone their eighteenth-century German equivalents—*Laune, Witz* etc. For such a differentiation, see Gretchen A. Wheelock, *Haydn's Ingenious Jesting with Art: Contexts of Musical Wit and Humor* (New York, 1992), ch. 2.

106. Quintilian VI.iii.1.

107. "Was die *Musici* so wol von sich selbst/ als auch andere Leute von ihnen zu judiciren pflegen?—Ob ein *Componist necessario* müsse studirt haben." See Johann Beer, *Musikalische Diskurse*, ch. 17, 16 and 41.

108. Quintilian VI.iii.23.

109. See Lucie Olbrechts-Tyteca, *Le comique du discours*, p. 8.

110. This practice became widespread in scholastic rhetoric, especially in preaching.

111. This observation falls in line with Hardin's: "Countless passages in Beer's novels satirize neoscholastic syllogistic methods that had lost their pedagogical value and had become mere exercises in hairsplitting." See James Hardin, *Johann Beer*, p. 5.

112. See Somfai, *The Keyboard Sonatas*, p. 302.

113. The pianistically awkward parallel thirds of mm. 19–20 may be intended by the orator as a kind of tongue twister so that, at the level of *pronuntiatio*, he mocks his opponent's lack of technical mastery. I thank Robert Winter for this observation. In my own performances, I have always found mm. 19–20 much harder to perform than mm. 77–78, when the passage recurs for the second time and the hand has become more relaxed. Then, the orator takes responsibility for his words, which he now executes well enough to impress his audience. Stumbling the first time around, thus, is for the performer nothing to be ashamed of; on the contrary, it totally fits the context of irony.

114. Making this point in my own performance, I repeat mm. 9–87 only, leaving the definitive conclusion of mm. 88–101 to the very end. See Tom Beghin, *Joseph Haydn. Sonaten voor Pianoforte/Sonatas for Fortepiano* (CD Eufoda 1230; Louvain, 1996).

115. See Johann Nikolaus Forkel, "Commentar über die 1777 gedruckte Abhandlung über die Theorie etc.," partly reproduced in Andreas Liebert, *Die Bedeutung des Wertesystems der Rhetorik für das deutsche Musikdenken im 18. und 19. Jahrhundert* (Frankfurt am Main, 1993), p. 305. On this commentary, a manuscript not in Forkel's hand but probably written by someone who attended his lectures, see Wolfgang Auhagen, "Meine Herren! Die Sympathie der Töne . . . " in *Concerto* 2/4 (1985), p. 34.

116. Wheelock, *Haydn's Ingenious Jesting with Art*, p. 68. The distinction between wit and judgment is made by John Locke in his *Essay Concerning Human Understanding* (1690), quoted by Wheelock p. 21: Wit is the "assemblage of ideas, and putting those together with quickness and variety, wherein can be found any resemblance or congruity." *Judgment*, on the other hand, requires "separation of ideas wherein can be found the least difference, thereby to avoid being misled by similitude, and by affinity to take one thing for another."

The Demise of Philosophical Listening: Haydn in the 19th Century

LEON BOTSTEIN

I. Peculiar Agreements: The Consensus Regarding Haydn.

The history of the critical and cultural reception of music remains inextricably bound to shifting conceptions of what, in the final analysis, constitutes the work of music. When a historically discrete musical public—that is, listeners and amateur performers—maintains over time particular conceptions of how music functions, what music means, and what the essence of the musical experience is, expectations about music become a crucial factor in the formation of musical culture. Indeed, major shifts in reigning attitudes alter the course of compositional ambitions; they also force a reconstruction of the narrative of music history.[1]

The nineteenth century, for example, saw a shift away from the initial early Romantic emphasis on music as an aesthetic experience in real time tied to the imagination and the nearly inarticulate inner self—music as performed, heard, and remembered—a concept best described in the late-eighteenth-century writings of such early Romantics as Jean Paul and Wackenroder. The premium they placed on instrumental music, similar to the approach to the instrumental music of Beethoven evident in E.T. A. Hoffmann, was based on a normative expectation of what the impact of music ideally ought to be. Although "music as experience" retained its prestige with particular composers and sectors of the public, later in the century the emphasis shifted to an allegiance to music as text, to the printed score, which became analogous to a book that might be sampled, read, studied, and returned to at will. The character of this approach to music demanded of the listener and amateur a self-conscious awareness of history, tradition, and precedent. An attitude towards music as a mirror of the historical moment, representative of the generation of Eduard Hanslick and Johannes Brahms, was not uppermost in the early Romantic enthusiasm for music.

Despite such shifts in fundamental expectations and norms of reception over the nineteenth century, the critical response to Haydn's music—whether understood as a performed event or as a text to be studied and re-read—did not change. The significant disputes during the nineteenth century involving musical taste and culture altered the view of Bach, Mozart, and Beethoven, but not the understanding of Haydn. In the case of no other major composer was there as little evolution, so much consistency, so little genuine shift in aesthetic judgment and response. And until quite recently, this static and recalcitrant nineteenth-century perception seemed to have left an indelible mark on twentieth-century assessments of Haydn as well.

Consider, for example, the contrast between the shifting reception of Mozart's music and the stasis in attitudes towards Haydn. In the 1881 revision of his classic 1854 tract on the inherent autonomy of music, *On the Beautiful in Music*, Eduard Hanslick used the change in Mozart reception, and thus in the representation of Viennese classicism itself, as a way of strengthening the anti-Wagnerian argument that emotion could not serve as the essential content of music. Whereas a few generations earlier Mozart's symphonies had been seen as vehicles of "vehement passion, bitter struggle, and piercing agony" that contrasted with the "tranquillity and wholesomeness of Haydn," the two composers now had become amalgamated as part of an "Olympian classicism."[2] Mozart, once favored by the early-nineteeth-century Romantics, had become more like Haydn. By the end of the nineteenth century, this distanced image of Mozart was abandoned again, as witnessed by the Mozart revival of the fin de siècle.[3] But Haydn stayed in the same place.

Throughout the nineteenth century, no one sensed a need to challenge the predominant view of Haydn's music. The perception of Haydn as innocent, naive, cheerful, healthy, supremely well-crafted but essentially entertaining and emotionally distant, if not irrelevant, displayed a tenacious constancy. E.T. A. Hoffmann had set the stage with his claim that "Haydn's compositions are dominated by a feeling of childlike optimism. . . a world of love, of bliss, of eternal youth. . . no suffering, no pain; only sweet, melancholy longing for the beloved vision." In this sense Haydn becomes the basis upon which "Mozart leads us deep into the realm of spirits." And, of course, Beethoven "sets in motion the machinery of awe, of fear, of terror, of pain and awakens the infinite yearning which is the essence of romanticism."[4] This interpretation was reinforced by Carpani's epistolary Haydn biography of 1812, and from the evident restraint and caveats in Stendhal's version of Carpani a decade later.[5] These two writers compared Haydn to a master genre or landscape painter—to Claude Lorrain, the great seventeenth-century painter—whose canvases, despite their virtues, did not provide the beholder with an evident subjective viewpoint or the self-conscious opportunity to invent a passionate, interior response. By 1812, Haydn was already distanced and historical. The isolated individual placed within the landscape and the outer world, the figure to be found or implied in the paintings of Caspar David Friedrich, was absent from this conception of landscape painting. While Beethoven would be routinely linked with Friedrich, Haydn would rather be compared with Tintoretto (as he was by Schumann)[6] or (stylistically) with David. He would not be compared with Delacroix. One explanation for this was offered by Adolf Bernhard Marx, who pointed to Haydn's relative monothematicism, as opposed to the greater dialectical tension of contrasting themes in the sonata forms of Mozart and Beethoven later favored by Romanticism.[7]

Critical comparisons of Haydn to a distant but honored precursor such as Lorrain or Tintoretto allowed nineteenth-century composers and commentators to lavish praise on Haydn's technical command and his role in the development of instrumental music, particularly the sonata, quartet, and symphony. Yet Haydn was condemned to a form of aesthetic and cultural irrelevance. Where the Bach revival led to a revaluation of Bach as a figure at once historical and contemporary, Haydn served throughout the nineteenth century as a merely historical one. He was the acknowledged master, the father of autonomous instrumental musical discourse. Meanwhile his music was said to be bereft of profound emotional inspiration or narrative significance.

The search for meaning in Haydn did not get very far beyond formalism. Schopenhauer may have been inspired by Haydn's music to discover the possibilities of self-referential meaning, autonomy, and significance in music, but he overlooked Haydn's overt attempts to convey extramusical meaning. Johann Friedrich Herbart rejected altogether the significance of the text in *The Creation* and *The Seasons*, declaring, "fortunately, [Haydn's] music needs no text; it is mere curiosity that impels us to know what he has tried to illustrate. His music is simply music, and it needs no meaning to make it beautiful." An admirable but bloodless notion of formal perfection was conceded, but that was all.[8]

Haydn conceivably could have provided a rallying point for mid-century proponents of so-called absolute music, the ideal of purely musical meaning. Indeed, to them Haydn's consummate craftsmanship was preferable to fashion and philistinism. In comments made in 1839, Schumann hailed "Altvater" Haydn as welcome relief from "this chronically diseased era of music," in which one only rarely could be "inwardly satisfied." Haydn, whose music offered satisfaction because of its conservative integrity, provided relief from a painful awareness of inadequacy by being "clear as sunlight . . . bereft of any sense of ennui with life, and inspiring nothing except for joy, love of life, and a childlike happiness about everything. . ." Still, Haydn's virtues did not connect to the sensibilities that led Schumann to embrace Thomas Moore's "Lalla Rookh" as an inspiration for his *Das Paradies und die Peri*.[9] In January 1841 Schumann displayed his usual weariness with the old master, complaining that "Haydn's music has always been played here often and one can no longer experience anything new with him. He is like a familiar friend of the family [*Hausfreund*] whom one meets always with respect and gladly. But a deeper relevance for today's world he does not possess."[10]

Schumann's heirs—Hanslick and other anti-Wagnerians—struck the same note. Writing in November 1856, just two years after the completion of his magnum opus, Hanslick noted in a review of quartet concerts:

> One began as usual with Haydn, the father of the quartet, a praiseworthy custom, so long as one does not neglect the sons in relation to the father. The representation of the old master with two works in a cycle of six evenings is entirely sufficient. In the first place, on account of nearly one hundred years of unrivalled attention, Haydn's quartets are so deeply rooted in our blood, not only on the part of amateurs but Haydn's successors as composers, that we feel, in the case of every one of these clear and cheerful musical works, that we are encountering an old friend. Furthermore, it was part of the historical character of the Haydn era that his quartets represented much more the common elements of a genre than a differentiated, sharply defined individuality. It is revealing that one always refers to "a Haydn quartet" whereas one is precise with regard to the specific work one is talking about in the case of Beethoven. It is important for the hearer of Beethoven which of the series of Beethoven quartets he wishes to hear, because they are all distinctly individual, which is not the case with Haydn. The rea-

> sons do not lie exclusively with the fundamentally different personalities of the two masters. The manner of composition was entirely different in their respective times. Anyone who wrote more than one hundred symphonies and came close to that in terms of quartets, could not possibly invest in each of these works a distinct richness of individuality. Insofar as Beethoven wrote ten times less, he was able to put into a work ten times more.[11]

Familiarity, the saying goes, breeds contempt. Hanslick's views never changed. In 1891 he commented with some irony on Haydn's choral madrigal "The Storm" that, since the world had experienced a wholly new set of storms in the hundred years since the work's composition, Haydn's representation of calm was more boring than comforting. In 1896 Hanslick seemed more intrigued by the revival of Gassmann than in hearing Haydn again.

The "opposition" during the nineteenth century, the so-called New German School and the Wagnerians who dominated the end of the century, paid Haydn the master slightly different compliments, but hardly more appreciative ones. Franz Liszt seems to have given no attention to Haydn at all, except for a passing interest in *The Creation* and by using a Haydn sonata to demonstrate how he could make a modern piano sound like a spinet.[12] In 1850 Hans von Bülow, during his early Wagnerian phase, spoke again of Haydn's "childlike immediacy." In 1856 Bülow followed Schumann's use of Haydn, defending him against the fake connoisseurship of the general public which, seeing music as an aspect of affirmative cheerfulness, liked hearing Haydn too much and for the wrong reasons.

In an essay on Wagner's *Faust* Overture in 1858, Bülow spelled out the right reasons for praising Haydn: his "populist simplicity" and "richness of motives of high nobility." Years later, in correspondence from the 1880s about concert programming, Bülow reiterated the familiar view of Haydn as rulemaker and precursor. His choice of a Haydn symphony on a program that also featured the "Jupiter" Symphony and the *Eroica* was contingent on how it related to the Mozart and prepared the audience for the Beethoven.[13]

Richard Wagner paid homage to Haydn in a comparable, if not equally perfunctory, manner. He reserved what little enthusiasm he had for music before Beethoven for Mozart, who added "the passionate breath of the human voice" to instrumental music. Haydn was the composer who stressed the dance and the populist roots of art music—another commonplace and oft-repeated idea (which competed with the notion of the childlike) in nineteenth-century historical narratives. Haydn reflected "the blithesome freshness of youth" and the "simple song tune of the folk." Wagner followed Hoffmann, who credited Haydn with being congenial and comprehensible to the majority. For Wagner, as for Hoffmann, Beethoven was the logical historical outgrowth, the composer who "opened up the boundless faculties of instrumental music for expressing elemental storm and stress."[14]

Insofar as Haydn was important, it was as precursor in two respects: in his regard for the music of the populace at large, not merely the aristocracy, and in his use of dance forms—though the courtly dance was not favored in the nineteenth century. For Wagner, Haydn's craftsmanship lay in hiding "contrapuntal ingenuity" in the "rhythmic dance melody" so that the "the character of the dance peculiar to a dance ordained by the laws of freest Phantasy . . . the actual breath of Joyous human life," was illuminated. Nonetheless, Beethoven was to Haydn "as the born adult to the man in second childhood." In Haydn's instrumental music, the demonic essence of music is "playing with its fetters, with the childishness of a greybeard born."[15]

For all the ink that has been spilled on the aesthetic controversies of the mid-nineteenth century regarding program music and "absolute" music, both camps viewed Haydn in much the same way. This commonality offers an opportunity to challenge the idea that the overt split in nineteenth-century aesthetic approaches was as stark as their proponents and subsequent defenders wanted posterity to think. Underlying the divide between absolute and program music are shared notions of what constituted music of significance for the contemporary listener.

One might have thought that the respect Herbart and Hanslick paid to the purity of Haydn's music would have inspired a certain allegiance to Haydn's oeuvre on the part of the most committed anti-Wagnerians. Yet all that Clara Schumann and Joseph Joachim could seem to hear in Haydn was a foreshadowing of Beethoven, particularly in Haydn's adagios, or an exotic cheerful folksiness in his closing rondos.[16] Brahms presents a more complex case. In his extensive library, amidst the manuscript and first-edition treasures, there is very little Haydn to be found, in contrast to the extensive collection of works by Beethoven, Mozart, and Schubert. He did copy out a few works by Haydn, and he also varied the St. Antoni Chorale, which he believed to be by Haydn. The Serenade, Op. 11, opens with a striking resemblance to Haydn's London Symphony, No. 104, and it has been argued that Haydn was crucial to Brahms's compositional struggle in the 1850s as he searched for models and sources that might differentiate himself from Schumann.[17] Nonetheless, for both pro- and anti-Wagnerians, the underlying expectation remained the same: music was supposed to be capable of inspiring and commanding the interior of one's soul, and Haydn's music failed to do so, whereas Bach's and Mozart's, not to speak of Beethoven's, did.

One slight reason may have been the extent to which Haydn's music was a crucial component of serious musical education, given that what we learn in school often emerges tainted by the brush of official approval. Familiarity with Haydn was an indispensable part of nineteenth-century self-cultivation (*Bildung*), and his work retained a visible place in concert life throughout the century. *The Seasons* and *The Creation* remained staples of the amateur choral tradition in German-speaking Europe.[18] A limited but nonetheless varied array of Haydn's symphonies—twenty-one, to be precise—were part of the Vienna Philharmonic repertoire between 1860 and 1910.[19] A somewhat more generous selection, including excerpts from operas and choral works, marked the Leipzig Gewandhaus repertoire during the same period. But even in Leipzig, Haydn stood behind Beethoven and Mozart. Owing in part to the influence of English taste, Haydn retained a stable place in the repertory of American symphony orchestras until the last quarter of the nineteenth century, when performances of his music experienced some decline.

Friedrich Nietzsche wrote that "to the extent that the temperament of genius [*Genialität*] can coexist with a thoroughly good man, Haydn possessed it. He goes to the very edge of the line which morality prescribes for the intellect; he just makes music that has 'no past'."[20]Nietzsche, in his post-Wagnerian phase, put the collective nineteenth-century view in its most profound form. Haydn's achievement was as the figure in history who was universally credited with developing classical forms and instrumental music, the artist whose normative achievement retrospectively transcended the historical. His music sounded as if it had no precursors and, in the sense of Nietzsche, successfully defied the nasty nineteenth-century habit of historicization.

At the same time, a residual sense of blandness and excessive respectability remained; insofar as conventional middle-class morality could ever be associated with the aesthetic realm, Haydn managed it. Nietzsche's formulation was his own gloss on the widely accepted link between innocence-childhood-purity and Haydn. His use of the word "Genialität" is conscious, as is his use of "Moralität." As Nietzsche knew, both words overtly suggest parallel English words, which carry different meanings explicitly relevant to Haydn's London years. The

German use of geniality suggests both greatness and creativity, as well as the English meaning of an unobjectionable cheerfulness. Haydn as a "personality" in the nineteeth-century sense was nowhere to be found: he had transcended the mundane and the purely human by writing himself out of his own music. He invented music as a formal, abstract enterprise—without however developing its capacity to be profound and therefore transcend conventional morality.

Neither Wagnerians nor anti-Wagnerians seemed to need to delve beyond this position. Hearing Haydn as the composer without a past meant there was no historical persona to approach, and no need to "undo" the way in which his music had been heard from the beginning of the century on, as had been the case with Bach, Mozart, and Beethoven. In the mid-1880s, when Nietzsche penned his aphorism, Haydn had "no past," in part because the reception of his music had never evolved.

Perhaps Haydn's most crucial formal contribution was that he had realized, as the historian Emil Naumann put it, "the great natural law of organic development" in musical language and form in ways independent of non-musical narrative patterns. His music seemed as normative as it was unobjectionable; it was cheerful, wholesome, eminently healthy.[21] It prepared the way for other composers who would engage and capture the imagination. Ludwig Nohl, writing in 1866, allowed that Haydn, as the developer of the sonata, set the stage for Mozart and Beethoven to invest the form with "truly ennobled and grandiose pictures of humanity and life," thereby lifting it out of the realm of "mere wordless play of sounds." Nohl used practically the same language as Nietzsche would later use in describing Haydn's inspiration as "genial" and his work as a "source of pleasure and edification."[22] In an era beset by controversy, hostility, and a nearly obsessive reflection on originality, historical precedent, and the nature and character of music, such ritual praise was damning indeed. Bach, Handel, Mozart, and Beethoven were reheard, rethought, and actively fought over—but not Haydn.

This late-nineteenth-century consensus regarding Haydn seemed so all-pervasive that it motivated Hermann Kretzschmar to weigh in with a long dissent about the composer's profundity and emotional depth. In the introduction to his discussion of the Haydn symphonies in his classic guide to the concert repertoire, *Führer durch den Konzertsaal*, he took issue with the conventional view. "An astonishingly large number of music lovers and musicians, including names possessed of the most celebrated reputations, believe that they can honor 'Papa' Haydn with a mixture of condescension by considering him 'genial' and 'childlike'. . ." To understand Haydn, Kretzschmar believed, one had to concentrate on how he transformed the mundane and rendered his material majestic and mythic. In Kretzschmar's view, Haydn should be compared to Aeschylus and Sophocles.[23] Like the great Greek tragedians, he transformed the simple into the profound.

Indeed, Kretzschmar's association of Haydn with Aeschylus and Sophocles was a rare perception. Though nineteenth-century music critics were obsessed with the relationship between formal procedures and narration and representation, the "master" of form, Haydn, was excluded from the discussion. Mozart, Beethoven, and Schubert were seen as using Haydn's strategies, and in the process achieving a narrative-through-music that appeared compelling. Meanwhile the narrative in Haydn's music—either subjective (in the listener) or objective (in the music itself)—had no import. This view persisted despite the acceptance of programmatic titles for many symphonies. The controversies aroused in Haydn's lifetime by the late oratorios on account of the use of descriptive techniques and tone painting ended abruptly in the early nineteenth century. The clear relationship between Haydn's music and so-called extramusical meaning—the entire late-eighteenth-century complex of attitudes toward music as pictorial, characteristic of emotions, and narrative—was deemed irrelevant to the Lisztian-Wagnerian agenda. More surprising was the fact that the proponents of the ideology of absolute music set aside Haydn's extramusical aspirations as essentially naive, separable from, and therefore not problematic or integral to his greatness.

Advocates of program music in the nineteenth century cited Beethoven's *Pastoral* Symphony as a model and recognized an emotional content in Mozart. Yet Haydn's efforts at tone painting and the profound philosophical content of many of his instrumental works produced no resonance. Richard Strauss had only a marginal interest in Haydn, though Mozart always rivaled Wagner as a source of inspiration for him. And even a Haydn defender such as Leopold Schmidt, the Berlin critic and enthusiastic Straussian, unconsciously ended up reinforcing the picture of Haydn's music as somehow sterile and distant.

In his highly successful popular 1898 Haydn biography,[24] Schmidt argued that Haydn properly should be seen more as a "youthful revolutionary" than as "an old man in a wig." By this he meant that the example of Haydn's command of musical form might well have a larger influence on future generations than it seemed to exert on contemporary composers. Picking up on a similar theme struck fifty years earlier by Schumann, Schmidt lamented the contemporary circumstance in which music is "freed from old traditions," yet strives in confused ways to "unclear objectives." As he put it, "the pressure to originality, which is not based on historical evolution or transcendent creative talent, too quickly takes on the symptoms of the sickly. It is therefore desirable that so pure and fundamentally healthy an artistic spirit as Haydn's should function for a long time as a productive inspiration." For Schmidt, Haydn understood that the point of all music was the spreading of joy: "The naturalness of his musical inspiration and realization should remain a model for us."[25] Once again Haydn was held up as the antidote to philistinism and excess (of the kind audible in Mahler). Schmidt's language linking Haydn to medicinal and moral purity is totally unlike the prose applied traditionally to Beethoven or Mozart. As with Nietzsche and Wagner, Schmidt's emphasis on health reveals the weakness of Haydn's position in the fin de siècle.

The many musical handbooks written for the musical public during the nineteenth century further confirm this impression. In the *New Musical Lexicon of Music* of 1857, Adolf Bernhard Marx and the editors once again stressed the affirmative qualities of Haydn, including his innocence, purity, clarity, and unsullied naturalness. Though Marx also talked about Haydn's "natural inwardness and profundity," he explicitly delimited, as did Hoffmann, Haydn's attribution of emotional and intellectual meaning, pointing out that even when Haydn deals with the sorrowful and the grim, he does so as a "loving father" for whom balance and moderation are never lost.[26] Two lexica from the 1880s, one by August Reissman, the multi-volumed *Mendel Lexicon*, and the supplemental *Lexicon* to the Cologne *Neue Musikzeitung*, repeat these ideas, adding only that Haydn's historical role was primary as the father of instrumental music and the "true creator of the sonata form." As Reissman put it, Haydn didn't so much invent any new forms. Rather he brought "order" by creating "regulated organization"[27] that resulted in the mature forms of instrumental music.

The impediment that nineteenth-century attitudes posed for an ambitious re-evaluation of Haydn was not entirely lost on the scholars who gathered in Vienna in 1909 to celebrate the Haydn centenary. The stultifying insistence on the formal and foundational merits of his work to the exclusion of any larger meaning or significance, however, was countered in a disappointing manner. Feverish nationalisms and political rivalries were raging on the continent in the years just before World War I. One might have wished for a serious reinterpretation that would have asserted a new relevance for Haydn in such a context. Instead the 1909 conclave made a virtue out of the seeming absence of controversy regarding Haydn's music and its historical place.

Alexander Mackenzie exclaimed that he was proud to honor the memory of Haydn as the father of all "cosmopolitan musicians. . . . The childlike simplicity of Haydn's music still delights us all," he noted as he called for a "closer union and more perfect harmony between musicians of all countries."[28] Guido Adler's opening speech to the congress celebrated Haydn's connection with populism, his roots in folk music, and his unique place in connecting Viennese classicism to the immanent and essential universalism of music.

As the twentieth century progressed, nineteenth-century notions of Haydn continued to exercise influence in the aesthetic sphere, despite the post-World War I context of neoclassicism.[29] How can one interpret, for example, the fact that in Arnold Schoenberg's 1911 *Theory of Harmony*, there is barely a mention of Haydn and, in contrast to Mozart, not a single Haydn musical example is used?[30] An intense new musicological interest, sparked by the first modern complete edition of Haydn's works,[31] sought to untangle a dense growth of authenticity problems and at the same time dust off works by Haydn not performed since the eighteenth century. Writing in 1951, John H. Mueller noted that this effort at a revival in the early twentieth century could be explained in part because Haydn's symphonies spoke "directly to the twentieth-century era," because they "are possessed of the utmost lucidity and elegance . . . and an integrity absolutely unmarred by any affectation, exaggeration, or bombast" and offer "scintillating relief from the congested orchestration of the late Romantics."[32] In fact, Mueller was only partially correct: the twentieth century has seen not one Haydn revival, but at least three. The first, early in the twentieth century, occurred precisely in reaction against late Romanticism, but was overshadowed by an even greater resurgence of interest in Mozart. The second, after the Second World War, was sparked by another attempt at a new edition and the first modern performances of many works, often organized by H. C. Robbins Landon. And during the third, in the twenty some years since the Haydn festival-conference in Washington in 1975 (followed by the Haydn Year 1982, his 250th birthday), the musicological era met the early-performance era in ways that sought to reclaim Haydn as a composer of passion and intensity to match Haydn the composer of elegance and refinement. But there is a long way to go: Haydn still fails to speak as directly to us as he might, because Mozart and Beethoven continue to dominate our conception of him. The notion of Haydn as precursor lingers.

Why, then, did the nineteenth century consistently define Haydn's compositional mastery in terms of simplicity, humor, cheerfulness, geniality, folksiness, order—all implying an absence of passion and a lack of emotional, narrative, and psychic relevance?

II. Four Dimensions of the Paradox: Haydn's Deification into Irrelevance

The explanation for the respectful but bland deification of Haydn in the nineteenth century—as a composer of more crucial historical significance than continuing aesthetic and cultural valence—possesses four dimensions of increasing complexity. First is what might be called the "touchstone" approach: the use of Haydn as a stable and neutral measure of cultural criticism. Second are the rituals of nineteenth-century biography that made Haydn both an unfortunate victim of the *ancien régime* and a populist figure, and therefore easier to set to the side. Third is the larger subject of nineteenth-century attitudes toward the aesthetics of the eighteenth century, which reveals the diminishment of one of the eighteenth century's great achievements and pleasures, that which might be called philosophical listening. Finally comes the transformation of late-eighteenth-century views on music-making and musical communication, in which we see a new ideology of connoisseurship that reflected the need to create a normative and hierarchical classicism in response to the enormous increase in the size of music's audience. These dimensions of Haydn reception will be taken up in turn.

Haydn as Touchstone

Haydn served as a constant instrument of cultural self-criticism for nineteenth-century figures from Schumann to Schmidt. Unlike Bach, Handel, Mozart, and Beethoven, however, Haydn was not appropriated as a source of inspiration and emulation. Precisely because he was not an object of contemporaneity, he and his music could function as a clear-cut contrast. As we have seen, Haydn was effectively and reflexively used as a symbol of cultural criticism because, as Hanslick pointed out, he was considered a neutral and nearly unobjectionable part of standard musical education. One passed through Haydn on the way to musical maturity just the way music history passed through Haydn on the way to Mozart and Beethoven. Taking the wrong turn—a descent into philistinism—meant failing to learn the lessons of history.

The comparative neutrality of Haydn within the nineteenth-century construct of the classical canon, his availability as a symbol of cultural criticism and contrast, is perhaps best highlighted by one of the recurring peculiarities of nineteenth-century Haydn scholarship: the emphasis placed on the change in Haydn's music after his encounter with Mozart. Gustav Hoecker and Leopold Schmidt were unequivocal in their view that the most lasting part of Haydn's repertory, particularly the later symphonies and oratorios, reflected Mozartean influence. This was one way in which Haydn's place in the repertory continued to be justified.[33] Another way to earn Haydn a place of honor was to argue his relation to Beethoven. In this way, Haydn's role as touchstone revealed him to be an influence that was already completely absorbed.

Biographical Assumptions

The issue of greatest concern to nineteenth-century biographers was that Haydn had not been a free artist but the servant of the aristocracy. This point may be painfully obvious, but unfortunately it is poorly understood. Nineteenth-century biographies of Mozart focused on his rebellion against the Archbishop of Salzburg, as well as on his conflict with his father and the presumed snubbing of Mozart by the Viennese aristocracy. These biographical episodes gave Mozart the aspect of a neglected romantic genius whose frustrations lent his music an interior depth and secret melancholy. Such depths seemed absent from the consistently public and overt meanings of Haydn. There seemed to be an inner Mozart, but commentators either refused or failed to find significant sub-texts in Haydn, a man who wore the Esterházy livery with apparent willingness. As Wagner put it, Haydn's greatest achievements were his late works, written independently of Esterházy but under foreign patronage, whereas Mozart never "arrived at comfort: his loveliest works were written between elation of one hour and the anguish of the next."[34]

It turns out that Haydn's private life and the dynamics between personal happiness and the writing of music were far more interesting and complicated than any nineteenth-century biographer was willing to emphasize. Although both Haydn and Mozart married on the rebound, so to speak—that is, to the sisters of the women with whom they really were in love—the commonplaces of Haydn's life story, as seen by the nineteenth century, make no allowance for the image of Haydn the artist as abandoned, lonely, troubled, or psychically complex (even if Carpani, for one, was explicit on the matter of Haydn's unhappy marriage). His poignant comment of 1790 to his friend Marianne von Genzinger on the restrictions to which he had to submit—"it is indeed sad always to be a slave"—was not assimilated into a more complicated picture of Haydn's psyche.[35] The absence of a powerful nineteenth-century biographer of the stature of Otto Jahn (Mozart) or Alexander Wheelock Thayer (Beethoven) further reinforced the popular stereotypes about Haydn and helped set him apart. Carl Ferdinand Pohl's death in 1887 meant that the two volumes of his important biography of Haydn (1875–1882) brought Haydn up only to the end of the Eszterháza years in 1790; the third volume dealing with the most popular and well-known works had to wait until Hugo Botstiber completed the book in 1927.

But issues of Haydn's employment and the quantity of music he wrote remained uppermost in nineteenth-century attitudes. There seemed to be something socially deferential and perhaps even superficial about Haydn's music. Obeisance to formalities and manners, to the public aspect of music as entertainment for aristocrats, was first derided by the generation of composers who came of age after the fall of Napoleon. Berlioz was typical in assuming that Haydn's music was composed as the occasion demanded, not as the composer might have wished, and that its inner spirit was not the result of any subjective search for self-expression. The historian and aesthetician Heinrich Köstlin, in his 1874 history of music, delighted in recounting that Haydn, in order to write music, first had to dress in a socially acceptable manner and become "*salonfähig*" (fit for the salon).[36] To nineteenth-century critics, only the late Haydn, the one liberated from direct servitude, betrayed hints of a truly personal language or a search for the infinite.

As Wagner's characterization suggested, the image of Haydn as servant of an aristocratic public extended to his London years, when he was feted by English high society. Haydn's status suffered from nineteenth-century aesthetic reactions to the French Revolution, especially the effort to transform the sensibility for music into a middle-class achievement reflective of individuality rather than a mark of aristocratic cultivation and manners. The ambitions of the generation of 1809/10—Schumann, Mendelssohn, Chopin—can be understood in terms of an ambitious non-aristocratic individual such as Julien Sorel, the hero of Stendhal's *The Red and the Black*. Such a superior talent could invent himself through the conceits of intense aesthetic response, genius, and originality. The public of this generation, seeking to delineate the ways in which aesthetic achievement could redefine an elite, looked to Jean Paul instead of Goethe in this regard. Indeed, Stendhal's comparative lack of enthusiasm for Haydn stemmed in part from his affection for the personality of Mozart, who, unlike Haydn, seemed bent on establishing his independence and individuality.

Late Haydn appealed to subsequent generations of listeners not only because the music appeared to conform to an evolutionary scheme of increasing differentiation and complexity. The late Haydn was also the Haydn emancipated, if not from his wig, at least from the Esterházy livery. Nevertheless, the embrace of this late music by the English could not compete with the romantic image of Mozart as misunderstood by the Viennese court and aristocracy. Likewise, despite the facts, Beethoven's eccentricities and apparent overt challenges to social conventions fit the Romantic prejudices, as did the myth of Schubert's extreme poverty and obscurity.

By the mid-nineteenth century, the Wagnerian prejudice against success in one's own time, particularly with a philistine, self-satisfied public, also militated against a reconsideration of Haydn. The obvious contrast, of course, was Beethoven, who was seen as the ambiguous, striving, emotionally expressive romantic artist cast adrift by society, in constant conflict with the philistines around him. His stature grew in the later nineteenth century with the notion that his late music—unlike Haydn's—had experienced opposition and bewilderment in its time, only to be accepted by later generations. The nineteenth century could take credit for truly understanding Beethoven. As for Haydn, neither his success in his own time nor his music was considered incomprehensible or opaque and therefore progressive.

With the possible exception of *The Seasons*, which had been criticized for its tone painting, nineteenth-century critics took as a given the idea that there had never been anything difficult or controversial in Haydn's work, or that not a single piece in the Haydn canon had been misunderstood in its own time. And as for *The Seasons*, these same critics saw no reason to dispute the discomfort among Haydn's contemporaries with his efforts at naturalistic description, despite their engagement in their own time with program music.[37] It was Beethoven's *Pastoral Symphony* that became the starting point for a new ideology of the way music might relate to illustration and narration. The continuity of aesthetic ambition and approach between Haydn and Beethoven emphasized in the beginning of the nineteenth century was obliterated by the end of the century. Later critics saw Beethoven's programmatic ambitions, particularly in the *Ninth Symphony*, as representing a sharp historical discontinuity.

One element in Haydn's biography held unusual attraction for nineteenth-century attitudes, however: his origins. This was his status, unique within the classical pantheon, as a simple "man of the people," a quality seen as exemplified by *The Seasons*. In the 1930s Ernst Kris and Otto Kurz developed a pathbreaking theory on the origins and function of the different types of artists' biographies. Taking their interpretive lead, we can see that the accepted version of Haydn's life story fits a familiar biographical pattern for artists that dates back to classical antiquity. Haydn's story is that of the extraordinary talent fortuitously discovered, despite his humble origins: Here was a simple peasant genius who, after an early rescue from his village by a perceptive relative (leading to choir school at St. Stephen's in Vienna), just happened to live in the same building in Vienna as the famous Italian composer-conductor Nicola Porpora. Porpora recognized the greatness of the young man and gave him his first opportunity. Like the great painters of the Renaissance discovered by chance, Haydn overcame the obstacles created by the poverty and obscurity of his birth.[38]

This story held tremendous appeal for a nineteenth century nostalgic for simpler times, before industrialization and urbanization. Mozart, Beethoven, and C. P. E. Bach all had fathers who were musicians themselves, so they fell into the less attractive and certainly more mundane pattern of the musician as artisan who is trained in the father's workshop. The fact that Haydn's ancestors were of no social significance and had no connection to anything artistic added an aura to his achievement. He was therefore credited with a unique capacity to speak to ordinary people. His use of the dance and the simple tune lent him a lasting connection to an illiterate, uneducated populace; he remained, rhetorically, a symbol of inspiration for the lower classes. Félix Clément, the music historian and composer writing in the 1860s, identified, among other virtues, Haydn's remarkable discipline and capacity for and devotion to work as part of his idealized image: an example that contrasted sharply with the self-indulgent modern pseudo-artistic personality.[39]

This helps to explain recurrent references by nineteenth-century critics to the folk roots of Haydn's music and his use of apparently Hungarian, Croatian, and Austro-German folk material.[40] The dance rhythms and vitality of his music were readily associated with glorified memories of a fast-vanishing village and rural culture. Haydn's many dances for courtly consumption had no place in this account, but his acknowledged capacity for wit was incorporated into the general line of argument. By the 1820s the urban, middle-class artist and his audience had begun to romanticize the rural world as a place of cheerfulness, happiness, innocence, and vitality: precisely the terms associated with Haydn's music. The misreading of Rousseau and the distinction between nature and civilization assisted, ironically, in the nineteenth-century reception of Haydn as, of all the composers, the least artificial and the most natural.

The Seasons helped to make this point for the nineteenth century. In a great work of music, Haydn managed to ennoble the simple people, the ordinary landscape, and daily life. This populist affinity, which was not evident in *The Creation*, made *The Seasons* a potent symbol.[41] Since naturalness, however attractive, was no longer accessible to artists trapped in the lonely spaces of the nineteenth-century urban European world, Haydn became a bittersweet vehicle of nostalgia and a remembrance of things long past.[42] This point was underscored by the sustained popularity of *The Seasons* in the programs of choral societies.

The Shift Away from Philosophical Music

Partly because of this "simple peasant" myth, it has been assumed that Haydn, unlike Beethoven or most subsequent composers, was poorly educated and had very little interest in matters literary or philosophical.[43] Mozart's letters reveal an individual with a profound and reflective intelligence. Beethoven's intellectual ambitions were never doubted and were confirmed by his library. Though Haydn's music, particularly his operas, amply satisfies a search for a connection between music and ideas, his ambiguous legacy as an opera composer and the absence of a compelling written record on the order of the Mozart letters have helped to obscure his view of music and musical meaning.

However, as recent scholars have made evident, Haydn was engaged with the relationship between aesthetics and ethics, and the intersection between art and morality, even beyond his statement that he had often "tried to portray moral characters in his symphonies."[44] The conception of a piece of instrumental music as making a philosophical argument recognizable and significant from the point of view of the listener was not part of the Romantic complex of listening habits, but it was integral to Haydn's work from the 1760s and 1770s on and particularly to his late instrumental music, the work most familiar in the nineteenth century.

Haydn's achievement lay in the creation of music that fulfills, perhaps as closely as any, an eighteenth-century theoretical view of what music should be as an art form, perhaps especially in contrast to painting. Insofar as music was not about any form of imitation or, as Adam Smith put it, the "reflective disposition of another person," it was abstract, in effect the closest equivalent to pure thought and self-reflection. Smith argued that instrumental music was "a complete and regular system," that it filled up "completely the whole capacity of the mind so as to leave no part of its attention vacant for thinking of anything else. . . . The mind in reality enjoys . . . a very high intellectual pleasure, not unlike that which it derives from the contemplation of a great system in any other science."

Smith's notion of the hearing of music as totally occupying the mind is comparable to Sulzer's foray into that favorite eighteenth-century debate regarding whether music or painting has a more lasting impact. Although music's impact was transient, its capacity to engage the whole individual, to envelop the mind and soul by appealing to reason through emotion, was unique. Although the sort of philosophical pleasure Smith described was understood as a source of emotional satisfaction and joy (which is why Haydn's wit was so well appreciated in its own time) music was no mere "pleasurable pastime for the leisured." It was a powerful, all-encompassing weapon with a strong impact on the body and mind, and susceptible even to political use.[45]

The sense of total engagement that results in a welcome and satisfactory emotional and aesthetic conclusion aptly characterizes the response to Haydn's music in London.[46] It fits Edmund Burke's notion of the sublime as "astonishment," with gradations including awe and terror. The power of the sublime was that it "entirely filled the mind" with its object. By virtue of its temporality, its creation of tension through sound, and the impact of vibrations on the body, music created the possibility of "a succession of great parts," a vehicle that could instill emotionally a sense of vastness and greatness and thus create the "artificial infinite." Music can "anticipate our reasonings, and hurries us on by an irresistible force." This is a virtual description of the role of expectation and memory in listening to Haydn's late symphonies. What Haydn had added was what Burke regarded as the "positive pleasure" of beauty, which was the result of a "mechanical" intervention of qualities evident in works of music, and which included the virtues of consistency and formal balance created by resolution of contrast. A work of music, particularly one by Haydn, excited many passions, utilized variety, loudness, and "quick transitions," and demanded a strategy that ultimately left the listener with a languorous contemplative sense of "melancholy."[47]

Haydn's music satisfied the expectation put forward by Christian Gottfried Körner, who applied to music his friend Schiller's idea of an aesthetic education. Körner argued that to achieve a sense of beauty through music, the ear had to be trained. If music was to achieve its goals as an instrument of beauty and ultimately ethical ennoblement, the listener needed to have an understanding capable of discriminating form within the sounds of instrumental music. This required explicit instruction. Precisely because music "forgoes the advantages of the other arts" and in effect "gives us nothing to think about," whatever meaning we are able to find in it is of a high order, since it is created freely by us, the listeners. Music, when given form, shapes its own visceral emotional power into self-sufficiency, permitting the composer and listener to invest music with order, clarity, and wide-ranging meaning.[48]

Music as an art was the taming of the acknowledged emotional power of hearing and sound. The eighteenth century placed a premium not only on form but on the symbolic achievement of resolution within the musical experience. Resolution meant the reconciling of the disparate and conflicting elements of an emotional experience, as mirrored by contrasts in the music. The sublime and the beautiful could be achieved through a formal structure that was designed around music's "regaining the home tonic," as Körner put it. In his later symphonies, Haydn revealed what Schroeder has described as the capacity not only to "persuade" but to engage the listener in a unique and powerful emotional narrative that finally becomes a philosophical and cognitive experience.[49]

The all-encompassing nature of the musical experience made it possible for eighteenth-century theorists to claim that music possessed an argument in and of itself, without any reference to pictorialism. Even so-called extramusical meanings were welcome, since they did not detract from the overpowering impact of sound and hearing. The argument of instrumental music could be analogous to other systems of thought that ultimately influence the passions and reason. Such deductive systems as logic and mathematics for example, where a concept of beauty can be argued whose recognition depends on the same "very great sensual pleasure" and "intellectual pleasure" that Adam Smith believed listening induced, were analagous to music. Epistemology and even empirical science could demand the "contemplation of a great system," just as music did.

The much-talked-about link in eighteenth-century philosophy between truth and beauty rested in part on the capacity of the perceiver to recognize and respond to intrinsic structural parallels between truth and beauty. As Zelter wrote to Goethe in 1826, Haydn's works "are the ideal language of truth . . . they might be exceeded but never surpassed. His genius is nothing less than the expression of a soul born free, clear, and innocent."[50] If the discovery of clear, consistent, and complete laws lay beneath the differentiated and imperfect appearance of nature as understood by Newton and Locke, then the perception of beauty in music composed, as well as music perceived by the listener, required the working-out and recognition of the musical argument. That argument, in turn, had to reflect laws analogous to those of the mind and the physical universe. The praise lavished on Locke and Newton for revealing the laws of nature and human understanding framed the objective for instrumental music. A Haydn symphony therefore became a philosophical argument whose command of the sense of beauty and the sublime, the rational and the emotional, mirrored back to the listener through total engagement in the moment of hearing (associationist connections with the extramusical included, as in Haydn's "The Storm") the fundamental coincidence of truthfulness and rationality in the world and in the mind. Insofar as this line of argument survived into the nineteenth century, it became associated with religion. Clément, whose classicist tastes and anti-Wagnerian sentiments were unabashed, noted that Haydn achieved "a Christian serenity" in music, in which truth and virtue were so evident that they demanded admiration from all of posterity.[51]

Haydn's achievement therefore responded to the eighteenth-century debate about whether the beauty resided in the object or in fact was the result of the act of perception by the imagination. If it were the latter, then only as a subjective act of interpretation could the link be sustained between truth and beauty or, in the world of human behavior, morality and beauty. If the subjective reaction to the work provided the sense of beauty, then any sense of the objectivity of aesthetic categories was lost. If, for example, one heard music in an associationist manner and the associations were contingent on the experience of the listener in a Lockean manner, and not on the work, then the inherent beauty of the object was suspect. One solution to re-establishing objectivity was the development of a system of linkages between musical procedures and meaning that fixed the associations into the work itself.

If music was only about itself, in Smith's terms, and required a pure act of self-reflection without associationist imitation, then the connoisseurship of music enabled the individual to grasp, in some "free, clear, and innocent" manner (to use Zelter's terms), the triumph of the objective over the subjective and the subordination of the individual imagination to the unity explicit in the divine and mirrored in perceived reality. If within the eighteenth-century world of total comprehensive philosophical systems, morality—like knowledge and truth—was rational, then in hearing music the connoisseur would confront a rational imaginative experience related to ethics and morals. A Newtonian law or a Lockean principle itself is never visible. The mind must deduce the abstract law from the concrete transitory event. Music as a system, although not directly imitative of nature, retained the individualized materiality of a specific musical work and the transitory specificity of the time of hearing. That specificity and materiality had to be penetrated by the listener to grasp the abstract principles of the system of music inherent within them. That system made itself clear through the formal acts of presentation, argument, development, return, and reconciliation.

This explains why eighteenth-century composers like Haydn had no difficulty with the idea of descriptive music or tone painting. Since music could never imitate nature except by symbol and analogy, the acceptance of clearly artificial parallelisms between affect and sound did not interfere with the demand that the imagination travel from the transitory and materially particular in each single work to an abstract truth. Such a demand created an extreme premium on the formal treatment of musical ideas and effects within a single piece of music. It also allowed a composer such as Haydn to use the systematic "truth" of musical structure to reconcile seemingly contradictory phenomena. This systematic truth could emerge from any particular set of themes, keys, or instrumental agglomerations. It was revealed through the elaboration of the musical material in the work and was underscored by the structure of endings and the very shape of musical memory, which is why wit, surprise, and delayed or interrupted expectations within a piece were part of the compositional strategy.

For the eighteenth-century connoisseur, hearing a Haydn symphony was a way not *into* subjectivity, but a way to *transcend* subjectivity. Music's abstract language permitted the experience of the sublime and the beautiful that issued from the recognition of moral truth inherent in all parts of the universe. The pre-Kantian link between ethics, epistemology, and reason and in turn the eighteenth-century fusion of reason and religion (as in the notions of natural religion and Deism) made music plausible as an art of moral argument. Instrumental music was particularly well-suited to this task, because unlike vocal or dramatic music, its effects upon the reflective listener's mind depended entirely on the composer's ability to reveal an underlying systematic coherence of truth and beauty. The English audience that heard Haydn's symphonies in the late eighteenth century had known how to appreciate his quite religiously based ambition to realize in music a medium for philosophical and moral contemplation. As Burke and Smith realized, such an ambition demanded music's access to both the sensual and the intellectual, the emotional and the rational, the sublime and the beautiful.

The nineteenth century, in contrast, had lost fundamental sympathy for this rational philosophical project. As a result, it found the music of Haydn cold, lacking in the human qualities most often linked to the perception of subjectivity. Mozart and Beethoven, never identified in the same way as part of the eighteenth-century rage for music as a philosophical system, did not suffer the same fate. The shift is most clearly forecast in the views expressed by Herder, who challenged the idea that music was self-sufficient in Smith's sense. He wrote:

> You, painting, have the lightest, most beautiful, strongest and lasting effect. You speak to the imagination and through it to reason and the heart. You open the portals of creativity. You relax the ones you love and render them content. You, music, on the other hand, wave the magic wand over the human heart. You move the feelings and passions, but in a darker way. And you need a guide and an explanation to approach the human mind in a precise way and to satisfy our moral and physical sensibility.[52]

It was no longer enough for the listener simply to respond and recognize: a guide, a critic, an interpreter was needed now to grapple with the "darker" way. In Herder we observe the beginnings of a new philosophical treatment of music as an aspect of the infinite and the individual linked to willing and to the irrational.

As the nineteenth century evolved, it took its cue from Herder's perception that the indeterminate and darker nature of music deprived it of its immediate function as a symbolic system of morality. For the Romantics, the boundlessness of music was connected to a non-rational act of imagination conceived as the subjective transformation of experience. The Romantics posited an ontology and ultimately a cultural conception of music radically different from the assumptions under which Haydn worked. The underlying culture now rejected the idea of music as a complete philosophical system. There is perhaps no better example of this shift away from the eighteenth-century mode of hearing in the nineteenth century than Stendhal's assessment of Haydn. Stendhal took a dim view of instrumental music and viewed it as inferior. Carpani and Stendhal may even have borrowed a page from Herder. Music was physical and emotional, which made it more "profoundly essential than satisfaction of the intellect." Although Haydn was the master of "the art of landscape," he was no Raphael, because he "failed" at vocal and operatic music. And, for the early German Romantics, Haydn's variety of instrumental music could never command the emotional element of vocal music, or reach the "heights of grandeur" and "gentle melancholy" of Mozart and his melodic gift.[53]

With Hoffmann, Herder, and Stendhal, the nineteenth century turned to newly-conceived links between poetry and music on the one hand, and the connection between word and sound on the other, all the while acknowledging the unique power of the musical. Indeed soon, by some mysterious alchemy, and despite Carpani, instrumental music, with its indeterminacy of meaning and hence very wide field of possible poetic associations, often would be valued more highly than vocal music.[54] But the pre-Wagnerian nineteenth-century evolution of a new rhetoric of meaning and a new type of program music began quickly. Despite the extensive praise of instrumental music, it was precisely Beethoven's and Mozart's (not Haydn's) adaptability to a subjective, personal, emotive, non-philosophical narrative—the link between the musical and the extramusical, particularly the literary—that helped to define nineteenth-century taste. Wagner represented the apogee of this shift in expectations, just as Schumann and Schubert mirrored its beginnings. This is why the turn away from the eighteenth-century view of music as a philosophical system was as significant for Schumann and Hanslick as it was for Liszt and Wagner. Hanslick's ideology of the autonomy of music—of absolute music—did not involve a return to philosophical listening, but rather to a different construct of subjective appropriation.

The genuine pleasure of the philosophical contemplation of music at which Haydn excelled had become a lost habit. Both the music of Haydn and the idea of reason behind it suffered in the nineteenth-century dichotomy between emotion and reason, the rational and irrational, and the collapse of the eighteenth-century philosophical psychology of rationality and enlightenment.

The Ideology of Connoisseurship and the Need for a Normative Classicism

If nineteenth-century music critics were keenly aware of Haydn's presumed status as a servant composing on demand at the behest of the aristocracy, they were equally conscious of the transformation of the audience and public role of music in its own time. Because they assumed that the sensibility toward music resided within the perceiver as well as the creator, they considered the consciousness of the listener crucial. As the century developed, the evolution of a refined musical consciousness was soon linked to the ideal of *Bildung*, or self-cultivation, as once exemplified exclusively by the cultivated aristocrat.[55] Although the aristocrat as employer was easily vilified, the aristocrat as connoisseur became idealized. *Bildung* emerged as an ambivalent category of middle-class self-assertion, ambition, and insecurity. In nineteenth-century accounts of Beethoven's career, for example, aristocratic patrons were viewed not as employers, but as connoisseurs and amateurs. The fact that Beethoven "stood up to" such men did not diminish admiration for the aesthetic foresight and discrimination displayed by Razumovsky, von Fries, Lobkowitz, and Waldstein. Such aesthetic connoisseurship became a model for subsequent middle-class notions of sophisticated musicality.

As early as the 1830s, a perceptible line of argument questioned whether the expansion of high culture and the audience for the arts was salutary. The growth of literacy in the late eighteenth century had occasioned the subsequent spread of musical culture visible by the 1830s. The deification of Beethoven in the 1830s ran parallel with Heinrich Heine's attacks on contemporary culture and Robert Schumann's virulent campaign against the philistine superficiality of contemporary musical life, a line of argument that Wagner would continue.

The formation of the Society of the Friends of Music in Vienna during the Napoleonic era represented an unusual alliance between the high aristocracy and an elite middle class. In Vienna the Society became the basis of an ever-expanding world of participants in musical life who took on roles as amateurs, patrons, and listeners. The explosion of the choral movement in the 1840s and 1850s mirrored the further growth of public musical life in German-speaking Europe. Musical culture on the continent, especially in Paris and Vienna during the 1830s and 1840s, generally approximated the scale of public musical life that Haydn encountered in London in the early 1790s. Before 1848, during the period of restoration, this new musical public constituted a mix of an old aristocracy and an urban middle class. Within the new non-aristocratic public, music benefited from its heritage as a form of aristocratic entertainment. Arno Mayer has argued that the values of the old regime were never entirely displaced during the nineteenth century, despite the radical political and economic changes (and Marxist ideas about cultural formation).[56] Music constitutes a powerful case in point. Self-cultivation, as an ideal of middle-class education, involved approximating and appropriating the connoisseurship that was historically associated with Nicolaus Esterházy. The discerning listener assumed through culture the pose and manner of the eighteenth-century aristocrat.

This nineteenth-century ideology of connoisseurship depended on the creation of a normative classical past, one historically linked to an era of aristocratic privilege in which music was a narrowly distributed and highly refined social instrument and ritual. At the same time, a set of new expectations was placed on the music of the present. These new expectations, which we usually identify as characteristic of Romanticism, defined new music as emerging from Beethoven, the composer who extended the normative procedures of a classicism associated with a closed circle of aristocrats into a language accessible to the educated individual, irrespective of social origins.

From the beginning of the Romantic era, an uneasy tension existed between the demand that music be understood as an independent, abstract form of communication and the thought that music possessed a deep relationship to some psychological geography of human expressiveness and inner reflection. Music making and listening became analogous to the experience of reading alone. Precisely because of this analogy to reading, music had to connect with the subjective imagination in a way that reflected itself in so-called non-musical meanings, either of narration or representation.

This was true of instrumental music as much as vocal. Beethoven was clearly a composer of drama and rhetoric, in which the gestures of instrumental music in relation to extramusical meaning seemed profound but unstable.[57] The widely held Wagnerian perception that Mozart's genius lay in his operas and vocal music led to the idea that his instrumental music also had a vocal and therefore human cast to it. Because of this, its line and structure were susceptible to Romantic listening: one could hear in Mozart an interior narrative. In Haydn, on the other hand, there seemed to be only the playfulness of sound. That Haydn was a composer of drama and rhetoric was a view that lay in the past—and future.

The perception of the absence of extramusical profundity in Haydn's instrumental music, despite its acknowledged exemplary virtuosity in techniques of musical elaboration, transformation, and variation, has remained almost second-nature throughout the history of Haydn reception. Here biography and social history intersect. Being cheerful and telling jokes that result from the virtuosic manipulation of self-consciously simple building blocks did not satisfy the expectation of inner boundlessness. However, it did seem to fit the desire for entertainment associated with a discredited historical elite—and to satisfy a later generation's sense of its sophisticated musical and aesthetic judgment. Understanding Haydn was considered a mark of cultivation, a prior condition to being able to discern truth in one's own time. Since Beethoven had to be saved from philistine reductionism, it was critical that he be evaluated not just on emotional terms, but through a recognition of his greatness in purely musical terms—i.e., in relation to the procedures established by Haydn. Just as Haydn was understood as a necessary precursor to Beethovenian Romanticism, the individual in the cultivation of his own taste had to recapitulate the encounter with Haydn, and therefore the formal language of music that lay beneath any attempt at expressiveness.

This elite redefinition of connoisseurship required an embrace of classicism because the new educated urban elite needed to retain its exclusivity on the capacity to respond to music. Therefore it spawned an ideology of implicit cultural criticism of contemporary fashion (i.e., the popularity of particular works of opera and virtuosic instrumental music that were viewed as superficial). One direction in which this growing obsession with declining standards of taste led was the essentially conservative ideology of the autonomy of music. The other direction, set by Wagner (who chose to stress Haydn's links to the simple folk), attempted to open the experience of music to a wider public through the integration of symphonic musical procedures with drama.

True connoisseurship, Hanslick suggested, was being able to know the causes of music's power and to be able to appreciate the autonomy of music and yet respond to it with a powerful emotion, without confusing correlation with causality. Formal elegance and structural complexity permitted great music to be appropriated by each individual differently. The Lisztean ideology of poetic instrumental program music seemed to devalue the inherent protean character of great music by limiting its potential meaning. The point was not that one should not respond with passion or even an associationist mode of listening to Brahms, Chopin, Mendelssohn, or Schumann. The source of their music to inspire such a deep response, however, rested in formal achievements, understood in some way as "purely musical" and linked to classical models.

However, the accusation that in the end Liszt and Wagner were subordinating music's inherent and unique powers to mere storytelling and surface emotional manipulation failed to revive interest in Haydn as more than a dimension of history. The highly personalized interpretive act of listening became idealized, and the connection to Haydn's music was lost, except for the amateur performer. Haydn, elevated into the model of pure formalism, could not help but fail to capture the imagination of the new kind of listener.

Meanwhile, Haydn's great oratorios remained beloved as works in which amateurs could participate. Despite the greatness of the music in them, the extramusical significance of *The Creation* and *The Seasons* seemed mere surface phenomena that did not disturb the formal integrity of the compositional method. The same was alleged with respect to the symphonies with descriptive titles. The moments of illustration in which Haydn indulged were no longer controversial, but obvious; and whatever deeper extramusical intent Haydn wished to convey was no longer interesting or audible.[58] Joachim singled out Haydn's adagios because they sounded the most like Mozart and Beethoven. Slow movements in Haydn seemed most susceptible to the highly prized habits of subjective appropriation. The outer movements of the sonatas, quartets, and symphonies appeared as cheerful formal exercises that established the essential normative rules of future musical games and communication. Haydn had become the lawgiver of classicism.

• • •

The cultural conservatives of the 1840s and 1850s failed to realize that in rescuing the formal part of the eighteenth-century musical tradition, they were abandoning the philosophical ambitions from which it had sprung. In order to rethink Haydn, the stubborn veneer of nineteenth-century habits of reception, which have extended well into this century, must be dissolved and scraped away. When we try to understand Haydn from the perspective of the eighteenth century rather than the nineteenth, we rapidly realize that Haydn's music carried for its listeners and contemporaries gravity, philosophical depth, passion, and complex beauty. His formal achievements, celebrated as such by nineteenth-century criticism, engendered in his own lifetime precisely that emotionally intense response later generations considered somehow missing.[59] And this means, of course, that formal achievements—as Haydn himself did not fail to point out—were never only what Haydn was about.

NOTES

1. See Hans Robert Jauss, *Toward an Aesthetic of Reception* (Minneapolis, 1982); *Die Theorie der Rezeption-Rückschau auf ihre unerkannte Vorgeschichte* (Konstanz, 1987); and Lydia Goehr, *The Imaginary Museum of Musical Works* (Oxford, 1992) for the most recent and frequently cited introduction to the historical and philosophical issues. I am deeply indebted to the invaluable criticism and assistance of Elaine Sisman and to the writing and encouragement of James Webster.

2. Eduard Hanslick, *Vom Musikalisch-Schoenen. Historisch-kritische Ausgabe*, ed. Dietmar Strauss, (Mainz, 1990), pp. 31–33. The fact that Mozart's music permitted a variety of subjective responses that varied over time was evidence, according to Hanslick, that music was objective: that there was no inherent emotional meaning to the work of music itself. Implicit in this argument was Hanslick's criticism of modern Wagnerian emotionalists who, as they relentlessly pursued contemporary musical fashion, either lost or never possessed the capacity to grasp the visceral intensity that Mozart might properly inspire. Hanslick may have been aware that during the mid-nineteenth century, particularly in France, Mozart's symphonic music was considered inferior to Haydn's and certainly subordinate in importance to Mozart's operas. Despite this Parisian preference for Haydn, Berlioz had little use for him, and could barely sit through a performance of one of his symphonies. See Katharine Ellis, *Music Criticism in Nineteenth Century France. La Revue et Gazette musicale de Paris 1834–1880* (Cambridge, 1995), pp. 84–93.

3. See Gernot Gruber, *Mozart and Posterity*, trans. R. S. Furness (Boston, 1994); also Heinrich Schenker, "Ein Wort zur Mozartrenaissance" (reprinted from the *Neue Revue* 1897), pp. 252–256, in Hellmut Federhofer, ed., *Heinrich Schenker als Essayist und Kritiker* (Hildesheim, 1990).

4. Cited from the essays on Beethoven's Fifth Symphony and Beethoven's instrumental music in David Charlton, ed., *E.T.A. Hoffmann's Musical Writings*, trans. Martyn Clarke (Cambridge, 1989), pp. 97–98 and pp. 237–38.

5. See the excellent introduction and edition by Richard N. Coe of Stendhal, *Lives of Haydn, Mozart and Metastasio* (London, 1972). For a good but brief context for Stendhal see Robert Alter and Carol Cosman, *A Lion for Love. A Critical Biography of Stendhal* (Cambridge, Mass., 1986).

6. Robert Schumann, *Tagebücher*, ed. Georg Eisman, vol. 1, 1827–1838 (Leipzig, 1971), p. 281, took this comparison from Carpani, in Stendhal, op. cit., p. 141.

7. Adolf Bernhard Marx, *Die Lehre von der musikalischen Komposition*, 5th edition (Leipzig, 1879), vol. 3, pp. 595–96. Thanks to Scott Burnham for the reference.

8. Cited in Peter le Huray and James Day, eds., *Music and Aesthetics in the Eighteenth and Early-Nineteenth Centuries* (Cambridge, 1981), p. 454.

9. Robert Schumann, *Gesammelte Schriften*, ed. Martin Kreisig, (Leipzig, 1914), vol. 1, p. 450. It is possible that Schumann, like others, sought to downplay Haydn as a model, particularly for this work, which can be heard as deriving from Haydn's achievements in the late oratorios.

10. Ibid., vol. 2, p. 54.

11. Eduard Hanslick, *Sämtliche Schriften. Historisch-kritische Ausgabe*, ed. Dietmar Strauss, vol. 1/3, *Aufsätze und Rezensionen 1855–1856* (Vienna, 1995), pp. 306–307.

12. Haydn is totally absent from August Goellerich's diary of Liszt's piano master classes. See the English-language edition of Wilhelm Jerger's text in Richard Louis Zimdars, *The Piano Master Classes of Franz Liszt 1884–1886* (Bloomington, 1996); and

Alan Walker, *Franz Liszt*, vol. 3, *The Final Years 1861–1886* (New York, 1996), p. 287.

13. Hans von Bülow, *Briefe*, Band 7 1886–1894, ed. Marie von Bülow (Leipzig, 1908), pp. 126, 129, and 420–421; and *Ausgewählte Schriften 1850–1892* (Leipzig, 1911), p. 208.

14. Richard Wagner, "The Art Work of the Future," in *Prose Works*, ed. William Ashton Ellis, (New York, 1892/1966), vol. 1, pp. 120–21. For reasons of historical consistency I am using the standard Wagner translation.

15. Wagner, "Beethoven," in *Prose Works*, vol. 5, p. 82.

16. Joseph Joachim, *Briefe*, vol. 1, 1842–1857 (Berlin, 1911), pp. 288, 295, 308; vol. 3, 1869–1907 p. 342. Also Johannes Brahms and Joseph Joachim, *Briefwechsel*, vol. I (Berlin 1908/1974) p. 221; *Clara Schumann–Johannes Brahms. Briefe aus den Jahren 1853–1896*, ed. Berthold Litzmann (Leipzig, 1927), vol. 1, pp. 118–19.

17. Brahms made a copy of the slow movement of an early Haydn symphony, no. 16 in B flat (1762), in about 1870 and copied it out for Joachim a year later. He also copied out a vocal pastorella attributed to Haydn, possibly in 1863, and chose the *St. Antoni Chorale* as the theme of his orchestral variations, Op. 56b. See Margit L. McCorkle, *Johannes Brahms: Thematisch-Bibliographisches Werkverzeichnis* (Munich, 1984), Anhang V1 Nr. 4, nos. 63, 67, 68, p. 723.

18. See, for example, notices of performances throughout German-speaking Europe in the Viennese *Neue Musikalische Presse* from the mid-1890s on, and in the *Neue Musik-Zeitung* published in Stuttgart and Leipzig from the same period.

19. See Richard von Perger, *Fünfzig Jahre Wiener Philharmoniker* (Vienna, 1910).

20. Friedrich Nietzsche, *Menschliches, Allzumenschliches*. Zweiter Band, in *Werke*, vol. 3, ed. Karl Schlechta, (Munich, 1954), pp. 934–35.

21. Emil Naumann, *Deutsche Tondichter* (Berlin, 1882), p. 147.

22. Ludwig Nohl, *Musikalisches Skizzenbuch* (Munich, 1866), pp. 150–51.

23. Hermann Kretzschmar, *Führer durch den Konzertsaal*, vol. 1 (Leipzig, 1919), p. 113.

24. Schmidt's biography appeared in Heinrich Reimann's popular series *Berühmte Musiker. Lebens- und Charakterbilder nebst Einführung in die Werke des Meisters*.

25. Leopold Schmidt, *Joseph Haydn* (Berlin, 1898), p. 116.

26. See, for example, Marx on Haydn in A. B. Marx, *Die Musik des neunzehnten Jahrhunderts und ihre Pflege. Methode der Musik* (Leipzig, 1873), p. 178.

27. The lexica are August Reissman and Hermann Mendel, eds. *Musikalisches Conversations-Lexicon* (Berlin, 1880); Eduard Bernsdorf, ed., *Neues Universal Lexicon der Tonkunst* (Dresden, 1857); P. J. Tonger, *Conversations-Lexicon der Tonkunst.* Beilage der neuen Musikzeitung (Cologne, n.d.).

28. See Guido Adler, ed., *Haydnzentenarfeier. Bericht III. Kongress der internationalen Musik Gesellschaft Wien 25–29 Mai* (Vienna, 1909), pp. 41, 45, 52–53. This view is strikingly reminiscent of Joachim's letter to his nephew Harold in 1898, in which he remarked, in response to Henry Hadow's view of Haydn, that he "lifts the material into a higher sphere and has the German gift to assimilate so that it becomes a universal, ideal thought, intelligible to all nations." To Joachim's credit, he argued that the slow movements of Haydn were equal in their depth and religiosity to those of Bach and Beethoven, but in making this claim he knew that his view was distinctly a minority one. Joachim, *Briefe*, op. cit., vol 3, pp. 481–82.

29. Scott Messing, *Neo-Classicism in Music. From the Genesis of the Concept through the Schoenberg/Stravisnky Polemic* (Ann Arbor, 1988), p. 62.

30. Schoenberg's pedagogical writings later in his career give somewhat more space to Haydn, but Mozart and Beethoven overwhelm Haydn as representatives of classical

procedures in composition. See Arnold Schoenberg, *Fundamentals of Musical Composition*, ed. Gerald Strang and Leonard Stein, (New York, 1970).

31. This edition, by Mandyczewski and others (Leipzig), was begun belatedly in 1907 (compared to the series of *Gesamtausgaben* of Bach, Mozart, Beethoven, and others begun decades earlier, in some cases already in the 1850s) and broke off in the 1930s after the publication of only a small portion of Haydn's works

32. John H. Mueller, *The American Symphony Orchestra: A Social History of Musical Taste* (Bloomington, 1951), p. 212.

33. Gustav Hoecker, *Das Grosse Dreigestirn: Haydn, Mozart, Beethoven* (Glogan, n.d.), p. 130.

34. Wagner, op. cit, vol. 5, p. 88.

35. Letter of 27 June 1790, in H. C. Robbins Landon, *Haydn: Chronicle and Works*, vol. 2: *Haydn at Eszterháza, 1766–1790* (Bloomington, 1978), p. 745.

36. Heinrich Köstlin, *Geschichte der Musik im Umriss* (Leipzig, 1910), pp. 416–18.

37. See the reviews reprinted in Landon, *Haydn: Chronicle and Works* vol. 5: *The Late Years, 1801–1809* (Bloomington, 1977), pp. 182–95.

38. See Ernst Kris and Otto Kurz, *Die Legende vom Künstler. Ein geschichtlicher Versuch* (Vienna, 1934/Frankfurt, 1995). The tradition of biography for the great visual artists was well-developed, owing to the work of Vasari. In response to the growing audience for music, it was only in the nineteenth century that a comparable popular and general formula for composers came into being. It is ironic that Haydn had a partial unexpected benefit from the new industry of musician biographies that took its cue from the visual arts.

39. Félix Clément, *Les Musiciens célèbres depuis le seizième siècle jusqu'à nos jours*, 2d ed. (Paris, 1873), p. 121.

40. Laurence Berman, *The Musical Image. A Theory of Content* (Westport, 1993), pp. 182–85.

41. Landon, *Haydn Chronicle*, vol. 5.

42. It is not surprising, therefore, that in this context that runs from E.T.A. Hoffman to Hanslick, there is a curious absence of sympathy for Haydn's religious music. It seemed too mundane and earthbound. See Charlton; *Hoffmann*, pp. 370–71.

43. See László Somfai, *Joseph Haydn. His Life in Contemporary Pictures* (New York, 1969); and in contrast, James Webster, *Haydn's "Farewell" Symphony and the Idea of Classical Style* (Cambridge, 1991).

44. Haydn's remark to his biographer Griesinger, from the latter's *Biographische Notizen über Joseph Haydn* (Leipzig, 1810), in Vernon Gotwals, trans., *Haydn: Two Contemporary Portraits* (Madison, 1968), p. 62. See David Schroeder, *Haydn and the Enlightenment: The Late Symphonies and their Audience* (Oxford, 1990); Elaine Sisman, "Haydn's Theater Symphonies," *Journal of the American Musicological Society* 43 (1990): 292–352; and Webster, *Haydn's "Farewell" Symphony.*

45. Adam Smith, *Essays on Philosophical Subjects* (London, 1795), pp. 171–73.

46. Simon McVeigh, *Concert Life in London from Mozart to Haydn* (Cambridge, 1993), pp. 92–156.

47. Edmund Burke, *On the Sublime and Beautiful* (London, 1812), pp. 202, 234–35, 264–66. See the essay by James Webster in this volume; A. Peter Brown, "The Sublime, the Beautiful and the Ornamental: English Aesthetic Currents and Haydn's London Symphonies," in *Studies in Music History presented to H. C. Robbins Landon on his seventieth birthday*, ed. Otto Biba and David Wyn Jones, (London, 1996), pp. 44–71; Elaine Sisman, *Mozart: The "Jupiter" Symphony* (Cambridge, 1993).

48. Christian Gottfried Körner, "Über Charakterdarstellung in der Musik" in *Aesthetische Schriften*, ed. Joseph P. Bauke (Marbach, 1964) pp. 24–28, 45–48.

49. Schroeder, *Haydn and the Enlightenment*. See also the essay by Mark Evan Bonds in this volume.

50. *Briefwechsel zwischen Goethe und Zelter*, vol. 2, 1799–1827, ed. Max Hecker, (Frankfurt, 1987), p. 473.

51. Clément (p. 136) also compared Haydn to Ingres (who admired Haydn).

52. J. G. Herder, "Ob Malerei oder Tonkunst eine grössere Wirkung gewähre. Ein Göttergespräch," in *Herders Werke*, H. Duncker, ed. (Berlin, n.d.), vols. 2–3, pp. 249.

53. Stendhal, *Lives of Haydn, Mozart, and Metastasio*, p. 74.

54. See John Neubauer, *The Emergence of Music from Language: Departures from Mimesis in Eighteenth-Century Aesthetics* (New Haven, 1986); Bellamy Hosler, *Changing Aesthetic Views of Instrumental Music in Eighteenth-Century Germany* (Ann Arbor, 1981)

55. See Kevin Barry, *Language, Music and the Sign. A Study in Aesthetics, Poetics and Poetic Practice from Collins to Coleridge* (Cambridge, 1987), pp. 1–27.

56. Arno J. Mayer, *The Persistence of the Old Regime: Europe to the Great War* (London, 1981).

57. See George Barth, *The Pianist as Orator* (Ithaca, 1992); and Mark Evan Bonds, *Wordless Rhetoric. Musical Form and the Metaphor of the Oration* (Cambridge, Mass., 1991).

58. See the telling analysis of Haydn's program music (in which only the *Seven Last Words of Christ* is taken seriously) in Friedrich Niecks, *Programme Music in the Last Four Centuries* (London, 1906), pp. 73–78.

59. Compare the enthusiastic and perceptive reaction by the painter Philipp Otto Runge (1777–1810) to the symbolism of the *The Seasons*, quoted in Le Huray and Day, p. 522.

Part II

Documents

A Yearbook of the Music of Vienna and Prague, 1796

JOHANN FERDINAND RITTER
VON SCHÖNFELD, VIENNA 1796

TRANSLATED BY KATHRINE TALBOT

Johann Ferdinand Ritter von Schönfeld (1750–1821), originally from Prague and with a publishing house there, opened one in Vienna in 1783 and spent time in both places. His almanac lists him only as someone who holds private "dilettante academies," or amateur concerts, at which "strangers are welcome." He may or may not have written all the entries in this yearbook. In the preface he indicated that he hoped to follow up his effort with a regular series of such listings, but no more appeared under his name. The following translation comprises the preface and first three chapters of the yearbook, which gives a strikingly vivid picture of a diverse and highly social musical life in the Vienna of 1796; these chapters include listings (1) of musical patrons, (2) of performers and composers active in the city, and (3) of amateur concerts. ("Academies" sometimes referred to orchestras and more often to the occasions in which the orchestras played.) The remaining chapters on Vienna (there are fifteen very similar chapters devoted to Prague) include: (4) the imperial court musicians; (5) aristocratic house orchestras and wind bands; (6) music lovers who possess major collections of scores (only DuBeyne, Fuchs, Hess, and Kees, whose names appear already in the first chapters); (7) composers (a list extracted from Chapter 2); (8) people who conduct from the violin; (9) music dealers and publishers; (10) instrument- and organmakers; then listings of personnel in the orchestras of the (11) opera of the National Theater; (12) German theater; (13) Marinelli Theater in Leopoldstadt; (14) Schikaneder's Theater auf der Wieden; and finally (15) an outline of the state of music in Vienna, listing its elements as church music, concerts, military music, theater music, and dance music. Where supplementary first names or corrected spellings have been supplied in brackets, the source is Otto Biba's index to the volume. Haydn is spelled "Haiden" throughout; I have corrected it, except at the beginning of his entry. [Ed.]

[Source: *Jahrbuch der Tonkunst Wien und Prag 1796.* Facsimile edition, with Afterword and Index by Otto Biba. Munich-Salzburg: Emil Katzbichler, 1976]

Preface

Vienna and Prague now have so many enthusiasts, friends, and admirers of music, as well as great masters and amateurs, that we have felt the need for a comprehensive catalogue. For who would believe that there are more than two hundred people in Vienna who all seem united in wanting to bring the art of music to its highest level here.

Yet however modest an undertaking this will appear to some, it has been most difficult for someone interested in the truth to see something go into print which might appear incomplete or imperfect. This could so easily occur with such a document, especially in Vienna which has so many inhabitants that they often hardly know even those people who live in the same building. Many diverse means had to be employed before one could feel convinced that everything had been done, otherwise a meager list would have been printed.

The chief intention of this Yearbook is to give credit and reflect honor on those to whom it is due. We have registers of honest burghers, of scholars, and of artists of various kinds, yet the musicians are always forgotten. Those who have not had the good fortune to become known through their printed work have died and are lost to all fame as if they had never been.

From now on we want to take good care that not one of these beautiful spirits escapes us, and that their well-deserved reward does not fail to materialize.

Do not look for criticism—we only want to praise. Facts based on truth remain, therefore, our only criterion, and this we want to continue with much pleasure every year, if this first attempt is accepted as what it is, a contemporary history of the music of Vienna.

So as not to hurt anyone's feelings, we have listed everyone in alphabetical order, and have not become involved with complete forms of address, for you can find those only in an almanac or register of the nobility.

I. Special Friends, Protectors and Connoisseurs in Vienna

In this category we include those patrons who have not only celebrated, supported, and made known individual musicians in all kinds of ways, but have given music a new strength and luster which is especially important, since music is so little paid in comparison with other amateur activities. Among the number of these admirable persons are the following:

In Alphabetical Order

Count von Apony [Apponyi]
His Excellency Count von Balassa
Herr Court Councillor Baron von Dubain [Du Beyne Aeodat]
Herr Johann Count of Esterhazy
Countess Lady Gilfort, née Countess von Thun
Herr Court Councillor [*Hofrath*] von Greiner
Count Leonhard von Harrach
Her Excellency Countess von Hatzfeld
The House of Henikstein
Herr State Councillor [*Regierungsrath*] von Hess
Count von Kuefstein, Imperial Councillor [*k. k. Regierungsrath*]
Princess Lignowsky [Lichnowsky], née Countess von Thun
Fräulein von Martines
Herr Imperial Councillor von Mayer, Imperial Paymaster
Count von Oborsky
Herr State Councillor von Paradis
Baroness von Puffendorf [Pufendorf]
The House of Puthon
Countess von Schönfeld, née Countess von Fries
His Excellency Baron van Swieten
His Excellency Count von Ugarte

II. Virtuosos and Amateurs in Vienna

(In alphabetical order)

A

Herr Adamberger [Johann Valentin]. Since this excellent virtuoso has now become a private teacher, we shall dispense with our rule of exclusion and will not regard him as a theater virtuoso, for he has become too important in artistic matters to allow us to pass him over. Everyone knows what a splendid singer he is and recognizes the great contribution he has made to our German opera. He is one of the most perfect singing teachers, for he has exhaustively learned everything the Italian school requires, and we have to thank him for many delightful singers. He has composed a few arias and other pieces, and these have been favorably received.

Fräulein Adlersburg has often sung at his Excellency Vice-President von Kees's and in the Augarten where her singing was warmly applauded.

Herr Albrechtsberger [Johann Georg], director of music at St. Stephen's, he has written a well-known music textbook. His teaching is robust, thorough, and classical. Every musician who has studied under him has felt this to be an advantage. His main subject is church music, and his fugues are exceptional. He is no friend of modish music in the *galant* style *[Galanteriemusik].* He is an excellent organist.

Fräulein Charlotte and *Sophie von Alt,* daughters of the Imperial Privy Councillor's Agent. The former plays the pianoforte with much precision, while the latter has a very pleasing voice.

Fräulein Altemonte [Altomonte, Katharina], a real musical genius. Her truly Italian singing is very beautiful, full of feeling, flexibility and proper method. Her strengths are in the *adagio*, and her *recitative* is her particular forte and makes her one of our foremost amateurs. She also reads so well that she can accompany a *Partiture a Vista* [score at sight]. She sings brilliantly, and anyone who has heard her accompany herself on the piano will be enchanted by her singing, for then she is freer to use her frequent *tempi rubati*. She sings sentimental songs not only with great judgment but also with enthusiastic feeling.

Count Apony [Apponyi, Anton], a great lover of music who plays the violin very well, and does a great deal for music.

Frau von Arnstein (Fanny), the most powerful and difficult compositions are her favorites. She reads music very well, has light fingering and a masterly touch. She excels at fast passages. It is to be regretted that she seems to have lost the taste for it in the last few years and hardly every plays the pianoforte. People who have such a wealth of talent ought not to allow art to become impoverished, for it is in any case always in need of nourishing. She has a very agreeable and fluent voice. Her little daughter in her turn promises to have many musical talents.

Fräulein Auer[n]hammer, (Katton) [Katharina], daughter of the Herr Court War Councillor, sings alto with so much precision, depth, and genuine charm that one can rightly call her the only alto in Vienna.

Fräulein von Auer[n]hammer (Charlotte), her sister, plays the pianoforte with a great deal of taste and fluency.

Fräulein Auer[n]hammer (Theres) another sister, sings soprano with much natural charm thanks to her great musical talents.

B

Mademoiselle Bayer is a distinguished virtuoso on the violin. She wields a pleasant bow and plays sonatas as well as concertos with taste and skill.

Bartenstein, [Anton] Freyherr von, Imperial Councillor. Plays the violin well.

Beck, Herr [Johann] von, a post office administrator, is very musical and plays the basset horn very well.

Beck, J. U. C., knows a great deal about music. As a pupil of the excellent Zissler [Zistler], he made great progress on the violin. His bowing is gentle, he plays with much ease and taste, playing concertos and quartets and singing a kind of baritone in theatrical performances.

Berndt, Frau von, wife of the hospital administrator, plays the piano with brilliance.

Bethofen, [Beethoven, Ludwig van], a musical genius who has chosen to live in Vienna for the last two years. He is generally admired for his extraordinary speed and the ease with which he plays extremely difficult [music]. He seems recently to have entered deeper into the inner sanctum of music, and one notices this particularly in the precision, feeling, and taste of his work. It has heightened his fame considerably. His true love of art is revealed by the fact that he has become a student of our immortal Haydn, to be initiated into the sacred mysteries of composition. During the absence of [Haydn], this great master . . . has transferred his student to the great Albrechtsberger. Much can be expected when such a genius entrusts himself to the most excellent masters. We already have several beautiful sonatas from him; the most recent are particularly outstanding.

Bianchi, Fräulein von, is an excellent singer who knows a great deal about music.

Bitzenberg, Madame, née Huber, a very skillful pianist with correct fingering, accuracy, pace, and timing. She is musical in every respect, also plays the violin and sings. One can recommend her highly as a teacher.

Bose, Herr von [Böse, Joseph], Court Secretary to the Directorate, has the talent to sing nicely without actually being musical. He is able to sing in tune when tackling the greatest music, not only arias, but also duets, trios, and quartets and even *finali*.

Bösenhönig, Madame, née Auernhammer [Bessenig, Josephine Barbara], pupil of Richter, Kozeluch, and Mozart. One expects much of such masters. She has indeed become a great pianist, has taste and feeling, and it is now up to her to make her art truly distinguished. Young ladies are fortunate to be able to find such a talented female as a teacher. She has also composed variations and fashionable pieces for the piano which reveal fire and good taste.

Braun, Baron [Peter] von, son of the late Herr Imperial Councillor, a vigorous pianist and a painstaking musician who has produced powerful compositions, among others Bürger's *Leonore*.

Breindl [Preindl, Joseph], Deputy Choirmaster at St. Peter's. A man who is well thought of, produces good pianoforte students, and knows much about music. As well as church music, in which he is distinguished by his pleasing style, he also composes concertos and sonatas for the piano. Various small salon pieces, among which there are a few jocular songs, seem to be children of his leisure time. These pieces, however little worth he sees in them, show definite signs of a scholarly nature and a cheerful disposition [*Laune*].

Bridi, [Anton], a young wholesale merchant. He is without doubt the crowning glory of our amateur tenors. He sightreads any page without difficulty and has a gentle, soulful voice with which he expresses as much magic as he desires. In jocular songs he chuckles, he declaims dramatic arias with austere expression, and in the *adagio* his tones are melting. His *recitative* is strong, true, and thrilling. In short, he is a true child of nature, summoning music of his heart. But anyone who wants to hear him in his full splendor must hear him when accompanied by the piano. A large, full orchestra is less favorable to his ornaments and soft modulation.

Brunner, Demoiselle, daughter of the Herr Dentist, is a clever violinist both in quartets and concertos.

Buchhammer, I. U. C., plays the violin and cello and is a substantial double bass player.

C

Claus, a young medic, plays the flute quite charmingly and has a nice clear tone.

Clement, [Franz]. This darling of the muses, though still a boy, is an enraptured and fiery youth and, when practicing his art, becomes a man. He is surely one of those geniuses which nature produces only sparingly. His tone is soulful, thrilling, and melting, his quick notes clear, floating, and clean, and one sometimes thinks that his very soul inhabits the violin and dissolves into sound. He also has a great gift for wit and clowning which he often shows in the rondo. Once he has become a fully-fledged composer, it is to be hoped that he will enrich our music with witty and genial pieces in the manner of Haydn. We have not said too much about his great talent, since he has already been so much praised in the many parts of Europe in which he has traveled. It is to be hoped that all the flattery, sometimes carried to extremes, which has been heaped on him and will, no doubt, be continued to be heaped on him both in writing and by word of mouth, will not make him vain and egotistical. These are the most dangerous obstacles in his path and could interrupt the progress of his art.

But it is to be regretted that such an outstanding talent has to live without any assistance in impoverished conditions in a city where there are so many wealthy and powerful music lovers. Is there not one among the splendid houses of which we are so proud, which, for the sake of art, has enough enthusiasm and magnanimity to improve the position of this young genius to make it possible for him at least to continue his studies in an unhurried way? That would be sad!

Cornet, certainly one of our best singing teachers. His instruction stresses the most rigorous musical accuracy and exactitude, intonation, modulation, and method. He places much emphasis on *Canto steso* [sustained notes] and takes a great deal of care of the voice. He makes it a matter of principle to allow his students nothing but simple, natural singing for long stretches of time and always gives them arias appropriate to their voices so as not to strain them. For this reason he carefully restricts the performance of bravura arias. In general, he has the best Italian taste. He himself has a pleasant tenor voice, and he composes agreeable, tender, and expressive arias and songs.

D

Demuth, [Gottlieb], employed by the Imperial Lottery. A very worthy violinist, pupil of the late Zissler [Zistler], distinguished for his beautiful tone.

Del Georgio, Abbé. An artist who, as an amateur, has few equals on the violin and could easily make a living from his music if his circumstances demanded it. He conducted the former Kees concerts with fire and energy, and wields a strong bow. Moreover, he is equally proficient in concertos and quartets. He has a splendid tone, strong and melting, and one can hear at his first stroke that he is a true master. He carries the hearts away in his *adagio*.

Dienst, J. U. C., is very musical, has a good strong bass voice, also plays the viola and cello.

Dopelhofen, Baron von, jun. [Doblhof-Dier, Freiherr Josef von]. A strong violone player who has also written some well-wrought compositions, among which are several excellent choruses.

Dornfeld, Fräulein Josephine von, plays the violin very nicely.

Drostig, Fräulein Josephine von, daughter of the former Hungarian Court Agent. She plays the piano very well and has a beautiful alto voice.

Düran [Durand, A. F.], with the former Royal Grassalkowitz orchestra, a skillful concerto player on the violin.

E

Eberl, [Anton], a skillful pianist and composer who mostly sets literary works.

Eibler, [Eybler, Joseph], Choirmaster at the Schottenkirche [Scots church], is very talented on the organ and pianoforte. He plays quickly and pleasantly and improvises quite well. He does not seem to like teaching, however, for he has neglected some of his lectures and given others up. He has written some fine quartets for the violin, also some quintets for an oboe *principale*, but they are not in general use, since they were especially written for Herr Däumer [Teimer] and therefore teem with difficulties. One would hope, for the sake of music, that he does not allow himself to be blinded by the current madness which looks for beauty in bombast, extreme speed, and a superabundance of notes. It would be a pity if such a man, with his talent, were to forget that music, as a fine art, must follow nature's principles and that nature, far from overloading her works, uses rules of the strictest economy and, in her simple way, reaches that grace which moves us so deeply. At last November's great ball his minuets and German dances were received with great applause. He is moreover one of our best French horn players, and he plays the viola and various other instruments.

Eichinger, [Ignaz], in the princely Schwarzenberg chancellery. Plays the pianoforte very nicely.

Eppinger, [Heinrich]. He is one of our most excellent amateur violinists, especially in concertos and quartets. He is one of Zis[t]ler's best pupils. His tone is agreeable and pleasing, and he has plenty of speed.

Esterhazy, Johann Graf von, a valuable friend of music who plays the oboe with feeling and delicacy.

Eyb, Herr von, at the Imperial General Directorate, sings a fine bass.

F

Faber, Joseph, merchant, a skillful flute player.

Flamm, [Franz Xaver] von, dispatcher for the municipal authority, is very musical and plays various instruments, especially the viola.

Flamm, Fräulein [Margarethe] von, daughter of the above, is a skillful alto singer.

Förster, [Emanuel Alois], one of our good pianists who has also written beautiful piano sonatas, violin quartets, and similar music.

Fribert[h], Karl, director of music of both the upper and lower Jesuit Church as well as at the so-called Italian Chapel. His compositions, which comprise mostly church music and some arias, are chiefly distinguished by being clear, strictly correct, very agreeable to the ear and heart and, without being overloaded, dazzling for the voice. In them he follows a deeply felt aesthetic. His vocal line is flexible and fluent and never either empty nor too darkened by instrumentation. When he teaches singing, he is anxious to protect the voice.

Fribert[h], Mademoiselle Antoinette, his daughter. Though weak and sickly, she nevertheless has a very beautiful voice and, using the pleasant Fribert method, sings delightfully.

Fribert[h], Mademoiselle Therese, an excellent musician with a fundamental understanding of music, reads music easily and fluently and plays the pianoforte well. In her youth, during her residence with the Salesian nuns, she was already a teacher.

Fuchs, [Peter], a member of the Court orchestra, an excellent violinist. His bowing is strong and pleasant, and his students learn to keep precise time. He produces good students.

Fuchs, [Joseph Franz], in the lower Austrian government, is very musical. His special gift as a pianist is to communicate well and produce excellent students.

G

Geissler, Frau von, née von Türkheim, is a skillful pianist.

Gellenick, [Gelinek] Abbé [Joseph], a great friend of music and strong pianist who gives lessons himself but often puts speed before expression. He has written some pieces for the piano and some beautiful variations on favorite themes.

Gilford, Lady [Guilford de Gillhall, Maria Karoline], née Countess von Thun, is one of our best amateur guitarists, an instrument she plays with tender feeling, delicacy, and taste. Her singing is melting, soulful, and harmonious, with pleasant modulation and method.

Giulliani, [Cecilia] von, née Bianchi, a wonderful singer with a strong clear orchestra voice. Her throat has a great deal of fluency and her tone is flexible.

Greiner, Karoline von, daughter of the Herr Court Councillor. This excellent woman combines remarkable qualities which grace head and heart with a high degree of musicality. She is one of Vienna's foremost lady pianists with a masterly touch, strong in execution, and is undaunted by the greatest difficulties. She is the mainstay of the compositions of the great Steffan, and in her hands the works of this old master (whose student she is) shine most brightly. Although she sings in a fine clear voice, she considers singing a trifling matter and has no taste for bravura arias. She prefers to sing ariettas and songs of an artless kind which she likes to accompany on the piano, and then she sings charmingly. She also plays the zither very well.

Griessbacher, [Anton] director of the wind band of Count Grassalkowitz, an excellent concert performer who plays the clarinet with great delicacy and purity.

Grohmann is in the chorus of the National Theatre and has a good tenor voice. He teaches the rudiments of singing.

Grünwald, Professor at the Theresianum and a very popular pianist who has written quartets and various other pieces which have received acclaim.

Gyrowetz, [Adalbert], a young artist who does not yet seem to have found his direction. He reads music and plays the piano with skill, and also plays the violin very well. The compositions he has written, quartets, sonatas, and Italian ariettas, are generally popular, especially abroad. The latter have very pleasant themes and good form and aesthetic. We can probably expect much of his genius.

H

Haiden [Haydn], Joseph. Who in the whole of Europe has not heard of this great master in the last twenty years? However numerous his symphonies, one still longs daily, with insatiable thirst, for new ones. Yet while one has to say that his symphonies are unequaled and, as many imitators have found, inimitable, it is equally true that they are his greatest works and have added more to his immortality than all his other compositions. But there is many a man of taste who will listen to his older products of this kind with greater pleasure than to his younger ones, and it is possible that Haydn himself may secretly agree. Perhaps he has been wanting to show that he too can wear the garments of the latest musical fashion.

Who is as fortunate as he in the invention of happy, witty, and delightful melodies, and who else has the gift to develop them so naturally and yet so unexpectedly, so simply and yet so artistically? If the saying *il facile è difficile* were thought to hold good, it is eternally wrong. His piano pieces are mostly pleasant, simple, and easy to play, and for this reason so much more useful than those written by today's composers who depend on difficulties and make such hard demands on the student that they are often arduous even for the master. His quartets are full of bewitching harmonies, and they have this special quality of immediately attracting one's attention, holding it and moving on, as in a labyrinth, through flowering meadows, past babbling brooks, alongside roaring streams. His themes often fall into two seemingly contradictory [parts] which, in their very opposition, come to a wonderful agreement and, unnoticed, weave themselves into perfect concord. This stamp of a great genius can particularly be found in the newer quartets [Op. 71, Op. 74 (1793)] which he wrote for Count von Apony [*sic*]. He does not, on the other hand, seem as comfortable with the treatment of songs; with the exception of a few arias, one notices a kind of awkwardness in his vocal music. However beautiful his cantata *Ariadne* is, one misses that sublimity which Benda established so beautifully in his melodramas. We also have no epoch-making opera by him yet. He is happier in his beautifully wrought music and in his immortal Seven Last Words *[Sieben letzten Worte]*.

Haimerle, von jun., son of the Lichtenstein Court Councillor, blows the oboe very nicely. His enthusiasm for this instrument makes us expect much of him.

Häring, [Johann Baptist] von, a splendid talent on the violin. This young man can be put at the head of the amateurs who play that instrument. Since there are some contenders to this title who may make equal claims, one immediately realizes there are some disagreements amongst the adherents of these geniuses. Yet when it is a question of competition, nothing is more difficult to determine than the greatness of a master in the fine arts. One musician may, for example, have more speed, another more precision; one more strength, one more gracefulness; one may evoke more admiration with his high notes, another more feeling with melting intonation, etc. Of two musicians, both are masters, but who dares decide which is the greater? Each possesses artistry, and the variation in taste is likely to crown now one, now the other. Once one accepts this fundamental principle, artists of every kind will be considered with more justice. Were one to put the countless numbers of our good women pianists into an order of merit, how difficult it would be to determine the first and the last. Kindly excuse this digression, for which we might be reproached that it does not appear in its proper place. In any case, the excellence of this popular amateur is so well known that it does not need a lengthy analysis.

Harold, surveyor, gives piano lessons and has sound principles.

Harold [Harolt, Johann Michael], the elder, has become known among connoisseurs through his substantial church compositions, in which his fugues have been especially praised.

Harrach, Count Leonhard, not only a great friend of music, but also an excellent amateur performer. He plays the flute with delicacy and speed, his tone is pure, and when he gives a concert one listens to him with pleasure.

Hasselbeck, von, Hungarian Court Agent. A very skillful amateur on the violin who used to lead the second violins in the well-known large-scale concerts of Vice-President von Kees.

Hatzfeld, Countess [Hortense] von. This lady is a special lover, connoisseur, and protector of music. She has one of the strongest and clearest chest voices, has a great deal of fluency in passagework, a wonderful trill, and beautiful ornaments. She is just right for great sublime songs and bravura arias. She lifts the heart with her energy. In opera (in the private theatre) she evokes admiration and in the concert hall she gives pleasure. Her execution surpasses the usual ability of the amateur.

Haugwitz, Countess Sophie, née Countess Fries, a great lover of music with cultivated taste. She sings a charming alto with agreeable technique.

Hauschka, [Vinzenz], employed by the Imperial Treasury, is one of our best cellists. He is in demand in the most distinguished orchestras, not only as an accompanist but also as a concerto soloist. He plays his instrument with virtuosity and expressiveness.

Haynemann, [Florian], doctor of surgery, is one of our best flute players. His embouchure is very pleasant, his tone clear and melting. His speed makes him able to use double-tonguing without difficulty. Since the flute is played by fewer musicians than other instruments, it is easy to see how such a skillful man is much in demand in musical circles.

Henikstein, Joseph von, this talented young man shows himself to advantage in various kinds of music. His is one of the best basses among our amateurs. His voice is strong and flexible, suitable for all modulations. In witty, jesting, and satirical pieces no one but our *Benucci* is a match for him. He has the great musical advantage that he can read everything at sight. He has brought the mandolin back from oblivion and plays it quite brilliantly. He plays the cello skillfully in all the great orchestras and quartets.

Henikstein, Frau [Elise Hönig] von, née Sonnenstein, his wife. A charming singer. Her voice has an especially melodious sound and is graceful, flexible, and fluent. As Fräulein von Sonnenstein she had already gained many honors in musical circles.

Henikstein, Josepha von. Music is certainly not the least of this lady's many distinctions, for she has brought this art to special perfection. She reads music very well, has excellently cultivated taste, and though she does not have one of the strongest voices, it can be heard above trios, quartets, quintets, choruses, and finales, which she very often sings. Her modulation and technique are beautiful, rich, and correct, and she has the still greater advantage of being able to accompany herself in every type of song.

Henikstein, Karl von. Though he also plays the violin and viola, his main distinction is his ability to play the mandolin with speed, lightness, delicacy, and taste.

Henikstein, Johann von, also a member of this musical family. He plays the violin, viola, and is beginning to sing bass.

Henneberg, [Johann Baptist], director of music at Schickaneder's theater, a clever master of the pianoforte. Though no complete opera of his is known, few operas are given at the Theater auf der Wieden to which he has not made excellent contributions.

Hermann, [Johann Franz] von Hermannsdorf, a singular admirer of music, plays the transverse flute with exceptional lightness, purity, and precision.

Hess, Frau von, wife of Councillor Hess. She is an excellent pianist, a student of Clement. She relishes powerful and sublime compositions, sight reads particularly well, plays with expression, delicacy, swiftness, and has a masterly touch. It is a pity that one of our foremost pianists has so little leisure for her art.

Hilgar, [Hilger, Niklas] von, bank teller. Of all our amateurs the most famous violinist. He sight reads superbly, has a good, solid, pure tone, and his bowing is substantial.

Hirsch, Mademoiselle, daughter of a bookkeeper in Henikstein's currency exchange. A graceful flower which blooms in secret. It seems that in her seclusion there is no encouragement for her talent but her father's great love of music. She plays the piano with vigor, taste, and speed. With the great number of her scores, she plays the music of all the masters, but particularly the works of the immortal Mozart.

Hochmayer, [Peter] von, a great friend of music who plays the oboe with delicacy. He is a pupil of the great Däumer [Teimer] and plays concertos.

Hof[f]meister, [Franz Anton], a composer who seems to be better known and liked abroad than in his own home town. Nobody but Haydn has written as much and for so many instruments. There are symphonies, sonatas, duets, trios, quartets, quintets, for violin, viola, flute, piano, etc.

Hummel, [Johann Nepomuk], a pleasant youth of fifteen. A born genius on whom the Muse already smiled in his childhood. He is already a skillful pianist whom everyone who hears has to admire since he is at this moment such an artist that his equal can only be sought [not found]. It is generally believed that he may well claim a talent like Mozart's. Yet sensitive listeners miss the light and shade as well as the soul in his playing, and since these are an integral part of music they prefer the young Clement. But nobody can dispute his manly fire. He has written some sonatas which have been received with approval. Nobody is more able to produce variations on a given theme on the spot.

K

Kapol, von, is very musical and plays the cello well.

Karoly, Countess [Elisabeth] von, née Countess von Wallenstein, [Waldstein-Wartenberg], a very skillful artist on the piano which she plays with delicacy, expression, virtuosity, and taste. She is an excellent pupil of Imperial Director of Music Kozeluch.

Kauer, [Ferdinand], director of the Marinelli orchestra. Though he has had less success with his operas than [Wenzel] Müller, director of the same orchestra, one cannot in all fairness judge them inferior. He has also written various clever variations and other piano music.

Kees, [Franz Bernard Ritter] von, Councillor in the Upper Judiciary, plays the viola and cello very skillfully.

Kees, Fräulein Mimi, daughter of the above, plays the piano very nicely and is a pupil of Herr Breindel's.

Kernhofer, [Anton] von, Councillor, plays the flute with much delicacy.

Kessler, [Christoph] von, Court Secretary. He has written some very pleasing fantasies for the piano.

Kirzinger, [Kürzinger, Paul]. A composer who is little known here. He has not only studied at all the best Italian schools in Italy itself, but has also studied all the masters who have written about music right back to Rameau. He has then chosen a system of his own which has given him a special facility for judgment and treatment, especially of operas and songs. It is a pity that his stoical, high-minded philosophy keeps him too much hidden from the public.

Kneusel, played for the former orchestra of Count Grassalkowitz, a very skillful musician both on the violin and on the viola.

Knobloch, [Johann], doctor of medicine, a keen and skillful violinist as well as concerto and quartet player and accompanist. Occasionally he allows himself to be carried away by his ardor, but wields a splendid bow.

Kollonitsch, Countess von, the younger, is a great music lover and plays the pianoforte.

Kollowrath, Countess [Maria Theresia] von, daughter of His Excellency the Directorial Minister. Plays the pianoforte with true skill, delicacy, and feeling.

Kopey, in the Lower Austrian Government. Plays the cello very well and has thus made himself very acceptable to musical society.

Kozeluch, Leopold, Imperial Director of Music, born in Bohemia and known as a distinguished musician all over Europe for the last ten years. Few composers have written as much for the fortepiano. He has composed some very beautiful symphonies. His concertos have the advantage of following a definite system and being written with the greatest clarity. His solo passages are never eclipsed or smothered by other instruments; just as rarely does it happen that the subsidiary *concertante* instruments struggle for precedence with the principal voice, as is all too common with many writers. The accompanying instruments are always very pleasant, harmonic, and set well together. His subjects are pleasing and sweetly caressing in the *adagio*. He has written many cantatas and arias which prove that he has a great capacity for handling vocal music, and they reveal his ability to write operas. He also appears to be well able to write ballet music, and it would be fortunate for our ballet dancers if he acquired more influence. His sonatas, both for solo piano and for piano accompanied by the violin and cello, are very numerous and universally popular. Unfortunately, he is accused of being too pleased with himself, and that he therefore repeats himself or dwells too long in one place. There is less justice in the opinion that he plagiarizes parts of his own work though some passages may resemble each other. This can, after all, be seen as a characteristic of his style—and which classical composer may not be recognized by his style?

He does not perform any more, though he once played very well. On the other hand, his school is without doubt the best as far as true musical feeling is concerned. It is to him that the fortepiano owes its emergence. The monotony and the confusion of the harpsichord do not fit in with the clarity, delicacy, and light-and-shade which he demands in music. He therefore did not take any pupils who would not work on the fortepiano, and it appears that he took no small share in the reform of taste in keyboard music. For it is from that moment that the notes have been valued more for their quality than their quantity. His students have had much success, and they love a true feeling in music. It is a pity that this great master has almost completely given up teaching in the past years.

Kraft, [Anton and *Nikolaus]*, father and son, formerly members of Count Grassalkowitz's orchestra. Both play the cello extremely well and belong, without a doubt, to the masters of this instrument in Vienna. They have also been much honored on their travels abroad.

Kramer, director of Count Grassalkowitz's house orchestra. A very skillful violinist, not only in quartets and concertos but also as leader of a whole group. He has composed many quartets and symphonies, and they bear the stamp of a pleasantly original character.

Krämer, Joseph, cavalry officer, is a skillful cellist.

Kracky, [Anton], plays the violin.

Kraus, Nanette von, daughter of the Imperial War Councillor, has a very nice voice and sings with special feeling.

Krees, member of the Imperial Court War Council, has a pleasant tenor voice, intonation, and technique. He also plays the violin and various other instruments.

Kreibig, [Greibig, Franz], director of the Court Orchestra. A genius on the violin which he plays with soulful expression, all possible precision, and appropriate speed. It is only a pity that one hears him so seldom; an exaggerated modesty, and perhaps an over-lively imagination of hidden artistic hurdles, has made him fearful of doing wrong. Anyone who, unnoticed, has the good fortune to hear him improvise in his room would be enraptured by the magic of his playing. Since if anyone knows how to love and treasure the great worth of the sensitive, melting music for the heart, it is certainly Kreibig. No musical tricks can be made to look like truth to him, whether from the features of the composition or from its execution; he knows much too exactly the secret sympathetic strings of the harmony that touches the heart to be deceived by them. But when an artist sets these strings in motion, he dissolves to such an extent in sweet rapturous feelings, that he forgets himself, so to speak. When he conducts his orchestra all bows are just one bow, all notes are but one note, everything seems brought to life by the same ardor. Not the smallest nuance is lost, the most imperceptible *piano* soars through the most precise gradations to the strongest *forte* or else leaps with the greatest energy from extreme to extreme. He is the best model of the often too little respected art of conducting.

Krois, [Johann Baptist], of the Imperial Custom house, is a very good orchestral violinist. He plays pleasantly with much skill and delicacy, reads very well, though his ardor drives him sometimes too strongly in his tempi.

Kruft, Freyinn [Maria Anna] von, is very musical and plays the piano with such excellence that she taught her children herself, the two most distinguished being:

Kruft, Catton [Katharina], who reads music very well and is a really strong pianist and,

Kruft, Justine, who distinguishes herself by her gentleness, purity, and precision. Both have been for some time pupils of Fräulein Paradis.

Kubik, Fräulein von, has a good voice and sings very nicely.

Kuefstein, Count [Ferdinand]. This great friend and protector of the fine arts and especially of music is one of our foremost violinists, demonstrating much art and feeling. He is also an especially good conductor which he has proved when conducting *Axur* in the princely Auersperg Palace.

Kuffner [Küffner], in minting and mining. He is a good violinist, a very useful member in musical academies.

Kurzbeck, Magdalene von, one of our best pianists. She reads music well, has speed, clarity, and gentleness. But her special gift is her ability to grasp and remember music, so that when she has heard a piece a few times, be it a large-scale orchestral work such as a symphony, or a piano sonata which she likes, she is able to repeat it on the pianoforte.

L

Laccusius, Fräulein von [Lagusius, Franziska], is a good forte-piano player.

Lang, Fräulein Catton [Katharina] von, daughter of Baron v. Lang, owner of a factory in Ebreichsdorf. She plays the pianoforte with a great deal of feeling and precision and promises to become an excellent artist.

Lange, Madame [Aloysia, née Weber, Mozart's sister-in-law]. Woe the good reputation of our taste and knowledge, that such a great virtuoso should live amongst us as an amateur! And woe if she has finally to seek her bread abroad! The misers ransack the bowels of the earth to find treasure, in order to stuff their coffers with dead gold. Vienna searches all of Italy for singers and keeps such a paragon idle within its walls. Any composer whose work she performs will gain immeasurably. She will surprise him by anticipating his feelings with her own. Who else can summon such sounds out of her heart? And whose tones master our hearts so irresistibly as hers? What clarity of tone, what suspenseful waxing and waning, what subtle shading, what melting transition through the minor keys, what pearly triplets and runs, what pure trills from quietest *piano* to strongest *forte* and back to dying-away piano, what *recitative* full of vigor, warmth, honesty, lively aesthetics! In short, everything that can be created out of the most sensitive soul will be created by her.

Lipawsky, [Joseph], a skillful master of the piano amongst whose compositions the opera *Die Silberquelle* (The Silver Spring), which was performed at the Theater auf der Wieden, has become a special favorite.

Lignowsky, Baroness, [Lichnowsky, Christianne] née Countess von Thun, is a good artist. She plays the pianoforte with expression and feeling.

Litt, Baron van der, son of the former Anspach Bayreut Resident, is a very strong bass singer.

Lobkowitz, Prince [Joseph von], a great lover of music who also plays the violin himself very nicely.

Lorenz, plays the bassoon and is a strong and substantial violone player.

Löwenau, [Ludwig], with the police, plays the violin and viola.

M

Manka, formerly with the Grassalkowitz orchestra, a good cellist who has played many times in private academies.

Margelik, Her Excellency Freyinn [Antonia Josepha] von, née Zänker, a great lover of music and very skillful pianist.

Martines, Fräulein Nanette von, is one of the greatest connoisseurs among our many amateurs. She sight reads, accompanies from the score, is a splendid singer, very grammatical in composition and execution. Her taste is mainly for pieces in the older Italian manner. She almost always has a singing school of her own which she keeps for her entertainment and out of love for the art of music, and here she trains excellent singers, among whom Frau von Dürfeld, née Fräulein von Hacker, distinguished herself, though she died too young. She has composed masses and many arias which sometimes approach Jommelli's style, and is in every way a great champion of music.

Maschek, [Paul], a skillful pianist who is very musical. Besides several other instruments, he plays the musical glasses. Because he loves art, he is quite willing to join in playing on any occasion with no thought of furthering his own interests. He has composed pleasant motets and quartets, and we expect much of his diligence.

Mayern, Freyinn von, plays the piano with much feeling.

Menzel, [Zeno Franz], member of the Imperial Chamber Orchestra, is a skillful orchestral violinist and also teaches. He has already traveled a little.

Messner, J. U. C., is one of our strongest pianists of stupendous speed. He mostly plays compositions by Mozart and Brendt and, as he likes variations, he has written some himself. He attracted a great deal of attention as a boy, now one hears him much less frequently.

Messner, Fräulein [Mesmer, Maria Anna], lady-in-waiting to Her Imperial Majesty the Empress. A singer with a very beautiful, clear voice and pleasant modulation. She knows a great deal about music. Her performance is flattering and true.

Montecucoli, Count [Peregrin] of the Knightly Order of Malta, plays the oboe with much diligence and enthusiasm.

Mozart, Madame [Constanze, née Weber, Mozart's widow], plays the piano and sings quite nicely.

Müller, [Wenzel], chief conductor and director of the Marinelli Theatre in the Leopoldstadt. There is probably no one else in the world who has written so many operas in such a short time. There are over twenty. One might expect this fact and the ease with which the work is written to preclude much originality, but that is not necessarily so, for he is a folk composer, producing opera texts of the kind his public requires.

Just as good people are pleased when they meet many old acquaintances in unexpected places or in company, it is equally charming for the obliging ear to hear, in a new opera, themes and passages made popular by frequent repetition. The composer can be sure that such pieces, familiar by time and habit, will have the best reception and will be garlanded by masses of flowers in every garden and meadow. The fatherland also has many folksongs and dances which fit such a purpose. Herr Müller takes precedence in this, which no one can object to, because he not only selects well these permissible aids, but he also knows how to use them in the most suitable way. This is proved these days by making operas out of old Hafner plays, which receive an enormous amount of applause.

Müller, Mademoiselle [Josepha], also a remarkable genius. As the daughter of a middle-class family without the opportunity to educate her taste by going about in superior circles, her feeling for harmony awakened of itself, and she rose so high in the art, that she is considered the greatest harpist in Vienna. She therefore gives the royal archduchesses lessons on this instrument.

Münich, Baron von, son of the Imperial Councillor, plays the cello.

N

Natorp, Fräulein Klarette von, daughter of the Herr Wholesale Merchant. A pupil of the great Maffoli, sings alto with much technique.

Ni[c]kelsberg, [Heinrich Nickl] von, son of the Herr Court Secretary, is a good pianoforte player and also plays the cello.

Ni[c]kelsberg, Fräulein von, his sister, pupil of Herr Steffan, plays the piano very nicely.

Nikorowitsch Frau von [Nikorowicz, Maria Anna] née von Bourgignon, has a fine, pleasant voice. She has become known chiefly through Lamentations which she has sung several times.

O

Osler, at the Municipal Authority, is popular for his cello playing and is often called on by private academies.

P

Palf[f]y, Countess Theres, daughter of His Excellency Count Leopold von Palf[f]y, has a strong voice and sings with much expression.

Panschap, [Leopold], a chorister who, since he has a good tenor voice, often sings to a great deal of applause at musical gatherings.

Paradis, Fräulein [Marie] Theres, daughter of the Herr State Councillor. This pianist who is famous over half of Europe, is a pupil of Richter and Kozeluch. Her touch is that of a master rather than a student, for she makes demands on herself which are neither sleight of hand nor bursts of noisy speed but are nourishment for the spirit and the heart. What is most praiseworthy in the way she plays is the feeling, taste, nuance, clarity, and precision she shows. She is especially strong in the so-called pearly style *(giuoco granito)* in which all the notes in a run stand in the same relationship to each other in power, clarity, and tempo. She uses rubato sparingly and appropriately, and in her *adagios* the notes float almost like a voice in song. She carefully eschews all copying in her compositions and, a child of nature, tries to go her own way, striving for honesty in feeling, and seeking to express all passions and phenomena of nature through melody. Since this is her main aim, she does not take much notice of the higher principles of composition but only observes the necessary rules.

Her greatest works are the best-known: the opera *Der Schulkandidat (*The School Candidate); a melodrama *Ariadne and Ba[c]chus,* and a cantata on the death of the king of France. She has been reproached for being too eloquent in some places. Whether this shows too much striving for tone-painting or whether a wealth of ideas is the cause, we don't know.

Pfeiffer, [Leopold]. He is not mentioned here as a good bass singer in the Marinelli Theatre, for in this role he does not, according to our plan, fit in this list, but as an excellent amateur violone player, in which capacity he even plays concertos.

Philebois, Mesdemoiselles, two talented sisters, both amateur singers. The elder has a fluent voice and sings in a fairly high register but with literal exactitude. The younger has an agreeable alto voice and sings with pleasant sensibility. We deduce from this that bravura arias are more suitable for the elder than the younger, and that the latter should sing moving adagio arias. It appears that both ladies tend to sing mainly in amateur performances of operas.

Puffendorf [Pufendorf], Baroness [Anna] von, wife of the Imperial Councillor. It is a real pleasure to listen to this amiable lady when she sings with the full force of her fine feelings. While her voice is not particularly strong, her ornaments, her performance, her taste, her feelings are superb. She is an enthusiastic lover of music, not just of the fashionable pieces or the so-called *morceau du jour* as is so common amongst amateurs, but also of old and serious pieces. She is always delighted to join in singing choral church music and fugues. This shows that she reads fluently and gives the music the correct intonation.

Puthon, Fräulein Julie. This young woman shows a remarkable talent for the mandolin, which she plays with enchanting delicacy, clarity, purity, feeling, and taste.

R

Raphael, [Ignaz Wenzel], works at the official statistical office. He is a true musical genius whose talent matures daily. Of the many instruments he plays, his proficiency on the fortepiano is particularly admirable, for he has much fluency and delicacy. Few equal him in accompanying from the score. He reads so exceptionally easily that he lets all the instruments be heard together with the piano, and at the same time he sings in a pleasant tenor voice in quartets, quintets, and choruses. He does not play in orchestral concerts but plays fashionable pieces, fantasies, and variations very charmingly. He is the author of some diverse pieces which are much to be recommended. His *canons* are quite unique and give universal satisfaction in all the houses where he plays them. For some time now his pieces have been performed by all quartets as a matter of course. People were not happy and the musical entertainment was not complete until some of his canons were heard. His most recent ballet called *Das Veilchen* (The Violet), contains much eloquent music, a feat nobody is likely to better in a hurry.

Rath, J. U. C., a young man most useful in musical society who plays the violin, viola, and cello.

Rathmeyer, J. U. C., has a very fine and exceptionally strong tenor voice, a very good ear and a special facility in reading music. But one could wish that he put more care into a gentle flexibility of the voice (which would be so easy for him), for then he could compete with tenors of the first rank as his voice is very pleasant and rightly receives much applause.

Reschny, a skillful amateur cellist and very useful in quartets.

Röllig, [Leopold], employed in the Imperial Court Library. This great artist has become famous as the inventor of the keyboard glass harmonica which is played like a pianoforte. Though it cannot be said that he plays this instrument in an exemplary manner, he certainly understands the spirit of musical glasses better than most.

Rombec, Her Excellency Countess, née Countess Kobenzl, has a great mastery of the pianoforte, playing with precision, taste, and speed, so that she can be counted among the greatest artists of the instrument.

Rudolph, a young man who is a very talented violinist and is known and appreciated in every musical society. He plays the instrument superbly, both in concertos and quartets, has a strong stroke, solid bowing, and a fine tone. He is a good conductor and always directs the band in the Augarten.

S

Saffran, Baroness [Anna] von, née von Hartenstein. One of Kozeluch's most excellent students. She plays the pianoforte with great delicacy, purity, and feeling, and reads music with consummate skill.

Salieri, Anton, Imperial Director of Music, is a student of the great Gassmann, his predecessor, and is a great admirer of the immortal Gluck on whose style he models his work. When one adds this to his own genius, one understands the source of his greatness. While we have a few piano and organ concertos, and he has written some church music, the Italian Opera is his chief field, and all Europe is grateful for his output. Whatever differences of opinion and obsessions with innovation there may be, there is no doubt that his operas stand out among all others with their wit, tone-painting, humor, gracefulness, fire, and good, unartificial instrumental writing. He knows so well how to fit his music to the actions of the singers, so that he not only makes their acting easier but often shows them in which direction to go. A good opera composer has to study the starting point of human passions and its course meticulously—he himself must be the orator and the actor. Among Salieri's many operas, *Fiera di Venezia* and *Grotte di Tronfonio* are special favorites, *Axur* is generally admired, and the opera seria (written for Paris) *Les Danaides* is a brilliant masterpiece. It is to be regretted that he has given us few new works in the last years.

Sauer, Countess, née von Heisenstein, sings with remarkable feeling and is skillful in reading music.

Scheidl, son of the admirable cellist [actually, violinist] in the Court Orchestra. His special talent as a pianist has been known since early youth. He plays with great skill.

Schenk, [Johann], Director of the house orchestra of Major General Prince von Auersperg. He has become known for his symphonies and German operas.

Schindelecker, [Philipp], plays with the Imperial Chamber Orchestra and is thought to be our greatest master on the cello.

Schmitt, [Johann Adam], Doctor of Medicine, and excellent violinist who used to be welcomed with open arms in all our private academies, and especially in quartets, for his charming tone and dazzling expression but, to the dismay of our true friends of music, has recently withdrawn from public life.

Schönfeld, Countess, née Countess von Fries. A student of Kozeluch. She is one of those pianists who seek the beauty of music in clarity, precision, taste, and feeling and therefore find the surest way to the heart.

Schönfeld, Fräulein Nanette, daughter of Herr von Schönfeld of Trnowa, plays the piano with much merit. Her expression is very full of sensibility. One can count on the feeling of her superb heart.

Schuhmann, von, Court Agent, a great lover of music who, within the circle of his closest friends, plays the flute and the cello.

Schupanzig, [Schuppanzigh, Ignaz], son of Professor Schupanzig who teaches at the high school. This young man seems to have quite given himself over to the service of Apollo. He loves all good music and does not give exclusive preference to one instrument, one composition, or one master. His own instrument is really the viola which he plays excellently, but he seems recently to have shown a preference for the violin. He has played it with feeling, grace, and true art in concertos and quartets. He also enjoys conducting a whole group, which happens with precision, nuance, feeling, and fire. He is therefore known and sought after in all musical circles, for he is willing and helpful.

Schwab, Frau [Katharina Edle] von, née von Häring, a great music lover who plays the piano and sings.

Schwingenfeld, von, is very musical, has a pleasant and flexible tenor voice and much good taste. He usually sings with piano accompaniment and other voices, trios, quartets, finales, etc.

Sebottendorf, Baroness [Josepha Henrica] von, née Königsburg, another skillful pianist who plays only occasionally and then in seclusion. Anyone who wants to hear her will have to listen at her boudoir door, nor will she use her pleasant voice full of feeling.

Seidschek, Fräulein von, niece of the Court Architect von Cerini. A new ornament but lately added to the number of Vienna's fine musicians. As one of the strongest students of our unforgettable Mozart, much is expected of her. As well as great speed, she shows much taste and feeling and uses a good deal of rubato.

Selinger, Doctor of Medicine, one of our best amateur cellists who is always in demand in all the respected academies. Apart from being a great technician, he has the advantage of producing a pleasant and soulful performance.

Sonnleitner, Fräulein von, daughter of the former jurist, a good pianist who has performed in various public academies, making a good impression. She is a pupil of Breindel's.

Sonnleitner, Ignaz von, has studied music and sings with a full, pleasant and strong bass voice.

Spangler, [Johann Georg], Director of the church choir at St. Michael's, he has a very pleasant style and setting in his church music and knows how to lead the choir in the best possible way. As a singer he has a fine tenor, sweet, comfortable, and flexible, and his soft voice and wonderful modulation awakens the most pleasant feelings.

Stadler. The brothers Stadler [Anton and Johann] play with the Imperial Court Orchestra, are exceptionally skilled artists both on the usual clarinet as well as on the basset clarinet, which difficult instrument they have completely in their power in terms of tone, delicacy, expression, and ease.

Steffan, [Joseph Anton], a master who has outlived the taste of his era. He is a clever man who has a great deal of music in him. He has written many piano concertos.

Steinert, [Johann], Imperial Court Secretary at the Privy Chancellery, is an exceptional pianist and indeed such a good musician that he writes excellent compositions for his own entertainment.

Stock, works in the police department. A strong violinist in the symphony orchestra who is very useful in musical circles.

Strassoldo, Countess Theres, daughter of His Excellency the Imperial Councillor, a great friend of music who sings with a beautiful clear voice and much feeling.

Strassoldo, Countess Josephe, a very strong and talented pianist who reads well and who gives a fiery and expressive performance.

Streicher, [Johann Andreas]. Vienna has made a new and certainly very valuable acquisition with the arrival of this very skillful man. He has only recently moved here from Munich. His compositions are rich, pleasant, and grateful to play, much liked abroad but not yet known here. They are especially suitable for the fortepiano and will give pleasure to our amateurs. He himself plays splendidly and knows well how to manage the instrument. While playing with great skill and speed, he never disregards lucidity and the most accurate expression. For those music lovers who care for true music he will be welcome, and as far as teaching is concerned, he is perhaps the only possible replacement for Herr Kozeluch.

Streicher, Madame [Nanette], his wife, a daughter of the famous instrument maker Stein from Augsburg. She is a very skillful amateur pianist, who is so perfect in her power over this instrument that all the feelings of her heart are at her disposal. Under her fingers sounds grow and melt and lose themselves until they are inaudible. Anyone who wants to get to know the qualities of a good piano must listen to her.

Stubenrauch, Frau [Ant.] von, wife of the Imperial Agent, formerly very well known as Fräulein Karger. She is one of the amateurs who used to sing in many of the academies, especially that of Kees where she received much applause. Her voice is strong and clear, and her special advantages are great fluency and an exceptionally high pitch. Her willingness to sing for anyone who asks to hear her makes her many friends.

Süssmayer, [Franz Xaver], the second director of the Hoftheater. He has recently become popular by writing several German operas. His opera *Moyses* is written in an elevated style and perhaps not very suitable for the Theater auf der Wieden for that very reason. But he has had a great deal more luck with his *Spiegel von Arkadien* (Mirror of Arcadia) which, apart from some very well-thought-out pieces, including several trifling and well-known arias which he has inserted in suitable places, so that the whole thing caused a sensation. What serves to recommend him is that he is a student of Mozart, who valued him greatly. Indeed, he worked on some of the unfinished pieces of that great genius.

Sommer, [Georg], organist at the Hofkirche and St. Peter's, he has for so long been known as a great master of the piano but, because of other commitments, does not teach anymore.

T

Täuber, [Teyber, Anton], a composer of taste who is less known than his skill deserves. His settings for voices are particularly dazzling. He has written quartets and other compositions.

Teimer, [Johann and *Philipp]*, two brothers. Who in Vienna does not know these famous oboe virtuosos? They grace our most distinguished orchestras. Their tone is melting and their playing so distinguished that some of our composers have written pieces especially for them. They are also masters of the English horn.

Tepper, von. Though this nice young man must be considered an amateur, he has studied music for more than eight years and through his travels has profited much in knowledge and taste. He has stupendous speed on the fortepiano. His innumerable runs are fast, and everyone listening has to admire his pace.

Trnka, Frau [Theresa] von, née von Lang, an enthusiastic lover of music who has risen high in the art of singing. She accompanies herself very correctly on the piano, reads well, and sings with so much taste, technique, and feeling, that every note betrays her ardent heart. Though she has not one of the strongest voices, all orchestras find it to their advantage to welcome her.

Trübensee, [Triebensee, Johann Georg and *Josef]*, father and son, play in the National Orchestra; two splendid oboists who play this instrument with great feeling. The son has written several beautiful compositions principally for wind band.

Tschoffen, Frau [Barbara Edle] von, née von Puthon, one of Kozeluch's best students, a quite exceptional pianist who combines much delicacy and taste with a very pure performance.

Türke, Franz, a young merchant, pupil of Herr Anton Wranitzky, an excellent violinist who distinguishes himself by his strong bowing, a pure and lovely tone, and clear performance, and proves beside that he is no stranger to elaborate passages.

U

Ugarte, His Excellency Count [Johann Wenzel], a great admirer of music who plays the violin very well.

Ulbrig, [Maximilian], a Lower Austrian Government bookkeeper. Though he is only an amateur, he is a very useful musician. His compositions are excellent, especially his symphonies. They are pleasant on the ear, very fiery, rich, and appropriate in part-writing, full of seriousness, dignity, and sublimity. They might be used more effectively than some of Haydn's symphonies at a popular festival or on a solemn occasion at court.

Umlauf, [Ignaz], Director of Music at the Imperial Court Orchestra, and piano teacher of the younger archdukes. He has composed church music, piano concertos, and German operas; among the latter are *Die schöne Schusterinn*, *Die Bergknappen*, and *Das Irrlicht*. His operas are very well liked. Nobody knows whether it is because of lack of time or whether there is some other reason why we have not had any new work from him.

V

Vanhal, [Johann Baptist], one of our oldest composers who, it seems, has fallen out of fashion. But this is not so abroad, where his work is still much appreciated. He has written a great deal for most instruments, but nothing new has appeared for some time, and it may be thought that he himself has wished to be forgotten.

Vogel, a skillful, very musical singer with a good bass voice.

W

Wallenstein, Countess von, plays the pianoforte with much taste and feeling and is also one of those of Kozeluch's pupils who are distinguished by their precision and feeling.

Walterskirchen, Freyinn von, one of our best known amateur singers. Her voice is clear, full, and flexible, her method pleasant, and her feeling true. She shines not only in the great bravura arias, but also sounds pleasing in smaller fashionable pieces, and the most difficult church music is easy for her. She is also an excellent pianist though without ever wanting to make such a claim. She plays the most difficult passages with skill. She was taught by Herr Riegler of Pressburg.

Weigel, [Weigl, Joseph], Director of Music who also conducts from the piano at the Court Opera and Hoftheater. A promising composer of vocal music who has matured before our eyes. From Albrechtsberger's textbook, he learned the principles of solid composition, and he learned expression, taste, and practical application under Salieri. His passion for the art is burning and his diligence untiring, which is proved by his many operas following one upon the other and becoming ever longer and more rich and perfect. This energetic young man may well presently put an end to the delusion that no German could ever treat Italian song with dignity. His latest opera, *Giuliette and Pirotto*, received great praise from impartial experts who particularly liked the finale of the first act. It is a pleasure to watch him conduct with attention, fire, and liveliness. It can be said of him that he works with body and soul.

Weigl, [Anna Maria], mother of the composer, was at one time the foremost singer at the German Hoftheater which she left in disgust to the annoyance of all music lovers and, much to their chagrin, has never been heard again. Having to do without her pleasant, soulful singing has been a great loss to music.

Wetzlar, Raimund Freiherr von, plays the guitar beautifully and with feeling and sings with it in a pleasant voice.

Wissdorf, [Martin], Councillor at the Court War Council Accounts Department. A first-rate amateur violinist, very musical, who also conducts big pieces very well.

Wölfl, Herr [Joseph], a truly dexterous pianist whose skill one does not find every day. He sight-reads anything he sees with incredible accuracy, and his opera *Der Höllenberg* (The Mountain of Hell) brought him much praise.

Wranitzky, Ant[on], Director of the princely Lobkowitz Orchestra, one of our foremost violinists. He has trained excellent students, clearly proved by [the skill of] Herr Schupanzig and Herr Türk.

Wranitzky, Paul, Director of the opera orchestra at the Imperial National Theatre, brother of the above. Also a splendid violinist who has written quartets, symphonies, and operas.

Z

Zois, Freyinn [Katharina] von, née von Auenbrucker [Auenbrugger], was formerly one of our foremost pianists, an instrument she played not only with skill but also with taste. But she has not played in academies for some years. She has one of the most pleasing singing voices and combines with it a great number of ornaments that are not only elegant but full of feeling.

III. Amateur Concerts

The following are the best-known of our music lovers who occasionally or at fixed times give large concerts or even only quartets:

Count [Anton] von Ap[p]ony[i]. This hardworking music-lover, who loves the violin and vocal music particularly, often gives [concerts with] quartets. He enjoys bringing together a variety of singers who will sing all kinds of choral works and other pieces. He has taken part, in place of Count Franz Esterhazy, in the great concerts of Baron van Swieten.

Count [Franz de Paula] von Ballassa puts a great deal of effort into the weekly concerts he gives, usually through almost the entire winter.

Frau Baroness von Buffendorf [Pufendorf, Anna] has a weekly musical salon which serves the excellent purpose of helping participants with the study of music by making them more and more familiar with it. This is a closed salon, confined to those who will sing, for there is only singing and piano playing on these occasions. The pieces are mostly fugues, choral works, and church music. Apart from the Baroness herself, the participants are Baroness Walterskirchen, Henikstein, Bridi, Raphael, Schwingelfeld, etc. All great music lovers.

Count Franz von Esterhazy. This great music lover gives beautiful concerts at certain times of the year, when mostly great and exalted pieces are performed, especially Handel choruses, the *Heilig Sanctus* by Emmanuel Bach, Pergolesi's *Stabat Mater* and similar pieces. A variety of our most eminent virtuosos is always present.

Herr Court Councillor [Franz Sales] von Greiner, who values music greatly, whose daughter is an incomparable pianist and who has a fine bass voice himself, gives a great annual concert on his Feast Day (Franciscus Salesius) and that of his wife and daughter (Karolina). He also has excellent quartets performed every Tuesday in Advent and during Lent.

Herr [Joseph Hönig, Edle] von Henikstein. The Muse of the art of music has taken up her quarters in this house. Apart from the fact that the eldest son holds a weekly evening of instrumental music where only the participants are invited, there is singing every evening all the year round, and since a greater part of our most skillful amateurs as well as many masters of the profession meet here, there is always an opportunity to hear beautiful music.

Fräulein [Nanette] von Martines. At the home of this skillful musical artist is a great salon every Sunday evening, and on these occasions there is much singing and playing on the piano. Sometimes there is also a band of wind instruments which plays right through the evening.

Herr Court Councillor Baron von Mayern gives beautiful quartet concert during Lent when one can occasionally hear his wife at the piano.

Herr Court Councillor von Meyer, who is a civil paymaster, is such a special music lover that the whole complement of personnel in the chancellery is musical, Raphael and Hauschka being among them. It is thus easy to see why a great deal of music is made here in town, and when the Herr Court Councillor is in the country. His Imperial Majesty the Emperor has himself been present at such musicales.

Herr State Councillor [Joseph Anton] von Paradis, or rather his daughter, has been giving weekly quartet concerts throughout the winter. These are intended to give young amateurs practice and taste as well as pleasure in the art. There is always much singing and piano playing, and one can find promising talents there. Some big concerts are also held.

His Excellency [Gottfried] Freiherr van Swieten, Imperial Privy Councillor and Senior Librarian. This man must be regarded as the patriarch of music. His taste is solely for the great and sublime. Many years ago he wrote twelve beautiful symphonies himself. When he is present at a concert, our half-connoisseurs don't let him out of their sight, so that they can guess from his expression (which isn't always easy to read) what judgment they should pronounce on what they have heard. Every year he give some grand and magnificent concerts, where only pieces by the old master are performed. His great love is for the Handel style from which great choruses are often performed. He gave such a concert just this past Christmas at the Prince von Paar's, where an oratorio by this master was performed.

Baroness [Katharina] von Zois usually has a small select group at her home on Sunday morning, where there is singing at the piano.

There are many other houses where large or small concerts are held at various times throughout the year. Among them are the houses of His Highness Prince von Lobkowitz, His Princely Grace von Lignowsky [Lichnowsky], His Excellency Count Strassoldo, Count von Hoyos, Herr State Councillor von Isdenzy, Herr Imperial Councillor Baron von Partenstein, Herr Court Councillor von Kraus, Herr Court Councillor von Schröder, Herr von Puthon, Herr von Natorp, wholesale merchant; Herr von Buchberg, wholesale merchant; Baron von Lang and others.

A feature of some of these private concerts is that strangers who have come to Vienna are allowed easy access, and that they are kindly received. This is so in the houses of Herr von Henikstein, Herr Court Councillor von Greiner, Fräulein von Martines and Herr von Schönfeld from Prague.

In the summer there have also been amateur concerts under the direction of Herr Rudolph in the Augarten hall. A number of amateurs contributed the necessary money, the late Vice President von Kees provided the scores and instruments, and all local inhabitants and strangers of any standing were given free admission.

Similar concerts were arranged by the much loved Herr Schupanzig. He gave musical entertainment by amateurs every Thursday in the early summer from six to eight

Remarks on the Development of the Art of Music in Germany in the Eighteenth Century

JOHANN KARL FRIEDRICH TRIEST

TRANSLATED BY SUSAN GILLESPIE

Pastor Triest of Stettin (1764–1810) had a small but important role to play in music history. His ambitious serialized article on eighteenth-century German music appeared in the relatively new but influential periodical (*Allgemeine musikalische Zeitung*), put out by the important firm of Breitkopf & Härtel in Leipzig. It was significant in at least three respects. First, it argued for the pre-eminence of Johann Sebastian Bach in establishing a "German music," and thus was preparatory to the "Bach revival" of the nineteenth century. Second, it applied Kant's aesthetic ideas to music, especially in the idea of "pure" and "applied" music, much as Michaelis did (though on different aspects of music) in the two decades after the publication of the *Critique of Judgment* in 1790. Finally, in its nationalist appropriation of composers like Bach, Mozart, and Haydn, it created a vision of German music emerging as a critical force over the course of the eighteenth century, especially in instrumental music. Germany obviously includes Austria. And for instrumental music ("pure" music, to Triest), Haydn was the *ne plus ultra.* It is interesting to note, given the focus of the first essay in this volume, that Triest compares Mozart to Shakespeare, and criticizes both for the same transgressions—rule-breaking and inappropriately combining comic and serious elements—for which Haydn was criticized by many others. Here, however, it is Mozart's operatic music that is the focus, not his instrumental music. Because of this, and because opera buffa in this period routinely conflated comic and serious elements, the comparison seems less personal.

Musicologists cite Triest frequently, but selectively; the whole of his article is rarely considered, and has never before been translated. Carl Dahlhaus is the only scholar to have looked at his view of the entire century, in the article "Zur Entstehung der romantischen Bach-Deutung" (in *Bach-Jahrbuch* 64 [1978]: 192-210). Dahlhaus points out Triest's binary oppositions that play out in a kind of dialectical development over the period: rhetorical/poetic, mechanical/aesthetic, harmonic/melodic, pure music/applied music, strict style/free style. The relatively common tendency to view the century in these terms awaits further study. Headings have been added to identify the main topic of each of the segments of the serialized article, and the main composers and theorists mentioned by Triest have been given some identifying detail in brackets. Footnotes are the author's, unless otherwise noted. [Ed.]

Triest uses the terms *Tonart* and *Musik* in ways that are not always quite synonymous. In general, *Tonart*, with its etymological root *Ton* (tone) seems to be the more evocative of the acoustic nature of musical experience. In the translation, *Tonkunst* generally appears as "art of music." [Trans.]

[Source: "Bemerkung über die Ausbildung der Tonkunst in Deutschland im achtzehnten Jahrhundert," *Allgemeine musikalische Zeitung* 3 (January 1–March 25, 1801), no. 14 (cols. 225–35), no. 15 (241–49), no. 16 (257–64), no. 17 (273–86), no. 18 (297–308), no. 19 (321–31), no. 22 (369–79), no. 23 (389–401), no. 24 (405–10), no. 25 (421–32), no. 26 (437–45).]

[No. 14. Introduction. On music as a fine and applied art, and a brief survey of its broadest developments.]

The entry into the new century evokes powerful emotions in anyone who not only takes an interest in the private matters that concern him during his brief time on earth, but also thinks seriously and often about what humankind in general has gained, and what it lacks. And where might we find a better opportunity to depict the value of our life's purpose than when we survey a long time-span, in which we observe the many lovely fruits of previous centuries' efforts, while its final decade offers the wondrous preview of a new drama whose outcome we cannot foresee! —What an inducement to cosmopolitan glances into the past and future! What immeasurably rich material for a philosophical survey of the part played in these events by Nature (or fate) and that played by the free actions of men! —Truly an instructive undertaking, which, in these days, is rendered both easier and more difficult than in earlier times. Easier, because human history is not limited, as it once was, to the most eminent events (the fates of rulers and their wars), but also follows the course of culture in its various tributaries and includes, in particular, the development of the sciences and arts. It is made more difficult, on the other hand, by the great ferment in which the latter are to be found at this moment (because of their broad dissemination). Consequently, every historian who wishes neither to harm the truth nor to risk his reputation must become mistrustful of himself; namely, whether he has chosen the right perspective for his portrayal. But even a modest attempt of this kind, no matter how unsuccessful, can always be useful, for at least it will impel people who are skilled and well-informed to correct or add to his portrayal, and to bring the target closer, as it were, as a result of this exchange of ideas and information. So, then, these pages, too, may contain (as many a reader might think us duty-bound to provide) a brief "Survey of the Course of Development that the Art of Music has Taken during the Last Century in Germany," in the course of which no one, undoubtedly, will fail to note that the conclusions arrived at therein are merely the personal opinions of one individual, and insofar as they contain praise or criticism of famous men, only reluctantly (for the sake of the coherence of the whole) emerge into the light of day.

At the same time, this portrayal is meant to be *pragmatic* (i.e. aesthetic-historical), since a merely narrative recounting of historical events would be quite pointless or at any rate superfluous here, and hence it will have to be preceded by "A Few Glances at the Development of the Musical Art in General, Leading up to the Present." This will lead to the above-mentioned perspective, from which, in turn, to examine the very different shape that German music assumed in the last century.

The need of human beings to bring their mental and emotional powers into harmony, or to represent them in such a way, produced the *fine* arts [*die* schönen *Künste*]. Sensuality gave the imagination material for free play, and understanding tried to bring this play into conformity with its rules. The importance of such inner cultivation became clear in the expression of feelings; it was probably the wish to please others, or to transport them to a similar state, along with the experience that sensual depictions reflect back on their creator, that impelled human beings to bring forth *beautiful forms*. They used the latter to express or awaken emotions and later also to deceive other people with the mere semblance of these emotions. Thus every fine art (including music) had a dual definition. It was partly *pure* art (existing for itself), the transformation of sensual material into the free and beautiful play of the imagination; and partly (in keeping with its *empirical* origins) it was only an aesthetic means to other ends, especially the more beautiful portrayal of one or several individual subjects (their feelings and actions), in which case it was *applied* art.[1] Now Nature provided three different means by which human beings can express their feelings: gestures, tones, and concepts. Hence mime, music, and the verbal arts (poetry and rhetoric). These accomplished their ends all the more surely, the more they were combined in the portrayal of feelings. This was easier in previous eras than it is now—as a quick glance at our theatrical forms and effects, among others, persuades us. But why? —The answer to this question sheds a bright light on the fate of the fine arts. It provides the key to surveying the course that music has followed until now, and at the same time gives us a standard for judging the cultivation not only of individuals, but of whole periods and peoples. Therefore it will probably be worthwhile to spend a few moments on this subject. In the preparatory period of culture, imagination and understanding are only the impotent servants of sensuality and have little effect on its refinement. In the next period, imagination rises to a level equal with that of sensuality (the Heroic Age). In the third period, understanding is in balance with the other powers of the soul (the Age of Pericles), and it is here that we find the most delicious fruits of the fine arts. Later on, understanding senses the superiority that is a function of its (i.e. not merely human) nature and its propensity for infinity. It struggles to gain unlimited power over the senses and the imagination, but experiences the fate of the child who will not suffer the leash. It spins around on its axis, loses itself in dreamy reveries and baroque notions, looks down upon the other two powers of the soul, and consequently undermines the sense of beauty and distorts culture, which must, as a result, take an entirely different course and retreat (at least seemingly) from its previous gains. This, without respect to the physical causes, is how the barbarism of the Middle Ages came about, in which the fine arts were all but eliminated, and after which they long retained such a dry, impotent form that they almost completely failed to accomplish their higher purpose, that of ennobling the heart. But even this seeming disfigurement of mankind is like the sleep of Nature. It is followed by a vast general fruitfulness; sensuality and imagination are cultivated once again, making use of the remains of a more beautiful Antiquity; and understanding, which has been liberated even earlier and is no longer estranged from itself, matures along with them, until, sooner or later, it becomes their benevolent leader rather than their opponent. Hence it would seem that only our impatience, our narrow point of view, or occasionally the habitual arrogance of *isolated* understanding, are responsible if we perhaps feel displeased by the great ferment that occurred during the second half of the last century; without it to prepare the way no great and lasting humanity can flourish.

Although this sketch may fall short in several respects, it seems to me, nevertheless, that it follows rather closely the course of development of music itself. The latter, as was mentioned above, had value, at first, only as an applied art; i.e. it was used to express the sentiments of an individual subject. Quite a long time was required before it began to be practiced as a pure art, i.e. the melody, harmony, etc., were cultivated as beautiful play without reference to a text. Hence the almost inseparable link, in earlier days, between music and its sister arts, mimetic drama and poetry, and the resulting miracles of art based on the myths of Antiquity. However, [music itself] already contained the seeds of an inevitable separation, in the period when human understanding, in its treatment of the fine arts, would begin to disdain the fetters with which it had been bound, until then, by sensuality and imagination. And these seeds were—the *mechanism* of the musical art itself.[2] Here, in its treatment of the fine arts, understanding had the most natural opportunity to elevate itself above the other powers of the soul; here a broader field was open to it than to the other arts. The mechanism of mimetic drama and poetry attained quite early its more complete development,[3] which it owed primarily to music.[4] But the art of music had not yet perfected its mechanism, and would surely not have done so without the well-known cultural decline that plunged the sciences and arts into a long night. For if it consisted only of melody and rhythm, our imagination would not have much room for play. But the experience that Nature produces musical tones independent of mankind (singing), whereas poetry and mimetic gesture (which will probably be defined in such a way as to exclude the trained dance of animals, etc.) came about only through and by human beings, was the cause of *instrumental music*; and the observation that several musical tones of varying pitch may resound well together, or that (as was noticed later) there is in nature no entirely simple musical tone, led to the discovery of *harmony*. This infinitely enlarged the mechanism of the art of music, lent new charm to melody, lightened and strengthened the expression of the emotions, created pure artistic products (existing for their own sake), and, finally, through the conviction that the relationships between tones could be broken down into numbers and calculated, not only gave harmony itself inner consistency but also made music amenable to scientific treatment. In this way, Nature herself endowed the art of music with a power that the other arts did not enjoy to *the same* extent, making it a gift of the purest, most powerful enchantment that we as humans, i.e. as sensual-rational beings, with some cultivation of our mental and emotional powers, can experience. Music was not always capable of producing this ecstasy (which is generally considered to be the strongest touchstone of a work of art, despite the fact that this touchstone is profoundly ambiguous, since there can be thousands of incalculable causes of emotion outside of art); but its power was a result, partly of the great breadth and versatility of the musical mechanism, and partly of the new course of development taken by culture during its revival. This (mechanical) course provided an opportunity for each of the various parts of music to experience its separate development, so that the one was often forgotten and neglected for the other (the melody, for harmony; singing, for instrumental music, and vice versa). The new course did not spring, as in Antiquity, from the senses, but rather from the understanding, which, crippled by the chains of hierarchy, long hesitated to recognize any claims to cultivation by sensuality and imagination, even though it could not do without them. Hence sensuality remained crude, imagination flat, and art became mere artifice. Instead of genius and wit, people contented themselves with dry reflection and calculations. They wanted to make art into a science before it had once more ripened into art, i.e. to study the foundation of the rules before gathering them from Nature; in short, they took a plant that was meant to refresh and ennoble them and carved it into—a toy. This was especially true of music. People devoted themselves to it who either (as a result of climate, etc.) originally lacked aesthetic feeling or had abandoned it for religious obscurity. Even much later, after a brave man had torn the dreadful chain asunder,[5] the art of music still felt this compulsion. Nor could it have been otherwise. Human understanding had sunk too low. The rays of the new dawn had to tempt the understanding to pay attention to itself alone, in order to break free of the still unchecked pressure. Science benefited a great deal from this, and rapidly; but art, which needs more than merely intellectual assistance, did not quite keep pace with this development. As an *applied* art, music lagged behind, for its companion, poetry, hardly deserved the name in Germany, where language, too, was still in its childhood. As a *pure* art, by contrast, music made quite good progress, not only in practice but also in that aspect of its internal mechanism that best occupies the understanding, namely *harmony*. All of music's art and erudition were united in harmony, and a knowledge of counterpoint was the single and greatest thing a master who had accomplished everything could do to attract the admiration of his fellow artists, so long as he could not be accused of any errors in his grammar (strict counterpoint). Melody and rhythm were accorded less attention. The former was held back by the close attachment to psalmody and the old sacred modes; nor could it gain anything from a music that was written more for the eye (in the score) than for the ear. And the development of rhythm was retarded not only by the prevailing, dragging [style of] choral singing, but also by the spirit of the nation in general.

This is how things stood with the German art of music *on the whole* toward the end of the century *before last*. The warming rays cast in our direction from Italy and France were still striking a very cold earth, which was producing only erudition and scholastic criticism instead of art. Harmony, the only thing that was held in high esteem, had little to recommend it to the ear, because the lack of purer temperament could not be replaced or made less obvious by singing, as in Italy and France. In a word, the old German ponderousness and lack of a sensitive ear contrasted too strongly with the fire and sense of beauty of those Italian and French masters who dared to visit Germany (in individual bands), or whose works had spread their fame abroad, for them not to inspire in the great multitude a stubborn resistance to the new manner. —It remained for the eighteenth century to give the German art of music a mighty impetus. Thanks to the fact that it attempted, midway in its course, to bring Italy's emotional grace and France's energy together with German thoroughness, and that German geniuses, like busy bees, carried the pollen of foreign art into their country and labored over it with their peculiar strength—thanks to all this our fatherland succeeded, in the eighteenth century, in arousing in both these nations a respect for German music that might have been even greater and more widespread, had our own respect for foreign artists not been all too evident.

What, now, became of music in Germany during the past century? And *how* did it become what it did? The answer to these two questions, which always go hand in hand, can be approached from various perspectives. The most natural one is probably the one that is closely linked to *important* men who exercised a *prominent* influence on the course of music's development and were epoch-making in this regard.[6] The notion of a history of the fine arts already demands this. What the latter became, we owe to the genius and diligence of outstanding human beings; whereas history portrays other events as much more dependent on Nature and fate. Should we, then, simply name in passing those individuals who had such a significant effect, even long after their death? Should we not, in a survey like this, regard them rather as the principal figures in a painting, which a non-partisan and grateful posterity does not seek to rob of the light in which they already appeared to their contemporaries? —Certainly, this tribute is our duty, and can coexist very well with the conviction that a great distance remains between us and the goal of perfection that lies before us. Yet as much as those men may have done, there were still quite a few circumstances contributing to the development of the art of German music in the last century that must not be ignored. These include the influence exerted on German music by Italian and French music, the gradual transformation of people's thinking about ethical questions, as well as the character of those arts that are related to music (especially poetry and rhetoric), and more. It is necessary to examine these things if we want to explain the enthusiasm for some artists and artistic works, on the one hand, and their critique, on the other. —So much for the preview; now to the survey itself, which can most conveniently be divided into *three* periods, as follows:

1. From the beginning of the century (i.e. from Fux, Keiser, Telemann *et al.*) to the death of Joh. Seb. Bach.
2. From Graun, Hasse, C. P. E. Bach *et al.* to J. Haydn and Mozart.
3. From Mozart to the end of the century.

• • •

[No. 15: On the sitution of German culture and music at the beginning of the eighteenth century.]

"Do the Germans have and have they ever had a music of their own?" This question used to be asked by many German natives and foreigners who, familiar with the German drive to imitate, have not considered that every cultivated nation forges its own peculiar path in the treatment of the arts and sciences under the confluence of a thousand circumstances, even if this peculiarity is not always so evident or exemplary as in other countries that are more favored by Nature. The composition of Germany reveals, at a single glance, that here there can be no generally binding artistic taste such as exists, for example, in France and England. On the other hand, this aggregation of peoples who have little in common except for their written language results in a true artistic democracy (or federalism), with all the attendant disadvantages and advantages. These include the strange, sometimes blameworthy but for the *future* perhaps healthy mixture of heterogeneous things in one and the same work (for example the lachrymose comedy [*weinerliches Lustspiel, comédie larmoyante*], the heroic-comic opera, the theatrical church-music and churchlike theater music, and so forth), at which foreign taste not infrequently takes umbrage. Further, the attention paid to everything foreign, and then also a greater slowness, which, again, is easily explained by the general spread of new important ideas and works, from which another, surely laudable characteristic arises, namely *thoroughness*. This, at least, is ascribed to the Germans, and it is indeed the thing that, from the beginning to the end of the last century, distinguished German music *in comparison* to other nations. Who can deny (as was mentioned earlier) that the Germans, taken as a whole, can compete neither with the Italians in regard to depth of emotion, nor with the French in regard to the liveliness of their ideas and portrayals! For what happens in big cities is, in our case, the least appropriate standard against which to measure the whole. Sober-minded and dry in both our social and our private lives, intending more toward counting and calculating than toward feeling, no one can be surprised if, among us, the fine arts appear more bodily, or if from the first period of German composers of the last century we have few if any works to show for ourselves that manifest an aesthetic spirit that treats the mechanism of music not as an end, but as the means. This is why we were (and are) so overly rich in all kinds of instrumental pieces,[7] among which, apart from the legions of quite amateurish products, one finds so many in which one can criticize either the confused imitation of famous masters—to the point of the most obvious plagiarism—or a bizarre and meaningless artificiality that makes us look in vain for an aesthetic idea. This is why (as was mentioned above), even as late as the third period the proper application of the rules of harmony was the only thing considered necessary for someone to earn the right to be a master of music, and in the applied art of music, i.e. in sacred and theatrical pieces, it is not difficult, despite our great fruitfulness, to tot up the compositions of genius, if we exclude Graun, Hasse, Mozart (also Naumann, Homilius, G. Benda, Hiller, Rolle, and a few others)—for Handel and Gluck did not compose for Germany, nor have they, up to now, had an effect on German music in general. In a word, the peculiarity of the German art of music consisted, at least in the first half of the last century, in the fact that it was treated more as a mechanical art, which only pleases when it provides stuff for thinking (i.e. calculating).

Why is this? —Besides the above-mentioned causes, the following appear on closer examination. France and Italy, which have always preceded Germany in culture, did so in respect to music as well. In those regions, Nature had done everything to win them for the art of music. Climate, national character, language,[8] and the easier familiarity with the relics of ancient Greek and Roman art and science all combined to make Italy, in particular, the natural homeland of the more recent nobler music. The latter reached Germany as early as the seventeenth century, where, for example in Dresden, Munich, and other cities, Italian masters set the tone. It took root, despite all resistance, because it suited the German spirit in the form the latter had assumed at that time, as follows. Since the general revival of the sciences and arts, the latter had remained, until the second half of the eighteenth century, under the tutelage of the *church*, except possibly for the beneficence of princely extravagance. This circumstance, combined with the tendency (mentioned in the introduction) for the arts to provide material for the play of reason alone, explains why, at that time, in both Italy and Germany, only harmony, among the three main aspects of the internal mechanism of music (melody, harmony, and rhythm), attracted prominent admirers. The organ was the principal instrument, for it, above all others, could show harmony in all its brilliance. The achievements of [fifteenth- to seventeenth-century theorists] Bernhardo [Bernhard], Gafforio, or Zarlino, etc., were an enticement to polyphonic singing and playing and to exploring the relationship of the intervals. Although Lud. Viadana [c. 1560–1627] introduced solo singing, he did not put an end to contrapuntal artificiality. [Jacopo] Peri and Orazio Vecchio [Vecchi] did not achieve significantly better results in their operas [around 1600], although they did lay the groundwork for later changes in taste. In a word, melody and rhythm could not always keep pace with harmony. This was the condition in which music entered Germany from Italy. Here, too, it could find protection only under the aegis of religion. The Germans, by nature cooler and less songful, but thorough, now immersed themselves in the study of harmony, in which they soon caught up with or surpassed the Italians; however, for a long time after this the Germans confined themselves almost exclusively to this area, while musicians in Italy, following Leon. Leo [1694–1744] and others, were not only composing more melodiously (following their natural bent), but even falling into the opposite extreme and neglecting harmony. [The tendency described here] was especially evident in protestant Germany, specifically the region that was farthest from Italy. Here religion (outside which any involvement with music was considered, if not sinful, at least no more than a useless diversion) cast a scornful eye on the mixture of the theatrical style with the original sacred style, as it was beginning to be adopted in the Catholic regions (to lure the populace and the Protestants). Worship, in this (northern) part of Germany, was not supposed to be enthusiasm engendered by the stimulation and intoxication of the senses, but solemn, melancholy reflection. To support it, the cultivation of harmony was exceedingly important; for what could sustain this reflection better than a fugue or similar piece, which, when performed *well* on the organ, is pleasing even to the neophyte. The transcendent nature of the subject matter and a suitable (often unpoetic and even incomprehensible) text allowed free play to all the arts of counterpoint, for the words scarcely meant more than the syllables of Solmization.[9] What mattered was not, as in the theater, the characterization of singing individuals, and all attempts in this direction, namely the ecclesiastical dramas, produced unfortunate results, with the possible exception of the choruses, where harmony was able to shine. —*Opera music*, it is true, did not have quite the same psalmodic cut as in France in the age of Lully, but there was such emptiness, such awkwardness of rhythm, in short, such ponderousness that it was impossible not to recognize the influence of sacred music. Admittedly, this gave singers of both sexes more opportunities to show off all of their art. They made of the piece, which except for the counterpoint was only a sketch, what they would and could. Just as one ordinarily gives a position to a man, and only inadvertently a man to a position, so operas, at this time, existed almost entirely for the singers, and not singers for the opera.[10] The composer, who undoubtedly deserves first place,[11] often had to cede his position to the actors, and would have had to do so more frequently if it had been possible to do without him. All these constraints contributed more than a little to the fact that applied music had no aesthetic character, for the composer was certain to earn the applause of connoisseurs if he knew how to handle and make use of double counterpoint; while the applause of the great multitude was something only the singers could win for him.

Still, to form a clearer general picture of the course of development of German music at the beginning of the last century, one must also consider the state of its chief helper, poetry. Without poetry, the art of music does not reach its more perfect development. But at that time, what kind of German poetry was worthy of the name that was not rhymed prose, or that was fit for music? —Our language was groaning under the almost general contempt in which it was held by more cultivated people. In church, despite Luther's sincere efforts, Latin held sway, at least for music. Among scholars it was dominant. At court, it was beginning to be less common; it was giving way to French, and in theaters that were worthy of the name one heard only

Italian singing. —German national modesty toward things foreign was not entirely responsible for this situation. Our language, when it comes to richness of vocabulary and elegance of construction for the more precise distinction among concepts, probably ranks as one of the first among all now living tongues, and therefore the most convenient for philosophy; but in respect to sonority it can reliably be said—whatever patriotism may think—to be less good. A clear proof is provided by the many impure vowels, harsh diphthongs, and especially the number of sibilants and gutturals. Furthermore, the very advantage mentioned just above stands in the way of the energy and naiveté that are necessary for poetry—qualities that make many a poorer language so charming, and whose lack is made all the more glaring by the strivings of contemporary poets (who often give us stilted or flat language in their stead). Be that as it may, one thing remains certain: more recent music, especially German music at the beginning of the last century, was not formed (as Greek music probably was) in imitation of *poetry*, but rather of *rhetoric*. Anyone who is even somewhat familiar with the rules of rhetoric and of composition, as well as with the general pattern of our musical works, will not doubt this for a moment. Only since the introduction of the accompanying recitative, of finales, etc., has our art of music become more poetic, although in pure music C. P. E. Bach made energetic attempts in this direction—of which more later. Now, rhetoric is distinguished from poetry, in general, by the fact that in the former the understanding is more active and dominant than the imagination. This character was given to music, as well. The lack of lively, vivid imagination, of sonorous language and familiarity with the *spirit* of the art works of other nations, old and new, all combined to make applied music (combined with poetry) so insignificant and desiccated that later on, when taste became more refined, the mere skeletons of such works could serve as an amusement for musical anatomists. The rare exceptions, among which Reinhard Keiser [1674–1739] in Hamburg is probably the most eminent, if one does not consider the definitive praise by a Mattheson, Hasse, and Reichardt to be overly enthusiastic, were so lost, that of 116 works written by this famous man little or nothing has survived for posterity. Thus it was the *natural* destiny of German music, at the beginning of the last [eighteenth] century, to be confined only to the mechanisms of the art of music and specifically to the isolated treatment of harmony.

• • •

[No. 16: On J. S. Bach.]

But now the time has come to examine the other side of the coin. If a person seeks only sensory stimulation from music, or only wants to look at its most perfect examples, it is true that the condition of German music described above may well provide an excuse to poke fun at the German tendency to sober, melancholy reflection; the true cosmopolitan and friend of the arts, however, will recognize this one-sidedness as the solid foundation of the later greatness of German music. The mechanism of any art must first have been developed to a very high level before it can become sufficiently mature to have an effect on *cultivated* individuals that is as powerful as the one its first appearance had on coarser folk who felt more than they thought. What kind of works are still being written today by composers who are not profoundly familiar with the rules of harmony? Either borrowed or insipid pieces, which, when performed in concert or at the piano, all too often move the listener to exclaim "*claudite rivos,*" etc.[12] Far from disparaging our worthy predecessors for the ponderousness and pettiness they exhibited in their artistic works, we should rather thank them for the laborious efforts by which they developed the rules of harmony by means of examples. For what the philosopher is without logic, the painter without drawing, or the architect without pure mathematics, a musician is without harmony—a sounding brass and a tinkling bell. He may, by accident or talent, hit on some natural expressions, but his products are never *genuine* works of art, merely (despite the fleeting applause of the ignorant mob) ephemera, in which training too often takes revenge for the neglect it has suffered. The transition from harmony to melody, on the other hand, is much easier, and it is only by taking this path that the composer, if he is sufficiently well versed in harmony, and his youthful drive to pour out his wealth of ideas in all directions has moderated, can achieve that genuinely thrilling simplicity that can never be confounded with triviality or poverty of ideas. It would be going too far, as our predecessors did (and some still do), were one to see the treatment of harmony and especially counterpoint as the *only* thing that distinguishes a musician; to do so would be to settle for the scaffolding rather than the building, and for dry artifice rather than an art that ennobles the heart. But it would be even sadder if mere emotion or—which is the same thing—the taste of ignorant listeners were to serve as the highest standard for art.[13] There could be no shorter or more certain road to barbarism than this. Thanks, therefore, heartfelt thanks to those men who at the beginning of the last century put their ingenuity to work to bring the most difficult part of the pure art of music closer to perfection. — — And now—what joy it is for patriotic citizens of our fatherland to know that the greatest, most profound musical harmonist of all times, who surpassed everything that Italy, France, and England had done for *pure* music, was a German! This man who astonished his contemporaries, accustomed as they were to learned works, who gave posterity examples that to this day have not been surpassed, examples that were looked upon as miracles (unfortunately they still are for many composers!), which no one, even with an uncommon degree of preparation, could approach without a secret shudder! —Lofty and noble, the name of Johann Sebastian Bach shines brightly above all German musicians of the first half of the last century. With a Newtonian spirit, he embraced everything in harmony that had been thought or made an example of; he stirred up harmony's depths so completely and with such good effect that he is regarded as the legislator of genuine harmony, whose laws are still in force today. He has yet to be surpassed by any composer in the world in the field in which he was most brilliant, strict counterpoint, and whatever anyone has tried to say or do in recent years to reduce his stature finds little or no acceptance, however easy it ordinarily is to belittle a great man by making him responsible for the taste of the times! In his early years Bach already studied the works of famous men such as Frohberger, Pachelbel, etc., but his greatest gain came from a fortunate turn of fate that made him acquainted with the French music of the period and its energy.[14] In France, the harpsichord had been especially cultivated, alongside the organ, which was the principal instrument. [François] Couperin's works, above all, gave our Bach a chance to explore new perspectives and treatments of harmony. His searching character and his German persistence made use of the creative hints of the French in a manner that raised him above his contemporaries and made him, so to speak, the person who perfected the harmonic edifice, and to whom most of the good composers who followed him either avowedly or secretly owed the greatest debt of gratitude. Because of his talent and his hard work, he did with great facility things that other people found amazingly difficult. This reliable characteristic of great artists was joined by another. He did not write for the applause of the great multitude, nor did his compositions follow his hand's aptitude; instead he made his hand (often working all night) become accustomed to his compositions (—in sharp contrast to many more recent virtuosos who compose to suit their technique). He ceaselessly pursued his artistic ideal, laid the groundwork for a freer unity between the diatonic and chromatic species of sound, and in this way compelled a purer temperament. In the process, he discovered a fingering (more fully developed by his great son C. P. E. Bach) that is incontestably the most natural. All this already made him the great benefactor of the musical world—and then [there are] his compositions, of which Gerber has said so nicely "that they resemble Odysseus' bow, on which we should try our strength!" —In fact, they are for music what Homer's songs were for the epic. From the *Iliad* and the *Odyssey*, people abstracted the rules of the epic, and from J. S. Bach's fugues, etc., those of modern harmony. How fortunate for us that these works were not lost! Even if anarchy, with its usual consequences of disdain for solidity and effort, were to reign in music for a time, sooner or later the distaste aroused by soft foods will lead back to these worthy men, and if this century were to bring forth a genius who made it unnecessary to study the works of J. S. Bach, then we would like to make a deep, deep bow before that individual in advance.

If some people should find me excessively enthusiastic in speaking of this patriarch of the new harmony (for no friend of the art of music, if he does not want to be accused of ignorance or jealous vanity, can speak of such a man without enthusiasm), they should reflect on the fact that I am not claiming that J. S. Bach did *everything* there was to do for music. His accomplishments really only embrace pure music, i.e. the mechanism of music, especially harmony and the strict style. In the field of applied music, free style, or the like, not only his contemporary Handel, but also his successors, his son C. P. E. Bach as well as [Carl Heinrich] Graun, [Johann Adolph] Hasse, and later J. Haydn, Mozart, and others, found a path that he had not trodden. Whether he *might* have done so, as well, if he had been not merely a performer and contrapuntist, but also a *singer*, like several of the above-named men (for example Graun, Hasse, Haydn), is something we cannot judge. Enough that he earned immortal merit in one of the most important parts of music.

Meanwhile, however great the influence was that J. S. Bach had on the development of the German art of music, because he directed his extraordinary powers at something that had to be especially welcome to the German spirit and way of thinking, which concerns itself so gladly (at least at that time) with difficult and even melancholy reflections; nevertheless there were also other circumstances that combined with him to bring music in Germany into flower, even if *as a whole* it still could not compete with Italian or French music. At the beginning of the last century, Germany had begun to recover from the terrible destruction of the Thirty Years' War, so much so that even Emperor Leopold's wars with France and the Turks did not noticeably retard the new life that was beginning to stir everywhere. Leopold himself, along with other German princes (from Saxony and Bavaria, among others) was a protector of the sciences and arts (even a virtuoso in his time). In Vienna, Dresden, Prague, Leipzig, and Munich, as in Hamburg, where Apollo ruled along with Mercury, people greatly valued and encouraged the art of music. The great external religiosity raised music up in the Catholic churches and monasteries, and in the Protestant churches it continued to hold a place of honor (partly out of respect for Luther). The above-mentioned[15] luxury of the princes opened the door to Italian operas and operettas. The French refugees brought to Germany a more perfect instrumental music, which had more liveliness than the slow church style had previously permitted. Both were to prove useful for melody and rhythm in the future. In addition, the French emigrés had introduced the Italian notation, and began, though only gradually at first, to increase the tempos somewhat, egged on by theatrical music; in this process the shorter notes (thirty-second and sixty-fourth notes) that had been invented at the beginning of the century were more than a little helpful. Above all, however, music was helped along by the purer temperament, which had become increasingly necessary because of the desire for polyphonic instrumental music and J. S. Bach's method of employing the keyboard. The employment of all the keys, wherein people had previously not ventured to modulate because of their attachment to the old church modes, the invention of double-flats and -sharps, etc., together led to the improvement or abandonment of instruments that either did not have all the notes or were incapable of producing them purely, i.e. in proper intervals of the improved temperament, or that were not suitable for a larger orchestra. This is what happened to the shawm, the recorder, the dulcimer, etc.; while the lute, the theorbo, the pandura-zither, and others declined in popularity. Instead of the viola da gamba, the 'cello (invented by Tardieu in Paris in 1708) was employed, along with the clarinet (invented by J. C. Denner in 1700), the French horn (invented in 1680 in France), and especially the violin as the principal instrument, along with the organ and the harpsichord.

If one considers these things, which are only briefly hinted at here, and which all occurred in the first half of the last century, it is clear that the only thing lacking for the rise of German music toward the end of the last century was a few men who would nourish the splendid seed, pick up and elaborate on the improvements made in Italy, France, and Germany in harmony and melody, church and dance music; who would be very familiar with the rules of harmony but would not think they were the only thing pertaining to a perfect musical mechanism, but would provide beautiful melodies, as well—in a word, men who would take the great progress already made in pure music and use it with genuine artistic sensibility in applied music (which, after all, always has the greatest charm); or who, even without texts, would show through original tone paintings what delicate but strong fabrics could be woven from the riches that had now been created. Germany was fortunate to have such men in the middle of the past century. They impressed their contemporaries with great power, not only here but to some extent also abroad. They continued to influence their successors for a long time, captivated otherwise fickle taste for quite a while, and would perhaps have done so even longer if a number of great geniuses of later eras had not happily succeeded in filling in the few gaps they had left in their treatment of music (which were partly only the result of their times and other circumstances). What friend of the art of music does not speak with gratitude of Graun, Hasse, C. P. E. Bach, *et al.*, even if he no longer has much or indeed anything to do with their works? —Who does not confess that it was they who transformed the budding plants into beautiful blossoms, and magically inspired the gay spring that now spread so pleasantly over German music and made it possible for music, which until then had been almost only mechanical, to claim to be a *fine art*? — Indeed, it is probably only right if we date the second period of the development of German music in the last century from these justly venerated men, and take a closer look at their influence on it!

• • •

[No. 17: Vocal music at midcentury.]
Second Period: *from Graun, Hasse, and C. P. E. Bach to J. Haydn and Mozart.*

Pragmatic history, especially the history of a fine art, does not always advance in step with chronology or, more precisely, with the chronicle of artists. One great man often has a more immediate effect on his contemporaries, and hence on the development of his art, while another who is living at the same time does not create a new school until later. This occurs when the former does not attempt to alter the national taste, while the second, intentionally or unintentionally, gives the course of artistic development a direction that does not quite mesh with the old gears. The first case is that of J. S. Bach, the second of Graun and Hasse.

The latter two men lived and worked at almost the same time as Bach, but Bach concerned himself almost exclusively with something that German industriousness and the national spirit had already treated; he only perfected and solidified the harmonic edifice as such. For this, what was required was not so much a lively and delicate sensibility as a finely developed ear and a profound, persistent spirit of inquiry; not so much the view *outside* of himself as that *within*; not so much foreign nourishment as his own original power. He impressed people quickly because he excited their admiration, and triumphed even over great artists, so to speak. Only a man of this type had the ability and the necessity to lift *pure music* (see the explanation of this term in the introduction) high, very high. For such music is a kind of archetype of art, bestowed from a higher realm, and the man who exhibits such an intimate relationship with it seems like a magician to whom one tends to ascribe supernatural powers. On the other side, the man who uses art only as a means for the more beautiful portrayal of human emotions and actions reaps for his efforts not only immediate amazement, but love and satisfaction. He attracts these in proportion to his works' faithfulness to Nature, i.e. the more closely he—even if unintentionally—follows human beings' most interesting ideas and emotions, which are thrilling even to the uninitiated. If this naturalness is the product not merely of chance and talent, but also of hidden, yet genuine artistry (*artis est, celare artem* [it is art to conceal art]) as well, only then does he have a powerful effect on the development of art and make a name for himself. But this does not happen immediately, for the great multitude may regard works by this kind of artist as beautiful, praiseworthy, and even as something unusual, but on account of their very naturalness (*ut sibi quivis speret idem* [as anyone likewise hopes]), they will not pay him the respect he deserves. Only later, when they have become convinced that this composer also had a complete command of artistry and forbore to use it only because he was pursuing other aims that do not separate the artist from the man; only then will the contemporary world, and even more posterity, shower him with praise. Such a widespread following can seldom, if ever, be inspired by an artist whose merely melancholy brilliance shines in pure music. It is possible only in applied music, which takes the more *specific* portrayal of human emotions and actions and embodies and elevates them in connection with poetry (and drama); for these are works not only for the connoisseur, but for the layman as well.[16]

In the middle of the last century (actually even earlier, but their fame was only solidly established later on), Graun and Hasse made their entrance onto this German stage. They elevated vocal music, which had been neglected until then, to an even higher level. Well versed in the rules of harmony (Graun even more than Hasse), they nevertheless used them only to support the melody, which, as the original language of sentiment, they never put last, but regarded as that part of the tonal mechanism that could and must have the greatest effect on the heart. This distinguished them from other composers of their time. They composed much, both for the church and for the theater, gave German music a more beautiful and graceful shape, and earned great fame even in the fatherland of music. —How and by what means did this occur? —As is usual with men who are destined to be demagogues (in the artistic as well as the political realm), many things combined to place the driving wheel of German art in their hands. In part they lifted themselves, and in part they were uplifted. Natural talent in melody was the first source of their greatness. Before them, all the important singers who were known in Germany came from Italy. These foreigners arrived with too lofty a notion of the advantages of their homeland when it came to music for them not to have viewed the lean, though skillful, skeleton of German music with contempt. Nor was their pride entirely baseless. For some time, Italy had exercised the right of an artistic tutelage over Germany. The foster child had imitated its foster parent with great success when it came to harmony. But at this very moment, Italy's music was in the throes of a great revolution. It no longer wanted to be counted and admired, it wanted to move its listeners too, and the only way it could do this was by cultivating the melodious song. On this path, it was more difficult for the German spirit to keep pace with its model. The Germans felt the beneficent effect of the change, they honored it, but—their dependence on Italy only increased. Hence if someone wanted to distinguish himself in Germany, he had to mold himself to the new shape, to the extent that he was composing for the voice. He also had to possess a thorough knowledge of harmony, in order not to offend the grammarians, and had to combine this with an active imagination and a passionate character or exceptional delicacy of feeling. The former was characteristic of Hasse, the latter of Graun. The fiery character of the first and the gentle one of the latter were indispensable for the effects they aroused. (Almost like Luther and Melanchthon [the rhetorician].) Their study of composition elevated them when they were still only singers, although in that era virtuosos knew more about composition than they do today. But the works of a Keiser, a Porpora, etc., awakened their enthusiasm for natural expression, while their familiarity with harmony and counterpoint served merely as a means. The first and most thrilling kind of music, which will remain so as long as human beings exist, because man himself is the vehicle for it and its tones not only can be combined with concepts but are also the most easily and perfectly assimilated with our feelings, and which can never be surpassed by an instrument, even though thousands more should be invented[17]—in a word, *song* was always the chief concern of the two men. For it they sacrificed many—and of Hasse one can say perhaps too many—of the other powers of music. But they never deserved the reproach that, like Leo's followers who were not entirely faithful to their master, or like most Italians of the most recent period, they went to the other extreme and, for the sake of a sweet, pleasing melody, treated harmony as something secondary. All this was the fruit of their genius, their knowledge, and their character. At the same time, these qualities could probably never have advanced so far if favorable conditions and encouragement had not also contributed a great deal. Even the greatest spirit requires an external impetus for the development of its power, whether it be extraordinary pressure or an especially fortunate destiny. Hasse and Graun experienced the latter. While they were still young, destiny led them to places where the music of that time was in its greatest flower, to Hamburg, Braunschweig, and Dresden.[18] Hasse [1699–1783], as was mentioned above, was educated first in Hamburg in the tradition of the famous, melody-rich Keiser. He then trained as a singer at the theater in Braunschweig, and after that went to Italy, where he became a pupil of the great Aless. Scarlatti and subsequently married the famous singer Faustina [Bordoni], who greatly augmented his genius and his fame. Graun found nourishment for his talent in Dresden, where several skilled men, above all that most insightful of all music directors, [Johann Georg] Pisendel [1687–1755], were in their glory. The theater in Hamburg offered him, too, a marvelous opportunity to raise himself up—even more than Hasse, since he arrived there with a greater knowledge of harmony. —But up to this point, both Hasse and Graun remained within the glittering but narrow circle of virtuosos. Men of greater weight were needed to lead them onto a higher path, where they could make their contribution to the course of German music as composers, as well. They found them; Hasse in King Augustus of Poland, Graun in Frederick II. The love of ostentation that reigned at the court of the first, where they saw, or desired to see, Versailles in Germany, naturally could not do without the art of music. Music had taken root there long before; now it was a matter of surpassing the other courts in musical recognition, as well. In this they succeeded. It was during this period that Hasse arrived in Dresden, armed with everything the new taste had produced in Italy. Adroit and fiery in both the secular and the theatrical style, he soon made Dresden into a leading site for applied music in Germany. On the whole, however, he had a greater effect on southern Germany, and he spent the last years of his life in Italy. —With [C. H.] Graun [1704–1757] it was different. He first went to Italy, after having educated himself in Germany, although with the help of Italian masters and Italian works. His gentle, calm character, as well as his destiny, which did not drive him so restlessly from place to place as Hasse, made him more inclined toward and more skilled in the depiction of gentle, delicate sentiments, while Hasse surpassed him when it came to heroic and harsh character portrayals and also seemed to have the theatrical effect of great multitudes more in his power. —Graun was always impeccable in respect to strict composition, and he impressed connoisseurs in this way at the same time as he moved audiences with his sweet melodies. He was not as powerfully thrilling as Hasse, but his enchantment lasted longer. —Yet all of this might not have been so useful to the musical world, had not the man who did so extraordinarily much for his people, for Germany, indeed for the cultivation of humanity in general, had not Frederick II taken Graun under his protection and placed him at the head of his musical institutions. From now on Graun never lacked opportunities to apply his qualifications. Working with him on the improvement of taste were men who not only, as practical musicians, numbered among the greatest virtuosos of the day, but who also were possessed of thoroughgoing insights into the theory of music—men like [Johann Joachim] Quantz, Franz Benda, C. P. E. Bach, etc. The great male and female singers—Astrua, Salimbeni, etc.—contributed no less. In this way, *Berlin*, which until then would not have survived the comparison with other cities when it came to music, quickly rose to the first rank and was, from then on, the musical authority, at least for the northern half of Germany, although Graun's works were applauded even in Italy. Berlin was now the place where in the theater, in church, and in concerts both the grammarians and the sensitive friends of art could find satisfaction. The former, by seeking out the compositions that were written with intent to be strict, i.e. in keeping with the rules of harmony; the latter, by having an opportunity both to hear more than contrapuntal artifice (although the latter still seemed to be the only thing required of a non-vocal musician), and also, as a result of the increasingly appropriate application of the musical mechanism, to learn to love music in its newer, more beautiful form. It was no longer a dry skeleton that he was expected to admire, it was a body endowed with flesh and blood, and one that did not conceal any errors or infirmities under the pleasant exterior of its sturdy parts. The Berlin School was characterized by its combination of noble melodies with correct harmonies, and its success in bringing the two together to faithfully express feelings, especially those that do not stray too far from the normal course of human life (for the wild and the bold did not succeed as well as the soft and the inward). The main initiators of this course of musical development were, in other words, *Germans*, a German prince and German artists. The prince [succeeded in this] by combining a great spirit with the passionate love of music and by gathering these important men around him and nourishing their artistic sensibilities; but above all by the fact that he was revered not only as the miracle of his time, its model in the arts of war and government, but also as its leader in matters of taste—and that he defied all the old prejudices. From now on the defenders of piety dared revile the theater as a sinful entertainment only in private. And yet, despite the authority of Frederick II, theatrical music would hardly have raised itself up without a significant struggle against the old ideas, had it not been introduced to Germany (and here one finds another opportunity to admire the cautious, but sure workings of reason!) under the protection of a foreign language that was unknown to the common people, and was therefore regarded as nothing but a royal plaything.

There was a still more significant factor that facilitated music's rise. According to the definition of theater, poetry (in both the broader and the stricter sense) is always the principal thing; music is only supposed to be its helper, and to appear neither as an autocratic ruler nor as a slave. It followed that Poetry herself was not meant to appear (as is so often the case nowadays) in a revealing and often even rather soiled negligee, nor was she meant to have such an awkward gait (full of unsonorous words or phrases) that it would provoke her obliging sister to abandon her. Hence our great artists, who did so much for the development of applied music, our Hasse and Graun would never have reached their goal, despite their talents, knowledge and hard work, if they had not been supported in this by a man whose truly musical poetry aroused their enthusiasm, and who today still occupies such a unique place in music. Who else but—Metastasio? Inspired by the powerful spirit he imbibed from the ruins of beautiful Antiquity, he breathed the same noble and friendly spirit into his immortal works. This euphony, this rounding of details and of the whole, this strength of the characters, this distancing from opulence and bombast, on the one hand, and from boring sobriety, on the other; in short, this inner and outer poetry, which seems to sing itself, taking us back to the time of Euripides and recalling the spirit of Greek drama from its banishment (unfortunately only briefly)—all this must have given new strength, as it were, to those composers who were bold enough to approach it with genuine artistic sensibility, and could not but make Metastasio a great benefactor of the German art of music.

Now, in a word, applied music in Germany stood revealed in all its youthful charm. Its two principal branches, *sacred* and *theater music*, had achieved *equal dignity*, without being *mingled together* (as has so often occurred in recent times, despite the essential difference between them).[19] Each gained more than a little from the other. Sacred music assumed greater inner, appropriate simplicity and outer richness. *Theatrical* music, which was dissolving its bonds with the former, so to speak, was prevented from excessive luxuriousness by the thoroughness that was demanded of it, and by the serious and significant matters it took for its content. This must not be forgotten if one wants to do justice to the works of Graun, among others. For posterity does not always judge fairly; it is often excessive in praise or blame. And it almost cannot be otherwise, for the works that it is criticizing remain, while the circumstances under which they were created perish.[20] Thus, for example, the awkwardness of the rhythm, the uniformity of the melodic figures, their almost constant repetition, the drum bass, which encouraged the despotism of the obbligato voices; in short, the entire square-cornered cut of the arias and choruses (analogous to the dress fashions of the time)—all weaknesses that even the most enthusiastic admirer of Graun and his contemporaries cannot deny in his works for the theater—were a consequence less of the inner limitations of the artist than of the predominant taste, which even the most original spirit can only defy up to a certain point. — Besides, Frederick the Great, whose achievements in the realm of German art have already been mentioned, did impose some restraints on its inner development. He developed an affection for the melodious Graun, but probably did not treat him consistently enough; for he made this gentle man create portrayals of heroic characters and scenes. The opera, as is well known, was seen as a means of promoting the military spirit for which the foundation had already been laid by Frederick William I. Hence everything was concentrated on this subject, and Graun had to bend to the king's will. That he would probably have worked differently and thus given German music, on which he had such a powerful effect, a different direction, is shown by the one work of his that has survived longer than all the others, and that even now is always received with appreciation despite the changes in taste, namely his [oratorio] *Tod Jesu*. Every great artist who works under significant external influence tries to convey to posterity one or two works in which he is able to concentrate the power of his spirit and artistic cultivation as freely as possible. Inspired by the sweet presentiment that these works will be the ineradicable root of his fame, even if its other branches should wither, he devotes his greatest efforts to them and—reaches his goal.[21] So too with Graun. In his operas he accommodated the one-sided taste of his king and was more obliging than Mozart[22]; only with his Passion could he be sure that the king would be only slightly, if at all interested, since the subject and language were too far removed from the monarch's own taste. This was bolstered by Graun's own tendency to religiosity and the really poetic text, which, despite its errors, is almost the only *musical* poem that we Germans possess. No wonder he worked on it so utterly *con amore*, and in the process created a lasting national work (as someone recently called it, with justification).

• • •

[No. 18: Instrumental music and music theory at midcentury.] While *applied* music was being given such a pleasing form by Hasse and Graun,[23] *pure* music was also undergoing a significant change. Until now, an artistic harmonic progression was the only thing people appreciated in products of this kind. Its forms, even more than those of applied music, were thoroughly *rhetorical*, not *poetic*. Concertos, sonatas, toccatas, preludes, and even so-called "fantasies" all betrayed this anxious character. If a piece contained only one theme, which, however, could be reproduced in ten different permutations, people gave no further thought to the question whether it had anything to say. The *ideal*, which pure music, by its very nature, has more within its power than applied music, and whose *suggestion* is pure music's greatest charm, lay completely outside the composers' field of vision; when they composed they were merely calculating. In short, this frosty play of tones lacked spirit and life. But the injection of Italian song into Germany was not without its effect even on purely instrumental compositions. The growing infatuation with music remained fixed, as it was everywhere, on beautiful melodies. But not everyone could sing, nor could they perform Italian arias, in particular! And instrumental music came first. Hence they felt the need to compose for the keyboard, etc., in ways that would fall pleasantly on their ears. In home music, as well as in concerts, contrapuntally worked movements were now replaced by the theatrical style—excepting choruses and the like. However, the former were not entirely abandoned, instead people attempted to combine them with the latter. The result was the *chamber style [Kammerstyl]*, which the strict grammarians and church composers derisively termed the *galant style*. In the process,

naturally, some of the old rules had to be broken, and because even leading musicians did so it helped prepare the ground for the mischief that has most recently gained such currency; namely the madness that it is possible to do without studying the rules altogether and [simply] write down one's ideas, so long as they don't sound unpleasant. —This transplanting of the theatrical style to the art of pure music had the effect of producing a great emptiness and monotony in the accompanying voices. Just as, in the theater, singing ruled and—at least at that time—had to rule alone; so it was in pure music, with an obbligato instrument or with the right hand on the keyboard. As rolling passages gradually came be used more regularly in the theater, so here, too, they increasingly began to cast their shadow over noble song, so that, for example, Franz Benda's [1709–1786] art in his adagio now almost seems, with few exceptions,[24] to be among the things that, like painting on glass, have been lost. With this transition of pure music from harmonic artifice to merely melodic emptiness more, in fact, would have been lost than had been gained, since the change was caused by the inappropriate use and imitation of the theatrical style and not by gradual inner development, had not one man fortunately stood up to seize the reins of music as it foundered—someone who combined originality with profound study and opened a path for pure music that could otherwise hardly have been anticipated. Like Ossian, he touched the strings, and the empty tinkling—did not entirely die away, but shrank before his magical power as long as the latter held sway. For such an upward thrust of pure music, what was absolutely necessary was the superior cultivation of an instrument that can portray, not just melodies, but harmonies as well, and can do so in such a way that a single individual has all aspects of the *inner* tonal mechanism in his power. Of old this was the *organ*, in more recent times the *piano*.[25] The former has the advantage of colossal, overwhelming power and lasting tones, while the latter is superior in the production of fine nuances and in imitation of the kind of feelings and ideas that come from within human beings more than they are imposed from without. The former is made for the sublime, the latter only for the beautiful and gentle. But enough; Carl Philipp Emanuel Bach [1714–1787], worthy of his great father, attracted the attention of all the connoisseurs and half-connoisseurs with his compositions for the keyboard. Among the former, this soon turned to enthusiasm, for they admired the novelty and boldness of his phrases, his light treatment of rhythm, and his beautiful combination of noble melodies with the most powerful harmony. They were glad that he wanted to put an end to the theatrical thrumming, which was so poor in harmonies and was beginning to dominate in sonatas and the like; and that the effort required to perform his works would rescue the study of music from falling into mere frivolity that tickled the ears. The half-connoisseurs, as usual, followed the opinion of the connoisseurs. They secretly disliked Bach's works, which they found dark and difficult, but the charm of novelty and their vanity, which made them loathe to be left behind, made them try their luck with it. Both groups missed the perspective from which Bach ought to have been viewed. The connoisseurs, by admiring in him only the strong and bold harmonist; the half-connoiseurs, by believing that his greatness lay only in the difficulties caused by the performance of his works. —No, Bach did not make an effort to compose in a dark and difficult manner; instead these characteristics flowed naturally from his ideas, in which the mechanical (merely reckoning) musician was as incapable of following him as was the musician who sought only sensual delight. What was stirring in him was a kind of *aesthetic* idea, i.e. one that combines concepts and emotion, and that does not allow itself to be expressed in words, although it comes very *close* to the *specific* emotion that song can depict for us, and of which it is, as it were, the archetype. He translated this to his keyboard (or into notes), whereby his intimate familiarity with the tonal mechanism almost automatically furnished him with the necessary forms. Since his *poetic spirit* avoided common ideas whenever he was permitted to compose freely, it was inevitable that those people who did not possess a kindred spirit would fail to understand it, and even with repeated practice barely recognized what a rich trove of ideas it contained. Bach was another Klopstock, who used tones *instead of* words. Is it the fault of the singer of odes if his lyrical ardor seems to the rough multitude like nonsense? —In this way, Bach's dithyrambs, i.e. his fantasies and keyboard sonatas (for what was said above applies only to these, although he did not entirely deny his original power in any of his works), had to have an effect on most music lovers that was more alarming than inviting. This does not outweigh, but rather adds to his great achievement, namely his demonstration that pure music is no mere shell for applied music, or abstraction from it, but that it could achieve great aims by itself. He showed that it had no need to contort itself prosaically, or at best rhetorically, as a mere game for the senses or the intellect, but instead had the capacity to raise itself up to the level of poetry, which is the more pure, the less it is dragged down into the realm of common perception by words (which always contain secondary meanings). But here we can observe something remarkable. Such a man, such a poetic musician, ought, one would think, to have excellent success in composing works for voice; —and yet this was not the case. With the exception of isolated original beauties, songs would hardly have secured his great fame, which, as noted, is actually based solely on his *sonatas* and *fantasies* (for even his concertos, despite a number of beautiful solo movements, cannot be compared with these. Among other things, connoisseurs have criticized a certain dryness and emptiness in their accompaniment, which admittedly might be excused, in part, by the custom of the times and the inadequate cultivation of the instruments, etc.). How might this be explained? It seems to me, by the following. In his sonatas and fantasies his ideas were transmitted *directly* to the keyboard, without having to adapt themselves to anyone else. But to compose vocal music one must have a pliability of spirit that demands a certain self-denial, as it thinks itself fully into the poet's train of thought and never leaves it.[26] This characteristic was lacking in our Bach, and it had to be lacking; for he was too self-sufficient, too original, too poetic to set a text successfully; and he did not yet know or did not use the stratagem of more recent years, namely to select poor texts that, thanks precisely to their poor quality, would not impose any constraints on him. —At the same time, the abovementioned benefits were not the only ones through which he made such a great contribution to German music. —As Michel Angelo Buonarotti gained fame as a builder, sculptor, and painter, so our Bach, not only as a composer and keyboard-player, but also as—a *theoretician*. And now the time has come to say something about the state of musical theory in Germany during the last century, since the most important figures in this field lived and worked, for the most part, in the second period.

Fundamental theories are a reliable measure of the development of an art, even where there has previously been no lack of similar *attempts*. Germany had experienced quite a few of the latter during the sixteenth and seventeenth centuries, if one is willing to consider one-sided scholastic examinations of scales and sacred song as such. But for a theory to be *fundamental*, it must rest on *firm* principles, and must not have any great gaps; in other words it must be comprehensive, while not overstepping the boundaries of its field. Moreover, there is, for every fine art, a *dual* theory: 1) a *mechanical* theory, which treats its mechanism and is more *negative* than positive for the practical artist, i.e. makes him adept *only* at avoiding mechanical mistakes; and 2) an *aesthetic* theory, which presupposes the existence of the other, and deals *philosophically* with the *actual aims of the art*.[27] As long as the tonal system itself was still in great ferment, no comprehensive theory could emerge from it. J. S. Bach was the first to put an end to this ferment.

Until then, people had made do with isolated remarks that, despite their systematic form, did not deserve the name of theory (according to the definition given above). It was also inevitable that people would mix the two types of theory, and this mingling was one of the chief reasons for the oft-repeated complaint that the principles of music were so shaky. —Hence in the first half of the last century there was no *actual* theory of music in Germany. For the works in this direction by the almost superhumanly prolific writer [Johann] Mattheson [1681–1764], while they contain a large number of beautiful, original, and witty observations, are too fragmentary, too polemical, and too overloaded with cleverness (although it is often apt and naive), and at the same time, as befits the taste of that era, too playful and trivially hair-splitting *[mikrologisch]*, so that one can immediately recognize the colorful multitude of ideas thronging in the head of their rapid-writing originator. —Kirnberger, Marpurg, and C. P. E. Bach were the first to give Germany theories of music, which were naturally of the first type, and through which they cleared the way for those of the second type, with which we hope the new century will provide us. Their works still have (as proof of their excellence) the force of law. All the theoreticians and practical musicians who came after them built upon their work, with the (real or apparent) exception of one individual, whose system, however, has *not yet* found *great* acceptance among us.[28]

Through their writings, the first two musicians ([Friedrich Wilhelm] Marpurg [1718–1795] and [Johann Philipp] Kirnberger [1721–1783]), made Berlin the capital of theoretical music and music criticism. Even their bitter feuds with each other, while they may not have done honor to their character, were all the more salutary for art. They forced both sides to go to great lengths and study the difficult materials more deeply, although it is not to be denied that sometimes mere obstinacy and devotion to preconceived ideas (which should be the farthest thing from a critic's mind) made them focus their cleverness on details. Apart from this, the feuds performed a great service, especially for beginning artists, by assuring that the latter did not, as is usual, swear so readily by what their teachers said, but instead were forced to test things out for themselves. —Meanwhile, Kirnberger, although compared to Marpurg he wrote very little, was victorious in the end, i.e. he maintained the greatest reputation as a theoretician. This came about very naturally. Marpurg, who was far superior to Kirnberger intellectually, was not satisfied with developing the mechanical aspect of music; he also made *excursions* into aesthetic theory, for which the art of music was not yet sufficiently mature. Like Mattheson, he too was burdened with a great throng of ideas about art, which often poured out in merely fragmentary descriptions. With the exception of his classical essay on the fugue, and perhaps a couple of other writings, his works, for all that they contain much excellent and instructive material, do not bear the stamp of completeness. His other activities also militated against this. In the process, he betrayed too great a predilection for French theory, which he reproduced in condensed form with all its advantages and—imperfections, and which did not coincide with the practical theories of J. S. Bach, to which the Germans were attached. —Kirnberger, on the other hand, confined himself to the mechanism of the art of music, which always remained the main thing for the Germans. Thus it was easier for him to bring to his work the unity, logical consistency, and completion that are necessary to found a school. He followed the principles of his great teacher J. S. Bach fully, and since he felt that he himself was not capable of style, he attached himself to great men who helped him achieve order, present his ideas in a transparent manner, and examine the subjects of his reflection exhaustively. These men were [Johann Georg] Sulzer [1720–1779], Lambert, and others. To all these circumstances we owe the fact that we possess the important work *The Art of Strict Musical Composition* [1771–1779], which, thanks to the above-mentioned characteristics, especially its logical consistency and clarity, surpasses and may perhaps long surpass everything of a similar nature, and which no *real* contemporary composer can do without.

What these two men (Marpurg and Kirnberger), and here and there a few others, did for a scientifically based theory of the art of music,[29] C. P. E. Bach did for piano practice. Since this instrument, as noted above, served at that time as the principal support of pure music, he did a great service with his instructions on how to use it properly, in his *Essay on the True Art of Playing Keyboard Instruments,* [1753–1762]. —Above all else, he tried to bring clarity to the theory of finger placement, which until then had been inconsistent. In this he followed his father, who had been forced by his own works to come to terms with the difficulties of performing them; he did this by searching out the easiest and surest, and consequently also the most natural fingering. Initially this remained a secret of the school; it was C. P. E. Bach who first made it generally known. He, too, felt that his works, which were far removed from the relaxed pace of the theatrical style that had now been transplanted into pure music, demanded uncommon strength if they were not to be deformed. Aware of the richness and delicacy of his ideas, he had good reason to fear that they would be translated faithfully only by a few people other than himself. To make these efforts as easy as possible, he tried in his theory of fingering to remove at least the mechanical hindrances. In this way, he opened a path to greater and more *reliable* skillfulness, which consists not in high-wire acrobatics but in the power to represent every playable series of tones the way their creator conceived them. But he went even further. The wish to keep the fine nuances of his expression from being muddied by a dull, awkward performance, or at the opposite extreme by a performance overloaded with flourishes, resulted in his lovely comments about performance and the ornaments *[Manieren]*. His theory of accompaniment also showed that he was both a grammarian and a man of aesthetic feeling. In this, as well (in the chapter on ornaments), he sought to encourage a *speaking* performance in general. But only a tiny group of genuine artists followed him *truly* in this. Most of them were seduced by the guttural and running manner of theatrical singing, and by the addiction to celebrity, i.e. to astonishing the mob with a skillfulness that had nothing to say. As a result, they misused and exaggerated these flourishes; and the later superficiality in learning music utterly ruined the good that Bach had intended. Be that as it may, this success, which was so regrettable from the point of view of art, did have the effect that Bach increasingly stood out as unique. Indeed, he and his father towered over most of the musicians of their time (where *pure* music is concerned) like a pair of cloud-high mountains over little foothills. They seemed to carry the musical firmament on their shoulders; and ever since then there has been no *serious* pilgrimage to their holy places from which it was not possible to return home with a rich harvest for one's knowledge of art.

• • •

[No. 19: The spread of music in Germany.]

Up to this point, it has been rather easy to survey the course of development taken by German music in the last century. It still remained in rather elevated regions. It went its way—serious, thoughtful, noble, and full of feeling—and among the handful of its leaders it counted only men of rare power. The demands imposed on newcomers by the initiated were generally great and strict. Only definite connoisseurs (alongside the voices of educated patrons) were permitted to exercise critical judgment; everyone else repeated what they said. The populace was prevented from having any intimate involvement with *practical* music by the artificiality of sacred music and the Italian language of the theater. Concerts and private musicales were still a rarity. The middle class still had too little cultivation, and dance music was either too coarse, too unharmonic and unmelodic, or its rhythm was too heavy. Hence it remained separated from the noble, higher art of music by a distance as great as the political gulf between the estates. In addition, the prejudice that considered music outside the church to be useless or even sinful made many mothers and fathers, in their desire to be respectable, hesitate to teach it to their children. —But now came the point in time where music would no longer be cultivated as a hothouse plant, but would be set out among the other fruits for life's enjoyment and distributed along with them. Frederick II, by his example and the regard in which he was held, scattered the seed of enlightenment quickly and widely. Here and there, agreeable theater melodies found their way even to remote towns. Sacred music also became—with the exception, perhaps, of solo organ works—simpler, more melodious, and more dazzling to the populace through the use of multiple instruments. The oratorios were gradually transformed into something midway between theater and sacred music, contributing, in this way, not a little to the decline of the prejudice against non-sacred music. Above all, however, [sacred music] appealed to the ears of the people by imitating the graceful, accessible theatrical style of instrumental music, which made the latter so easy to perform, and as a result of which ordinary dance music, too, took on increased vitality and singability. Now the natural facility for music that is so common in certain of Germany's provinces (especially *Saxony*, *Bohemia*, *Schleswig*, and *Swabia*) began to develop apace. But from this point on it also becomes more and more difficult to survey the whole of this new course of development of the art of music in Germany at a single glance. To fully describe all the elements that belong within it, one would have to examine the progress or regression of each province separately, and would, in the end, find it difficult to form a single conclusion about the whole, perhaps for the reason that, especially since *that* era, the various different German peoples were growing more and more separate in regard to culture, customs, and taste. To do all this would require not a sketchy description like this one, but a thick, thick volume. There is nothing left to do but to examine those changes in the art of music in which a large number, if not all, of the German provinces participated, namely the ones that had a reputation for outstanding intellectual culture; and to speak of *those* artists whose works had the greatest effect on it.

Here one is immediately confronted by a noticeable change in the *external* form in which the art of music developed. At the beginning of the century, *sacred music* was the most important thing to work on. Later, it was forced to concede equal rank to theatrical music. *Pure* (or, if one prefers, merely instrumental) music at first bore a greater resemblance to the style of sacred music, and was only of secondary importance. But as the latter followed the melodious theater style, as it came to be treated in a way more suited for the senses and the heart than for the understanding, as the love of music became widespread everywhere, in short, as the above-mentioned causes of the change in taste and customs occurred, sacred music also began to falter, and the *theater* and *concert* became the most important levers of the musical art. In *Catholic* Germany, plenty of sacred works were performed; but almost all the Missas, Kyries, Misereres, etc., were given such a theatrical form that practically nothing but the locale and the text distinguished these performances from an opera or a concert. In *Protestant* Germany, the zeal for outward religiosity was increasingly beginning to cool. To this were added the relative lack of encouragement, the scanty recompense—no longer adequate for daily wants, as it had once been—paid to cantors and organists, who could only make do by giving private lessons or playing in concerts. Who, under such circumstances, could want to continue writing seriously for the church? Who would want to take an interest in the despised choirs, which were practically only retained out of habit? And what skilled professional musician with a love of honor and art would not, under such circumstances, have chosen the theater or the house orchestra *[Kapelle]* above service to the church? There he would not be paid especially well either, on account of the ever-increasing competition, but at least he would do better and often reap greater honors than in the church. —Truly, it required a rare and vigorous artistic sense when men like Hiller, Rolle, etc., took the neglected area under their wing and tried, in part, to preserve choral song, and in part to find *noble* means of embracing the theatrical style so as to protect sacred music and prevent the even more rapid loss of credit that it would otherwise have suffered.

Concerts and *plays*, on the other hand, aroused an enthusiasm that was all the greater. Instrumental music increasingly became separated from vocal music and was enlarged thanks to the gradual cultivation of the *wind instruments*, which had previously only been used as a means of *enhancing* expression. *Virtuosos* and *dilettantes* materialized in large numbers and demanded a greater variety of pieces with which to amuse themselves and the public, for example sonatas, duets, trios, quartets, concertos, symphonies, etc. Since, at the same time, most of the compositions of this kind still left people missing *real* song, they attempted to replace this lack with *skillfulness* and in this way engendered a greater rapidity in the *tempo*, whereby, however, they also laid the groundwork for the later loss of simple, meaningful delivery and powerful, noble vocal music.

At the same time, two elements were still lacking to make the art of music into more of a popular possession, namely the easy and inexpensive spread of musical manuscripts and the use of theater music for more tasteful presentations of *German* mores in the *German* language. This too occurred. *Leipzig*, which already counted J. S. Bach among its citizens, had the good fortune also to be home to those men who deserve the credit for this. Joh. Gottlob Emanuel Breitkopf, through his shop and his new music press, which his successors continued to perfect, laid the groundwork for a more rapid distribution of new musical works, which served the art of music in more or less the same way as the art of book printing served the sciences. Consideration of the place where these pages are being printed [Leipzig, *chez* Breitkopf] forbids me to say more on the subject. The public, through its ever greater participation, has passed judgment.

But the most remarkable change in this interim period, which had such an impact on the increasing cultivation of the middle class and its current receptivity to better music, and which among other things also made the most significant contribution to leading the art of music out of the realm of the initiated and socially prominent into that of the common people, so that it became, as it were, *common property*, was brought about principally by J. A. Hiller [1728–1804]. Here we are not concerned with the man's thoroughgoing musical scholarship; the work he did for the church; his salutary patronage of the works of *Handel*, along with others in the more elevated style; his instructive writings, which could be so immensely useful for the future creator of an aesthetic theory of music; or, finally, his many and diverse efforts toward the preservation of both regular solo and polyphonic singing, especially the latter, by means of which this dignified old gentleman, who is still alive, and whose active love of art persisted through the end of the last century, has earned the veneration and gratitude of the musical world. It was his *operettas* that caused such a great sensation in his time that one is justified in making them into leading characters in any portrayal of the changes undergone by the art of German music in the past century. —The more justified the reproach that was often levelled against the German nation, namely that on the whole it was not susceptible to natural but beautiful song (a reproach that might still be made with undiminished force but for an amalgamation with more southern peoples toward which the nineteenth century, in a kind of reverse migration, seems to be leading us), the more indebted we are to Hiller's successful attempts to create a taste for it among the people. This could only happen by means of the theater. Until then, the populace had little benefit from the latter. Only with difficulty were the popular dramas *[Haupt- und Staatsaktionen]* and harlequinades displaced, first, by starchy transplants of French and Italian tragedies and comedies on German territory, and by Lessing's contributions. All this, however, did more for the understanding than for sensuality and the heart. The Italian opera, which in any case was performed only in the big cities, and then only rarely, entertained only the more highly educated. The populace was more dazzled than moved, partly by the splendor and expense, partly by the foreign language, and partly by the ancient subjects, which require a knowledge of history and antiquity if one is to be touched by them. Besides, only their *lyrical* part, the arias and choruses, could generally transport the audience. The reciting and declaiming parts of the text (the recitative), in which the dialogue and the actual plot were clothed, could (especially since they were frequently presented without a descriptive accompaniment) fail to be fatiguing only to an Italian, who sings when he speaks and speaks when he sings—and of late it may fatigue him too. Hence the *French* had previously opted for another manner in their *vaudeville* and other theaters. They presented comedies interspersed with songs, whereby the latter were meant to express either lasting feelings or a maxim. In this way the so-called operettas were created. —Our *Hiller* now embarked upon this path. He found in his noble friend Weisse[30] a man who provided just the sort of texts that were needed for this purpose, namely to disperse the music among the populace and, in so doing, ennoble their emotions. What could be more fitting than scenes from the *world of the idyll*, the mere description of which suffices to touch the hearts of all human beings who have not been spoiled? This necessarily had to awaken the enthusiasm of the middle and lower estates, which were gradually feeling their human worth. In addition, the pieces themselves had a coherent plan, developed characters, and a language that was as natural as it was noble. All of this outweighed the comments made by earnest critics about specific poetic lapses and shortcomings. Then came gentle Hiller to pour the most noble melodies over these friendly texts—melodies that seemed so completely drawn from nature that they appeared almost throughout to be the genuine language of sensibility, and that were as pleasing to the ear as to the heart. He also supported them with proper, if not brilliant harmonies; which latter, even if he had been so inclined, would not have been permitted either by the taste or by the state of instrumental music at that time. He also knew how little could be demanded of German singers in respect to artistic delivery (for even now, except for the opera houses and here and there the national theaters, true *bravura* singing is a rarity); in other words, he accomplished his aim more easily by expressing his ideas in a way that was more syllabic than melismatic. —Under all these circumstances, Hiller's operettas could not but be very beneficial for the general taste in music, and to date (admittedly partly for reasons that will be discussed in the description of the third period) no modern operetta set piece that achieved rapid popularity has lasted, as a popular song, as long as many of Hiller's.

But here, too, the well-known saying applies: nothing is so good that is does not also have its shortcomings. Thus, this popularization of music led (and the man so highly respected will not take the following comment amiss, if he should happen upon it, since he could hardly foresee such success) to a certain retardation of the higher inner perfection that it would probably have attained if it had descended only gradually to the popular level, i.e. by transforming the great Italian opera into a similar, somewhat less brilliant German one, and its heroic text into not a provincial, but an upper-bourgeois one. It fell too *rapidly* into the opposite extreme. For the characters, as well as their sensibilities and actions, for all their psychological truth and ethical appropriateness, remained too *ordinary* and too *common* to be adequate for the real demands of art, which can only maintain its *dignity*[31] at a certain level by holding fast to the *ideal*. In this way the whole assumed a skimpy, awkward, prosaic character, and, because the composer followed the poet all too closely, an awkward rhythm; all of which put art *as such* in danger of paying dearly for the joy it gave the populace. For now the great multitude, for whom art should never appear without a cloak of magic, because their destiny is only to pray silently at the altar [of art], thought that they could make judgments about works of art, and as a result the swarm of imitators, who ordinarily mistake the shell for the kernel and seek only the applause of the crowd, was induced to cobble together a tasteless mixture of high and low, emotional and sober, of the ideal and raw Nature, such as the third period has provided in such superfluity. The tendency toward this kind of mixture is already innate in the German character. Was it good to provide an excuse for it? Was it good to lead the better artist, who carries his ideal within his breast, into temptation to succumb to an addiction to *popularity*, this cliff that so often leads art, if not to destruction then at least to the loss of its solidity? — — All these remarks are probably permissable given the current state of aesthetics and after the passage of nearly forty years; but they in no way detract from Hiller's merit, since, as we have said, it would have been almost impossible for him to have foreseen that his efforts would be crowned with such success. —

But even at that time, or shortly thereafter, there were composers who chose a different path and attempted, as it were, to compensate for this leap of art by leading it back to a higher plane. No one did this with greater success than Georg Benda [1722–1795]. What German friend of music does not know the works of this artist, who feels so truly, profoundly, and beautifully? Who can boast of having refined taste without, after the motley modern operettas and the wild noise-making of *most of* their intended-to-be emotional finales, sitting down at his piano, at least occasionally and in secret, to experience refreshment and profound pleasure from Benda's sketches of human nature, as faithful as they are noble? —He, too, combined the sweetest melodies with the most correct harmony and a rhythm that was already very flexible. He knew (and it is this that most greatly enhances his worth as an artist) the fine line of demarcation between an overwrought style and boredom. Everything, from his *ritornellos* to his *bravura* passages, was meaningful.[32] In the process, he wisely limited himself only to those things that suited his powers and inclinations. The latter no more included the grand, the bold, or the powerfully heart-wrenching than the burlesque or the comical. His strength lay in the aria (or rather cavatina) and the emotional recitative; the latter belongs, in terms of *musical* declamation (for *rhetorically* it is not without flaws), among the most excellent we have to show for ourselves. With this he opened a path to the heart, and he could be sure of hitting his target wherever there was a heart to be found. For he lived so completely for art, which did not serve as an adjunct to his vanity, but rather ruled in his mind as a sublime goddess and filled his entire being to the point of rapturous transcendence of the real world. Oh, when will Germany make us the gift of another Georg Benda! —I am moved to this exclamation by the interest—so flattering for our audience—that his works have awakened. If this interest later gradually faded, the responsibility lay, *among other things*, with the continually growing realm of the art of music and the need to hear *new* works that nourished the senses more than the heart. At least there was, afterward, only one individual whose almighty power was so great that Benda deserved to fade away before him like the moon before the sun.

As, in this way, the theatrical music of the *second* and *third* type sought its proper form, the theatrical music of the *first* type (the serious Italian opera) did not sit idly by. It made especially good use of the already more advanced development of instrumental music, which it employed both in groups of players and in individual obbligato passages; it combined greater variety and internal and external brilliance with the advances that had already been made; and it attempted to achieve greater emotional effect through a harsher depiction of the passions with all the means of pure and applied music—and for the most part it succeeded. Among the composers who achieved excellence in this realm I will mention only Reichardt and Naumann; the former being especially gifted when it came to expressing the great and the bold (and who moreover enriched the art of music partly as a writer of instructive comments and partly as a composer of songs); and the latter being blessed by nature and art with the ability to give dignified expression to soft and tender sentiments. Both men are still alive and working, as ornaments of German music. Their actions, before and after, speak for themselves and need no further elaboration.

Now we have come to the two final decades of the last century, which still provide us with many remarkable perspectives on the development of our music. It is true that it now becomes ever more difficult to follow its chameleon shapes; but here we see appearing two stars of the first magnitude, which shed their light over all of Germany (and even today over distant lands). The first was already the object of great veneration early [in his career], although his sanctification has only reached its apogee in our time. The other may have departed some years ago for the orbit of higher spheres, but his sunlight still penetrates down to us and often awakens us to lofty enthusiasm. Gratitude demands that we devote extensive consideration to their great influence on the recent and future course of music.

• • •

[No. 22: The increase in music and musical life.]
Third Period: *from J. Haydn and W. A. Mozart to the End of the Last Century*

If one wanted to characterize the final fifth or tenth of the last century with a single word, one could perhaps find no better term than "ferment." Almost all human knowledge and activity are affected by it, and to an ever increasing degree. Not only political opinions and theories, but scientific ideas and systems as well (even logic), have been shaken to their foundations; indeed, what is more, and is at the same time a distinguishing characteristic of the present era, these changes did not remain merely objects of knowledge or playthings for scholars and idle world-watchers, but have been translated unusually rapidly into practical life. Would it not be a miracle if the fine arts, which are so closely connected with those things, i.e. with both scientific and practical ideas, were not infected by this kind of ferment? —If the *arts alone* remained on their old track, where none but experienced men were permitted to hold the reins, and their great value was not fully amenable to common perception and understanding? —In fact, we find, after even the most cursory glance at the more recent state of the art of music, that the latter, far from not participating in the general ferment, could well serve as an emblem or model of important occurrences. —*Fermentation* (in physical as well as moral matters) occurs when slumbering forces are awakened, or subordinate ones seek to rise to the same level as others that have dominated them. Good is then mingled with bad; and this is how it was with the art of music at the end of the last century. — —At the beginning of the second period described above, *song*, which had been injected into Germany, had almost replaced the former, merely calculating music. In this seemingly regal position, it long retained the power that Nature herself had given it. Instrumental music appeared either as song's mere accompanist, or, if it wanted to reign alone, borrowed the latter's pleasantness and brilliance. But gradually instrumental music began to crave a higher rank. It relied (drawing, like the populace, on its physical superiority and the level of culture achieved by the formerly lower estates) on the increasing number and development of its tools. Thus, the ruled were first transformed into rulers, i.e. song was forced to adapt itself to instrumental music, and was not infrequently outshone where it had been supposed to play the leading role. From this—as is customary in democracies—there later developed a struggle of *all against all*, which, in our modern operas, is so frequently—thrilling or numbing?[33] Music, in other words, gained in *quantity*. —The growing love of music; the Germans' greater talent for instrumental as against vocal music; the overshadowing of the church by the theater, with its natural tendency to variety; and the imitation of the theatrical style in works of pure music—all this inevitably had to turn the supposedly golden and silver age of art, *as art*, into a period of inferior value, or at least so it seemed. For anyone who still recalled the impression that the masterworks of the second period had made on him in his youth, this inevitably led to complaints about the decline of genuine taste, because he could not find his way out of the tangle of mediocre, superficial, bad, insubstantial compositions. —Whether these complaints are justified, and to what extent—of this more later. For now, only a brief description of the course of development taken by the German art of music, in general, in this period.

Sacred music was increasingly hastening toward its inevitable fate, which had been prepared long before. Where attempts were made to sustain it in its old form, people paid it less and less attention, and the cantors and organists had a very easy time of it. The spirit of the age did not accord quite so well with what the first half of the century had still considered holy. People of cultivation and taste even began to feel ashamed of being affected by it. Wherever sacred music was still maintained, however, it assumed a theatrical guise, both inwardly and outwardly. Significant works of this genre were performed only in concerts; and it was only to find room for large orchestral masses, or to earn ample income, that they were sometimes moved to the churches on weekdays. Just as, at the beginning of the century, almost no composer could lay claim to fame and virtuosity who was not at home on the organ, so at its end genuine and thorough organists had become increasingly rare in comparison to other instrumentalists. Only a tiny group of connoisseurs paid men like Häsler the respect that their organ playing deserved, and the latter were often forced to try their fortunes abroad. Even a [Georg Joseph] Vogler would scarcely have had so many listeners at his church concerts if he had not possessed a great skill in the registration that helped him to make the organ into a kind of panorama for the ear, so that one could enjoy the cannonades, thunderstorms, terrifying winds, etc.; while he played the fugues, etc., only as a second thought, for the sober-minded connoisseurs or half-connoisseurs who had heard that such things are especially suited for the organ (on account of its lasting tones and pedal).[34] —In a word, sacred music is no longer a thing that exists in its own right. With the exception of the chorales for Sunday performance, and here and there on holidays a few fragments from the old generation of cantors, or in Catholic regions an occasional Missa, Kyrie, etc., few traces of the former brilliance are to be found. In the meanwhile, however, in the most recent period, people seem to feel that it is a shame to see the energy of this style being lost, and thus sacred music is almost suffering the fate of a well-known Eastern nation whose ruins are being carried through all of Christendom. Nowadays one often hears sacred settings not only in instrumental pieces, but even in comic operettas, and there will probably be no lack of imitations of the recent piece that brought us old chorales on, behind, and underneath the stage. Whether sacred music will have its revenge (as the above-mentioned nation responded to the pressure of Christianity through trade), by forcing its way into theatrical performances and distorting artistic taste—this is something about which aestheticians may speak with *one* voice.

But what a confusing swarm comes into view as soon as we try to shed more light on the *theater* and its music toward the end of the past century. From the Alps to the North Sea and the Baltic, from the old borders of France to the new ones of East Prussia, there was and is almost no city of moderate size that is not home to a wandering troupe of players during at least a few weeks of the year. And what must these players perform most frequently? —*Operettas*; for they give more food for sensuality than theater alone. —It is a well-known experience that serious (and older) people prefer comedy to tragedy; hence the *comic* operetta would have to fare better among the Germans than the *serious* opera. Best of all would be the *low-comic* operetta, which would be excellently suited to our taste and manners. But even in this regard, Germany was not the model. Italy's *Arlecchino* gave birth to our *Hanswurst*, and its *opera buffa* gave rise to our comic operetta. It is true that France also had and has some similar things, but more refined, wittier, and less bawdy. The Italians and Germans, on the other hand, love harsh contrasts, have less appreciation for fine satire, and consider a piece to be amusing only if it makes them laugh. What role does music play in all this? —The role of painted decoration. If one examines it closely, it arouses disgust, and the ill-informed person does not understand the effects that are caused by such rough lines and dots when they are seen, at the proper distance, as integral masses. It is similar with low-comic music. If a person versed in grammar, in counterpoint, analyses the score, he finds common melodies, coarse rhythm, trivial (or even bizarre) modulations, and to accompany them usually a text that cannot make the slightest pretense to poetry. "Such stuff," he says, is only for the "tasteless beginner in music;" it is suited "at best for gutter songs and love songs." But he allows himself to be talked into going to the operetta. Resolving to treat it with contempt, he enters the theater. But, just look, the sober-minded critic is laughing along. It does him no good to feel ashamed on the way home; he comes back a second time (if the performance was otherwise not bad), and finally he even feels comfortable. —What is the basis for this? —Partly it lies in the nature of *human beings* and *music*, partly in the fact that the latter appears here as a *genuinely helping art*, which neither rules nor slavishly obeys. —Accustomed as we are to bringing our worries and business cares into the life of society, we find this kind of relaxation of the mind so refreshing that in these hours of recreation we prefer a tasteless farce (if only it occupies the senses and does not constantly fly in the face of reason) to the most intelligent tragedy.[35] —Moreover, it seems clear that of the two types of emotion—*sadness* and *joy*—music has broader scope within the latter.[36] The former is dissolved by musical expression into melancholy, while the latter is fortified by singing and playing. In the theatre this is especially important. Here the expression of a *long lasting* suspension of feelings (in minor keys), or their suppression, cannot but be distasteful, on account of the *closer* relationship we bear to the suffering subject and because his feelings are too far removed from the natural, unemotional, or pleasure-seeking mood of the listeners; it must cause pain rather than pleasure. For this reason, major harmonies predominate, and who would be likely to sit through an opera made up of nothing but minor harmonies?[37] —It would be easier with unbroken major harmonies, because they are less tiresome to the populace than to the connoisseur.[38] —Finally, the pleasure people take in comic operettas is based on the fact that here (namely in the really comic passages) the music exerts a great influence on sensuality, without making this influence as obvious as when other things are being expressed. Let us consider, for example, the fine nuances of feeling that the art of music is meant to depict when it deals with loftier subjects. If the music is faithful and beautiful, it outshines the other arts, or challenges them to a contest with it, which divides the attention. If it is not faithful, then neither the connoisseur nor the public knows what to make of it, and they feel bored during a composition that might have been pleasing without words or when joined with another text. In the comic opera, on the other hand, the composer—*seemingly*—has an easier and a safe task. He need not worry about putting his work into the hands of a mediocre orchestra and singers, because in this case the public would rather forgive the latter's clumsy singing than a poor plot. He must also avoid all traces of anything academic or stilted if he wants to achieve his aim. —No wonder, then, that what *seems* easy is considered to be so in reality, and that the comic muse has been so fruitful among us! —What good is it, then, to possess a fine aesthetic sense, a knowledge of poetry, a profound theory of music? —A subject that provides an occasion for coarse jokes and a variety of stage decorations, steeped in waltz melodies, is enough for the comic opera. — —Though the muse may avert her face—people make fun of her sensitivity, for after all the rough mob has been invited by Thalia's own priests to sit in judgment, and the artist who is lazy or who seeks only tumultuous applause can brush off the criticism of the more tasteful connoisseur by saying that it is hard to swim against the tide. —A vain excuse! For is not comedy, too, the stuff of *art*? And is it permissable to confuse the latter with Nature? Should art settle for a baroque mixture of half tragic and half comic performances? And must music in the theater, then, either be *everything*, or, on the contrary, be less than the painted stage decorations? — —But it seems as if the Germans, who once looked to works of art almost exclusively for rational pleasure, wearied of this habit in the final part of the last century, for they accepted and enjoyed the most ridiculous theatrical nonsense, if only it tickled their senses. *Southern* Germany set the tone. The *northern* part resisted longer. Given the ravenous hunger for new works resulting from the widespread amateur engagement with music and the relative unfruitfulness of theatrical composers, northern Germany retained a more lasting loyalty to the better compositions of the French, for example [opera composers] Grétry or Monsigni. —As a result, both the understanding and the more refined sensibility still had something to do. But it wasn't long before our countrymen, always hungry for imported delicacies, allowed themselves to be seduced by the enjoyment of pieces in the modern Italian style. The compositions of Paisiello, Martin, *et al.*, as truly lovely and accessible as some of them were, made people overlook the mindless content of the text. Now the southern Germans, who, as noted above, had always admired Italian taste, had secured their triumph. Soon the fantastic offspring of the Viennese suburban theaters began to flood all of Germany, and so it went without interruption until the end of the last century. Among the crowd of pseudo-composers only a few stood out who did honor to the art of music. The best popular composer was unquestionably Dittersdorf [1739–1799]. He could have defended Germany's honor against the probably not undeserved reproach of foreigners, namely that the trend toward comedy had appeared among us without our having any natural talent for or real concept of it. Dittersdorf's insights into the inner nature of music, and his knowledge in general, were above the ordinary. Nature had provided him with musical wit and a sure sense that seldom caused him to strike a wrong note in the comic mood. These characteristics, taken together, would surely have been most useful, not only for musical taste but also *in* music itself, particularly in light of the huge and well-deserved applause that this composer's works elicited. But he both wrote too much, on the one hand, and succumbed too easily to the general tendency to write mixed compositions, on the other; moreover his unlucky star several times led him to tasteless, poetically poorly realized subjects, whereby he may have hoped (in vain) that his pleasant music could charm cultivated men and prevent them from feeling annoyed. Hence he allowed himself to be taken in by the prejudice resulting in part from the poor state of our *musical* poetry and the vanity of our composers—and which, of late, some people have even defended—namely, that the text of an operetta is relatively irrelevant, and even that the caliber of the music would be all the higher, the less thought was given to the text. —I may be permitted a few observations on this point. —The audience, in fact, has become accustomed to paying little attention to the text, as long as the music sounds good, or the stage decorations provide entertainment for the eye. However, one cannot blame the *audience* for this. What true poet is not ashamed, nowadays, to devote his energies to the production of a poetic changeling of the sort that operettas, in their natural unaesthetic form, must almost inevitably be? —The poets who did so generally came to grief, that is they robbed the senses to give to the intellect. Moreover, the composers themselves have too little understanding of the essence of dramatic poetry, or they are happy to be able to attract the attention of their listeners to their work alone. Then they exploit the great, almost voluptuous development of instrumental music, which often outshines the vocal music, not to mention the content of the piece. The superficial way in which the music is studied also plays a role, as does, finally, the desire for more sensual than rational pleasure and recreation—something that, for its part, has its basis in the increasing crush of events and cares. —On closer look, it appears that the composers and poets are more to blame for these maltreatments of art than the listeners. For it is the latter who are supposed to be educated by the former; composers and poets should not overstep the bounds of music as an applied or *helping* art; they should consider that to destroy taste in such a mischievous way is a sin that is far too little redeemed by the ephemeral nature of the product. In a word, they should not lose sight of art's *aim*, and should seek more honor *in* than *outside of* themselves. —Nor should anyone try to justify himself by pointing to one of the great musicians of the last century, whose operetta texts are mostly bad, too. Not everything a great man does necessarily invites praise or imitation! One must also ask whether he had any choice in the matter, and whether there were especially compelling reasons that excuse his behavior as an *exception* to the rule? —

—With this question, I have now cleared the way for commenting on a man who is too great, too singular not to be recalled in detail; but also too great, too singular for the weak voice of a single individual to dare to express, in the name of thousands and thousands of friends of music, the profound enthusiasm and veneration that his works awaken in them. However, the gap in this survey would be too great, too unpardonable, if I were to content myself with the mere mention of his name, and the conviction that it will not be difficult, given the lasting enjoyment and study of his works by connoisseurs, to correct any mistakes right away, gives me courage not to withhold my own remarks about him.

• • •

[No. 23: Mozart as opera composer; Germany's pre-eminence in instrumental music.]

W. A. Mozart, then, who was indisputably the greatest theatrical composer produced by Germany in the final period of the last century, was only a child when he exhibited the extraordinary genius by which he astonished his contemporaries and, to an even greater extent, posterity. Like C. P. E. Bach, he was raised by an excellent father, and in general he had, as an artist, much in common with that famous man, setting aside the different taste of the period and the broader field that Mozart cultivated. What strength, what versatility were required to stand out so clearly in the most recent period, when one virtuoso, one work of art was constantly outshining the previous one, and to secure the kind of lasting admiration that Mozart has earned for himself! For an artist's fame to reach this height, he could not, as had once been possible, limit himself to *one* genre; he had to try his luck in all of them. Thus Mozart. He wrote little songs and great sacred works, comic and serious operas, piano concertos, sonatas, quartets, symphonies, etc. If they were not all masterpieces, and were often even unpolished juvenalia, nevertheless even the most insignificant piece contained individual beauties and original traits that made it precious to the friends of his muse. I will leave it to Mozart's *musical* biographer (whom we still lack), to dissect his works and weigh their relative merits. Here I can only comment that his *fame* is based primarily on his *dramatic* works and after that on his works for the *fortepiano [sic]*. There are different opinions about the relative value of the dramatic works when they are ranked comparatively, but even connoisseurs agree (apart from the fact that Mozart himself said so) that *Don Giovanni* is probably his best opera. He had written it for his "*friends*," i.e. for people who not only were familiar with the art of music *per se*, but who were also in a position to comprehend the great degree of *idealization* that he brought to *this particular* work. His genius sought a subject in which he could not only reveal his abundant musical knowledge, showing that the whole mechanics of music (melody, harmony, and rhythm) came easily to him; but through which he could also portray the most *diverse* characters both individually and *collectively*, in polyphonic passages in which each one remained unmistakable and characteristically true to himself. The childlike faithful daughter, the melancholy deserted beloved, the naive country maiden, the loyal but jealous peasant, and the urban lad pining for his love; the cowardly, womanish simpleton and the reckless, skillful libertine; and then the ghost, as it is constructed by the imagination, and the lusty peasants, the terrifying spirits of hell—everything is painted in such a (*genuinely* musical) way that one can almost dispense with words if one only knows what characters are on stage.[39] Of the two main characters, *D. Giovanni* and *Leporello*, the latter, in particular, is so unique and suffuses the whole opera with such a genuinely comic mood that (assuming the orchestra and the musicians do their part) one can hardly grow weary of repeated visits to refresh one's spirit in the contemplation of this ideal. —Truly, however tastes may change, this opera will still be regarded as a masterwork at the close of the next century, and with a—soon to be expected—better text it will arouse the same enthusiasm among listeners that connoisseurs of classic Roman poetry may feel when they read their *Horace*. — —Is, then, an answer to the question still required whether the good music compensates for the miserable text? —Do you know how to portray characters with as much truth, power, perfection, and *idealization* as Mozart in his *Don Giovanni*? In this case, and only then, allowances can be made for your lack of taste (or, in some cases, your mischievous disdain?) in choosing shallow subjects (assuming that you were given the choice). —Since the actual niveau that an artist has achieved can best be judged from those of his works that are produced *voluntarily* and *con amore*, *Don Giovanni* also serves as a measure of Mozart's greatness. He was, to put it succinctly, one of the greatest *poetic* (or *musically poeticizing*) musicians that Germany experienced in the last century. How this should best be understood will be clear to anyone who recalls what has been said above concerning C. P. E. Bach. Indeed, I dare say that among our famous musicians of the past century there are only three men to whom this quality can be ascribed in any significant degree—E. Bach, Mozart, and J. Haydn. But Mozart embraced more disciplines than Bach. The latter wrote poetically for the keyboard, for pure instrumental performance. Mozart did this too, but he was perhaps even more outstanding in applied music. Bach *tended* more toward the French, Mozart toward the Italian genius of music. Bach lost [something] as soon as he proceeded to attach his ideas to words; Mozart's fertile imagination, by contrast, required this restraint in order to show itself in a clear and more beautiful, all encompassing light.[40] This explains the bizarre ideas in many of his instrumental works, which have attracted the criticism of a number of grammarians; as well as the excessive decoration in the accompaniment, which only a very few orchestras are able to soften properly and to perform in such a way that Mozart's intentions do not get lost in an incomprehensible tangle. With all this in mind, the following conclusion might be drawn: in pure instrumental music Mozart was great, very great, but not unsurpassable; but when it came to the loftier demands of art (from the point of view of aesthetics), his accomplishment is even greater in applied music, i.e. above all in music for the theater. In the latter, he outshines almost all those who preceded or were contemporaneous with him, even though he not infrequently makes one regret his failure to polish his work, and in many of his compositions his genius did not follow its own lead completely, but conceded more to local and temporal circumstances than one might wish. But by bringing together these two qualities (as an instrumental and a theatrical composer), he may perhaps long stand in such a unique position that only weak or cross-eyed people may look upon him without the admiration that his overwhelming strength requires of our understanding and our feelings. Oh, without a doubt, the laments over the loss of this *divine* genius, who matured early but also departed early, will increase as our hope of ever *fully* replacing him fades, despite the great number of contemporary composers. Still, at the moment of his leaving us, he must have been consoled over his brief career by the happy thought that the artist has *the* advantage over many other men that he is often more useful and more greatly honored after his death than during his lifetime. —Mozart's legacy to art, and through art to humankind, was equally great and exquisite. It carries his name even to proud foreign countries. May they *duly* appreciate his worth! And may this appreciation never, here or there, be profaned by a blind, *vain rage for imitation*. — —Unfortunately, experience has already shown that the latter wish belongs to the realm of pious hopes. In almost all the recent German operettas that are not composed in the tone of a Kasperle-theater [puppet-theatre] (and often even in these), the desire is audible to compose in a manner that is *Mozartish*. Quick, vehement digressions, huge finales and the use of all possible instruments for obbligato accompaniment—and presto, you have a piece *à la Mozart*. In other words, the shadow and the shell are taken for the body, with little sense of the spirit that animated it. A Mercury is not carved from every piece of wood! and imitating a genius seldom produces a tolerable result if one looks closely. But it was and is a peculiarity of our epoch that the rage for imitation is so often found in close juxtaposition with the desire to be original. Nor should it be difficult to discover the key to this phenomenon. Every composer, when he is setting out, feels that the legions of musical pieces with which we are endowed make it difficult for him to distinguish himself. There are only two ways for him to do so, either by producing something new and striking, or—by walking in the footsteps of a famous man who is fashionable at that precise moment. He believes that the first is true of his ideas, and many a composer probably hopes that his supposed originality will protect him from accusations of carelessness or shallowness of knowledge. —But at the same time, he is either completely carried away by the works of that well-known individual, or has at least learned that the public is extremely well disposed toward the latter's manner. Hence the composer imitates him, often without desiring or even being aware of it, and nothing is more natural than that we are served up so many unoriginal, flabby, incomplete compositions, which—something that *seems* strange but is not[41]—become more so, the sharper the criticism becomes. —And once someone has achieved even a modicum of success with his works, he knows no better method for maintaining his fame than—writing *quite a lot.* What art or even the *true* honor of an artist gains from this is too clear for it to be necessary to say anything further.

In spite of all this, it would be wrong to claim that Mozart, the unsurpassed, had no worthy successors at all. Who does not pay homage to the excellent works of [Peter] Winter [1754–1825], who has no need to be ashamed of his "Son pittore anch' io"? Who does not take pleasure in [Joseph] Weigl's [1766-1846] ingenuous compositions? Who does not hope for many more beautiful things from Weber, whose previous works have made it clear that he resides in Berlin, where they are in the habit of polishing their compositions? —Equally well recognized are the talents of [Johann Rudolf] Zumsteeg, *et al.*, which promise us many an artistic pleasure; and surely the last years of the previous century would have blessed us with even more powerful theatrical works of genius, had not the Muses been starved and intimidated by the raging of an unfortunate war in southern Germany, and, in the north, by the more restricted public and private economy that resulted, in part, from this conflict.

Maybe better days are just around the corner. —Meanwhile, we would like to turn our attention to another principal aspect of the practical art of music, which displayed such fruitfulness in the latter part of the previous century, and by means of which Germany—one can say this in all candor, with no danger of being accused of political grandiloquence—distinguishes itself above all the other nations of the earth. If it is true that our applied art of music, to the extent that *song* is required, leaves much to be desired in both composition and execution—things that are superior in Italy and France; and if our theater music, in particular, must compete for recognition with works composed in the above-named countries, especially France, in respect not only—please note—to the *inner* content of the *music*, but also to the aesthetic arrangement and treatment of the *whole*; nevertheless, in instrumental music (as regards the number as well as the merit of the compositions) they can be counted upon to be inferior to us. —Who would wish to keep track of the innumerable symphonies, quartets, sonatas, concertos for all kinds of instruments, etc., that were published, especially in the third period; or to keep a list of the virtuosos and dilettantes whose talent often makes it difficult to decide to whom to give first priority? —Admittedly, what is excellent and good is mixed in together—how could it be otherwise?—with what is mediocre and bad. But one can say frankly that, with few exceptions, our *mediocre* instrumental works are comparable to works that in other countries, toward the end of the last century, were considered *good*. — The reason for this lies in the Germans' outstanding talent for instrumental music, which talent, for its part, derives from many other things mentioned earlier in these remarks, *viz.* climate; political organization; a melancholy national character that looks to the fine arts more for the pleasures of the understanding than for those of the heart; etc. —For reasons that are equally easy to explain, the Italians and the French prefer song to all other music. Yet it should be noted that toward the end of the last century Germany did more to respect and develop vocal music than it had at the beginning of that period; while France and Italy were introducing our instrumental luxury to their countries. As much as there is to say on this subject, I must skip over it in order to have room to address a more important issue, namely the answer to the question of how the German instrumental music of the last period differed from that which came before, and what qualities are deserving of praise or criticism *in general*. —Here, everything depends on what *purpose* it is intended to achieve and achieves. The *applied* art of music (combined with song) expresses *specific* feelings and ideas, and wants to influence the *heart more than the imagination [Phantasie]*. *Purely instrumental music,* which relates to the former more or less as speculative philosophy relates to practical philosophy, is not in a position—even in its most beautiful products—to represent more than an *analogue* of sentiment, even though it is often capable of producing in a mediated way, i.e. through the mood of the listener, emotional responses that are just as powerful as the ones stimulated by music combined with words. Its actual purpose, then, is to assist the participant, by means of the *indefinite* quality of its phrases (which must never be confused with the muddled, the boring, or the insipid), to make *freer* use of his imagination *[Einbildungskraft]*, and then to leave it up to him (or the circumstances) to determine which *more specific* ideas and feelings this play of tones may lead him to. The *least* effect of the latter is mere *sensual stimulus* (a pleasant motion of one's hearing, less as an organic than as a vital sense). A greater effect is created when the understanding is stimulated to examine the correctness, beauty, or artistic skill of the series of tones (for example in the case of works or passages in strict counterpoint). The greatest effect, however, is when the listener—even without auxiliary elements such as ballet, marches, etc.—believes that he perceives, in the composition that is being performed, the expression of specific ideas or feelings that have simply not been expressed, and easily supplements the text, as it were, with his thoughts. —This last is something on which only *the* instrumental composer can count who has achieved complete or near complete mastery of the tonal mechanism—both internal and external—; who knows how to apply it skillfully and has discovered, through genius and study, the universal, natural character, as it relates to that analogue [of feeling], of all the tones, keys, series of keys, harmonies, rhythms, instrumental combinations, etc., that he wishes to use; and who, finally, in the design and execution of his works, has not chosen the first best-sounding or skillful phrase, but has taken the trouble to express some idea or sentiment that is *as specific as possible*—and to remain faithful to it. Such a composer can never be embarrassed by [Fontenelle's old] question: *"Sonate, que me veux-tu?"*

With this, I think I have given the standard for the *aesthetic* value of every possible kind of instrumental music, and at the same time have made it clear that instrumental music had to be more perfect in the final period of the last century than in the two preceding periods. By its very nature, namely, it has a larger territory within the tonal realm than vocal music, which cannot, for this reason, avoid greater similarity and uniformity in its figures and forms (for example in the concluding bars of its arias). But at the same time, this large scope of instrumental music also gave the grammatical critics the right to be more strict. In the *first* period, people wanted to avoid this criticism, and—encouraged stiff devotion to strict counterpoint, with which, naturally, they could achieve only the second effect of instrumental music; its higher purpose had to be lost. —In the *second* period, as was mentioned above, instrumental music tended to follow the theatrical style and seemed, as a result, to take on a more emotional character. But in fact it only *seemed* to do this. For just as the mechanism of the art of music had previously been treated not as a *means* but as an *end*, so it now remained, with the difference that in the first period skillful harmony, and in the second an easily comprehensible melody was preferred. Hence, with the exception of the works of E. Bach and a few others, the letter still ruled without the spirit, and only habit or enthusiasm for then-famous men could bring critics to ignore the fact that the limiting of instrumental music, as wise as it may have been when accompanying vocal music (in the applied art of music), would not exactly be an absolute advantage when instrumental music was seeking to achieve its effect alone. Seeking simplicity, they fell into dragging monotony, without reflecting that even simplicity only elevates a work of art under certain circumstances. For since instrumental music, by its very nature, is directed more to the understanding and the imagination, as vocal music is to the heart; so instrumental music must also provide enough material to exercise those mental powers—especially since it does not have the support of poetry. It must, then, shine by means of *variety*, which, however, must not make things too difficult for the understanding in its search for unity. Instrumental composers of the third period strove to correct all these shortcomings, and instrumental works assumed a fuller, more voluptuous form. Those artists who either clearly recognized or intuited the true destiny of this musical genre now combined in their works the thoroughness of the first period with the songfulness of the second, adding striking new elements in the process. They took advantage of the more developed internal and external tonal mechanism to transform voices that had been mere accompaniments into more obbligato parts. This was done both in works for solo instruments (for example, in piano sonatas, with the bass and later even the middle voices) and in combinations of several instruments, for example in symphonies, quartets, etc., where the intent was to achieve a result more or less the same as that produced by beautiful groups of figures in paintings or on the stage. —But only a few trod this path with *the* power that it demands. So many lacked either a deep and broadly comprehensive knowledge of the essential nature of music, or aesthetic sense and inventiveness. Others composed only as *virtuosos*, i.e. they worked for *artists*, not for *art*. This occurred not only in concertos, where one forgives it because concertos are the special proving ground of virtuosity, and hardly one in a hundred can claim to possess any inner artistic value (so that, for example, the ritornellos, etc., are nothing but rests for the lungs or the fingers); but also in pieces that, supposedly, are intended to elevate all the participating instruments to an equal or near equal rank, for example in quartets (literally: musical conversations for four voices). Here either the first violin, flute, etc., dominates throughout, and the solo passages of the others are once again just rest stops for the former, or, in the best case, one voice follows the other with its passages and roulades, while the others, in true theatrical manner, do nothing more than—round out the harmony. When it comes to beautiful combinations among the voices, or a characteristic and significant role for each of them, etc.—how many composers think about this, or remain equally far removed from triviality and from stilted modulations that are meant to be something, but on closer inspection are nothing but—empty artifice! —This is less obvious in *symphonies*. —What is charming about this kind of composition resides precisely *in the variety, in the assembage of the whole mass of instruments for the development of the beauty and meaning that lies within the main theme, which is, in itself, easily comprehensible and often seemingly simple*. —Here, to compose something that is wholly *pure* and yet *powerful* is admittedly more difficult, but the shortcomings, unless one is a very expert connoisseur, are more noticeable when reading the score than when listening. The outcome is the same as with all colossal figures, which one gladly forgives for unevenness in the details if only the whole is imposing and achieves its purpose. But whether this applies to so many symphonies, whether they possess the above-mentioned qualities or are not more often deafening, through chaotic noise in which the timpani gradually play a more and more principal role (for nowadays who composes a symphony without timpani?)—this is a question that can best be answered by experience. —Still, all these shortcomings should probably not permit the lovers of the old to declare that the symphonies of the second or even the first period are more suitable than more recent symphonies. While everything having to do with *this* kind of musical composition may not be quite what it should be, nevertheless good taste (grounded in aesthetics) will probably coexist better with the excessive fullness and voluptuousness of the current symphonies than with the leanness of the earlier ones, whose movements' purity is inadequate recompense for their boring monotony and awkward rhythms.

The more outstanding new works include, among others, those of Rosetti, [né Franz Anton Roesler, c. 1750–1792] who was snatched away from music too soon, and some by [Franz Christoph] Neubauer, among others, in which one finds more of a splendid tumult of instruments.

• • •

[No. 24: Haydn as composer of instrumental music.]

But all the composers of symphonies and quartets lag behind *the* man who has plied his craft for almost an entire half century with ever new, inexhaustible, genuinely amazing power, and became the greatest benefactor of German instrumental music in the third period of the last century. All of Germany has long since paid its tribute to the exceptional genius of our great J. Haydn. And the hoarse voices of pedantic gnatslayers, who will gladly condemn an entire work, endowed with a thousand beauties, the moment they stumble across a couple of forbidden fifths and octaves, even though the latter are concealed, and who teased even Haydn about such things, have long since been silenced, for people have realized that even in his knowledge of musical grammar Haydn was superior to many a proud master of counterpoint. And who does not rejoice that at the end of the century the name Haydn is still repeated with reverence abroad, that London and Paris are competing in their praise of one of his most recent works, which was not required for him to be elevated to the loftiest level of musical fame here at home. —But why should I add my drop to the ocean by merely declaiming on the subject of his immortal achievements—although admittedly this is a tempting thing to do. —I would rather risk the attempt to clarify for myself (and perhaps for the occasional reader who has not yet reflected on it), on what, actually, Haydn's greatness is based. — —

Everything is united in him to make him the greatest of all instrumental composers. —In his youth, he (like Graun, Hasse, J. A. P. Schulz, [1747–1800] etc.) was a very popular singer. He studied the great Italian masters, and so who would be surprised that he gave us such splendid melodies, that everything in his works, even the most complex passages, sings so beautifully; that his principal movements, whether in the serious or in the comic style, have such a meaningful, powerful simplicity, by which the feelings of connoisseur and amateur alike are immediately swept along. With this he combined the most profound study of harmony (nourished by Bach's works, among others), whose fruits are the boldest, most surprising, and yet by no means Baroque modulations, with which he arouses our enthusiasm. Add to this a knowledge of the particular character of the instruments and their effects, and all this combined with the rarest originality of a mind that does not, even in the huge number of his works, copy others or himself, although he does have his own unmistakable manner (as anyone, if he has even a passing acquaintance with Haydn, will hear when a piece by another composer is substituted)—for this reason alone our great master stands before us as admittedly deserving of our veneration, but not incomprehensible. —Yet this does not exhaust the reasons for his greatness. The quintessence thereof seems to me to lie in the exceptionally light treatment of rhythm, in which no one can compete with him, and in what the English call humor, and for which the German word *Laune* does not quite provide an exact equivalent). The latter characteristic explains his tendency to comic turns of phrase and the even greater success he achieves with these than with more serious passages. —If one wanted to find a parallel with other famous men, J. Haydn might perhaps be compared, in respect to the fruitfulness of his imagination, with our Jean Paul [Richter, 1763–1825] (omitting, evidently, the chaotic design, for transparent representation *(lucidus ordo)* is not the least of Haydn's virtues); or in respect to his humor, his original wit (*vis comica*) with Lor. Sterne. —If, moreover, one wanted to describe the character of Haydn's compositions in just two words, they would be—it seems to me—*artful popularity, [kunstvolle Popularität]* or *popular* (easily comprehensible, effective) *artfulness [populäre Kunstfülle]*. —But in what genre of musical works might Haydn be greatest and most masterful? —This question must be posed in the case of almost every significant composer of the third period, for he is asked not only to write a lot, but to write diverse things. Now it is admittedly certain that a *genuine* artist arouses interest in every facet of the art in which he works, but there is equally general agreement that even the greatest original genius can only work with *superior* good fortune in one or a few parts of that art, particularly in an era when art has grown from a little plant into a tree with many branches. And thus I am not afraid of offending the majority of connoisseurs and critics if I propose the following classification of Haydn's works. —Undoubtedly, the first place belongs to his *symphonies* and *quartets*, in which no one has yet surpassed him. The second, to his compositions for *piano*. The latter, however, stand out only as filled with sentiment, tender, and easy to comprehend despite their great artistry, for in *other* respects many a recent piano composer (other than Mozart) may challenge him for the first prize, especially Muzio Clementi with his fiery spirit (indeed, in time, when the wild enthusiasm has subsided, perhaps a Beethoven). After this come his *sacred works*, and finally his *works for the theater*, to the extent that these have become known. The proof of this last observation is provided, among others, by the very work that is arousing such an extraordinary sensation (almost as much as Mozart's *Magic Flute*), namely—the *Creation*. Of this work, I dare to assert that it will neither detract from nor augment Haydn's *genuine* fame as an artist—by which something quite different is meant than the fame conferred by the great multitude.[42] Reverence for a great man must not blind us to the requirements of aesthetics vis-à-vis *such* a work of art. And what can aesthetics have to say to a natural history, or geogony, set to music, where objects pass before us as in a magic lantern; what can it say to the constant object-paintings, to the mixture of sacred and theatrical styles (which shows us just how far things have gone with the latter)—in a word, to the tendency of the whole? —Must it not be painful for every admirer of Haydn's to see the man's great powers wasted, *to the detriment of art* (for *such* examples are often dangerous), on a text that is not worthy of him? —Truly, the originator of the old Mosaic Sabbath song probably did not dream that it would be such a great success at the end of the eighteenth century, bedecked with all the pomp of the modern art of music! —The exceptionally beautiful, splendid choruses may compensate us for the aesthetic blunders of most of the other parts only if we mentally subtract (as many a listener may have desired to do on hearing it) the text. —Enough. My own conviction (which can be defended in detail if necessary) is that this work, *as a whole*, cannot increase Haydn's fame. But—it can also detract only a little, if at all. For the text did not originate with him, and it was therefore not his fault that it forced him into a constant portrayal of objects, instead of the subject. Besides, he actually wrote this oratorio (and this circumstance is one that should not be overlooked, in light of the man's great achievements), for the *English*, who are still accustomed to Handel's rain and snow paintings, and who, if they mean to be true to their taste, must find in this *Creation* one of the greatest masterpieces they have ever heard. — —In sum, no composer of the last century has done so much for the development of *instrumental music* as our father J. Haydn. No one made such use of its internal and external power; no one but he was capable not only of giving it the appropriate equal weight with vocal music, but even of forcing the latter, toward the beginning of the new century, to summon all its strength in order not to be left behind.

• • •

[No. 25: Vocal music at the end of the century.]

In fact, at the end of the last century, *vocal music* seemed to occupy a similar position in relation to instrumental music as it had at the beginning of the century, with the one difference that whereas it had formerly been threatened by the development of a part of the internal mechanism of music (harmony), now it was being threatened by the development of its external mechanism (the increased number and cultivation of the instruments). There were plenty of singers, both male and female, but what is there to praise about most of them? — In the *grand opera* (the model for the others), *castratos* became increasingly rare, and if, on the one hand, this reflected greater respect for the rights of *Nature*, still it cannot be denied, on the other hand, that art is suffering as a result, at least in the beginning, i.e. for as much time as it will take for—there to be enough natural singers available who strive to achieve through diligence and hard work what comes so easily to castratos: firmness, flexibility, strength, evenness, and purity of voice. These qualities were indispensable at a time when song attracted attention almost exclusively to itself. But now the instruments had gained as much ground, if not more. They supported the singer *too* much for him to have still found it necessary to expend much diligence on *pure, sure pitch*. The practice of *solfeggio*, which, when practiced *appropriately*, performs such useful service, seemed pointless to most of them; they started in with arias, rehearsed them mechanistically, and then strode boldly onto the stage, for it was rare that was there not an instrument to accompany the singer's voice. The revenge taken by the neglected art, as soon as the singers were supposed to sing anything other than the main part (i.e. a middle part), was considered less important, because wherever possible they turned such parts down, or relied, in following the easy thirds, on the sound of the instruments. Purity of intonation also suffered from the concealment of the voice under the instruments, as anyone will readily attest who knows how difficult it can be to tune an orchestra *purely* when there is not (as there is in good bands) solid tuning and training of the ear as a result of much practice. But it was *vocal performance* that suffered the most; partly because the singers paid less mind to theory (female singers, as one can imagine, least of all), and partly because for one thing the ornamentation was almost entirely written out by the composers (and what better evidence can be adduced against the singers than this justified mistrust of their knowledge and taste?), and for another the varied instrumental accompaniment left no room for vocal performance, or misled the singers to produce empty flourishes, with which they even disfigured the recitative.[43]

All this applies, admittedly, only to the great mass of singers, for on the stages of the opera and the national theaters there are many laudable exceptions, including Hurka, Schik[aneder], etc. Up to now, overall, their example has provoked more admiration than imitation, however, and one can easily imagine what a toilsome position the *repetiteur* must occupy in many theaters, when one notices the anxious glances that the singers, who are oft *entirely* innocent of reliable pitch and beat, cast toward their music director. Worst of all was the situation of choral music in the third period. The decline of sacred music brought it, too, into neglect. In schools where it had been exceedingly well nourished people were paying it less and less attention, and then mainly to support street singing, which—to the detriment of both health and morals—provided a means of subsistence for poor boys and youths during their school years, and for which our era, occupied as it is with more interesting matters, has not yet found a more reasonable alternative. Only one institution stands out positively—the *Thomasschule* in Leipzig, which, to the honor of its founders and supporters, was still flourishing at the end of the century under the supervision of the worthy Hiller.[44]

But the lack of *skilled* singing masters, who when compared with the huge army of instructors for instruments, especially the piano, numbered scarcely five in one hundred, had to make the existence of trained voices and *pure*, *sure*, *beautiful* delivery ever rarer in most localities in Germany. In any case, no one was thinking of means to make it easier for the main source of singers, the female sex, to learn the dry fundamentals, or to restrain their natural preference for the soprano voice. Hence even in concerts that did not feature experienced orchestral or theatrical vocalists, the thing that is of the greatest interest to the audience, namely the *singing*, lagged behind, and did more to ruin than to develop taste. Above all, the choruses that were put together in this way were considered the "*parties honteuses*" of the concerts, and would have been even more so had they not been drowned out by the instruments, even though the conductors worked their hardest on them. —Amid these sad prospects for vocal music, one institution gradually emerged that set out on the only correct path to bring vocal music more into balance with instrumental music, namely the so-called *Singakademie* in Berlin. A large group of dilettantes and professional vocalists soon took a warm interest in it, even though they practiced only works in a sacred style (chorales and the like) and did this (in the interest of pure and sure intonation) without instrumental accompaniment—except for the piano. This proved that pleasure in noble, powerful singing had by no means died out, but was only waiting for a knowledgeable and—humane leader, someone who would enjoy general confidence, in order to be quickly revived and spread. This man was a much revered veteran of the art of music—C[arl Friedrich] Fasch [1736–1800]. In the second period he, along with Bach, had already been one of the ornaments of the Berlin

Kapelle, and since then he had been quietly educating many an excellent student by teaching and example. Certainly there have, until now, been extremely few musicians who, like him, combined the most profound musical scholarship with the most refined taste, and—what is rarest of all—with very great *modesty*. This last quality, which prevented him from writing a large quantity of works, was probably the only reason why his merits did not become even more generally known, because he lived in an era when one had to make oneself important, had to thrust oneself upon the public by means of new, brilliant works in order to be admired. Not so our Fasch. In his heart there ruled not vanity, but genuine love of art and feeling for *true* artistic honor. His works bore traces of the most careful polishing throughout, without being boring or ordinary. They had all the advantages of the old school, and yet they showed that their creator had always moved forward with the spirit of the times. This lovely *attitude* in his works is what makes them so exemplary. But he also garnered profound respect as a teacher and a supporter of *nobler* singing. This respect was paid him by all who knew him and his works and had an appreciation for true artistic and human value. The final year of the now bygone century removed him from his former circle of activities. Then many an admirer of his, near and far, heard this news with wistfulness; then he achieved what Cato had wished for: some observers asked why no one had raised a monument, such as had often been erected for less important artists, to the noble Fasch? One day, when what is now new will seem old and—as is so often the case—what is now old will once again appear new, pilgrimages to the great composers of the previous century will not omit this man who composed and accomplished not many different things, but much (*multum, non multa*). Meanwhile, it is to be wished and hoped that the institute he founded, which has been so faithfully maintained by his talented and knowledgeable assistant Zelter, will long continue to flourish and bear fruit, without falling prey to the usual fate of such *voluntary* societies—weariness, jealousy, etc.! Wouldn't it also be lovely if this institute, to the benefit of German music, were emulated in cities large and small *wherever possible*? Admittedly, this requires men who combine insight into the nature of the vocal art and a sure ear with unselfish love of music, and especially with patience and friendliness, in order not to grow tired during the elementary phase and frighten off the often shy dilettantes. But are such men really as rare as one thinks? Will attempts in this direction really be so unsuccessful as one fears? Will the struggle against inertia, vanity, and envy be too difficult for *those* individuals who undertake such an effort? I think not. One need only take the usefulness of such institutes properly to heart, and not be led astray by their initially slow progress, by the early difficulties, and they will prosper reliably.

For only in this way, as it seems, it is possible to solve the most important need now confronting the *practical* art of music for us in Germany. Instrumental music, given our naturally outstanding talent for it, needs nothing; but *song, beautiful and artistic* (not artificial) *song*!! —The latter, as noted above, is not an entirely native German, especially northern German fruit and therefore needs all the more very careful nurturing. —Manifest proof of this can be found in the *folk songs* and the state of *songs* in general. Several provinces in Germany have almost no original folk songs of their own. What the burgher or peasant sings on solemn or happy occasions is either borrowed from operettas or of such a nature that the melody and text offend the more experienced eye and ear, understanding, and moral sensibility; and, besides, the impure performance is painful to listen to. Why is this? The leading causes are probably partly natural clumsiness when it comes to singing, partly the complete neglect of the latter in the public schools, or—something that is even more damaging—the horrid blubbering at the beginning and end of the lessons. In addition: the still very great *political* gap between the lower and the higher estates, which is extremely oppressive not only for the intellectual development of the former, but for their aesthetic development (their sense of beauty, their feeling for art), as well; although there is no denying that in the last decade of the previous century the *harsh* differences between classes were greatly ameliorated, and one should not fail to take advantage of these workings of fate and reason. Finally, folk songs are in a sad state by reason of the fact that our poets and composers are unable to divest themselves, *up to a certain point*, of their artistic training for this purpose, and therefore so seldom find the right tone for such songs—or sustain it. Meanwhile, this effort, too, may well be for naught, as long as care is not taken to awaken the *desire* to sing at all, which depends on neither the poet nor the composer. For among the lower classes, *if* they want to sing, the issue is more *that* they are singing (i.e. expressing their emotions) than *what*, and least of all *how* they are doing it. From this it appears that, for the moment, this genre of music must be left to chance.

Something *entirely different*, however, are those songs that serve to provide happy hours for *cultivated* (not yet spoiled) people, either in solitude or in intimate, more refined circles where one does not need to leave one's heart at the door. These songs must absolutely not be *confounded* or *mixed up* with actual folk songs, in either their poems or their compositions. They are unquestionably among the most powerful means that the art of music can employ for its higher purpose, the ennobling of the heart. Here it is least acceptable for art to degenerate into artifice and, as a result, weaken sentiment; here all the pleasures of the senses and the understanding are subordinated to those of the heart. But precisely because of this *condensed* power, the composition of a *song* demands not just adequate knowledge of the theory of music and poetry, but also a knowledge of mankind, i.e. of the manner in which man expresses his sentiments *free* of compulsion and art. Above all, it requires the composer to have his own lively sense of what is good and noble. Let no one dare to occupy himself with the composition of a song who lacks this last quality! Even if he were to know more about harmony than [J.] S. Bach, he will only be able to produce an awkward, dispirited, and shoddy patchwork. Experience is only too good a teacher in this regard. How many people, especially in the third period, allowed themselves to be persuaded to make their debut with a collection of songs, as if the first best ideas sufficed for this purpose! No, just as not everyone who has mastered the first rules of versification and followed them in manufacturing some occasional poems can make a good sonnet, even one with just a few stanzas; so only the practiced composer who is rich in emotions can give us songs that we may sing more than once without boredom. And there is, perhaps, no other genre with respect to which musical criticism should be stricter, than this one. —But there are a number of significant and beloved collections of lieder that have become known in the most recent period, and that have more than passing value. Such songs were given to us by Mozart, Haydn, Naumann, Hurka, Reichardt, and Schulz. Of these, those of the last-named composer have found the greatest acceptance, *in their own time*, in home entertainment.[45] —What might the reason have been? I am convinced that it is the fact that Schulz's lieder, *for the most part*, are far removed in tone and content from the *ordinary folk song*, on the one hand, and from the *more elevated* songs (for whose enjoyment an exceptional degree of cultivation of both art and feeling is required, as for example with Reichardt's songs), on the other; so that they represent a kind of *middle genre*. On first glance, and as the title indicates, they are designed to imitate the popular tone—naturally in a nobler form. But their actual purpose, as one soon notices, is with the aid of music to awaken *purer* feelings in the breast of those human beings who are often aware of the disadvantages that culture so easily causes for the heart, especially in the urban tumult, and that either leads them to quarrel with humanity in general or, after a futile struggle, to be swept along with the tide. Voss and Schulz (like Weisse and Hiller, with their operettas, before them), believed they could best achieve this intrinsically beautiful aim by taking as the subject of their songs the world of the idylls in German dress; and if it were possible to describe and measure the invisible workings of art we would surely hear some people admitting that Schulz's songs did not fail to have this effect on them. Assuming that these means were the right ones, the composition of these songs could probably have fallen into no better hands than those of our Schulz. As is well known, he possessed a very profound and comprehensive knowledge of the theory of music, one that had advanced to *the level where it did not drag him involuntarily into affectation, but was entirely at his beck and call.*[46] —Melody and harmony, as carefully as he knew how to use them, were for him only means to an end, and Germany can probably point to no composer who was more aware of the relationship that should obtain between poetry and music in applied music. His sensitive and lively feelings also brought him to the point where every turn of phrase, even every tone corresponded to the *total idea* and sentiment that he wanted to express. Only in this way was it possible for him to give his songs a simultaneously *specific* and *ideal* character, so that the unprejudiced observer must exclaim: This is exactly the way it should be! —But would it be a good thing, *at this time*, to imitate *this* genre of lieder? I think not; and not only because the ghost of a Schulz will not necessarily sit comfortably on every singer of Lieder, but rather because the most *immediate* tendency of these songs no longer suits our era, and because art itself generally gains little from middle genres of its products. The political and civil ferment of the third period seems to have made us Germans too insensitive or too overripe for the enjoyment of Arcadian pleasures and feelings. To ignite our feelings, we now require a stronger dose of artificial means than can be provided by the view of unspoiled but also *uncultivated* human beings, into whose situation such songs are meant to transport us. The understanding, which is so variously excited and engaged, increasingly blocks those paths to the heart that lead otherwise than through itself, and increasingly—*even* in our *imagination*—the man of artiface takes the place of the mere man of *nature*, who is very limited in his forms and in the range of his activities. In a word, we seek art—quite anti-Rousseauishly—even in those places where we once believed and felt happy that we could do without it. To go backwards is no longer possible, even if it were desirable; we must work our way through to the goal, which—is still far off. But even this—namely this ferment, if it is to be used to bring us more rapidly to the goal, makes it our duty in our future works of art, both large and small, to avoid as much as possible *vacillating* between the common and the noble, the rough (merely natural) and the finely cultivated. And from all this it follows: that Schulz's lieder had to grow old sooner than they deserved by virtue of their inner excellence. These remarks, moreover, by no means apply to him, who remains unforgettable, but only to—his imitators. For he also acquired abilities that raised him to the level of the best, if not the most brilliant German composers of the previous century. *Simplicity* and *truth* are the most salient characteristics of his works. He was led to them by the natural tendency of his heart, combined with his great knowledge of art. This made him especially adept at portraying the *sublime* (above all the religious sublime, in which he is perhaps first after Handel) and at expressing the *innocent* and (in short songs) the *childlike*, which, from the standpoint of aesthetics, is very close to the sublime, even though in respect to artistic effort they seem to be two opposite extremes. The things that fall in between, namely the portrayal of the fiery, the comic, and so on, to which a voluptuous imagination and hence greater power and variety of instrumental accompaniment etc. belong, were not his forte. He also knew himself too well to undertake anything of this kind except when compelled by circumstances. How much we owe to this man, who is also distinguished by a profound, *pure* love of art, is something that his biographer (his friend and also his near relation in spirit and feelings) will, we hope, elaborate for us. The last year of the previous century snatched him away, too, after fate had already forced this equally outstanding man and artist, as a result of illness, to renounce almost all participation in music. Oh, how many people there were and still are for whom no sacrifice would have been too great to preserve him longer for the musical world![47]

• • •

[No. 26: Conclusion. Where German music has been and is now.] These, then, would be the most important changes that the *practical* art of music experienced toward the end of the past century. During this general expansion of the amateur engagement with music, which put only sacred music to sleep, but brought new life to the remaining genres, the *theory* and the *literature* of music did not entirely fail to progress, even if they have had only slight influence, *until now*, on the *course* of music itself. For this reason I shall touch on them only briefly here. The cause of this slight influence probably lay primarily in the fact that the experienced musicians so rarely had any scholarly

education and the scholars who may have devoted some attention to music seldom, for their part, had a sufficiently profound knowledge of art. For this reason we are not much more advanced in the theory of the *mechanism* of music than they were at the time of Marpurg and Kirnberger; and in regard to the *aesthetic* treatment of music we have almost nothing but—*fragments* to show for ourselves. True, among them one can find excellent observations and valuable materials, as well as hints for future aesthetic theoreticians of music; for example, from the earlier period, in Sulzer's *General Theory of the Fine Arts* in the writings of [Johann Friedrich] Reichardt and [Johann Gottlieb Karl] Spazier, and in Kramer's magazine and other works. —A number of worthy men also contributed to the closing of gaps in musical *instruction*. Thus, M. D. Furth in Halle made a not inconsiderable contribution through his practical *Klavierschule* and other works, which, under the guidance of a *skilled* teacher, surely encourage not superficiality but thoroughness in the easiest way. Next to them, we ought not to forget Petri's *Introduction to Practical Music* which contains a kind of musical encyclopedia and would be even more appreciated if its author had brought his great store of knowledge (especially historical knowledge) into greater order and presented it more tastefully. A new important work that is free of these shortcomings is the *Primer of Theoretical Music* by H. A. Klein, which responds to a not inconsiderable need. Its compendium form makes it especially suitable as a guide for teachers; it is only too bad that its *technical* section (with the exception of the organ) is so brief. Could the reason for this have do with the German *public*, which especially in works of scholarship and art demands the greatest possible—*inexpensiveness*, and in this way forces writers to adopt an excessive condensation of their ideas? —Still, works that only *German* toil and diligence could produce have also found a place among us, and they have earned greater respect for the literature of music—until now always one of the least respected among the disciplines. Above all, Forkel's writings, and even in the first period the discoveries from the realm of old church music reported by the learned abbot M. Gerbert, as well as, finally, E. L. Gerber's *Lexicon of Musicians* (this work which is so useful and unique of its kind) are telling proof that among us, with proper support, there would be no lack of men who, by portraying the past, could give our insight into the future a more specific and firmer direction than the present ferment of the *practical* art of music would otherwise lead one to suspect.

Now there remains only the important question: What has the German art of music gained or lost *on the whole, from the beginning to the end* of the previous century? —I would gladly avoid this question, for I know how awkward or nearly impossible it is for an unknown writer to try to guide the judgment of the public, especially when it comes to subjects in the fine arts, without being criticized, and justifiably, for reckless self-conceit. On the other hand, it seems to be the duty of everyone who steps forward with any type of criticism to justify his starting perspective by providing a concluding judgment, especially since modesty would not have him believe that readers have paid such close and unflagging attention to his comments that they can deduce the results for themselves. In this ambivalent state, between speaking and remaining silent, one experience proves decisive, namely that with respect to the value of older and newer music the voices of the public are in fact—here and there certainly to the disparagement of art—still too divided not to excuse a modest attempt to put these judgments to the test. Nothing would seem to lead more directly to it than an essay like this one; so let us try!

Devotion to the old on the one side and the *charm of novelty* on the other have always been two perilous cliffs upon which science, like art, has often foundered. The former, by suppressing the desire to inquire into the merit of new discoveries and forms; the latter, by rejecting, contrary to the nature of reason, what has *always* been good and beautiful along with what was inadequate and bad among the products of earlier eras. This often led to a later revision—or to straying even farther from the goal. Both [tendencies] have their uses, in individual instances, but these uses do not reliably compensate for the harm they do to humanity. But there is probably no field in which it is *more difficult* to defend oneself against the *deleterious* influence that the *charm of novelty* has on us than an art that, by its very nature, cannot prosper without it. In the *visual arts*, for example, the encounter with beautiful works generally produces a *greater* pleasure, the *older* they are; because sensual apperception plays a lesser role in this kind of artistic pleasure than does reflection, and the thought "So mankind had already progressed that far!," which increases our admiration, is not interrupted by any new observation. With music it is different. Music has greater sensual charm and maintains it through a continuous variation of the feelings, thus *subjecting reflection to apperception*. Musical works of *significance* are therefore often only appreciated by connoisseurs after repeated hearing or during their *reading* of the score. This applies especially to *pure* music, because it is not abetted by any *specific concepts* to make the *longer duration* of one and the same *feeling* endurable. But one should take all the more care not to let the natural desire for novelty degenerate to the point where one pays less attention to the eternal laws of the true and the beautiful, which are independent of our volition and mood, than to that desire. *When art is not dependent on fashion, but fashion on art, only then are both in good condition! Only then can human beings derive truly lasting benefit from them!* May those people take this to heart who seek only the *new*, praise only the *new*, without being *desirous* or *capable* of comparing it *in detail* with the old! May they consider that it is often nothing but *self-deception* (lack of ability to remember or of sufficient experience or insight) when some things *seem* new to them that are only distinguished by *accidental* or *insignificant* secondary characteristics from things that have already been thought, done, and written! —But others, who are so *attached to the old* that they are suspicious of every new form, every unusual turn of phrase, are no less mistaken in their judgment of the course of musical development and of incidental changes in taste. Like the friend of the merely modern, when it comes to the past, the lover of the old often does an injustice to the contemporary world. This, too, results from self-deception, which is constantly nourished by the disinclination to step out of the old rut and to examine the value of the new precisely and in a non-partisan way. For one forgets that the ancients were once modern too, and that the concepts "ancient and contemporary" have nothing to do with human arbitrariness (which is what one has in mind when one criticizes the modern). But above all, this represents a sin against Nature and the natural purpose of our intelligence, which betrays its inborn tendency to infinity precisely through the unending drive to push aside old *forms*. —I direct these observations not only at people who do not like any music that is not written in the style of Graun or Bach—for by now the latter has more or less died out or is no longer heard,—but as a warning for the future, namely when our great masters of the third period will also be old-fashioned, when the increased veneration of them and their works might lead, in the same way, to injustice toward new geniuses.

So long as no more powerful means are found than in the past to bind the human spirit with chains; so long as the culture that has been achieved is not destroyed root and branch by horrible destruction of the entire earth (for example by mass migrations and crusades, although even their destructive power is generally thought to be much greater than pragmatic history teaches); until then it seems to me to be equally foolish to speak of the *decline* of an art *per se*, or to claim that it has reached its *loftiest peak*. No, it can happen (and really does happen) that in a particular period one important aspect of an art is less respected and worked on than another. It can be that people tend, at one moment, to sacrifice *thoroughness* to *liveliness* in their portrayals, and then before long to sacrifice the latter to the former; but does it follow from this that a whole art is in decline? —It is true that *taste* is not such an arbitrary matter as some people suppose; but art only falls into a state of lethargy when taste—*does not* change. In the opposite case, when people become aware of various improvements in the most recent period, when they feel tempted to look down pityingly on our ancestors who did not know any such advantages, when they observe with astonishment and satisfaction the more general interest that art awakens in recent times—is it then already time to rest on some imagined laurels? It is time to speak of perfection, which could be followed by nothing but—decline? —Perhaps all these errors could be prevented by a single question: What is the highest goal of every fine art? —*Humanity*, and not merely of individual human beings, but of our entire species. Have we already reached this goal? —We can no more answer with "yes" than we could claim that there has not yet been any progress in approaching the goal. It seems to me, rather, where the latter is concerned, that even in the course of development of the art of music from the beginning to the end of the last century, this progress is perceptible. The progress of the human spirit often occurs in a way that is similar to the one Nature follows in the creation of material beings. The nobler the fruit she is creating is meant to be, the longer she ordinarily spends working on its raw seed, separating and mixing its primal materials. The time of *blossoming* is bracing but short. From then until the complete ripening of the *fruit* Nature requires even more extensive influence of the elements, which often challenges the patience of the person who, above all, demands *immediate, practical* usefulness from everything that happens in the world. And how often something appears to our shortsighted eyes to be destructive but is nothing but an indispensable means to a *higher*, generally useful purpose. So too with art. At first its development only treats the *organization of its more solid parts* (for example harmony). That was the fate of German music up until almost the middle of the last century. This was followed in the second period by its blossoming. It gave evidence of *life force*, which now *began* to stir, and which did not simply allow itself to be led by the mechanism of the musical art (like the melancholy masters of counterpoint), but subordinated this mechanism to more far-ranging purposes. But this *balance* could not last long. Music became too broadly dispersed for it not to suffer losses in specific instances as a result of the differing treatment to which it was subjected. If we judge it according to *this* criterion, we will admittedly be tempted to declare that the third period is not exactly the best. But if we consider that the very ferment of intellectual and moral forces brings the same benefits for our culture *as a whole* that the struggle of the earth's elements produces, then we will be reconciled with it as easily as we recognize that there is still much—*very much* to hope and to do before one can—not speak of goals and peaks—but even excuse a pause along the path that we have begun to tread.

This, now, would be *my* profession of faith regarding the value that music acquired among us in the previous century. The *first* period was dominated by thorough but, compared to the other branches of music, one-sided treatment of harmony. In the *second*, people sought to add grace and loveliness by means of more melodious, comprehensible compositions. In the *third*, variety, richness, and liveliness were characteristic qualities of our music, but often at some cost to the advantages of the first two periods.[48] What the new century will give us we do not yet know; but, I repeat, in the individual case, where art is dependent on genius, study, and taste, it is the work of human beings, who may be praised or criticized for their advances or their steps backward; *as a whole*, we can only think of it as the work of a higher power, which *never, never* can take *real* steps backward—or else the noblest thing in the world is a soap bubble.[49]

Let us then, you loyal and profound admirers of the divine art, which is so often praised as a foretaste of celestial bliss, look back with joy and gratitude on the path that it so admirably traversed even in the previous century! Deafened neither by the trumpet call of blind enthusiasm nor by the hoarse croaking of envious critics, let us honor our great masters by continued study of their richly varied works, without claiming that they are infallible and unsurpassable. —Let us never lose sight of the *true* needs of art, and never confound it with the demands of arbitrariness and capriciousness! —Finally, let us be ever more strict toward the maltreatment to which art is subjected, mainly by unknowing, vain, and careless or untalented composers; but let us also lavish all imaginable attention on those who, by thorough insight, genius, and toil, demonstrate their inner vocation for the development and elevation of an art that has pretensions to greater value than as a fleeting means of sensual pleasure; and that even, like the spirit that works in it, is capable of perfectibility toward the infinite! —

NOTES

1. This division of music, formed by analogy to pure and applied mathematics, may well be more aesthetically important nowadays, given the great expansion and mixing of its various branches, than the division into instrumental and vocal music. The latter actually refers only to the tools of the art of music, and reveals, if we are speaking of the expression of emotions, nothing further than that vocal music deals with it *directly*, and instrumental music only *indirectly*. The division that is utilized here (and for which more precise terms may perhaps be found) is intended primarily to respond to the proclamations about the apparent decline of the art of music that are so frequent nowadays. If one wanted to allow, as genuine music, only that which concretely portrays the sentiments of a particular [human] subject (although this is the original and also the highest goal of the art of music), it would condemn all voiceless compositions (as, in painting, Raphael's arabesques and other non-referential artistic play); and hence all or most sonatas, fugues, concertos, symphonies, etc., would be only meaningless games. But no, the music gives pleasure and, if the philosophers will permit me, —also cultivates the heart, even if not so manifestly as in church or in the theater, through works like these; the latter are nothing but beautiful (i.e. formed according to the rules of art) play, which already has appropriate usefulness *[Zweckmässigkeit]* as soon as an aesthetic, if indistinct idea dominates the whole. This is what I understand by *pure* music, to which one may even reckon all vocal pieces whose text says nothing, merely serving as a vehicle for the employment of the voice. In contrast to which, the sensual portrayal in music of a [human] subject (his emotions and actions), where poetry and mimetic gesture, etc. take first place, is called *applied* music. The latter, in a certain sense, also includes the characteristic instrumental works such as those composed by C. P. E. Bach, J. Haydn, Dittersdorf, etc., which are related to the original word-music as pantomime to drama. So much for the explanation of these expressions; more on this subject on another occasion.

2. By "mechanism" is meant the essence of the natural means through which a fine art is able to produce its *forms*, and through which it also becomes an art in its own right. It is *developed* as soon as 1) its individual parts stand in a natural relationship and balance and give mutual support to each other, and 2) these parts are of such a nature that they suffice for every possible purpose of this particular art. The mechanism of music is partly an *internal* one (melody, harmony, rhythm), and partly an *external* one (the material composition of the tone-producing tools).

3. A clear proof of this is that we are still no more advanced in it than the Greeks were. The suppleness of their versification has still not been attained, and in regard to mime perhaps only the Paris opera can provide a few exceptions.

4. Poetry entirely (melodic language and rhythm), mimetic gesture in part, namely rhythmic movement. The latter drew the other, admittedly more important part of its development, from the visual arts, or vice versa.

5. Palestrina and Luther were the guardian angels of the art of music in the sixteenth century. The former (1555) for the southern German (Catholic), the latter for the northern (Protestant) church.

6. Since it is not our intent to provide a *comprehensive* history of the German art of music in the eighteenth century—an undertaking that awaits a Forkel—but we are merely talking about the general *course* of its *development*, only those German musicians can be named here who, at least for a time, gave a dominant direction to our music and were considered as generally venerated models. Germany possessed, and still possesses, a number of skilled, even famous men whom probably only the confluence of particular cir-

cumstances prevented from being the same kind of authoritative figures in the realm of music as those who earned such great fame.

7. One need only recall the practice of arranging (castrating) operas and operettas, from *Don Juan* to *Sonntagskind*, for two flutes, violins, in short for all kinds of string and wind instruments! —Are the French and English our predecessors or imitators in this? I almost think, the latter. In Italy, so far as I know, they do not engage in this—mischief.

8. Here a short comparison of *Italian* and *French* music, for the purpose of clarifying the influence on German music of the former in regard to song, and of the latter in regard to instrumental music (at least in the first half of the last century). —The *sensual* charm of the notes is limited by the words, for the consonants muffle the sound. That this occurs in as limited a way as possible is the peculiarity of *Italian* vocal music and is made easier by the number and purity of the vowels in this language. *French* music, although not so guttural as German music, can nevertheless not compare with Italian in regard to *sonority*. Furthermore, it belongs to a nation which compares to the former as wit to emotion. The Italian would like to say everything that he feels; the Frenchman often says more than he thinks. The senses dominate the arts of the former, the understanding [reason] the arts of the latter. Hence in singing the Italian relies more on the *tone*, the Frenchman on the *idea*. Hence Italian singing is by its nature more melismatic, French singing more syllabic (compare Lully and Gluck). An apparent contradiction to what has been said is provided by Italian *buffo singing*. But this can be resolved by recalling that the buffo originally served as a contrast to the all too melismatic music (or, if you will, as a satire against the all too syllabic music), when opera ceased to be mere recitative; that the pliant language made it lighter; and that in general a wise Nature gave the Italians their drollness as an antidote to melancholy. —In instrumental music, the French were and are, on the whole, quicker, cleverer, more artificial, while the Italians have more solidity. If this *natural* difference between French and Italian music has not always been evident in recent years, if the two nations seemed to exchange their musical taste, this was the result of particular causes whose examination would lead us too far afield.

9. The *Amen fugues*, of which Petri speaks so amusingly in the *Introduction to Music*, p. 88, were long a beloved and much praised hobby horse of cantors and church composers.

10. A circumstance that has not disappeared and that is only somewhat assuaged by the preponderance of instrumental music, and that even Mozart was able to overcome only in his *Don Giovanni* and *Requiem*.

11 .The relationship between the *composer* and the *performing musician* (where the two are not one and the same) deserves special study in our time, when so many nimble-fingered virtuosos boast of being *artists*. What the writer of plays is in relation to the actor, the architect in relation to the carpenter, is more or less what the composer is in relation to the performer of his works. The former starts from the whole and adds the detail; the latter portrays the detail and leads through it toward the whole. The former sets to work synthetically, the latter analytically. Only physical limitations (including an often very excusable lack of mechanical skill) prevents the composer from performing his work himself in the most perfect manner. By contrast, the greatest worth of a performing musician consists in correctly grasping the sense of the composer and knowing how to portray it. *He*, in other words, should not invent anything *new*, and if he adds decorations that are not prescribed they must not contradict the content and spirit of the composition. Only in a case where the latter are flat or the composer (as the playwright often does) has only sketched out his ideas can the performer make improvements or additions; but not without insight into the rules of composition and refined taste. Under this condition alone does the performing musician have a right to the title of fine artist; otherwise—no matter how much skill, sureness, agility, beauty of tone, etc., he may possess—he only deserves

that of craftsman, although with various degrees of artistry. —This is a topic about which it would certainly be worthwhile to write a *separate treatise*.

12. *Claudite iam rivos, pueri; sat prata biberunt* (Now close the sluices, lads; the fields have drunk their fill) is the last line of Virgil's Third Eclogue. Its meaning, after the singing contest that comprises the eclogue, is "That's enough!" See Virgil, *The Eclogues*, trans. Guy Lee (Hammondsworth, Middlesex, England, 1984), p. 53. Thanks to Michael Long for the reference. [Ed.]

13. Is effect—as is so widely claimed nowadays—really the highest law of art or the most important goal of the artist? Would it not be good to be cautious in applying this maxim and—to discuss it in detail?

14. A proof of the claim that we are more indebted to the French for our instrumental music, and to the Italians more for our song.

15. The fine arts flourish in most places only as a result of the luxury of the powerful and the rich. As depressing as this remark may be for the enthusiastic friend of the arts, who so fervently wishes for people to love art not as a mechanism of vanity, but for its own sake, and who, quite justifiably, finds in this dependency the so frequent paralysis of art; still, on the other hand, one should recall with a sense of gratitude that the overwhelming taste for the fine arts is the best means to limit the natural excesses of the rich and powerful. Fortunate is the land whose prince and nobility converse, if not more gladly, at least as gladly with the nine sisters as with Diana and Bellona!

16. In the same way as the painter is related to the mere draftsman, so the composer of truly poetic song is related to the mere writer of counterpoint, even if the latter utilizes a text, but only as a vehicle. The former gives us the illuminated elevation of the building, the latter merely the dry blueprint according to its dimensions. The former gives us the human body in all its carnality and the expression of passion; its secondary figures are also full of life and significance. The latter only gives us the outline or the skeleton, and the decorations are there only for concealment.

17. Why, if our nerves are at all sensitive, are we unable to tolerate the interrupted sounds of the musical glasses [glass harmonica] for very long? Indeed, why does protracted music by wind instruments, even if it is pure, tire us more quickly than less pure music made by stringed instruments or human voices? —The reason lies primarily in the following. Every tone, even every sound, is perceived by us in two relations, a *material* and an *arithmetical* one. The *arithmetical* relation (the uniformity of the movements of air) is what makes the tone a tone, i.e. the musical sound in its various gradations. The *material* relation is to the material composition of the *sounding tools*, which depends in turn on their size, construction, chemical mixture, etc. Music *in itself*, to the extent that it is perceived by the *inner* sense, has to do, it is true, only with the former (arithmetical) relation. But since it is our auditory organs that first excite this (inner) sense, the *material* composition of the tones is also very important. Here it depends on their relation to our auditory organs; for example how much greater or smaller the *density* of our inner organs is (on which, as is well known, the degree of their elasticity depends), related to the density of composition of the tones. The resulting *material purity* makes it easier, on the one hand, to comprehend arithmetical purity and thus tenses our nerves (wherein the reason for its sensual charm lies); however, if the former *too greatly* exceeds the material purity of *our* organs, an excessively strong tension results that soon exhausts the power of our senses. This is the case in which we find ourselves with the glass harmonica. Similarly, strings on wood reduce the material purity, which is greater where the wood is made to sound through air alone. By contrast, there is probably no greater *material* conformity than that between the organs of the voice and the ear, so that the charm of singing is based not only on its mental origin, but also on the above-mentioned homogeneity with our *external* senses,

to which, admittedly, the activity of our *intellectual* powers must be added if a sustained, simple song is to provide us the greatest possible pleasure. — —How immeasurably much can be deduced from all that, for example for the ease of listening to a many-hued orchestral body, for the appropriate choice of instruments for diverse performances, for their mechanical perfection, etc., as well as, further, for the explanation of the pleasure that crude and wild peoples find in their music, which sounds barbaric to us, etc., etc., is something that anyone can probably comprehend who considers these carelessly tossed off remarks to be worthy of some reflection.

18. Until the most recent times, with the exception of J. Haydn and Mozart (who also only count as exceptions), the music in southern Germany was almost nothing except a—*colony of Italian music*, which loyally followed all the changes in taste of the homeland. But here we are actually speaking only of theater music. There were and are important men there who distinguished themselves in sacred music, especially in monasteries, but also outside them. Who, for example, does not know and revere the learned Albrechtsberger? —But they could not stem the flood that was pressing in upon them from Italy.

19. I may be allowed a few comments here, which for reasons of space are only aphoristic. —The *essential* (aesthetic) difference between *theatrical* and *church* music (of which style, whose forms depend more on the stage of development of the tonal mechanism, etc., is only a consequence) is based on the differences between

1) the *subject* to be portrayed

2) the *objects* to which the portrayal refers

3) the *effect* that each of these types of music seeks to create.

1) In church music, the *subject* is generalized; sacred music expresses the sentiments of all the people who have come together there; whereas theater music only expresses those of the individuals on the stage (singly or in groups).

2) The *object* of church music is an *ideal* that bears the character of the eternal (the godhead or its representatives, and virtue as a means of approaching it). —The object of *theater music* is also an ideal, but not presented as such. —The former depicts men as more independent of, the latter as more dependent on Nature. —Both are concerned with what human beings *should be*, the church *directly*, the theater *indirectly*.

3) The most natural tendency of church music is to concentrate the feelings of the participants in a single emotion (devotion). The latter, however, because it creates extraordinary tension in the heart, thanks to the generalization of the subject and the idealization of the object, soon ceases to be emotion with consciousness—where it is really present—and either numbs the inner sense or is transformed into a mere operation of the understanding (deep melancholy reflection).

Hence the material power, the shattering mass of tones, hence the slowness of movement (i.e. the longer duration of the same note), hence the skillful interweaving of tones (counterpoint and fugue), which invites reflection, and the *concealment of the rhythm*, which is intended to guard against the change of emotions.

Theater music has as its goal the creation of a *diversity* of emotions. —It does not want (and this is the essence of *illusion*) to engage the understanding at the *expense* of the senses; in this it is greatly supported by entertainments for the visual sense, among other things. —Here *melody* and *rhythm* are the main thing, and far freer—both in the greatest possible variety (for example passagework, ballets, etc.). It intoxicates without numbing and does not depress the emotions, but excites them. —The theater of the Greeks had a more *ideal quality*, more *energy* and *poetry* than ours and was therefore more effective. —*Church music* is more susceptible to theatrical admixtures, the more *anthropomorphism* (the character of all positive religion) there is in theoretical and practical religion. —One need only examine Catholic and Protestant church music as a whole. More on this subject, perhaps, on another occasion.

20. The sources of such judgments, which lie *within us*—and of which we will say more at the conclusion of this essay—namely the attachment to the old, on the one hand, and the charm of novelty on the other, will not be broached here.

21. How wonderful it would be for art, what high, perhaps even double degree of development would it have achieved, if artists' most original, freest products were not usually their *first*, when they are not yet initiated into the secrets of art. — —Wounded by the stings of criticism, to which they have revealed weaknesses, or drunk with the incense that was strewn at them, or else pressured by frequent commissions, etc., they soon take to the main highways but work less for art than for the populace. —Only *those* artists deserve (and are given) *constant* admiration who have understood how to preserve their originality until the time of their greatest artistic development.

22. One need only remember Mozart's witty retort to Emperor Joseph in response to his criticism of the [too] many notes.

23. As indicated above, I mention only the *supreme command*, for the other, in part very meritorious men either followed in their footsteps or did not do as much for art as *a whole*, which is the sole subject of discussion here. Those who judge this essay will, I hope, not forget that I set out to write a sketchy history of *art*, not *artists*, and have mentioned the latter only for the sake of the first.

24. Among whom K. M. Haak in Berlin is one of the best.

25. Triest uses *Klavier* throughout to refer most often to harpsichord or simply keyboard. Sometimes, however, the sense suggests clavichord or even piano. It seems awkward to use the generic term "keyboard" when it is placed in opposition to "organ." Thus the term is variously translated here. [Ed.]

26. For this reason one seldom sees great instrumental composers who would be equally great for songs, and vice versa. Only Mozart, if one is not *too* particular about it, can be considered a significant exception. —But of this more later.

27. In the *visual arts* this separation is not so necessary as in the *art of music*, because in the latter the mechanism itself is so large that it demands constant study.

28. It is not fitting for the author of this essay to make any judgment, regarding a living, famous, and in quite a few respects (among others, the mechanism of the organ) unquestionably deserving man, which is not yet based on the opinions of *all* important critics and that hence—as his *own* opinion—might be faulted as arrogance. He can and would only like to make note of the existing situation.

The revolution that Abbot Vogler intends to bring about in music seems to be suffering a fate that is similar to that of the Browneian theory in medicine. It has friends and opponents. The *former* believe "that as a consequence of the removal of all stiff, useless, pedantic rules (as they call them), it could happen that sacred music is given more energy and simplicity, the theatrical style greater dignity, and pure music greater brilliance. The *latter* are of the opinion" that what is lasting and good about the new theory, despite the invectives against Bach, etc., is —nothing new, and sometimes just expressed differently. The remaining teachings and supposed improvements (as they say) are often in conflict with the most natural and generally valid principles, and are the fruits of the usual craving for paradox that one would expect in an eccentric thinker (who does not like to suffer anyone next to, much less above himself), and whose originator vainly seeks to avoid criticism by claiming to be misunderstood. This, they claim, is less true of his compositions, but more of his performance, which is more dazzling than thorough and moreover does not fully cohere with the theory he has established, etc."

Who is correct is something that may be reliably decided soon, in the new century.

29. All of mankind's *practical* knowledge can be divided, from the point of view of the *subject,* into three classes. The mere craftsman (in the broadest sense) knows, *as such,* nothing but the practical means of producing a work, and what he does is more the fruit of a merely mechanical practice and blind imitation (of a routine) than of original reflection. There are such men, as is well known, in music, just as in theology and law, among other fields. —The craftsman is elevated to an *artist,* the more familiar he is with the rules on which his works are based (with theory), and, it should be noted, the more this knowledge of the rules forms a *coherent whole* in his understanding. —*Scholarship* is concerned with the *reasons* for human knowledge—here, in other words, for practice—with the *reasons* for the rules, which are derived from the real sciences (mathematics and philosophy, which of late are competing for the rank of sciences). —For the same genre, one sometimes finds one, sometimes two, or even all three levels together in one head. —What result this leads to, especially for *criticism,* I do not need to say.

30. There may perhaps be only two instances, in addition to these two men, where *German* poets and composers worked in such lovely unison—Gotter with Benda and Voss with Schultz.

31. It would be a serious misunderstanding if the reader were to believe me to be saying that I would like to see everything *comical* or *burlesque* banished from the theater. On the contrary, it quite properly belongs there. But *how* should it be conveyed *musically*? —I know of no better answer to this than to study Mozart's Leporello! —I say *study,* for merely seeing and hearing him might not be sufficient.

32. Take, as just one example, the great aria in *Walder,* "Wer dem Schiffbruch," in which can be found not just the painting of objects, as required by the text, but at the same time in most coloraturas a beautiful expression of *human* feelings and their changes, such as one seeks in vain in many other works of art that shine only through instrumental pomp and meaningless runs.

33. If it were allowable to make jokes about things that are only too serious, one might, at this juncture, draw a far-reaching, perhaps not unwitty parallel between the most recent political changes and those occurring in music. But I will leave this to the person who, in the next century, will write the history of the present one (and including the preparatory phenomena from the most recent one). It could well be that he would then demonstrate from the results that the course of development followed by the art of music was just as important for its *higher* aim (the ennobling of the emotions and hence of humanity) as political revolutions were for theirs—except that the former, praise the Lord, had no bloody consequences.

34. There is still one country in which the organ is especially honored, and that is *England,* —which, in respect to language, customs *(mutatis mutandis),* etc., one could actually call the old Germany. —Here one finds organs and positives everywhere. After England, they are probably most greatly valued in Holland.

35. Among the French, the former (namely that when they are in society they constantly have their business and domestic concerns in mind) is more rare; hence they also have less need of coarse farces to cheer them up. Hence, barring other circumstances, they will always be the masters of more refined drama (*haute comédie*).

36. The inner mechanism of music already leads in this direction, for example that the first *natural* modulation of the minor tones is into the major scale of the mediant. Further, the rules that freely occurring dissonances are only permitted in certain cases,—that their resolution cannot be postponed for too long, etc.

37. Gluck's operas with tragic subject matter will therefore on average only arouse enthusiasm among Frenchmen and educated Germans, and as long as our national character does not change, pieces like the *Zauberzither* or the *Sonntagskind* will fill the theater

coffers better than an *Iphigenie*, since the latter, in any case, can only be performed in the better theaters.

38. Proof is provided by Wenzel Müller's products. —Also, there are even grand operas of this kind, for example *Dario von Alessandri*, which in Berlin has jokingly been called the *Opera Made of D Major*.

39. Hence even the dreadful German text with which this excellent work has so far been deformed almost everywhere (so far as I know), to the shame of the theater directors, has not been able to reduce the pleasure in this work, as long as the performance was tolerably pure and precise.

40. Comparisons of famous men have a number of uses, if only by virtue of the fact that they increase the veneration for the one who lives longest, because people are in the habit of *admiring* what is old and far away more than what is new and present, even if they should feel a greater love for the latter. —It was possible to read in these pages (by another hand) an excellent parallel between Rafael and Mozart. —I may be allowed to cite another famous man of the past, between whose *spirit* as an artist and the spirit of Mozart I believe I discern a number of similarities, namely—Shakespeare. Profound, bold, fortunate inroads into the human heart and lively portrayal of the emotions are common to both men. Similarly the *tendency* and the talent for the grotesque, in both tragedy and comedy. Both have been criticized for a certain disregard of the old rules of art—for example in Shakespeare breaches of poetic unity, in M. of strict composition *[den reinen Satz]*. Both had profound aesthetic *feeling* without an entirely refined *taste*, because of a lack of scientific education. Hence the frequent disregard of good usage, —in Sh. through anachronisms and scenes of horror, —in M. through too frequent contrasts between the comic and the tragic and through bizarre tonal sequences. (It is true that their public bore a large share of responsibility for this.) On the other hand, Sh. drowns out the voice of criticism by striking situations, M. by striking modulations, etc. —A detailed parallel between *entire* works of the two artists, for example between *Don Giovanni* and *Lear* or *Hamlet*, *Othello*, etc. and between individual characters like *Falstaff* and *Leporello* (the *musical* Leporello) might perhaps be not unuseful for aesthetics.

41. For the judges whose opinions the modern composer fears and respects are ordinarily not the very small, strict, bothersome handful of definite connoisseurs, but—the public at large.

42. With all respect to the public; —I know of no worse judge in artistic *matters* than the public when it makes judgments *en masse*.

43. As a result, the so-called *cadenzas* have also fallen almost completely out of favor. Previously, they had been added on almost every occasion, which was undoubtedly wrong. Now the way most of the bravura arias are structured, the ignorance of the singers, and similar factors are increasingly pushing these tricks aside. Only in grand operas are they still occurring. Whether this is entirely a good thing is a question. For if they were nothing but a way to test of the skillfulness of the singers, where the instruments cannot help them, at least they would compel the latter to end their laziness in studying the pieces. But they [the cadenzas] are also something more. Their real purpose is to portray the course of the emotions that have dominated the aria, but in a *concentrated* way (on a reduced scale), without being constrained by the fetters of the rhythm, etc. This by no means always happens through roulades, but is often achieved better through single meaningful tones. For this, however, one needs not merely a knowledge of the musical mechanism (how one *can* treat and vary a theme), but also taste and feeling of one's own, as well as the gift of imagination. But because nowadays one seldom finds all this in combination, the composers do not do badly to avoid cadenzas in the arias.

44. Certainly a description of this institute, which would go into detail concerning both its *internal* and *external* aspects, its advantages and possible shortcomings, etc., in an *extensive* and *nonpartisan* way, would be very useful and welcome among the friends of the German art of music. In case it should not yet have appeared, it is hoped that men of *substantive expertise*, who are at the source, will soon give us one. I am so bold as to make a public request for it here.

45. I say, *in their own time*. For even if the charm of novelty is not and cannot be as powerful in any other art as it is in music; still a little song that only expresses emotions and gives vanity very little to do cannot make any great claims to longlasting interest.

46. This theory is revealed in his songs, among other things, by a seemingly small but important circumstance, namely the appropriate choice of *keys*. One should try playing just one of his songs in another key, and with a little attention one will sense how the character of the song loses part of its naturalness.

47. He took many beautiful wishes and good intentions for the improvement of art with him to the grave. Thus he told the author of this essay, among other things, quite often that he would have liked to write a *popular* handbook of the art of music, especially singing, for the use of *teacher seminaries* and teachers in *small* schools, so that they could help themselves with it, because he too had an interest in improving song among all classes of the people. Perhaps another capable man will realize this ambition, someone who has sufficient knowledge of art and the gift of avoiding the merely academic, which only the professional musician needs to know, without leaving significant gaps. —May it come to pass soon!

48. Here it would be possible, to find a standard for judging the value and development of the German art of music *outside* of itself, to adduce a number of comparisons. Among other things, one could say that in the first period of the last century music in Germany resembled a *Dutch* garden, where solidity and effort dominated to the point of the most anxious and costly care. —In the second period it had similarity with the *French-Italian* art of gardening, which at first pleases the eye with its compass-drawn forms, but also soon causes a certain emptiness in the emotions. The third period imitated the *English* garden, whose principal character is the concealment of art in great masses that cannot be seen at one glance, but which often also reveals really (not only seemingly) unregulated or Baroque combinations. One could also compare pure music with a flower garden and applied music with an orchard—but enough for the lover of such flights of fancy! — —

49. Only with some effort can I resist the temptation to say a few words about what the art of music most particularly needs. For example, as was mentioned above, we are still lacking a proper *aesthetic* theory of music. Moreover, it is probably time to look at music *metaphysically*. The most important thing, however—I state it brazenly—is the almost *complete* lack of *genuinely musical German poems*, i.e. poems that not only have a beautiful, really poetic content and form, corresponding to the essence and aim of the art of music, but also are distinguished by the careful choice of sonorous, singable words, etc. However, let someone else pay more detailed attention to such—hopefully not pious—wishes! For I hold it to be my duty to hasten to a conclusion. Perhaps these remarks have already fatigued some readers and stolen space from more important essays. The reason for this, however could only lie not in the significant material, but in its incorrect treatment. May the *initiated* — (for I have not written for musical or philosophical laymen, as is quite evident) — find it worth the trouble of showing me on occasion, with reasons, whether and where I have left significant gaps in my views! —This wish, one may believe it or not, grows only out of *pure, deep* love of art.

Joseph Haydn's Library: Attempt at a Literary-Historical Reconstruction

MARIA HÖRWARTHNER

TRANSLATED BY KATHRINE TALBOT

In the ground-breaking 1976 volume of the Yearbook for Austrian Cultural History, Herbert Zeman edited a collection of essays and documents called *Joseph Haydn and the Literature of His Time*. By revealing the intellectual and social contexts and institutions surrounding Haydn—the literary salons, correspondence, relationship to English literature, development of theater singing, and the like—the authors in the volume uncover Haydn as an involved and aware participant. The extent of this participation is palpably evident when we are permitted a glance—indeed, a long and intimate look—at the books on Haydn's shelves. While Haydn's books on music (theory, practice, history) have long been known, the reconstruction of the riotous diversity of philosophy, poetry, history, travel writing, even occult science, that he bought or received had to wait until Maria Hörwarthner's dissertation on Haydn's engagement with the literary life of his time (University of Vienna, 1979), previewed in the lengthy article for the Yearbook translated here.

Presentation of such an ongoing bibliographical project in English translation poses particular challenges for the translator and editor. To make Hörwarthner's article both more comprehensible to the general reader and more useful to the scholar, we have: 1) for works in languages other than English, provided the principal title of each work in the original language as well as translation; 2) wherever practical, added authors', editors', and/or translators' names at the outset of each entry; 3) distinguished among bibliographical elements through punctuation, style, and word order, particularly in translations, when to do so did not distort the flavor and spirit of the volume in question. [Ed.]

[Source: "Joseph Haydns Bibliothek—Versuch einer literarhistorischen Rekonstruktion," in *Joseph Haydn und die Literatur seiner Zeit,* ed. Herbert Zeman, *Jahrbuch für Österreichische Kulturgeschichte* 6 (1976): 157–207.]

Preface

The following literary-historical documentation is based on the handwritten catalogue of books[1] which was part of the estate documents of Joseph Haydn and which is now in the city archive of Vienna (Wiener Stadtarchiv, Mag. Abh. 2436/1809). It was drawn up by the Imperial Book Audit Office soon after the composer's death and was officially certified by the auditor Joseph Köderl on 19 December 1809.

It is clear that the list of books was not recorded until after the auction sale had been concluded, since both the valuation and the sale prices are noted in two columns to the right of the books as entered, and added up sequentially at the end of each of the seven pages of the list.

As was customary, details about the individual books are mostly fragmentary. The apparently hastily drafted notes are limited to either the surname of the author or do not even mention one, then list a distinguishing—often abbreviated—title fragment along with place of publication and year. Spelling and other errors are common.

The aim of the following survey is:

1. to give complete bibliographical documentation of all the books listed in the handwritten index of the library;[2]
2. to discuss the certain or possible relationship of the various works with Haydn's personality and work;
3. to present the literary-historical situation in Vienna around 1800 from the perspective of the intellectual interest of Haydn and the circle close to him.

This triple undertaking is served by 1) the following bibliographical list (the sequence and numbering correspond to the handwritten original) with commentary accompanying the individual titles, and 2) by an afterword summarizing the research findings.

I

[1] [Gray, W. and Guthrie, W., editors].

Allgemeine Weltgeschichte. Im Englischen herausgegeben von Wilhelm Guthrie und Johann Gray (General world history. Edited, in English, by William Guthrie and John Gray). Translated and improved by various German scholars. Troppau, Brünn, Vienna: Trassler, Schrämbl 1784–94.

The work comprises ninety-one volumes, of which Haydn owned sixty-five.

It appears from the preface that this is a reprint of a German translation of the English original, which was published between 1764 and 1767.

The work considers the history of the world to be the result of an act of creation, and accords the history of culture and the intellect a central place. It is one of those publications intended to advance general education, works which more or less inundated the Austrian book market in the last third of the eighteenth century. The state's educational propaganda aimed at awakening a historical consciousness in an increasingly large section of the population.[3]

[2] [Krünitz, D. Johann Georg, translator/editor].

Oekonomische Encyklopädie, oder allgemeines System der Land- Haus- und Staats-Wirtschaft, in alphabetischer Ordnung (An encyclopedia of economics or general system of the economics of agricultural-, household-, and national-economy, in alphabetical order). Translated from the French with notes and additions, . . . by D. Johann Georg Krünitz. Berlin, Joachim Pauli 1773–1858.

Johann Georg Krünitz (1725–1798)[4] published the first seventy-two volumes of this monumental, and at the time leading, reference work. After his death it was added to by Friedrich Jakob Flörke, among others. By 1858 it had increased to 242 volumes.

Haydn's library contained a reprint of the first part as far as volume 78, published in Brünn (1787–1804) and nowadays almost impossible to obtain.

[3] [Burney, Charles.]

A General History of Music, from the Earliest Ages to the Present Period. To which is prefixed a dissertation on the Music of the Ancients. By Charles Burney, Mus. D. F. R. S.

Volume the first, London. Printed for the Author: And sold by T. Becket, Strand; J. Robson, New Bond Street; and T. Robinson, Paternoster Row, 1776.

Volume the second, London. Printed for the Author: And sold by J. Robson . . . and G. Robinson . . . 1782.

Volume the third. Printed for the Author: And sold by Payne and Son . . . Robson and Clark . . . and G. G. J. and J. Robinson . . . 1789.

Haydn's name is mentioned several times with much approval in the fourth volume of this extensive, illustrated ("with cuts") music history.[5]

The fact that music scholar Charles Burney (1726–1814)[6] held Haydn in high regard is much in evidence in the more detailed discussion of the composer's work: "I am now happily arrived at that part of my narrative where it is necessary to speak of HAYDN! the admirable and matchless HAYDN!"[7]

Haydn was on friendly terms with Burney during his stay in London; Burney had announced the composer's arrival in London with a poem,[8] and was instrumental in Haydn's receiving an Honorary Degree in Music.

[4] Adelung, Johann Christoph.

Versuch eines vollständigen grammatisch-kritischen Wörterbuches / Der Hochdeutschen Mundart, mit beständiger Vergleichung der übrigen Mundarten, besonders der oberdeutschen. Dem noch beygefüget ist des Herrn M. Fulda Preisschrift über die beyden deutschen Haupt-Dialecte (Attempt at a complete grammatical-critical dictionary of High German with diligent comparisons to other dialects, especially Upper German. In addition M. Fulda's prize essay on the subject of the two principal German dialects). Leipzig, Bernhard Christoph Breitkopf & Son, 1774–1786.

Johann Christoph Adelung's (1732–1806)[9] famous five-volume dictionary carried on Gottsched's work and was a pivotal factor in the

German-speaking part of Austria in the second half of the eighteenth century because of the official linguistic "purification" begun at the time of Maria Theresia. *Adelung* was particularly widely distributed in Vienna, for hand-in-hand with the school reforms and the broadening and consolidating of German language-teaching, *Adelung's* language and grammar instruction was widely used in all Viennese educational institutions. The fact that *Adelung* was so frequently reprinted by Johann Thomas Trattner[10] shows how much his books were used for reference. But more than anything, *Adelung* became an indispensable reference book of correctness for many Austrian writers in their endeavor to compete with authors from other German-speaking cultures.[11]

[5] [Shakespeare, William.]

> *The Plays of William Shakespeare.* In ten Volumes. With corrections and illustrations of various commentators; to which are added notes by S. Johnson and G. Steevens. The third edition, revised and augmented by the editor of Dodsley's Collection of Old Plays. 10 Vol. London: C. Bathurst etc. 1785.

It is impossible to establish how generally this edition (current until the nineteenth century) was available in Vienna. It is possible that Haydn acquired it in England.

The works of Shakespeare became known in Vienna gradually during the 1770s. The Vienna National Theatre put on only German adaptations or parodies,[12] but the catalogues of the lending libraries[13] of the time have several entries of Shakespeare's plays both in the original language and in German translations and are proof of his popularity.

Worth remarking on is the extent of Shakespeare's reputation in western Hungary, the result of performances by Carl Wahr's theatrical troupe. This company put on plays at Eszterháza during the summer seasons of 1772–1777 and in the winter season in Pressburg (Bratislava), where the company performed *Hamlet* in the German adaptation by the Viennese dramatist Heufeld, and in 1774 *Macbeth* and *Othello,* presumably in the translations by Wieland. They also performed *King Lear* in the German translation by the troupe's dramatist Christoph Seipp. Haydn evidently composed incidental music for *Hamlet*.[14]

[6] [Cook, Captain James.]

A New, Authentic and Complete Collection of Voyages round the World, undertaken and performed by Royal authority. Containing . . . an authentic . . . history of Captain Cook's first, second, third, and last voyages . . . Now publishing under the direction of G. W. Anderson, Esq., assisted by a principal officer who sailed in the Resolution Sloop, and by many gentlemen; etc. London: A. Hogg, 1784.

Like many people of his time, Haydn greatly valued books about travel. Several travel writers appear in the list of his books.[15] James Cook's (1728–1779) famous *Voyages* were popular in Vienna. Franz Anton Schrämbl published the work in a German translation in 1792.

[7] [Cardano, Hieronymus.]

Offenbarung der Natur vnnd Natürlicher Dingen auch mancherley subtiler würckungen. Durch den hochgelerten Hieronymum Cardanum, etc. (The Revelation of nature and natural things, as well as various subtle effects. First written in Latin by the learned Hieronymus Cardano), doctor of medicine at Weyland. By which the whole area of the world, both the heavenly and the elemental spheres are indicated as well as comets, stars, all of the earth, rocks and plants and strange flowers, animals and people. Everything that moves and grows, of natural and artificial things such as fire, common arts and crafts, also other minor arts and hidden things about which one wonders whether they go against nature. Also all kinds of strange customs, peoples and towns or other such as have so far been little written about or described. Such things will be found at greater length and complete in the catalogue.

All this translated diligently and faithfully into good German by Heinrich Pantaleon, doctor of medicine.

Printed in Basle by Heinrich Petri. [1559]

The 17 books are bound together in a valuable folio. The translation by Heinrich Pantaleon (1522–1595)[16] is based on Cardano's *Opus physicum de rerum varietate.* The date of publication is not reliably established in the copy. The foreword by Pantaleon, the translator, is dated 1559. The date mentioned in Haydn's estate (1554) seems wrong, since the above preface makes no mention of an earlier German translation.

The Italian mathematician, doctor, and philosopher Gerolamo Cardano (1502 or 1506–1571) equates the light of the world soul with the eternally ruling principle of generation and motion.

Cardano's work was available in the bookshops of Vienna in the second third of the eighteenth century. The 1760 printed catalogue of the bookshop Zum goldenen Vliess lists the main works of Cardano, including the above translation.[17]

[8] [Xanthopulos, Nikephorus Callistus.]

> *Kirchen Histori Nicephori Callisti Deß Hochberuembten Kirchenscribenten,* etc. (The church history of Nicephori Callisti the much famed church writer), published in eighteen books. Heretofore translated from Greek into Latin by the late learned Herr Johann Lange, Imperial Councillor, [Röm. Kön. May. Rath.] etc. For the use and pleasure in our common native country and to compare our present church with the ancient Catholic church of God, also all sorts of examples of Christian belief and life to learn therefrom, it has been translated into German through the faithful diligence of Herr Max Fugger the elder, Freiherr von Kirchberg and Weissenhorn, with several necessary annotations and glosses and a useful index. The first part comprises the first nine books of this history, from the birth of Christ until approximately the year 367. The above is followed by another part. Printed in Ingolstadt by David Sartorius anno MDLXXXVIII. [1588]

The church history by Nikephorus Callistus Xanthopulos (ca. 1256–1335), ending with the death of the Emperor Phocas (610), was originally published in Greek in eighteen volumes and was translated by Johann Lange into Latin. The German translation by Max Fugger the elder contains the eighteen books in a lavish folio.

While the work was rejected by the Protestant church, it had a great following among Catholics and was much used as a source by scholars of the Church.[18] The work was available in Viennese bookshops in Haydn's lifetime.[19] It is not known how the folio came into Haydn's possession.

[9] and [80]

[9] [Hübner, Johann, editor].

Johann Hübners reales Staats- Zeitungs-[20] *und Conversations-Lexicon.* (Johann Hübner's specialist state-, newspaper-, and conversation-encyclopedia). New, improved and much augmented edition. Leipzig, in the Gleditsch Bookshop, 1782.

This is a new edition of the first edition of the same name of 1704 (further editions 1706, 1708, 1709, 1711, and 1713).

[80] [Hübner, Johann, editor].

Curieuses[21] *Natur- Kunst- Gewerck- und Handlungs-Lexicon.* (Curious nature-, art-, craft- and business-encyclopedia) . . . With a detailed preface by Herr Johann Hübner. . . Leipzig, Joh. Friedrich Gleditsch & Sohn, 1712.

Haydn owned the second edition of 1714.

The *Handlungs-Lexicon* (Business encyclopedia) is the continuation of the original *Conversations-Lexicon* of 1704, which is supposed to be based on a work written by Christian Weise.[22] The Hamburg pedagogue Johann Hübner (1668–1731) is merely the editor.

[Hübner's] two works together form a general reference work relevant to the educational needs of the eighteenth century. The popular form of presentation aims for the broadest possible influence.

In response to turn-of-the-eighteenth century enthusiasm for encyclopedias that spread into Germany from the French Enlightenment, the Leipzig bookdealer Johann Heinrich Zedler (1706–1763) had published in mid-century the 64-volume *Grosse vollständige Universal-Lexicon aller Künste und Wissenschaften* (Great universal encyclopedia of all arts and sciences). In consideration of the cost, the *Hübner* was probably preferred to the *Zedler* for private libraries.

[10] [Society of Citizens of the Imperial Capital, translators & editors.]

Französische Mord- und Unglücksgeschichten, wie sich solche seit den Unruhen in Frankreich wirklich zugetragen haben. (Tales of murder and misfortune as they have really occurred in France since the unrest). Translated from the French and promoted for publication by a Society of Citizens of the Imperial Capital. Vienna and Prague, Schönfeld Verlag, 1794.

According to Haydn's estate list, he had only six volumes of the seven-volume publication—assuming the clerk did not count wrong.

This is an anti-revolutionary propaganda work, a collection of faked documents, bogus letters, and tales of so-called "true events" made into a mosaic nightmare picture of the horrors of the French Revolution and the destruction of the French state.

Considering that Jacobinism was being vigorously persecuted by the government of the Austro-Hungarian monarchy and that leaders of secret revolutionary movements were executed in 1795,[23] the distribution of this work was probably publicly encouraged.

[11] [Hiller, Gottlieb.]

Gottlieb Hillers Gedichte und Selbstbiographie (Gottlieb Hiller's poems and autobiography).

Volume 1: Köthen, printed and published by the Anesch Court bookstore, 1805; Volume 2. [As above.] 1807.

Haydn probably owned only the first volume, in which his name was printed among the subscribers, in the front. His decision to subscribe to this volume (his only known subscription) shows his general interest in literature on the one hand and his search in the 1780s for suitable song texts on the other.

Hiller (1788–1826)[24] was a so-called "nature poet." A discursive autobiography in the first volume is followed by a section of poems of a predominantly devotional-pathetic, sometimes ballad-like kind. The second volume contains impressions and events from Hiller's *Reisen durch einen Theil von Sachsen, Böhmen, Österreich und Ungarn* (Travels to a part of Saxony, Bohemia, Austria and Hungary).

[12] [Aesop.]

Favole d'Isopo Greco elegantissime e de molti altri tradotte nuovamente di Latino in Lingua Italiana. In Venetia MDXLIIII. Co'L Privilegio del summo Pontefice Paulo III. et dello Illustris. Senato Venetiano per anni dieci.[25] (Fables by Aesop the most elegant Greek and many others, translated from Latin into Italian. In Venice, 1543. Privilege of his Highness the Pontiff Paulo III and of the illustrious Venetian senate for 10 years).

A new edition of this book, dated 1568, was in Haydn's library.

[13] Knigge, Adolph Franz Friedrich Ludwig Freiherr von.

Über den Umgang mit Menschen (On dealing with people). In three parts. 4th expanded and improved edition, Vienna, Franz Haas, 1793.[26]

Original edition: Hannover: Schmidt's Bookshop, 1788.

A. F. Knigge (1752–1796)[27] was a dilettante in various fields, wrote plays, novels and most important of all, his widely known book, *Über den Umgang mit Menschen,* in which he endeavors to instruct the reader in the "art of making himself noticed, important and respected" (p. 9), leading to an *"esprit de conduite"* as he calls it (pp. 9 and 25).

It should not be assumed that Haydn looked seriously for inspiration in "Knigge," which was typical household reading in Vienna. He must have been sixty-one when he acquired the book, and by then he had long been established in society.

[14] [Hagedorn, Friedrich von.]

Die sämtlichen poetischen Werke des Herrn Friedrichs von Hagedorn. (The complete poetical works of Friedrich von Hagedorn). Vienna, printed and published by Joseph Edler von Baumeister, 1789. [2 volumes].[28]

Original publisher: Hamburg, J. C. Bohn, 1757.

The Hamburg poet of the early rococo, Friedrich von Hagedorn (1708–1754) was well-known in Austria, and especially in Vienna, his odes and songs as well as his fables having been reprinted several times.

Trattner had already reprinted the *Sämmtlichen poetischen Werke* (Complete poetical works) in 1765[29] as well as 1780, and Schrämbl reserved volumes 12 to 16 of his series *Sammlung der vorzüglichsten Werke deutscher Dichter und Prosaisten* (Collection of the most excellent works of

German poets and prose writers) (1790–91) for Hagedorn. Hagedorn's writings can also be found in the third volume of the literature collection *Der Jugendfreund oder die deutschen Schriftsteller in einer Auswahl für die deutsche Jugend* (The friend of youth, or a selection of German writers for German youth) (St. Pölten: Laitré, 1792). The Viennese lending libraries, which reflected the current taste and literary demand pretty accurately, also had Hagedorn's books on their shelves.[30]

[15] and [62]

[15] [1. Kleist, Ewald von.]

1. *Die Sämmtlichen Werke des Herrn Ewald von Kleist.* (The collected works of Herr Ewald von Kleist). First volume of the series, *Sammlung der vorzüglichsten Werke deutscher Dichter und Prosaisten* (Collection of the most excellent works of German poets and prose writers). Vienna. Printed and published by Joseph Edler von Baumeister, 1789.

First volume. The complete works of Ewald von Kleist.

Vienna, printed and published by Joseph Edler von Baumeister, 1789.

This series was clearly undertaken as a competitive enterprise to Schrämbl's identically-named *Sammlung . . . deutscher Dichter*—also begun in 1789.

Ewald von Kleist (1715–1759) was a poet who wrote in the sentimental rococo style and who became famous with his poem, "Der Frühling" (Spring). He enjoyed great popularity in Vienna which can be seen by the number of reprints of his books.[32] The works are also available in the lending libraries of Zahlheim and Trattner.[33]

Joseph von Baumeister's reprint follows the Berlin first edition (published in 1761 by Voss) in most respects. But there are a few additions from Ramler's revised edition (Berlin, 1778).

[62] [Kleist, Ewald von.]

Des Herrn Christian Ewald von Kleist sämtliche Werke. (Complete works of Christian Ewald von Kleist). Reutlingen, published by Johann Georg Fleischhauer, 1775.[34]

Since the publication date is given as 1785 in the index of Haydn's library, this is either an error or it is a later, no longer available edition.

The contents and order of the pieces follow almost exactly that of the Berlin first edition of 1761.

[15] [2. Haller, Albrecht von.]

2. Volume 2 of Baumeister's *Sammlung . . . deutscher Dichter* (see above) consists of the writings of Albrecht von Haller. It appeared in 1789 or 1790.[35]

The Swiss poet of nature and ideas, Albrecht von Haller (1708–1777), famous chiefly for his poem, "The Alps," was early a favorite of Viennese readers.[36]

[15] [3. Lichtwer, M. G.]

3. *Fabeln in vier Büchern.* (Fables in four books.) Vienna, printed and published by Joseph Edler von Baumeister, 1790.

Magnus Gottfried Lichtwer (1719–1779), who, as a poet of fables, stood without doubt in the shadow of Gellert, was repeatedly reprinted in Vienna.[37]

Originally published as *4 Bücher Aesopischer Fablen in gebundener Schreib-Art* (Four books of Aesopian fables in verse). Leipzig: W. Deer, 1748.

In his series of secular canons, Haydn set to music the didactic verses concluding eleven of Lichtwer's fables.[38]

[16] See entries and commentary under [39].

[17] [a) Barthélemy, Jean Jacques.]

a) *Reise des jüngern Anacharsis durch Griechenland, vierthalb 100 Jahre vor der gewöhnlichen Zeitrechnung* (Journey of the younger Anacharsis through Greece, four hundred fifty years before the common era). From the French of Herr Barthélemy. Vienna, printed and published by F. A. Schrämbl, 1792–93. [7 parts in 12 volumes: 1st and 2nd part, 1792; 3–7 parts, 1793]

or
b) [Title as above.] Vienna and Prague, by Franz Haas, 1792–1976. [7 parts in 7 volumes].

The individual volumes of both editions have a copperplate engraving on their title pages (this is the reason for the handwritten note "m. k."—mit Kupfern) i.e., with copperplate.

Since both publishers, F. A. Schrämbl and F. Haas, began the reprint of the novel by Jean Jacques Barthélemy (1716–1795) in the same year (1792) we cannot be certain which of the editions was in Haydn's library. The book index lists seven volumes, and the date of publication is usually that of the first volume; it is therefore most likely the (b) edition.

Franz Haas produced a complete reprint of the German translation by Johann Erich Biester (1749–1816),[39] published 1790–93 by the Berlin publishing house of F. Lagarde. The second to seventh part of the edition by Schrämbl also uses the translation by Biester, while the first part contains a version translated by Schrämbl himself.

Anacharsis, a Greek of the 4th century BC., recounts his many years of travel in the various regions of ancient Greece in which the description of historico-cultural conditions form the core of the novel. One can characterize *Anacharsis* as a kind of *Bildungsroman* interspersed with elements of the contemporary literature of friendship and its institutions.[40]

[18] Tasso, Torquato.

Das Befreyte Jerusalem [Jerusalem Delivered]. Also a life of the author; Italian and German text, Mannheim by the Publishers of Great Foreign Minds, 1781.

If 1787, the date in the handwritten index, is correct, the work must have been reprinted in that year.

The German translation of the Italian Renaissance epic is by Wilhelm Heinse.

[19] [Retzer, Joseph von, editor.]

Choice of the Best Poetical Pieces of the Most Eminent English Poets. Published by Joseph Retzer. Volume 1 and 2: Vienna, Sonnleithner & Hoerling, 1782; Volume 3: Vienna, John David

Hoerling, 1785; Volume 4: Vienna, John David Hoerling, 1786; Volumes 5 and 6: Vienna, Trattner, 1786.

The editor Joseph von Retzer (1754–1824)[41] included the following writers in his anthology of excerpts from English literature:[42] Joseph Addison (1672–1718), James Thomson (1700–1748), Alexander Pope (1688–1744), Arthur Collins (1690–1760), John Milton (1608–1674), George Steevens (1736–1800), Ben Jonson (1572–1637), John Sheffield (1648–1721), Samuel Johnson (1709–1784), John Dryden (1631–1700), William Congreve (1670–1729), Anthony Ashley Cooper, Earl of Shaftesbury (1671–1713), Evan Lloyd (1734–1776), Lady Mary Worthley Montague (1689–1762), William Shenstone (1714–1763), Philip Dormer Stanhope, Earl of Chesterfield (1694–1733), Edward Young (1683–1765), George Lyttleton (1709–1773), Oliver Goldsmith (1730–1774), Jonathan Swift (1667–1745), Richard Lovelace (1618–1658), Henry Fielding (1704–1754), William Whitehead (1715–1785), Thomas Parnell (1679–1718), John Armstrong (1709–1779), Thomas Shepard (1605–1649), Alexander Barclay (1475?–1522), Richard Cumberland (1732–1811), Thomas Chatterton (1752–1770), John Wilmot Rochester (1647–1680), John Hawkesworth (1715–1773), Samuel Richardson (1689–1761), Richard Steele (1672–1729), Henry Brooke (1703–1783), Robert Barclay (1648–1690), Christopher Pitt (1699–1748), Robert Wolsley (1649–1697), William Walsh (1663–1708), Anthony Hamilton (1646–1720), George Granville, Lord Landsdowne (1667–1735), among others.

[20] Reichart, Christian.

Christian Reicharts Land- und Garten-Schatz (Christian Reichart's country and garden treasury). 6 parts in 3 volumes. Erfurt, published by Heinrich Rudolf Nonne, 1753–55. Part 1: Of all kinds of seeds; Part 2: The cultivation of trees; Part 3: Of cabbages, roots and onions used as food; Part 4: Which deals with kitchen, herb and medicinal plants; Part 5: on the use of the land without fallow periods and repeated fertilizing. With a preface by J. G. Daryés; Part 6: On the growing of hops and flowers.

This encyclopedia of plants is probably related to Haydn's leaning to a diet-based way of life.

[21] Metastasio, Pietro Antonio Domenico Bonaventura.

Poesie (Poems). Edited by d'Calsabigi: 10 volumes, Paris, 1755–1769.[43]

According to the list of the books in Haydn's library, the fifth and tenth volumes were missing. That the date is given as 1765 is explained by the fact that the author of the list took the date not from the first but from a later volume.

The dramatic works of the Viennese Court poet Metastasio were extremely popular in the Imperial City, and many composers wrote music for them: Vinci, Caldara, Predieri, Hasse, Bonno, Fux, Reutter, Wagenseil, Gassmann, Gluck, and others.[44] In 1779 Haydn composed the opera *L'isola disabitata* (The uninhabited island), using Metastasio's libretto.

Haydn may have begun to buy the individual volumes of *Poesie* as a young man, probably on the installment plan, particularly since the composer already considered the poetry of Metastasio as the only reading matter worth its name in the years of his early struggles to get ahead.[45]

[22] [Klopstock, Friedrich Gottlob.]

Der Messias (The Messiah). Altona, David Adam Eckardt, 1780.

The Emperor Joseph II heads the printed lists of subscribers followed by the Austrians de Luca, Seibt, Haschka, Kurzböck, Riegger, Schrämbl, Zahlheim, etc.

The Messiah became a much-read book in Vienna as far back as the 1760s. The wide popularity of Friedrich Gottlob Klopstock (1724–1803) in Austria (cf. also his connection to the literary circle of the Greiner family, n. 148) did not end at the turn of the nineteenth century. Trattner is known to have published the following: *Schriften* (Writings), 1765;[46] *Der Messias*, 1765, 1773, 1775, and 1798; *Hermanns-Schlacht* (The battle of Arminius), 1769; *Salomo* and *Der Tod Adams* (The death of Adam), 1775 and 1798; *David,* 1798; *Oden* (Odes) and *Lieder* (Songs), 1798. The publisher Schrämbl also included

Klopstock in his *Sammlung . . . deutscher Dichter* (41st to 45th volume, Vienna, 1794–95). The Viennese lending libraries also offered their readers several of Klopstock's works.[47]

[23] Pérau, Gabriel Louis Calabre.

L'ordre des Franc-Maçons trahi (The order of the freemasons, betrayed.) [n.p., n.d.]

This book on the subject of the Freemasons was first published in 1744 and was then reprinted many times.[48]

[24] Wezel, Johann Karl.

Lebensgeschichte Tobias Knauts des Weisen, sonst der Stammler genannt. Aus Familiennachrichten gesammlet (The life story of Tobias Knaut the Wise, otherwise known as "the Stammerer." Collected from family papers). Leipzig, published by Siegfried Lebrecht Crusius. Volume 1, 1773; Volume 2, 1774; Volume 3, 1775; Volume 4, 1776.

The author of this anonymously published novel, Johann Karl Wezel (1747–1819)[49] was a dramatist in Vienna from 1782. Wurzbach reports that he "was said to enjoy the favor of the Emperor Joseph."[50]

Tobias Knaut embodies the type of German humorous novel based on the English comic novel, a style that spread throughout Germany in the last thirty years of the eighteenth century. The theme of the work is the physical and psychological development of an eccentric.

The third volume of the four-volume work was on the index of forbidden books in Vienna.[51] It is nonetheless included in Trattner's lending library catalogue for 1780.[52]

[25] [Gotter, Friedrich Wilhelm.]

Gedichte von Friedrich Wilhelm Gotter (Poems of Friedrich Wilhelm Gotter). [2 volumes].

Friedrich Wilhelm Gotter (1746–1797),[53] who edited the *Göttinger Musenalmanachs* (Göttingen almanach of the muses) in 1768, was already highly regarded in the Vienna of the 1770s as a dramatist, or rather a writer of comedies in the French manner. His poetry was also published in Vienna.[54]

The text of Haydn's song, *Auch die Sprödeste der Schönen* (Even the most obdurate of beauties), came from Gotter.[55]

[26] [Bürger, August.]

Gedichte von Gottfried August Bürger (Poems of August Bürger). Carlsruhe, published by Christian Gottlieb Schmieder, 1779.[56]

The year noted in the library index, 1789 (instead of 1779), is either another mistake, or this is a later reprint.

First edition: Poems by G. A. Bürger, with eight copperplate engravings by Chodowiecky, drawn and engraved by Göttingen, printed on commission by Johann Christian Dietrich, 1778.[57]

Viennese readers were familiar with this writer of popular lyric poetry. He was best known for his ballads. Schrämbl reprinted Bürger's poems in 1789.[58]

Haydn set three pieces of Bürger's to music.[59]

[27] [Wieland, Christoph Martin.]

Wielands Neueste Gedichte. Vom Jahre 1770–1777 (Wieland's latest poems. From the years 1770–1777). New, improved edition. Carlsruhe, published by Christian Gottlieb Schmieder, 1777.

The first edition came out in the same year as the reprint listed in the Haydn Library index—1777. The second part did not appear until 1779.[60]

This work contains a series of rococo epyllions, a short form of the epic which was favored by Wieland at this time.

Wieland, a poet who lived in Weimar, was the most widely read and most popular poet in German-speaking Austria—and especially in Vienna—in the second half of the eighteenth century, although Austrian book censorship had put his *Agathon, Don Sylvio de Rosalva,* and *Neuen Amadis* on the Index of prohibited books.[61] Those works of Wieland's which were not on the Index were much reprinted in the eighties and nineties. In 1784 Trattner printed *Musarion oder die Philosophie der Grazien* (Musarion or the philosophy of the graces) and

Die Grazien (The graces); in 1785 *Oberon* followed. Another considerable reprint project was Schrämbl's 86-volume complete edition of Wieland's writings.[62]

The catalogues of the Viennese lending libraries list *Der Goldenen Spiegel* (The golden mirror),[63] *Geschichte der Abderiten* (History of the Abderites), *Musarion,* and twelve volumes of the *Teutschen Merkur*[64] as well as a three-volume edition of the *Poetischen Schriften.*[65] The relationship between Wieland and Haydn rested on mutual esteem. In 1800 the Weimar poet honored the composer with verses on his *Creation,*[66] whereupon Haydn asked Wieland for a text for an oratorio. Haydn's request, conveyed by Griesinger to the publisher Breitkopf & Härtel, may not have been passed on to Wieland.[67]

[28] [de Comte, translated by] Johann Ernst Zeiher.

> *Vollständiger Unterricht von Küchengewächsen, der Beschaffenheit des Erdbodens, den ihm dienlichen Lagen und Himmelsstrichen, erforderliche Wartung, ihre Nutzbarkeit, wie sie zu vermehren, ingleichen die Art und Weise, die Mistbeete einzurichten, zu jeder Jahreszeit Schwämme zu ziehen usw.* (Complete instruction in kitchen plants, the composition of the soil and useful siting and regions thereof, necessary maintenance and uses of them, how to propagate them, as well as the art and manner of constructing compost heaps, growing mushrooms in every season, etc.). By de Comte, translated from the French (with footnotes), two parts, Leipzig 1756.[68]

Haydn's ownership of this translation by Johann Ernst Zeiher (1720–1784)[69] was motivated by his predilection for a dietetic way of life.[70]

[29] Sintenis, Christian Friedrich.

> *Reden in dem Augenblick der Veranlassung. Ein Impromtu vom Verfasser der Menschenfreuden.* (Orations at a moment's notice. An extemporization from the author of "Mankind's Joys."). Leipzig, published by Siegfried Lebrecht Crusius, 1779.[71]

This work by Sintenis (1759–1829),[72] a Protestant pastor, contains morally edifying and didactic reflections in sentimental-poetic language. The form of the oration, which develops from the chosen themes, generally approaches the character of the religiously moralizing speech, that is: a kind of sermon.

Sintenis's Disquistions' were familiar to the Viennese. In the *Provinzialnachrichten* (provincial newspaper) of 1785, Trattner announced a forthcoming reprint, and the book was also available in Trattner's lending library.[73]

[30] [Wilmsen, Friedrich Ernst.]

Vermischte Gedichte von Friedrich Ernst Wilmsen (Miscellaneous Poetry by Friedrich Ernst Wilmsen). Berlin, published by Arnold Wever, private bookseller.[74]

The volume holds mostly "occasional poems" by Wilmsen (1736–1797),[75] partly in an archaic manner, partly following English nature poetry (Thomson etc.), often imitating Klopstock; the sentimental character predominates.

[31] [Banchieri, Adriano; Giulio Cesare della Croce; and others]

Bertoldo, con Bertoldino e Cacasenno in ottava rima ("Bertoldo," along with "Bertoldino" and "Cacasenno" in octave verse). With subjects, allegories, annotations and copper engravings. Venice, 1739.[76]

"Bertoldo" and "Bertoldino" are by Giulio Cesare della Croce (1550–1609); "Cacasenno" is by Adriano Banchieri (pseudonym of Canullo Scaliero della Fratta; 1567–1634); put into verse by Riva, Balbi and others.

This comic epic is based on the *Torpeide* and the *Batrachomyomachia*.

[32] [Ramler, K.W., editor.]

Lyrische Bluhmenlese, (Lyrical flower harvest). Edited by K. W. Ramler. Leipzig by Weidmann heirs, and Reich. 1st volume 1774; 2nd volume, 1778.

This is the third anthology of poetry edited by Ramler, the first two being *Oden mit Melodien* (Odes with melodies) (1753–1755), and *Lieder der Deutschen* (Songs of the Germans) (1766).

The first volume of *Lyrische Bluhmenlese* appeared in 1774 (in five books, each with 52 songs) and contains poems of the Anacreontic movement (Gleim, Uz, Gotz) and later rococo period (Hagedorn) as well as verse of poets from the *Göttinger Musenalmanachs* and the group know as the Hainbund (Blum, Boie, Burger, Claudius, Gotter, Voss, etc.). The second volume of 1778 (in four books) can be taken as a reworking of *Lieder der Deutschen,* since 75 percent of the contents is the same[77] and only individual poems have been replaced by contributions from the younger generation (Goeckingk, Miller, Bürger, Stolberg, Eschenburg, Lenz, Pfeffel, etc.).

Ramler is notorious for his highhanded changes and modifications of published poems.

The texts for Haydn's part songs are based primarily on pieces from *Lyrische Bluhmenlese.* Five lieder texts were also taken from this anthology.[78]

[33] [Siebigke, Ludwig Anton Leopold.]

Museum berühmter Tonkünstler. In Kupfern und schriftlichen Abrissen vom Prof. C.A. Siebigke. Oder Museum deutscher Gelehrten und Künstler (Museum of famous musicians. In etchings and written outlines by Prof. C. A. Siebigke. Or museum of German scholars and artists). Second volume. Breslau, by August Schall, 1801.

I. *Johann Sebastian Bach.* Including a short account of his life and style. [1801]

II. *Joseph Haydn.* Including a short account of his life and style. [1801]

II. *Wolfgang Gottlieb Mozart.* Including a short account of his life and style. [1801]

Muzio Clementi. Including an account of his style. [n.p.] (1801)[79]

Musical biographies I–III also appeared as individual small volumes. Since the volume on Haydn does not appear in the catalogue of his books, it can be assumed that it was either overlooked by the compiler of the estate or that it was lost on an earlier occasion. It is certain that Haydn owned it.[80]

It is known that Haydn was on friendly terms with Mozart and knew Clementi (1752–1832) personally.

[34] [Goldoni, Carlo.]

Le Commedie del Signor Avvocato Carlo Goldoni. (The comedies of Attorney Carlo Goldoni, Esq.). 13 volumes. Bologna 1762, 1754–1763[81]

There is no indication whether Haydn ever owned the 13 volumes, since the estate booklist mentions only volumes 1–3, as well as 5, 10, and 12. But it appears probable that the composer took the texts for the operas *Lo speziale* (1769), *Le pescatrici* (1770), and *Il Mondo della luna* (1777) from the above edition.[82]

[35] [Robertson, William.]

The History of America. By William Robertson D. D. Principal of the University of Edinburgh, Historiographer to his Majesty for Scotland and Member of the Royal Academy of History at Madrid. 3 vol. Vienna. Printed for F. A. Schrämbl 1787.[83]

First edition:
London. Printed for W. Strahan;, T. Cadell in the Strand and J. Balfour, At Edinburgh, 1777.

A German translation was published in Leipzig by Weidmann the same year as the first [English] edition.
The above reprint edition by Schrämbl is evidence of the demand for the book in Vienna.

[36] [Young, Edward.]

Eduard Young, Klagen oder Nachtgedanken über Leben, Tod, and Unsterblichkeit (Edward Young: Lamentation or night thoughts on life, death and immortality). English and German. 2 volumes. Hanover: Hahn 1760–1761.[84]

This is probably a reprint of the first four sections of the translation by Arnold Ebert (1723–1795),[85] published in 1751 in Braunschweig and Hildesheim. Presumably Haydn owned a later edition, from the Hanover printing of 1765.

Edward Young's (1683–1765) partly didactic poem (separate editions: London, 1742–1745; first complete edition: London 1747) exerted a lasting influence on German sentimentalism by its combination of superabundant emotionalism and sober reflection, and came to be accepted in Austria because of its own corresponding literary trends. According to Joseph von Retzer, Young belonged beside Shakespeare, Milton and Pope as one of the most popular British poets in the second half of the eighteenth century.[86]

[37] [Merrick, James, and W. W. Tattersall.]

> *A Version or Paraphrase of the Psalms., originally written by the Rev. James Merrick, A. M. Divided into stanzas, and adapted to the purposes of public or private devotion.* By the Rev. W. W. Tattersall, A. M. Vicar of Wotton under Edge, Gloucestershire, and Chaplain to the Hon. Mr. Justice Buller, London: Printed for Thomas Payne and Son, at the Mews Gate; Benjamin White and Son, Fleet Street; Robson and Clarke, New Bond Street; G. G. J. and J. Robinson, Paternoster Row; Mr. Fletcher and Mr. Prince, Oxford; Mr. Merrill, Cambridge; and Joseph Bance, Wotton under Edge. 1789.[87]

This edition is based on James Merrick's (1720–1769) adaptation of the psalms, *The Psalmes, Translated or Paraphrased in English Verse* (Reading 1765).[88]

Haydn, who probably brought the work back from London, composed six pieces from it for a collection of psalms for three voices which Tattersall published under the title "Improved Psalmody" in 1793.[89]

As a token of appreciation for his collaboration on the collection of psalms, Haydn received a plate with the following inscription: "Dr. Haydn, Dr. Arnold, Mr. John Stafford Smith and Mr. Atterbury declared their readiness to cooperate with Dr. Cooke, Dr. Hayes, Dr. Dupuis, Dr. Pearson, Mr. Calcott, the Rev. Osborne Wight, Mr. Webber, Mr. Shield and Mr. Stevens in their exertions towards perfecting a Work for the Improvement of Parochial Psalmody; as a [small] Token of esteem for his abilities and of gratitude for his services, this Pice of Plate is presented to Dr. Haydn by W. D. Tattersall."[90]

[38] [Rabener, Gottlieb Wilhelm.]

Gottlieb Wilhelm Rabeners Satiren. (Gottlieb Wilhelm Rabener's satires) 1st–4th part [in two volumes]. 4th improved edition. Vienna, Johann Thomas Edl. von Trattner, 1776.

First edition:
Sammlung satyrischer Schriften (Collection of satirical writings) Leipzig, by J. G. Dycks, publisher, 1751–55.

The work collects satirical prose essays on a wide variety of subjects. Rabener (1724–1771) follows the Enlightenment premises of reason and wit, for which the satire is a particularly suitable literary form.

The following indicate the breadth of Rabener's influence in the Viennese cultural sphere:

(a) Trattner's going back to press at least four times for *Rabeners Satiren* (see above)[91]

(b) the publication of a weekly periodical entitled *Satiren nach dem Geschmacke Rabeners* (Satires in the style of Rabener). Nos.1–13. Vienna: Trattner, 1778.

(c) Rabener's works being in the Viennese lending libraries.[92]

[39] and [16]

[39] [Gellert, Christian Fürchtegott.]

C. F. Gellerts sämmtliche Schriften (C. F. Gellert's collected works.) New improved edition, 10 parts, Vienna, printed by Joh. Thomas Edler von Trattner, Imperial Court Printer and Bookseller, 1782.

[1st volume:] *Fabeln und Erzählungen* (Fables and tales)

[2nd volume:] *Moralische Gedichte. Vermischte Gedichte. Geistliche Lieder und Oden* (Moral poems. Miscellaneous poems. Religious songs and odes.)

[3rd volume:] *Lustspiele* (Comedies.)

[4th volume:] *Briefe, nebst einer praktischen Abhandlung von dem guten Geschmacke in Briefen* (Letters, accompanied by a practical treatise on good taste in letter-writing.)

*Leben der Schwedischen Gräfinn von G*** (The life of the Swedish countess von G**.)

[5th volume:] *Abhandlungen und Reden* (Discourses and speeches.)

[6th volume:] *Moralische Vorlesungen* (Moral lectures) (Lectures 1–15).

[7th volume:] *Moralische Vorlesungen* (Moral lectures) (Lectures 16–25).

[8th and 9th volumes:] *Briefwechsel Gellerts aus den nachgelassenen Schriften* (Gellert's posthumously published correspondence.)

[10th volume:] *Christian Fürchtegott Gellerts Leben von Johann Andreas Cramer* (Christian Fürchtegott Gellert's life by Johann Andreas Cramer).

All parts of the Trattner reprint edition follow the Augsburg original edition—also in ten volumes—of Gellert's *Sämmtlichen Schriften* (Collected writings) (originally 1769–1774; further editions: 1775 and 1783f.)[93]

[16] [Gellert, Christian Fürchtegott.]

Poetische Schriften von Christian Fürchtegott Gellert (The poetical writings of Christian Fürchtegott Gellert). Vienna, printed and published by F. A. Schrämbl 1792.

These are Volumes 25 to 28 of Schrämbl's *Sammlung . . . Deutscher Dichter* etc. The edition contains only the fables and tales, and moral poems.

Gellert's work, with its ethos rooted in the German pietism of the Enlightenment close to Bodmer in its literary intentions, was a practically obligatory part of every private library during Haydn's lifetime. Trattner arranged for numerous reprints of Gellert, who was especially highly regarded as a sentimental poet.[94] His books were found in the Viennese lending libraries as a matter of course.[95]

Haydn called Gellert his favorite poet[96] and used his texts for canons and his part songs.[97]

[40] Arnold, Theodor.

A Compleat Vocabulary, English–German; and German–English . . . Newly amended by J. B. Rogler. 3rd edition Züllich 1790.[98]

Haydn owned three English dictionaries (see below, [77] and [79]).

[41] [Sterne, Laurence.]

The Select Works of Laurence Sterne M.A. In nine Volumes. Vienna, Printed for R. Sammer, Bookseller, 1798.

Volumes 5 and 6: *A Sentimental Journey through France and Italy by Mr. Yorick. With an Account of the Author's Life. To which are Added Several Pieces by the same Author.* Complete Ed. in four Volumes.

The first and second parts of Sterne's (1713–1768) *Sentimental Journey* can be found in volume 5, the third and fourth parts in volume 6.

While the *Sentimental Journey* had an enormous influence on the development of the German novel,[99] there were at first considerable barriers to the distribution of Sterne's work because of its prohibition under the book censorship.[100] Once the prohibition was relaxed, *A Sentimental Journey* was received with enthusiasm.[101]

[42] Eckartshausen, Carl von.

Sittenlehren für alle Stände und Menschen zur Bildung junger Herzen (Instruction in ethics for all classes and people, for the education of young hearts). Munich: Mayr 1784–85 [2 vols.].[102]

There is no evidence of an edition published in Berlin in 1783 as mentioned on the estate list.

Eckartshausen's (1752–1803)[103] moral concerns have a didactic and reflective tone in this work of essays presented in the form of tracts and epistles. The reader is given guidelines to enable him to keep the divinely inspired ethical law. The work appeals particularly to the human emotions, which is the reason for the "sentimentalist" style in the prose as well as in the poems interspersed throughout.

Eckhartshausen's writings were reprinted by the Brünn publisher J. S. Siedler, in 1788.

[43] [Klopstock, Friedrich Gottlob?]

Herrmanns Schlacht. (The battle of Arminius).

It has not been possible to ascertain unambiguously the volume in question which, according to the book catalogue, was published in Leipzig in 1753.

Among the many literary works of the time about Hermann or Arminius, none of those investigated accord with the title, place, and year of publication given in the estate list.

Klopstock's *Hermannsschlacht* was not published until 1769, in Hamburg and Bremen. Nevertheless it is this book that has to be considered first, along with the dramatization of Klopstock's text by Johann Gottfried Dyk, printed in Leipzig in 1784.

[44] Smith, Adam.

A Theory of Moral Sentiments, or an Essay towards an Analysis of the Principles by which Men naturally judge concerning the Conduct and Character, first of their Neighbours, and afterwards of themselves. To which is added a Dissertation on the Origin of Language. A new Edition. Basil: Tourneisen, 1793 [2 vols.][104]

The author uses the analytical method in his ethical treatise, distancing himself from Shaftesbury's synthesis-based theory. He repudiates the doctrine of "moral sense" as not being very rationally accessible and, coming closer to Hume's view, contrasts it with sympathy as the fundamental factor in ethical consciousness—which suggests a certain resonance in the realm of the spiritual with educated Austrian readers and their civilization.[105]

[45] Cooper, Anthony Ashley, Third Earl of Shaftesbury.

Characteristicks of Men, Manners, Opinions, Times. In three Volumes. Vol. I (1.) A Letter concerning Enthusiasm. (2.) Sensus Communis, or an Essay on the Freedom of Wit and Humour. (3.) Soliloquy, or Advice to an Author. Vol. II (4.) An inquiry concerning Virtue and Merit. (5.) The moralists; a Philosophical Rhapsody Vol. III (6.) Miscellaneous Reflections on the said Treatises, and other critical Subjects. With

Collection of Letters. Basil: J. J. Tourneisen & J. L. Legrand, 1790.[106]

Shaftesbury (1671–1713), whose philosophic system combines ethics and aesthetics under a universally understood principle of harmony, coined the concept of "moral sense," i.e. the natural moral dispositions of human beings which, at the same time as the feeling for harmony, represents an inborn aesthetic principle. The revival of the Platonic ideal of *kalos ka'gathas* found a lively resonance in German literary intellectual life.[107]

Shaftesbury's work was still among the prohibited books in the 1770s.[108]

The fact that Haydn owned the above edition of Shaftesbury in the original language rather than in the only German translation of the "philosophical works" by Holty, Benzler, and Voss[109] published in 1776–1779, seems significant in that it indicates the composer's involvement, traceable to the 1790s, with English philosophical aesthetics. This is also true for his possession of the works of Burke and Smith (see [46] and [44]).[110]

[46] [Burke, Edmund.]

A philosophical Inquiry into the Origin of Our Ideas of the Sublime and Beautiful. With an introductory Discourse concerning Taste and several other Additions. A new Edition. Basil, Printed and sold by J. J. Tourneisen, 1792.[111]

Burke's (1729–1797) aesthetics divides the concept of the sublime and the beautiful into two separate spheres, each with autonomous value. This work, first published in 1756, exerted a lasting influence on German aesthetics and poetry in the second half of the eighteenth century. It was chiefly Lessing, Kant, Mendelssohn, and Schiller who carried on the discussion of the concept of the sublime and the beautiful in Germany.

The lack of an Austrian edition as well as other factors make it likely that knowledge of this work was limited in Austria. On the other hand, it was indirectly disseminated widely through Meinhard's German translation of Henry Home's *Elements of Criticism*,[112] a book based on Burke's aesthetic theories.

[47] [Casti, Giambattista.]

Poesie liriche di Gio. Battista Casti poeta di sua altezza reale il gran-duca di Toscana. Dedicate alla real gran-duchessa Maria Luisa arci-duchesa d'Austria ec. ec. ec. (Lyric poetry of Gio. Battista Casti, poet to His Highness the Grand Duke of Tuscany. Dedicated to the Grand Duchess Maria Luisa, Arch-Duchess of Austria, etc., etc., etc.). In Florence, for lo Stecchi and Pagani, all'Insegna del Giglio/Con Approvazione. 1769.

The Abbott Giambattista Casti (1721–1803), whose poetry was based on rococo subject matter which Haydn regarded so highly for its attitude to the human spirit and to life, was Court poet in Vienna from 1790 to 1796 under Leopold II and Franz II.

It may be that Haydn, who knew Casti personally,[113] had received the volume, with its dedication, as a gift from the author.

[48] Höslin, Jeremias.

Meteorologische Witterungsbeobachtungen (Meteorological observations) Tübingen: Cotta, 1784.[114]

The date of publication noted in the library list (1780) may be wrong, since no reference to an earlier printing exists.

[49] [Horapollon Niliacus.]

Hieroglyphica Horapollinis, a Davide Hoeschelio Fide Codicis Augustiani ms. correcta, suppleta, illustrata. Augustae Vindelicorum ad insigne pinus. Cum privilegio Caes. perpetuo. Anno 1595. (The hieroglyphics of Horapollon, etc.).

The *Hieroglyphica*—from the fourth and fifth century AD—of Horapollon Niliacus, presumably an Alexandrian scholar-priest which was originally translated from the Egyptian into Greek by a certain "Philippus," was published and provided with a commentary by David Hoeschel (1556–1617). A Latin translation by Merkler is printed side by side with the Greek text.

A manuscript of the *Hieroglyphica,* acquired in 1419 through Christofori de Buondelmonti for the humanistic research into hieroglyphics of the Florentine circle around Cosimo de Medici in 1419, was first printed in its original Greek text by Aldus in 1505. The work was printed forty times between then and 1727, mostly in a Latin translation, sometimes complete, sometimes amalgamated with other texts.

The work contains indexes and interpretations of so-called enigmatic hieroglyphics which depict ideographs based on traditional symbols. The hieroglyph collection of Horapollon did not only determine the classical interpretation of hieroglyphics which interpreted the pictographic writing as an esoteric expression of *sapientia veterum* [the wisdom of the ancients], but also affected the development of a specifically Renaissance hieroglyphics. From this grew the genre of emblematic allegorical art during the sixteenth century, reaching its peak in the seventeenth, and continuing to have an effect until the end of the eighteenth, when Johann Joachim Winckelmann was still working on Horapollon.[115]

While one must doubt whether Haydn was able to read this work, given that his knowledge of Latin was not very deep, the mere ownership of it shows the magnetism which the strange and esoteric character of the *Hieroglyphica* must surely have exerted on him and many of his contemporaries.[116]

[50] Ovid.

> *Ovidii Nasonis Metamorphosis, oder Verwandlungs-Bücher* [Ovid's *Metamorphoses]*. With 150 engravings devised by Johann Wilhelm Bauer and engraved in copper by Jean Andry. In oblong folios. Nürnberg.[117]

This practically inexhaustible work, which with its poetical-mythological pictures and material must have had a stimulating effect on Haydn's imagination, was available in Vienna also in a French edition as: *Les Methamorphoses d'Ovide réprésentées en figures, dessinés et gravées par J. Wilh. Bauer, Wien 1641.*[118]

[51] [Garzoni, Tomaso.]

> *Il Serraglio De gli Stupori del Mondo, di Tomaso Garzoni da Bagnacavallo.* (The seraglio of the wonders of the world, by Tomaso Garzoni of Bagnacavallo.) Divided into ten sections

according to the various wonderful subjects; that is monsters, prodigies, conjuring tricks, fortunes, oracles, sibyls, dreams, astrological curiosities, miracles in general and wonders in particular. Told by the most celebrated historians and poets, how they sometimes occur, also considering their probability and improbability according to nature.

A work both learned and curious for theologians, preachers, scholars of the scriptures, experts in the law, and for philosophers, academicians, astrologers, historians, poets and others.

Annotated by three tables of information by M. R. P. D. Bartolemeo, his brother, ...

With three most informative indexes and the permission of the superiors and privileged. Venice, printed by Ambrosio and Bartolomeo Brothers, at the bookstore of San Marco. 1613.

This work, compiled by Tomaso Garzoni (1549–1589), was probably already a rarity in Haydn's time. It is a kind of anthology of literary curiosities and supernatural objects. It probably belongs alongside [49] and [50] in its significance for Haydn.

[52] [Schwarzkopf, Wolfgang, publisher.]

Natürliches Zauber-Buch. Oder Neu-eröffneter Spielplatz rarer Künste (Book of natural magic. Or newly-opened playground of rare arts). First part, in which not only all kinds of conjuring tricks and other curious mathematical and physical arts, but also the most common card, dice, billiards, draughts, and other games are most accurately described and lavishly illustrated. New and improved edition. Nuremberg, Wolfgang Schwarzkopf, 1762.

This is a game and leisure time book that also contains instructions for simple conjuring tricks.

Party games as a leisure activity among intimate friends as well as within so-called "games societies" were very fashionable in Haydn's lifetime, and took the place of "reading institutes" when these were prohibited, [119]

[53] Sacchi, Giovenale.[120]

Delle Quinte successive nel contrapunto e delle regole degli accompagnamenti. (On parallel fifths in counterpoint and on the rules of accompaniment.) Milan, 1789.

All other musicological works are listed in the estate listing of Haydn's music.

[54] [Gerber, Ernst Ludwig, editor.]

Historisch-Biographisches Lexicon der Tonkünstler (The historical & biographical dictionary of musicians). Which contains information about the life and work of writers about music, about famous composers, singers, instrumental virtuosos, amateurs, organ and instrument makers. Put together by Ernst Ludwig Gerber, Chamber Musician to the Prince of Schwarzburg-Sonderhausen and Court Organist of Sonderhausen.

Volume 1: A–M: Leipzig by Joh. Gottlob Immanuel Breitkopf 1790;

Volume 2: V–Z: Leipzig by Joh. Gottlob Immanuel Breitkopf 1792.

This relatively comprehensive musical encyclopedia—first planned as a sequel to J. G. Walther's Musical Encyclopedia (Leipzig, 1732)—devotes four columns to the work of Joseph Haydn.[121] Haydn's brother Michael also rates a few lines.

A letter of Haydn's to Gerber (1746–1819)[122] about *The Seasons* dated 23 September 1799[123] testifies to at least a brief contact between the composer and the author of the encyclopedia.

[55] Beckendorf, Karl Friedrich von.

Grab der Chikane, worin gezeigt wird, daß häufiger Processe das größte Uebel eines Staates sind. (The Grave of chicanery, in which it is shown that frequent lawsuits are the greatest evil for a State.) Berlin: Reimer 1781–1785. [3 volumes].[124]

This work, now practically impossible to find, was presumably aimed against malicious litigation following the reforms in civil jurisdiction that Joseph II had instituted under the influence of the Enlightenment, the effects of which had been an increase in legal proceedings.[125]

[56] Luca, Ignaz de.

Das gelehrte Österreich. Ein Versuch. (Scholarly Austria. An Essay.) Volume 1: printed by von Ghelen 1776; Volume 2: printed by Joh. Thomas Edler von Trattner 1778.

This encyclopedia of scholarship and the arts by de Luca (1746–1799),[126] which emulated such works published in other countries, is typical of the enlightened spirit of the time of the Empress Maria Theresia. It testifies to the great encyclopedic diligence of the author and was much consulted, especially in Vienna.

Joseph Haydn's "Autobiographical Sketch" was included in the second volume, with some additions.[127]

[57] [Nicolay, Ludwig Heinrich.]

Vermischte Gedichte von Herrn Ludwig Heinrich Nicolai, Kabinettssekretär und Bibliothekar Sr. Kaisserl. Hoheit des Großfürsten aller Reußen (Miscellaneous poems by Herr Ludwig Heinrich Nicolai, Secretary of the Cabinet and Librarian to His Imperial Highness the Grand Duke of all Russias). Latest edition. Vienna, Johann Thomas Edler von Trattner 1785.[128]

The original edition appeared in nine volumes in 1778–1786 in Berlin and Stettin, published by Friedrich Nicolai. Trattner's reprint of all nine volumes cannot have been completed until 1786 at the earliest.

Ludwig Heinrich Nicolay (1737–1820),[129] who lived in St. Petersburg and was incidentally in close correspondence with Ramler, was very much part of the rococo tradition—partly in the "sentimental" style— with his fables, elegies and epics of medieval knights in the manner of Ariosto. Parallels with Wieland are apparent in his treatment of romantic-heroic themes of knighthood.

The Trattner reprint demonstrates Nicolay's popularity in Vienna.

[58] Friedel, Johann.

Heinrich von Walheim oder Weiberliebe und Schwärmerey. Vom Verfasser der Eleonore, kein Roman, eine wahre Geschichte. (Heinrich von Walheim or the love of women and visions of rapture. From the author of "Eleonore," not a novel but a true story). 2 Parts, Frankfurt & Leipzig [n.p.] 1785.

The author of this novel, Johann Friedel (1755 or 1751–1789),[130] was a writer much read throughout Austria who joined Schikaneder's theater company in 1783 and became director of the Theater auf der Wieden. He became famous following a series of his comedies *Eleonore* and *Karl und Klärchen,* written under the influence of Richardson. His last novel, *Heinrich Walheim,* endeavors to highlight emotional nuances while showing the development of a young man under the influence of the educational methods of the Jesuits. It also sketches a realistic picture of the life and customs of the Vienna in the age of Maria Theresia.

Typically enough, *Heinrich Walheim* was prohibited in Vienna.[131]

[59] Campe, Joachim Heinrich.

Erste Sammlung merkwürdiger Reise-beschreibungen für die Jugend (First collection of remarkable travel tales for young people). 12 parts, with etchings. Hamburg 1785–1793.[132]

According to the catalogue, Haydn owned only eight of the twelve volumes.

Joachim Heinrich Campe's (1746—1818)[133] aim in this modified summary of the most renowned contemporary travel literature was primarily educational.

Trattner took on several publications by this writer for young people—also incidentally the tutor of Alexander and Wilhelm von Humboldt—in his reprint project of 1784 and 1785.[134]

[60] [Baumberg, Gabriele von.]

Sämmtliche Gedichte Gabrielens von Baumberg (The collected poems of Gabriele von Baumberg). Vienna, Joh. Thomas Edler von Trattner 1800.

Gabriele von Baumberg, a Viennese (her married name was Bacsany; 1775–1839),[135] was the author of elegiac lyrical poetry and "occasional poetry."

The volume in question contains among others the prize poem "To the Great Immortal Haydn, on the Occasion of the Performance of that Musical Masterpiece *The Creation* at the Imperial National Theater" (page 268f).

[61] [Ramler, Karl Wilhelm.]

Karl Wilhelm Ramlers lyrische Gedichte. (Karl Wilhelm Ramler's lyric poetry). Berlin, by Christian Friedrich Voss 1772.

Ramler's (1725–1798) authority in relation to questions of literary forms was recognized among Viennese writers chiefly because of his odes after Horace, some written in the sentimental style. This edition of the *Lyrische Gedichte*, which includes, besides the odes, the *Musikalische Gedichte* (Musical Poems) and *Geistlichen Kantaten* (Spiritual Cantatas), was reprinted by Trattner in 1783. The 1776 catalogue of the Viennese lending library lists Ramler's odes in a 1768 edition from Berlin.[136]

[62] See entries and commentary under [15].

[63] Mendelssohn, Moses.

Morgenstunden oder Vorlesungen über das Daseyn Gottes (morning hours or lectures on the existence of God). Frankfurt & Leipzig 1790.[137]

A later printing of the reprint edition of 1792 was in Haydn's library.

Moses Mendelssohn (1729–1786) was a popular philosopher of the German Enlightenment. At the center of his *Morgenstunden* stands the proof for the existence of God. The certainty of an absolute and eternal mind is derived from the necessity that the world, i.e. everything real, has to be founded in thought. At the same time the work contains a refutation of Spinoza's epistemological system and is biased towards Leibniz's principle of a deistic rationalism.

Mendelssohn's works achieved considerable influence on those involved in the Austrian Enlightenment, especially those of a Freemasonic cast, and were especially widely disseminated in Vienna and Bohemia. Trattner brought out a reprint of the *Philosophischen Schriften* (Philosophical writings) in 1783, *Phädon* followed in 1784, and *Kleine philosophischen Schriften* (Short philsophical writings) in 1792. The *Abhandlung von der Unkörperlichket der menschlichen Seele* (Treatise on the incorporeality of the human soul) was first published in Vienna in 1785.[138] Copies of the *Philosophischen Schriften* were in the Viennese lending libraries.[139]

The fact that Haydn owned this work provides important insights regarding his world view.

[64] Martial.

> *Marcus Valerius Martialis in einem Auszüge* (Marcus Valerius Martialis, a selection). In Latin and German. Collected by Karl Wilhelm Ramler from the translations in verse by various authors
>
> Volume 1: Leipzig by Weidmann heirs and Reich 1787;
> Volume 2: Leipzig, in the Weidmann Bookstore 1788;
> Volume 3: Leipzig, in the Weidmann Bookstore, 1789;
> Volume 4: Leipzig, in the Weidmann Bookstore 1790;
> Volume 5: Leipzig, in the Weidmann Bookstore 1791.

This edition of the [first century Roman epigrammatist] Martial, edited, with commentary, by Ramler, has a German translation facing the original text, which presumably helped the composer widen his knowledge of Latin—not to mention the pleasure he must have taken from the satire and rationalistic wit of Martial.

[65] [Reichardt, Johann Friedrich.]

> *Briefe eines aufmerksamen Reisenden die Musik betreffend* (Letters of an observant traveler, about music). Written to his friends by Johann Friedrich Reichardt. Frankfurt & Leipzig 1774–1776 [2 volumes].

In this volume Johann Friedrich Reichardt (1752–1814),[140] the composer and writer about music, reported, partly critically, on the way in which music was performed in Germany, as well as on the famous singers and composers of his time. The musical life of Austria is not considered in this account. Among other things the author makes a brusque attack on the English musical scholar Charles Burney.[141]

[66] [Griesinger, Georg August.]

Denkwürdigkeiten aus der Geschichte der österreichischen Monarchie. Auf jeden Tag des Jahr gesammlet. Historisch-mahlerisches Taschenbuch von und für Österreich (Memorabilia from the history of the Austrian monarchy. Collected on every day of the year. Historical-pictorial diary about and for Austria). By G. A. Griesinger. Vienna, by J. V. Degen 1804.

Georg August Griesinger (1769–1845)[142] also known as Haydn's first biographer, presents for each of the 365 days of the year "one man or fact from Austrian History which deserves to be snatched from oblivion."[143] In this way he paints a kaleidoscope picture of the distant and immediate past within the Austro-Hungarian Empire. The slim volume includes a short article about Haydn.[144]

[67] [Voss, Johann Heinrich.]

Johann Heinrich Voß vermischte Gedichte und prosaische Aufsätze (Johann Heinrich Voss, miscellaneous poems and prose essays). Frankfurt and Leipzig, at the expense of the publisher (Giessen by Krieger) 1784.[145]

Johann Heinrich Voss (1751—1826) was a realistic, and somewhat socially-critical portrayer of bourgeois life on the one hand and country life on the other. His poetry did not have a great following in the literary circles of Vienna, as opposed to that of such Hain poets as Bürger and Hölty, which was reprinted by Schrämbl as well as Trattner.

It is typical that Haydn owned an edition of even this poet.

[68] [Schönfeld, Johann Ferdinand von.]

Jahrbuch der Tonkunst von Wien und Prag. (Yearbook of the music of Vienna and Prague). Schönfeld's publishing house. 1796.

This small music handbook provides information about the musical institutions, musicians, composers, and amateur musicians of Vienna and Prague. It contains an appreciation of Haydn.

[A translation of part of the work is included in the present volume. Ed.]

[69] [Lubi, Michael.]

Gedichte von Michael Lubi (Poems by Michael Lubi). Grätz, printed by the Brothers Tanzer 1804.

The volume contains occasional poems in the form the odes, as well as songs in the rococo manner. It also contains a poem honoring Joseph Haydn as the composer of *The Creation* (Pages 49ff.).

[70] [Alxinger, Johann Baptist.]

Alxingers Sämmtliche Gedichte (Alxinger's complete poems). Klagenfurth and Laybach, by Ignaz Edler von Kleinmayer 1788 [2 volumes].

Johann Baptist Alxinger (1755–1779),[146] who was in contact with many scholars and poets both inside and outside Austria (including among others Wieland, Uz, Gessner, Ramler, Gleim, Goeckingk, Adelung, Nicolay, etc.), shows himself dependent on German models in all his literary production. His poems are in the sentimental rococo style.

Alxinger was not only a member of the Freemason's lodge Zur wahren Eintracht (Of True Concord), which Haydn joined in 1785,[147] but frequented Court Councillor von Greiner's literary salon, where no doubt he had personal contact with Haydn.[148] In the 1790s he sympathized with the Illuminati.

[71] and [72]

[71] Matthisson, Friedrich von.

Gedichte (Poems). 4th printing. Zurich 1797.[149]

[72] Matthisson, Friedrich von.

Gedichte von Matthisson (Poems by Matthisson). 5th, enlarged edition. Zurich, by Orell, Füssli & Co. 1802.

Matthisson's (1761–1813)[150] poetry is made up of partly antique-sounding odes and charming-sentimental as well as melancholy songs. It does not seem to have attained any considerable readership in Vienna by around the turn of the eighteenth century. No reprints are known. Ludwig van Beethoven, however, left a lasting memorial to the poet in his 1796 setting of "Adelaide." The fact that a volume of his work was in Haydn's library shows the composer's interest in lyrical poetry.

[73] [Claudius, Matthias.]

Asmus omnia sua secum portans, oder sämmtliche Werke des Wandsbecker Bothen (Collected works of the Wandsbeck messenger). Carlsruhe, by Christian Gottlieb Schmieder 1791 [5 volumes].

This is a reprint of the *Sämmtlichen Werke* (Collected works) of Asmus— pseudonym of Matthias Claudius (1740–1815), as well as the name of the journal he published, also known as the *Wandsbecker Bothe* (Wandsbeck messenger). This original edition was self-published as follows: Parts I and II: Hamburg, printed by Bode 1775; III and IV: by the author, and on commission by Gottlieb Lowe in Breslau 1778 and 1783, respectively; Part V: by the author on commission by Carl Ernst Bohn in Hamburg 1790.[151]

The reprint edition of 1791 contains the five volumes cited above. The last three volumes of the complete edition appeared in 1798, 1803, and 1812, and were no longer printed by Schmieder.

In this collection the poems of Claudius alternate with critical essays, fictitious letters and reviews.

Since the works of Claudius were not printed in Austria, it must be assumed that his work was little known there. There was a copy of the *Sämmtlichen Werke* in Trattner's lending library.[152]

Haydn had received the work as a present from the Swedish diplomat Silverstolpe, with whom he was on friendly terms.[153] It fits in well with the currents of German literature as absorbed by Haydn, particularly as regards poetry.

[74] [Castelli, Nicolo di.]

La Fontana della Crusca Overo; il Dizzionario italiano-tedesco e tedesco-italiano / Aumentato, corretto, & accentuato per tutto, con somma Diligenza, in questa quinta Edizione, dall' Autore proprio; cioè da Nicolo di Castello. (The fountain of the Crusca [literary academy in Florence] That is: Italian-German and German-Italian dictionary for the thorough study of the Italian language, previously produced for the German and now augmented and improved with great diligence, also thoroughly accentuated in this fifth edition by the author himself, Nicolo di Castelli). With Roman, Imperial Polish, Electoral Saxon, privileges, Leipzig, Weidmann, 1741.[154]

Haydn owned a later, 1749 edition.

[75] [Robertson, William.]

Wilhelm Robertsons Geschichte von Schottland unter den Regierungen der Königinn und des Königs Jakobs VI. bis auf die Zeit, da der Letztere den englischen Thron bestieg. Nebst einem Abrisse der schottischen Historie vor diesem Zeitabschnitte (William Robertson's history of Scotland under the reign of the Queen and King James VI until the time when the latter ascended the throne of England. As well as an outline of earlier Scottish history). Translated from the English with a critique by a distinguished Englishman, accompanied by some comments, explanations and a preface. Two parts: Ulm & Leipzig in the Gaumisch Book Company 1762.

This work, originally published in London, was translated by Georg Friedrich Seiler (1733–1807).[155]

[76] [Pope, Alexander.]

Essay on Man. Der Mensch, ein philosophisches Gedicht von Alexander Pope (Man, a philosophical poem by Alexander Pope). German translation. With the English text of the most recent augmented edition. Altenburg, in the Richter Book Company 1759.

The compiler of the book catalogue has once again made a mistake regarding the date, noting it as 1750 instead of 1759.

The translation is by Heinrich Christian Kretsch.[156]

Pope's work was much read in Vienna, especially towards the turn of the century. Trattner had reprinted selections from Pope's work in French translation as far back as 1761. This was followed at the turn of the century by a series of reprints devoted to Pope from the Viennese publisher Sammer. Many of Pope's works could be found in the Viennese lending libraries.

[77] Ludwig, Christian.

The complete Dictionary, english-germ. and germ.-english. — Vollständiges deutsch-Englisches und englisch-deutsches Wörterbuch. Newly revised by J. B. Rogler. Leipzig 1790 (2 volumes).[157]

The second volume was probably not published until 1791, as noted in the Haydn estate list.

[78]

Dictionnaire nouveau français-allemand et allemand-français à l'usage des deux nations (New French-German and German-French dictionary for the use of both nations) (7th edition) 2 volumes. Strassbourg (1818).[158]

The 1762 edition that Haydn owned according to the estate list is probably an earlier edition of the dictionary.

[79] [1. Klausing, Anton Ernst and Nathan Bailey.]

[Volume 1.] *A Compleat English Dictionary oder vollständiges Englisch–Deutsches Wörterbuch,* First published by Nathan Bailey but now revised, augmented and improved by Anton Ernst Klausing, public instructor in philosophy and antiquities at Leipzig and the smaller *Fürstencollegii* of the same *Collegiat.* Seventh edition. Leipzig and Züllichau, by Nathanael Sigismund Fromann's heirs, 1788.

[2. Klausing, Anton Ernst and Theodor Arnold.]

[Volume 2.] *Vollständiges Deutsch–Englisches Wörterbuch,* (Complete German-English dictionary). Originally compiled with much diligence by Theodor Arnold and now improved and augmented by Anton Ernst Klausing P. P. Seventh edition, Leipzig and Züllichau, by Nathanael Sigismund Fromann's heirs, 1788.

Haydn must have owned a later edition of 1792.

[80] See entries and commentaries under [9].

[81] [Meidinger, Johann Valentin.]

Practische Französische Grammatik, wodurch man diese Sprache auf eine ganz neue und sehr leichte Art in kurzer Zeit gründlich erlernen kann (Practical French grammar, by which one can learn that language thoroughly in a new and very easy way in a short time). By Johann Valentin Meidinger, intructor of French and Italian in Frankfurt am Main. Thirteenth edition, improved throughout, Frankfurt am Main, 1798.

[82]

Tour of the Isle of Wight. The drawings taken and engraved in Aquatinta by J. Hassell. Dedicated, by permission, to his Royal Highness the Duke of Clarence. In two volumes. London:

Printed by John Jarvis; for Thomas Hookham, in New Bond Street 1790.[159]

No doubt Haydn brought this work back from England as a memento of an excursion of several days to the Isle of Wight.

The description of the journey through Southampton, Southwick, and Portsdown to the Isle of Wight throws light on many historical, art-historical, and scenic details.

[83] a) Schenk, Karl.

Beschreiburg der warmen und kalten Bäder der Stadt Baden in Niederösterreich; nebst Anleitung zu deren Gebrauch (Description of the warm and cold baths of the town of Baden in Lower Austria, including instructions for their use). Vienna 1794.

b) Schenk, Karl.

Abhandlung über die warmen Quellen und Bäder der Stadt Baden in Niederösterreich; nebst zweijähriger Beobachtung über die vorkommenden Krankheiten der Badegäste (Discourse on the warm springs and baths of the town of Baden in Lower Austria, including a two-year inquiry into the illnesses occurring among the visitors of the spa). Vienna: Schaumburg 1799.[160]

The fragmentary details in the catalogue allow us to identify the volume in question only as either a) or b).

It is possible that the acquisition of this work arose from the illness of Haydn's wife. In her last years she had to take the cure in Baden several times.

[84] [Trötscher, Christian Friederich, publisher.]

Der Grätzerische Secretär, oder gründliche Anleitung, alle Arten schriftlicher Aufsätze, welche im bürgerlichen Leben vorkommen, nach den Regeln einer guten Schreibart und den in den k.k. Staaten bestehenden Vorschriften zu verfassen (The Graz secretary, or a thorough guide to the drafting all manner of written compositions needed in the life of a citizen, also rules of a good way of writing and of drawing up documents for the Austrian Imperial

State). Grätz 1800. By Christ. Friede. Trötscher, book and music store proprietor in the Bendlisch house no. 156.

The secretary in question is a letter-writing manual. Such a text- and specimen- book for letter-writing was something no bourgeois library could be without.

Why Haydn should own the *Grätzerische Secretär* rather than the *Wienerische Secretär*[161] remains unknown. Presumably however this manual, published in 1800, was at the time the most modern Austrian work in its field. Before 1800 Haydn probably used another.

[85] [Holcroft, Thomas.]

The Adventures of Hugh Trevor. Vols. I–III. London; Printed for Shepperson and Reynolds, No. 137, Oxford-Street, 1794.

Three further volumes of the 6-volume novel appeared in London in 1797. The book catalogue shows clearly that Haydn owned only the first three. Holcroft (1745–1809), a man of radical politics who was arrested for revolutionary activities in 1794, had personal contact with Haydn (!) and probably personally presented the three volumes of this socio-critical novel to the composer.

According to a note of Haydn's to Holcroft in the text, he supposedly gave him a canon and two songs. Part of the note (dated 1794) says: "I track me the liberty to send you the Canon, and the 2 songs and if it is *possible*, I *self* will *come to you to day, o [or] to morrow.*"[162]

[86] [Rochlitz, Johann Friedrich.]

Allgemeine Musikalische Zeitung (Universal Musical Review).[163]
First year, from 3 Oct. 1798 to 25 Sept. 1799
Second year, from 1 Oct. 1799 to 24 Sept. 1800
Third year, from 1 Oct. 1800 to 23 Sept. 1801
Fourth year, from 1 Oct. 1801 to 22 Sept. 1802
Fifth year, from 1 Oct. 1802 to 21 Sept. 1803
Sixth year, from 1 Oct. 1803 to 26 Sept. 1804.

All issues for the years listed were published in Leipzig by Breitkopf & Härtel.

In each of the six volumes are several discussions of compositions by Haydn, announcements of the publication of scores of his works, as well as a series of reviews, etc. Wieland's poem to Haydn was also published in the journal.[164]

It is certain that Haydn read every single issue of the *Allgemeine Musikalische Zeitung* with special interest. Hermann von Hase reports that when some issues did not arrive punctually, the composer asked Griesinger to "heartily urge Breitkopf & Härtel to let him have the missing issues, since he liked to read them." When Griesinger brought replacements, he "embraced him warmly and thanked him most kindly."[165]

[87] and [88]

[87] Homann, Johann Baptist.

Großer Atlas von 46 illum. Tafeln über die ganze Welt (Large atlas of 46 illuminated plates of the whole world). Nuremberg 1716.

[88] Homann, Johann Baptist.

Kleiner Atlas scholasticus von 26 Charten (Small school atlas with 26 maps). Merseburg [ca. 1717].

Homann's (1664–1724)[166] atlases were in general use during the eighteenth century.

[89] *Journal de la Tour de Temple* (Journal of the tour of the Temple).
This is presumably a text about the Templars, but was impossible to identify.

[90] [Schubert, Theodor.]

Populäre Astronomie (Popular Astronomy). By Theodor Schubert, Member of the Imperial Academies of Science of St. Petersburg and Stockholm. First part. History of Astronomy and Celestial Astronomy. St. Petersburg. Printed by the Imperial Academy of Science 1804.

This popular-science text is based on Theodor Schubert's (1758–1825)[167] *Lehrbuch der theoretischen Astronomie* (Textbook of theoretical astronomy), St. Petersburg, 1798.

[91] Burton, John.

An account of the Life and Writings of Herman Boerhaave, Doctor of Philosophy and Medicine; Professor of the Theory and Practice of Physic; and also Botany and Chemistry in the University of Leyden; President of the Chirurgical College in that City; Fellow of the Royal Academy in Paris. In Two Parts. With an Appendix. London: Printed for Henry Lintot 1743.

Beside the account of the life of the Leyden professor of medicine Hermann Boerhaave (1668–1738), the book also contains an appreciation of his work written in a popular manner. Boerhaave's teachings were the foundation on which the English doctor Thomas Sydenham (1624–1689) constructed his rehabilitation of Hippocratism as well as the revival of clinical discipline. Boerhaave, as the teacher of Ger[h]ard van Swieten (1700–1772), contributed crucially to the training of the older Viennese school of medicine.

As administrator of the botanical gardens in Leyden, Boerhaave stayed in friendly correspondence with Vienna-based Doctor Johann Baptist Bassand, and used him as intermediary for obtaining plants from Vienna and the Austrian mountains.[168]

[92] Three separate texts are incorporated in one item.

[a]

Osservazioni sopra la musica ed il Ballo Milano (Observations on music and the Milanese *ballo*).

The publisher and date of publication of this work could not be traced.

b) [Forkel, Johann Nikolaus.]

Musikalisch-kritische Bibliothek (Musicological library). By Johann Nikolaus Forkel. Gotha, by Carl Wilhelm Ettinger 1778/1779 [3 volumes].[169]

According to the book catalogue Haydn owned only the second volume, which contained musical treatises, reviews, and also an ode by Haschke.

c) Kolof, Lorenz Christoph Mizler von.[170]

Musikalische Bibliothek, oder gründliche Nachricht, nebst unparteyischem Urteil von alten und neuen musikalischen Schriften und Büchern (Musical Library, or a thorough report, and impartial opinion, on old and new musical writings and books). 1st part, Leipzig 1736, —2nd and 3rd part, ibid, 1737. —4th and 5th part, ibid, 1738. —6th part, ibid, 1739. — 2nd volume 1st part, ibid, 1749. —2nd part, with 10 copperplates, ibid, 1742. —3rd and 4th part, with 12 copperplates, ibid, 1743. . . 3rd volume. . . 4th volume, 1st part, with 4 copperplates, ibid, 1754.[171]

Only the second volume was found in Haydn's library .

[93] Miscellaneous.

II

Joseph Haydn acquired more than half of his library in the 1780s and 1790s. We know this chiefly from the publication dates of the books: twelve works appeared before 1750 (of which six came out before 1650), another six appeared in the fifties, eight in the sixties, twelve in the seventies, twenty-seven in the eighties, twenty-six in the nineties, and nine after 1800.[172] After that year, the number of acquisitions falls to approximately a third compared with the eighties and nineties. According to these figures, at least three quarters of the books became the composer's property after the middle of the 1770s.

The chronology of the *belles lettres* in German shows that Haydn did not own the works of German poets before the end of his fortieth year, and that, according to the dates of the appearance of the books, he did not become deeply involved in German poetry until the 1780s, a time when he frequented the salon of Imperial Councillor Greiner.

The question arises why Haydn's library increased particularly in the eighth and ninth decade of the eighteenth century. The reason may well be as follows:

a) Haydn obviously shared the enormous advance in literary education and culture in Austria, the achievement, to a great extent, of the Freemasons and, especially in Vienna, that of the Freemason-oriented salon of von Greiner.[173]

b) Haydn's search in the eighties for suitable texts for songs to set to music was the result of his connection with Greiner, and no doubt led to the composer acquiring the volumes of verse.

c) The fashion among the sophisticated bourgeoisie in the second half of the century of owning a library will surely also have influenced Haydn in the acquisition of books.

This general readiness to be actively interested in literature was to a great extent the result of the program of culture and education initiated at the time of the Empress Maria Theresia which prepared the ground, especially in the Imperial city of Vienna, for the tenets of the German Enlightenment. Owning books was evidence of bourgeois education. The expansion of the freedom of the press under Joseph II in 1781 brought about the greater availability of literature. In his *Beobachtungen über österreichische Aufklärung und Litteratur* (Observations on Austrian enlightenment and literature) of 1782, Aloys Blumauer reported: "Reading has become a necessity for us; almost every halfway well-off private person owns a small library—if only to cover a few walls—and anyone who can read has at least half a dozen books."[174] Privately owned libraries became a specifically social phenomenon among the middle classes toward the end of the eighteenth century.

In view of this reading epidemic, it is no doubt also true that books as gifts became increasingly popular in the course of the eighteenth century. It is likely that Haydn's library grew considerably through gifts of books in the eighties, when his name began to become famous both in Austria and abroad.

Only in retrospect do we know how a small number of the books came into the possession of the composer. Tradition has it that the Swedish diplomat Silverstolpe presented Haydn with the works of the *Wandsbecker Bothe*.[175] According to the prepayment list printed in it, he acquired the volume of verses by Gottlieb Hiller by subscription.[176] The composer probably also bought the numerous reference books himself, while the luxury editions were probably given to him as presents to enhance his library.[177] In the same way it is likely that the more valuable of the volumes published in London came from his generous English friends and admirers.[178] The books which contained a contribution about Haydn's person or work may well have been complimentary copies.[179] The same may be true of the volumes of verse by Michael Lubi [69] and Gabriele von Baumberg [60], in each of which a poem in homage of Haydn and *The Creation* was printed. He obviously collected these gifts and the books he had bought which praised him or his work.

Haydn certainly used his library regularly in later years and enjoyed reading. Albert Dies, Haydn's biographer, reports that the composer kept a rigorous timetable (presumably according to dietary principles) and mentions his reading habits: "The hour between two and three was set aside for his midday meal. Afterwards he always did some small domestic chore or went into his library and took down a book to read. . . At eight o'clock in the evening he usually went out but got back at nine and either sat down to write a score, or he took a book and read until 10 o'clock." [180]

Haydn's library was therefore not simply acquired for reasons of prestige, nor merely for show as a bourgeois status symbol, but was something in which the composer found education and pleasure. The contents of the library are not difficult to arrange into various fields and areas.[181] They throw a significant light on Haydn's intellect, lifestyle, and understanding of art.

I. General Literature and Reference Books

1. **Dictionaries**

a) Five foreign language dictionaries: Theodor Arnold's German–English, English–German dictionary [40]; Christian Ludwig's German-English, English–German dictionary [77]; Anton Ernst Klausing's *Compleat English Dictionary* [79]; *Dictionnaire français-allemand et allemand-français* [78] and Nicolo di Castelli's *Dizzionario italiano-tedesco e tedesco-italiano* [74].

b) A German dictionary: Johann Chrisoph Adelung—*Wörterbuch der Hoschdeutschen Mundart* (Dictionary of High German) [4].

2. **Grammars, Letter-writing Manual**

Johann Valentin Meidinger's *Practische Französische Grammatik,* including a course in French [81] and *Der Grätzerische Secretär* (The Graz secretary) [84].[182]

3. **Reference Books**

a) General: Johann Hübner's almanac-style encyclopedia, *Reales Staats- Zeitungs- und Conversations-Lexicon* [9] and its sequel about nature, art, craft and trade, *Curieuses Natur- Kunst- Gewerck und Handlungs-Lexicon.* [80]

b) Special Subjects: 78 volumes of Johann Georg Krünitz's economic encyclopedia, *Oekonomische Encyklopädie* [2] and Christian Reichart's "country and garden treasury," *Land- und Garten-Schatz* [20].

c) Biographical: Ernst Ludwig Gerber's musical dictionary *Historisch-Biographisches Lexicon der Tonkünstler* [54], and Ignaz de Luca's *Gelehrtes Österreich* (Scholarly Austria) [56].

4. **Popular Science**

a) Horticulture, agriculture, & herbology: Reichart's *Land- und Garten-Schatz* [20], and Johann Ernst Zeiher's translation about kitchen plants, *Vollständiger Unterricht von Küchengewächsen* [28].[183]

b) Medicine and chemistry: John Burton's *An Account of the Life and Writings of Herman Boerhaave* [91].

c) Geography and History: Johann Baptist Homann's large and small atlases [87] and [88]; *Tour of the Isle of Wight* [82]; Guthrie and Gray's *Allgemeine Weltgeschichte* (General world history) [1]; William Robertson's *History of America* [35] as well as his *Geschichte von Schottland* (History of Scotland) [75]; also Haydn's biographer Griesinger's daybook of memorabilia, *Denkwürdigkeiten aus der Geschichte der österreichischen Monarchie* [66].

d) Meteorology: Jeremias Höslin's *Metereologische Witterungsbeobachtungen* (Meteorological observations) [48].

e) Balneology: Either of Karl Schenk's books on the baths of Baden [83].

f) Astronomy: Theodore Schubert's *Populäre Astronomie* (Popular astronomy) [90].

5. **Works on Music**

a) History of Music: Charles Burney's *A General History of Music* [3].

b) Biographies of, or monographs on musicians: Siebigke's *Museum berühmter Tonkünstler* (Museum of famous musicians), with portraits of Johann Sebastian Bach, Haydn, Mozart, and Clementi. [33]

c) Giovenale Sacchi's musical theory treatise, on parallel fifths in counterpoint, *Delle Quinte successive nel contrapunto* [53].[184]

d) Writings on contemporary musical life: Johann Friedrich Reichardt's *Briefe eines aufmerksamen Reisenden die Musik betreffend* (Letters of an observant traveler, about music) [65]; Johann F. von Schönfeld's *Jahrbuch der Tonkunst von Wien und Prag* (Yearbook of the music of Vienna and Prague) [68]; Johann Nikolaus Forkel's musicological library, *Musikalisch-kritische Bibliothek* [92]; and the first six years' issues of the *Allgemeine Musikalische Zeitung* (Universal musical review). [86]

6. **Literature with Social Content**

a) Entertainment: *Natürliches Zauber-Buch* (Book of natural magic) [52].

b) Personal and moral education: Knigge's *Über den Umgang mit Menschen* (On dealing with people) [13]; Christian Friedrich Sintenis's *Reden in dem Augenblick der Veranlassung* (Orations at a moment's notice) [29]; Carl von Eckartshausen's *Sittenlehren für alle Stände und Menschen zur Bildung junger Herzen* (Instructions in ethics for all classes and people, for the education of young hearts) [42];[185] also Joachim Heinrich Campe's *Erste Sammlung merkwürdiger Reisebeschreibungen für die Jugend* (First collection of remarkable travel tales for young people) [59].

7. **Political Writings**

Französische Mord- und Unglücksgeschichten, we sich solche seit den Unruhen in Frankreich wirklich zugetragen haben (Tales of murder and misfortune as they have really occurred in France since the unrest) [10], and Karl Friedrich von Beckendorf's attack against the overly-litiginous effects of Joseph II's reforms, *Grab der Chikane* [55].

8. **Writings on Freemasonry and the Literature of Esoteric Lore**

Gabriel Louis Calabre Pérau, *L'Ordre des Franc-Maçons trahi* (The order of Freemasons, betrayed) [23]; the *Journal de la Tour de Temple* [89]; the *Hieroglyphica Horapollinis* [49]; Tommaso Garzoni's collection of drolleries, *Il Serraglio De gli Stupori del Mondo* [51] and Gerolamo Cardano's *Offenbarung der Natur* (Revelation of nature) [7].[186]

9. **Theology**

Nicephorus Callistus' church history, *Kirchen Histori* [8], and Reverend William Tattersall's adaptation of James Merrick's *A Version or Paraphrase of the Psalms* [37].

10. **Works of Popular Philosophy or Aesthtics**

a) German: Moses Mendelssohn's *Morgenstunden oder Vorlesungen über das Daseyn Gottes* (Morning hours or lectures on the existence of God) [63].

b) English: Adam Smith's *A Theory of Moral Sentiments* [44]; Shaftesbury's *Characteristicks of Men, Manners, Opinions, Times* [45] and Edmund Burke's *Philosophical Inquiry into the Origin of Our Ideas of the Sublime and Beautiful.* [46]

II. Belles Lettres

1. **English Literature**

a) Drama: *The Plays of William Shakespeare* [5].

b) Poetry and Epic Verse: Joseph von Retzer's selection, *Choice of the Best Poetical Pieces of the Most Eminent English Poets* [19]; Alexander Pope's *Essay on Man* [76]; and, in translation, Edward Young's *Klagen oder Nachtgedanken über Leben, Tod und Unsterblichkeit* (Lamentation or night-thoughts on life, death and immortality) [36].

c) Novels or Travel Writing: Captain Cook's *Voyages* [6]; Laurence Sterne's *Sentimental Journey Through France and Italy by Mr. Yorick* [41]; and Thomas Holcroft's *The Adventures of Hugh Trevor* [85].

2. **French Literature**

Translation of Jean Jacques Barthélemy's novel, *Reise des jüngern Anacharsis durch Griechenland* (Journey of the younger Anacharsis through Greece) [17].

3. **Italian Literature**

a) Drama: Pietro Metastasio's *Poesie* [21][187] and Carlo Goldoni's *Commedie* [34].

b) Poetry and epic verse: Giambattista Casti's *Poesie liriche* [47]; Torquato Tasso's *Jerusalem Delivered,* in German translation[18]; and Giulio della Croce, *Bertoldo* [31].

4. **Latin Literature**

a) Satirical epigrams: Karl Wilhelm Ramler's bilingual (Latin and German) edition of Martial [64].

b) Mythological epic: Ovid's *Metamorphoses* [50].

5. **German Literature**

a) Secular poetry and epic verse: Friedrich von Hagedorn's complete poetical works [14]; Ewald von Kleist's collected works [15. 1]; Albrecht von Haller's writings [15. 2]; Magnus Gottfried Lichtwer's *Fabeln in vier Büchern* (Fables in four books) [15. 3]; Christian Fürchtegott Gellert's fables and tales, moral poems, and "miscellaneous" poems [16] and [39]; Gottfried August Bürger's poems [26]; Christoph Martin Wieland's *Neueste Gedichte* (Latest poems) [27]; Friedrich Ernst Wilmsen's "miscellaneous" poems [30]; Karl Wilhelm Ramler's anthology, *Lyrische Bluhmenlese* (Lyrical flower harvest) [32]; Ludwig Heinrich Nicolay's "miscellaneous" poems [57]; Gabriele von Baumberg's collected poems [60]; Ramler's lyric poetry [61]; Johann Heinrich Voss's "miscellaneous" poems [67]; Johann Baptist Alxinger's complete poems [70]; Friedrich von Matthisson's poems [71] and [72]; poems from Matthias Claudius's collected works of the *Wandsbecker Bothe* [73]; poems by Gottlieb Hiller [11] and Michael Lubi [69].[188]

b) Religious poetry and epic verse: Gellert's "religious songs and odes" (see [39]) and Ramler's "spiritual cantatas" (see [61]).

c) Satire: Gottlieb Wilhelm Rabener's satires [38].

d) Drama:[189] Gellert's comedies, the third volume of his collected works (see [39]) specifically including the following: *Die Zärtlichen Schwestern* (The affectionate sisters); *Das Orakel* (The oracle), *Die Betschwester* (The devotee); *Das Loos in der Lotterie* (The ticket in the lottery); *Die Kranke Frau* (The sick woman); and *Das Band* (The ribbon). The second volume of Gotter's poems (see [25]) contains the tragedies, *Elektra, Merope, Alzire,* and *Medea.*

e) Novels: Johann Karl Wenzel's *Lebensgeschichte Tobias Knauts* (The life story of Tobias Knaut) [24]; Johann Friedel *Heinrich von Walheim* [58]; also Gellert's novel on the life of the Swedish countess von G**[39]. [190]

Haydn's collection of books can be seen as almost completely characteristic of his time. Practically all the works were part of the cultural heritage of the social class to which he belonged. Even foreign language literature enjoyed considerable popularity in Vienna: French was much used, Italian widely known, and English gained much influence toward the turn of the century.

Haydn owned a remarkable number of books in English and Italian. His knowledge of foreign languages was quite respectable: "He was not very skilled in French, but he liked to speak Italian, and he spoke it fluently, he learned to make himself understood in English when the need arose during his two journeys to England, and he understood all the Latin that appeared in the Roman Catholic rites."[191]

Griesinger's account is on the whole accurate. But it must be assumed that Haydn was not only able to "make himself understood in English when the need arose," but that, in the three years he spent in England, he became fairly fluent in speaking the language as well as reading English. The letters to Luigia Polzelli show his fluency in Italian, which at that time was not only the language of musicians, but also of the Austrian aristocracy and the Imperial Court, and was in many ways preferred to French. Haydn learned Latin, if only to a modest extent, during the time he spent at the monastic school while he was a choirboy at St. Stephen's from 1740 on.

Speaking several languages gave the composer a certain aura of cosmopolitanism, contrary to the traditional view, or at least reveals a personal versatility based on the many-sided gifts of a solid personality. This is another way in which the widely circulated legend of the composer's cheerful naiveté is unsatisfactory if not altogether misleading. For the moment it will suffice to mention a few facts.

We are surprised to find that Haydn, apparently without having known Meinhard's widely-circulated German translation of Home's *Elements of Criticism,*[192] went direct to Home's source, Edmund Burke's *Philosophical Inquiry into the Origin of Our Ideas of the Sublime and Beautiful.* The fact that he owned the philosophical works of Shaftesbury and Smith[193] is unexpected in the same way. Burke's works on aesthetics in particular make clear that we must not underestimate Haydn's intellectual interests in favor of a mythological naiveté. It is obvious from Haydn's *The Creation,*[194] and his collaboration with Gottfried van Swieten, that he knew everything there is to know about two central points of artistic creation: the basic motivating force of "the sublime" and "the beautiful." It is more than probable that particularly Haydn's later work rests on a solid base of philosophical and aesthetic culture, an education to which the texts in his library bear witness.

The great number of popular scientific works in a variety of disciplines prove Haydn's wide interests. It is remarkable that beside his professional and artistic activities he was able to find the energy to expand his general knowledge through an autodidact's regular schedule of reading (see above), a pattern based on a way of living guided by enlightened, diet-conscious habits.

The question of Haydn's religious beliefs has so far not been conclusively resolved. Even the more recent biographers tell us without exception of his almost naive faith, his unquestioning Catholicism.[195] But it is striking that there was no Catholic devotional literature in his library. The question therefore arises whether certain periods of his life were influenced by forces other than Catholicism. Besides the lack of devotional Catholic works in his possession, we know that between 1782 and 1796 he produced hardly any religious compositions; this suggests that Haydn did not shy away from the secularizing tendencies of the Enlightenment in the age of Joseph II, but rather that the intellectual spirit of the Enlightenment—as seen in the Masonic circles around Imperial Councillor Greiner[196]— greatly influenced his mode of living and his musical creativity. The secularization of originally sacred subjects is most noticeable in the composition of *The Creation* under the influence of Gottfried van Swieten. The oratorio was banned from performance in churches during Haydn's lifetime.

All told eight of the books in Haydn's library were owned illegally.[197] These books were not allowed to go to auction after his death, and were confiscated by the authorities. They included: Knigge's *Über den Umgang mit Menschen,* Pérau's *L'ordre des Franc-Maçons trahi,* Wenzel's *Lebensgeschichte Tobias Knauts,* della Croce's *Bertoldo, con Bertoldino e Cacasenno,* Eckartshausen's *Sittenlehren für alle Stände und Menschen,* Friedel's *Heinrich von Walheim,* and Campe's *Sammlung merkwürdiger Reisebeschreibungen für die Jugend.*[198]

Here we see the composer's inclination to step beyond the boundaries drawn by the Index, in favor of enlightened literature. What is more: an interest even in metaphysical currents seems to have been present—consider the works in the library that come close to the occult sciences. At any rate what is clear are personality traits that clearly show a world outlook distancing itself from the traditional way of looking at things, and leading in directions little noticed before now.

As we know, Haydn particularly loved German lyric poetry, especially poetry of the rococo period, and of a sentimental turn. The preponderance of volumes of verse in his library can be put down to his search for texts for songs. In a letter to the Viennese publisher Artaria (October 18, 1781) he asks to be sent, as a contrast to the songs of a cheerful nature, "Three new tender texts for songs."[199] It is known that he approached Franz Sales von Greiner for help on the same subject.[200] He knew rococo literature intimately, and it appealed to his aesthetic sensibility and philosophical understanding more than any other kind of verse. The authority of the heart in the (literarily) enlightened sense—here perhaps best implied by the concept "tender"—characterized Haydn's work from the eighties on. And thus the composer did have a one-sided relationship with German literature of the eighteenth century. Typical of his day, he confined his fondness to the literature of the rococo, remaining untouched by *Sturm and Drang,* by the Weimar classicism of Goethe and Schiller, or by the romantic movement that came into existence within his lifetime. This is why all books relevant to these movements are missing from his bookshelves.

What might have motivated such literary conservatism? The viscosity of the reigning dynamics in the reception of German literature in Austrian territories seems to have been decisive in this respect: In Vienna, Gellert (1716–69) was still fashionable,[201] verses in the rococo manner still much loved, bardic songs in the manner of Klopstock were still being produced, as were knightly epics in the wake of Wieland, and local poets continued to follow the example of the Saxon school. This conservatism continued even as Werther-fever ebbed and Germany's Sturm und Drang disappeared, even after Goethe's *Iphigen*ie (1787) and *Tasso* (1790) and Schiller's *Don Carlos* (1787).[202] It is true that toward the end of the eighties Goethe and Schiller[203] were accepted in Vienna, but they did not replace the older literary styles.

The apparently backward-looking trend of literary life in German Austria, oriented as it was toward permanence rather than progress, is the reason for the conservative line of the German literary books in Haydn's estate. Another underlying factor was Haydn's circle of acquaintances, who continued to support this form of literature: such figures as [Michael] Denis, Alxinger, the Greiners, Retzer, Ratschky, Leon, and many others carried their enthusiasm for late-rococo literature (Klopstock, Wieland) well into the nineteenth century. The rational clarity and the resulting awakening of the soul lent rococo poetry (also its language) a lucidity and accessibility that Haydn could make his own— despite his well-known lack of formal schooling.

In the 1780s he was glad to embrace the stimuli offered in Greiner's salon. He was brought face to face with the kind of literature he was able to follow both linguistically and intellectually. The linguistic transparency and discursiveness of the poetry of the Enlightenment, the playful simplicity of rococo forms, and the artlessness of a poet like Bürger or Claudius all lay within Haydn's possibilities for understanding literature, and he reacted only to those impulses that were likely to be fertile territory for his intellect or creativity. For lack of time and personal reasons, all other developments and transitional stages in German literature—even contemporary ones—remained foreign to him. According to his biographer Griesinger, Haydn was himself very conscious of this limitation: "Haydn knew the poets of the latest period only very little, and he gladly admitted that he could not come to terms with their ideas and their way of expressing themselves."[204]

For Haydn, *belles lettres* were indeed the literature of the "beautiful," a literature that was achievable in an age of enlightenment and in the sophisticated bourgeois society in which he moved: a source of pleasure and edification and, finally and particularly, a support in his artistic and musical aspirations.

NOTES

Abbreviations used in this note section:

ADB	*Allgemeine Deutsche Biographie.* 56 volumes, Leipzig: 1875–1912.
Behrisch	Behrisch, Heinrich Wolfgang von. *Die Wiener Autoren. Ein Beytrag zum gelehrten Detuschland.* N.p., 1784.
Czikann-Gräffer	Czikann-Gräffer, Johann Jacob Heinrich. *Österreichische National-Encyklopädie oder alphabetische Darlegung der wissenswürdigsten Eigenthümlichkeiten des österreichischen Kaiserthumes. . . .* 6 volumes. Vienna, 1835–1837.
Goedeke	Goedeke, Karl. *Grundriss zur Geschichte der deutschen Dichtung* 4/1 (Dresden, 1916) and 5/2 (Dresden, 1893).
Jöcher	Jöcher, Christian Gottlieb. *Allgemeines Gelehrten-Lexicon.* 11 volumes. Leipzig: Gleditsch, 1750/51.
Kayser	Kayser, Christian Gottlob. *Vollständiges Bücher-Lexicon, enthaltend alle von 1750 bis zu Ende des jahres 1832 in Deutschland und in den angrenzenden Ländern gedruckten Bücher. . . .* 6 volumes. Leipzig, 1834–1838.
Meusel, Gel. T.	Meusel, Johann Georg. *Das gelehrte Teutschland, oder Lexicon der itzt lebenden teutschen Schriftsteller.* 23 volumes. Lemgo, 1796–1834.

Meusel, Lex.	Meusel, Johann Georg. *Lexikon der vom Jahr 1750 bis 1800 verstorbenen teutschen Schriftsteller.* 16 volumes. Leipzig, 1802–1816.
Wurzbach	Wurzbach, Constant von. *Biographisches Lexicon des Kaiserthums Österreich, enthaltend Lebensskizzen der denkwürdigsten Personen, welche 1750–1850 in Kaiserstaate und seinen Kronländern gelebt haben.* 60 volumes. Vienna, 1856–1890.
UB	Universitätsbibliothek.
ÖNB	Österreichische Nationalbibliothek.
StB	Wiener Stadtbibliothek.

1. This article derives from my doctoral dissertation, "Die Beziehung Joseph Haydns zum Literarischen Leben seiner Zeit. Aspekte seiner Geistesbildung und weltanschaulicher Entwicklung" (Ph.D. diss., Vienna; 1979).

2. I owe special thanks to the long distance lending facilities of both the Vienna Universitätsbibliothek and the Österreichische Nationalbibliothek for their kind support.

3. Cf. Walter Götze, *Die Begründung der Volksbildung in der Aufklärungsbewegung* (Langensalza, 1932); Fritz Valjavec, *Geschichte der abendländischen Aufklärung* (Vienna–Munich, 1961), pp. 271f, 284–94; Eduard Winter, *Barock, Absolutismus und Aufklärung in der Donaumonarchie* (Vienna, 1971).

4. *ADB* 17, 253.

5. Burney, *A General History of Music,* Volume IV, Chapter X ("Of the Progress of Music in Germany, during the Present Century"), pp. 579, 584, 591, 596.

6. On Charles Burney, see Hugo Riemann, *Musik Lexikon.* 12. rev. ed., 3 vols. ed. Wilibald Gurlitt (Mainz, 1959–1972), 2:254.

7. Burney, *General History,* IV, 599.

8. "Verses on the Arrival of the great Musician Haydn in England" (January, 1791), published in *The Monthly Revue* or *Literary Journal* (London, 1791), V, 223.

9. *ADB* 1, pp. 80ff.

10. In the *Catalogus der von Johann Thomas Edlen von Trattnern . . . auf eigene Kosten verlegten Bücher* (Vienna, 1798), the following works of Adelung are listed: *Deutsche Sprachlehre* (1782); *Auszug aus der deutschen Sprachlehre* (1782); *Vollständige Anweisung zur deutschen Orthographie* (1790); *Kleines Wörterbuch für die Aussprache, Orthographie, Biegung und Ableitung als der 2te Theil zur deutschen Orthographie* (1791).

In the *Provinzialnachrichten* of January, 1785, Trattner announced a large-scale reprint series (I, pp. 136–41). In the chart of works planned, Adelung's *Wörterbuch der hochdeutschen Mundart* is also cited.

11. The Austrian writer Johann Baptist Alxinger, for instance, depended to a great extent on Adelung's dictionary. Gustav Wilhelm remarks in a footnote to Alxinger's letter of March 8th (1788): "In the preface to *Doolin [von Mainz]* Alxinger showed his gratitude to the great linguist for all that he had learned from him, but he sometimes disagreed with Adelung's propositions in his footnotes . . . Alxinger's language in his epics is in many ways dependent on Adelung's dictionary. . . . The influence of the dictionary is particularly strong in the revision of *Doolin.*" See Gustave Wilhelm,

"Letters of the poet Johann Baptis Alxinger" (Minutes of the Imperial Academy of Sciences in Vienna 140, 1898), p. 43f.

12. See also Nagl-Zeidler-Castle, *Deutsch-Österreichische Literaturgeschichte* 2 (Vienna, 1914), 443 and 515f, and William Steedman, "Die Aufnahme der englischen Literatur im 18. Jahrhundert in Österreich" (Ph.D. diss., Vienna, 1938), pp. 125ff.

13. These lending libraries were open to everyone, and the public would borrow books for a fixed amount of money or read them in a suitably equipped room. Franz Jakob Bianchi founded the first Viennese library in 1772; Karl von Zahlheim took it over in 1776, and soon after this it passed into the hands of the publisher Trattner who obtained a license to sell books from the library. The publisher Kurzböck also ran a library. There are still catalogues of the books available at the time of Bianchi and Zahlheim, and there are two from Trattner's time. They are in the Vienna Stadtbibliothek. (Signatures according to the order indicated: A 10.922; A 11.809; A 71.163; and A 71.164). The stock of books in the lending libraries is historically important, since the libraries had to offer what was suited to the general public's literary taste. At the same time they introduced the readers to new literary trends, and in this way formed public taste.

14. Cf. the compilation [of evidence] in: Mátyás Horányi, *Die Esterházysche Feenreich. Beitrag zur ungarländischen Theatergeschichte des 18. Jahrhunderts* (Budapest, 1959), p. 93f. [See also the essay by Elaine Sisman in this volume. (Ed.)]

15. Cf. [17], [41], [59].

16. On Pantaleon see *Jöcher* 3, p. 1227; *ADB* 25, pp. 128ff.

17. *Catalogus librorum facili adscripto pretio promercalium. In der Buchhandlung zum goldenen Vliess auf der Hohen Brucken* (Viennae: Fr. A. Kirchberger, 1760) pp. 109f. (ÖNB 122, 125–A).

18. See Günther Gentz, *Die Kirchengeschichte des Nicephorus Callistus und ihre Quellen*. Revised and enlarged by Friedhelm Winkelmann (Berlin, 1966) pp. 192f.

19. Cf. *Catalogus librorum . . . zum goldenen Vliess*, p. 734.

20. The description *Zeitungs-Lexicon* refers to information value it contains about notable current events and recent facts.

21. *Curious* here means remarkable in the sense of "worth knowing," "enlarging knowledge."

22. See the introduction to the *Conversations-Lexicon*.

23. Cf. Alfred Körner, *Die Wiener Jacobiner—"Homo Hominibus"* (Franz Hebenstreit): Translation and commentary by Franz-Joseph Schuh (Stuttgart, 1972).

24. About Hiller see *ADB* 12, 420; *Meusel, Gel. T.* 22, II, 761; *Goedeke* V/2, 543.

25. Biblioteca Nazionale Marciana (Venice).

26. Further editions of the Vienna reprint by Franz Haas of 1798, 1801, and 1804 are recorded in *Goedeke* IV/1, 615.

27. See *ADB* 16, p. 288ff.

28. This edition, which has become very rare, is in the Universitätsbibliothek Graz (I.332).

29. Cf. the *Avertissement*, which reads: "Johann Thomas von Trattnern, Imperial Knight, Imperial Court Printer and Bookseller, has printed the following books at his own cost. Vienna 2 May 1765."

30. a) *Plan des mit dem k. k. Realzeitungs-Komptoir vereinbarten Lekturkabinete . . . Zu finden im k. k. allerg. privil. Kunst und Realzeitungs Komptoir auf dem Kohlmarkt* (Vienna: Joseph Kurzböck, 1772), 246. (St.B. A1 10.922). [Hereinafter *Plan*]

b) *Einrichtung des Neuen Lectur Cabinets zu Wien im Jahr 1776. Nebst einem angehängten Verzeichniß der vorhandenen Zeitungen, Broschuren und Bücher* (Vienna: E. F. Bader, 1776), (St. B. A1 11.709). [Hereinafter *Einrichtung*]

c) *Catalogue des livres latins, français, italiens, anglais et allemands, qui servent de premier fond au cabinet litteraire privilegié à Vienne. De Jean Thomas Nob. de Trattner, dans sa maison au Graben.* (Vienna, 1780), No. 815 and 856. (St.B. A7 7.164). [Hereinafter *Catalogue des livres*]

31. The two editions of Kleist in Haydn's library are dealt with together for the sake of clarity.

32. a.) by Trattner, 1765 (see *Avertissement)*, 1784 and even 1798; b) by Schrämbl as the first volume of the *Sammlung . . . deutscher Dichter* (1789).

33. Cf. a) *Einrichtung* (1776), p. 16; b) *Catalogue des livres*, (1780), No. 831.

34. The volume appeared within the series, *Sammlung der poetischen und prosaischen Schriften der schönen Geister in Teutschland.*

35. The reprint in question is, unfortunately, not available anywhere.

36. a) The catalogue of the bookstore Zum goldenen Vliess (Vienna, 1760, p. 302) records Haller's *Versuch Schweizerischer Gedichte* in a Göttingen edition of 1753. b) Haller's work also appeared in the *Jugendfreund* (see commentary to [14]): 1st volume, *Versuch Schweizerischer Gedichte;* 2nd volume: *Alfred, König von Angelsachsen.* c) Trattner reprints: *Gedichte* (1765—see *Avertissement); Fabius und Cato und Alfred* (1783); *Usong* (1798). d) Schrämbl reprint: *Versuch Schweizerischer Gedichte* (29th and 30th volumes of *Sammlung der vorzüglichsten Werke deutscher Dichter und Prosaisten* of 1793). e) Lending libaries: *Plan* (1772), No. 245; *Einrichtung* (1776), 4 and 5; *Catalogue des livres* (1780), No. 1408.

37. a) Trattner reprints: *Fabeln in vier Büchern* (1772–73); *Das recht der Vernunft* (1773). b) Schrämbl reprint: *Poetische Schriften* (*Sammlung* 34–35, 1793). c) Lending library; *Catalogue des livres* (1780), No. 780 and 825.

38. Presumably Haydn used the texts of the volumes for the setting of the closing sentences of the following fables: "Der Kobold" (p. 156); "Der Fuchs und der Marder" (p. 149); "Das Reitpferd" (actual title: "Das Reisterpferd") (p. 10); "Phöbus und sein Sohn" (p. 32); "Die Tulipane" (p. 39); "Der Hirsch" (p. 146); "Der Esel und die Dohle" (p. 37); "Der Bäcker und die Maus" (p. 58); "Die Flinte und der Hase" (p. 148); "Der Nachbar" (p. 190) and "Der Fuchs und der Adler" (p. 110).

39. See *ADB* 2, p. 632f.

40. Cf. Wolfdietrich Rasch, *Freundschaftskult und Freudschaftsdichtung im Deutschen Schrifttum des 18. Jahrhundert vom Ausgang des Barock biz zu Klopstock* (Halle A.S., 1936), pp. 101ff, pp. 108f. [Thanks to Dorothea von Mücke on this entry. (Ed.)]

41. See *Wurzbach* 25, pp. 343ff; de Luca 2, p. 49ff; *Behrisch* p. 180; *ADB* 28, p. 275f.

42. A number of English writers included in Retzer's collection were prohibited in Vienna before the relaxation of book censorship

43. See British Museum, *General Catalogue of Printed Books 158* (London, 1962), p. 770.

44. See Carl Ferdinand Pohl, *Joseph Haydn,* 1, (Berlin, 1875), p. 162.

45. "His hours passed with teaching and studying. Everything had to relate to music, and for that reason he never touched another book at that time; the only exception was the poetry of Metastasio." See Albert Dies, *Biographische Nachrichten von Joseph Haydn.* With footnotes, in a new edition by Horst Seeger (Berlin, 1964), p. 42.

46. See *Avertissement.*

47. The catalogues list: a) *Plan* (1772): *Klopstocks Werke* (No 225–228); b) *Einrichtung* (1776), *Die deutsche Gelehrten-Republik* (4) and *Hermannsschlacht* (55); c) *Catalogue des livres* (1780): *Gelehrten-Republik* (No. 702) and *Messias* (No. 765).

48. Cf. Denis Silagi, *Jakobiner in der Habsburger-Monarchie. Ein Beitrag zur Geschichte des aufgeklärten Absolutismus in Österreich.* (Vienna, 1962), p. 220.

49. *Wurzbach* gives the following various ways of writing the name: Wetzel, Wexel, Wözel, Wötzel, or Wezl, but Wezel seems to be the most common. See *Wurzbach* 52, p. 183f; ADB 42, p. 292f; *Meusel Gel. T*, p. 8, *Behrisch*, p. 248f.

50. *Wurzbach* 52, p. 183f.

51. *Catalogus librorum a commissione Caes. Reg. Aulica prohibitorum* (Vienna: Gerold, 1776), p. 173 (ÖNB 227.875–A).

52. *Catalogue des livres* (1780), No. 1389.

53. See *Meusel, Lex.* 4, p. 292ff; *ADB* 9, p. 450f.

54. The following dramas or singspiels by Friedrich Wilhelm Gotter were reprinted, sometimes repeatedly, in Vienna: *Orest und Elektra*, a tragedy in verse in five acts, after Voltaire and Crebillon (1773); *Die falschen vertraulichkeiten*, a comedy in three acts, after Marivaux (1774); *Der Kobold*, a comedy in four acts, after Breton and Collé, and "nationalized" by F. W. Gotter (1778); *Der Faschingsstreich*, a comedy in five acts (1779); *Juliane von Lindorak*, a drama in five acts, after Gozzi (1780); *Der argwöhnische Ehemann*, a comedy in five acts (1781); *Romeo und Julie. Ein ernsthaftes Singspiel in 3 Aufzügen von Herrn Gotter. . .* (Brünn: Swoboda, 1791); *Die Mutter*, a comedy in five acts, after the Countess of Genlis (1782); *Alzire*, a tragedy in verse in five acts (1783); *Der Ehescheue*, a comedy in five acts (1783); *Veit von Solingen*, a comedy in four acts (1784); *Mariane*, a middle-class tragedy in three acts (1789); *Der Erbschleicher*, a comedy in five acts (1790); *Das öffentliche Geheimnis*, a comedy after Gozzi (1792); *Die Basen*, a comedy in three acts (Grätz, 1796); *Medea*, a drama with music (Text J. J. Engel and F. W. Gotter; music George Benda, 1806). Gotter's *Gedichte* was published by Rudolph Gräffer in 1787, a reprint of the Gotha edition of the same year; and again in 1803 in Vienna and Prague by Franz Haas.

55. The poem with the title "Lohn der Treue" (The reward of fidelity) is on p. 212 of this edition.

56. See *Goedeke* IV/1, p. 1005.

57. Cf. ibid.

58. *Gedichte von G. A. Bürger* (=*Sammlung* 2–3, 1789).

59. Bürger's epigram, "Herr Gänsewitz zu seinem Kammerdiener" (Herr Gänsewitz to his valet), was set by Haydn as a canon. The source for the text was presumably Karl Heinrich Joerdens's *Blumenlese deutscher Sinngedichte* (Flower harvest of German sentimental verses), (Berlin: publ. by the Royal Realschulbuchhandlung, 1789–91, I, p. 139). He also set Bürger's verses, *Beherzigt doch das Diktum: cacatum non est pictum* (Heed the dictum: *cacatum*, etc.) as a canon. The text comes from the poem "Prinzessin Europa" (as Haydn himself noted in a autograph), which was published in Bürger's *Weltliche hochteutsche Reimen* (Secular High German rhymes). Cf. the "critical report" on the publication of the canon by Otto Erich Deutsch in the as yet uncompleted *Haydn-Gesamtausgabe* (Munich-Duisburg: 1959). Among the part songs, Haydn used other texts of Bürger's, among them the second "ode of Anakreon" entitled "Auf die Frauen." These were presumably taken from Ramler's *Lyrischer Bluhmenlese* (see [32]). In Haydn's song the title is "An die Frauen."

60. See *Goedeke* IV/1, p. 561.

61. *Catalogus librorum. . . prohibitorum* (1776), above all nos. 6, 9, 24, and 117.

62. Wieland's *Sämtliche Werke* (Vienna: Schrämbl, 1797–1808) in 86 volumes.

63. *Plan* (1772), No. 198.

64. *Einrichtung* (1776), 5 and 25. [Wieland's journal of the arts, drama, and culture, the *Teutsche Merkur*, was extremely influential. Ed.]

65. *Catalogue des livres* (1780), No. 1527

66. Johann Nikolaus Forkel delivered to Haydn Wieland's poem, "Wie strömt dein wogender Gesang . . . " (How your surging song flows. . .), which was printed in the *Allgemeine musikalische Zeitung* (3rd year. no. 50 [Sept. 9, 1801]: p. 852). See also my commentary on [86]; also Hugo Botstiber, *Joseph Haydn* 3 (Leipzig: 1927; 1 and 2 by Pohl), p. 188.

67. Cf. Botstiber, pp. 198ff.

68. Cited from: *Meusel, Lex.* 15, p. 376; also *Kayser* 4, p. 318.

69. See *Meusel, Lex.* 15, p. 376f.

70. See commentary to [20].

71. Universitätsbibliothek Leipzig; see also *Goedeke* IV/1, p. 598.

72. See *ADB* 24, p. 401f.

73. *Catalogue des livres* (1780), no. 1509.

74. Bayerische Staatsbibliothek. The volume that has been scrutinized has a handwritten dedication dated 1762. According to Meusel (*Lex.* 15, p. 180), the volume was published in that year.

75. See *Meusel, Lex.* 15, p. 180ff.

76. Cf. British Museum 16 (1965), p. 423.

77. Karl Wilhelm Ramler, *Lieder der Deutschen* (Songs of the Germans). Facsimile print of the edition of 1766 (Berlin: G. L. Winter). With an epilogue by Alfred Anger (Stuttgart, 1965), Appendix A, p. 17ff.

78. The texts to the following *Mehrstimmige Gesänge* come from *Lyrische Bluhmenlese:* "Der Augenblick" (The moment), by J. N. Götz; II, 224; "Die Harmonie in der Ehe" (The harmony of marriage), by J. N. Götz; II, 224; "Alles hat seine Zeit" (Everything has its time), from the Greek, translated by A. Ebert; II, 376; "Die Beredsamkeit" (Eloquence), by G. E. Lessing; II, 22; "Der Greis" (The old man), by J. W. Gleim; I, 422; "An den Vetter" (To the cousin), by Ch. F. Weisse; I, 338; "Daphnens einziger Fehler" (Daphne's only fault), by J. N. Götz; I, 287; and "An die Frauen" (translation of the second "ode of Anakreon" by G. A. Bürger; I, 334—see note 59). The following texts are taken from the *Bluhmenlese:* "Minna," I 303; "Der Verdienstvolle Sylvius" (Deserving Sylvius), by J. N. Götz; I, 14; "Eine sehr gewöhnliche Geschichte" (A very ordinary story), by Ch. F. Weisse; I, 27; "Die zu späte Ankunft der Mutter" (Mother arriving too late), by Ch. F. Weisse; I. 407; and "Lob der Faulheit" (In praise of laziness), by G. E. Lessing; II, 127.

79. Part 5 of volume 1 of *Museum deutscher Gelehrten und Künstler.* The author is not named, but is probably also Ludwig Anton Leopold Siebigke.

80. See Riemann I, p. 321f.

81. Compare British Museum 88 (1961), p. 232. Volumes 1 and 2 of this reprint are part of a third printing. For this reason the date of the edition, 1753, noted in Haydn's book catalogue points to Haydn owning an earlier edition of the first two volumes.

82. The edition in question is not available.

83. Universitätsbibliothek Graz (I.14183)

84. Cf. *Kayser* 6, p. 306.

85. See *ADB* 5, p. 586f; *Meusel, Lex.* 3, p. 15ff.

86. Cf. Retzer's foreword to the first volume of the collection *Choice of the Best Poetical Pieces of the Most Eminent English Poets* (1783), VI.

87. British Library (Microfilm PS, 765714).

88. Cf. Bibliotheca Britannica, II, No. 666d.

89. The work is catalogued in the music part of Haydn's estate.

90. Quoted from Dies, p. 158.

91. Haydn owned the 4th printing! The satires were reprinted by Trattner in 1765 (see *Avertissement)*.

92. *Plan* (1772), no. 185 and 214; *Catalogue des livres* (1780), no. 1513.

93. See *Goedeke* IV/1, p. 78.

94. *Sämmtliche Werke,* 1765 (see *Avertissement); Sämmtliche Schriften;* 1773, 1782 (see commentary to [39], and 1789; *C. F. Gellert's Briefe,* 1775; *Moralischen Vorlesungen,* 1776; *Briefe, nebst einer praktischen Abhandlung vom guten Geschmack,* 1778.

95. *Plan* (1772), nos. 181–184; *Einrichtung* (1779), 19 and 21; *Catalogue des livres* (1780), nos. 832 and 869.

96. Cf. the report by the Swedish diplomat Frederik Samuel Silverstolpe, who visited Haydn in 1798. "In the same room as the instrument there was a bookcase with glass doors. In it I especially noticed a collection of the best German poets, and when we spoke of them, Gellert seemed to be his hero."—Quoted from Georg Feder, "Joseph Haydn als Mensch und Musiker," [in *Joseph Haydn und seine Zeit*], *Jahrbuch für Österreichische Kulturgeschichte* 2 (1972): 47. See also Botstiber, p. 119; Silverstolpe, Några Återblicker (Stockholm, 1841).

97. Haydn set the following texts of Gellert's as canons: "Der Menschenfreund" (The philanthropist), the setting of a pair of verses from the piece of the same name from *Moralischen Gedichte,* Trattner edition: II, p. 11; Schrämbl edition: III, p. 58; "Gottes Macht und Vorsehung" (God's might and providence), the setting of the last verse of the fifteen-verse poem from *Geistliche Lieder und Oden,* Trattner edition: II, P. 161 and "Die Liebe der Feinde" (The love of enemies), the setting of the first verse of the ten-verse poem from *Geistlichen Liedern und Oden* for Haydn's part songs; "Betrachtung des Todes" (Contemplation of death), the setting of the second of thirteen verses, Trattner edition: II, p. 221; "Wider den übermut" (Against high spirits, the setting of the first of six verses. Trattner edition: II, p. 111; "Aus dem Danklied zu Gott" (From a song thanking God), the setting of the first of thirteen verses, and "Abendlied zu Gott" (Evening song to God), the setting of the first five verses of the poem simply called "Abendlied" (Evening song) in Gellert. Trattner edition: II, p. 195.

98. Cf. *Kayser* 1, 110, British Museum 205 (1963), p. 454; see also commentary to [79].

99. Cf. Peter Michelsen, *Laurence Stern und der deutsche Roman des 18. Jahrhundert,* Palästra vol. 232 (Göttingen, 1962).

100. *Catalogus librorum. . . prohibitorum* (1776), pp. 171 and 354.

101. See Roswitha Strommer "Die Rezeption der englischen Literatur im Lebensumkreis und zur Joseph Haydn," in *Joseph Haydn und die Literatur seiner Zeit,* ed. Herbert Zeman, *Jahrbuch fur österreichisher Kulturgeschichte* 6 (1976):135f.

102. cf. *Kayser* 2, p. 94; *ADB* 5, p. 610.

103. See *ADB* 5, p. 608ff.

104 . Cf. British Museum 224 (1964), p. 17.

105. Strommer, "Rezeption der englischen Literatur," p. 153.

106. Cf. British Museum 4 (1965), p. 1235.

107. Cf. Oskar F. Walzel, "Shaftesbury und das deutsche Geistesleben," in *Germanische-Romanische Monatsschrift* 1 (1909): 416–37.

108. See *Catalogus librorum . . . prohibitorum* (1776) 15, pp. 296 and 298.

109. *Des Grafen Shaftesbury philosophische Werke* (Lord Shaftesbury's philosophical works). From the English. Leipzig, Weygand, 1776–1779. (3 volumes). The translation is mostly by Ludwig Heinrich Chrisoph Hölty and Johann Lorenz Benzler; Johann Heinrich Voss was also involved (see *Goedeke* IV/1, pp. 1043 and 1066).

110. See Strommer, "Die Rezeption der englischen Literatur," p. 152.

111. Schweizerisches Landesbibliothek.

112. See Strommer, "Die Rezeption," p. 124. We know of one reprint by Trattner and one by Schrämbl of *Grundsätze der Kritik*, the Johann Nikolaus Meinhard translation of Henry Home's *Elements of Criticism* (Vienna, Trattner 1785/86). Schrämbl published the work in 1790. [But see the essays by James Webster and Mark Evans Bonds in this volume. —Ed.]

113. Cf. Pohl II, p. 22.

114. Cf. *Kayser* 3, p. 199.

115. Andreas Alciatus' *Emblematum liber* was first printed in 1531 and reprinted for the last time in 1781. For the *Hieroglyphica Horapollinis* see Dietrich Walter Jöns, *Das "Sinnen-Bild." Studie zur allegorischen Bildlichkeit bei Andreas Gryphius* (Stuttgart, 1966), 4ff; Ludwig Volkmann, *Bilderschriften der Renaissance. Hieroglyphik and Emblematik in ihren Beziehungen und Fortwirkungen* (Leipzig: 1923), pp. 8f, 84–94, 112 and 114f.

116. The two following catalogue items, [50] and [51], show some parallels with the ideas addressed in this work.

117. Quoted from the library catalogue of the bookstore Zum goldenen Vliess (1790), p. 783.

118. Quoted from Johann Christoph Adelung, *Fortsetzung und Ergänzungen zu Ch. G. Jöcher's allegemeinem Gelehrten-Lexicon* . . . (Leipzig: Gleditsch, 1784) I, p. 1527f.

119. Cf. Franz Kadrnoska, "Der Almanach im gesellschaftlichen and literarischen Leben Österreichs" (1770–1848). (Ph. D. diss., Vienna, 1973), p. 122f. Beside many almanacs which mainly contained instructions for games, many "games books" were also sold in Vienna, for example, the *Neueste Spielbuch. Nebst einer gründlichen Anweisung zu einer leichten Erlernung des l'Hombre, Quadrille, Cinquille, Whist, Tarock* . . . Vienna: by Mössle, 1802.

120. See Riemann II, p. 561.

121. Gerber, *Historisch-Bibliographisches Lexicon der Tonkünstler.* I, pp. 609–612.

122. See Riemann, I. p. 607f.

123. Cf. Joseph Haydn. *Gesammelte Briefe,* ed. Dénes Bartha (Kassel, 1965), p. 339.

124. See also *Kayser* 3, p. 416.

125. Cf. Hermann Conrad, *Deutsche Rechtsgeschichte II (Neuzeit)* (Karlsruhe: 1966), p. 466f.

126. See *ADB* 19, pp. 335ff; *Meusel, Lex.* 8, pp. 360ff; *Wurzbach* 16, pp. 119ff; de Luca 1, pp. 300ff.

127. Ignaz de Luca, *Das gelehrte Österreich* II, pp. 309ff.

128. Only the first two volumes of 1785 could be scrutinized.

129. Correct spelling: Nicolay; cf. *Goedeke* IV/1, p. 618; *ADB* 23, p. 631: *Meusel, Gel. T.* 5, p. 428f.

130. See *Wurzbach* 4, p. 257f; *Meusel, Lex.* 3, p. 511f; *Behrisch*, p. 71f. Gustav Gugitz puts Johann Friedel's date of birth as 1751 or 1752 in his essay on the writer (*Jahrbuch der Wiener Grillparzer Gesellschaft* 15 [1905]: pp. 186–250).

131. Cf. *Wiener Blättchen* of 25 February 1788. In reference to Haydn's owning prohibited books, see p. 448 below.

132. See *Kayser* 1, p. 408.

133. See *ADB* 3, p. 734f.

134. For example: *Robinson der jungere, zur angenehmen und nützlichen Unterhaltung* (1784); *Theophron, oder der erfahrene Ratgeber für die unerfahrene Jugend* (1784). A *Kinderbibliothek* and a "little book of manners" were advertised in the *Provinzialnachrichten* of 1785.

135. See *Wurzbach* 1, p. 112ff; *Czikann-Gräffer* 1, p. 200; Nagl-Zeidler-Castle II, p. 326f.

136. *Einrichtung* (1776), p. 17.

137. See British Museum 157 (1962), p. 835; *Goedeke* IV/1, p. 490.

138. Mendelssohn, *Abhandlung von der Unkörperlichkeit der menschlichen Seele*. Itzt zum erstenmal zum Druck befördert (Vienna: Hartl, 1785).

139. *Einrichtung* 1776), 4; *Catalogue des livres* (1780), No. 1371.

140. See Riemann II. p. 480; *ADB* 27, pp. 629ff.

141. See commentary to [3].

142. See Hermann von Haase, *Joseph Haydn und Breitkopf & Härtel* (Leipzig, 1909); Edward Olleson, "G. A. Griesinger's Correspondence with Breitkopf & Härtel," *Haydn Yearbook* 3 (1965): 5ff; Günter Thomas, "Griesingers Briefe über Haydn. Aus seiner Korrespondenz mit Breitkopf & Härtel," *Haydn-Studien* 1 (1966): 49ff.

143. See the preface to this work.

144. "1st of April, 1732. Joseph Haydn born." (Pp. 120–22).

145. *Goedeke* IV/1, p. 1086) cites the edition as unauthorized.

146. See *Wurzbach* 2, p. 23; *ADB* 1, p. 379f; *Behrisch*, p. 11f.

147. Prominent members of the lodge were, among others, Josef von Sonnenfels, Councillor von Greiner, Gottfried van Swieten, Reinhold, Aloys Blumauer, Retzer, Ratschky, Leon and Wieland; Haydn joined the lodge in 1785.

148. See Roswitha Strommer, "Wiener literarische Salons zur Zeit Joseph Haydns," in *Joseph Haydn und die literatur seiner Zeit*, p. 106.

149. Cf. *Goedeke* V/2, pp. 106, 429. This edition no doubt came out from the same publisher as [72].

150. See *ADB* 20, p. 681f.

151. Cf. *Goedeke* IV/1. p. 978.

152. *Catalogue des livres* (1780), no. 1573.

153. Cf. no. 96.

154. See p. 448f.

155. See *ADB* 33, p. 647f.

156. *Meusel, Lex.* 7, p. 350f.

157. Cf. *Kayser* 3, p. 604.

158. Cf. *Kayser* 2, p. 43.

159. Landesbibliothek Coburg.

160. A) and b) cf. *Kayser* 5, p. 72.

161. *Der Wienerische Secretär auf alltägliche Fälle. Zum Gebrauch für jeden der in schriftlichen Aufsätzen und Briefschreiben Unterricht verlangt.* Vienna: Joseph Gerold, 1786.

162. Haydn, *Gesammelte Briefe*, p. 303f.

163. Johann Friedrich Rochlitz was the editor of the *Allgemeine musikalische Zeitung* from 1798 to 1819, and a collaborator until 1835.

164. Cf. note 66.

165. Hase, p. 9f.

166. See *ADB* 13, p. 35ff.

167. See *ADB* 32, p. 630.

168. Cf. *Hermann Boerhaave's Letters to Johann Baptist Bassand. Chosen and introduced by Ernst Darmstaedter* (Munich, 1927). See also Strommer, *Die Rezeption*, pp. 125, 152.

169. Cf. Riemann I. p. 532f.

170. See Riemann II, p. 228f; *Meusel, Lex.* 9, p. 193ff.

171. See *Meusel, Lex.* 9, p. 194; *Kayser* 4, p. 123.

172. Works in several volumes that appeared over two decades are counted in both decades. For this reason the total number is one hundred.

173. See Strommer, *Wiener literarische Salons*, p. 97–121. It is known that Greiner also belonged to the lodge *Zur wahren Eintracht*.

174. Aloys Blumauer, *Beobachtungen über Österreichische Aufklärung und Literatur* (Vienna: Kurzböck, 1782), p. 54. Other writers also report on the writing epidemic and the increased desire to read after the arrival of a greater freedom of the press. Compare this also with Christoph Friedrich Nicolai's *Beschreibung einer Reise durch Deutschland und die Schweiz im Jahre 1781. Nebst Bemerkungen über Gelehrsamkeit, Industrie, Religion und Sitten.* (Description of a journey through Germany and Switzerland in the year 1781. As well as remarks on erudition, industry, religion, and manners). 2 (Berlin: Nicolai, 1783–1796), 118f; see also Franz Gäffer, *Aus dem Wien des Kaiser Joseph* (From Vienna at the time of the Emperor Joseph), introduced and newly edited by Paul Wertheimer (Vienna, 1919), p. 42.

175. Cf. commentary to [73].

176. Cf. commentary to [11].

177. I.e., above all Cardano's *Offenbarung der Natur* [7], Callistus's *Kirchen Histori* [8], Cook's *Voyages* [6], Klopstock's *Messias* [22], Ovid's *Metamorphoses* [50], etc.

178. The volumes in question: Burney's *History of Music* [3]; Shakespeare's *Plays* [5]; [Merrick's and] Tattersall's *A Version or Paraphrase of the Psalms* [37]; perhaps also Robertson's *History of America* [35].

179. Cf, de Luca's *Gelehrtes Österreich* [56]; Gerber's *Historisch-Biographisches Lexicon der Tonkünstler*, [54] and *Jahrbuch der Tonkunst von Wien und Prag* [68].

180. Dies, p. 209f.

181. No rigid system was used; works which belong to several groups are only cited once, the decision as to where to place them decided in each case by the greater affinity with the overall group.

182. The letter-writing manual, *Briefe nebst einer praktischen Abhandlung von dem guten Geschmacke in Briefen*, which was very popular in Vienna, is included in the 4th volume of Gellert's *Sämmtliche Schriften* (see [39]).

183. The fact that Haydn owned these texts confirms the theory that Haydn was, like many of his contemporaries, interested in diet. A great many writings on this subject, suitable for various professions, living conditions, etc., appeared as far back as the eighteenth century.

184. About two dozen other works on music theory are included in Haydn's musical estate. [For a list, see H. C. Robbins Landon, *Haydn Chronicle and Works*, vol. 5: *Haydn: The Late Years* (Bloomington: 1980), pp. 314–16.]

185. The *Reden* by Sintenis, as well as Eckartshausen's *Sittenlehren* show a distinctive religious-pietist tendency and are stylistically influenced by sentimental literature. The texts are therefore considered to be literature in a wider sense.

186. Only part of the work deals with matters of crypto-scholarship: astrology, mysticism, animism, etc.

187. This ten-volume edition also contains Metastasio's poetry.

188. Hiller and Lubi's works lack literary worth.

189. According to Elssler's catalogue, *J. Haydn's Verzeichnis musicalischer Werke theils eigener, theils fremder Compositionen,* (which can be found in the British Museum, London), Haydn had accumulated, before his death, "175 various little books of operas, oratorios, marionettes, and cantatas." These are not listed in the estate book catalogue. Compare also Haydn's handwritten list of titles of libretti (in the Wiener Stadtbibliothek).

190. Gellert's novel is reprinted in the 4th volume of his *Sämtlichen Schriften* (see [39]).

191. Georg August Griesinger, *Biographische Notizen über Joseph Haydn,* ed. Franz Grasberger (Vienna, 1954), p. 52.

192. See commentary to [46].

193. See commentary to [44] and [45].

194. Cf. Paula Baumgärtner, "Gottfried van Swieten als Textdichter von Haydn's Oratorien" (Ph. D. diss., Vienna, 1930); Edward Olleson, "The Origin and Libretto of Haydn's 'Creation,'" *The Haydn Yearbook* 4 (1968): 148–68; Anke Riedel-Martiny, "Die Oratorien Joseph Haydns" (Ph. D. diss., Göttingen, 1965); Anke Riedel-Martiny, "Das Verhältnis von Text und Musik in Haydns Oratorien," *Haydn-Studien* 1 (1967): 205–240; Martin Stern, "Haydns 'Schöpfung.' Geist und Herkunft des van Swietenschen Librettos. Ein Beitrag zum Thema 'Säkularisations' im Zeitalter der Aufklärung," *Haydn-Studien* 1 (1966): 121–98; Hans-Jürgen Horn, "Fiat lux. Zum Kunsttheoretischen Hintergrund der Erschaffung des Lichtes in Haydn's 'Schöpfung,'" *Haydn-Studien* 3 (1974): 65–84.

195. Cf. Erich Schenk, *Das Weltbild Joseph Haydns. Vortrag in der feierlichen Sitzung der Österreichischen Akademie der Wissenschaften am 3. Juni 1959* (Vienna, 1959), p. 249f; Rosemary Hughes, *Haydn* (London, 1950), p. 58; Karl Geiringer, *Joseph Haydn* (Mainz, 1959), pp. 125f and 299; Leopold Nowak, *Joseph Haydn. Leben, Bedeutung, und Werk* (Vienna, 1959), p. 298; Heinrich Eduard Jacob, *Joseph Haydn, Seine Kunst, seine Zeit, sein Ruhm* (Hamburg, 1969), pp. 30, 155, 291, 305, and 309; Horst Seeger, *Joseph Haydn* (Leipzig: 1970), p. 125; H. C. Robbins Landon, *Haydn* (London, 1972), p. 28.

196. See Strommer, *Wiener Literarische Salons,* p. 118.

197. Printed lists of books prohibited by the Imperial Censorship Commission have come down to us from the time before 1777. *Catalogus librorum a commissione . . . Aulica prohibitorum, Viennae, Officina Kaliwodiana 1762–1767* (ÖNB 13.897–A.H.); *Catalogus librorum* (as above) *Vienna,* Leopold Kaliwoda 1768 (ÖNB 180.698–A); *Catalogus librorum* (as above) 1774 (ÖNB 70.Bb. 205–H) and an edition of the Index with a supplement for 1777 (see note 51). It seems that the index was not printed during the time of increased press freedom (1781–1795). We have no definite proof of its being printed again until 1796: *Verzeichniß der Bücher welche bei der K.K. Bücherzensur in Wien . . . verboten worden sind* (Vienna: 1796–1865—UB II, 256 527 I).

198. The works mentioned are crossed out by hand, and at the end there is the official entry: "The deleted books are to be delivered as here instructed."

199. Haydn, *Gesammelte Briefe,* p. 104.

200. See Strommer, *Wiener literarische Salons,* pp. 97f, 118f.

201. A reprint of Gellert's work was published by Trattner in 1789. In the same year, Schrämbl began to publish a compilation in 45 volumes: *Sammlung der vorzüglichsten . . . ,* which contains works by Kleist, Bürger, Gessner, Hölty, Uz, Hagedorn, Michaelis, Pfeffel, Thümmel, Gellert, Haller, Weiss, Lichtwer, Willamov, Gerstenberg, and Klopstock.

202. Cf. also Friedrich Rosenthal, "Wieland in Österreich," *Jahrbuch der Grillparzer Gesellschaft* 24 (1913): 55–102.

203. Viennese editions of Schiller's dramas from before 1800: *Die Räuber* (1790); *Die Verschwörung des Fiesco zu Genua* (1787); *Kabale und Liebe* (1789). Viennese editions of Goethe's plays, *Die Leiden des jungen Werthers* (1788); *Clavigo* (1785) and 1795); *Faust. Ein Fragment* (1796); *Claudine und Villa Bella* (1789); *Die Geschwister* (1787); *Erwin und Elmire* (1776 and 1796).

204. Griesinger, *Biographische Notizen,* p. 63.

Alphabetical Listing of the Authors in Haydn's Library [Ed.]

Adelung, Johann Christoph [4]
Aesop [12]
Alxinger, Johann Baptist [70]
Arnold, Theodor [40]
Banchieri, Adriano, et al. [31]
Barthélemy, Jean Jacques [17]
Baumberg, Gabriele von [60]
Beckendorf, Karl Friedrich von [55]
Bürger, August [26]
Burke, Edmund [46]
Burney, Charles [3]
Burton, John [91]
Campe, Joachim Heinrich [59]
Cardano, Hieronymus [7]
Castelli, Nicolo di [74]
Casti, Giambattista [47]
Claudius, Matthias [73]
Cook, Captain James [6]
Cooper, Anthony Ashley, Earl of Shaftesbury [45]
de Comte [28]
Eckartshausen, Carl von [42]
Forkel, Johann Nikolaus [92b]
Friedel, Johann [58]
Garzoni, Tomaso [51]
Gellert, Christian Fürchtegott [16, 39]
Gerber, Ernst Ludwig [54]
Goldoni, Carlo [34]
Gotter, Friedrich Wilhelm [25]
Griesinger, Georg August [66]
Guthrie, William, and John Gray [1]
Hagedorn, Friedrich von [14]
Haller, Albrecht von [15.2]
Hiller, Gottlieb [11]
Holcroft, Thomas [85]
Homan, Johann Baptist [87, 88]
Horapollon Niliacus [49]
Höslin, Jeremias [48]
Hübner, Johann [9, 80]
Klausing, Anton Ernst [79]
Kleist, Ewald von [15.1, 62]
Klopstock, Friedrich Gottlob [22, 43]
Knigge, Adolph, Freiherr von [13]
Krünitz, Johann Georg [2]
Lichtwer, M. G. [15.3]
Lubi, Michael [69]
Luca, Ignaz de [56]
Ludwig, Christian [77]
Martial [64]
Matthison, Friedrich von [72]
Meidinger, Johann Valentin [81]
Mendelssohn, Moses [63]
Merrick, James, and W.W. Tattersall [37]
Metastasio, Pietro [21]
Mizler, Lorenz Christoph [92c]
Nicolay, Ludwig Heinrich [57]
Ovid [50]
Pérau, Gabriel Louis Calabre [23]
Pope, Alexander [76]
Rabener, Gottlieb Wilhelm [38]
Ramler, Karl Wilhelm [32, 61]
Reichardt, Johann Friedrich [65]
Retzer, Joseph von [19]
Reichart, Christian [20]
Robertson, William [35, 75]
Rochlitz, Friedrich [86]
Sacchi, Giovenale [53]
Schenk, Karl [83]
Schönfeld, Johann Ferdinand von [68]
Schubert, Theodor [90]
Schwarzkopf, Wolfgang [52]
Shakespeare, William [5]
Siebigke, Ludwig Anton Leopold [33]
Sintenis, Christian Friedrich [29]
Smith, Adam [44]
Society of Citizens of the Imperial Capital [10]
Sterne, Laurence [41]
Tasso, Torquato [18]
Trötscher, Christian Friedrich [84]
Voss, Johann Heinrich [67]
Wezel, Johann Karl [24]
Wieland, Christoph Martin [27]
Wilmsen, Friedrich Ernst [30]
Xanthopulos, Nikephorus Callistus [8]
Young, Edward [36]

Index

Index

Haydn's musical compositions

Index of names

Please note: Further names can be found on pages 395–462, in Maria Hörwarthner's "Joseph Haydn's Library." Because it is an extensive bibliography, this chapter has not been indexed here.

List of Contributors

Tom Beghin is Assistant Professor of Music at the University of California, Los Angeles. He received a D.M.A. in Historical Performance Practice from Cornell University. As a soloist on fortepiano he has played numerous recitals in the United States and Europe. His CD recordings include Haydn sonatas (Eufoda), Haydn's *Ariadne a Naxos* and German songs (Bridge, with Andrea Folan), and two recordings of Beethoven Sonatas (Claves, Eufoda).

Mark Evan Bonds is Professor of Music at the University of North Carolina, at Chapel Hill. He is the author of *Wordless Rhetoric: Musical Form and the Metaphor of the Oration* (1991) and *After Beethoven: Imperatives of Originality in the Symphony* (1996), both published by Harvard University Press.

Leon Botstein is the President of Bard College, where he is also Leon Levy Professor in the Arts and Humanities. He is the author of *Judentum und Modernität* (Vienna, 1991) and *Music and Its Public: Habits of Listening and the Crisis of Modernism in Vienna, 1870–1914* (Chicago, forthcoming), as well as *Jefferson's Children: Education and the Promise of American Culture*, forthcoming later this year from Doubleday. He is also music director of the American Symphony Orchestra and Editor of *The Musical Quarterly*.

Susan Gillespie is Vice President for Public Affairs at Bard College. She has contributed translations of music-historical essays, reviews, letters, and memoirs to many of the previous volumes published in conjunction with the Bard Music Festival. Her translations of essays by Theodor W. Adorno have appeared in *Grand Street, Raritan,* and *Musical Quarterly.*

Rebecca Green received her Ph.D. from the University of Toronto with a dissertation on "Power and Patriarchy in Haydn's Goldoni Operas." She has taught cultural studies and music at Trent University and was Killam Post-Doctoral Fellow at Dalhousie University. She has contributed an essay to *Goldoni and the Musical Theatre,* ed. Domenico Pietropaolo (Legas) and is currently at work on a book about Haydn's operas.

Mary Hunter is Professor of Music at Bowdoin College. She has written on Haydn's and Mozart's operas, and on the wider repertory of opera buffa in the late eighteenth century. She is the author of *The Poetics of Entertainment: Opera Buffa in Vienna, 1770–1790* (Princeton University Press, forthcoming), and co-editor with James Webster of *Opera Buffa in Mozart's Vienna* (Cambridge University Press, in press).

Elaine Sisman is Professor of Music at Col
author of *Haydn and the Classical Variation* (Ha
and the Cambridge Handbook *Mozart: T*
(Cambridge University Press), she specializes
thetics of the eighteenth and nineteenth centu
on such topics as Haydn's theater symphonies,
music, Beethoven and the meaning of *pathe*
Brahms's variations.

Kathrine Talbot is a novelist, poet, and tr
Sussex, England. Among her novels are *F*
Innermost Cage; her translations include *T*
Manfred Bieler, *When the Nightbird Cries,* by Lil
the tales by Leonora Carrington in her *The H*

James Webster is Goldwin Smith Professo
University. He is the author of *Haydn's "Fa*
Idea of Classical Style: Through-Composition and
Instrumental Music (Cambridge University Press) and the article on Haydn in the forthcoming revised *New Grove Dictionary of Music and Musicians*, and an editor of *Haydn Studies: Proceedings of the International Haydn Conference, Washington, D.C., 1975* and *Opera Buffa in Mozart's Vienna* (Cambridge University Press, in press). He has published on many aspects of Haydn's life and music, as well as on Mozart, Beethoven, Brahms, and other eighteenth- and nineteenth-century composers.